THE LENIN ANT

Books by Robert C. Tucker

Philosophy and Myth in Karl Marx

The Soviet Political Mind

The Great Purge Trial (Co-Editor)

The Marxian Revolutionary Idea

The Marx-Engels Reader (Editor)

Stalin as Revolutionary, 1879–1929:
A Study in History and Personality

Stalinism: Essays in Historical
Interpretation (Editor)

THE
LENIN
ANTHOLOGY

Edited by

ROBERT C. TUCKER

PRINCETON UNIVERSITY

W · W · NORTON & COMPANY

New York · London

W. W. Norton & Company, Inc., 500 Fifth Avenue, New York, N.Y. 10110
W. W. Norton & Company Ltd., 37 Great Russell Street, London WC1B 3NU

Library of Congress Cataloging in Publication Data
Lenin, Vladimir Il'ich, 1870–1924.
    The Lenin anthology.
    Includes bibliographical references.
    I. Tucker, Robert C., ed. II. Title.
DK254.L3A5787 1975   335.43′092′4   74–14933

This book was designed by Robert Freese.
The typefaces are Deepdene and Electra,
set by Maryland Linotype Co.

The book was printed by The Murray Printing Co.

PRINTED IN THE UNITED STATES OF AMERICA

0

ISBN 0-393-09236-X

Contents

vii

Preface

Pavel Axelrod, who before he became a Menshevik worked closely with Lenin, said of him in 1910 that "there is not another man who for twenty-four hours of the day is taken up with the revolution, who has no thoughts but thoughts of revolution, and who even in his sleep, dreams of nothing but revolution."[1] He might have added: writes of nothing but revolution. For revolution was, and remained, the leitmotif of all that Lenin wrote. And he was astonishingly prolific as a writer. He was three months short of fifty-four years old when he died in 1924, and much of his fairly short life was invested in practical leadership of the Bolshevik Party and in directing the regime it created, and the Communist International, after the party came to power in Russia in 1917. Yet, his total literary output in the latest, fifth, Soviet edition of his collected writings,[2] comprising speeches, correspondence, and preparatory materials as well as published books, pamphlets, and articles, comes to fifty-five solid volumes.

The paradox of an extremely active political leader whose writings far exceed in volume (not to mention influence) those of most full-time scholars is partly explained by the nature of most of what he wrote. Not only the speeches and correspondence but also a great many of the articles and longer treatises are addressed to practical problems of the revolutionary movement and its politics, both before and after 1917. The work that has claim to be considered his masterpiece, his modern *Prince*—*"Left-Wing" Communism—An Infantile Disorder*—was a manual of strategy and tactics for Marxist revolutionary movements. His theoretical analysis of imperialism in the treatise of that title was also an apologia for the revolutionary political line that he followed during the World War. His great work of Marxist political theory, *The State and Revolution*, was an effort to legitimize in Marxist terms his revolutionary politics of 1917 in Russia. In an important sense, the whole corpus of Lenin's writings could be published under the title of the work of 1902 that more than any other laid the foundations of Bolshevism as a movement and hence was instrumental in his becoming prob-

1. Quoted in Bertram D. Wolfe, *Three Who Made a Revolution: A Biographical History* (New York, 1948), p. 249.
2. V. I. Lenin, *Polnoe sobranie sochinenii*, 55 vols. (Moscow, 1958–65). An English translation based mainly on the fourth Soviet edition (V. I. Lenin, *Sochineniia*, 45 vols. [Moscow, 1946–67]) is available under the title *Collected Works*.

ably the most history-making single individual of this century: *What Is to Be Done?*

A well-known person whose name escapes me has said that one should speak for one's contemporaries but write for posterity. Marx and Engels instinctively followed that maxim most of the time. One feels that when Marx wrote the superb first lines of *The Eighteenth Brumaire of Louis Bonaparte,* he knew that his publicistic essay was going to be an historical classic. With Lenin it is different: his classics-to-be are often written as though he were simply dealing with issues of the revolutionary here-and-now with hardly any sense of their lasting importance. Not only his extended and sometimes rather arid polemicizing with opponents whose names would now be forgotten if not for these very polemics of his, but a good deal else besides, is dated and of little permanent interest. Consequently, even *What Is to Be Done?* can be slightly abridged, as I have done, to a reader's potential advantage, and the same is true of other writings of Lenin's. For this reason as well as because of the inevitable limitation of space in placing the enduringly significant Lenin within the covers of a single volume, even a bulky one, I have made bold to be his editor here and there, seeking, however, to bring out the substance and plan of argument of each major writing. Nevertheless, such key works as *The State and Revolution* and *"Left-Wing" Communism* (minus an appendix), not to mention a large number of his shorter writings, speeches, draft resolutions, etc., are presented here unabridged. Throughout, asterisks have been used to indicate breaks in the text due to abridgement. (Within the texts, interpolations in brackets are Lenin's, unless otherwise indicated.)

In this anthology I have followed the organizational principle and techniques employed in my previous edited volume, *The Marx-Engels Reader.* The materials are organized under chronologically successive major themes of Lenin's thought, a procedure made all the more natural in this instance because of the 1917 watershed. This combination of thematic and chronological grouping has been modified only in Part VI (Revolution and Culture) for reasons which will be plain to the reader. Each selection is preceded by a note offering essential background information and, in most instances, a brief interpretive comment. The Introduction is a general interpretation of Lenin's career as a revolutionary leader and thinker. A chronology of his life appears at the beginning of the book and a short bibliographical essay at the end.

With Marx, the central fact that we have slowly and painfully, but conclusively, established during this scholarly generation is the fundamental underlying unity of his thought from the 1844 manuscripts to *Capital* and beyond. With Lenin our task as scholars and teachers is, in my opinion, to make more clear and distinct the fact that his thought underwent change and development over the years. Much mischief has resulted, and continues to result, from a tendency to treat the theme of a particular period as a timeless position. There *are* certain basic constants in Lenin's thinking, such as the stress on leadership, and in particular party leadership, in revolutionary politics. But there are changes of great significance too. Thus, the Lenin of the Civil-War and foreign-intervention year of 1919 who could see nothing but apocalyptic conflict ahead in Soviet Russia's relations with the surrounding capitalist world, gave way to the Lenin of 1921–22, who found, partly in response to changes in the actual situation, that a certain "equilibrium" had emerged in Soviet relations with the West. The Lenin of the early aftermath of the October Revolution who saw internal class war as the main content of the proletarian dictatorship, and who advocated revolutionary violence and terror, gave way to the Lenin of the NEP who counseled "reformist" instead of revolutionary methods of building socialism in Russia and prescribed educational measures amounting to a "cultural revolution" rather than coercive class struggle for the realization of that goal. The philosophical Lenin who wrote *Materialism and Empirio-criticism* in 1908 underwent a certain change under the influence of a war-time study of Hegel which is reflected in his *Philosophical Notebooks*. In choosing the materials that make up this volume, I have attempted to convey to the reader some sense of the significant changes as well as constants of Lenin's thought.

With the exception of three selections ("The Symptoms of a Revolutionary Situation," "Against Futurism" and "On Bureaucracy: From Lenin's Correspondence"), which I translated, the writings of Lenin contained in this volume are English translations put out by either Progress Publishers or the Foreign Languages Publishing House in Moscow prior to the Soviet Union's signing of the International Copyright Convention. In a few places I have made slight alterations in wording in order to render a phrase more concretely or vividly. The footnotes to the texts, save where explicitly designated as either Lenin's or mine, are those provided by the editors of the Soviet English translations. I have abridged these notes where possible in the interest of conserving space, but have made no additions.

My thanks go particularly to Professor Rolf H. W. Theen of Purdue University for advice related to this volume, as well as to my editors at W. W. Norton & Company, James L. Mairs and Emily Garlin, for their many-sided assistance. Professor Theen appraised my choice of materials and generously shared with me his outstanding expertise in Leniniana, for example by suggesting the representative comments from Lenin's correspondence about bureaucracy in the Soviet system. I am likewise, as so often before, greatly indebted to my colleague, Professor Stephen F. Cohen, for his counsel on various aspects of the book. Professor Norman Levine provided a most useful appraisal of the proposed selections, and Professor Alexander Rabinowitch kindly discussed with me the problem of what to include of Lenin's 1917 writings. I am grateful to A. T. Ferguson, Jr., for his assistance in selecting material from Lenin's *Philosophical Notebooks*. I am indebted to Thomas Robertson, Shaheen Dil, Monica Mosler, and Michael Kraus for research assistance, and to Lorna Giese for her skillful typing. My wife, Evgenia Tucker, has given me, as always, moral support as well as expert advice on questions relating to the Russian language.

R.C.T.

A Lenin Chronology[1]

1870	April 10 (22). Lenin (Vladimir Ilyich Ulyanov) was born at Simbirsk (now Ulyanovsk), on the Volga River.
1879	August 16 (28). Lenin entered the first grade at the Simbirsk classical *gymnasium*.
1886	January 12 (24). Death of Lenin's father, Ilya Nikolaevich Ulyanov.
1887	March 1 (13). Arrest of Lenin's elder brother Alexander in Petersburg for participation in an attempt on the life of Tsar Alexander III. He was sentenced to death and on May 8 (20) was executed.
	May 5 (17)–June 6(18). Lenin took final examinations in the *gymnasium*.
	June 10 (22). Lenin graduated from the *gymnasium* with a gold medal.
	August 13 (25). Lenin entered the University of Kazan to study law.
	September–November. Lenin took part in the activities of a revolutionary student circle.
	December 4–5 (16–17). Lenin was arrested for participation in student disorders.
	December 5 (17). Lenin was expelled from the University.
	December 7 (19). Lenin was exiled from Kazan to the village of Kokushkino, in Kazan Gubernia, under unofficial police surveillance.
1888	May 9 (21). Lenin applied to the minister of education for permission to re-enter the University of Kazan. His application was denied.
	September 6 (18). Lenin applied to the minister of

1. This chronology has been drawn from the more detailed one in Lenin, *Polnoe sobranie sochinenii*. Prior to February 1918, when Russia adopted the Gregorian calendar, the Julian calendar was used. The dates accordingly were thirteen days earlier than our calendar. Thus April 10, 1870, on the Julian calendar, the day of Lenin's birth, was April 22 on the Gregorian calendar. In the chronology here presented, the dates prior to 1918 are given old style, with the corresponding new-style date shown in parentheses. (All footnotes to this chronology are R.C.T.'s.)

internal affairs for permission to travel abroad to continue his education. His application was denied.

Early October. Lenin was given permission to reside again in Kazan, where the Ulyanov family joined him. Police surveillance continued.

Autumn. Lenin studied Marx's *Capital* and spoke in a Marxist circle.

1889   May 3–4 (15–16). Lenin moved from Kazan to a village in Samara Gubernia.

May. Lenin applied for permission to go abroad for medical treatment. The Department of Police denied him a passport for foreign travel.

May–June. Lenin advertised in the *Samara Gazette* his availability for giving lessons.

October. Lenin moved to Samara (now Kuibyshev) and gave lessons.

1890   Early months. Lenin continued the study of Marx and Engels, translated the *Communist Manifesto* into Russian.

May 17 (29). Lenin's mother requested the minister of education to permit him to take final examinations at a university. The request was granted, and Lenin received permission to take law examinations at the University of Petersburg without having been a student there.

1891   April 4 (16)–April 24 (May 6). Lenin passed the spring-term examinations of the law faculty of the University of Petersburg.

September–November. Lenin passed the fall-term and written law examinations at the University of Petersburg.

October 20 (November 1). Lenin was given an audience by the vice-director of the Department of Police with reference to travel abroad. His request was turned down.

November 12 (24). Lenin returned from Petersburg to Samara.

November 15 (27). The examining commission of the law faculty of the University of Petersburg awarded Lenin a diploma first class.

1892   January 30 (February 11). Lenin became assistant to attorney A. N. Khardin in Samara.

February 28 (March 11). Lenin petitioned the Samara District Court for the right to plead cases as an attorney.

June. Lenin appeared in the Samara District Court as attorney for the defense in the cases of peasants Bambukov, Chinov, and others.

1893   January–August. While working as an attorney in Samara, Lenin took part in clandestine revolutionary circles and wrote anti-populist tracts.

August–September. Moving to Petersburg, Lenin became assistant to attorney M. F. Volkenstein. He appeared as an attorney in the Petersburg District Court.

Autumn. Lenin entered and became active in a Marxist circle and made the acquaintance of some local factory workers.

1894   Spring–summer. Lenin wrote his first major work, *Who Are the "Friends of the People" and How Do They Fight Against the Social Democrats?*

1895   April–September. Lenin went abroad, made contact with the Emancipation of Labour group in Switzerland, traveled and made contacts in France, Austria, and Germany.

Autumn. Lenin returned to Petersburg and there helped to organize the St. Petersburg Union of Struggle for the Liberation of the Working Class. He remained active in clandestine revolutionary circles.

December 8–9 (20–21). Lenin and his associates in the Union of Struggle were arrested.

1896   Lenin was in prison in Petersburg. Between interrogations, he made contact with relatives and friends outside, who sent books he requested; he started preparatory work on his book about the development of capitalism in Russia, wrote a draft program of the Social-Democratic Party, an article entitled "Friedrich Engels," a May Day leaflet, etc.

1897   February 13 (25). Lenin was sentenced to three years of exile under police surveillance in East Siberia and given permission to proceed there at his own expense under the system of police-certified passage from place to place enroute.

February 14 (26)–17 (March 1). Given four free days in Petersburg, Lenin held meetings with members of the Union of Struggle.

February 18 (March 2)–February 22 (March 6).

Lenin stopped in Moscow enroute to Siberia, visited his mother there, and went to the main library.

March 4 (16). Lenin arrived in the West Siberian city of Krasnoyarsk.

March 6 (18). Lenin petitioned the governor general of Irkutsk Gubernia in East Siberia, on the grounds of weak health, to be allowed a place of exile in West Siberia in Krasnoyarsk Gubernia or the Minusinsk District of Yenisei Gubernia.

March–April. By special arrangement, Lenin was given access in Krasnoyarsk to the large personal library of a wealthy merchant, G. V. Yudin, and worked there on materials for his study of the development of Russian capitalism.

April 30 (May 12). Lenin, having received assignment in the area he had requested, left Krasnoyarsk, via Minusinsk, to his place of exile—the village of Shushenskoe.

1898   July 10 (22). Lenin was married to Nadezhda Konstantinovna Krupskaya, who had joined him in exile.

1898–1900   While in Siberian exile, Lenin completed *The Development of Capitalism in Russia*, which was published in Russia under the pseudonym "Ilin," and produced numerous other writings, some of which were sent abroad for uncensored publication.

1900   January–February. Upon completion of the term of exile, Lenin—prohibited from residing in the capital, university towns, or large worker centers—chose Pskov, not far from Petersburg, as his place of residence. Upon arrival there he resumed intense Social-Democratic activities, with occasional illegal travels to Moscow, Petersburg, Riga, etc.

May 21 (June 3). Lenin was arrested while on an illegal visit to Petersburg. After interrogation, he was sent to the town of Podolsk, near Moscow.

July 16 (29). Having received in May a passport for foreign travel, Lenin went abroad.

August–December. Living mostly in Geneva and Munich, Lenin worked with Plekhanov, Axelrod, and others to organize the all-Russian Marxist party paper *Iskra*, the first issue of which came out at the end of 1900 with three articles in it by Lenin.

1901–2   Living in Munich and (from April 1902) in London, Lenin continued his émigré party activities as an *Iskra* editor, and wrote *What Is to Be Done?*

1902   April 27 (May 10). Lenin placed an advertisement in *The Athenaeum* of London: "Russian doctor of law and his wife would like to take English lessons from an Englishman (or an Englishwoman) in exchange for Russian lessons."

Autumn. First meeting between Lenin and Trotsky, following the latter's arrival in London from Russia.[2]

1903   End of April. Lenin took up residence in Geneva.

July–August. Lenin took part in the Second Congress of the Russian Social-Democratic Workers' Party, held in Brussels and London. The Bolshevik-Menshevik division emerged there.

August 11 (24). Lenin, accompanied by congress supporters, visited Karl Marx's grave in Highgate Cemetery.

1903–4   Lenin was active in émigré party affairs. His writings included *One Step Forward, Two Steps Back*.

1905   January 12 (25). Responding to Russia's "Bloody Sunday" (January 9), Lenin wrote an article, "The Beginning of Revolution in Russia," in which he called for preparation of an armed uprising.

April. The Bolshevik-dominated Third Party Congress was held in London under Lenin's guidance.

June–July. Back in Geneva, Lenin wrote *Two Tactics of Social Democracy in the Democratic Revolution*.

Early November. Lenin returned to Russia and plunged into party and journalistic activities.

1906   April–May. Lenin took part in the Fourth Party Congress, held in Stockholm—a congress of attempted Bolshevik-Menshevik unification.

Late August. Lenin moved to Finland, where he resided until December 1907 while continuing his party activities.

1907   April–May. Lenin took part in the Fifth Party Congress, held in London.

December 25 (January 7, 1908). Lenin moved to Geneva, beginning his second emigration.

1908   Mid-December. Lenin moved to Paris to continue party work and his writing; he worked on *Materialism and Empirio-criticism*.

2. This item is not supplied in the chronology contained in Lenin, *Polnoe sobranie sochinenii*.

1909–11	Residing in Paris, Lenin continued his party and journalistic activities, with occasional travels, e.g., in June 1910 to visit Maxim Gorky on the isle of Capri.
1912	January. Lenin took the leading part in the all-Bolshevik Sixth Party Conference, held in Prague, at which the Bolshevik faction organized itself as a separate party, the Russian Social-Democratic Workers' Party (Bolshevik).

April. Lenin directed the organizing of the Bolshevik party's daily paper *Pravda* (*The Truth*), published legally (though not without difficulties with the state censors) in Russia starting April 22 (May 5), 1912.

June. Lenin moved from Paris to Cracow (then in the territory of the Austro-Hungarian Empire) in order to establish closer ties with Russian affairs.

November. Lenin met with Stalin in Cracow.[3]

1914   After the start of the World War, Lenin moved to Berne, in neutral Switzerland, where he continued his émigré and journalistic activity, defending a radical anti-war position oriented toward a politics of social revolution in the warring countries.

1915   September. Lenin took part in the First International Socialist Conference, held in Zimmerwald, Switzerland, with thirty-eight participants from European countries, including Germany, Russia, and France. Although the conference took an anti-war position, only a minority supported the radical line of Lenin, who wanted to break with the Second International and form a new, revolutionary Third International.

1916   April. Lenin took part in the Second International Socialist Conference, held in Kienthal, Switzerland, and again was in the more radical minority.

July 12 (25). News reached Lenin of the death of his mother in Petrograd.

1917   March 2 (15). Lenin, living in Zurich, learned of the February Revolution in Russia.

March 24 (April 6). Lenin received word of the German government's agreement to permit him and other Russian political émigrés to cross Germany enroute to Russia.

March 27–30 (April 9–12). Lenin traveled by train

---

3. This item is not supplied in the chronology contained in Lenin, *Polnoe sobranie sochinenii.*

across Germany, then embarked by a Swedish ship for Sweden.

April 3 (16). Lenin arrived by train at the Finland Station in Petrograd, where he gave speeches to welcomers inside the station and standing atop an armored car in the square in front of the station.

April 4 (17). Having drafted his "April Theses" while enroute to Petrograd, Lenin read them before party meetings and sent them to *Pravda* for publication.

April 4 or 5 (17 or 18). Lenin became editor of *Pravda*.

April–June. Lenin engaged in many-sided activities as a journalist, speaker at mass meetings, and leader of the Bolshevik Party at its conferences and in sessions of its Central Committee.

July 5–October 24 (July 18–November 6). Lenin was forced to go into hiding (in Petrograd and later in Finland) after a mass political demonstration which the Provisional Government used as a pretext to seek his arrest and trial. He remained in constant contact with leading members of the Bolshevik Party and wrote, *inter alia, The State and Revolution.*

Night of October 24–25 (November 6–7). Lenin arrived at revolutionary headquarters in the Smolny Institute as the Bolsheviks' armed action against the Provisional Government and takeover of power was in progress.

Night of October 26–27 (November 7–8). Lenin appeared before the Second All-Russian Congress of Soviets, which approved his decrees on peace and land. A new government, the Council of People's Commissars, was formed, with Lenin as its chairman.

1918   August 30. Lenin was wounded by a pistol shot fired by Fanya Kaplan, a member of the Socialist Revolutionary Party, as he was leaving a Moscow factory after giving a speech.

1919   March 2. Lenin opened the First Congress of the Communist International, and chaired its first session.

1921   July 13. Lenin went on a month's holiday at his country house in Gorki, a village not far from Moscow, on his doctors' advice.

December 6. Lenin moved to Gorki for rest.

December 31. By Politburo decision, Lenin was ordered to take a six-week leave for his health, not coming to Moscow for work without the Central Committee Secretariat's permission. He remained in active touch with state affairs while living outside Moscow.

1922   March 25. Lenin returned to Moscow for regular work.

April 23. Lenin went into a hospital in Moscow to be operated on for removal of the bullet fired by Fanya Kaplan. He resumed work the following day.

May 25–27. Lenin suffered his first stroke, causing partial paralysis of the right arm and leg, and speech impairment.

Mid-June. Lenin's health improved, permitting contact with state affairs, visits by associates, some writing.

September 11. A concilium of medical professors decided to permit Lenin to resume work from October 1.

November. Lenin addressed the Fourth Comintern Congress and a plenary session of the Moscow Soviet —his last public speeches.

December 13. Lenin had two further strokes, and was persuaded to give up all work for the time being.

Night of December 15–16. An acute worsening took place in Lenin's condition.

Night of December 22–23. A further worsening; paralysis of the right arm and leg.

December 23. Lenin asked the doctors to allow him to dictate to stenographers for five minutes because he was "concerned about one question." He then dictated the first part of his "Letter to the Congress."

December 24. Lenin demanded permission to dictate a "diary" for at least a brief time each day. After a conference of Stalin, Kamenev, and Bukharin with the doctors, it was decided that he should be allowed to dictate for five to ten minutes daily, but not to engage in correspondence; that no visitors would be allowed; and that he should not be kept informed of political matters.

December 25–26. Lenin finished dictating the "Letter to the Congress."

December 1922–February 1923. Lenin went on dictating his final notes and articles.

1923   January 24. Lenin requested his secretary, L. A. Fotieva, to ask Dzerzhinsky or Stalin for the materials of the Politburo's commission on the Georgian question; he instructed her and two other assistants to study the materials and prepare a report for him, saying that he "needed this for the Party Congress."

February 14. Lenin requested Fotieva to rush completion of all his assignments, particularly on the Georgian question, and instructed her to transmit to A. A. Sol'ts, a member of the presidium of the Central Party Control Commission (concerned with matters of party discipline) his opinion on the Georgian question.

March 5. Lenin dictated letters to Trotsky and Stalin.

March 6. Lenin dictated a letter to the Georgian Communists Mdivani and Makharadze. Later in the day his health took a sharp turn for the worse.

March 10. Lenin suffered a new stroke, which caused intensified paralysis of the right side of the body and loss of speech.

May 15. Lenin was moved to his Gorki country house.

Second half of July. Lenin's condition improved; he could walk and practiced writing left-handed.

October 19. Lenin went by automobile through the Kremlin and streets of Moscow, returned to the Kremlin and took books from its library, then returned to Gorki.

Late November–December. Lenin received several visitors, including Bukharin, Preobrazhensky, and Krestinsky.

1924   January 17–18. Krupskaya read to Lenin a report from *Pravda* on the Thirteenth Party Conference proceedings.

January 19. Lenin went for a sleigh-ride in the woods.

January 19–20. Krupskaya read to Lenin, from *Pravda*, the resolutions of the Thirteenth Party Congress. She later reported that he became disturbed during the reading.[4]

January 21. A sudden sharp worsening of Lenin's condition. Death came at 6:30 P.M.

---

4. The disturbance is understandable, since one of the conference resolutions attacked Trotsky and the "opposition" as representing a "petty-bourgeois deviation in the party"—from which Lenin could see that his fear of a party split caused by the Stalin-Trotsky feud, a fear he had expressed in the "Letter to the Congress," was well-founded; and, further, that Stalin, whom he had planned to unseat from power at the coming Party Congress, had already gained the upper hand in the intra-party struggle.

Introduction

Lenin and Revolution[1]

ROBERT C. TUCKER

Revolutionary politics is that special form of political activity whose object is the radical reconstitution of the political community itself, for which purpose the overthrow of the existing regime and institutions associated with it is usually necessary. For very many reasons—including wars, decolonization, technological change, and the spread of communications—the twentieth century has been a time of revolutionary politics throughout much of the world. Among the revolutionary leaders and theorists who have come to the fore during this time, the most remarkable in many ways and the most influential is Lenin. When the centenary of his birth was officially marked in his homeland, Russia, in 1970, one could see signs in many places saying: "Lenin lived, Lenin lives, Lenin will live." Whatever the truth of that prophecy, and whatever the form of his present survival, the twentieth-century world has been profoundly and pervasively affected by the fact that "Lenin lived."

It is no cause for surprise that this greatest revolutionist of his age was a Russian. The *ancien régime* of the tsardom had held firm long after most other great European states underwent their modern revolutionary renovations. The popular insurrection of 1905 (Lenin would later call it the dress rehearsal for 1917) made plain already that Russia had a rendezvous with revolution. No other country, moreover, with the sole exception of France, had such a rich tradition of revolutionary politics. If a revolutionary politician and thinker of genius was to emerge in the early twentieth century, Russia was the logical place for it to happen.

---

1. This introductory essay has been drawn in large measure from material in Chapter Two of my book *Stalin as* *Revolutionary, 1879–1929: A Study in History and Personality* (New York, 1973).

Lenin and Russian Jacobinism

Lenin must be understood both as the creator of a distinctive version of Marxism as a revolutionary theory and also as a person steeped in the native Russian, non-Marxist revolutionary tradition. He was clearly conscious of himself as a representative and in some sense a continuer of this tradition. In an article of 1912, commemorating the centenary of the birth of the nineteenth-century Russian radical Alexander Herzen, Lenin pictured his own contemporary revolutionary generation as being in direct line of succession to two earlier ones: the generation of revolutionary nobles and landlords whose representatives, the Decembrists,[2] had awakened Herzen, and the later generation of revolutionary commoners (*raznochintsy*) whom Herzen had called "the young helmsmen of the gathering storm." Among the latter Lenin singled out for special mention Nikolai Chernyshevsky, a writer and critic who assumed intellectual leadership of the Russian radicals during the eighteen-fifties, and the heroes (as he called them) of the Narodnaya Volya (People's Will). The People's Will was the secret revolutionary organization whose leaders had carried out the assassination of Tsar Alexander II in 1881.

Between the eighteen-fifties and the eighties the various groups of intellectuals who made up the Russian revolutionary movement were loosely subsumed under the general title of "populists" (*narodniki*). They subscribed to a distinctively Russian socialist ideology the foundations of which had been laid by Herzen. In the intellectual debates of the eighteen-forties between the Russians who called themselves "Slavophiles" and those who were known as "Westerners," Herzen had been a leading Westerner—one of those who saw it as Russia's destiny to progress in the direction already being taken by the most enlightened European nations. However, disillusioning contact with European reality during and after the 1848 Revolution in France (where he had taken up exile) led Herzen to revise his earlier Westernism. Taking his departure from the old Slavophile image of the Russians as a "social people," he propounded the idea that the Russian peasant was an instinctive socialist and that the *mir* (the traditional communal village in Russia) was the nucleus of a future Russian socialist society. If the man of the future in France was the industrial worker, the man of the

---

2. A group of high-born guards officers, influenced by Western constitutional ideas (in some cases while serving abroad after the Russian defeat of Napoleon's army), who made an unsuccessful attempt to stage a troop rising in Petersburg on December 14, 1825, following the death of Tsar Alexander I. In later years their action was seen as the opening episode of the Russian revolutionary movement of the nineteenth century.

future in Russia was the peasant, the *muzhik*; and economically backward, not-yet-capitalist Russia, blessed by the survival of its archaic village commune, might in fact be destined to lead the world to socialism.[3]

The populist belief in Russia's special path and in a "Russian socialism" based on the village commune was not a part of the legacy of Russian revolutionism that found a continuer in Lenin. What he found enduringly valuable in the native revolutionary tradition was something else of importance: its model of the dedicated professional revolutionist and its wealth of experience and lore of clandestine political organization. These aspects of the tradition were associated, in turn, with a doctrine that became known as "Russian Jacobinism." It held that a revolutionary seizure of power from below should be followed by the formation of a dictatorship of the revolutionary party, which would use political power for the purpose of carrying through from above a socialist transformation of Russian society.

One of its early formulations appeared in a populist proclamation circulated in 1862 under the title "Young Russia." The author, P. G. Zaichnevsky, was leader of a secret group at Moscow University. The theory was more fully elaborated by such major figures of the populist movement of the seventies as Pyotr Tkachev and Pyotr Lavrov. According to Tkachev, a ruling elite of revolutionary intellectuals who had conquered political power through "destructive" revolutionary activity from below would utilize this power for "constructive" revolutionary activity from above. Relying chiefly on persuasion of the masses through propaganda rather than on coercion, they would gradually transform the country on socialist lines —building the *mir* into a genuine commune, expropriating private property in the means of production, fostering equality, and encouraging popular self-government to the point where the revolutionary dictatorship would itself no longer be needed. Similarly, the leadership of the People's Will envisaged the establishment of a "provisional revolutionary government" that would carry through a socioeconomic revolution from above, which would be ratified by representatives of the people meeting in a national assembly. Such was Russian Jacobinism in the setting of the populist movement. It had an enduring effect upon history owing to the influence that it exerted upon the political thought of Lenin.

The populists of the seventies had been divided over revolutionary tactics, some advocating the gradual conversion of the peasants

3. For this reasoning see particularly his essay "The Russian People and Socialism," in A. I. Gertsen (Herzen), *Izbrannye filosofskie proizvedeniia* (Moscow, 1946), II, 128–59. For a survey of the populist movement, see Franco Venturi, *Roots of Revolution: A History of the Populist and Socialist Movements in Nineteenth-Century Russia* (New York, 1960).

to their cause through propaganda (as in the "going to the people" movement of that decade) and others arguing for propaganda "by deed," meaning terrorist action. The latter group saw the Russian peasant as a potential rebel against authority, and reasoned that an act like the assassination of the tsar might spark a general conflagration in the countryside, a greater and successful Pugachev movement. The assassination of Alexander II in 1881 aroused no such peasant response, however, and led to more severe reaction under his successor, Alexander III. In the sequel many radicals from the populist camp turned away from the tactics of terrorism and lost faith in the peasantry as a revolutionary constituency. Meanwhile, another potential constituency was appearing in the still small but growing Russian industrial worker class, which numbered upwards of three million before the end of the century.[4] Given all these conditions, it is not surprising that a section of the intelligentsia grew receptive to the ideology of proletarian socialist revolution being propagated by Karl Marx and Friedrich Engels. In a number of European countries there existed by this time Social-Democratic parties professing Marxism as their program and acting in the name of the industrial working class as their principal constituency. In 1883 a populist turned Marxist, Georgi Plekhanov, launched Russian Marxism on its career as an organized movement by forming a group for "The Liberation of Labor" in Geneva, Switzerland, where he resided.

The initial impulse of the movement, which had in Plekhanov a mentor as well as organizer, was the search for new ways in Russian revolutionary politics. The founding documents were Plekhanov's anti-populist tract *Socialism and the Political Struggle* and its continuation, *Our Differences*. In them he concentrated his attack squarely upon Russian Jacobinism. The conception of a seizure of power by a secret conspiratorial organization was a "fantastic element" in the People's Will program. The very notion of a "provisional revolutionary government" exercising tutelage over the people in the process of building a socialist society was objectionable. A dictatorship of the revolutionary party was unnecessary and undesirable; the workers would not want to exchange one form of tutelage for another, and would no longer need "tutors" by the time of their future graduation from the historical school of revolutionary political self-education. Meanwhile, a premature capture of power by an organization like the People's Will, even supposing it to be feasible, would either collapse for want of popular support or

---

4. J. L. H. Keep, *The Rise of Social-Democracy in Russia* (London, 1963), p. 6. The total population of Russia in 1897 was 129 million. Peasants constituted four-fifths of the total. Emilian Pugachev was a Cossack who led a large peasant rebellion in the Volga region in 1773–75. He was ultimately executed.

else issue in a "patriarchal and authoritarian communism" or "Peruvian [that is, hierarchical and authoritarian] communism" should the government survive and try to introduce socialism from above by decree. Hence the revolutionary movement should cease conspiring to seize power and give up all idea of carrying out "social experiments and vivisections" upon the Russian people under the dictatorship of a revolutionary party.[5] As for Russia's Marxists, they should join with other oppositionist strata of society, including liberals, in a political struggle to overthrow tsarist absolutism and establish free political institutions in their country. This democratic revolution would accelerate the pace of Russian economic development and permit a growing industrial proletariat to build its own independent political party like the Social-Democratic parties of Western Europe. In a future socialist revolution the workers would take power as a class.

In these early writings, as it turned out, Plekhanov was laying the theoretical foundations not of the Russian Marxist political movement as a whole but of its Menshevik wing. The opposing, Bolshevik, wing, of which Lenin became leader, showed the influence of some of the very ideas Plekhanov was attacking. But not until much later did all this become clear.

When *Socialism and the Political Struggle* appeared in Geneva in 1883, the future Lenin was a carefree boy of thirteen growing up as Vladimir Ilyich Ulyanov in the town of Simbirsk (now Ulyanovsk), on the Volga. His father, who was school inspector for Simbirsk province and as such a minor member of the nobility, died in 1886. In the following year Vladimir's older brother Alexander, a student at Petersburg University, joined a new People's Will group in a plot to mark the sixth anniversary of Alexander II's assassination by assassinating Alexander III. The plot was foiled. The young man was hanged, having refused on principle, and despite his mother's entreaties, to ask the tsar for clemency. This event greatly helped to propel Vladimir onto his own revolutionary career. His martyred brother became his hero and the annihilation of tsarism his implacable aim.[6]

Soon after entering Kazan University in the fall of 1887 to study

5. G. V. Plekhanov, *Sotsializm i politicheskaia bor'ba. Nashi raznoglasiia* (Moscow, 1939), pp. 59, 60, 65, 88–89.
6. This is not to suggest that his motivation in later life may be summed up under a simple formula. On Vladimir's reaction to Alexander's execution, see Bertram D. Wolfe, *Three Who Made a Revolution* (Boston, 1948), pp. 65–66. For the earlier relations between Alexander and Vladimir, their clash of personalities, see Nikolai Valentinov (N. V. Volski, *The Early Years of Lenin*,

translated by Rolf H. W. Theen (Ann Arbor, Mich., 1969), pp. 118–22. On Vladimir's hero-worship of his executed brother, see Louis Fischer, *The Life of Lenin* (New York, 1964), p. 17. Fischer plausibly speculates that Vladimir's shock and wrath over Alexander's fate were enhanced by "regret not to have been close to the hero brother." On this issue see also Rolf H. W. Theen, *Lenin: Genesis and Development of a Revolutionary* (Philadelphia, 1973).

law, Vladimir was expelled for participation in a student demonstration. The police then exiled him to his grandfather's country estate in Kazan province. In late 1888 he received permission to reside in the city of Kazan, where his mother, sisters, and younger brother joined him. A year later the family moved to Samara (now Kuibyshev), farther south on the Volga. He read for the law examinations on his own, passed them in Petersburg in 1891, and later practiced law briefly in Samara. During all this time, however, his obsessive interest, and the main subject of his reading, was not law but revolution. Among the materials into which he plunged were the populist writings of the sixties and seventies. One that had been his brother's favorite, and now became Vladimir's, was the socialist novel that Chernyshevsky wrote upon being incarcerated in the Peter and Paul Fortress prison in Petersburg in 1862: *What Is to Be Done? Stories about New People.*

In the novel's gallery of radical men and women, the legendary character of Rakhmetov particularly stands out. He is the scion of a landowning family of ancient aristocratic lineage. Soon after arriving in Petersburg at the age of sixteen to study in the university, he undergoes a complete conversion through a meeting with a young man of radical views, and dedicates the remainder of his life to the revolutionary cause. He reads prodigiously. On a trip to Western Europe he insists upon giving away the bulk of his inherited fortune to a poverty-stricken, great thinker and father of a new philosophy, "a German." He cultivates extraordinary physical strength through strenuous exercise, by keeping to a diet of semi-raw beefsteak and black bread, and even by working as a Volga boatman on his wanderings through Russia. He lives ascetically, taking no wine and rejecting the love of a young woman whom he would have wished under normal conditions to marry. On one occasion he tests his capacity to bear pain by spending the night on a bed of sharp nails. Of Rakhmetov and others like him, Chernyshevsky writes in the novel: "They are few in number, but through them flourishes the life of all; without them it would die out and go sour. They are few in number, but they enable all people to breathe; without them people would suffocate. Such ones are few in the great mass of good and honest people, but in that mass they are as the flavor in the tea, the bouquet in the fine wine; the strength and the aroma come from them. They are the flower of the best people, the movers of the movers, the salt of the salt of the earth."

This novel furnished inspiration for several generations of Russian radicals. That it furnished inspiration also for Vladimir Ulyanov is well attested to by, among other things, the fact that he entitled his own revolutionary treatise of 1902—the most important of all his works in historical influence—*What Is to Be Done?* Conversing with friends in a Geneva cafe in January 1904, he confirmed that he had done so with the novel in mind. He angrily rejected a disparaging remark about the literary quality of Chernyshevsky's work, and confessed that it had influenced him profoundly, particularly when he reread it after his brother's execution: "It captivated my brother, and it captivated me. It *made me over completely.* . . . It's something that charges you up for the whole of your life." He went on to explain that "the greatest merit of Chernyshevsky lies not only in showing that any right-minded and truly decent person must be a revolutionary, but also something still more important: he showed what sort of person a revolutionary should be, what rules of conduct he should follow, how he should proceed to his goal, and by what means he should attain it."[7]

Ulyanov's Marxist self-education began in the fall of 1888 in Kazan, where he studied Marx's *Capital* and made contact with a Marxist "circle" (as clandestine study groups were called). It continued intensively after the family's move in the following year to Samara. There too he involved himself in the activities of Marxist circles. But these were not the only contacts that he made. He also sought out and conversed at length with former members of the People's Will who were living in Samara as political exiles. In these conversations with surviving representatives of populism's heroic period, he showed special interest in the old Russian Jacobinists, beginning with Zaichnevsky and his program of revolutionary dictatorship in the manifesto "Young Russia." "In talks with me," wrote one of the exiles much later, "Vladimir Ilyich often dwelt on the question of the seizure of power, one of the points of our Jacobin program. . . . Now more than ever I come to the conclusion that already at that time he was developing the idea of the dictatorship of the proletariat."[8]

There is much to be said for this view. Though initially Lenin accepted Plekhanov's notion of a two-stage revolution in Russia, the thrust of his thinking all along was toward the creation without delay of a revolutionary party dictatorship dedicated to the transformation of Russian society along socialist lines—the dictatorship that he founded in 1917. Thus in 1905 he opposed the Menshevik tactic of supporting the liberals in a strictly bourgeois-democratic revolution against tsarism, and gravitated to the tactic of telescop-

7. N. Valentinov, *Vstrechi s Leninym* (New York, 1953), pp. 103, 108. The author of this invaluable memoir was in 1904 a constant companion of Lenin in Geneva. He later broke with Lenin and joined the Mensheviks. After the Revolution he returned to Russia and worked in the early twenties for a Soviet newspaper, then went abroad and spent the remainder of his long life in emigration. For further biographical particulars see the introduction by Michael Karpovich and foreword by Leonard Schapiro to the English translation, *Encounters with Lenin* (London, 1968), and the introduction by Bertram D. Wolfe to Valentinov's *The Early Years of Lenin.*
8. Valentinov, *Vstrechi,* p. 117.

ing the two stages of revolution under a "democratic dictatorship of the proletariat and peasantry."[9] And when he returned from emigration in April 1917 to a Russia in upheaval, he advocated a strategy of pressing forward from the stage of democratic revolution represented in the Provisional Government to that of socialist revolution via the seizure of power and establishment of a "dictatorship of the proletariat." In an effort to validate this position ideologically, Lenin went back to his Marxist texts during an interval of forced inactivity during 1917 and wrote *The State and Revolution*, his principal work of political theory.

The aim of *The State and Revolution*, as he put it, was to restore to Marxism the "revolutionary soul" that had been let out of it by such leaders of contemporary Social-Democratic Marxism as Karl Kautsky in Germany. The soul of the classical Marxism of Marx and Engels was the teaching that the revolutionary proletarian dictatorship was the necessary political instrument of a society's transition to socialism and future communism. To be a genuine Marxist it was not enough to accept the theory of the class struggle; one also had to accept the doctrine of proletarian dictatorship as the goal and terminal point of this struggle. In practice, moreover, a proletarian dictatorship would mean a dictatorship of the revolutionary party *on behalf* of the proletariat. "By educating the workers' party," as Lenin expressed it, "Marxism educates the vanguard of the proletariat capable of assuming power and *leading* the whole people to socialism, of directing and organizing the new system, of being the teacher, the guide, the leader of all the working and exploited people in organizing their social life without the bourgeoisie and against the bourgeoisie."[1] Consequently, it would be in no sense un-Marxist for the party to seize power and rule dictatorially in the interest of building a socialist society in Russia. This was the practical political conclusion implicit in every line of Lenin's seemingly scholastic theoretical treatise on Marxist views about the state.

It was a very Russian revolutionary soul that he breathed back into Marxism. Admittedly, the teaching on proletarian dictatorship had a significant place in classical Marxism, and one which later Social-Democratic Marxists, including even Engels in his old age, were inclined to downgrade. But it had not the central place accorded it in Lenin's Marxism, nor was the proletarian dictatorship conceived by Marx and Engels as a dictatorship of a revolutionary party on behalf of the proletariat. They did not imagine that the working people, once in power, would have need of a party as their

9. On this see his *Two Tactics of Social-Democracy in the Democratic Revolution*, pp. 120–147, below.

1. See *The State and Revolution*, pp. 311–398, below.

"teacher, guide, and leader" in building a new life on socialist lines. The elevation of the doctrine of the proletarian dictatorship into the "essence" of Marxism, as Lenin later called it,[2] and the conception of this dictatorship as a state in which the ruling party would exercise tutelage over the working people, were a sign of his deep debt to the Russian populist revolutionary tradition. Leninism was in part a revival of Russian Jacobinism within Marxism. Lenin himself must have been well aware of this. It is less clear whether he was aware that indirectly, therefore, his outlook showed the influence of the Russian autocratic tradition that seemed, in 1917, to have reached its end.

The First Decade

Ulyanov moved to Petersburg in 1893, ostensibly to practice law but in fact to engage in socialist activity, and quickly acquired a certain reputation as a learned Marxist from the Volga.[3] Among those whom he met in Marxist circles of the capital were two future Menshevik opponents, Julius Martov and Alexander Potresov, and his future wife, Nadezhda Krupskaya, a young noblewoman involved in after-hours socialist activity while holding a clerical job in the railway administration.

In early 1895, he went abroad for four months, going first to Switzerland, where he met and made a strong impression upon Plekhanov and the latter's associate P. B. Axelrod. On his return he undertook with Martov and others to organize a "St. Petersburg Union of Struggle for the Liberation of the Working Class." These efforts led to his (and Martov's) arrest at the end of 1895. After a year of imprisonment in Petersburg, he was sentenced to three years of exile in eastern Siberia. He and Krupskaya were married when she joined him there in 1898.[4] In July 1900, several months after completing the term of exile, he went abroad again and entered the recently founded Russian Social-Democratic Workers' Party's leadership as one of the editors of *Iskra* (*The Spark*)—a new foreign-based party organ that he himself had done much to organize. Except for his return to Russia during the insurrectionary turmoil of 1905–7, he remained in emigration until 1917, living mainly in Switzerland. Such are the unrevealing externals of his revolutionary biography.

2. For his argument on this point, see his treatise *The Proletarian Revolution and the Renegade Kautsky*, pp. 461–76, below.

3. Nadezhda K. Krupskaya, *Reminiscences of Lenin* (New York, 1970), p. 1.

4. For Krupskaya's life see Robert H. McNeal, *Bride of the Revolution: Krupskaya and Lenin* (Ann Arbor, Mich., 1972), and her own *Reminiscences of Lenin*. Their marriage was childless.

In Petersburg in the early nineties, socialist activity meant discussions in the "circles," writing on issues before the movement, and propagating socialist ideas among workmen. Ulyanov's colossal capacity for work, combined with his powerful and prolific pen, brought him to the fore as a pamphleteer for revolutionary Marxism during that time of controversy between the populist and Marxist branches of the socialist movement, and between militants and moderates within the Marxist branch. In 1894 he struck out at Pyotr Struve, a leading figure among the so-called "Legal Marxists," in a critique nearly as long as the book of Struve's it attacked; and he wrote a book-length polemical reply to an anti-Marxist article in a populist journal.[5] The polemic, entitled *Who Are the "Friends of the People" and How Do They Fight Against the Social-Democrats?*, went through three illegal hectographed editions and seven "printings" between July and November 1894.[6]

Openly political socialist writings, not legally publishable under then-prevailing censorship practices, would either be published abroad and smuggled back into Russia or, as in this instance, duplicated and circulated clandestinely (a forerunner of the present-day *samizdat*, or "self-publishing," as the circulation of uncensored writings in typescript is called in Soviet Russia). Writings of academic style and bulk, such as Struve's book and Ulyanov's long review of it, were publishable legally although various circumlocutions and code words, known to the radicals as "Aesopian language," frequently had to be used. As an example, Plekhanov's influential book of 1895 on *The Development of the Monist View of History* came out legally in Russia. "Monism" was a code word for "Marxism," and the author's name appeared as "Beltov." Among the pen names that Ulyanov used during the first decade were "Ilyin," "Tulin," and "Lenin." Some have suggested that in using the latter his inspiration may have been the Lena, a river in eastern Siberia. "Lenin" would thus carry the connotation of "man from the Lena." Recent Soviet sources confirm this.

The populist-Marxist debates of the nineties were dominated by other issues than those Plekhanov had raised against Russian Jacobinism in his works of the early eighties. The People's Will tradition of conspiratorial terrorism, which still had some support, was only one of several trends among the populist groups that finally united to form the peasant-based party of Socialist-Revolutionaries (SR's) in 1901–2. In the nineties, the two socialist camps were divided chiefly by the *narodnik* rejection of Marxism as a socialist ideology

5. The former was "The Economic Content of Populism and Its Criticism in Mr. Struve's Book," the book in question being Struve's *Critical Remarks on the Question of Russia's Economic Development* (1894). On this controversy see Keep, *Rise of Social-Democracy*, pp. 29–31, 36–37.

6. Lenin, *Polnoe sobranie sochinenii*, I, 656–57.

for Russia, and by a series of economic issues. Lenin's contributions to the debate were notable for their uncompromising defense of the Marxist class-struggle interpretation of history as the only correct theory for the Russian (or any other) revolutionary movement, and for their heavy concentration upon economic issues. He especially opposed the populists' view of capitalism in Russia as a regressive tendency that could and should be stopped, and their belief—associated with idealization of the peasant commune—in Russia's exceptionality.[7] His principal attempt to refute these views was *The Development of Capitalism in Russia*, a treatise produced during his Siberian years on the basis of books consulted in libraries that he was able to visit on the way to the place of exile and other materials brought to him by Krupskaya or sent through the mail by his sister. It sought, in Marxist fashion, to refute the populist position by giving statistical proof that Russian capitalism, which it saw as historically "progressive" no matter how painful its impact, had already undermined the old economy, even in the countryside. "The Russia of the wooden plough and flail, of the water mill and hand loom," it concluded, "has entered upon rapid transformation into a Russia of the metal plough and threshing machine, the steam mill and steam-powered loom."[8]

In the Marxist-populist debates of the nineties Lenin trained his polemical fire upon his populist contemporaries; he did not attack the early Russian populism of Chernyshevsky and his generation. As if to underline how much importance he attached to this distinction, he constructed one of his essays around the theme that the Marxists had more claim than the populists to the intellectual legacy of that early generation. This thesis was based on the highly strained argument that the thinkers of the sixties (whom Lenin called "enlighteners" rather than populists), neither believed in Russia's special character (*samobytnost'*) nor idealized its village life, but desired its "assimilation into general European culture."[9] Evidently it was through this kind of reasoning that Lenin recon-

---

7. Lenin, *Polnoe sobranie sochinenii*, II, 532–33. On the populist-Marxist debate, see Keep, *Rise of Social-Democracy*, pp. 28–38. For later populist thought see James H. Billington, *Mikhailovsky and Russian Populism* (Oxford, 1958).
8. Lenin, *Polnoe sobranie sochinenii*, III, 597–98. This book was sufficiently historical and statistical to pass the censorship, and was legally published in Petersburg in 1899. Lenin, who was still in Siberia then, signed it "Vladimir Ilyin."
9. "What Legacy Do We Renounce?" in Lenin, *Polnoe sobranie sochinenii*, II, 533. Written in Siberia in 1897, this essay was published legally in Petersburg in

the following year. To assure its approval by the censors, Lenin had to use considerable Aesopian language. Thus he chose as a representative figure of the men of the sixties an obscure writer of liberal persuasion named Skaldin. In a letter of 1899 to Potresov he revealed that he had used Skaldin as a code-word for Chernyshevsky, and also that he had overstated the case. On these points see *Polnoe sobranie sochinenii*, IV, 544, and Keep, *Rise of Social-Democracy*, p. 38. Although Chernyshevsky had died in 1882, after twenty years of prison and exile, his name remained unmentionable from the censors' point of view.

ciled his adamant opposition to contemporary populism with his continuing conviction that the Marxist party had much to learn from the pre-Marxist Russian revolutionary tradition. He simply refrained from identifying the latter as populist.

His political writings around the turn of the century reflect the emergence of Leninism (a word he himself never used) as an amalgam of the Russian revolutionary heritage and Marxism. One of his themes was the paramount importance of the practical side of the movement—program, organization, and tactics. This he emphasized in *The Tasks of the Russian Social-Democrats*, a pamphlet written in Siberia in 1897 for uncensored publication abroad and, appropriately, the first of his writings to appear under the name "Lenin." True, he took issue here with a surviving great figure of the populist movement of the sixties and seventies, Pyotr Lavrov. Now living abroad, Lavrov had recently questioned the possibility of creating a workers' party in Russia without organizing "a political *conspiracy* against absolutism" in the tradition of the People's Will. Respectfully referring to him as "a veteran of revolutionary *theory*," Lenin rejected the idea of confining the revolutionary political struggle to a small group's conspiracy to seize power. The battle against absolutism should consist, he said, not in hatching plots but in training, disciplining, and organizing the workers, in propaganda and agitation among them. But save for its focus on workers instead of peasants, this approach also formed a part, as Lenin well knew, of the populist heritage. So did his way of identifying "absolutism" as the supreme enemy. After observing that bureaucracy ("a special stratum of people specializing in government and placed in a privileged position vis-à-vis the people") existed everywhere, he remarked that nowhere was this institution so unchecked as in "absolutist, semi-Asiatic Russia." Consequently, not only the proletariat but many other elements of the people were arrayed against "the omnipotent, irresponsible, corrupt, savage, ignorant, and parasitic Russian bureaucracy."[1] It has been observed that one common characteristic of "classical populism" in all its forms was the feeling that the "Russian state of bureaucratic absolutism has been the primordial enemy of the popular masses and their intrinsic communal-socialist tendencies."[2]

In the editorial of the first issue of *Iskra*, published in December 1900, Lenin again underlined the cardinal importance of practical organizational questions, and added: "In this respect we have lagged

1. For *The Tasks of the Russian Social-Democrats* see pp. 3–11, below.
2. Theodore Dan, *The Origins of Bolshevism* (New York, 1964), p. 143. A prominent figure among the Russian Mensheviks, Dan took part in the Russian Revolution, was deported in 1922, and lived abroad for the remainder of his life. This book was originally published in a Russian edition in New York in 1946.

greatly behind the old figures of the Russian revolutionary movement." The party should recognize the deficiency, he said, and direct its efforts to devising a more conspiratorial arrangement of its affairs, to systematic propaganda of the rules of procedure and methods of evading the police, and to the training of people prepared to devote to revolution not just their free evenings but their whole lives.[3] Lenin returned to organizational questions in his editorial for *Iskra*, No. 4, in May 1901. This time he spoke of the party's need for a fully worked out "plan" of revolutionary organization, and outlined some features of a plan that he promised to present in greater detail in a booklet then being prepared for the press.

"Organizational questions," Lenin's views on them in particular, were a fateful bone of contention when fifty-seven delegates from Russia and abroad met in Brussels in July 1903 for the Russian Social-Democratic Workers' Party's Second Congress—a meeting with more claim than an earlier one in Minsk to be considered the constituent congress. When it came time to adopt the party's rules, Lenin and Martov submitted different drafts of clause one, which defined the meaning of membership in the party. Though superficially their formulas were very much alike,[4] the small difference reflected a large issue. Lenin's was the "hard" position, Martov's the "soft." Martov at first had a majority, but lost it owing to the withdrawal from the congress of the delegates of the Jewish Workers' Bund and one other small group of his supporters. (The Bund was an organization founded in 1897 to represent the interests of Jewish workers in Lithuania, Poland, and Russia. It entered the Russian Social-Democratic Workers' Party at its founding congress in 1898, but subsequently withdrew.) Consequently, Lenin and his followers went down in history as the *Bolsheviki* (majorityites); their opponents, as the *Mensheviki* (minorityites).

The Beginning of Bolshevism

In the aftermath of the congress the split widened as those involved grew more clearly aware of the depth of the divergence over Lenin's centralistic conception of the revolutionary party. Ple-

3. Lenin, *Polnoe sobranie sochinenii*, IV, 376.
4. For details, plus an account of the congress and preceding events, see Leonard Schapiro, *The Communist Party of the Soviet Union* (New York, 1959), ch. 2. The difference was that Lenin's draft required, along with acceptance of the party's program and material support, the member's "personal participation in one of the party organizations," whereas this portion of Martov's draft provided only that the member must give the party "his regular personal cooperation under the direction of one of the party organizations." The party's First Congress was held clandestinely in Minsk in 1898, with only a handful of participants.

khanov, who now joined Martov, Axelrod, Trotsky, and others in the anti-Lenin camp, questioned the authenticity of Lenin's Marxism and drew a comparison between him and Bakunin with respect to their centralism.[5] Trotsky contended that Lenin was more of a Jacobin than a Marxist and made his often-quoted prediction that "these methods lead, as we shall yet see, to this: the party organization is substituted for the party, the Central Committee is substituted for the party organization, and finally the 'dictator' is substituted for the Central Committee."[6] Soon the friction between "hards" and "softs" took on organizational form as a division between factions. During a few years of unpeaceful factional coexistence there were efforts, sponsored by Trotsky among others, toward unification. The split became formal and irrevocable in 1912 when Lenin called an all-Bolshevik meeting in Prague, where his faction constituted itself the "Russian Social-Democratic Workers' Party (Bolshevik)."

Born in strife, the original party of Russian Marxists died in schism. But this account of events is no adequate explanation of the origin of Bolshevism as a political movement. Underlying the division at the Second Congress was Lenin's organizational "plan." This he set forth prior to the congress in the booklet promised in "Where to Begin." Printed in Stuttgart in March 1902, under the title *What Is to Be Done? Burning Questions of Our Movement*, the booklet went into Russia by the usual clandestine methods and was soon circulating among Marxists all over the country. During 1902–3, copies of it were found in searches of Social-Democrats arrested in Petersburg, Moscow, Kiev, Nizhnii Novgorod, Kazan, Odessa, and elsewhere. Reactions to it were strong.

The Russian Marxist movement was then experiencing serious internal malaise following its rapid growth during the controversy with the populists during the nineties. It had entered a period of "dispersion, dissolution, and vacillation," as Lenin observed in the booklet. The vacillation was reflected in the appearance of "Economism," a school of Marxist thought which held that revolutionary struggle for socialist aims was premature in underdeveloped Russia and that her Marxists should therefore confine themselves for the present to assisting the workers in their fight for economic benefits. This of course was deeply dispiriting counsel for militant Marxists impatient to get on with the political task of overthrowing the

5. G. V. Plekhanov, *Sochineniia*, XIII (Moscow and Leningrad, 1926), pp. 116–33 and 134 n. The article, entitled "The Working Class and the Social-Democratic Intelligentsia," appeared in *Iskra* in July–August 1904.
6. For this see Robert V. Daniels, *The*

Conscience of the Revolution: Communist Opposition in Soviet Russia (Cambridge, Mass., 1960), p. 13. Another critic, cited here by Daniels, denounced Lenin in *Iskra* for his "cult of the professional revolutionary."

autocracy. To renounce revolutionary political action for the fore-seeable future was completely repugnant to them. Consequently, in the prevailing atmosphere of uncertainty and doubt, they were all the more receptive to the prospectus for political action and the vibrant message of revolutionary hope and faith which came to them in *What Is to Be Done?*

Every page of this pamphlet reflected a Hannibalian hate for "the shame and curse of Russia," as Lenin called the tsarist autoc-racy. It poured scorn on the "tailism" that invited Marxists to drag along in the rear of the workers' movement instead of marching in the van and giving it direction. It summoned militant Marxists to form a "new guard" under whose aegis Russian Social-Democracy would emerge from its crisis into the full strength of manhood. It breathed a spirit of revolutionary voluntarism, of confidence in the capacity of such a small but well-organized elite of Marxist revolu-tionaries to build up an oppositional mass movement in Russian society and lead it to victory over the seemingly impregnable tsarist government. Most important of all, it prescribed in clear and defi-nite terms that should be *done* towards this end, and thus it pointed the way for Russian Marxists from revolutionary talk to revolu-tionary action, gave them a practical plan and tasks to perform.

What was to be done, first of all, was to create the right kind of revolutionary party organization for Russia's special conditions. As if to reveal the inspiration that his plan drew from the populist tradition, Lenin devoted some glowing lines in this connection to the memory of "the magnificent organization which the revolution-aries had in the seventies, and which should serve us all as a model." He argued that the Russian Marxist party, unlike its coun-terparts in Germany and other freer countries in the West, should not seek a mass working-class membership, although it should strive to link itself with masses of workers and other discontented elements of society through party-infiltrated trade unions, study circles, and similar intermediate groups. To meet the needs of con-spiratorial operation in the tsarist police state, the party should consist chiefly of persons trained in the art of revolutionary activity and prepared to make it their full-time occupation. It was of course this idea that underlay Lenin's draft of clause one of the rules at the Second Congress. His and Martov's differing formulations on party membership were predicated upon differing conceptions of the party itself. But only one of these—Lenin's—was clearly thought out.

The theme of the pamphlet was the necessity of leadership for successful revolution. The party was conceived as a leadership group that would play an essential part in "making" the political revolution by giving ideological guidance to the masses and directing the revolutionary movement. In Lenin's Archimedean metaphor, "Give us an organization of revolutionaries, and we shall overturn the whole of Russia!" If classical Marxism proclaimed the imminence of world proletarian revolution, Leninism (or "Marxism-Leninism," as it became known in the Soviet Union after Lenin's death) originated in the proposition that there is no proletarian revolution except through the party. But it also advanced a further thesis: the leadership to be furnished by the elite party must be heroic in caliber. To be able to overturn the whole of Russia, the organization must consist of revolutionaries of special mold. Social-Democrats should take as their ideal not the trade union secretary but the "tribune of the people, able to react to every manifestation of tyranny and oppression." They should be prepared to accomplish, as individuals, great revolutionary deeds. Lenin invoked the name of the German Social-Democratic leader Bebel and those of famous Russian populist revolutionaries of the seventies—Alexeyev, Myshkin, Khalturin, and Zhelyabov—to show what "miracles" individuals could perform in the revolutionary cause.[7] Clearly, in taking the title of Chernyshevsky's *What Is to Be Done?* as his own, Lenin was saying that the contemporary struggle against tsarism had need of men like Rakhmetov.

This call to revolutionary heroism sounded a new note in Russian Marxist writings. The historical role of individuals was one of the subjects of the earlier controversy with the populists. The latter contended that Marxist economic determinism precluded their opponents from recognizing the influence of great men upon historical events. The Marxists, for their part, accused the populists of disregarding class analysis of social phenomena in favor of a theory of "hero and crowd" according to which historical progress issues from the impingement of outstanding individuals' thought upon the minds of the uncreative mass of humanity. Such, indeed, had been the theme of Lavrov's *Historical Letters*, a series of articles originally published in a Russian journal in 1868–69. For Lavrov the prime movers of change and advance in history were critically thinking, justice-seeking individuals whose awareness of the imperfection of existing social forms was forever disturbing the sleepy peace of the "human ant-heap." Answering the imaginary objection that mere individuals could never avail against the custom-bound mass of people, he wrote: "But how has history proceeded? Who has moved it? Solitary fighting personalities. And how have they managed to do this? By becoming, as they had to become, a force." Then he visualized the method of becoming a force. A small num-

7. For *What Is to Be Done?* see pp. 11–119, below. Andrei Zhelyabov (1850–81) was an organizer and leader of the People's Will. August Bebel (1840–1913) was one of the founders of the German Social-Democratic party.

ber of critically thinking, committed, and energetic personalities, realizing that "only through organization is victory possible," would form a "social party" of struggle for truth and justice, seeking in the process to enlist the support of allies among the masses "who have not reached the point of critical thought but suffer from the very same social ills that the party is being organized for the purpose of eliminating."[8] This book became the Bible of young Russian radicals of the seventies and a major influence on populist thought.

Presenting the contrary, Marxist, view in a pamphlet of 1898 on *The Role of Individuals in History*, Plekhanov argued that the personal qualities of historical figures could affect only individual features of events, not the general trend. Had Napoleon Bonaparte been struck down by a bullet early in life, some other individual of comparable capacity would have come forward to accomplish his life work and the course of history would have been the same. But in an effort to show how Marxism could take account of the "particle of truth" in the great-man theory, Plekhanov allowed that individuals could make a mark upon history by *accelerating* the socioeconomically predetermined course of human development. "A great man is great not because his personal qualities give individual features to great historical events," he explained, "but because he possesses qualities that make him most capable of serving the great social needs of his time."[9] This became the generally accepted Russian Marxist position.

Although Lenin did not directly take issue with it, his own outlook differed radically. The novel whose title he took for the exposition of his revolutionary plan could well be described as a dramatization of Lavrov's philosophy of revolution, and the Lenin of *What Is to Be Done?* as a Marxist Lavrov. He too believed that only through organization is victory possible. He too wanted to organize a party of struggle for change whose influence would spread out in concentric circles from a nucleus of committed, energetic, and enlightened leaders—in this case enlightened by Marxist theory. He too saw the social ills of the great, backward, bureaucratically misruled Russian Empire as sources of material suffering that made it possible for the party of heroes to attract a mass following to its banners. Despite his sincere and fervent acceptance of Marxism, Lenin was so much the prototypical radical Russian intellectual, so

8. P. L. Lavrov, *Filosofiia i sotsiologiia. Izbrannye proizvedeniia* (Moscow, 1965), II, 112, 119, 126–28. Lavrov, it may be noted, had presented the main kernel of this philosophy in his *Outlines of Questions of Practical Philosophy* (1859). For this see *ibid.*, I, 459–60. The Lavrovian point of view finds clear expression in Chernyshevsky's *What Is to Be Done?*
9. G. V. Plekhanov, *The Role of Individuals in History* (New York, 1940), pp. 48–52, 56, 59. On the issue with the populists, see *The Development of the Monist View of History*, in Plekhanov, *Selected Philosophical Works* (Moscow, n.d.), I, 647–49, 742–43, 787, 823.

steeped in the Russian revolutionary lore of the sixties and seventies, that his plan of revolution came out with a striking underlying structural resemblance to that offered in the *Historical Letters*. And like the earlier work, it was received by some as a gospel.

To Plekhanov, Lenin's mode of reasoning was bound to seem, on reflection, un-Marxist. There was no place in Plekhanovist thinking for an exuberant faith in the power of Social-Democratic Rakhmetovs to work wonders in the revolutionary cause and thereby make history. Not surprisingly, Plekhanov charged that Lenin was reviving the old populist theory of heroes and the crowd, with the sole difference that Lenin's revolutionary heroes were to lead a proletarian rather than a peasant crowd. He explained the belatedness of his critical reaction to *What Is to Be Done?* by saying that only *after* the Second Congress had it become clear to him what an "enormous influence" the pamphlet was having upon the party's practical workers, and to what an extent it owed this influence to its very errors. "Lenin," he is also reported to have said, "wrote a catechism for our practical workers, not a theoretical but a practical work, as a result of which many began to revere him and proclaim him a Social-Democratic Solomon."[1]

The older man's acid comment paid unwitting tribute to the strength of Lenin's work, its electric appeal to many of the "practical workers" in the movement. Particularly at that time of demoralization, they most needed what Lenin offered: a practical plan and program designed to further the realization of the party's revolutionary goal. It gave the activists in the movement the clear revolutionary perspective that they craved, and an invitation to carry on revolutionary activities not only among the factory workers but in all strata of the population with grievances against an oppressive regime. More important still, it encouraged them to believe that a people's victory over tsarism was a real possibility—as, indeed, 1905 soon showed it to be. No wonder, then, that Lenin's booklet evoked an ardent response from many Russian Marxists. A report from the *Iskra* organization to the Second Congress said that according to their own testimony numerous persons inside Russia were becoming *Iskra* adherents because of this work. "It gave us practical workers what we particularly needed," recalled a younger brother of Martov's who at the time was a committeeman in Kharkov.[2] Valentinov, then a member of a circle of young Social-

---

1. Plekhanov, *Sochineniia*, XIII, 133–34, 139. The comment on Lenin's "catechism," quoted by N. Valentinov in *Vstrechi s Leninym* (New York, 1953), p. 55, may have been made orally. (See note 7, p. xxxi, above.)
2. Quoted in Keep, *Rise of Social-Democ-* racy, p. 93, from Levitsky, *Za chetvert' veka* (Moscow and Leningrad, 1926), p. 122. The original family name of Martov and Levitsky was Tsederbaum. On the report of the *Iskra* organization to the Second Congress, see Lenin, *Polnoe sobranie sochinenni*, VI, 465.

Democrats in Kiev, remembers that the whole group greeted the appearance of *What Is to Be Done?* with great enthusiasm and even began to view Lenin as the logical man to become leader of the party at the coming Second Congress. He also recalls how receptive the group was to Lenin's theme of individual revolutionary heroism.[3]

However foreign it may have been to the spirit of historical materialism, this appeal to herculean efforts by revolutionary heroes made heady reading for young Marxist revolutionaries carrying on clandestine political activity in the Russian provinces under conditions that were often drearily discouraging. One such person was the future Stalin, then an obscure practical worker in Transcaucasia. He was one of those who began to revere Lenin as a Social-Democratic Solomon. In a letter of 1904 to a fellow Georgian revolutionary living in Leipzig, he unreservedly associated himself with Lenin's views and confessed that Lenin was his chosen leader. He scornfully dismissed Plekhanov's criticisms of *What Is to Be Done?* What he found particularly attractive in Lenin's pamphlet was the doctrine of leadership, the theory that it was the mission of the Marxist intelligentsia to raise the proletariat to a consciousness of the socialist ideal rather than "break this ideal up into small change or adjust it to the spontaneous movement."[4]

It is generally accepted that the beginnings of Bolshevism as a separate movement within the Russian Social-Democracy date from around 1903. But this development, as suggested earlier, is not to be satisfactorily explained by the conflict to which the movement owed its name. What gave Bolshevism its original impetus, indeed what brought it into being, was not the quarrel at the Second Congress; it was the appearance of *What Is to Be Done?* Even prior to this Lenin was the author of widely read writings and a figure to be reckoned with among Russian Marxists. But it was the inspirational power of his pamphlet of 1902 that elevated him in the eyes of many and made him the central figure of an actual movement. What was reflected in all this, apart from the cogency of Lenin's ideas to the minds of some of his contemporaries, was the appearance on the Russian revolutionary horizon of a charismatic leader-personality.

The Leader-Centered Movement

Charismatic authority, which Max Weber contrasts with "traditional" and "rational-legal" types of authority, is described by him

3. Valentinov, *Vstrechi*, pp. 53–55.
4. I. V. Stalin, *Sochineniia*, 13 vols. (Moscow, 1946–52), I, 56–58.

as repudiating the past and representing a "specifically revolutionary force." It comes into the world proclaiming the need for and
possibility of profound change. The classical manifestation is the
outlook of the religious prophet who says, "It is written . . . , but I
say unto you. . . ." Weber's implication is that charismatic authority occurs in the context of a social movement that may arise
outside of and in any event is in some manner opposed to the
existing order—a radical movement, be it of religious, political,
cultural, or other complexion. Such movements typically attract
persons who are experiencing some form of acute distress—social,
economic, psychic, or a combination of these—and who respond
eagerly to the promise of deliverance from it. An individual in
whom this promise appears to be embodied, whether by virtue of
his coming forward with a gospel of radical change or his ability to
show the way to change, is a candidate for the role of charismatic
leader.

Imbued with a sense of mission, he offers himself as one especially qualified to be the leader of a movement for change. His
followers, who are also typically his disciples, freely accept his
leadership because they perceive him to be the possessor of extraordinary qualities or powers; and this "recognition" of his special
qualification is seen by Weber as decisive for the validity of charisma.[5] To say this is not to imply any irrationality on the part of
either leader or followers, but only that his charismatic authority
has a definite messianic quality. It therefore arouses their intense
and enthusiastic devotion. The strong emotional bond that grows
up in these circumstances may find expression, either during his
lifetime or after his death, in a cult of the leader. Indeed, we may
hypothesize that the followers' spontaneous emotional tendency to
surround the leader with a personality cult is one of the characteristic signs of charisma.

The narrowly based revolutionary movement of nineteenth-
century Russia produced its heroes, who also in most cases became
its martyrs, but no pronounced charismatic leadership emerged.
However, there was in the Russian intelligentsia a definite receptiv-
ity to such leadership. A profound alienation from official Russian
society and commitment to visionary social goals characterized the
radical intellectual as a human type. Conditions of life in Russia so
filled him with revulsion that fundamental revolution became, in
very many instances, an acutely felt personal need, a cause worth

5. Max Weber, *The Theory of Social
and Economic Organization* (New York,
1947), pp. 359–62. Also, Max Weber,
"The Three Types of Legitimate Rule,"
*Berkeley Publications in Society and In-
stitutions*, IV, 1 (Summer 1958), 1–11;
and *From Max Weber: Essays in Sociology*, ed. H. G. Gerth and C. Wright Mills
(New York, 1958), p. 52. For a discussion of the charisma concept and the
literature pertaining to it, see Robert C.
Tucker, "The Theory of Charismatic
Leadership," *Daedalus* (Summer 1968),
pp. 731–56.

dedicating or even sacrificing one's life to. Persons of such outlook were to be found in all sections of the revolutionary milieu, including Marxist circles, and were capable of responding with passionate devotion to a revolutionary leader of extraordinary or charismatic quality when one at last appeared.

Far more than Menshevism and other Russian radical groups of the time, Bolshevism was a leader-centered movement. As a faction and later as an independent party, it was essentially Lenin's political following in Russian Marxism. As Menshevik opponents liked to say, it was "Lenin's sect." Certain currents of political thought and ideology were, to be sure, associated with it. But to be a Bolshevik in the early years was not so much to accept a particular set of beliefs as it was to gravitate into the orbit of Lenin as a political mentor, revolutionary strategist, and personality.

The gravitational pull of Lenin as a personality appears to have been very strong. In a book of sketches of Bolshevik leaders written many years later, A. V. Lunacharsky, one of Lenin's Old Bolshevik companions, spoke of his "magnetism" (*ocharovanie*). "This magnetism is colossal," he asserted. "People who come into his orbit not only accept him as a political leader but in some strange fashion fall in love with him. This is true of people of the most varied caliber and mental disposition—from such a delicately vibrating enormous talent as Gorky to some clumsy *muzhik* from Penza Gubernia, from first-class political minds like Zinoviev to some sailor or soldier who only yesterday belonged to the Black Hundred gangs and today is ready at any time to lay down his wild head for 'the leader of world revolution—Ilyich.' "[6] Testimony from a multitude of sources supports this comment.

The historical core of Lenin's following was a little group of political émigrés in Geneva who became known as the "Bolshevik colony." A vivid picture of this group and of Lenin as its central figure comes from Valentinov. Having been won to Lenin's views from afar by his reading of *What Is to Be Done?* this young revolutionary made his way to Geneva in early 1904, after escaping from a Kiev jail, and was received into the Bolshevik colony. It proved to be a group of people who regarded themselves as Lenin's disciples and were worshipful in their attitude towards him. Although he was then only thirty-three years old, they habitually referred to him as the "Old Man" (*starik*), thereby expressing profound respect for his Marxist erudition and his wisdom in all matters pertaining to revolution. "The *starik* is wise," remarked one

6. A. V. Lunacharsky, *Revoliutsionnye siluety* (Moscow, 1923), pp. 12–13. (English translation: *Revolutionary Silhouettes* [New York, 1968].) The phrase "Old Bolshevik," used above of Luna-charsky, refers in Soviet usage to one who joined the Bolshevik Party before 1917 and took part in its revolutionary activity.

member of the group to Valentinov. "No one before him has taken apart so delicately and well the levers and screws of the mechanism of Russian capitalism." A belief in Lenin's great historical mission was also expressed. As one member of the group put it: "Ilyich will show us all who he is. Just wait, just wait—the day will come. Then everyone will see what a big, what a very big man he is." Despite his own enthusiasm for the leader, Valentinov was abashed at first by the almost religious "reverential atmosphere" that surrounded Lenin in the colony. Then, little by little, he too became greatly enamored of Lenin: "To say that I 'fell in love with him' would be a little comical, but this verb probably expresses best the attitude that I felt toward Lenin for many months."[7]

Not all the revolutionaries who came into direct contact with Lenin had this reaction, and among those who did there were some, like Valentinov himself, who later broke away and rejected Lenin as a mentor and leader. Yet it attests to the remarkable strength of Lenin's magnetism that it at least temporarily drew into his orbit not only those who responded positively to his way of political thinking but even some whose tendency was to oppose it. Martov, to cite a particularly significant example, is said to have "fallen under the spell of Lenin's personality" during the time of their collaboration as editors of *Iskra*, "scarcely realizing whither he was being led."[8] Another fellow editor and subsequent Menshevik leader, Potresov, published much later a memoir that is remarkable both as a personal confession and as a diagnosis of Lenin's charismatic quality:

> No one could so fire others with his plans, no one could so impose his will and conquer by force of his personality as this seemingly so ordinary and somewhat coarse man who lacked any obvious sources of charm. . . . Neither Plekhanov nor Martov nor anyone else possessed the secret radiating from Lenin of positively hypnotic effect upon people—I would even say, domination of them. Plekhanov was treated with deference, Martov was loved, but Lenin alone was followed unhesitatingly as the only indisputable leader. For only Lenin represented that rare phenomenon, especially rare in Russia, of a man of iron will and indomitable energy who combines fanatical faith in the movement, the cause, with no less faith in himself. If the French king, Louis XIV, could say, *L'état c'est moi*, Lenin, without putting it into words, always had the feeling, *Le parti c'est moi*, that in him the will of the movement was concentrated in one man. And he acted accordingly. I recall that Lenin's sense of mission to be the leader at one time made an impression upon me also.[9]

7. Valentinov, *Vstrechi*, pp. 72–73, 75, 79.
8. Keep, *Rise of Social-Democracy*, p. 126.
9. A. I. Potresov, *Posmertny sbornik proizvedenii* (Paris, 1937), p. 301. The article on Lenin in which this passage appears was originally published in Germany in the journal *Die Gesellschaft*, Book II (1927).

As Potresov pointed out, there was little in Lenin's appearance to explain his "hypnotic effect upon people." Short, stocky, and bald, he struck some as resembling a Russian peasant. Aside from the driving physical energy and strength he exuded, the only physical attribute that particularly impressed others was his eyes, which were variously described as "penetrating," "flashing," "all-seeing," "unusual," and "emitting little blue sparks in the corners."[1] He was, it is universally agreed, totally unpretentious in manner, a person of utmost directness and sincerity.

It was on the speaker's platform that Lenin showed the special powers by virtue of which his followers set him apart from ordinary men. These were not gifts of brilliant oratory such as those for which Trotsky became famous. Lenin's speaking style was completely free of histrionics and striving for effect. Speaking in matter-of-fact tones, although articulately and with concentrated intensity, Lenin would launch directly into the subject at hand and present a clear, logically reasoned analysis replete with supporting facts. The effect upon his listeners was often quite extraordinary. Over and over he demonstrated the power to raise his party audiences to a pitch of excitement, a veritable state of exaltation. Listening to his two speeches at the Bolshevik conference of 1905 in Tammerfors, for example, the normally reserved Stalin, like the rest of the company, was carried away. "I was captivated by that irresistible force of logic in them which, although somewhat terse, thoroughly overpowered his audience, gradually electrified it, and then, as the saying goes, carried it away completely," he recalled. "I remember that many of the delegates said: 'The logic of Lenin's speeches is like a mighty tentacle which seizes you on all sides as in a vise and from whose grip you are powerless to tear yourself away: you must either surrender or make up your mind to utter defeat.' "[2] Similar reminiscences abound in the memoir literature. To cite a vivid one, Max Eastman was moved to a state of "Pindaric rapture" while watching Lenin speak in public for the next to last time, in November 1922, and afterwards described him in a note as "the most powerful man I ever saw on the platform." Lenin appeared to him "a granite mountain of sincerity" of whom "you feel that he is all there for you—you are receiving the whole of the man." It was as though a selfless intellectual had at last appeared on the scene of history, and "he was taking us inside his mind and showing us how the truth looks."[3]

1. *Zhivoi Lenin. Vospominaniia pisatelei o V. I. Lenine*, ed. N. I. Krutikova (Moscow, 1965), p. 48; *Takim byl Lenin. Vospominaniia sovremennikov*, ed. G. Zhuk (Moscow, 1965), pp. 104, 118, 499, 500. Louis Fischer writes that Lenin's eyes had "an X-ray quality" (*The Life of Lenin* [New York, 1964], p. 625).

2. I. V. Stalin, *Sochineniia*, VI, 55.
3. Max Eastman, *Love and Revolution: My Journey Through an Epoch* (New York, 1964), pp. 334–35. Eastman came to Moscow in the early twenties as an enthusiast of the Revolution. He married the sister of a prominent Bolshevik and was befriended by Trotsky, among others.

Since Lenin wrote as he spoke, his political writings had something of the compelling quality of his political speeches. Not surprisingly, the genre in which he expressed himself to greatest effect was the lengthy pamphlet on the order of *What Is to Be Done?* At intervals in the years after 1902, he produced a whole series of them: *One Step Forward, Two Steps Back; Two Tactics of Social-Democracy in the Democratic Revolution; The Right of Nations to Self-Determination; Imperialism, the Highest Stage of Capitalism; The State and Revolution; The Proletarian Revolution and the Renegade Kautsky;* and *"Left-Wing" Communism—An Infantile Disorder.* These pamphlet-treatises shaped the strategy and outlook of Bolshevism and were landmarks in its history. Although they contained many excursions into Marxist theory, basically they subordinated theoretical concerns to the practical needs and problems of the revolutionary movement. In this they continued the tendency of *What Is to Be Done?*, which made the Marxist theory of revolution into a theory of how to make a revolution. It might therefore be said that they elevated the practical needs and problems of the movement to the level of theory. Even in his one abstract philosophical treatise, *Materialism and Empirio-criticism* (1909), Lenin was preoccupied with practical needs of the movement as he perceived them, in this case with the need for a doctrinaire Marxist theory of the universe as an ideological foundation; and, appropriately enough, one of the book's themes was the "party character" of philosophy itself. Some Russian Marxist minds of speculative theoretical bent were repelled. But this and other writings of Lenin exerted a hypnotic power over many others precisely *because* of the spirit of partisan practicality that permeated them.

There shone through in Lenin's speeches and writings not only an inflexible will to revolution but a belief in it, a confidence that a socialist revolution would come about in Russia and that he and his followers would lead it. Potresov rightly pointed to this quality of revolutionary faith as a prime source of Lenin's charisma. To appreciate its full significance, we must recall how hard it was in the early years of the century for Russian revolutionaries to preserve faith in the success of their cause. In Chekhov's Russia, as the poet Valery Briusov recalled in 1920, people like himself had pictured the revolution as a far-off event that they were not likely to see in their own lifetimes: "Now, for example, there is talk of travel to other planets, but few of us hope to see them. That is exactly how far away the Russian Revolution seemed to us then. To foresee that the Revolution was not so far away and that now was the time to be moving towards it—this was possible only for a man of colossal wisdom. And this is what astonishes me most of all in Lenin."[4]

4. *Zhivoi Lenin*, p. 238. Briusov gave the speech in the Press Club in Moscow on the occasion of Lenin's fiftieth birthday.

Lenin had managed to communicate to people who yearned for socialist revolution without seriously expecting it a feeling that such a revolution was a real possibility, and in doing this he was ministering to their deep-seated need for confidence in their own commitment.

It is true that the upheaval of 1905 exposed the inner weakness of the monarchy behind its imposing façade of power, and showed that mass revolution was a potentiality in Russia. But as this revolutionary wave receded and the tsarist regime consolidated itself, the rank-and-file of the revolutionary parties deserted en masse. Many members of the radical intelligentsia began to question the revolutionary beliefs by which they had lived. Russian Marxists showed a tendency to renounce clandestine political activity, thereby succumbing to what Lenin saw as the heresy of "liquidationism." The revolutionary movement as a whole experienced a period of disintegration, stagnation, and decline. And another time of severe trial ensued with the coming of the World War in 1914.

Later testimony from prominent Bolsheviks suggests that Lenin's faith and fortitude during those times of adversity may have been of decisive importance for the Bolshevik movement. Stalin, for one, places great stress on Lenin's instilling of confidence in his dispirited Bolshevik followers after their defeat at the Stockholm "Unity Congress" in 1906 at the hands of a Menshevik majority. Defeat, he says, "transformed Lenin into a spring of compressed energy which inspired his followers for new battles and for future victory." He further recalls how the Bolshevik delegates huddled dejectedly together, gazing at Lenin and expressing discouragement, and how "Lenin bitingly replied through clenched teeth: 'Don't whine, comrades, we are bound to win, for we are right.' "[5] Zinoviev, to take another example, gives—from intimate personal memory—the following account of Lenin's role during the ensuing "dark era" of counter-revolution: "He alone contrived to collect a close and intimate circle of fighters, whom he would cheer up by saying: 'Don't be disheartened; these dark days will pass, the muddy wave will ebb away; a few years will pass and we shall be borne on the crest of the wave, and the proletarian revolution will be born again.' "[6]

A significant strand in Lenin's revolutionary faith was belief in the imminence of socialist upheavals in Europe, and his visions of Russian revolution drew added inspirational strength from a tendency to picture it as part of a larger, international revolutionary scene. Already in *What Is to Be Done?* he envisaged the Russian proletariat making itself the "vanguard of the international proletariat" by overthrowing tsarism. Subsequently he gravitated, as did

5. Stalin, *Sochineniia*, VI, 56.
6. G. Zinoviev, *Lenin. Speech to the Petrograd Soviet Celebrating Lenin's Recovery from Wounds Received in the Attempt Made on His Life on August 30, 1918* (London, 1966), p. 29.

Trotsky, to the notion of a dialectical link between Russian and European revolution. In 1905 he presented an alluring image of the "great perspectives" that a seizure of power in Russia would open up: "The flame of our revolution will set light to Europe; . . . then the revolutionary upsurge in Europe will have a reciprocal effect upon Russia, and will change an epoch of several revolutionary years into one of several revolutionary decades. . . ."[7]

The belief in the ripeness of the major European nations for socialist revolution was one of the factors behind Lenin's espousal of a radical policy in the wake of the February Revolution of 1917, which deposed the tsar and created a Provisional Government in Russia. When news of this revolution reached Lenin in Zurich, he immediately adumbrated a radical position in a set of "theses" dispatched to Stockholm for the guidance of Bolsheviks then on their way back to Russia. Shortly afterwards, in the first of a series of "Letters from Afar," he declared that the revolution in Russia was only the first of the revolutions to be engendered by the World War, and then went on to say that the Russian Revolution itself was still only in its "first stage."[8] These two propositions were intimately interlinked in his mind. And the imminence of European socialist revolutions was a prominent theme of his messages to the Bolshevik Central Committee in October, demanding that the party proceed without delay to carry out the armed rising and seizure of power.

According to Max Weber, a charismatic leader must from time to time furnish "proof" of his charisma. He must demonstrate in action the extraordinary powers with which he is endowed in his followers' minds. In the case of a revolutionary political leader, charisma will be most clearly proved by the demonstration of extraordinary revolution-making powers. Lenin furnished this proof to the Bolsheviks in 1917.

On a party questionnaire of 1921, Lenin gave his pre-1917 occupation as "writer" (*literator*). But the years of literary activity were spent in preparation for the role of revolutionary command that he assumed on his arrival at the Finland Station in Petrograd (as St. Petersburg had been renamed in 1914) in April 1917. To participate in revolution was the highest of his aspirations. As he put it in a subsequent postscript to *The State and Revolution*, which he wrote while in hiding in August and September of that year and left unfinished when he returned to Petrograd in October to take charge of the revolution, "It is more pleasant and useful to

---

7. Lenin, *Polnoe sobranie sochinenii*, X, 14.
8. Lenin, *Polnoe sobranie sochinenii*, XXXI, 11. For the "theses" dispatched to Stockholm, see the same volume, pp. 1–6.

go through the 'experience of the revolution' than to write about it."[9] As it turned out, however, "writing about it" was for Lenin a primary means of "going through" it.

His direct personal involvement in the developing revolutionary events was terminated in July after an abortive mass outbreak for which he and his party were held responsible by the authorities. In the ensuing anti-Bolshevik terror, he decided to go into hiding, along with Zinoviev, so as to escape probable assassination. In his absence, overall leadership of the Bolsheviks in the capital devolved upon Trotsky, who only now, at long last, became a member of the Bolshevik Central Committee and formally merged his small personal political following, the so-called Inter-Borough organization, with the Bolshevik Party. Elected president of the Petrograd Soviet (revolutionary council) in September, Trotsky used this key position to carry out a series of masterly political maneuvers in preparation for the events of late October. Meanwhile, his spellbinding oratory worked its effect upon the masses. As the climax drew near, he directed the organization of the armed rising and capture of power. When Lenin reached the headquarters of the insurrection at the Smolny Institute on the evening of October 24, he found operations proceeding swiftly and effectively under command of the Military Revolutionary Committee, headed by Trotsky. The following evening, the Bolshevik leaders appeared before the Congress of Soviets, meeting in the Smolny, to inaugurate the new regime. As John Reed describes the scene of Lenin's first appearance on the rostrum, "he stood there waiting, apparently oblivious to the long-rolling ovation, which lasted several minutes. When it finished, he said simply, 'We shall now proceed to construct the socialist order!' Again that overwhelming human roar. . . . His great mouth, seeming to smile, opened wide as he spoke. . . . For emphasis he bent forward slightly. No gestures. And before him, a thousand simple faces looking up in intent adoration."[1]

Despite his physical absence from Petrograd during the climactic period, Lenin played a decisive part in the October Revolution. From the beginning, when news of the first revolution reached him in Switzerland, he grasped that a more radical Russian revolution was possible. His political instinct informed him that the war-weary soldiers, discontented workers, and land-hungry peasants would give increasing support to a revolutionary party that appealed to them with slogans like "Peace, Bread, and Land" and "All Power to the Soviets!" No sooner had he set foot on Russian soil than he unfolded in his "April Theses" a political strategy aiming at a more radical revolution. Having persuaded the Bolshevik leadership to

9. See below, pp. 397–98.
1. John Reed, *Ten Days That Shook the World* (New York, 1960), p. 172.

adopt this strategy as the party line, he then took charge of the efforts to put it into practice. Nor did his leadership of the Bolsheviks lapse when he went into hiding in July. While Trotsky took command in Petrograd, Lenin went on making the revolution in the familiar role of a writer.

His essential contribution was to *nerve* the Bolsheviks into making their decisive revolutionary move when the time came. This fundamental concern inspired all of Lenin's writings and messages from his hiding-place. His seemingly theoretical treatise on *The State and Revolution* pursued a supremely practical end: to persuade the Bolsheviks (including, perhaps, himself) of the full Marxist legitimacy of taking power by force and violence and then setting up a "dictatorship of the proletariat" which would suppress the bourgeoisie and other counter-revolutionary elements. His subsequent pamphlet, *Can the Bolsheviks Retain State Power?*, sought to quell doubts and refute the fearful thought that the party might not be able to hold onto political power if it succeeded in attaining it. If 130,000 landlords could rule Russia repressively after 1905, he argued, surely 240,000 Bolsheviks could rule it in the interests of the lowly, particularly if they took swift steps to expand the social base of Bolshevik rule by enlisting millions of the poor in the everyday work of administration through such organizations as the Soviets.[2] In *Marxism and Insurrection*, a letter to the party written at the end of September, he maintained forcefully that a Bolshevik victory was now assured, since all objective conditions existed for a successful insurrection: majority support for the Bolsheviks in both the Petrograd and Moscow Soviets, a nationwide rising revolutionary spirit, great vacillation in the ranks of the other parties, and the advantage of a party that firmly knew the path it must follow. Then, in a series of further messages in October, he virtually bludgeoned the party leaders into taking the historic decision despite the doubts that afflicted some and the objections of such prominent figures as Zinoviev and Kamenev. "We must not wait! We may lose everything!" he exclaimed in a final appeal to the Central Committee written on October 24. "History will not forgive revolutionaries for procrastinating when they could be victorious today (will certainly be victorious today), while they risk losing much, in fact, everything, tomorrow."[3]

Whether or not the Bolshevik Revolution would have taken place without Lenin's leadership is one of those historical questions that people feel driven to pose in spite of their ultimate insolubility. The opinion that Trotsky expressed in his diary in exile in 1935 is all the more significant since he himself was the one other individual

2. See below, pp. 399–406.
3. "Advice of an Onlooker," pp. 413–14, below.

whose contribution may have been decisive. In the absence of both himself and Lenin, he reasoned, there would have been no October Revolution. In his own absence the Revolution would have taken place on condition that Lenin was present and in command. Without Lenin, however, he alone would probably not have been able to bring the irresolute Bolshevik leadership to the crucial decision.[4] Something similar had been said by Zinoviev many years earlier. Speaking before the Petrograd Soviet in 1918, shortly after the near-fatal attempt on Lenin's life by a former Socialist-Revolutionary, Fanya Kaplan, he said: "The October Revolution—insofar as even in a revolution one may, and indeed, *must* speak of the role played by the individual—the October Revolution and the part played in connection with it by our party are to the extent of nine-tenths the work of Lenin. If anybody could bring into line all those who doubted or hesitated, it was Lenin."[5] Whatever their historical validity, these judgments tell a great deal about the Bolshevik perception of Lenin's role in the October Revolution.

But it was not only in the taking of power that he gave his followers "proof" of his extraordinary quality; he went on doing so in the exercise of power—as a revolutionary from above. One might argue, at the risk of some exaggeration, that it was in the role of revolutionary statesman that Lenin finally found his true element and demonstrated the full measure of his political genius. With that composed self-assurance which had characterized him from youthful years, he began his career in power by drafting and putting before the Congress of Soviets in the first hours the decrees on peace and land by which the new government established its revolutionary credentials and ringingly appealed for mass support in Russia and beyond its borders. Then he took charge of the beleaguered Bolshevik regime in its epic struggle to survive. No sooner had the Revolution been made than it needed to be defended, and its pros-

4. *Trotsky's Diary in Exile, 1935* (New York, 1963), p. 46. This statement is consistent with the picture that Trotsky gives in his *History of the Russian Revolution* (Ann Arbor, Mich., 1957). Isaac Deutscher summarizes as follows the point of view of the *History*: "His [i.e., Lenin's] shrewdness, realism, and concentrated will emerge from the narrative as the decisive elements of the historic process, at least equal in importance to the spontaneous struggle of millions of workers and soldiers. If their energy was the 'steam' and the Bolshevik party the 'piston box' of the revolution, Lenin was the driver" (*The Prophet Outcast: Trotsky, 1929–1940* [London, 1963], pp. 240–41). Taking issue with Trotsky's view that Lenin's presence was a *sine qua non* of the October Revolution, Deutscher points out that this view ill accords with Trotsky's Marxist *Weltanschauung*, and adds that if it were true, ". . . then the leader cult at large would by no means be preposterous; and its denunciation by historical materialists, from Marx to Trotsky, and the revulsion of all progressive thought against it would be pointless" (*ibid.*, p. 244). That the view ill accords with Trotsky's *Weltanschauung* may speak against the *Weltanschauung* rather than against the view. Nor is this view invalidated by the consideration that its acceptance would make the Lenin cult seem other than "preposterous." For an argument that Lenin's presence was decisive for the outcome of the Revolution, see Sidney Hook, *The Hero in History* (Boston, 1955), ch. X.
5. Zinoviev, *Speech to the Petrograd Soviet*, p. 43.

pects for salvation were unclear during the critical first two years of turmoil, civil war, and foreign intervention. At the outset, a German ultimatum in the peace talks that Trotsky conducted at Brest-Litovsk plunged Lenin's regime into a grave crisis that was both external and internal. Overcoming the opposition of Bukharin and others in a "Left Communist" faction that was calling for revolutionary war, he finally forced through an acceptance of the German terms in the hope of trading space for time, a policy subsequently vindicated by events. On this ground alone, some Bolsheviks came to regard him not only as the *sine qua non* of the Revolution but its savior as well. Needless to add, Lenin had no monopoly upon heroic leadership of the Bolshevik cause during the revolutionary period. Many others rendered exceptional service in saving the Revolution and constructing the new Soviet order. It is particularly noteworthy that Trotsky rose to great heights as the organizer of the Red Army and chief manager of its operations on the far-flung fronts of the Civil War.

The Leader in Power

In deviation from the historic pattern of Russian autocracy, the Soviet Russian state arose as a novel form of party rule. Political power in the one-party system was vested in collective bodies such as the Party Congress, which met annually in the early years, and its elected interim surrogate, the Central Committee. Yet, the revolutionary party dictatorship had in Lenin an acknowledged individual supreme leader of such pre-eminence that it could properly be described as a "Lenin regime." What was the nature of his role as leader, and on what basis did he exercise his great authority?

It was not on the basis of his tenure of a particular office. Indeed, no office of supreme leader was established in the Soviet system. True, Lenin held the premiership. He was chairman of the Council of People's Commissars, the central Soviet government. But it was the higher party organs, notably the Central Committee and its subcommittee, the Politburo, that decided Soviet policy in both internal and external affairs, and the government evolved as the party's main executive agency. Lenin was an advocate of this arrangement and took care to uphold it in practice. In 1923, he praised the established procedure under which foreign-policy moves were decided in the Politburo for implementation by the Foreign Affairs Commissariat, and held up this "flexible amalgamation" of party and government institutions as a model of the way in which the Soviet party-state ought to function.[6] There were instances in

6. See *Better Fewer, But Better*, pp. 734–46, below.

which he would resolve differences between himself and a subordinate government leader not by invoking his superior power as premier but rather by referring the disputed issue to the Politburo for decision by a majority vote. It must be stressed, though, that he gave strong leadership in his role as presiding officer in the government. A participant in sessions of the Council of People's Commissars later recalled: "Lenin was not merely a chairman but a recognized chief to whom everyone brought his thorny problems. The commissars quarreled among themselves in their daily work, but here Lenin had the last word; and all alike left these meetings reassured, as though their quarrels had been those of children now pacified by a wise parent."[7]

Since the party was the ruling political authority in the Soviet state, it was not as chief of government but as head of the party that Lenin acted as supreme leader. On the party side, however, his primacy was not institutionalized in a post corresponding to the premiership in the government. Officially he was merely one of the members of the higher party organs: the Central Committee, which in the early twenties had about twenty-five full members and fifteen or so non-voting candidate members, and the Politburo. The latter in 1922 had a membership of ten (Lenin, Trotsky, Kamenev, Zinoviev, Stalin, Alexei Rykov, and Mikhail Tomsky, with Bukharin, M. I. Kalinin, and Viacheslav Molotov as candidate members). In filling out a questionnaire as a delegate to the Tenth Party Congress only a year earlier, Lenin gave his party office as "member of the Central Committee."[8]

The Central Committee, like the Politburo, operated as a collegial body, taking decisions by majority vote. In neither was Lenin chairman. Formally, he was on a par with the other full members; his vote counted for no more than theirs. There was a great discrepancy, however, between the formality and the reality of his position in these policy-making bodies. In fact he was the dominant individual and his influence was very great. He was *primus inter pares*, recognized by all the other members of the ruling group as their own and the party's supreme leader.

But what did his acknowledged leadership of the party, and

7. Simon Liberman, *Building Lenin's Russia* (Chicago, 1945), p. 13. An ex-Menshevik, Liberman worked for the Soviet government as a non-Communist specialist in the first post-revolutionary years and in this capacity attended meetings of the Council of People's Commissars. He testifies (pp. 180–81) from his own experience on Lenin's practice of referring decisions on disputed issues to the Politburo. When he directly asked Lenin's help in arranging permission for his son to accompany him on a business trip abroad, over opposition from the heads of the Cheka (secret police), Lenin, instead of over-ruling the latter in his capacity as premier, referred the question to the Politburo, where the issuance of the passport was approved by a vote of three to two.

8. *Desiatyi s''ezd RKP/b/. Mart 1921 goda. Stenograficheskii otchet* (Moscow, 1963), p. 643.

hence of the party-state, mean in practice? It may be useful to approach the question from the negative side. The acceptance of Lenin's authority did not mean that the other leaders were indisposed to disagree with him or oppose him on specific policy questions. As supreme leader, he did not simply issue commands to the ruling group; he did not rule by arbitrary *Diktat*. Automatic acquiescence in his position was not expected; the whole previous history of Bolshevik leadership politics militated against any such dictatorial relationship of the leader to his followers. It was not that Lenin hesitated to impose his views or was easily given to compromise when his position and that of his followers diverged, as happened rather frequently. On the contrary, he was a strong-willed and very self-confident leader who repeatedly set himself against the main current of party opinion in questions of revolutionary strategy and politics. He did not compromise with those who opposed him on matters that he deemed of critical importance for the movement. The point is that the powers on which he chiefly relied in exercising this forceful individual leadership were his powers of persuasion. It was so in the long preparatory period before Bolshevism came to power, and it remained so after the Bolshevik Revolution.

Lenin's ascendancy is illustrated by the military debate at the Eighth Party Congress in March 1919. In closed session, powerful forces in the Bolshevik leadership mounted a determined attack upon the military policy of Trotsky, who had left Moscow before the debate in order to direct operations against Admiral Kolchak's forces on the eastern front. The defeat of this military opposition became a foregone conclusion, however, when Lenin put in a strong plea on Trotsky's behalf; so much so that Lenin did not even remain at the congress to await the outcome.[9] Again, the ill-fated decision of July 1920 to launch the Red Army on an invasion of Poland—a decision for which Lenin himself was largely responsible—did not even shake his commanding authority in the party, although the results proved disastrous. As Zinoviev remarked at the Thirteenth Party Congress, some months after Lenin's death, no one but Lenin would have been able to go before a Party Congress (as he did in March 1921) and confess responsibility for such an error with complete political impunity.[1] Finally, it may be noted that Lenin, without holding office in the Communist International, dominated its decisions through his personal influence over the Russian representatives who gave leadership to the organization. They quarreled amongst themselves, recalls a former German Communist who

9. Isaac Deutscher, *The Prophet Armed: Trotsky, 1879–1921* (London, 1954), p. 431.

1. *Trinadtsatyi s"ezd RKP/b/. Mai 1924 goda. Stenograficheskii otchet* (Moscow, 1963), p. 256.

took part in the Comintern executive's sessions in 1921, but "when Lenin had had his say, the question was settled. His authority was simply taken for granted by his comrades. I don't mean they just obeyed mechanically or were under any kind of threat. I'll admit even today that his position was the result of his undoubted superiority."[2]

How was Lenin able to dominate the party without being an all-powerful chief executive who could give orders to its leading organs? Some might explain it by the prestige accruing to him as the one who had founded the Bolshevik Party and accomplished the astounding feat of leading it to power in the Revolution of 1917. Although not without merit, such an explanation can scarcely be accepted as adequate. For it leaves open the question of how he acquired his authority in the beginning and how he held onto it at the end; and here we must recall that the prestige of many an historical leader has declined very quickly after reaching its peak. In the final analysis, Lenin's phenomenal authority in the party derived from his extraordinary qualities as a revolutionary leader and political personality. We may express this in terms suggested earlier by saying that he conformed to Weber's conception of the charismatic leader who enjoys his authority not through enacted position or traditional dignity but owing to gifts of grace (charisma) "by virtue of which he is set apart from ordinary men and treated as endowed with supernatural, superhuman, or at least specifically exceptional powers or qualities" (the "supernatural" and "superhuman" being excluded in this instance.)[3] Alternatively, we may refer back to words that Lenin used in 1902 in a "Letter to a Comrade on Our Organizational Tasks." After describing the kind of revolutionary organization that his plan envisaged, he declared that its task was to "preserve *leadership* of the whole movement, preserving it, of course, not by force of power but by force of authority, by force of energy, by greater experience, greater versatility, and greater talentedness."[4] This formula for the party's preservation of its leadership of the mass movement may be taken as a fair description of how Lenin himself preserved leadership of the party during the following two decades.

He was the veritable hub of the Bolshevik regime in the five years of active life remaining to him after the taking of power. His authority, energy, and tact as a leader enabled him to manage the

2. Bernard Reichenbach, "Moscow 1921. Meetings in the Kremlin," *Survey*, No. 53 (October 1964), p. 17. Reichenbach was a co-founder of the German Communist Party.

3. Weber, *Theory of Social and Economic Organization*, p. 358.

4. Lenin, *Polnoe sobranie sochinenii*, VII, 14. The letter at first circulated among party members in Russia through the then-existing network of *samizdat*. The Siberian Social-Democratic organization put it out in hectographed form in June 1903, and it was published as a pamphlet in Geneva in the following year.

various strong-willed personalities among the Bolsheviks and to keep the work from being too greatly disrupted by the animosities that developed, as for example between Stalin and Trotsky in the course of the Civil War. He exercised supreme direction of Bolshevik policy and action in the Civil War, in external affairs, in economic life and the organizing of the new system. In March 1921—a time of profound crisis for the Revolution—he sponsored one of those abrupt and far-reaching shifts of line by which his political style was characterized. The White armies had been defeated by then, but inside the weary and war-torn country the peasants were vocally and in places violently in revolt against the forcible grain requisitions to which the beleaguered regime had regularly resorted under "War Communism." While the Tenth Party Congress was in session in Moscow, sailors and workers at the Kronstadt naval base, on an island outside Petrograd harbor, rose in armed rebellion and issued inflammatory appeals, like "Soviets without Bolsheviks!" The rising was crushed by the Red Army, but its political implications were taken into account by the Lenin regime. Under his leadership the Tenth Congress inaugurated the "New Economic Policy" (NEP) by abolishing forcible grain requisitions in favor of a graduated tax in kind on the peasant proprietors of the approximately twenty-five million small private farms then existing in Russia. It became a congress of transition not only from war to peace but likewise from the "military-proletarian dictatorship"[5] of the first years to a period of civil peace under the NEP, which lasted through most of the twenties.

Basic Soviet strategy in foreign affairs, under which the Comintern and the Foreign Commissariat operated as two arms of a dual policy, one working to overthrow capitalist governments while the other tried to conduct business with them, was essentially Lenin's creation, as was the notion of a Soviet diplomacy designed to reduce the insecurity of the revolutionary state by aggravating the discords between its enemies. Moreover, he closely supervised the conduct of foreign relations, even dictating to Foreign Commissar Georgi Chicherin, on occasion, the texts of diplomatic notes to be sent to foreign governments.[6] In the midst of all these labors of direct political leadership, he prepared and delivered a multitude of speeches, wrote articles for the Soviet press, and produced such major political treatises as *The Immediate Tasks of the Soviet Government*; *The Proletarian Revolution and the Renegade Kautsky*; and *"Left-Wing" Communism—An Infantile Disorder*. Toward the end, after illness partially incapacitated him, he set forth guidelines for post-Lenin Soviet policy in a series of shorter writings that

5. *Desiatyi s"ezd*, p. 560.
6. G. Chicherin, in *Izvestia*, January 30, 1924.

Bukharin would later call his "political testament." They had to do chiefly with the great problem of how to transform backward "NEP Russia" into a country that could properly be described as socialist.

It is hardly surprising in the light of all this that Lenin's stature in Bolshevik eyes grew to gigantic proportions. He came to appear the very personification of the miracle of their survival in power, and of the further promise of the Communist revolution at home and abroad. Not only by close associates but by great numbers of party members he was not simply admired but quite literally idolized. The strongest evidence of this is the testimony of those who observed party audiences on occasions when he spoke in public. One such report comes from Walter Duranty: "I have seen Lenin speak to his followers. A small, busy, thick-set man under blinding lights, greeted by applause like thunder. I turned round and their faces were shining, like men who looked on God. Lenin was like that, whether you think he was a damnable Antichrist or a once-in-a-thousand years' prophet. That is a matter of opinion, but when five thousand faces can light up and shine at the sight of him, as they did, and I saw it, then I say he was no ordinary individual."[7] Similar reports abound in the memoir literature. "Their faces shone," said a Russian Communist who was in the audience at one of Lenin's post-revolutionary public speeches. "It was truly an intellectual revel."[8] Ignazio Silone, who first saw Lenin at the Comintern congress in Moscow in 1921, recalls that "whenever he came into the hall, the atmosphere changed, became electric. It was a physical, almost a palpable phenomenon. He generated contagious enthusiasm the way the faithful in St. Peter's, when they crowd around the Sedia, emanate a fervor that spreads like a wave throughout the basilica."[9]

The hero-worship of Lenin was manifested in a tendency of his followers to make him the center of a personality cult. It appeared, for example, in the reactions when he was shot on August 30, 1918, and his recovery remained temporarily uncertain. The Soviet newspapers were filled at that time with messages expressing devotion to him and fervent wishes for his recovery. Trotsky, who in later years was to condemn the cult of Lenin, declared in a speech of September 2, 1918, to the Executive Committee of the Soviets: "Never has the individual life of one or another among us seemed to be of such secondary importance as it does now at a moment when the life of the greatest man of our age is in peril. Any fool can shoot Lenin's head to pieces, but to create this head anew

7. Walter Duranty, *Duranty Reports Russia* (New York, 1934), p. 170. Duranty was the *New York Times* correspondent in Moscow in the twenties.

8. *Zhivoi Lenin*, p. 283.
9. *Dissent*, September–October 1970, p. 429. The article appeared originally in *Corriere della sera*, April 22, 1970.

would be a problem for nature herself." And Lunacharsky quotes Trotsky as saying, presumably at this same time although not in public, "When you think that Lenin might die, all our lives seem useless and you stop wanting to live."[1] A few days later, in the speech to the Petrograd Soviet cited above, Zinoviev said that the Soviet state had found in Lenin "not only its chief political leader, practical organizer, ardent propagandist, poet and singer, but also its principal theoretician, its Karl Marx," and characterized him as follows: "Take the fanatical devotion to the people which distinguished Marat; take his integrity, his simplicity, his intimate knowledge of the soul of the people, take his elemental faith in the inexhaustible strength of the 'lowest of the lowly,' take all this and add to it the first-class education of a Marxist, an iron will, an acute analytical mind, and you will get Lenin such as we know him now."

Nothing could have been more displeasing to Lenin himself—to whom any craving for personal glory was foreign—than this great public outpouring of emotion and encomium. Consequently, when his health improved sufficiently to enable him to return to work, he was horrified to read what had been printed in the Soviet press after the shooting. V. D. Bonch-Bruevich, his aide in the Council of People's Commissars, recalls being urgently summoned into Lenin's office and listening to him exclaim:

> What is this? How could you permit it? Look what they are saying in the papers. Makes one ashamed to read it. They write that I'm such-and-such, exaggerate everything, call me a genius, a special kind of man. And look at this piece of mysticism: they collectively wish, demand, and desire that I get well. Next they'll be holding public prayers for my health. Why, this is horrible! And where does it come from? All our lives we have carried on an ideological struggle against the glorification of personality, of the individual. We long ago solved the question of heroes, and now we are again witnessing the glorification of personality. This is no good at all.[2]

Not content with privately voicing dismay, Lenin ordered Bonch-Bruevich and two other aides to visit the editorial offices of Soviet newspapers, starting with *Pravda* and *Izvestia,* and explain that the glorification of personality must stop immediately. "The very next

1. *Revoliutsionnye siluety*, p. 13. For the text of the speech of September 2, 1918, see Leon Trotsky, *Lenin* (Garden City, N.Y., 1959), pp. 196–205.
2. V. D. Bonch-Bruevich, *Izbrannye sochineniia*, III, *Vospominaniia o V. I. Lenin 1917–1924 gg.* (Moscow, 1963), pp. 296–98. The statement shows a curious forgetfulness on Lenin's part concerning his own earlier views on the decisive role of revolutionary heroes. In Lunacharsky's remembrance of this episode, Lenin, in ordering Bonch-Bruevich and two other aides to make the rounds of the newspapers, added: "It would not be convenient for me to forbid this kind of thing myself, for that would also be absurd and pretentious in its way. But you must surreptitiously put a brake on this whole business" (*Izvestia*, February 14, 1960).

day the newspapers were altogether different in tone," continues the memoir, "and Vladimir Ilyich never raised this question again."

A little over a year later, however, Lenin's followers again showed in public their tendency to place him on a pedestal. In speeches at a party meeting in April 1920 in honor of his fiftieth birthday, and in articles published in the Soviet press for this occasion, they acclaimed him as the *vozhd'*[3] of the Russian and world revolution. Maxim Gorky compared him as a history-making figure to Christopher Columbus and Peter the Great. Evgeni Preobrazhensky called him "the soul and brain of the October Revolution." A. Sol'ts portrayed him as a new kind of hero in history, a leader of consciously acting masses whose need was no longer for a hero to whom they could bow but for one who was, like Lenin, "flesh of their flesh, thought, and word." Trotsky described Lenin as a blend of Marxist internationalist and Russian revolutionary statesman with "something about him that is strongly suggestive of a peasant." Since Russia had never experienced a great revolution or reformation at the hands of its bourgeoisie, Trotsky said, its national revolution had devolved upon the working class, led by Lenin: "Our historical past knows neither a Luther, nor a Thomas Münzer, neither a Mirabeau, nor a Robespierre. For that very reason the Russian proletariat has its Lenin." Bukharin paid tribute to Lenin as a teacher who had developed a new theoretical school of Marxism, and on this account spoke of the other party leaders as his "disciples." Stalin, who was one of the last to speak at the meeting, commented that the others had left him with little to say and then devoted his remarks to the modesty of Lenin, recounting two episodes in which "that giant" had erred (one was in not having wanted to await the convening of the Congress of Soviets in October 1917 before launching the coup) and later courageously admitted erring. But in his *Pravda* article for the occasion, Stalin offered a general assessment of Lenin as the "organizer and *vozhd'*" of the Russian Communist Party. He concluded by contrasting Lenin with two lesser types of proletarian leaders known to history —those who were outstanding practical leaders in times of stress but weak in theory, like Lassalle and Blanqui, and those who were strong in theory but weak in organizational and practical work, like Plekhanov and Kautsky. The greatness of Lenin as a leader lay in combining both kinds of talent.[4]

Lenin responded to the birthday celebration by registering once

---

3. This strong Russian word for "leader" lacks a precise English equivalent. It could be rendered "supreme leader" or "Leader" (capitalized).
4. Stalin, *Sochineniia*, IV, 314–15. This and other articles commemorating Lenin's birthday appeared in *Pravda* on April 23, 1920. Ferdinand Lassalle (1825–

64) was a prominent German socialist leader. Louis-Auguste Blanqui (1805–81) was a French revolutionary leader who favored a seizure of power by a small, disciplined minority operating conspiratorially. Such tactics became known as "Blanquism."

again, this time publicly, his aversion to being an object of adulation. He absented himself from the jubilee meeting until the speeches in his honor were over. When he appeared after an intermission and was met by an ovation, he drily thanked those present, first for their greetings and secondly for excusing him from listening to them. Then he pointedly expressed the hope that in time a "more fitting" way of marking anniversary dates would be found, and he concluded his talk with a discussion of routine party problems. Even in this part of the short talk, he warned the party against permitting success to go to its head and becoming a "conceited party."[5]

Thus the Bolshevik Party, in spite of the great expansion of its numbers resulting from the Revolution, continued, in power, to be essentially what it had been in its small beginnings around the turn of the century—a leader-centered movement. But what was the relation of the masses of non-party people in Russia to Lenin as a political leader? We know that Russian workers and peasants who met him individually or in small groups felt the magnetic spell of his personality. For example, M. A. Landau-Aldanov, a Russian socialist who was politically opposed to Lenin, tells the following story of a worker who spoke briefly with him on the occasion of delivering a message: "I saw this workman at the moment when he returned from his audience with Lenin. He was powerfully moved, not the same man. Usually a quiet and reasonable being, he spoke all at once like a man in ecstasy. 'That is a man,' he repeated over and over, 'that is a man for whom I would give my life! With him a new life begins for me! Ah, if we had had a tsar like him!' "[6] Other such examples could be cited. We must take care, however, in generalizing from such evidence. What can be said with confidence is that, despite the low development of the modern communications media in Russia at that time, Lenin as a personality made a very strong impression upon the masses of people and aroused passionate feelings—both positive and negative. The ambivalence of attitudes arose from the fact that ordinary Russians, aided by the old habit of personifying political power in the tsar, tended to see in Lenin the personification of Bolshevism, towards which feelings in the populace were deeply divided in the revolutionary period. Those for whom the Bolshevik Revolution represented a threat to religious and other values perceived in Lenin a demonic figure, whereas those to whom the Revolution meant hope of deliverance from

5. Lenin, *Polnoe sobranie sochinenii*, XL, 325–27.
6. Related by René Fülöp-Miller in *The Mind and Face of Bolshevism: An Examination of Cultural Life in Soviet Russia* (New York, 1928), p. 40. "The whole success of Lenin," adds Fülöp-Miller, "is plainly due entirely to the spell of his personality, which communicated itself to all who came into touch with him, and then penetrated into the cabins of the peasants in the remotest villages."

misery saw in him a deliverer. Consequently, Lenin in his own lifetime became, quite literally, a legendary figure and subject of folklore.

There were legends in Russian Central Asia, for example, which pictured him as a liberator sent by Allah to make the people happy.[7] In remote peasant villages in the Urals region, the poet Ludmilla Seifullina heard similar tales. One of them, constructed along the lines of an ancient Russian heroic legend, told of how a man "of unknown rank and title, without passport, and by name Lenin" had divided up the nation with "Tsar Mikolashka" (i.e., Nicholas II), taking all the common folk onto his side and giving the fine folk to the tsar, and of how Lenin was winning the struggle because the fine folk could do nothing without the common folk and the generals had no soldiers to do their fighting for them. Seifullina found that Lenin had both detractors and defenders in the country districts; all of them, however, were vehement in expressing their feelings. She heard devout Russian Orthodox peasants depicting Lenin as a monstrous evildoer. Reciting whole pages of the Bible in a screaming voice, they would attribute to Lenin the number of the beast, the number 666, the number of Antichrist. Others, likewise with abundant reference to Holy Scripture, would speak out in his favor, saying that Lenin was the bearer of the righteous wrath of God, that he had come to fulfill the prophecies of Isaiah, that he acted according to the Bible when he took away the "broad acres of the rich." In a village of Old Believers there was a thin redheaded man who professed his faith in Lenin by joining the party, slinging on a rifle which he brandished threateningly at every meeting, and bellowing out scriptural texts to prove the justice of Lenin's political acts.[8] So Lenin's following was swelled by numbers of simple Russians for whom Marxism remained as much a mystery as any system of theology. Not in all instances did these people join the party.

Lenin died on January 21, 1924, after having been incapacitated for many months by his third stroke. Since his illness had been announced, there had been time for people to make a mental adjustment in advance of the event. Nevertheless, there appears to have been a spontaneous and very widespread feeling of sorrow among the population as well as in the party. Memorial meetings in cities and villages throughout the country were attended by masses of people. In Moscow tens and hundreds of thousands of people braved some of the bitterest cold in living Russian memory to await their turns to file through the Hall of Columns, where the body was

7. E. H. Carr, *Socialism in One Country 1924–1926*, II (New York, 1960), p. 3 n.
8. L. Seifullina, *Sobranie sochinenii*, II (Moscow and Leningrad, 1928), pp. 271–75.

lying in state, and to come to Red Square on the day of the funeral. Eliena Eastman, the sister of a prominent Bolshevik, obtained a pass enabling her to spend two hours in the Hall of Columns. In a letter to her husband, who was absent from Moscow at the time, she described the scene: "Mothers lift up their children for one look at him, hysterical women fall on the floor crying 'tovarishch Lenin,' three strong men in white suits are there to lift them and carry them out, and they cry so terribly that your blood becomes cold." Outside, the city presented the following picture: "The red flags with black hems, the black-red sash on the right arm of many people, many people selling little picture-brooches of Lenin, and his small white bust and small white statue, the white bright snow, the thick cold air, the frosted hair and furs, white smoke from the mouths and red fires in the street at night. That is Moscow of these days."[9]

9. Eastman, *Love and Revolution*, p. 399.

PART I

The Revolutionary Party and Its Tactics

The Tasks of the
Russian Social-Democrats

Written at the close of 1897 while Lenin was in Siberian exile and published the following year in Geneva by the Emancipation of Labour group, this pamphlet received a wide clandestine circulation inside Russia. Its opening emphasis upon the key importance of the movement's "practical" tasks may be seen as an announcement of Lenin's own chosen role as a theorist of revolutionary practice, and the discussion of the revolutionary party's agenda of activity as a preview of the major treatise on this subject that Lenin was soon after to produce in *What Is to Be Done?*

The second half of the nineties witnessed a remarkable increase in the work being done on the presentation and solution of the problems of the Russian Revolution. * * *

At the present time (the end of 1897), the most urgent question, in our opinion, is that of the *practical* activities of the Social-Democrats. We emphasise the *practical* side of Social-Democracy, because on the theoretical side the most critical period—the period of stubborn refusal by its opponents to understand it, of strenuous efforts to suppress the new trend the moment it arose, on the one hand, and of stalwart defence of the fundamentals of Social-Democracy, on the other—is now apparently behind us. Now the *main and basic features* of the theoretical views of the Social-Democrats have been sufficiently clarified. The same cannot be said about the *practical* side of Social-Democracy, about its political *programme*, its methods, its tactics. * * *

* * *

The object of the practical activities of the Social-Democrats is, as is well known, to lead the class struggle of the proletariat and to organise that struggle in both its manifestations: socialist (the fight against the capitalist class aimed at destroying the class system and organising socialist society), and democratic (the fight against absolutism aimed at winning political liberty in Russia and democratising the political and social system of Russia). We said *as is well known*. And indeed, from the very moment they appeared as a separate social-revolutionary trend, the Russian Social-Democrats have always quite definitely indicated this object of their activities, have always emphasised the dual manifestation and content of the class struggle of the proletariat and have always insisted on the inseparable connection between their socialist and democratic tasks —a connection clearly expressed in the name they have adopted. Nevertheless, to this day you often meet socialists who have the most distorted notions about the Social-Democrats and accuse them of ignoring the political struggle, etc. Let us, therefore, dwell a little on a description of both aspects of the practical activities of Russian Social-Democracy.

Let us begin with socialist activity. One would have thought that the character of Social-Democratic activity in this respect had become quite clear since the Social-Democratic League of Struggle for the Emancipation of the Working Class in St. Petersburg began its activities among the St. Petersburg workers. The socialist activities of Russian Social-Democrats consist in spreading *by propaganda* the teachings of scientific socialism, in spreading among the workers a proper understanding of the present social and economic system, its basis and its development, an understanding of the various *classes* in Russian society, of their interrelations, of the struggle between these classes, of the role of the working class in this struggle, of its attitude towards the declining and the developing classes, towards the past and the future of capitalism, an understanding of the historical task of international Social-Democracy and of the Russian working class. Inseparably connected with propaganda is *agitation* among the workers, which naturally comes to the forefront in the present political conditions of Russia and at the present level of development of the masses of workers. Agitation among the workers means that the Social-Democrats take part in all the spontaneous manifestations of the working-class struggle, in all the conflicts between the workers and the capitalists over the working day, wages, working conditions, etc., etc. Our task is to merge our activities with the practical, everyday questions of working-class life, to help the workers understand these questions, to draw the workers' attention to the most important abuses, to help them formulate their demands to the employers more precisely and practically, to develop among the workers consciousness of their solidarity, consciousness of the common interests and common cause of all the Russian workers as a united working class that is part of the international army of the proletariat. To organise study circles among workers, to establish proper and secret connections between them and the central group of Social-Democrats, to publish and distribute working-class literature, to organise the receipt of correspondence from all centres of the working-class movement, to publish agitational leaflets and manifestos and to distribute them, and to train a body of experienced agitators—such, in broad outline, are the manifestations of the socialist activities of Russian Social-Democracy.

Our work is primarily and mainly directed to the urban factory workers. Russian Social-Democracy must not dissipate its forces; it must concentrate its activities on the industrial proletariat, who are most susceptible to Social-Democratic ideas, most developed intellectually and politically, and most important by virtue of their numbers and concentration in the country's large political centres. The creation of a durable revolutionary organisation among the urban factory workers is therefore the first and most urgent task confronting Social-Democracy, one from which it would be highly unwise to let ourselves be diverted at the present time. But, while recognising the necessity of concentrating our forces on the factory workers and opposing the dissipation of our forces, we do not in the least wish to suggest that the Russian Social-Democrats should ignore other strata of the Russian proletariat and working class. Nothing of the kind. The very conditions of life of the Russian factory workers very often compel them to enter into the closest relations with the handicraftsmen, the industrial proletariat scattered outside the factory in towns and villages, and whose conditions are infinitely worse. The Russian factory worker also comes into direct contact with the rural population (very often the factory worker's family live in the country) and, consequently, he cannot but come into close contact with the rural proletariat, with the many millions of regular farm workers and day labourers, and also with those ruined peasants who, while clinging to their miserable plots of land, have to work off their debts and take on all sorts of "casual jobs," i.e., are also wage-labourers. The Russian Social-Democrats think it inopportune *to send* their forces among the handicraftsmen and rural labourers, but they do not in the least intend to ignore them; they will try to enlighten the advanced workers also on questions affecting the lives of the handicraftsmen and rural labourers, so that when these workers come into contact with the more backward strata of the proletariat, they will imbue them with the ideas of the class struggle, socialism and the political tasks of Russian democracy in general and of the Russian proletariat in particular. It is impractical to send agitators among the handicraftsmen and rural labourers when there is still so much work to be done among the urban factory workers, but in numerous cases the socialist worker comes willy-nilly into contact with these people and must be able to take advantage of these opportunities and understand the general tasks of Social-Democracy in Russia. Hence, those who accuse the Russian Social-Democrats of being

narrow-minded, of trying to ignore the mass of the labouring population for the sake of the factory workers, are profoundly mistaken.
On the contrary, agitation among the advanced sections of the
proletariat is the surest and the only way to rouse (as the movement expands) the entire Russian proletariat. The dissemination of
socialism and of the idea of the class struggle among the urban
workers will inevitably cause these ideas to flow in the smaller and
more scattered channels. This requires that these ideas take deeper
root among the better prepared elements and spread throughout the
vanguard of the Russian working-class movement and of the Russian revolution. While concentrating all its forces on activity among
the factory workers, Russian Social-Democracy is ready to support
those Russian revolutionaries who, in practice, come to base their
socialist activities on the class struggle of the proletariat; but it does
not in the least conceal the point that no practical alliances with
other groups of revolutionaries can, or should, lead to compromises
or concessions on matters of theory, programme or banner. Convinced that the doctrine of scientific socialism and the class struggle
is the only revolutionary theory that can today serve as the banner
of the revolutionary movement, the Russian Social-Democrats will
exert every effort to spread this doctrine, to guard it against false
interpretation and to combat every attempt to impose vaguer doctrines on the still young working-class movement in Russia. Theoretical reasoning proves and the practical activities of the Social-
Democrats show that all *socialists* in Russia should become *Social-
Democrats*.

Let us now deal with the *democratic* tasks and with the democratic work of the Social-Democrats. Let us repeat, once again, that
this work is *inseparably* connected with socialist activity. In conducting *propaganda* among the workers, the Social-Democrats *cannot* avoid political problems, and they would regard any attempt to
avoid them, or even to push them aside, as a profound mistake and
a departure from the basic principles of international Social-Democracy. Simultaneously with the dissemination of scientific socialism,
Russian Social-Democrats set themselves the task of propagating
democratic ideas among the working-class masses; they strive to
spread an understanding of absolutism in all its manifestations, of
its class content, of the necessity to overthrow it, of the impossibility of waging a successful struggle for the workers' cause without
achieving political liberty and the democratisation of Russian's political and social system. In conducting *agitation* among the
workers on their immediate *economic* demands, the Social-Democrats inseparably link this with agitation on the immediate political
needs, the distress and the demands of the working class, agitation
against police tyranny, manifested in every strike, in every conflict

between workers and capitalists, agitation against the restriction of the rights of the workers as Russian citizens in general and as the class suffering the worst oppression and having the least rights in particular, agitation against every prominent representative and flunkey of absolutism who comes into direct contact with the workers and who clearly reveals to the working class its condition of political slavery. Just as there is no issue affecting the life of the workers in the economic field that must be left unused for the purpose of economic agitation, so there is no issue in the political field that does not serve as a subject for political agitation. These two kinds of agitation are inseparably connected in the activities of the Social-Democrats as the two sides of the same medal. Both economic and political agitation are equally necessary to develop the class-consciousness of the proletariat; both economic and political agitation are equally necessary for guiding the class struggle of the Russian workers, because every class struggle is a political struggle. By arousing the class-consciousness of the workers, by organising, disciplining and training them for united action and for the fight for the ideals of Social-Democracy, both kinds of agitation will enable the workers to test their strength on immediate issues and immediate needs, to wring partial concessions from their enemy and thus improve their economic conditions, compel the capitalists to reckon with the strength of the organised workers, compel the government to extend the workers' rights, to pay heed to their demands and keep the government in constant fear of the hostility of the masses of workers led by a strong Social-Democratic organisation.

We have pointed to the inseparably close connection between *socialist* and *democratic* propaganda *and* agitation, to the complete parallelism of revolutionary activity in both spheres. Nevertheless, there is a big difference between these two types of activity and struggle. The difference is that in the economic struggle the proletariat stands absolutely alone against both the landed nobility and the bourgeoisie, except, perhaps, for the help it receives (and by no means always) from those elements of the petty bourgeoisie which gravitate towards the proletariat. In the democratic, *political* struggle, however, the Russian working class does not stand alone; at its side are all the political opposition elements, strata and classes, since they are hostile to absolutism and are fighting it in one form or another. Here *side by side* with the proletariat stand the opposition elements of the bourgeoisie, or of the educated classes, or of the petty bourgeoisie, or of the nationalities, religions and sects, etc., etc., persecuted by the autocratic government. The question naturally arises of what the attitude of the working class towards these elements should be. Further, should it not combine with them in the common struggle against the autocracy? After all, all Social-Democrats admit that the political revolution in Russia must precede the socialist revolution; should they not, therefore, combine with all the elements in the political opposition to fight the autocracy, setting socialism aside for the time being? Is not this essential in order to strengthen the fight against the autocracy?

Let us examine these two questions.

The attitude of the working class, as a fighter against the autocracy, towards all the other social classes and groups in the political opposition is very precisely determined by the basic principles of Social-Democracy expounded in the famous *Communist Manifesto*. The Social-Democrats support the progressive social classes against the reactionary classes, the bourgeoisie against the representatives of privileged landowning estate and the bureaucracy, the big bourgeoisie against the reactionary strivings of the petty bourgeoisie. This support does not presuppose, nor does it call for, any compromise with non-Social-Democratic programmes and principles—it is support given to an ally against a *particular* enemy. Moreover, the Social-Democrats render this support in order to expedite the fall of the common enemy, but expect nothing *for themselves* from these temporary allies, and concede nothing to them. The Social-Democrats support every revolutionary movement against the present social system, they support all oppressed nationalities, persecuted religions, downtrodden social estates, etc., in their fight for equal rights.

Support for all elements of the political opposition will be expressed in the propaganda of the Social-Democrats by the fact that, in showing that the autocracy is hostile to the workers' cause, they will also point to its hostility towards various other social groups; they will point to the solidarity of the working class with these groups on *a particular issue, in a particular task,* etc. In agitation, this support will be expressed by the Social-Democrats' taking advantage of every manifestation of the police tyranny of the autocracy to point out to the workers how this tyranny affects all Russian citizens *in general,* and the representatives of the exceptionally oppressed social estates, nationalities, religions, sects, etc., in particular; and how that tyranny affects *the working class* especially. Finally, in practice, this support is expressed in the readiness of the Russian Social-Democrats to enter into alliances with revolutionaries of other trends for the purpose of achieving certain particular aims, and this readiness has been shown in practice on more than one occasion.

This brings us to the second question. While pointing to the solidarity of one or other of the various opposition groups with the workers, the Social-Democrats will always single out the workers from the rest, they will always point out that this solidarity is temporary and conditional, they will always emphasise the independent class identity of the proletariat, who tomorrow may find themselves in opposition to their allies of today. We shall be told that "such action will *weaken* all the fighters for political liberty at the present time." We shall reply that such action will *strengthen* all the fighters for political liberty. Only those fighters are strong who rely on the *consciously recognised* real interests of certain *classes*, and any attempt to obscure these class interests, which already play a predominant role in contemporary society, will only weaken the fighters. That is the first point. The second point is that, in the fight against the autocracy, the working class must single itself out, for it is the *only* thoroughly consistent and unreserved enemy of the autocracy, *only* between the working class and the autocracy is no compromise possible, *only* in the working class can democracy find a champion who makes no reservations, is not irresolute and does not look back. The hostility of all other classes, groups and strata of the population towards the autocracy is *not unqualified*; their democracy always looks back. The bourgeoisie cannot but realise that industrial and social development is being retarded by the autocracy, but it fears the complete democratisation of the political and social system and can at any moment enter into alliance with the autocracy against the proletariat. The petty bourgeoisie is two-faced by its very nature, and while its gravitates, on the one hand, towards the proletariat and democracy, on the other, it gravitates towards the reactionary classes, tries to hold up the march of history, is apt to be seduced by the experiments and blandishments of the autocracy (for example, the "people's policy"[1] of Alexander III), is capable of concluding an alliance with the ruling classes against the proletariat *for the sake of* strengthening its own *small-proprietor* position. Educated people, and the "intelligentsia" generally, cannot but revolt against the savage police tyranny of the autocracy, which hunts down thought and knowledge; but the material interests of this intelligentsia bind it to the autocracy and to the bourgeoisie, compel it to be inconsistent, to compromise, to sell its oppositional and revolutionary ardour for an official salary, or a share of profits or dividends. As for the democratic elements among the oppressed nationalities and the persecuted religions, everybody knows and sees that the class antagonisms within these categories of the population are much deeper-going and stronger than the solidarity binding all classes within any one category against the autocracy and in favour of democratic institutions. The proletariat

---

1. The policy pursued by N. P. Ignatyev, minister of internal affairs in 1881–82, which was intended, as Lenin put it, "to bamboozle" the liberals. Part of the policy was the calling of conferences of "knowledgeable people" which included marshals of the nobility, representatives of the *zemstvo* administrations and similar people to discuss problems relating to a reduction in land redemption payments, the proper organisation of migration, and local government reform. In 1882, however, Ignatyev resigned, and a period of extreme reaction followed.

alone can be—and because of its class position must be—a consistently democratic, determined enemy of absolutism, incapable of making any concessions or compromises. The proletariat alone can be the *vanguard fighter* for political liberty and for democratic institutions. * * *

We will illustrate what we mean by quoting the following example. Take the civil service, the bureaucracy, as representing a special category of persons who specialise in the work of administration and occupy a privileged position as compared with the people. We see this institution everywhere, from autocratic and semi-Asiatic Russia to cultured, free and civilised England, as an essential organ of bourgeois society. The *complete lack of rights* of the people in relation to government officials and the *complete* absence of control over the privileged bureaucracy correspond to the backwardness of Russia and to its absolutism. In England powerful popular control is exercised over the administration, but even there that control *is far from being complete*, even there the bureaucracy retains not a few of its privileges, and not infrequently is the master and not the servant of the people. Even in England we see that powerful social groups support the privileged position of the bureaucracy and hinder the complete democratisation of that institution. Why? Because it is in the interests of the proletariat alone to democratise it *completely*; the most progressive strata of the bourgeoisie defend certain prerogatives of the bureaucracy and are opposed to the election of all officials, opposed to the complete abolition of electoral qualifications, opposed to making officials directly responsible to the people, etc., because these strata realise that the proletariat will take advantage of such complete democratisation in order to use it *against* the bourgeoisie. This is the case in Russia, too. Many and most diverse strata of the Russian people are opposed to the omnipotent, irresponsible, corrupt, savage, ignorant and parasitic Russian bureaucracy. But except for the proletariat, *not one* of these strata would agree to the complete democratisation of the bureaucracy, because all these strata (bourgeoisie, petty bourgeoisie, the "intelligentsia" in general) have some ties with the bureaucracy, because all these strata are *kith and kin* of the Russian bureaucracy. Who does not know how easy it is in Holy Russia for a radical intellectual, or socialist intellectual, to turn into an official of the Imperial Government, an official who takes comfort from the thought that he does "good" within the limits of office routine, an official who pleads this "good" in justification of his political indifference, his servility towards the government of the knout and the whip? *The proletariat* alone is unreservedly hostile to the autocracy and the Russian bureaucracy, *the proletariat* alone has no *ties* with these organs of aristocratic-bourgeois society and the proletariat alone is capable of irreconcilable hostility towards them and of waging a determined struggle against them.

When we show that the proletariat, led in its class struggle by Social-Democracy, is the vanguard fighter of Russian democracy, we encounter the very widespread and very strange opinion that Russian Social-Democracy relegates political tasks and political struggle to the background. As we see, this opinion is the very opposite of the truth. * * *

* * *

Russian Social-Democracy is still faced with an enormous, almost untouched field of work. The awakening of the Russian working class, its spontaneous striving for knowledge, organisation, socialism, for the struggle against its exploiters and oppressors becomes more widespread, more strikingly apparent every day. The enormous progress made by Russian capitalism in recent times is a guarantee that the working-class movement will grow uninterruptedly in breadth and depth. We are apparently now passing through the period in the capitalist cycle when industry is "prospering," when business is brisk, when the factories are working at full capacity and when countless new factories, new enterprises, joint-stock companies, railway enterprises, etc., etc., are springing up like mushrooms. One need not be a prophet to foretell the inevitable and fairly sharp crash that is bound to succeed this period of industrial "prosperity." This crash will ruin masses of small owners, will throw masses of workers into the ranks of the unemployed, and will thus confront all the workers in an acute form with the problems of socialism and democracy which have long faced every class-conscious, every thinking worker. Russian Social-Democrats must see to it that when this crash comes the Russian proletariat is more class-conscious, more united, able to understand the tasks of the Russian working class, capable of putting up resistance to the capitalist class—which is now reaping huge profits and always strives to burden the workers with the losses—and capable of leading Russian democracy in a decisive struggle against the police autocracy, which binds and fetters the Russian workers and the whole of the Russian people.

And so, to work, comrades! Let us not lose precious time! Russian Social-Democrats have much to do to meet the requirements of the awakening proletariat, to organise the working-class movement, to strengthen the revolutionary groups and their mutual ties, to supply the workers with propaganda and agitational literature, and to unite the workers' circles and Social-Democratic groups scattered all over Russia into a single *Social-Democratic Labour Party*!

What Is to Be Done?

BURNING QUESTIONS OF OUR MOVEMENT

Written at the end of 1901 and beginning of 1902, and published in March 1902 in Stuttgart, *What Is to Be Done?* elaborated in a comprehensive way the ideas about the party which Lenin had broached in earlier shorter writings, including *The Tasks of the Russian Social-Democrats*. His polemic against "Economism," for all its importance in the treatise, was mainly a convenient backdrop for presenting his theory of the nature, structure, and activities of the revolutionary party organization. In essence this work was the platform of what became known as "Bolshevism" after the party's Second Congress (1903), where the Bolshevik-Menshevik split originated. For further interpretation of its historical significance, see the Introduction, pp. xxxviii–xliii, above.

Party struggles lend a party strength and vitality; the greatest proof of a party's weakness is its diffuseness and the blurring of clear demarcations; a party becomes stronger by purging itself.
—From a letter of Lassalle to Marx, June 24, 1852

I. Dogmatism and "Freedom of Criticism"

A. *What Does "Freedom of Criticism" Mean?*

"Freedom of criticism" is undoubtedly the most fashionable slogan at the present time, and the one most frequently employed in the controversies between socialists and democrats in all countries. At first sight, nothing would appear to be more strange than the solemn appeals to freedom of criticism made by one of the parties to the dispute. Have voices been raised in the advanced parties against the constitutional law of the majority of European countries which guarantees freedom to science and scientific investigation? "Something must be wrong here," will be the comment of the onlooker who has heard this fashionable slogan repeated at every turn but has not yet penetrated the essence of the disagreement among the disputants; "evidently this slogan is one of the conventional phrases which, like nicknames, become legitimised by use, and become almost generic terms."

In fact, it is no secret for anyone that two trends have taken form in present-day international[1] Social-Democracy. The conflict between these trends now flares up in a bright flame and now dies down and smoulders under the ashes of imposing "truce resolutions." The essence of the "new" trend, which adopts a "critical" attitude towards "obsolete dogmatic" Marxism, has been clearly enough *presented* by Bernstein and *demonstrated* by Millerand.

Social-Democracy must change from a party of social revolution into a democratic party of social reforms. Bernstein has surrounded this political demand with a whole battery of well-attuned "new" arguments and reasonings. Denied was the possibility of putting socialism on a scientific basis and of demonstrating its necessity and inevitability from the point of view of the materialist conception of history. Denied was the fact of growing impoverishment, the process of proletarisation, and the intensification of capitalist contradictions; the very concept, *"ultimate aim,"* was declared to be unsound, and the idea of the dictatorship of the proletariat was completely rejected. Denied was the antithesis in principle between liberalism and socialism. Denied was *the theory of the class struggle*, on the alleged grounds that it could not be applied to a strictly democratic society governed according to the will of the majority, etc.

Thus, the demand for a decisive turn from revolutionary Social-Democracy to bourgeois social-reformism was accompanied by a no less decisive turn towards bourgeois criticism of all the fundamental ideas of Marxism. In view of the fact that this criticism of Marxism has long been directed from the political platform, from university chairs, in numerous pamphlets and in a series of learned treatises, in view of the fact that the entire younger generation of the educated classes has been systematically reared for decades on this criticism, it is not surprising that the "new critical" trend in

1. Incidentally, in the history of modern socialism this is a phenomenon, perhaps unique and in its way very consoling, namely, that the strife of the various trends within the socialist movement has from national become international. Formerly, the disputes between Lassalleans and Eisenachers, between Guesdists and Possibilists, between Fabians and Social-Democrats, and between Narodnaya Volya adherents and Social-Democrats, remained confined within purely national frameworks, reflecting purely national features, and proceeding, as it were, on different planes. At the present time (as is now evident), the English Fabians, the French Ministerialists, the German Bernsteinians, and the Russian Critics—all belong to the same family, all extol each other, learn from each other, and together take up arms against "dogmatic" Marxism. In this first really international battle with socialist opportunism, international revolutionary Social-Democracy will perhaps become sufficiently strengthened to put an end to the political reaction that has long reigned in Europe. [*Lenin*] The "Russian Critics" were the so-called "legal Marxists" (Struve, Bulgakov, Berdyaev and others).

Social-Democracy should spring up, all complete, like Minerva from the head of Jove. The content of this new trend did not have to grow and take shape, it was transferred bodily from bourgeois to socialist literature.

To proceed. If Bernstein's theoretical criticism and political yearnings were still unclear to anyone, the French took the trouble strikingly to demonstrate the "new method." In this instance, too, France has justified its old reputation of being "the land where, more than anywhere else, the historical class struggles were each time fought out to a decision . . ." (Engels, Introduction to Marx's *Der 18 Brumaire*). The French socialists have begun, not to theorise, but to act. The democratically more highly developed political conditions in France have permitted them to put "Bernsteinism into practice" immediately, with all its consequences. Millerand has furnished an excellent example of practical Bernsteinism; not without reason did Bernstein and Vollmar rush so zealously to defend and laud him. Indeed, if Social-Democracy, in essence, is merely a party of reform and must be bold enough to admit this openly, then not only has a socialist the right to join a bourgeois cabinet, but he must always strive to do so. If democracy, in essence, means the abolition of class domination, then why should not a socialist minister charm the whole bourgeois world by orations on class collaboration? Why should he not remain in the cabinet even after the shooting-down of workers by gendarmes has exposed, for the hundredth and thousandth time, the real nature of the democratic collaboration of classes? Why should he not personally take part in greeting the tsar, for whom the French socialists now have no other name than hero of the gallows, knout, and exile (*knouteur, pendeur et déportateur*)? And the reward for this utter humiliation and self-degradation of socialism in the face of the whole world, for the corruption of the socialist consciousness of the working masses— the only basis that can guarantee our victory—the reward for this is pompous *projects* for miserable reforms, so miserable in fact that much more has been obtained from bourgeois governments!

He who does not deliberately close his eyes cannot fail to see that the new "critical" trend in socialism is nothing more nor less than a new variety of *opportunism*. And if we judge people, not by the glittering uniforms they don or by the high-sounding appellations they give themselves, but by their actions and by what they actually advocate, it will be clear that "freedom of criticism" means freedom for an opportunist trend in Social-Democracy, freedom to convert Social-Democracy into a democratic party of reform, freedom to introduce bourgeois ideas and bourgeois elements into socialism.

"Freedom" is a grand word, but under the banner of freedom for industry the most predatory wars were waged, under the banner of freedom of labour, the working people were robbed. The modern use of the term "freedom of criticism" contains the same inherent falsehood. Those who are really convinced that they have made progress in science would not demand freedom for the new views to continue side by side with the old, but the substitution of the new views for the old. The cry heard today, "Long live freedom of criticism," is too strongly reminiscent of the fable of the empty barrel.

We are marching in a compact group along a precipitous and difficult path, firmly holding each other by the hand. We are surrounded on all sides by enemies, and we have to advance almost constantly under their fire. We have combined, by a freely adopted decision, for the purpose of fighting the enemy, and not of retreating into the neighbouring marsh, the inhabitants of which, from the very outset, have reproached us with having separated ourselves into an exclusive group and with having chosen the path of struggle instead of the path of conciliation. And now some among us begin to cry out: Let us go into the marsh! And when we begin to shame them, they retort: What backward people you are! Are you not ashamed to deny us the liberty to invite you to take a better road! Oh, yes, gentlemen! You are free not only to invite us, but to go yourselves wherever you will, even into the marsh. In fact, we think that the marsh is your proper place, and we are prepared to render *you* every assistance to get there. Only let go of our hands, don't clutch at us and don't besmirch the grand word freedom, for we too are "free" to go where we please, free to fight not only against the marsh, but also against those who are turning towards the marsh!

B. *The New Advocates of "Freedom of Criticism"*

Now, this slogan ("freedom of criticism") has in recent times been solemnly advanced by *Rabocheye Dyelo* (No. 10), organ of the Union of Russian Social-Democrats Abroad,[2] not as a theoreti-

2. The Union of Russian Social-Democrats Abroad was founded in 1894 on the initiative of the Emancipation of Labour group on the condition that all members accepted the group's programme.

The First Congress of the R.S.D.L.P. (Russian Social-Democratic Labour Party), held in March 1898, recognised the Union as the Party's representative abroad. Later the Union became dominated by the "Economists," also known as the "Young." (The Economists held that revolutionary struggle for socialism was premature in underdeveloped Russia and that Marxists should therefore confine themselves, for the present, to assisting the workers in their fight for economic benefits.) They refused to support the Manifesto of the First Congress because it declared the winning of political liberty to be the immediate task of the Social-Democrats.

At the Second Congress of the R.S.D.L.P., in 1903, representatives of

cal postulate, but as a political demand, as a reply to the question, "Is it possible to unite the Social-Democratic organisations operating abroad?": "For a durable unity, there must be freedom of criticism" (p. 36).

From this statement two definite conclusions follow: (1) that *Rabocheye Dyelo* has taken under its wing the opportunist trend in international Social-Democracy in general, and (2) that *Rabocheye Dyelo* demands freedom for opportunism in Russian Social-Democracy. * * *

* * *

C. Criticism in Russia

The chief distinguishing feature of Russia in regard to the point we are examining is that *the very beginning* of the spontaneous working-class movement, on the one hand, and of the turn of progressive public opinion towards Marxism, on the other, was marked by the combination of manifestly heterogeneous elements under a common flag to fight the common enemy (the obsolete social and political world outlook). We refer to the heyday of "legal Marxism." Speaking generally, this was an altogether curious phenomenon that no one in the eighties or the beginning of the nineties would have believed possible. In a country ruled by an autocracy, with a completely enslaved press, in a period of desperate political reaction in which even the tiniest outgrowth of political discontent and protest is persecuted, the theory of revolutionary Marxism suddenly forces its way into the *censored* literature and, though expounded in Aesopian language, is understood by all the "interested." The government had accustomed itself to regarding only the theory of the (revolutionary) Narodnaya Volya as dangerous, without, as is usual, observing its internal evolution, and rejoicing at *any* criticism levelled against it. Quite a considerable time elapsed (by our Russian standards) before the government realised what had happened and the unwieldy army of censors and gendarmes discovered the new enemy and flung itself upon him. Meanwhile, Marxist books were published one after another, Marxist journals and newspapers were founded, nearly everyone became a Marxist, Marxists were flattered, Marxists were courted, and the book publishers rejoiced at the extraordinary, ready sale of Marxist literature. It was quite natural, therefore, that among the Marxian

the Union (the *Rabocheye Dyelo* group) adopted an extreme opportunist position and left the Congress after it had recognised the League of Russian Revolutionary Social-Democracy Abroad as the only Party organisation abroad. The Second Congress of the Party declared the Union dissolved.

neophytes who were caught up in this atmosphere, there should be more than one "author who got a swelled head. . . ."[3]

We can now speak calmly of this period as of an event of the past. It is no secret that the brief period in which Marxism blossomed on the surface of our literature was called forth by an alliance between people of extreme and of very moderate views. In point of fact, the latter were bourgeois democrats; this conclusion (so markedly confirmed by their subsequent "critical" development) suggested itself to some even when the "alliance" was still intact.[4]

That being the case, are not the revolutionary Social-Democrats who entered into the alliance with the future "Critics" mainly responsible for the subsequent "confusion"? This question, together with a reply in the affirmative, is sometimes heard from people with too rigid a view. But such people are entirely in the wrong. Only those who are not sure of themselves can fear to enter into temporary alliances even with unreliable people; not a single political party could exist without such alliances. The combination with the legal Marxists was in its way the first really political alliance entered into by Russian Social-Democrats. Thanks to this alliance, an astonishingly rapid victory was obtained over Narodism, and Marxist ideas (even though in a vulgarised form) became very widespread. Moreover, the alliance was not concluded altogether without "conditions." Evidence of this is the burning by the censor, in 1895, of the Marxist collection *Material on the Question of the Economic Development of Russia*. If the literary agreement with the legal Marxists can be compared with a political alliance, then that book can be compared with a political treaty.

The rupture, of course, did not occur because the "allies" proved to be bourgeois democrats. On the contrary, the representatives of the latter trend are natural and desirable allies of Social-Democracy insofar as its democratic tasks, brought to the fore by the prevailing situation in Russia, are concerned. But an essential condition for such an alliance must be the full opportunity for the socialists to reveal to the working class that its interests are diametrically opposed to the interests of the bourgeoisie. However, the Bernsteinian and "critical" trend, to which the majority of the legal Marxists turned, deprived the socialists of this opportunity and demoralised the socialist consciousness by vulgarising Marxism, by advocating the theory of the blunting of social contradictions, by declaring the idea of the social revolution and of the dictatorship of the proletar-

3. *The Author Who Got a Swelled Head* is the title of a story by Maxim Gorky.
4. The reference is to an article by K. Tulin directed against Struve. The article was based on an essay entitled "The Reflection of Marxism in Bourgeois Litera-ture." [*Lenin, 1907 edition*] Lenin here refers to his article "The Economic Content of Narodism and the Criticism of It in Mr. Struve's Book (The Reflection of Marxism in Bourgeois Literature)" published under the pseudonym K. Tulin.

iat to be absurd, by reducing the working-class movement and the class struggle to narrow trade-unionism and to a "realistic" struggle for petty, gradual reforms. This was synonymous with bourgeois democracy's denial of socialism's right to independence and, consequently, of its right to existence; in practice it meant a striving to convert the nascent working-class movement into an appendage of the liberals.

Naturally, under such circumstances the rupture was necessary. But the "peculiar" feature of Russia manifested itself in the fact that this rupture simply meant the elimination of the Social-Democrats from the most accessible and widespread "legal" literature. The "ex-Marxists," who took up the flag of "criticism" and who obtained almost a monopoly to "demolish" Marxism, entrenched themselves in this literature. Catchwords like "Against orthodoxy" and "Long live freedom of criticism" (now repeated by *Rabocheye Dyelo*) forthwith became the vogue, and the fact that neither the censor nor the gendarmes could resist this vogue is apparent from the publication of *three* Russian editions of the work of the celebrated Bernstein[5] (celebrated in the Herostratean sense) and from the fact that the works of Bernstein, Mr. Prokopovich, and others were recommended by Zubatov (*Iskra*, No. 10). A task now devolved upon the Social-Democrats that was difficult in itself and was made incredibly more difficult by purely external obstacles— the task of combating the new trend. This trend did not confine itself to the sphere of literature. The turn towards "criticism" was accompanied by an infatuation for Economism among Social-Democratic practical workers.

The manner in which the connection between, and interdependence of, legal criticism and illegal Economism arose and grew is in itself an interesting subject, one that could serve as the theme of a special article. We need only note here that this connection undoubtedly existed. The notoriety deservedly acquired by the *Credo*[6] was due precisely to the frankness with which it formulated this connection and blurted out the fundamental political tendency of Economism—let the workers carry on the economic struggle (it would be more correct to say the trade-unionist struggle, because the latter also embraces specifically working-class politics) and let the Marxist intelligentsia merge with the liberals for the political "struggle." Thus, trade-unionist work "among the people" meant fulfilling the first part of this task, while legal criticism meant fulfilling the second. This statement was such an excellent weapon against Econ-

---

5. Eduard Bernstein's book *Die Voraussetzungen des Sozialismus und die Aufgaben der Sozialdemokratie* (published in English as *The Principles of Socialism*) was published in Russia in 1901.

6. *Credo*, a manifesto of the Economists drawn up by Y. D. Kuskova, appeared in 1899. Along with Kuskova, S. N. Prokopovich was a prominent member of the Economist group.

omism that, had there been no *Credo*, it would have been worth inventing one.

* * *

D. *Engels on the Importance of the Theoretical Struggle*

"Dogmatism, doctrinairism," "ossification of the party—the inevitable retribution that follows the violent strait-lacing of thought" —these are the enemies against which the knightly champions of "freedom of criticism" in *Rabocheye Dyelo* rise up in arms. * * *

* * *

* * * [H]igh-sounding phrases against the ossification of thought, etc., conceal unconcern and helplessness with regard to the development of theoretical thought. The case of the Russian Social-Democrats manifestly illustrates the general European phenomenon (long ago noted also by the German Marxists) that the much vaunted freedom of criticism does not imply substitution of one theory for another, but freedom from all integral and pondered theory; it implies eclecticism and lack of principle. Those who have the slightest acquaintance with the actual state of our movement cannot but see that the wide spread of Marxism was accompanied by a certain lowering of the theoretical level. Quite a number of people with very little, and even a total lack of theoretical training joined the movement because of its practical significance and its practical successes. We can judge from that how tactless *Rabocheye Dyelo* is when, with an air of triumph, it quotes Marx's statement: "Every step of real movement is more important than a dozen programmes." To repeat these words in a period of theoretical disorder is like wishing mourners at a funeral many happy returns of the day. Moreover, these words of Marx are taken from his letter on the Gotha Programme, in which he *sharply condemns* eclecticism in the formulation of principles. If you must unite, Marx wrote to the party leaders, then enter into agreements to satisfy the practical aims of the movement, but do not allow any bargaining over principles, do not make theoretical "concessions." This was Marx's idea, and yet there are people among us who seek—in his name—to belittle the significance of theory!

Without revolutionary theory there can be no revolutionary movement. This idea cannot be insisted upon too strongly at a time when the fashionable preaching of opportunism goes hand in hand with an infatuation for the narrowest forms of practical activity. Yet, for Russian Social-Democrats the importance of theory is enhanced by three other circumstances, which are often forgotten:

first, by the fact that our Party is only in process of formation, its features are only just becoming defined, and it has as yet far from settled accounts with the other trends of revolutionary thought that threaten to divert the movement from the correct path. On the contrary, precisely the very recent past was marked by a revival of non-Social-Democratic revolutionary trends (an eventuation regarding which Axelrod long ago warned the Economists). Under these circumstances, what at first sight appears to be an "unimportant" error may lead to most deplorable consequences, and only short-sighted people can consider factional disputes and a strict differentiation between shades of opinion inopportune or superfluous. The fate of Russian Social-Democracy for very many years to come may depend on the strengthening of one or the other "shade."

Secondly, the Social-Democratic movement is in its very essence an international movement. This means, not only that we must combat national chauvinism, but that an incipient movement in a young country can be successful only if it makes use of the experiences of other countries. In order to make use of these experiences it is not enough merely to be acquainted with them, or simply to copy out the latest resolutions. What is required is the ability to treat these experiences critically and to test them independently. He who realises how enormously the modern working-class movement has grown and branched out will understand what a reserve of theoretical forces and political (as well as revolutionary) experience is required to carry out this task.

Thirdly, the national tasks of Russian Social-Democracy are such as have never confronted any other socialist party in the world. We shall have occasion further on to deal with the political and organisational duties which the task of emancipating the whole people from the yoke of autocracy imposes upon us. At this point, we wish to state only that the *role of vanguard fighter can be fulfilled only by a party that is guided by the most advanced theory*. To have a concrete understanding of what this means, let the reader recall such predecessors of Russian Social-Democracy as Herzen, Belinsky, Chernyshevsky, and the brilliant galaxy of revolutionaries of the seventies; let him ponder over the world significance which Russian literature is now acquiring; let him . . . but be that enough!

Let us quote what Engels said in 1874 concerning the significance of theory in the Social-Democratic movement. Engels recognises *not two* forms of the great struggle of Social-Democracy (political and economic), as is the fashion among us, *but three, placing the theoretical struggle on a par with the first two*. His recommendations to the German working-class movement, which had become strong, practically and politically, are so instructive from the standpoint of present-day problems and controversies, that we hope the reader will not be vexed with us for quoting a long passage from his prefatory note to *Der deutsche Bauernkrieg*,[7] which has long become a great bibliographical rarity:

The German workers have two important advantages over those of the rest of Europe. First, they belong to the most theoretical people of Europe; and they have retained that sense of theory which the so-called "educated" classes of Germany have almost completely lost. Without German philosophy, which preceded it, particularly that of Hegel, German scientific socialism —the only scientific socialism that has ever existed—would never have come into being. Without a sense of theory among the workers, this scientific socialism would never have entered their flesh and blood as much as is the case. What an immeasurable advantage this is may be seen, on the one hand, from the indifference towards all theory, which is one of the main reasons why the English working-class movement crawls along so slowly in spite of the splendid organisation of the individual unions; on the other hand, from the mischief and confusion wrought by Proudhonism, in its original form, among the French, and Belgians, and, in the form further caricatured by Bakunin, among the Spaniards and Italians.

The second advantage is that, chronologically speaking, the Germans were about the last to come into the workers' movement. Just as German theoretical socialism will never forget that it rests on the shoulders of Saint-Simon, Fourier, and Owen— three men who, in spite of all their fantastic notions and all their utopianism, have their place among the most eminent thinkers of all times, and whose genius anticipated innumerable things, the correctness of which is now being scientifically proved by us—so the practical workers' movement in Germany ought never to forget that it has developed on the shoulders of the English and French movements, that it was able simply to utilise their dearly bought experience, and could now avoid their mistakes, which in their time were mostly unavoidable. Without the precedent of the English trade unions and French workers' political struggles, without the gigantic impulse given especially by the Paris Commune, where would we be now?

It must be said to the credit of the German workers that they have exploited the advantages of their situation with rare understanding. For the first time since a workers' movement has existed, the struggle is being conducted pursuant to its three sides—the theoretical, the political, and the practical-economic (resistance to the capitalists)—in harmony and in its interconnections, and in a systematic way. It is precisely in this, as it were, concentric attack, that the strength and invincibility of the German movement lies.

Due to this advantageous situation, on the one hand, and to

7. *The Peasant War in Germany.*

the insular peculiarities of the English and the forcible suppression of the French movement, on the other, the German workers have for the moment been placed in the vanguard of the proletarian struggle. How long events will allow them to occupy this post of honour cannot be foretold. But let us hope that as long as they occupy it, they will fill it fittingly. This demands redoubled efforts in every field of struggle and agitation. In particular, it will be the duty of the leaders to gain an ever clearer insight into all theoretical questions, to free themselves more and more from the influence of traditional phrases inherited from the old world outlook, and constantly to keep in mind that socialism, since it has become a science, demands that it be pursued as a science, i.e., that it be studied. The task will be to spread with increased zeal among the masses of the workers the ever more clarified understanding thus acquired, to knit together ever more firmly the organisation both of the party and of the trade unions. . . .

If the German workers progress in this way, they will not be marching exactly at the head of the movement—it is not at all in the interest of this movement that the workers of any particular country should march at its head—but they will occupy an honourable place in the battle line; and they will stand armed for battle when either unexpectedly grave trials or momentous events demand of them increased courage, increased determination and energy.

Engels's words proved prophetic. Within a few years the German workers were subjected to unexpectedly grave trials in the form of the Exceptional Law Against the Socialists. And they met those trials armed for battle and succeeded in emerging from them victorious.

The Russian proletariat will have to undergo trials immeasurably graver; it will have to fight a monster compared with which an antisocialist law in a constitutional country seems but a dwarf. History has now confronted us with an immediate task which is the *most revolutionary* of all the *immediate* tasks confronting the proletariat of any country. The fulfilment of this task, the destruction of the most powerful bulwark, not only of European, but (it may now be said) of Asiatic reaction, would make the Russian proletariat the vanguard of the international revolutionary proletariat. And we have the right to count upon acquiring this honourable title, already earned by our predecessors, the revolutionaries of the seventies, if we succeed in inspiring our movement, which is a thousand times broader and deeper, with the same devoted determination and vigour.

II. The Spontaneity of the Masses and the Consciousness of the Social-Democrats

We have said that our movement, much more extensive and deep than the movement of the seventies, must be inspired with the same devoted determination and energy that inspired the movement at that time. Indeed, no one, we think, has until now doubted that the strength of the present-day movement lies in the awakening of the masses (principally, the industrial proletariat) and that its weakness lies in the lack of consciousness and initiative among the revolutionary leaders.

However, of late a staggering discovery has been made, which threatens to disestablish all hitherto prevailing views on this question. This discovery was made by *Rabocheye Dyelo*, which in its polemic with *Iskra* and *Zarya*[8] did not confine itself to making objections on separate points, but tried to ascribe "general disagreements" to a more profound cause—to the "different appraisals of the *relative* importance of the spontaneous and consciously 'methodical' element." *Rabocheye Dyelo* formulated its indictment as a *"belittling of the significance of the objective or the spontaneous element of development."*[9] To this we say: Had the polemics with *Iskra* and *Zarya* resulted in nothing more than causing *Rabocheye Dyelo* to hit upon these "general disagreements," that alone would give us considerable satisfaction, so significant is this thesis and so clear is the light it sheds on the quintessence of the present-day theoretical and political differences that exist among Russian Social-Democrats.

For this reason the question of the relation between consciousness and spontaneity is of such enormous general interest, and for this reason the question must be dealt with in great detail.

A. *The Beginning of the Spontaneous Upsurge*

In the previous chapter we pointed out how *universally* absorbed the educated youth of Russia was in the theories of Marxism in the middle of the nineties. In the same period the strikes that followed the famous St. Petersburg industrial war of 1896 assumed a similar general character. Their spread over the whole of Russia clearly showed the depth of the newly awakening popular movement, and if we are to speak of the "spontaneous element" then, of course, it

---

8. *Zarya* (*Dawn*) was a Marxist journal published by the *Iskra* editorial board in Stuttgart in 1901 and 1902.

9. *Rabocheye Dyelo*, No. 10, September 1901, pp. 17–18. *Rabocheye Dyelo*'s italics. [*Lenin*]

is this strike movement which, first and foremost, must be regarded as spontaneous. But there is spontaneity and spontaneity. Strikes occurred in Russia in the seventies and sixties (and even in the first half of the nineteenth century), and they were accompanied by the "spontaneous" destruction of machinery, etc. Compared with these "revolts," the strikes of the nineties might even be described as "conscious," to such an extent do they mark the progress which the working-class movement made in that period. This shows that the "spontaneous element," in essence, represents nothing more nor less than consciousness in an *embryonic form*. Even the primitive revolts expressed the awakening of consciousness to a certain extent. The workers were losing their age-long faith in the permanence of the system which oppressed them and began . . . I shall not say to understand, but to sense the necessity for collective resistance, definitely abandoning their slavish submission to the authorities. But this was, nevertheless, more in the nature of outbursts of desperation and vengeance than of *struggle*. The strikes of the nineties revealed far greater flashes of consciousness; definite demands were advanced, the strike was carefully timed, known cases and instances in other places were discussed, etc. The revolts were simply the resistance of the oppressed, whereas the systematic strikes represented the class struggle in embryo, but only in embryo. Taken by themselves, these strikes were simply trade union struggles, not yet Social-Democratic struggles. They marked the awakening antagonisms between workers and employers; but the workers were not, and could not be, conscious of the irreconcilable antagonism of their interests to the whole of the modern political and social system, i.e., theirs was not yet Social-Democratic consciousness. In this sense, the strikes of the nineties, despite the enormous progress they represented as compared with the "revolts," remained a purely spontaneous movement.

We have said that *there could not have been* Social-Democratic consciousness among the workers. It would have to be brought to them from without. The history of all countries shows that the working class, exclusively by its own effort, is able to develop only trade union consciousness, i.e., the conviction that it is necessary to combine in unions, fight the employers, and strive to compel the government to pass necessary labour legislation, etc.[1] The theory of socialism, however, grew out of the philosophic, historical, and economic theories elaborated by educated representatives of the propertied classes, by intellectuals. By their social status the founders of modern scientific socialism, Marx and Engels, them-

1. Trade-unionism does not exclude "politics" altogether, as some imagine. Trade unions have always conducted some political (but not Social-Democratic) agitation and struggle. We shall deal with the difference between trade union politics and Social-Democratic politics in the next chapter. [*Lenin*]

selves belonged to the bourgeois intelligentsia. In the very same way, in Russia, the theoretical doctrine of Social-Democracy arose altogether independently of the spontaneous growth of the working-class movement; it arose as a natural and inevitable outcome of the development of thought among the revolutionary socialist intelligentsia. In the period under discussion, the middle nineties, this doctrine not only represented the completely formulated programme of the Emancipation of Labour group, but had already won over to its side the majority of the revolutionary youth in Russia.

Hence, we had both the spontaneous awakening of the working masses, their awakening to conscious life and conscious struggle, and a revolutionary youth, armed with Social-Democratic theory and straining towards the workers. In this connection it is particularly important to state the oft-forgotten (and comparatively little-known) fact that, although the *early* Social-Democrats of that period *zealously carried on economic agitation* (being guided in this activity by the truly useful indications contained in the pamphlet *On Agitation,* then still in manuscript), they did not regard this as their sole task. On the contrary, *from the very beginning* they set for Russian Social-Democracy the most far-reaching historical tasks, in general, and the task of overthrowing the autocracy, in particular. Thus, towards the end of 1895, the St. Petersburg group of Social-Democrats, which founded the League of Struggle for the Emancipation of the Working Class, prepared the first issue of a newspaper called *Rabocheye Dyelo.* This issue was ready to go to press when it was seized by the gendarmes, on the night of December 8, 1895, in a raid on the house of one of the members of the group, Anatoly Alexeyevich Vaneyev,[2] so that the first edition of *Rabocheye Dyelo* was not destined to see the light of day. The leading article in this issue (which perhaps thirty years hence some *Russkaya Starina*[3] will unearth in the archives of the Department of Police) outlined the historical tasks of the working class in Russia and placed the achievement of political liberty at their head. The issue also contained an article entitled "What Are Our Ministers Thinking About?" which dealt with the crushing of the elementary education committees by the police. In addition, there was some correspondence from St. Petersburg, and from other parts of Russia (e.g., a letter on the massacre of the workers in Yaroslavl

2. A. A. Vaneyev died in Eastern Siberia in 1899 from consumption, which he contracted during solitary confinement in prison prior to his banishment. That is why we considered it possible to publish the above information, the authenticity of which we guarantee, for it comes from persons who were closely and directly acquainted with A. A. Vaneyev. [*Lenin*]

3. The leading article "To the Russian Workers" that Lenin wrote for the newspaper *Rabocheye Dyelo* has not been found. *Russkaya Starina (Russian Antiquary)* was a monthly magazine founded by M. I. Semevsky that carried articles on history; it was published in St. Petersburg from 1870 to 1918.

Gubernia⁴). This "first effort," if we are not mistaken, of the Russian Social-Democrats of the nineties was not a purely local, or less still, "Economic," newspaper, but one that aimed to unite the strike movement with the revolutionary movement against the autocracy, and to win over to the side of Social-Democracy all who were oppressed by the policy of reactionary obscurantism. No one in the slightest degree acquainted with the state of the movement at that period could doubt that such a paper would have met with warm response among the workers of the capital and the revolutionary intelligentsia and would have had a wide circulation. The failure of the enterprise merely showed that the Social-Democrats of that period were unable to meet the immediate requirements of the time owing to their lack of revolutionary experience and practical training. This must be said, too, with regard to the *St. Peterburgsky Rabochy Listok*⁵ and particularly with regard to *Rabochaya Gazeta* and the *Manifesto* of the Russian Social-Democratic Labour Party, founded in the spring of 1898. Of course, we would not dream of blaming the Social-Democrats of that time for this unpreparedness. But in order to profit from the experience of that movement, and to draw practical lessons from it, we must thoroughly understand the causes and significance of this or that shortcoming. It is therefore highly important to establish the fact that a part (perhaps even a majority) of the Social-Democrats, active in the period of 1895–98, justly considered it possible even then, at the very beginning of the "spontaneous" movement, to come forward with a most extensive programme and a militant tactical line.⁶ Lack of training of the majority of the revolutionaries, an entirely natural phenomenon, could not have roused any particular fears. Once the tasks were correctly defined, once the energy existed for repeated attempts to fulfil them, temporary failures represented only part misfortune. Revolutionary experience and organisational skill are things that can be acquired, provided the desire is there to

---

4. This refers to the suppression of the strike of Yaroslavl textile workers on April 27 (May 9), 1895. The strike, which involved over four thousand workers, was caused by the introduction of new rates, by means of which the administration of the mills reduced the wages of the workers.

5. *St. Peterburgsky Rabochy Listok* (*The St. Petersburg Workers' Paper*) was the organ of the St. Petersburg League of Struggle for the Emancipation of the Working Class.

6. "In adopting a hostile attitude towards the activities of the Social-Democrats of the late nineties, *Iskra* ignores the absence at that time of conditions for any work other than the struggle for petty demands," declare the Economists in their "Letter to Russian Social-Democratic Organs" (*Iskra* No. 12). The facts given above show that the assertion about "absence of conditions" is *diametrically opposed to the truth*. Not only at the end, but even in the mid-nineties, all the conditions existed for *other* work, besides the struggle for petty demands—all the conditions except adequate training of leaders. Instead of frankly admitting that we, the ideologists, the leaders, lacked sufficient training— the Economists seek to shift the blame entirely upon the "absence of conditions," upon the effect of material environment that determines the road upon which no ideologist will be able to divert the movement. What is this but slavish cringing before spontaneity, what but the infatuation of the "ideologists" with their own shortcomings? [*Lenin*]

acquire them, provided the shortcomings are recognised, which in revolutionary activity is more than half-way towards their removal.

But what was only part misfortune became full misfortune when this consciousness began to grow dim (it was very much alive among the members of the groups mentioned), when there appeared people—and even Social-Democratic organs—that were prepared to regard shortcomings as virtues, that even tried to invent a *theoretical* basis for their *slavish cringing before spontaneity*. It is time to draw conclusions from this trend, the content of which is incorrectly and too narrowly characterised as Economism.

B. Bowing to Spontaneity. Rabochaya Mysl

* * *

* * * [I]n the very first literary expression of Economism we observe the exceedingly curious phenomenon—highly characteristic for an understanding of all the differences prevailing among present-day Social-Democrats—that the adherents of the "labour movement pure and simple," worshippers of the closest "organic" contacts (*Rabocheye Dyelo's* term) with the proletarian struggle, opponents of any non-worker intelligentsia (even a socialist intelligentsia), are compelled, in order to defend their positions, to resort to the arguments of the *bourgeois* "pure trade-unionists." This shows that from the very outset *Rabochaya Mysl* began—unconsciously—to implement the programme of the *Credo*. This shows (something *Rabocheye Dyelo* cannot grasp) that *all* worship of the spontaneity of the working-class movement, all belittling of the role of "the conscious element," of the role of Social-Democracy, *means, quite independently of whether he who belittles that role desires it or not, a strengthening of the influence of bourgeois ideology upon the workers.* All those who talk about "overrating the importance of ideology,"[7] about exaggerating the role of the conscious element,[8] etc., imagine that the labour movement pure and simple can elaborate, and will elaborate, an independent ideology for itself, if only the workers "wrest their fate from the hands of the leaders." But this is a profound mistake. To supplement what has been said above, we shall quote the following profoundly true and important words of Karl Kautsky on the new draft programme of the Austrian Social-Democratic Party.[9]

Many of our revisionist critics believe that Marx asserted that economic development and the class struggle create, not only the

7. Letter of the Economists, in *Iskra*, No. 12. [*Lenin*]
8. *Rabocheye Dyelo*, No. 10. [*Lenin*]
9. *Neue Zeit*, 1901–2, XX, I, No. 3, p. 79. The committee's draft to which Kautsky refers was adopted by the Vienna Congress (at the end of last year) in a slightly amended form. [*Lenin*] (In the following quotation, and in all material quoted by Lenin, all bracketed comments are his. [*R. T.*])

conditions for socialist production, but also, and directly, the *consciousness* [K. K.'s italics] of its necessity. And these critics assert that England, the country most highly developed capitalistically, is more remote than any other from this consciousness. Judging by the draft, one might assume that this allegedly orthodox-Marxist view, which is thus refuted, was shared by the committee that drafted the Austrian programme. In the draft programme it is stated: "The more capitalist development increases the numbers of the proletariat, the more the proletariat is compelled and becomes fit to fight against capitalism. The proletariat becomes conscious" of the possibility and of the necessity for socialism. In this connection socialist consciousness appears to be a necessary and direct result of the proletarian class struggle. But this is absolutely untrue. Of course, socialism, as a doctrine, has its roots in modern economic relationships just as the class struggle of the proletariat has, and, like the latter, emerges from the struggle against the capitalist-created poverty and misery of the masses. But socialism and the class struggle arise side by side and not one out of the other; each arises under different conditions. Modern socialist consciousness can arise only on the basis of profound scientific knowledge. Indeed, modern economic science is as much a condition for socialist production as, say, modern technology, and the proletariat can create neither the one nor the other, no matter how much it may desire to do so; both arise out of the modern social process. The vehicle of science is not the proletariat, but the *bourgeois intelligentsia* [K. K.'s italics]: it was in the minds of individual members of this stratum that modern socialism originated, and it was they who communicated it to the more intellectually developed proletarians who, in their turn, introduce it into the proletarian class struggle where conditions allow that to be done. Thus, socialist consciousness is something introduced into the proletarian class struggle from without [*von Aussen Hineingetragenes*] and not something that arose within it spontaneously [*urwüchsig*]. Accordingly, the old Hainfeld programme quite rightly stated that the task of Social-Democracy is to imbue the proletariat [literally: saturate the proletariat] with the *consciousness* of its position and the consciousness of its task. There would be no need for this if consciousness arose of itself from the class struggle. The new draft copied this proposition from the old programme, and attached it to the proposition mentioned above. But this completely broke the line of thought. . . .

Since there can be no talk of an independent ideology formulated by the working masses themselves in the process of their movement,[1] the *only* choice is—either bourgeois or socialist ideology.

---

1. This does not mean, of course, that the workers have no part in creating such an ideology. They take part, however, not as workers, but as socialist

There is no middle course (for mankind has not created a "third" ideology, and, moreover, in a society torn by class antagonisms there can never be a non-class or an above-class ideology). Hence, to belittle the socialist ideology *in any way, to turn aside from it in the slightest degree* means to strengthen bourgeois ideology. There is much talk of spontaneity. But the *spontaneous* development of the working-class movement leads to its subordination to bourgeois ideology, *to its development along the lines of the Credo programme*; for the spontaneous working-class movement is trade-unionism, is *Nur-Gewerkschaftlerei*, and trade-unionism means the ideological enslavement of the workers by the bourgeoisie. Hence, our task, the task of Social-Democracy, is *to combat spontaneity, to divert* the working-class movement from this spontaneous, trade-unionist striving to come under the wing of the bourgeoisie, and to bring it under the wing of revolutionary Social-Democracy. The sentence employed by the authors of the Economist letter published in *Iskra*, No. 12, that the efforts of the most inspired ideologists fail to divert the working-class movement from the path that is determined by the interaction of the material elements and the material environment is therefore *tantamount to renouncing socialism*. If these authors were capable of fearlessly, consistently, and throughly considering what they say, as everyone who enters the arena of literary and public activity should be, there would be nothing left for them but to "fold their useless arms over their empty breasts" and—surrender the field of action to the Struves and Prokopoviches, who are dragging the working-class movement "along the line of least resistance," i.e., along the line of bourgeois trade-unionism, or to the Zubatovs,[2] who are dragging it along the line of clerical and gendarme "ideology."

Let us recall the example of Germany. What was the historic service Lassalle rendered to the German working-class movement? It was that he *diverted* that movement from the path of progressionist trade-unionism and co-operativism towards which it had been spontaneously moving (*with the benign assistance of Schulze-*

---

theoreticians, as Proudhons and Weitlings; in other words, they take part only when they are able, and to the extent that they are able, more or less, to acquire the knowledge of their age and develop that knowledge. But in order that working men *may succeed in this more often*, every effort must be made to raise the level of the consciousness of the workers in general; it is necessary that the workers do not confine themselves to the artificially restricted limits of *"literature for workers"* but that they learn to an increasing degree to master *general literature*. It would be even truer to say "are not confined," instead of "do not confine themselves," because the workers themselves wish to read and do read all that is written for the intelligentsia, and only a few (bad) intellectuals believe that it is enough "for workers" to be told a few things about factory conditions and to have repeated to them over and over again what has long been known. [*Lenin*]

2. S. V. Zubatov, a colonel in the Moscow gendarmerie, initiated "police socialism" by setting up police-run workers' organizations in Moscow and other cities in 1902–3.

Delitzsch and his like). To fulfill such a task it was necessary to do something quite different from talking of underrating the spontaneous element, of tactics-as-process, of the interaction between elements and environment, etc. A *fierce struggle against spontaneity* was necessary, and only after such a struggle, extending over many years, was it possible, for instance, to convert the working population of Berlin from a bulwark of the progressionist party into one of the finest strongholds of Social-Democracy. This struggle is by no means over even today (as might seem to those who learn the history of the German movement from Prokopovich, and its philosophy from Struve). Even now the German working class is, so to speak, split up among a number of ideologies. A section of the workers is organised in Catholic and monarchist trade unions; another section is organised in the Hirsch-Duncker unions,[3] founded by the bourgeois worshippers of English trade-unionism; the third is organised in Social-Democratic trade unions. The last-named group is immeasurably more numerous than the rest, but the Social-Democratic ideology was able to achieve this superiority, and will be able to maintain it, only in an unswerving struggle against all other ideologies.

But why, the reader will ask, does the spontaneous movement, the movement along the line of least resistance, lead to the domination of bourgeois ideology? For the simple reason that bourgeois ideology is far older in origin than socialist ideology, that it is more fully developed, and that it has at its disposal *immeasurably* more means of dissemination.[4] And the younger the socialist movement in any given country, the more vigorously it must struggle against all attempts to entrench nonsocialist ideology, and the more resolutely the workers must be warned against the bad counsellors who shout against "overrating the conscious element," etc. The authors of the Economist letter, in unison with *Rabocheye Dyelo*, inveigh against the intolerance that is characteristic of the infancy of the movement. To this we reply: yes, our movement is indeed in its infancy, and in order that it may grow up faster, it must become imbued with intolerance against those who retard its growth by their subservience to spontaneity. Nothing is so ridiculous and

3. Reformist trade unions founded in Germany in 1868 by Max Hirsch and Franz Duncker, prominent members of the Progressist Party.
4. It is often said that the working class *spontaneously* gravitates towards socialism. This is perfectly true in the sense that socialist theory reveals the causes of the misery of the working class more profoundly and more correctly than any other theory, and for that reason the workers are able to assimilate it so easily, *provided*, however, this theory does not itself yield to spontaneity, *provided* it subordinates spontaneity to itself. Usually this is taken for granted, but it is precisely this which *Rabocheye Dyelo* forgets or distorts. The working class spontaneously gravitates towards socialism; nevertheless, most widespread (and continuously and diversely revived) bourgeois ideology spontaneously imposes itself upon the working class to a still greater degree. [*Lenin*]

harmful as pretending that we are "old hands" who have long ago experienced all the decisive stages of the struggle.

* * * [T]he first issue of *Rabochaya Mysl* shows that the term "Economism" (which, of course, we do not propose to abandon, since, in one way or another, this designation has already established itself) does not adequately convey the real character of the new trend. *Rabochaya Mysl* does not altogether repudiate the political struggle; the rules for a workers' mutual benefit fund published in its first issue contain a reference to combating the government. *Rabochaya Mysl* believes, however, that "politics always obediently follows economics" (*Rabocheye Dyelo* varies this thesis when it asserts in its programme that "in Russia more than in any other country, the economic struggle is *inseparable* from the political struggle"). *If by politics is meant Social-Democratic politics*, then the theses of *Rabochaya Mysl* and *Rabocheye Dyelo* are utterly incorrect. The economic struggle of the workers is very often connected (although not inseparably) with bourgeois politics, clerical politics, etc., as we have seen. *Rabocheye Dyelo's* theses are correct, if by politics is meant trade union politics, viz., the common striving of all workers to secure from the government measures for alleviating the distress to which their condition gives rise, but which do not abolish that condition, i.e., which do not remove the subjection of labour to capital. That striving indeed is common to the English trade-unionists, who are hostile to socialism, to the Catholic workers, to the "Zubatov" workers, etc. There is politics and politics. Thus, we see that *Rabochaya Mysl* does not so much deny the political struggle, as it bows to its *spontaneity*, to its unconsciousness. While fully recognising the political struggle (better: the political desires and demands of the workers), which arises spontaneously from the working-class movement itself, it absolutely refuses *independently to work out* a specifically *Social-Democratic politics* corresponding to the general tasks of socialism and to present-day conditions in Russia. Further on we shall show that *Rabocheye Dyelo* commits the same error.

C. The Self-Emancipation Group[5] and Rabocheye Dyelo

We have dealt at such length with the little-known and now almost forgotten leading article in the first issue of *Rabochaya Mysl* because it was the first and most striking expression of that general

---

5. The Self-Emancipation of the Working Class group was a small circle of Economists that came into being in St. Petersburg in the autumn of 1898 and existed for a few months only. The group issued a manifesto dated March 1899 announcing its aims (printed in the magazine *Nakanune* [*On the Eve*], published in July 1899), its rules, and several proclamations addressed to workers.

stream of thought which afterwards emerged into the light of day in innumerable streamlets. V. I. was perfectly right when, in praising the first issue and the leading article of *Rabochaya Mysl*, he said that the article had been written in a "sharp and fervent" manner ("*Listok*" *Rabotnika*, No. 9–10, p. 49). Every man with convictions who thinks he has something new to say writes "fervently" and in such a way as to make his views stand out in bold relief. Only those who are accustomed to sitting between two stools lack "fervour"; only such people are able to praise the fervour of *Rabochaya Mysl* one day and attack the "fervent polemics" of its opponents the next.

We shall not dwell on the "*Separate Supplement*" to *Rabochaya Mysl* (below we shall have occasion, on various points, to refer to this work, which expresses the ideas of the Economists more consistently than any other) but shall briefly mention the "Appeal of the Self-Emancipation of the Workers Group" (March 1899, reprinted in the London *Nakanune*, No. 7, July 1899). The authors of the "Appeal" rightly say that "the workers of Russia are *only just awakening*, are just beginning to look about them, and are *instinctively clutching at the first available* means of struggle." Yet they draw from this the same false conclusion as that drawn by *Rabochaya Mysl*, forgetting that the instinctive is the unconscious (the spontaneous) to the aid of which socialists must come; that the "first available means of struggle" will always be, in modern society, the trade union means of struggle, and the "first available" ideology the bourgeois (trade union) ideology. Similarly, these authors do not "repudiate" politics, they merely (merely!) echo Mr. V. V. that politics is the superstructure, and therefore, "political agitation must be the superstructure to the agitation carried on in favour of the economic struggle; it must arise on the basis of this struggle and follow in its wake."

* * *

And so, we have become convinced that the fundamental error committed by the "new trend" in Russian Social-Democracy is its bowing to spontaneity and its failure to understand that the spontaneity of the masses demands a high degree of consciousness from us Social-Democrats. The greater the spontaneous upsurge of the masses and the more widespread the movement, the more rapid, incomparably so, the demand for the greater consciousness in the theoretical, political and organisational work of Social-Democracy.

The spontaneous upsurge of the masses in Russia proceeded (and continues) with such rapidity that the young Social-Democrats proved unprepared to meet these gigantic tasks. This unpreparedness is our common misfortune, the misfortune of *all* Russian

Social-Democrats. The upsurge of the masses proceeded and spread with uninterrupted continuity; it not only continued in the places where it began, but spread to new localities and to new strata of the population (under the influence of the working-class movement, there was a renewed ferment among the student youth, among the intellectuals generally, and even among the peasantry). Revolutionaries, however, *lagged behind* this upsurge, both in their "theories" and in their activity; they failed to establish a constant and continuous organisation capable of *leading* the whole movement.

In Chapter I, we established that *Rabocheye Dyelo* belittled our theoretical tasks and that it "spontaneously" repeated the fashionable catchword "freedom of criticism"; those who repeated this catchword lacked the "consciousness" to understand that the positions of the opportunist "Critics" and those of the revolutionaries in Germany and in Russia are diametrically opposed.

In the following chapters, we shall show how this bowing to spontaneity found expression in the sphere of the political tasks and in the organisational work of Social-Democracy.

III. Trade-Unionist Politics and Social-Democratic Politics

We shall again begin by praising *Rabocheye Dyelo*. "Literature of Exposure and the Proletarian Struggle" is the title Martynov gave the article on his differences with *Iskra* published in *Rabocheye Dyelo*, No. 10. He formulated the substance of the differences as follows:

> We cannot confine ourselves solely to exposing the system that stands in its [the working-class party's] path of development. We must also react to the immediate and current interests of the proletariat. . . . *Iskra* . . . is in fact an organ of revolutionary opposition that exposes the state of affairs in our country, particularly the political state of affairs. . . . We, however, work and shall continue to work for the cause of the working class in close organic contact with the proletarian struggle. [P. 63.]

One cannot help being grateful to Martynov for this formula. It is of outstanding general interest, because substantially it embraces not only our disagreements with *Rabocheye Dyelo*, but the general disagreement between ourselves and the Economists on the political struggle. We have shown that the Economists do not altogether repudiate "politics," but that they are constantly straying from the Social-Democratic to the trade-unionist conception of politics.

Martynov strays in precisely this way, and we shall therefore take his views as a *model* of Economist error on this question. As we shall endeavour to prove, neither the authors of the *"Separate Supplement"* to *Rabochaya Mysl* nor the authors of the manifesto issued by the Self-Emancipation Group, nor the authors of the Economist letter published in *Iskra*, No. 12, will have any right to complain against this choice.

A. *Political Agitation and Its Restriction by the Economists*

Everyone knows that the economic[6] struggle of the Russian workers underwent widespread development and consolidation simultaneously with the production of "literature" exposing economic (factory and occupational) conditions. The "leaflets" were devoted mainly to the exposure of the factory system, and very soon a veritable passion for exposures was roused among the workers. As soon as the workers realised that the Social-Democratic study circles desired to, and could, supply them with a new kind of leaflet that told the whole truth about their miserable existence, about their unbearably hard toil, and their lack of rights, they began to send in, actually flood us with, correspondence from the factories and workshops. This "exposure literature" created a tremendous sensation, not only in the particular factory exposed in the given leaflet, but in all the factories to which news of the revealed facts spread. And since the poverty and want among the workers in the various enterprises and in the various trades are much the same, the "truth about the life of the workers" stirred *everyone*. Even among the most backward workers, a veritable passion arose to "get into print"—a noble passion for this rudimentary form of war against the whole of the present social system which is based upon robbery and oppression. And in the overwhelming majority of cases these "leaflets" were in truth a declaration of war, because the exposures served greatly to agitate the workers; they evoked among them common demands for the removal of the most glaring outrages and roused in them a readiness to support the demands with strikes. Finally, the employers themselves were compelled to recognise the significance of these leaflets as a declaration of war, so much so that in a large number of cases they did not even wait for the outbreak of hostilities. As is always

6. To avoid misunderstanding, we must point out that here, and throughout this pamphlet, by economic struggle, we imply (in keeping with the accepted usage among us) the "practical economic struggle," which Engels, in the passage quoted above, described as "resistance to the capitalists," and which in free countries is known as the organised-labour syndical, or trade-union struggle. [*Lenin*]

the case, the mere publication of these exposures made them effective, and they acquired the significance of a strong moral influence. On more than one occasion, the mere appearance of a leaflet proved sufficient to secure the satisfaction of all or part of the demands put forward. In a word, economic (factory) exposures were and remain an important lever in the economic struggle. And they will continue to retain this significance as long as there is capitalism, which makes it necessary for the workers to defend themselves. Even in the most advanced countries of Europe it can still be seen that the exposure of abuses in some backward trade, or in some forgotten branch of domestic industry, serves as a starting-point for the awakening of class-consciousness, for the beginning of a trade union struggle, and for the spread of socialism.[7]

The overwhelming majority of Russian Social-Democrats have of late been almost entirely absorbed by this work of organising the exposure of factory conditions. Suffice it to recall *Rabochaya Mysl* to see the extent to which they have been absorbed by it—so much so, indeed, that they have lost sight of the fact that this, *taken·by itself*, is in essence still not Social-Democratic work, but merely trade union work. As a matter of fact, the exposures merely dealt with the relations between the workers *in a given trade* and their employers, and all they achieved was that the sellers of labour-power learned to sell their "commodity" on better terms and to fight the purchasers over a purely commercial deal. These exposures could have served (if properly utilised by an organisation of revolutionaries) as a beginning and a component part of Social-Democratic activity; but they could also have led (and, given a worshipful attitude towards spontaneity, were bound to lead) to a "purely trade union" struggle and to a non-Social-Democratic working-class movement. Social-Democracy leads the struggle of the working class, not only for better terms for the sale of labour-power, but for the abolition of the social system that compels the propertyless to sell themselves to the rich. Social-Democracy represents the working class, not in its relation to a given group of employers alone, but in its relation to all classes of modern society and

7. In the present chapter we deal only with the *political* struggle, in its broader or narrower meaning. Therefore, we note only in passing, merely as a curiosity, *Rabocheye Dyelo*'s charge that *Iskra* is "too restrained" in regard to the economic struggle (*Two Conferences*, p. 27, rehashed by Martynov in his pamphlet, *Social-Democracy and the Working Class*). If the accusers computed by the hundredweights or reams (as they are so fond of doing) any given year's discussion of the economic struggle in the industrial section of *Iskra*, in comparison with the corresponding sections of *Rabocheye Dyelo* and *Rabochaya Mysl* combined, they would easily see that the latter lag behind even in this respect. Apparently, the realisation of this simple truth compels them to resort to arguments that clearly reveal their confusion. "*Iskra*," they write, "willy-nilly [!] is compelled [!] to reckon with the imperative demands of life and to publish at least [!!] correspondence about the working-class movement" (*Two Conferences*, p. 27). Now this is really a crushing argument! [*Lenin*]

to the state as an organised political force. Hence, it follows that not only must Social-Democrats not confine themselves exclusively to the economic struggle, but that they must not allow the organisation of economic exposures to become the predominant part of their activities. We must take up actively the political education of the working class and the development of its political consciousness. *Now* that *Zarya* and *Iskra* have made the first attack upon Economism, "all are agreed" on this (although some agree only in words, as we shall soon see).

The question arises, what should political education consist in? Can it be confined to the propaganda of working-class hostility to the autocracy? Of course not. It is not enough *to explain* to the workers that they are politically oppressed (any more than it is *to explain* to them that their interests are antagonistic to the interests of the employers). Agitation must be conducted with regard to every concrete example of this oppression (as we have begun to carry on agitation round concrete examples of economic oppression). Inasmuch as *this* oppression affects the most diverse classes of society, inasmuch as it manifests itself in the most varied spheres of life and activity—vocational, civic, personal, family, religious, scientific, etc., etc.—is it not evident that *we shall not be fulfilling our task* of developing the political consciousness of the workers if we do not *undertake* the organisation of the *political exposure* of the autocracy *in all its aspects*? In order to carry on agitation round concrete instances of oppression, these instances must be exposed (as it is necessary to expose factory abuses in order to carry on economic agitation).

One might think this to be clear enough. It turns out, however, that it is only in words that "all" are agreed on the need to develop political consciousness, *in all its aspects*. It turns out that *Rabocheye Dyelo*, for example, far from tackling the task of organising (or making a start in organising) comprehensive political exposure, is even trying *to drag Iskra*, which has undertaken this task, *away from it*. Listen to the following: "The political struggle of the working class is merely [it is certainly not "merely"] the most developed, wide, and effective form of economic struggle" (programme of *Rabocheye Dyelo*, published in issue No. 1, p. 3). "The Social-Democrats are now confronted with the task of lending the economic struggle itself, as far as possible, a political character" (Martynov, *Rabocheye Dyelo*, No. 10, p. 42). * * *

* * *

What concrete, real meaning attaches to Martynov's words when he sets before Social-Democracy the task of "lending the economic struggle itself a political character"? The economic struggle is the collective struggle of the workers against their employers for better terms *in the sale of their labour-power*, for better living and working conditions. This struggle is necessarily a trade union struggle, because working conditions differ greatly in different trades, and, consequently, the struggle to *improve* them can only be conducted on the basis of trade organisations (in the Western countries, through trade unions; in Russia, through temporary trade associations and through leaflets, etc.). Lending "the economic struggle itself a political character" means, therefore, striving to secure satisfaction of these trade demands, the improvement of working conditions in each separate trade by means of "legislative and administrative measures" (as Martynov puts it on the ensuing page of his article, p. 43). This is precisely what all workers' trade unions do and always have done. Read the works of the soundly scientific (and "soundly" opportunist) Mr. and Mrs. Webb and you will see that the British trade unions long ago recognised, and have long been carrying out, the task of "lending the economic struggle itself a political character"; they have long been fighting for the right to strike, for the removal of all legal hindrances to the co-operative and trade union movements, for laws to protect women and children, for the improvement of labour conditions by means of health and factory legislation, etc.

Thus, the pompous phrase about "lending the economic struggle *itself* a political character," which sounds so "terrifically" profound and revolutionary, serves as a screen to conceal what is in fact the traditional striving *to degrade* Social-Democratic politics to the level of trade union politics. Under the guise of rectifying the one-sidedness of *Iskra*, which, it is alleged, places "the revolutionising of dogma higher than the revolutionising of life,"[8] we are presented with the *struggle for economic reforms* as if it were something entirely new. In point of fact, the phrase "lending the economic struggle itself a political character" means nothing more than the struggle for economic reforms. Martynov himself might have come to this simple conclusion, had he pondered over the significance of his own words. "Our Party," he says, training his heaviest guns on *Iskra*, "could and should have presented concrete demands to the government for legislative and administrative measures against economic exploitation, unemployment, famine, etc." (*Rabocheye Dyelo*, No. 10, pp. 42–43). Concrete demands for measures—does not this mean demands for social reforms? Again we ask the impar-

8. *Rabocheye Dyelo*, No. 10, p. 60. This is the Martynov variation of the application, which we have characterised above, of the thesis "every step of real movement is more important than a dozen programmes" to the present chaotic state of our movement. In fact, this is merely a translation into Russian of the notorious Bernsteinian sentence: "The movement is everything, the final aim is nothing." [*Lenin*]

tial reader: Are we slandering the *Rabocheye Dyelo*-ites (may I be forgiven for this awkward, currently used designation!) by calling them concealed Bernsteinians when, as their point of *disagreement* with *Iskra*, they advance their thesis on the necessity of struggling for economic reforms?

Revolutionary Social-Democracy has always included the struggle for reforms as part of its activities. But it utilises "economic" agitation for the purpose of presenting to the government, not only demands for all sorts of measures, but also (and primarily) the demand that it cease to be an autocratic government. Moreover, it considers it its duty to present this demand to the government on the basis, not of the economic struggle *alone*, but of all manifestations in general of public and political life. In a word, it subordinates the struggle for reforms, as the part to the whole, to the revolutionary struggle for freedom and for socialism. Martynov, however, resuscitates the theory of stages in a new form and strives to prescribe, as it were, an exclusively economic path of development for the political struggle. By advancing at this moment, when the revolutionary movement is on the upgrade, an alleged special "task" of struggling for reforms, he is dragging the Party backwards and is playing into the hands of both "Economist" and liberal opportunism.

* * *

"In addition to its immediate revolutionary significance, the economic struggle of the workers against the employers and the government [*"economic* struggle against the government"!] has also this significance: it constantly brings home to the workers the fact that they have no political rights" (Martynov, p. 44). We quote this passage, not in order to repeat for the hundredth and thousandth time what has been said above, but in order to express particular thanks to Martynov for this excellent new formula: "the economic struggle of the workers against the employers and the government." What a gem! With what inimitable skill and mastery in eliminating all partial disagreements and shades of differences among Economists this clear and concise proposition expresses the *quintessence* of Economism, from summoning the workers "to the political struggle, which they carry on in the general interest, for the improvement of the conditions of all the workers,"[9] continuing through the theory of stages, and ending in the resolution of the Conference on the "most widely applicable," etc. "Economic struggle against the government" is precisely trade-unionist politics, which is still very far from being Social-Democratic politics.

9. *Rabochaya Mysl,* "*Separate Supplement,*" p. 14. [*Lenin*]

B. How Martynov Rendered Plekhanov More Profound

"What a large number of Social-Democratic Lomonosovs[1] have appeared among us lately!" observed a comrade one day, having in mind the astonishing propensity of many who are inclined toward Economism to arrive, "necessarily, by their own understanding," at great truths (e.g., that the economic struggle stimulates the workers to ponder over their lack of rights) and in doing so to ignore, with the supreme contempt of born geniuses, all that has been produced by the antecedent development of revolutionary thought and of the revolutionary movement. Lomonosov-Martynov is precisely such a born genius. We need but glance at his article "Urgent Questions" to see how by "his own understanding" he *arrives at* what was long ago said by Axelrod (of whom our Lomonosov, naturally, says not a word); how, for instance, he *is beginning* to understand that we cannot ignore the opposition of such or such strata of the bourgeoisie (*Rabocheye Dyelo*, No. 9, pp. 61, 62, 71; compare this with *Rabocheye Dyelo's Reply* to Axelrod, pp. 22, 23–24), etc. But alas, he is only "arriving" and is only "beginning," not more than that, for so little has he understood Axelrod's ideas, that he talks about "the economic struggle against the employers and the government." For three years (1898–1901) *Rabocheye Dyelo* has tried hard to understand Axelrod, but has so far not understood him! Can one of the reasons be that Social-Democracy, "like mankind," always sets itself only tasks that can be achieved?

But the Lomonosovs are distinguished not only by their ignorance of many things (that would be but half misfortune!), but also by their unawareness of their own ignorance. Now this is a real misfortune; and it is this misfortune that prompts them without further ado to attempt to render Plekhanov "more profound."

Much water [Lomonosov-Martynov says] has flowed under the bridge since Plekhanov wrote his book [*Tasks of the Socialists in the Fight Against the Famine in Russia*]. The Social-Democrats who for a decade led the economic struggle of the working class . . . have failed as yet to lay down a broad theoretical basis for Party tactics. This question has now come to a head, and if we should wish to lay down such a theoretical basis, we should certainly have to deepen considerably the principles of tactics developed at one time by Plekhanov. . . . Our present definition of the distinction between propaganda and agitation would have to be different from Plekhanov's. [Martynov has just quoted Plekhanov's words: "A propagandist presents many ideas to one or a few persons; an agitator presents only one or a few ideas, but he

---

1. M. V. Lomonosov (1711–65) was the first prominent scientist in Russia.

presents them to a mass of people."] By propaganda we would understand the revolutionary explanation of the present social system, entire or in its partial manifestations, whether that be done in a form intelligible to individuals or to broad masses. By agitation, in the strict sense of the word [*sic!*], we would understand the call upon the masses to undertake definite, concrete actions and the promotion of the direct revolutionary intervention of the proletariat in social life.

We congratulate Russian—and international—Social-Democracy on having found, thanks to Martynov, a new terminology, more strict and more profound. Hitherto we thought (with Plekhanov, and with all the leaders of the international working-class movement) that the propagandist, dealing with, say, the question of unemployment, must explain the capitalistic nature of crises, the cause of their inevitability in modern society, the necessity for the transformation of this society into a socialist society, etc. In a word, he must present "many ideas," so many, indeed, that they will be understood as an integral whole only by a (comparatively) few persons. The agitator, however, speaking on the same subject, will take as an illustration a fact that is most glaring and most widely known to his audience, say, the death of an unemployed worker's family from starvation, the growing impoverishment, etc., and, utilizing this fact, known to all, will direct his efforts to presenting *a single idea* to the "masses," e.g., the senselessness of the contradiction between the increase of wealth and the increase of poverty; he will strive *to rouse* discontent and indignation among the masses against this crying injustice, leaving a more complete explanation of this contradiction to the propagandist. Consequently, the propagandist operates chiefly by means of the *printed* word; the agitator by means of the *spoken* word. The propagandist requires qualities different from those of the agitator. Kautsky and Lafargue, for example, we term propagandists; Bebel and Guesde we term agitators. To single out a third sphere, or third function, of practical activity, and to include in this function "the call upon the masses to undertake definite concrete actions," is sheer nonsense, because the "call," as a single act, either naturally and inevitably supplements the theoretical treatise, propagandist pamphlet, and agitational speech, or represents a purely executive function. Let us take, for example, the struggle the German Social-Democrats are now waging against the corn duties. The theoreticians write research works on tariff policy, with the "call," say, to struggle for commercial treaties and for Free Trade. The propagandist does the same thing in the periodical press, and the agitator in public speeches. At the present time, the "concrete action" of the masses takes the form of signing petitions to the Reichstag against raising the corn duties.

The call for this action comes indirectly from the theoreticians, the propagandists, and the agitators, and, directly, from the workers who take the petition lists to the factories and to private homes for the gathering of signatures. According to the "Martynov terminology," Kautsky and Bebel are both propagandists, while those who solicit the signatures are agitators. Isn't it clear?

The German example recalled to my mind the German word *Verballhornung*, which, literally translated, means "Ballhorning." Johann Ballhorn, a Leipzig publisher of the sixteenth century, published a child's reader in which, as was the custom, he introduced a drawing of a cock, but a cock without spurs and with a couple of eggs lying near it. On the cover he printed the legend, "*Revised* edition by Johann Ballhorn." Ever since then, the Germans describe any "revision" that is really a worsening as "ballhorning." And one cannot help recalling Ballhorn upon seeing how the Martynovs try to render Plekhanov "more profound."

Why did our Lomonosov "invent" this confusion? In order to illustrate how *Iskra* "devotes attention only to one side of the case, just as Plekhanov did a decade and a half ago" (39). "With *Iskra*, propagandist tasks force agitational tasks into the background, at least for the present" (52). If we translate this last proposition from the language of Martynov into ordinary human language (because mankind has not yet managed to learn the newly-invented terminology), we shall get the following: with *Iskra*, the tasks of political propaganda and political agitation force into the background the task of "presenting to the government concrete demands for legislative and administrative measures" that "promise certain palpable results" (or demands for social reforms, that is, if we are permitted once again to employ the old terminology of the old mankind not yet grown to Martynov's level). We suggest that the reader compare this thesis with the following tirade:

> What also astonishes us in these programmes [the programmes advanced by revolutionary Social-Democrats] is their constant stress upon the benefits of workers' activity in parliament [non-existent in Russia], though they completely ignore [thanks to their revolutionary nihilism] the importance of workers' participation in the legislative manufacturers' assemblies on factory affairs [which do exist in Russia] . . . or at least the importance of workers' participation in municipal bodies. . . .

The author of this tirade expresses in a somewhat forthright and clearer manner the very idea which Lomonosov-Martynov discovered by his own understanding. The author is R. M., in the "*Separate Supplement*" to *Rabochaya Mysl* (p. 15).

C. Political Exposures and "Training in Revolutionary Activity"

In advancing against *Iskra* his theory of "raising the activity of the working masses," Martynov actually betrayed an urge to *belittle* that activity, for he declared the very economic struggle before which all economists grovel to be the preferable, particularly important, and "most widely applicable" means of rousing this activity and its broadest field. This error is characteristic, precisely in that it is by no means peculiar to Martynov. In reality, it is possible to "raise the activity of the working masses" *only* when this activity *is not restricted* to "political agitation on an economic basis." A basic condition for the necessary expansion of political agitation is the organisation of *comprehensive* political exposure. *In no way* except by means of such exposures *can* the masses be trained in political consciousness and revolutionary activity. Hence, activity of this kind is one of the most important functions of international Social-Democracy as a whole, for even political freedom does not in any way eliminate exposures; it merely shifts somewhat their sphere of direction. Thus, the German party is especially strengthening its positions and spreading its influence, thanks particularly to the untiring energy with which it is conducting its campaign of political exposure. Working-class consciousness cannot be genuine political consciousness unless the workers are trained to respond to *all* cases of tyranny, oppression, violence, and abuse, no matter *what class* is affected—unless they are trained, moreover, to respond from a Social-Democratic point of view and no other. The consciousness of the working masses cannot be genuine class-consciousness, unless the workers learn, from concrete, and above all from topical, political facts and events to observe *every* other social class in *all* the manifestations of its intellectual, ethical, and political life; unless they learn to apply in practice the materialist analysis and the materialist estimate of *all* aspects of the life and activity of *all* classes, strata, and groups of the population. Those who concentrate the attention, observation, and consciousness of the working class exclusively, or even mainly, upon itself alone are not Social-Democrats; for the self-knowledge of the working class is indissolubly bound up, not solely with a fully clear theoretical understanding—or rather, not so much with the theoretical, as with the practical, understanding—of the relationships between *all* the various classes of modern society, acquired through the experience of political life. For this reason the conception of the economic struggle as the most widely applicable means of drawing the masses into the political movement, which our Economists preach, is so extremely harmful and reactionary in its practical significance. In order to become a Social-Democrat, the worker must have a clear picture in his mind of the economic nature and the social and political features of the landlord and the priest, the high state official and the peasant, the student and the vagabond; he must know their strong and weak points; he must grasp the meaning of all the catchwords and sophisms by which each class and each stratum *camouflages* its selfish strivings and its real "inner workings"; he must understand what interests are reflected by certain institutions and certain laws and how they are reflected. But this "clear picture" cannot be obtained from any book. It can be obtained only from living examples and from exposures that follow close upon what is going on about us at a given moment; upon what is being discussed, in whispers perhaps, by each one in his own way; upon what finds expression in such and such events, in such and such statistics, in such and such court sentences, etc., etc. These comprehensive political exposures are an essential and *fundamental* condition for training the masses in revolutionary activity.

Why do the Russian workers still manifest little revolutionary activity in response to the brutal treatment of the people by the police, the persecution of religious sects, the flogging of peasants, the outrageous censorship, the torture of soldiers, the persecution of the most innocent cultural undertakings, etc.? Is it because the "economic struggle" does not "stimulate" them to this, because such activity does not "promise palpable results," because it produces little that is "positive"? To adopt such an opinion, we repeat, is merely to direct the charge where it does not belong, to blame the working masses for one's own philistinism (or Bernsteinism). We must blame ourselves, our lagging behind the mass movement, for still being unable to organise sufficiently wide, striking, and rapid exposures of all the shameful outrages. When we do that (and we must and can do it), the most backward worker will understand, *or will feel,* that the students and religious sects, the peasants and the authors are being abused and outraged by those same dark forces that are oppressing and crushing him at every step of his life. Feeling that, he himself will be filled with an irresistible desire to react, and he will know how to hoot the censors one day, on another day to demonstrate outside the house of a governor who has brutally suppressed a peasant uprising, on still another day to teach a lesson to the gendarmes in surplices who are doing the work of the Holy Inquisition, etc. As yet we have done very little, almost nothing, *to bring* before the working masses prompt exposures on all possible issues. Many of us as yet do not recognise this as our *bounden duty* but trail spontaneously in the wake of the "drab everyday struggle," in the narrow confines of factory life. Under such circumstances to say that *"Iskra* displays a tendency to minimise the significance of the forward march of the drab everyday struggle in comparison with the propaganda of brilliant and complete ideas" (Martynov, *op. cit.,* p. 61), means to drag the Party back, to defend and glorify our unpreparedness and backwardness.

As for calling the masses to action, that will come of itself as soon as energetic political agitation, live and striking exposures come into play. To catch some criminal red-handed and immediately to brand him publicly in all places is of itself far more effective than any number of "calls"; the effect very often is such as will make it impossible to tell exactly who it was that "called" upon the masses and who suggested this or that plan of demonstration, etc. Calls for action, not in the general, but in the concrete, sense of the term can be made only at the place of action; only those who themselves go into action, and do so immediately, can sound such calls. Our business as Social-Democratic publicists is to deepen, expand, and intensify political exposures and political agitation.

A word in passing about "calls to action." *The only newspaper* which *prior to* the spring events[2] *called upon* the workers to intervene actively in a matter that certainly did not *promise* any *palpable results* whatever for the workers, i.e., the drafting of the students into the army, *was Iskra.* Immediately after the publication of the order of January 11, on "drafting the 183 students into the army," *Iskra* published an article on the matter (in its February issue, No. 2), and, *before* any demonstration was begun, forthwith *called upon* "the workers to go to the aid of the students," called upon the "people" openly to take up the government's arrogant challenge. We ask: how is the remarkable fact to be explained that although Martynov talks so much about "calls to action," and even suggests "calls to action" as a special form of activity, he said not a word about *this* call? After this, was it not sheer philistinism on Martynov's part to allege that *Iskra* was *one-sided* because it did not issue sufficient "calls" to struggle for demands "promising palpable results"?

Our Economists, including *Rabocheye Dyelo,* were successful because they adapted themselves to the backward workers. But the Social-Democratic worker, the revolutionary worker (and the number of such workers is growing) will indignantly reject all this talk about struggle for demands "promising palpable results," etc., because he will understand that this is only a variation of the old song about adding a kopek to the ruble. Such a worker will say to his

---

2. The events referred to were mass revolutionary actions by students and workers—political demonstrations, meetings, strikes—that took place in February and March 1901, in St. Petersburg, Moscow, Kiev, Kharkov, Kazan, and other cities in Russia.

counsellors from *Rabochaya Mysl* and *Rabocheye Dyelo*: you are busying yourselves in vain, gentlemen, and shirking your proper duties, by meddling with such excessive zeal in a job that we can very well manage ourselves. There is nothing clever in your assertion that the Social-Democrats' task is to lend the economic struggle itself a political character; that is only the beginning, it is not the main task of the Social-Democrats. For all over the world, including Russia, *the police themselves often take the initiative in lending* the economic struggle a political character, and the workers themselves learn to understand whom the government supports.[3] The "economic struggle of the workers against the employers and the government," about which you make as much fuss as if you had discovered a new America, is being waged in all parts of Russia, even the most remote, by the workers themselves who have heard about strikes, but who have heard almost nothing about socialism. The "activity" you want to stimulate among us workers, by advancing concrete demands that promise palpable results, we are already displaying and in our everyday, limited trade union work we put forward these concrete demands, very often without any assistance whatever from the intellectuals. But *such* activity is not enough for us; we are not children to be fed on the thin gruel of "economic" politics alone; we want to know everything that others know, we want to learn the details of *all* aspects of political life and to take part *actively* in every single political event. In order that we may do this, the intellectuals must talk to us less of what we already know[4] and tell us more about what we do not yet know

3. The demand "to lend the economic struggle itself a political character" most strikingly expresses *subservience to spontaneity* in the sphere of political activity. Very often the economic struggle *spontaneously* assumes a political character, that is to say, without the intervention of the "revolutionary bacilli—the intelligentsia," without the intervention of the class-conscious Social-Democrats. The economic struggle of the English workers, for instance, also assumed a political character without any intervention on the part of the socialists. The task of the Social-Democrats, however, is not exhausted by political agitation on an economic basis; their task is *to convert* trade-unionist politics into Social-Democratic political struggle, to *utilise* the sparks of political consciousness which the economic struggle generates among the workers, for the purpose of *raising* the workers to the level of *Social-Democratic* political consciousness. The Martynovs, however, instead of raising and stimulating the spontaneously awakening political consciousness of the workers, *bow to spontaneity* and repeat over and over *ad nauseam*, that the economic struggle "impels" the workers to realise their own lack of political rights. It is unfortunate, gentlemen, that the spontaneously awakening trade-unionist political consciousness does not *"impel"* you to an understanding of your Social-Democratic tasks. [*Lenin*]

4. To prove that this imaginary speech of a worker to an Economist is based on fact, we shall refer to two witnesses who undoubtedly have direct knowledge of the working-class movement and who are least of all inclined to be partial towards us "doctrinaires"; for one witness is an Economist (who regards even *Rabocheye Dyelo* as a political organ!), and the other is a terrorist. The first witness is the author of a remarkably truthful and vivid article entitled "The St. Petersburg Working-Class Movement and the Practical Tasks of Social-Democracy," published in *Rabocheye Dyelo*, No. 6. He divides the workers into the following categories: (1) class-conscious revolutionaries; (2) intermediate stratum; (3) the remaining masses. The intermediate stratum, he

and what we can never learn from our factory and "economic" experience, namely, political knowledge. You intellectuals can acquire this knowledge, and it is your *duty* to bring it to us in a hundred- and a thousand-fold greater measure than you have done up to now; and you must bring it to us, not only in the form of discussions, pamphlets, and articles (which very often—pardon our frankness—are rather dull), but precisely in the form of vivid *exposures* of what our government and our governing classes are doing at this very moment in all spheres of life. Devote more zeal to carrying out this duty and *talk less about "raising the activity of the working masses."* We are far more active than you think, and we are quite able to support, by open street fighting, even demands that do not promise any "palpable results" whatever. It is not for you to "raise" our activity, because *activity is precisely the thing you yourselves lack.* Bow less in subservience to spontaneity, and think more about raising *your own* activity, gentlemen!

D. What Is There in Common Between Economism and Terrorism?

In the last footnote we cited the opinion of an Economist and of a non-Social-Democratic terrorist, who showed themselves to be accidentally in agreement. Speaking generally, however, there is not an accidental, but a necessary, inherent connection between the two, of which we shall have need to speak later, and which must be mentioned here in connection with the question of education for revolutionary activity. The Economists and the present-day terrorists have one common root, namely, *subservience to spontaneity*, with which we dealt in the preceding chapter as a general phenomenon and which we shall now examine in relation to its effect upon political activity and the political struggle. At first sight, our assertion may appear paradoxical, so great is the difference between those who stress the "drab everyday struggle" and those who call

---

says, "is often more interested in questions of political life than in its own immediate economic interests, the connection between which and the general social conditions it has long understood." . . . *Rabochaya Mysl* "is sharply criticised": "It keeps on repeating the same thing over and over again, things we have long known, read long ago." "Again nothing in the political review!" (pp. 30–31). But even the third stratum, "the younger and more sensitive section of the workers, less corrupted by the tavern and the church, who hardly ever have the opportunity of getting hold of political literature, discuss political events in a rambling way and ponder over the fragmentary news they get about student riots," etc. The terrorist writes as follows: ". . . They read over once or twice the petty details of factory life in other towns, not their own, and then they read no more . . . dull, they find it. . . . To say nothing in a workers' paper about the government . . . is to regard the workers as being little children. . . . The workers are not little children." (*Svoboda*, published by the Revolutionary-Socialist Group, pp. 69–70.) [*Lenin*]

for the most self-sacrificing struggle of individuals. But this is no paradox. The Economists and the terrorists merely bow to different poles of spontaneity; the Economists bow to the spontaneity of "the labour movement pure and simple," while the terrorists bow to the spontaneity of the passionate indignation of intellectuals, who lack the ability or opportunity to connect the revolutionary struggle and the working-class movement into an integral whole. It is difficult indeed for those who have lost their belief, or who have never believed, that this is possible, to find some outlet for their indignation and revolutionary energy other than terror. Thus, both forms of subservience to spontaneity we have mentioned are nothing but *the beginning of the implementation* of the notorious *Credo* programme: Let the workers wage their "economic struggle against the employers and the government" (we apologise to the author of the *Credo* for expressing her views in Martynov's words. We think we have a right to do so since the *Credo*, too, says that in the economic struggle the workers "come up against the political régime"), and let the intellectuals conduct the political struggle by their own efforts—with the aid of terror, of course! This is an absolutely logical and inevitable *conclusion* which must be insisted on—*even though those* who are beginning to carry out this programme *do not themselves realise* that it is inevitable. Political activity has its logic quite apart from the consciousness of those who, with the best intentions, call either for terror or for lending the economic struggle itself a political character. The road to hell is paved with good intentions, and, in this case, good intentions cannot save one from being spontaneously drawn "along the line of least resistance," along the line of the *purely bourgeois Credo* programme. Surely it it no accident either that many Russian liberals—avowed liberals and liberals who wear the mask of Marxism—whole-heartedly sympathise with terror and try to foster the terrorist moods that have surged up in the present time.

The formation of the Revolutionary-Socialist *Svoboda* Group—which set itself the aim of helping the working-class movement in every possible way, but which included in its *programme* terror, and emancipation, so to speak, from Social-Democracy—once again confirmed the remarkable perspicacity of P. B. Axelrod, who *literally foretold* these results of Social-Democratic waverings *as far back as the end of 1897* (*Present Tasks and Tactics*), when he outlined his famous "two perspectives." All the subsequent disputes and disagreements among Russian Social-Democrats are contained, like a plant in the seed, in these two perspectives.[5]

5. Martynov "conceives of another, more realistic [?] dilemma" (*Social-Democracy and the Working Class*, p. 19): "Either Social-Democracy takes over the direct leadership of the economic struggle of the proletariat and by that [!] trans-

From this point of view it also becomes clear why *Rabocheye Dyelo*, unable to withstand the spontaneity of Economism, has likewise been unable to withstand the spontaneity of terrorism. It is highly interesting to note here the specific arguments that *Svoboda* has advanced in defence of terrorism. It "completely denies" the deterrent role of terrorism (*The Regeneration of Revolutionism*, p. 64), but instead stresses its "excitative significance." This is characteristic, first, as representing one of the stages of the break-up and decline of the traditional (pre-Social-Democratic) cycle of ideas which insisted upon terrorism. The admission that the government cannot now be "terrified," and hence disrupted, by terror, is tantamount to a complete condemnation of terror as a system of struggle, as a sphere of activity sanctioned by the programme. Secondly, it is still more characteristic as an example of the failure to understand our immediate tasks in regard to "education for revolutionary activity." *Svoboda* advocates terror as a means of "exciting" the working-class movement and of giving it a "strong impetus." It is difficult to imagine an argument that more thoroughly disproves itself. Are there not enough outrages committed in Russian life without special "excitants" having to be invented? On the other hand, is it not obvious that those who are not, and cannot be, roused to excitement even by Russian tyranny will stand by "twiddling their thumbs" and watch a handful of terrorists engaged in single combat with the government? The fact is that the working masses are roused to a high pitch of excitement by the social evils in Russian life, but we are unable to gather, if one may so put it, and concentrate all these drops and streamlets of popular resentment that are brought forth to a far larger extent than we imagine by the conditions of Russian life, and that must be combined into a *single* gigantic torrent. That this can be accomplished is irrefutably proved by the enormous growth of the working-class movement and the eagerness, noted above, with which the workers clamour for political literature. On the other hand, calls for terror and calls to lend the economic struggle itself a political character are merely two different forms of *evading* the most pressing duty now resting upon Russian revolutionaries, namely, the organisation of compre-

---

forms it into a revolutionary class struggle. . . ." "By that," i.e., apparently by the direct leadership of the economic struggle. Can Martynov cite an instance in which leading the trade-union struggle *alone* has succeeded in transforming a trade-unionist movement into a revolutionary class movement? Can he not understand that in order to bring about this "transformation" we must actively take up the "direct leadership" of *all-sided* political agitation? . . . "Or the other perspective: Social-Democracy refrains from assuming the leadership of the economic struggle of the workers and so . . . clips its own wings. . . ." In *Rabocheye Dyelo*'s opinion, quoted above, it is *Iskra* that "refrains." We have seen, however, that the latter *does far more than Rabocheye Dyelo* to lead the economic struggle, but that, moreover, it does not confine itself thereto and *does not narrow down* its political tasks for its sake. [*Lenin*]

hensive political agitation. *Svoboda* desires to *substitute* terror for agitation, openly admitting that "as soon as intensified and strenuous agitation is begun among the masses the excitative function of terror will be ended" (*The Regeneration of Revolutionism*, p. 68). This proves precisely that both the terrorists and the Economists *underestimate* the revolutionary activity of the masses, despite the striking evidence of the events that took place in the spring,[6] and whereas the one group goes out in search of artificial "excitants," the other talks about "concrete demands." But both fail to devote sufficient attention to the development of *their own activity* in political agitation and in the organisation of political exposures. And no other work can serve as a *substitute* for this task either at the present time or at any other.

E. The Working Class as Vanguard Fighter for Democracy

We have seen that the conduct of the broadest political agitation and, consequently, of all-sided political exposures is an absolutely necessary and a *paramount* task of our activity, if this activity is to be truly Social-Democratic. However, we arrived at this conclusion *solely* on the grounds of the pressing needs of the working class for political knowledge and political training. But such a presentation of the question is too narrow, for it ignores the general democratic tasks of Social-Democracy, in particular of present-day Russian Social-Democracy. In order to explain the point more concretely we shall approach the subject from an aspect that is "nearest" to the Economist, namely, from the practical aspect. "Everyone agrees" that it is necessary to develop the political consciousness of the working class. The question is, *how* that is to be done and what is required to do it. The economic struggle merely "impels" the workers to realise the government's attitude towards the working class. Consequently, *however much we may try to* "lend the economic struggle itself a political character," we *shall never be able to* develop the political consciousness of the workers (to the level of Social-Democratic political consciousness) by keeping within the framework of the economic struggle, for *that framework is too narrow*. The Martynov formula has some value for us, not because it illustrates Martynov's aptitude for confusing things, but because it pointedly expresses the basic error that all the Economists commit, namely, their conviction that it is possible to develop the class political consciousness of the workers *from within*, so to speak, from their economic struggle, i.e., by making this struggle the ex-

6. The big street demonstrations which began in the spring of 1901. [*Lenin, 1907 edition*]

clusive (or, at least, the main) starting-point, by making it the exclusive (or, at least, the main) basis. Such a view is radically wrong. Piqued by our polemics against them, the Economists refuse to ponder deeply over the origins of these disagreements, with the result that we simply cannot understand one another. It is as if we spoke in different tongues.

Class political consciousness can be brought to the workers *only from without*, that is, only from outside the economic struggle, from outside the sphere of relations between workers and employers. The sphere from which alone it is possible to obtain this knowledge is the sphere of relationships of *all* classes and strata to the state and the government, the sphere of the interrelations between *all* classes. For that reason, the reply to the question as to what must be done to bring political knowledge to the workers cannot be merely the answer with which, in the majority of cases, the practical workers, especially those inclined towards Economism, mostly content themselves, namely: "To go among the workers." To bring political knowledge to the *workers* the Social-Democrats must *go among all classes of the population*; they must dispatch units of their army *in all directions*.

We deliberately select this blunt formula, we deliberately express ourselves in this sharply simplified manner, not because we desire to indulge in paradoxes, but in order to "impel" the Economists to a realisation of their tasks which they unpardonably ignore, to suggest to them strongly the difference between trade-unionist and Social-Democratic politics, which they refuse to understand. We therefore beg the reader not to get wrought up, but to hear us patiently to the end.

Let us take the type of Social-Democratic study circle that has become most widespread in the past few years and examine its work. It has "contacts with the workers" and rests content with this, issuing leaflets in which abuses in the factories, the government's partiality towards the capitalists, and the tyranny of the police are strongly condemned. At workers' meetings the discussions never, or rarely ever, go beyond the limits of these subjects. Extremely rare are the lectures and discussions held on the history of the revolutionary movement, on questions of the government's home and foreign policy, on questions of the economic evolution of Russia and of Europe, on the position of the various classes in modern society, etc. As to systematically acquiring and extending contact with other classes of society, no one even dreams of that. In fact, the ideal leader, as the majority of the members of such circles picture him, is something far more in the nature of a trade union secretary than a socialist political leader. For the secretary of any, say English, trade union always helps the workers to carry on the economic struggle, he helps them to expose factory abuses, explains the injustice of the laws and of measures that hamper the freedom to strike and to picket (i.e., to warn all and sundry that a strike is proceeding at a certain factory), explains the partiality of arbitration court judges who belong to the bourgeois classes, etc., etc. In a word, every trade union secretary conducts and helps to conduct "the economic struggle against the employers and the government." It cannot be too strongly maintained that *this is still not* Social-Democracy, that the Social-Democrat's ideal should not be the trade union secretary, but *the tribune of the people*, who is able to react to every manifestation of tyranny and oppression, no matter where it appears, no matter what stratum or class of the people it affects; who is able to generalise all these manifestations and produce a single picture of police violence and capitalist exploitation; who is able to take advantage of every event, however small, in order to set forth *before all* his socialist convictions and his democratic demands, in order to clarify for *all* and everyone the world-historic significance of the struggle for the emancipation of the proletariat. Compare, for example, a leader like Robert Knight (the well-known secretary and leader of the Boiler-Makers' Society, one of the most powerful trade unions in England), with Wilhelm Liebknecht, and try to apply to them the contrasts that Martynov draws in his controversy with *Iskra*. You will see—I am running through Martynov's article—that Robert Knight engaged more in "calling the masses to certain concrete actions" (Martynov, *op. cit.*, p. 39), while Wilhelm Liebknecht engaged more in "the revolutionary elucidation of the whole of the present system or partial manifestations of it" (38–39); that Robert Knight "formulated the immediate demands of the proletariat and indicated the means by which they can be achieved" (41), whereas Wilhelm Liebknecht, while doing this, did not hold back from "simultaneously guiding the activities of various opposition strata," "dictating a positive programme of action for them"[7] (41); that Robert Knight strove "as far as possible to lend the economic struggle itself a political character" (42) and was excellently able "to submit to the government concrete demands promising certain palpable results" (43), whereas Liebknecht engaged to a much greater degree in "one-sided" "exposures" (40); that Robert Knight attached more significance to the "forward march of the drab everyday struggle" (61), whereas Liebknecht attached more significance to the "propaganda of brilliant and completed ideas" (61); that Liebknecht converted the paper he was directing into "an organ of revolutionary opposi-

7. For example, during the Franco-Prussian War, Liebknecht dictated a programme of action *for the whole of democracy*; to an even greater extent Marx and Engels did this in 1848. [*Lenin*]

tion that exposed the state of affairs in our country, particularly the political state of affairs, insofar as it affected the interests of the most varied strata of the population" (63), whereas Robert Knight "worked for the cause of the working class in close organic connection with the proletarian struggle" (63)—if by "close and organic connection" is meant the subservience to spontaneity which we examined above, by taking the examples of Krichevsky and Martynov—and "restricted the sphere of his influence," convinced, of course, as is Martynov, that "by doing so he deepened that influence" (63). In a word, you will see that *de facto* Martynov reduces Social-Democracy to the level of trade-unionism, though he does so, of course, not because he does not desire the good of Social-Democracy, but simply because he is a little too much in a hurry to render Plekhanov more profound, instead of taking the trouble to understand him.

Let us return, however, to our theses. We said that a Social-Democrat, if he really believes it necessary to develop comprehensively the political consciousness of the proletariat, must "go among all classes of the population." This gives rise to the questions: how is this to be done? have we enough forces to do this? is there a basis for such work among all the other classes? will this not mean a retreat, or lead to a retreat, from the class point of view? Let us deal with these questions.

We must "go among all classes of the population" as theoreticians, as propagandists, as agitators, and as organisers. No one doubts that the theoretical work of Social-Democrats should aim at studying all the specific features of the social and political condition of the various classes. But extremely little is done in this direction, as compared with the work that is done in studying the specific features of factory life. In the committees and study circles, one can meet people who are immersed in the study even of some special branch of the metal industry; but one can hardly ever find members of organisations (obliged, as often happens, for some reason or other to give up practical work) who are especially engaged in gathering material on some pressing question of social and political life in our country which could serve as a means for conducting Social-Democratic work among other strata of the population. In dwelling upon the fact that the majority of the present-day leaders of the working-class movement lack training, we cannot refrain from mentioning training in this respect also, for it too is bound up with the Economist conception of "close organic connection with the proletarian struggle." The principal thing, of course, is *propaganda* and *agitation* among all strata of the people. The work of the West-European Social-Democrat is in this respect facilitated by the public meetings and rallies which *all* are free to attend, and by the fact that in parliament he addresses the representatives of *all* classes. We have neither a parliament nor freedom of assembly; nevertheless, we are able to arrange meetings of workers who desire to listen to *a Social-Democrat*. We must also find ways and means of calling meetings of representatives of all social classes that desire to listen to *a democrat*; for he is no Social-Democrat who forgets in practice that "the Communists support every revolutionary movement,"[8] that we are obliged for that reason to expound and emphasise *general democratic tasks before the whole people*, without for a moment concealing our socialist convictions. He is no Social-Democrat who forgets in practice his obligation to be *ahead of all* in raising, accentuating, and solving *every* general democratic question.

"But everyone agrees with this!" the impatient reader will exclaim, and the new instructions adopted by the last conference of the Union Abroad for the Editorial Board of *Rabocheye Dyelo* definitely say: "All events of social and political life that affect the proletariat either directly as a special class or as *the vanguard of all the revolutionary forces in the struggle for freedom* should serve as subjects for political propaganda and agitation" (*Two Conferences*, p. 17, our italics). Yes, these are very true and very good words, and we would be fully satisfied if *Rabocheye Dyelo understood* them *and if it refrained from saying in the next breath things that contradict them.* For it is not enough to call ourselves the "vanguard," the advanced contingent; we must act in such a way that *all* the other contingents recognise and are obliged to admit that we are marching in the vanguard. And we ask the reader: Are the representatives of the other "contingents" such fools as to take our word for it when we say that we are the "vanguard"? Just picture to yourselves the following: a Social-Democrat comes to the "contingent" of Russian educated radicals, or liberal constitutionalists, and says, "We are the vanguard; the task confronting us now is, as far as possible, to lend the economic struggle itself a political character." The radical, or constitutionalist, if he is at all intelligent (and there are many intelligent men among Russian radicals and constitutionalists), would only smile at such a speech and would say (to himself, of course, for in the majority of cases he is an experienced diplomat): "Your 'vanguard' must be made up of simpletons. They do not even understand that it is our task, the task of the progressive representatives of bourgeois democracy, to lend the workers' economic struggle *itself* a political character. Why, we too, like the West-European bourgeois, want to draw the workers into politics, *but only into trade-unionist, not into Social-Democratic politics.*

---

8. Marx and Engels, *The Communist Manifesto.*

Trade-unionist politics of the working class is precisely *bourgeois politics* of the working class, and this 'vanguard's' formulation of its task is the formulation of trade-unionist politics! Let them call themselves Social-Democrats to their heart's content, I am not a child to get excited over a label. But they must not fall under the influence of those pernicious orthodox doctrinaires, let them allow 'freedom of criticism' to those who unconsciously are driving Social-Democracy into trade-unionist channels."

And the faint smile of our constitutionalist will turn into Homeric laughter when he learns that the Social-Democrats who talk of Social-Democracy as the vanguard, today, when spontaneity almost completely dominates our movement, fear nothing so much as "belittling the spontaneous element," as "underestimating the significance of the forward movement of the drab everyday struggle, as compared with the propaganda of brilliant and completed ideas," etc., etc.! A "vanguard" which fears that consciousness will outstrip spontaneity, which fears to put forward a bold "plan" that would compel general recognition even among those who differ with us. Are they not confusing "vanguard" with "rearguard"?

* * *

To proceed. Have we sufficient forces to direct our propaganda and agitation among *all* social classes? Most certainly. Our Economists, who are frequently inclined to deny this, lose sight of the gigantic progress our movement has made from (approximately) 1894 to 1901. Like real "tail-enders," they often go on living in the bygone stages of the movement's inception. In the earlier period, indeed, we had astonishingly few forces, and it was perfectly natural and legitimate then to devote ourselves exclusively to activities among the workers and to condemn severely any deviation from this course. The entire task then was to consolidate our position in the working class. At the present time, however, gigantic forces have been attracted to the movement. The best representatives of the younger generation of the educated classes are coming over to us. Everywhere in the provinces there are people, resident there by dint of circumstance, who have taken part in the movement in the past or who desire to do so now and who are gravitating towards Social-Democracy (whereas in 1894 one could count the Social-Democrats on the fingers of one's hand). A basic political and organisational shortcoming of our movement is our *inability* to utilise all these forces and give them appropriate work (we shall deal with this more fully in the next chapter). The overwhelming majority of these forces entirely lack the opportunity of "going among the workers," so that there are no grounds for fearing that we shall divert forces from our main work. In order to be able to provide the workers with real, comprehensive, and live political knowledge, we must have "our own people," Social-Democrats, everywhere, among all social strata, and in all positions from which we can learn the inner springs of our state mechanism. Such people are required, not only for propaganda and agitation, but in a still larger measure for organisation.

Is there a basis for activity among all classes of the population? Whoever doubts this lags in his consciousness behind the spontaneous awakening of the masses. The working-class movement has aroused and is continuing to arouse discontent in some, hopes of support for the opposition in others, and in still others the realisation that the autocracy is unbearable and must inevitably fall. We would be "politicians" and Social-Democrats in name only (as all too often happens in reality), if we failed to realise that our task is to utilise every manifestation of discontent, and to gather and turn to the best account every protest, however small. This is quite apart from the fact that the millions of the labouring peasantry, handicraftsmen, petty artisans, etc., would always listen eagerly to the speech of any Social-Democrat who is at all qualified. Indeed, is there a single social class in which there are no individuals, groups, or circles that are discontented with the lack of rights and with tyranny and, therefore, accessible to the propaganda of Social-Democrats as the spokesmen of the most pressing general democratic needs? To those who desire to have a clear idea of what the political agitation of a Social-Democrat among *all* classes and strata of the population should be like, we would point to *political exposures* in the broad sense of the word as the principal (but, of course, not the sole) form of this agitation. "We must arouse in every section of the population that is at all politically conscious a passion for *political* exposure," I wrote in my article "Where to Begin" [*Iskra*, May (No. 4), 1901], with which I shall deal in greater detail later.

We must not be discouraged by the fact that the voice of political exposure is today so feeble, timid, and infrequent. This is not because of a wholesale submission to police despotism, but because those who are able and ready to make exposures have no tribune from which to speak, no eager and encouraging audience, they do not see anywhere among the people that force to which it would be worth while directing their complaint against the "omnipotent" Russian Government. . . . We are now in a position to provide a tribune for the nation-wide exposure of the tsarist government, and it is our duty to do this. That tribune must be a Social-Democratic newspaper.

The ideal audience for political exposure is the working class, which is first and foremost in need of all-round and live political knowledge, and is most capable of converting this knowledge into active struggle, even when that struggle does not promise "palpable results." A tribune for *nation-wide* exposures can be only an all-Russia newspaper. "Without a political organ, a political movement deserving that name is inconceivable in the Europe of today"; in this respect Russia must undoubtedly be included in present-day Europe. The press long ago became a power in our country, otherwise the government would not spend tens of thousands of rubles to bribe it and to subsidise the Katkovs and Meshcherskys.[9] And it is no novelty in autocratic Russia for the underground press to break through the wall of censorship and *compel* the legal and conservative press to speak openly of it. This was the case in the seventies and even in the fifties. How much broader and deeper are now the sections of the people willing to read the illegal underground press, and to learn from it "how to live and how to die," to use the expression of a worker who sent a letter to *Iskra* (No. 7). Political exposures are as much a declaration of war against the *government* as economic exposures are a declaration of war against the factory owners. The moral significance of this declaration of war will be all the greater, the wider and more powerful the campaign of exposure will be and the more numerous and determined the social *class* that has *declared war in order to begin the war*. Hence, political exposures in themselves serve as a powerful instrument for *disintegrating* the system we oppose, as a means for diverting from the enemy his casual or temporary allies, as a means for spreading hostility and distrust among the permanent partners of the autocracy.

In our time only a party that will *organise* really *nation-wide* exposures can become the vanguard of the revolutionary forces. The word "nation-wide" has a very profound meaning. The overwhelming majority of the non-working-class exposers (be it remembered that in order to become the vanguard, we must attract other classes) are sober politicians and level-headed men of affairs. They know perfectly well how dangerous it is to "complain" even against a minor official, let alone against the "omnipotent" Russian government. And they will come *to us* with their complaints only when they see that these complaints can really have effect, and that we represent *a political force*. In order to become such a force in the eyes of outsiders, much persistent and stubborn work is required *to raise* our own consciousness, initiative, and energy. To accomplish this it is not enough to attach a "vanguard" label to rearguard theory and practice.

But if we have to undertake the organisation of a really nation-wide exposure of the government, in what way will then the class character of our movement be expressed?—the overzealous advo-

9. M. N. Katkov (1818–87), editor and publisher of *Moskovskiye Vedomosti* (*Moscow Recorder*), 1867–87, called himself "the faithful watchdog of the autocracy." V. P. Meshchersky (1839– 1914) published *Grazhdanin* (*The Citizen*), organ of the monarchist, anti-Semitic, terrorist Black Hundred organization.

cate of "close organic contact with the proletarian struggle" will ask us, as indeed he does. The reply is manifold: we Social-Democrats will organise these nation-wide exposures; all questions raised by the agitation will be explained in a consistently Social-Democratic spirit, without any concessions to deliberate or undeliberate distortions of Marxism; the all-round political agitation will be conducted by a party which unites into one inseparable whole the assault on the government in the name of the entire people, the revolutionary training of the proletariat, and the safeguarding of its political independence, the guidance of the economic struggle of the working class, and the utilisation of all its spontaneous conflicts with its exploiters which rouse and bring into our camp increasing numbers of the proletariat.

But a most characteristic feature of Economism is its failure to understand this connection, more, this identity of the most pressing need of the proletariat (a comprehensive political education through the medium of political agitation and political exposures) with the need of the general democratic movement. This lack of understanding is expressed, not only in "Martynovite" phrases, but in the references to a supposedly class point of view identical in meaning with these phrases. Thus, the authors of the Economist letter in *Iskra*, No. 12, state:

> This basic drawback of *Iskra* [overestimation of ideology] is also the cause of its inconsistency on the question of the attitude of Social-Democracy to the various social classes and tendencies. By theoretical reasoning [not by "the growth of Party tasks, which grow together with the Party"], *Iskra* solved the problem of the immediate transition to the struggle against absolutism. In all probability it senses the difficulty of such a task for the workers under the present state of affairs [not only senses, but knows full well that this task appears less difficult to the workers than to the Economist intellectuals with their nursemaid concern, for the workers are prepared to fight even for demands which, to use the language of the never-to-be-forgotten Martynov, do not "promise palpable results"] but lacking the patience to wait until the workers will have gathered sufficient forces for this struggle, *Iskra* begins to seek allies in the ranks of the liberals and intellectuals. . . .[1]

Yes, we have indeed lost all "patience" "waiting" for the blessed time, long promised us by diverse "conciliators," when the Economists will have stopped charging the workers with *their own* back-

1. Lack of space has prevented us from replying in detail, in *Iskra*, to this letter, which is highly characteristic of the Economists. We were very glad at its appearance, for the allegations that *Iskra* did not maintain a consistent class point of view had reached us long before that from various sources, and we were waiting for an appropriate occasion, or for a formulated expression of this fashionable charge, to give our reply. Moreover, it is our habit to reply to attacks, not by defence, but by counter-attack. [*Lenin*]

wardness and justifying their own lack of energy with allegations that the workers lack strength. We ask our Economists: What do they mean by "the gathering of working-class strength for the struggle"? Is it not evident that this means the political training of the workers, so that *all* the aspects of our vile autocracy are revealed to them? And is it not clear that *precisely for this work* we need "allies in the ranks of the liberals and intellectuals," who are prepared to join us in the exposure of the political attack on the Zemstvos, on the teachers, on the statisticians, on the students, etc.? Is this surprisingly "intricate mechanism" really so difficult to understand? Has not P. B. Axelrod constantly repeated since 1897 that "the task before the Russian Social-Democrats of acquiring adherents and direct and indirect allies among the non-proletarian classes will be solved principally and primarily by the character of the propagandist activities conducted among the proletariat itself"? But the Martynovs and the other Economists continue to imagine that "by economic struggle against the employers and the government" the workers must *first* gather strength (for trade-unionist politics) and *then* "go over"—we presume from trade-unionist "training for activity" to Social-Democratic activity!

* * *

Rabocheye Dyelo and the authors of the Economist letter published in *Iskra*, No. 12, should "ponder over the reason why the events of the spring brought about such a revival of revolutionary non-Social-Democratic tendencies instead of increasing the authority and the prestige of Social-Democracy."

The reason lies in the fact that we failed to cope with our tasks. The masses of the workers proved to be more active than we. We lacked adequately trained revolutionary leaders and organisers possessed of a thorough knowledge of the mood prevailing among all the opposition strata and able to head the movement, to turn a spontaneous demonstration into a political one, broaden its political character, etc. Under such circumstances, our backwardness will inevitably be utilised by the more mobile and more energetic non-Social-Democratic revolutionaries, and the workers, however energetically and self-sacrificingly they may fight the police and the troops, however revolutionary their actions may be, will prove to be merely a force supporting these revolutionaries, the rearguard of bourgeois democracy, and not the Social-Democratic vanguard. Let us take, for example, the German Social-Democrats, whose weak aspects alone our Economists desire to emulate. Why is there *not a single* political event in Germany that does not add to the authority and prestige of Social-Democracy? Because Social-Democracy is always found to be in advance of all others in furnishing the most revolutionary appraisal of every given event and in championing every protest against tyranny. It does not lull itself with arguments that the economic struggle brings the workers to realise that they have no political rights and that the concrete conditions unavoidably impel the working-class movement on to the path of revolution. It intervenes in every sphere and in every question of social and political life; in the matter of Wilhelm's refusal to endorse a bourgeois progressist as city mayor (our Economists have not yet managed to educate the Germans to the understanding that such an act is, in fact, a compromise with liberalism!); in the matter of the law against "obscene" publications and pictures; in the matter of governmental influence on the election of professors, etc., etc. Everywhere the Social-Democrats are found in the forefront, rousing political discontent among all classes, rousing the sluggards, stimulating the laggards, and providing a wealth of material for the development of the political consciousness and the political activity of the proletariat. As a result, even the avowed enemies of socialism are filled with respect for this advanced political fighter, and not infrequently an important document from bourgeois, and even from bureaucratic and Court circles, makes its way by some miraculous means into the editorial office of *Vorwärts*.

This, then, is the resolution of the seeming "contradiction" that surpasses *Rabocheye Dyelo*'s powers of understanding to such an extent that it can only throw up its hands and cry, "Mummery!" Indeed, just think of it: We, *Rabocheye Dyelo*, regard the *mass* working-class movement as the *corner-stone* (and say so in bold type!); we warn all and sundry against belittling the significance of the element of spontaneity; we desire to lend the economic struggle itself—*itself*—a political character; we desire to maintain close and organic contact with the proletarian struggle. And yet we are told that we are preparing the ground for the conversion of the working-class movement into an instrument of bourgeois democracy! And who are they that presume to say this? People who "compromise" with liberalism by intervening in every "liberal" issue (what a gross misunderstanding of "organic contact with the proletarian struggle"!), by devoting so much attention to the students and even (oh horror!) to the Zemstvos! People who in general wish to devote a greater percentage (compared with the Economists) of their efforts to activity among non-proletarian classes of the population! What is this but "mummery"?

Poor *Rabocheye Dyelo*! Will it ever find the solution to this perplexing puzzle?

IV. The Primitiveness of the Economists and the Organisation of the Revolutionaries

Rabocheye Dyelo's assertions, which we have analysed, that the economic struggle is the most widely applicable means of political agitation and that our task now is to lend the economic struggle itself a political character, etc., express a narrow view, not only of our political, but also of our *organisational* tasks. The "economic struggle against the employers and the government" does not at all require an all-Russia centralised organisation, and hence this struggle can never give rise to such an organisation as will combine, in one general assault, all the manifestations of political opposition, protest, and indignation, an organisation that will consist of professional revolutionaries and be led by the real political leaders of the entire people. This stands to reason. The character of any organisation is naturally and inevitably determined by the content of its activity. Consequently, *Rabocheye Dyelo*, by the assertions analysed above, sanctifies and legitimises not only narrowness of political activity, but also of organisational work. In this case, too, *Rabocheye Dyelo*, as always, proves itself an organ whose consciousness yields to spontaneity. Yet subservience to spontaneously developing forms of organisation, failure to realise the narrowness and primitiveness of our organisational work, of our "handicraft" methods in this most important sphere, failure to realise this, I say, is a veritable ailment from which our movement suffers. It is not an ailment that comes with decline, but one, of course, that comes with growth. It is, however, at the present time, when the wave of spontaneous indignation, as it were, is sweeping over us, leaders and organisers of the movement, that an irreconcilable struggle must be waged against all defence of backwardness, against any legitimation of narrowness in this matter. It is particularly necessary to arouse in all who participate in practical work, or are preparing to take up that work, discontent with the *amateurism* prevailing among us and an unshakable determination to rid ourselves of it.

A. What Is Primitiveness?

We shall try to answer this question by giving a brief description of the activity of a typical Social-Democratic study circle of the period 1894–1901. We have noted that the entire student youth of the period was absorbed in Marxism. Of course, these students were not only, or even not so much, interested in Marxism as a theory;

they were interested in it as an answer to the question, "What is to be done?," as a call to take the field against the enemy. These new warriors marched to battle with astonishingly primitive equipment and training. In a vast number of cases they had almost no equipment and absolutely no training. They marched to war like peasants from the plough, armed only with clubs. A students' circle establishes contacts with workers and sets to work, without any connection with the old members of the movement, without any connection with study circles in other districts, or even in other parts of the same city (or in other educational institutions), without any organisation of the various divisions of revolutionary work, without any systematic plan of activity covering any length of time. The circle gradually expands its propaganda and agitation; by its activities it wins the sympathies of fairly large sections of workers and of a certain section of the educated strata, which provide it with money and from among whom the "committee" recruits new groups of young people. The attractive power of the committee (or League of Struggle) grows, its sphere of activity becomes wider, and the committee expands this activity quite spontaneously; the very people who a year or a few months previously spoke at the students' circle gatherings and discussed the question, "Whither?," who established and maintained contacts with the workers and wrote and published leaflets, now establish contacts with other groups of revolutionaries, procure literature, set to work to publish a local newspaper, begin to talk of organising a demonstration, and finally turn to open warfare (which may, according to circumstances, take the form of issuing the first agitational leaflet or the first issue of a newspaper, or of organising the first demonstration). Usually the initiation of such actions ends in an immediate and complete fiasco. Immediate and complete, because this open warfare was not the result of a systematic and carefully thought-out and gradually prepared plan for a prolonged and stubborn struggle, but simply the result of the spontaneous growth of traditional study circle work; because, naturally, the police, in almost every case, knew the principal leaders of the local movement, since they had already "gained a reputation" for themselves in their student days, and the police waited only for the right moment to make their raid. They deliberately allowed the study circle sufficient time to develop its work so that they might obtain a palpable *corpus delicti*, and they always permitted several of the persons known to them to remain at liberty "for breeding" (which, as far as I know, is the technical term used both by our people and by the gendarmes). One cannot help comparing this kind of warfare with that conducted by a mass of peasants, armed with clubs, against modern troops. And one can only wonder at the vitality of the movement which expanded, grew, and scored victories despite the total lack of training on the part of the fighters. True, from the historical point of view, the primitiveness of equipment was not only inevitable at first, but *even legitimate* as one of the conditions for the wide recruiting of fighters, but as soon as serious war operations began (and they began in fact with the strikes in the summer of 1896), the defects in our fighting organisations made themselves felt to an ever-increasing degree. The government, at first thrown into confusion and committing a number of blunders (e.g., its appeal to the public describing the misdeeds of the socialists, or the banishment of workers from the capitals to provincial industrial centres), very soon adapted itself to the new conditions of the struggle and managed to deploy well its perfectly equipped detachments of *agents provocateurs*, spies, and gendarmes. Raids became so frequent, affected such a vast number of people, and cleared out the local study circles so thoroughly that the masses of the workers lost literally all their leaders, the movement assumed an amazingly sporadic character, and it became utterly impossible to establish continuity and coherence in the work. The terrible dispersion of the local leaders; the fortuitous character of the study circle memberships; the lack of training in, and the narrow outlook on, theoretical, political, and organisational questions were all the inevitable result of the conditions described above. Things have reached such a pass that in several places the workers, because of our lack of self-restraint and the ability to maintain secrecy, begin to lose faith in the intellectuals and to avoid them; the intellectuals, they say, are much too careless and cause police raids!

Anyone who has the slightest knowledge of the movement is aware that all thinking Social-Democrats have at last begun to regard these amateurish methods as a disease. * * *

B. Primitiveness and Economism

We must now deal with a question that has undoubtedly come to the mind of every reader. Can a connection be established between primitiveness as growing pains that affect the *whole* movement, and Economism, which is *one* of the currents in Russian Social-Democracy? We think that it can. Lack of practical training, of ability to carry on organisational work is certainly common *to us all*, including those who have from the very outset unswervingly stood for revolutionary Marxism. Of course, were it only lack of practical training, no one could blame the practical workers. But the term "primitiveness" embraces something more than lack of training; it denotes a narrow scope of revolutionary work generally, failure to understand that a good organisation of revolutionaries cannot be built on the basis of such narrow activity, and lastly—and this is the main thing—attempts to justify this narrowness and to elevate it to a special "theory," i.e., subservience to spontaneity on this question too. Once such attempts were revealed, it became clear that primitiveness is connected with Economism and that we shall never rid ourselves of this narrowness of our organisational activity until we rid ourselves of Economism generally (i.e., the narrow conception of Marxist theory, as well as of the role of Social-Democracy and of its political tasks). These attempts manifested themselves in a twofold direction. Some began to say that the working masses themselves have not yet advanced the broad and militant political tasks which the revolutionaries are attempting to "impose" on them; that they must continue to struggle for *immediate* political demands, to conduct "the economic struggle against the employers and the government"[2] (and, naturally, corresponding to this struggle which is "accessible" to the mass movement there must be an organisation that will be "accessible" to the most untrained youth). Others, far removed from any theory of "gradualness," said that it is possible and necessary to "bring about a political revolution," but that this does not require building a strong organisation of revolutionaries to train the proletariat in steadfast and stubborn struggle. All we need do is to snatch up our old friend, the "accessible" cudgel. To drop metaphor, it means that we must organise a general strike,[3] or that we must stimulate the "spiritless" progress of the working-class movement by means of "excitative terror."[4] Both these trends, the opportunists and the "revolutionists," bow to the prevailing amateurism; neither believes that it can be eliminated, neither understands our primary and imperative practical task to establish *an organisation of revolutionaries* capable of lending energy, stability, and continuity to the political struggle.

[One B—v has written in *Rabocheye Dyelo*, No. 6]: "The growth of the working-class movement is outstripping the growth and development of the revolutionary organisations." This "valuable remark of a close observer" (*Rabocheye Dyelo*'s comment on B—v's article) has a twofold value for us. It shows that we were right in our opinion that the principal cause of the present crisis in Russian Social-Democracy is *the lag of the leaders* ("ideologists," revolutionaries, Social-Democrats) behind *the spontaneous upsurge of the masses*. It shows that all the arguments advanced by the authors of

2. *Rabochaya Mysl* and *Rabocheye Dyelo*, especially the *Reply* to Plekhanov. [*Lenin*]
3. See "Who Will Bring about the Political Revolution?" in the collection published in Russia, entitled *The Proletarian Struggle*. Re-issued by the Kiev Committee. [*Lenin*]
4. *Regeneration of Revolutionism* and the journal *Svoboda*. [*Lenin*]

the Economist letter (in *Iskra*, No. 12), by Krichevsky and by Martynov, as to the danger of belittling the significance of the spontaneous element, of the drab everyday struggle, as to tactics-as-process, etc., are nothing more than a glorification and a defence of primitiveness. These people who cannot pronounce the word "theoretician" without a sneer, who describe their genuflections to common lack of training and backwardness as a "sense for the realities of life," reveal in practice a failure to understand our most imperative *practical* tasks. To laggards they shout: Keep in step! Don't run ahead! To people suffering from a lack of energy and initiative in organisational work, from a lack of "plans" for wide and bold activity, they prate about "tactics-as-process"! The worst sin we commit is that we *degrade* our political *and organisational* tasks to the level of the immediate, "palpable," "concrete" interests of the everyday economic struggle; yet they keep singing to us the same refrain: Lend the economic struggle itself a political character! We repeat: this kind of thing displays as much "sense for the realities of life" as was displayed by the hero in the popular fable who cried out to a passing funeral procession, "Many happy returns of the day!"

Recall the matchless, truly "Narcissus-like" superciliousness with which these wiseacres lectured Plekhanov on the "workers' *circles* generally" (sic!) being "unable to cope with political tasks in the real and *practical* sense of the word, i.e., in the sense of the expedient and successful *practical* struggle for political demands" (*Rabocheye Dyelo's Reply*, p. 24). There are circles and circles, gentlemen! Circles of "amateurs" are not, of course, capable of coping with political tasks so long as they have not become aware of their amateurism and do not abandon it. If, besides this, these amateurs are enamoured of their primitive methods, and insist on writing the word "practical" in italics, and imagine that being practical demands that one's tasks be reduced to the level of understanding of the most backward strata of the masses, then they are hopeless amateurs and, of course, certainly cannot *in general cope with any political tasks*. But a circle of leaders, of the type of Alexeyev and Myshkin, of Khalturin and Zhelyabov, is capable of coping with political tasks in the genuine and most practical sense of the term, for the reason and to the extent that their impassioned propaganda meets with response among the spontaneously awakening masses, and their sparkling energy is answered and supported by the energy of the revolutionary class. Plekhanov was profoundly right, not only in pointing to this revolutionary class and proving that its spontaneous awakening was inevitable, but in setting even the "workers' circles" a great and lofty political task. But you refer to the mass movement that has sprung up since that time in order *to degrade* this task, *to curtail* the energy and scope of activity of the "workers' circles." If you are not amateurs enamoured of your primitive methods, what are you then? You boast that you are practical, but you fail to see what every Russian practical worker knows, namely, the miracles that the energy, not only of a circle, but even of an individual person is able to perform in the revolutionary cause. Or do you think that our movement cannot produce leaders like those of the seventies? If so, why do you think so? Because we lack training? But we are training ourselves, we will go on training ourselves, and we will be trained! Unfortunately it is true that the surface of the stagnant waters of the "economic struggle against the employers and the government" is overgrown with fungus; people have appeared among us who kneel in prayer to spontaneity, gazing with awe (to take an expression from Plekhanov) upon the "posterior" of the Russian proletariat. But we will get rid of this fungus. The time has come when Russian revolutionaries, guided by a genuinely revolutionary theory, relying upon the genuinely revolutionary and spontaneously awakening class, can at last—at long last!—rise to full stature in all their giant strength. All that is required is for the masses of our practical workers, and the still larger masses of those who dreamed of practical work when they were still at school, to pour scorn and ridicule upon any suggestion that may be made to degrade our political tasks and to restrict the scope of our organisational work. And we will achieve that, rest assured, gentlemen!

* * *

But if the reader wishes to see the pearls of "Economist" infatuation with amateurism, he must, of course, turn from the eclectic and vacillating *Rabocheye Dyelo* to the consistent and determined *Rabochaya Mysl*. In its *Separate Supplement*, p. 13, R. M. wrote:

> Now two words about the so-called revolutionary intelligentsia proper. True, on more than one occasion it has proved itself prepared "to enter into determined battle with tsarism." The unfortunate thing, however, is that our revolutionary intelligentsia, ruthlessly persecuted by the political police, imagined the struggle against the political police to be the political struggle against the autocracy. That is why, to this day, it cannot understand "where the forces for the struggle against the autocracy are to be obtained."

Truly matchless is the lofty contempt for the struggle against the police displayed by this worshipper (in the worst sense of the word) of the *spontaneous* movement! He is prepared *to justify* our inability to organise secret activity by the argument that with the spontaneous mass movement it is not at all important for us to struggle against the political police! Very few people indeed would subscribe to this appalling conclusion; to such an extent have our deficiencies in revolutionary organisations become a matter of acute importance. But if Martynov, for example, refuses to subscribe to this, it will only be because he is unable, or lacks the courage, to think out his ideas to their logical conclusion. Indeed, does the "task" of advancing concrete demands by the masses, demands that promise palpable results, call for special efforts to create a stable, centralised, militant organisation of revolutionaries? Cannot such a "task" be carried out even by masses that do not "struggle against the political police" at all? Could this task, moreover, be fulfilled if, in addition to the few leaders, it were not undertaken by such workers (the overwhelming majority) as are quite *incapable* of "struggling against the political police"? Such workers, average people of the masses, are capable of displaying enormous energy and self-sacrifice in strikes and in street battles with the police and the troops, and are capable (in fact, are alone capable) of *determining* the outcome of our entire movement—but the struggle against the *political* police requires special qualities; it requires *professional* revolutionaries. And we must see to it, not only that the masses, "advance" concrete demands, but that the masses of the workers "advance" an increasing number of such professional revolutionaries. Thus, we have reached the question of the relation between an organisation of professional revolutionaries and the labour movement pure and simple. Although this question has found little reflection in literature, it has greatly engaged us "politicians" in conversations and polemics with comrades who gravitate more or less towards Economism. It is a question meriting special treatment. But before taking it up, let us offer one further quotation by way of illustrating our thesis on the connection between primitiveness and Economism.

In his *Reply*, Mr. N. N. wrote: "The Emancipation of Labour group demands direct struggle against the government without first considering where the material forces for this struggle are to be obtained, and without indicating *the path of the struggle*." Emphasising the last words, the author adds the following footnote to the word "path": "This cannot be explained by purposes of secrecy, because the programme does not refer to a plot but to *a mass movement*. And the masses cannot proceed by secret paths. Can we conceive of a secret strike? Can we conceive of secret demonstrations and petitions?" (*Vademecum*, p. 59.) Thus, the author comes quite close to the question of the "material forces" (organisers of strikes and demonstrations) and to the "paths" of the struggle, but, nevertheless, is still in a state of consternation, because he "worships" the mass movement, i.e., he regards it as something that *relieves* us of the necessity of conducting revolutionary activity and not as something that should encourage us and *stimulate* our revolutionary activity. It is impossible for a strike to remain a secret to those participating in it and to those immediately associated with it, but it may (and in the majority of cases does) remain a "secret" to the masses of the Russian workers, because the government takes care to cut all communication with the strikers, to prevent all news of strikes from spreading. Here indeed is where a special "struggle against the political police" is required, a struggle that can never be conducted actively by such large masses as take part in strikes. This struggle must be organised, according to "all the rules of the art," by people who are professionally engaged in revolutionary activity. The fact that the masses are spontaneously being drawn into the movement does not make the organisation of this struggle *less necessary*. On the contrary, it makes it *more necessary*; for we socialists would be failing in our direct duty to the masses if we did not prevent the police from making a secret of every strike and every demonstration (and if we did not ourselves from time to time secretly prepare strikes and demonstrations). And we *will succeed in doing this*, because the spontaneously awakening masses will *also produce* increasing numbers of "professional revolutionaries" *from their own ranks* (that is, if we do not take it into our heads to advise the workers to keep on marking time).

C. Organisation of Workers and Organisation of Revolutionaries

It is only natural to expect that for a Social-Democrat whose conception of the political struggle coincides with the conception of the "economic struggle against the employers and the government," the "organisation of revolutionaries" will more or less coincide with the "organisation of workers." This, in fact, is what actually happens; so that when we speak of organisation, we literally speak in different tongues. I vividly recall, for example, a conversation I once had with a fairly consistent Economist, with whom I had not been previously acquainted.[5] We were discussing the pamphlet, *Who Will Bring About the Political Revolution?* and were soon of a mind that its principal defect was its ignoring of the question of organisation. We had begun to assume full agreement between us; but, as the conversation proceeded, it became evident that we were talking of different things. My interlocutor accused the author of ignoring strike funds, mutual benefit societies, etc., whereas I had in mind an organisation of revolutionaries as an essential factor in "bringing about" the political revolution. As soon as the disagreement became clear, there was hardly, as I remember, a single question of principle upon which I was in agreement with the Economist!

5. This apparently refers to Lenin's first meeting with A. S. Martynov in 1901.

What was the source of our disagreement? It was the fact that on questions both of organisation and of politics the Economists are forever lapsing from Social-Democracy into trade-unionism. The political struggle of Social Democracy is far more extensive and complex than the economic struggle of the workers against the employers and the government. Similarly (indeed for that reason), the organisation of the revolutionary Social-Democratic Party must inevitably be of *a kind different* from the organisation of the workers designed for this struggle. The workers' organisation must in the first place be a trade union organisation; secondly, it must be as broad as possible; and thirdly, it must be as public as conditions will allow (here, and further on, of course, I refer only to absolutist Russia). On the other hand, the organisation of the revolutionaries must consist first and foremost of people who make revolutionary activity their profession (for which reason I speak of the organisation of *revolutionaries,* meaning revolutionary Social-Democrats). In view of this common characteristic of the members of such an organisation, *all distinctions as between workers and intellectuals,* not to speak of distinctions of trade and profession, in both categories, *must be effaced.* Such a organisation must perforce not be very extensive and must be as secret as possible. Let us examine this threefold distinction.

In countries where political liberty exists the distinction between a trade union and a political organisation is clear enough, as is the distinction between trade unions and Social-Democracy. The relations between the latter and the former will naturally vary in each country according to historical, legal, and other conditions; they may be more or less close, complex, etc. (in our opinion they should be as close and as little complicated as possible); but there can be no question in free countries of the organisation of trade unions coinciding with the organisation of the Social-Democratic Party. In Russia, however, the yoke of the autocracy appears at first glance to obliterate all distinctions between the Social-Democratic organisation and the workers' associations, since *all* workers' associations and *all* study circles are prohibited, and since the principal manifestation and weapon of the workers' economic struggle —the strike—is regarded as a criminal (and sometimes even as a political!) offence. Conditions in our country, therefore, on the one hand, strongly "impel" the workers engaged in economic struggle to concern themselves with political questions, and, on the other, they "impel" Social-Democrats to confound trade-unionism with Social-Democracy (and our Krichevskys,[6] Martynovs, and Co., while diligently discussing the first kind of "impulsion," fail to notice the

6. B. N. Krichevsky (1866–1919), a member of the Economist group, was the editor of *Rabocheye Dyelo* in 1899.

second). Indeed, picture to yourselves people who are immersed ninety-nine per cent in "the economic struggle against the employers and the government." Some of them will never, during the *entire* course of their activity (from four to six months), be impelled to think of the need for a more complex organisation of revolutionaries. Others, perhaps, will come across the fairly widely distributed Bernsteinian literature, from which they will become convinced of the profound importance of the forward movement of "the drab everyday struggle." Still others will be carried away, perhaps, by the seductive idea of showing the world a new example of "close and organic contact with the proletarian struggle"—contact between the trade union and the Social-Democratic movements. Such people may argue that the later a country enters the arena of capitalism and, consequently, of the working-class movement, the more the socialists in that country may take part in, and support, the trade union movement, and the less the reason for the existence of non-Social-Democratic trade unions. So far the argument is fully correct; unfortunately, however, some go beyond that and dream of a complete fusion of Social-Democracy with trade-unionism. We shall soon see, from the example of the Rules of the St. Petersburg League of Struggle, what a harmful effect such dreams have upon our plans of organisation.

The workers' organisations for the economic struggle should be trade union organisations. Every Social-Democratic worker should as far as possible assist and actively work in these organisations. But, while this is true, it is certainly not in our interest to demand that only Social-Democrats should be eligible for membership in the "trade" unions, since that would only narrow the scope of our influence upon the masses. Let every worker who understands the need to unite for the struggle against the employers and the government join the trade unions. The very aim of the trade unions would be impossible of achievement, if they did not unite all who have attained at least this elementary degree of understanding, if they were not very *broad* organisations. The broader these organisations, the broader will be our influence over them—an influence due, not only to the "spontaneous" development of the economic struggle, but to the direct and conscious effort of the socialist trade union members to influence their comrades. But a broad organisation cannot apply methods of strict secrecy (since this demands far greater training than is required for the economic struggle). How is the contradiction between the need for a large membership and the need for strictly secret methods to be reconciled? How are we to make the trade unions as public as possible? Generally speaking, there can be only two ways to this end: either the trade unions become legalised (in some countries this preceded the legalisation of the socialist and political unions), or the organisation is kept secret, but so "free" and amorphous, *lose,*[7] as the Germans say, that the need for secret methods becomes almost negligible as far as the bulk of the members is concerned.

The legalisation of non-socialist and non-political labour unions in Russia has begun, and there is no doubt that every advance made by our rapidly growing Social-Democratic working-class movement will multiply and encourage attempts at legalisation—attempts proceeding for the most part from supporters of the existing order, but partly also from the workers themselves and from liberal intellectuals. The banner of legality has already been hoisted by the Vasilyevs and the Zubatovs. Support has been promised and rendered by the Ozerovs and the Wormses, and followers of the new tendency are now to be found among the workers. Henceforth, we cannot but reckon with this tendency. How we are to reckon with it, on this there can be no two opinions among Social-Democrats. We must steadfastly expose any part played in this movement by the Zubatovs and the Vasilyevs, the gendarmes and the priests, and explain their real intentions to the workers. We must also expose all the conciliatory, "harmonious" notes that will be heard in the speeches of liberal politicians at legal meetings of the workers, irrespective of whether the speeches are motivated by an earnest conviction of the desirability of peaceful class collaboration, by a desire to curry favour with the powers that be, or whether they are simply the result of clumsiness. Lastly, we must warn the workers against the traps often set by the police, who at such open meetings and permitted societies spy out the "fiery ones" and try to make use of legal organisations to plant their *agents provocateurs* in the illegal organisations.

Doing all this does not at all mean forgetting that *in the long run* the legalisation of the working-class movement will be to our advantage, and not to that of the Zubatovs. On the contrary, it is precisely our campaign of exposure that will help us to separate the tares from the wheat. What the tares are, we have already indicated. By the wheat we mean attracting the attention of ever larger numbers, including the most backward sections, of the workers to social and political questions, and freeing ourselves, the revolutionaries, from functions that are essentially legal (the distribution of legal books, mutual aid, etc.), the development of which will inevitably provide us with an increasing quantity of material for agitation. In this sense, we may, and should, say to the Zubatovs and the Ozerovs: Keep at it, gentlemen, do your best! Whenever you place a trap in the path of the workers (either by way of direct provoca-

7. Loose.

tion, or by the "honest" demoralisation of the workers with the aid of "Struve-ism"[8]), we will see to it that you are exposed. But whenever you take a real step forward, though it be the most "timid zigzag," we will say: Please continue! And the only step that can be a real step forward is a real, if small, extension of the workers' field of action. Every such extension will be to our advantage and will help to hasten the advent of legal societies of the kind in which it will not be *agents provocateurs* who are detecting socialists, but socialists who are gaining adherents. In a word, our task is to fight the tares. It is not our business to grow wheat in flower-pots. By pulling up the tares, we clear the soil for the wheat. And while the Afanasy Ivanoviches and Pulkheria Ivanovnas[9] are tending their flower-pot crops, we must prepare the reapers, not only to cut down the tares of today, but to reap the wheat of tomorrow.[1]

Thus, *we* cannot by means of legislation *solve* the problem of creating a trade union organisation that will be as little secret and as extensive as possible (but we should be extremely glad if the Zubatovs and the Ozerovs disclosed to us even a partial opportunity for such a solution—to this end, however, we must strenuously combat them). There remain secret trade union organisations, and *we must* give all possible assistance to the workers who (as we definitely know) are adopting this course. Trade union organisations, not only can be of tremendous value in developing and consolidating the economic struggle, but can also become a very important auxiliary to political agitation and revolutionary organisation. In order to achieve this purpose, and in order to guide the nascent trade union movement in the channels desired by Social-Democracy, we must first understand clearly the absurdity of the plan of organisation the St. Petersburg Economists have been nursing for nearly five years. That plan is set forth in the "Rules for a Workers' Mutual Benefit Fund" of July 1897 (*"Listok" Rabotnika,* No. 9–10, p. 46, taken from *Rabochaya Mysl,* No. 1), as well as in the "Rules for a Trade Union Workers' Organisation" of October 1900 (special leaflet printed in St. Petersburg and referred to in *Iskra,* No. 1). Both these sets of rules have one main shortcoming: they set up the broad workers' organisation in a rigidly specified

8. I.e., "legal Marxism," whose chief representative was P. B. Struve.

9. Members of a patriarchal family of petty provincial landowners described in Gogol's *Old-Time Landowners.*

1. *Iskra's* campaign against the tares evoked the following angry outburst from *Rabocheye Dyelo:* "For *Iskra,* the signs of the times lie not so much in the great events [of the spring], as in the miserable attempts of the agents of Zubatov to 'legalise' the working-class movement. It fails to see that these facts tell against it; for they testify that the working-class movement has assumed menacing proportions in the eyes of the government." (*Two Conferences,* p. 27.) For all this we have to blame the "dogmatism" of the orthodox who "turn a deaf ear to the imperative demands of life." They obstinately refuse to see the yard-high wheat and are combating inch-high tares! Does this not reveal a "distorted sense of perspective in regard to the Russian working-class movement" (*ibid.,* p. 27)? [*Lenin*]

structure and confound it with the organisation of revolutionaries. Let us take the last-mentioned set of rules, since it is drawn up in greater detail. The body consists of *fifty-two* paragraphs. Twenty-three deal with the structure, the method of functioning, and the competence of the "workers' circles," which are to be organised in every factory ("a maximum of ten persons") and which elect "central (factory) groups." "The central group," says paragraph 2, "observes all that goes on in its factory or workshop and keeps a record of events." "The central group presents to subscribers a monthly financial account" (par. 17), etc. Ten paragraphs are devoted to the "district organisation," and nineteen to the highly complex interconnection between the Committee of the Workers' Organisation and the Committee of the St. Petersburg League of Struggle (elected representatives of each district and of the "executive groups"—groups of propagandists, groups for maintaining contact with the provinces and with the organisation abroad, groups for managing stores, publications, and funds").

Social-Democracy="executive groups" in relation to the economic struggle of the workers! It would be difficult to show more glaringly how the Economists' ideas deviate from Social-Democracy to trade-unionism, and how alien to them is any idea that a Social-Democrat must concern himself first and foremost with an organisation of revolutionaries capable of guiding the *entire* proletarian struggle for emancipation. To talk of "the political emancipation of the working class" and of the struggle against "tsarist despotism," and at the same time to draft rules like these, means to have no idea whatsoever of the real political tasks of Social-Democracy. Not one of the fifty or so paragraphs reveals even a glimmer of understanding that it is necessary to conduct the widest possible political agitation among the masses, an agitation highlighting every aspect of Russian absolutism and the specific features of the various social classes in Russia. Rules like these are of no use even for the achievement of trade union, let alone political, aims, since trade unions are organised by *trades*, of which no mention is made.

* * *

I could go on analysing the Rules, but I think that what has been said will suffice. A small, compact core of the most reliable, experienced, and hardened workers, with responsible representatives in the principal districts and connected by all the rules of strict secrecy with the organisation of revolutionaries, can, with the widest support of the masses and without any formal organisation, perform *all* the functions of a trade union organisation, in a manner, moreover, desirable to Social-Democracy. Only in this way can we secure the *consolidation* and development of a *Social-Democratic* trade union movement, despite all the gendarmes.

It may be objected that an organisation which is so *lose* that it is not even definitely formed, and which has not even an enrolled and registered membership, cannot be called an organisation at all. Perhaps so. Not the name is important. What is important is that this "organisation without members" shall do everything that is required, and from the very outset ensure a solid connection between our future trade unions and socialism. Only an incorrigible utopian would have a *broad* organisation of workers, with elections, reports, universal suffrage, etc., under the autocracy.

The moral to be drawn from this is simple. If we begin with the solid foundation of a strong organisation of revolutionaries, we can ensure the stability of the movement as a whole and carry out the aims both of Social-Democracy and of trade unions proper. If, however, we begin with a broad workers' organisation, which is supposedly most "accessible" to the masses (but which is actually most accessible to the gendarmes and makes revolutionaries most accessible to the police), we shall achieve neither the one aim nor the other; we shall not eliminate our rule-of-thumb methods, and, because we remain scattered and our forces are constantly broken up by the police, we shall only make trade unions of the Zubatov and Ozerov type the more accessible to the masses.

What, properly speaking, should be the functions of the organisation of revolutionaries? We shall deal with this question in detail. First, however, let us examine a very typical argument advanced by our terrorist, who (sad fate!) in this matter also is a next-door neighbour to the Economist. *Svoboda*, a journal published for workers, contains in its first issue an article entitled "Organisation," the author of which tries to defend his friends, the Economist workers of Ivanovo-Voznesensk. He writes:

It is bad when the masses are mute and unenlightened, when the movement does not come from the rank and file. For instance, the students of a university town leave for their homes during the summer and other holidays, and immediately the workers' movement comes to a standstill. Can a workers' movement which has to be pushed on from outside be a real force? No, indeed. . . . It has not yet learned to walk, it is still in leading-strings. So it is in all matters. The students go off, and everything comes to a standstill. The most capable are seized; the cream is skimmed— and the milk turns sour. If the "committee" is arrested, everything comes to a standstill until a new one can be formed. And one never knows what sort of committee will be set up next—it may be nothing like the former. The first said one thing, the second may say the very opposite. Continuity between yesterday and tomorrow is broken, the experience of the past does not serve as a guide for the future. And all because no roots have been struck in depth, in the masses; the work is carried on not by a hundred fools, but by a dozen wise men. A dozen wise men can be wiped out at a snap, but when the organisation embraces masses, everything proceeds from them, and nobody, however he tries, can wreck the cause. [P. 63.]

The facts are described correctly. The picture of our amateurism is well drawn. But the conclusions are worthy of *Rabochaya Mysl*, both as regards their stupidity and their lack of political tact. They represent the height of stupidity, because the author confuses the philosophical and social-historical question of the "depth" of the "roots" of the movement with the technical and organisational question of the best method in combating the gendarmes. They represent the height of political tactlessness, because, instead of appealing from bad leaders to good leaders, the author appeals from the leaders in general to the "masses." This is as much an attempt to drag us back organisationally as the idea of substituting excitative terrorism for political agitation drags us back politically. Indeed, I am experiencing a veritable *embarras de richesses*, and hardly know where to begin to disentangle the jumble offered up by *Svoboda*. For clarity, let me begin by citing an example. Take the Germans. It will not be denied, I hope, that theirs is a mass organisation, that in Germany everything proceeds from the masses, that the working-class movement there has learned to walk. Yet observe how these millions value their "dozen" tried political leaders, how firmly they cling to them. Members of the hostile parties in parliament have often taunted the socialists by exclaiming: "Fine democrats you are indeed! Yours is a working-class movement only in name; in actual fact the same clique of leaders is always in evidence, the same Bebel and the same Liebknecht, year in and year out, and that goes on for decades. Your supposedly elected workers' deputies are more permanent than the officials appointed by the Emperor!" But the Germans only smile with contempt at these demagogic attempts to set the "masses" against the "leaders," to arouse bad and ambitious instincts in the former, and to rob the movement of its solidity and stability by undermining the confidence of the masses in their "dozen wise men." Political thinking is sufficiently developed among the Germans, and they have accumulated sufficient political experience to understand that without the "dozen" tried and talented leaders (and talented men are not born by the hundreds), professionally trained, schooled by long experience, and working in perfect harmony, no class in modern society can wage a determined struggle. The Germans too have had demagogues in their ranks who have flattered the "hundred fools," exalted them above the "dozen wise men," extolled the "horny hand" of the masses, and (like Most and Hasselmann) have spurred them on to reckless "revolutionary" action and sown distrust towards the firm and steadfast leaders. It was only by stubbornly and relentlessly combating all demagogic elements within the socialist movement that German socialism has managed to grow and become as strong as it is. Our wiseacres, however, at a time when Russian Social-Democracy is passing through a crisis entirely due to the lack of sufficiently trained, developed, and experienced leaders to guide the spontaneously awakening masses, cry out with the profundity of fools: "It is a bad business when the movement does not proceed from the rank and file."

"A committee of students is of no use; it is not stable." Quite true. But the conclusion to be drawn from this is that we must have a committee of professional *revolutionaries*, and it is immaterial whether a student or a worker is capable of becoming a professional revolutionary. The conclusion you draw, however, is that the working-class movement must not be pushed on from outside! In your political innocence you fail to notice that you are playing into the hands of our Economists and fostering our amateurism. Wherein, may I ask, did our students "push on" our workers? *In the sense* that the student brought to the worker the fragments of political knowledge he himself possesses, the crumbs of socialist ideas he has managed to acquire (for the principal intellectual diet of the present-day student, legal Marxism, could furnish only the rudiments, only scraps of knowledge). There has never been too much of *such* "pushing on from outside"; on the contrary, there has so far been all too little of it in our movement, for we have been stewing too assiduously in our own juice; we have bowed far too slavishly to the elementary "economic struggle of the workers against the employers and the government." We professional revolutionaries must and will make it our business to engage in *this kind* of "pushing on" a hundred times more forcibly than we have done hitherto. But the very fact that you select so hideous a phrase as "pushing on from outside"—a phrase which cannot but rouse in the workers (at least in the workers who are as unenlightened as you yourselves) a sense of distrust towards *all* who bring them political knowledge and revolutionary experience from outside, which cannot but rouse in them an instinctive desire to resist *all* such people—proves you to be *demagogues*, and demagogues are the worst enemies of the working class.

And, please—don't hasten howling about my "uncomradely methods" of debating. I have not the least desire to doubt the purity of your intentions. As I have said, one may become a demagogue out of sheer political innocence. But I have shown that you have descended to demagogy, and I will never tire of repeating that demagogues are the worst enemies of the working class. The worst enemies, because they arouse base instincts in the masses, because the unenlightened worker is unable to recognise his enemies in men who represent themselves, and sometimes sincerely so, as his friends. The worst enemies, because in the period of disunity and vacillation, when our movement is just beginning to take shape, nothing is easier than to employ demagogic methods to mislead the masses, who can realise their error only later by bitter experience. That is why the slogan of the day for the Russian Social-Democrat must be—resolute struggle against *Svoboda* and *Rabocheye Dyelo*, both of which have sunk to the level of demagogy. We shall deal with this further in greater detail.[2]

"A dozen wise men can be more easily wiped out than a hundred fools." This wonderful truth (for which the hundred fools will always applaud you) appears obvious only because in the very midst of the argument you have skipped from one question to another. You began by talking and continued to talk of the unearthing of a "committee," of the unearthing of an "organisation," and now you skip to the question of unearthing the movement's "roots" in their "depths." The fact is, of course, that our movement cannot be unearthed, for the very reason that it has countless thousands of roots deep down among the masses; but that is not the point at issue. As far as "deep roots" are concerned, we cannot be "unearthed" even now, despite all our amateurism, and yet we all complain, and cannot but complain, that the *"organisations"* are being unearthed and as a result it is impossible to maintain continuity in the movement. But since you raise the question of *organisations* being unearthed and persist in your opinion, I assert that it is far more difficult to unearth a dozen wise men than a hundred fools. This position I will defend, no matter how much you instigate the masses against me for my "anti-democratic" views, etc. As I have stated repeatedly, by "wise men," in connection with organisation, I mean *professional revolutionaries*, irrespective of whether they have developed from among students or working men. I assert: (1) that no revolutionary movement can endure without a stable organisation of leaders maintaining continuity; (2) that the broader the popular mass drawn spontaneously into the struggle, which forms the basis of the movement and participates in it, the more urgent the need for such an organisation, and the more solid this organisation must be (for it is much easier for all sorts of

---

2. For the moment let us observe merely that our remarks on "pushing on from outside" and *Svoboda*'s other disquisitions on organisation apply *in their entirety to all* the Economists, including the adherents of *Rabocheye Dyelo*; for some of them have actively preached and defended such views on organisation, while others among them have drifted into them. [*Lenin*]

demagogues to side-track the more backward sections of the masses); (3) that such an organisation must consist chiefly of people professionally engaged in revolutionary activity; (4) that in an autocratic state, the more we *confine* the membership of such an organisation to people who are professionally engaged in revolutionary activity and who have been professionally trained in the art of combating the political police, the more difficult will it be to unearth the organisation; and (5) the *greater* will be the number of people from the working class and from the other social classes who will be able to join the movement and perform active work in it.

I invite our Economists, terrorists, and "Economists-terrorists"[3] to confute these propositions. At the moment, I shall deal only with the last two points. The question as to whether it is easier to wipe out "a dozen wise men" or "a hundred fools" reduces itself to the question, above considered, whether it is possible to have a mass *organisation* when the maintenance of strict secrecy is essential. We can never give a mass organisation that degree of secrecy without which there can be no question of persistent and continuous struggle against the government. To concentrate all secret functions in the hands of as small a number of professional revolutionaries as possible does not mean that the latter will "do the thinking for all" and that the rank and file will not take an active part in the *movement*. On the contrary, the membership will promote increasing numbers of the professional revolutionaries from its ranks; for it will know that it is not enough for a few students and for a few working men waging the economic struggle to gather in order to form a "committee," but that it takes years to train oneself to be a professional revolutionary; and the rank and file will "think," not only of amateurish methods, but of such training. Centralisation of the secret functions of the *organisation* by no means implies centralisation of all the functions of the *movement*. Active participation of the widest masses in the illegal press will not diminish because a "dozen" professional revolutionaries centralise the secret functions connected with this work; on the contrary, it will *increase* tenfold. In this way, and in this way alone, shall we ensure that

3. This term is perhaps more applicable to *Svoboda* than the former, for in an article entitled "The Regeneration of Revolutionism" the publication defends terrorism, while in the article at present under review it defends Economism. One might say of *Svoboda* that "it would if it could, but it can't." Its wishes and intentions are of the very best—but the result is utter confusion; this is chiefly due to the fact that, while *Svoboda* advocates continuity of organisation, it refuses to recognise continuity of revolutionary thought and Social-Democratic theory. It wants to revive the professional revolutionary ("The Regeneration of Revolutionism"), and to that end proposes, first, excitative terrorism, and, secondly, "an organisation of average workers" (*Svoboda*, No. 1, p. 66, *et seq.*), as less likely to be "pushed on from outside." In other words, it proposes to pull the house down to use the timber for heating it. [*Lenin*]

reading the illegal press, writing for it, and to some extent even distributing it, will *almost cease to be secret work*, for the police will soon come to realise the folly and impossibility of judicial and administrative red-tape procedure over every copy of a publication that is being distributed in the thousands. This holds not only for the press, but for every function of the movement, even for demonstrations. The active and widespread participation of the masses will not suffer; on the contrary, it will benefit by the fact that a "dozen" experienced revolutionaries, trained professionally no less than the police, will centralise all the secret aspects of the work—the drawing up of leaflets, the working out of approximate plans; and the appointing of bodies of leaders for each urban district, for each factory district, and for each educational institution, etc. (I know that exception will be taken to my "undemocratic" views, but I shall reply below fully to this anything but intelligent objection.) Centralisation of the most secret functions in an organisation of revolutionaries will not diminish, but rather increase the extent and enhance the quality of the activity of a large number of other organisations that are intended for a broad public and are therefore as loose and as non-secret as possible, such as workers' trade unions; workers' self-education circles and circles for reading illegal literature; and socialist, as well as democratic, circles among *all* other sections of the population; etc., etc. We must have such circles, trade unions, and organisations everywhere in *as large a number as possible* and with the widest variety of functions; but it would be absurd and harmful to *confound* them with the organisation of *revolutionaries*, to efface the border-line between them, to make still more hazy the all too faint recognition of the fact that in order to "serve" the mass movement we must have people who will devote themselves exclusively to Social-Democratic activities, and that such people must *train* themselves patiently and steadfastly to be professional revolutionaries.

Yes, this recognition is incredibly dim. Our worst sin with regard to organisation consists in the fact that *by our primitiveness we have lowered the prestige of revolutionaries in Russia*. A person who is flabby and shaky on questions of theory, who has a narrow outlook, who pleads the spontaneity of the masses as an excuse for his own sluggishness, who resembles a trade union secretary more than a spokesman of the people, who is unable to conceive of a broad and bold plan that would command the respect even of opponents, and who is inexperienced and clumsy in his own professional art—the art of combating the political police—such a man is not a revolutionary, but a wretched amateur!

Let no active worker take offence at these frank remarks, for as far as insufficient training is concerned, I apply them first and foremost to myself. I used to work in a study circle[4] that set itself very broad, all-embracing tasks; and all of us, members of that circle, suffered painfully and acutely from the realisation that we were acting as amateurs at a moment in history when we might have been able to say, varying a well-known statement: "Give us an organisation of revolutionaries, and we will overturn Russia!" The more I recall the burning sense of shame I then experienced, the bitterer become my feelings towards those pseudo-Social-Democrats whose preachings "bring disgrace on the calling of a revolutionary," who fail to understand that our task is not to champion the degrading of the revolutionary to the level of an amateur, but *to raise* the amateurs to the level of revolutionaries.

D. The Scope of Organisational Work

We have heard B—v tell us about "the lack of revolutionary forces fit for action which is felt not only in St. Petersburg, but throughout Russia." Hardly anyone will dispute this fact. But the question is, how is it to be explained? B—v writes:

> We shall not go into an explanation of the historical causes of this phenomenon; we shall merely state that a society, demoralised by prolonged political reaction and split by past and present economic changes, promotes from its own ranks *an extremely small number of persons fit for revolutionary work*; that the working class does produce revolutionary workers who to some extent reinforce the ranks of the illegal organisations, but that the number of such revolutionaries is inadequate to meet the requirements of the times. This is all the more so because the worker who spends eleven and a half hours a day in the factory is in such a position that he can, in the main, perform only the functions of an agitator; but propaganda and organisation, the delivery and reproduction of illegal literature, the issuance of leaflets, etc., are duties which must necessarily fall mainly upon the shoulders of an extremely small force of intellectuals. [*Rabocheye Dyelo*, No. 6, pp. 38–39.]

On many points we disagree with B—v, particularly with those we have emphasised, which most saliently reveal that, although weary of our amateurism (as is every thinking practical worker), B—v cannot find the way out of this intolerable situation, because he is weighted down by Economism. The fact is that society produces very *many* persons fit for "the cause," but we are unable to

4. Lenin refers to the circle of Social-Democrats (known as the "old members") in St. Petersburg; the circle formed the basis of the League of Struggle for the Emancipation of the Working Class, set up in 1895.

make use of them all. The critical, transitional state of our movement in this respect may be formulated as follows: *There are no
people—yet there is a mass of people.* There is a mass of people,
because the working class and increasingly varied social strata, year
after year, produce from their ranks an increasing number of discontented people who desire to protest, who are ready to render all
the assistance they can in the struggle against absolutism, the intol-
erableness of which, though not yet recognised by all, is more and
more acutely sensed by increasing masses of the people. At the
same time, we have no people, because we have no leaders, no
political leaders, no talented organisers capable of arranging extensive and at the same time uniform and harmonious work that
would employ all forces, even the most inconsiderable. "The
growth and development of the revolutionary organisations" lag,
not only behind the growth of the working-class movement, which
even B—v admits, but behind that of the general democratic movement among all strata of the people. (In passing, probably B—v
would now regard this as supplementing his conclusion.) The scope
of revolutionary work is too narrow, as compared with the breadth
of the spontaneous basis of the movement. It is too hemmed in by
the wretched theory of "economic struggle against the employers
and the government." Yet, at the present time, not only Social-
Democratic political agitators, but Social-Democratic organisers
must "go among all classes of the population."[5] There is hardly a
single practical worker who will doubt that the Social-Democrats
could distribute the thousand and one minute functions of their
organisational work among individual representatives of the most
varied classes. Lack of specialisation is one of the most serious
defects of our technique, about which B—v justly and bitterly
complains. The smaller each separate "operation" in our common
cause the more people we can find capable of carrying out such
operations (people who, in the majority of cases, are completely
incapable of becoming professional revolutionaries); the more difficult will it be for the police to "net" all these "detail workers," and
the more difficult will it be for them to frame up, out of an arrest
for some petty affair, a "case" that would justify the government's
expenditure on "security." As for the number of people ready to
help us, we referred in the preceding chapter to the gigantic change
that has taken place in this respect in the last five years or so. On
the other hand, in order to unite all these tiny fractions into one
whole, in order not to break up the movement while breaking up its

5. Thus, an undoubted revival of the democratic spirit has recently been observed among persons in military service, partly as a consequence of the more
frequent street battles with "enemies" like workers and students. As soon as
our available forces permit, we must without fail devote the most serious attention to propaganda and agitation among soldiers and officers, and to the creation
of "military organisations" affiliated to our Party. [*Lenin*]

functions, and in order to imbue the people who carry out the minute functions with the conviction that their work is necessary and important, without which conviction they will never do the work,[6] it is necessary to have a strong organisation of tried revolutionaries. The more secret such an organisation is, the stronger and more widespread will be the confidence in the Party. As we know, in time of war, it is not only of the utmost importance to imbue one's own army with confidence in its strength, but it is important also to convince the enemy and all *neutral* elements of this strength; friendly neutrality may sometimes decide the issue. If such an organisation existed, one built up on a firm theoretical foundation and possessing a Social-Democratic organ, we should have no reason to fear that the movement might be diverted from its path by the numerous "outside" elements that are attracted to it. (On the contrary, it is precisely at the present time, with amateurism prevalent, that we see many Social-Democrats leaning towards the *Credo* and only imagining that they are Social-Democrats.) In a word, specialisation necessarily presupposes centralisation, and in turn imperatively calls for it.

But B—v himself, who has so excellently described the necessity for specialisation, underestimates its importance, in our opinion, in the second part of the argument we have quoted. The number of working-class revolutionaries is inadequate, he says. This is perfectly true, and once again we stress that the "valuable communication of a close observer" fully confirms our view of the causes of the present crisis in Social-Democracy, and, consequently, of the means required to overcome it. Not only are revolutionaries in general lagging behind the spontaneous awakening of the masses, but even worker-revolutionaries are lagging behind the spontaneous awakening of the working-class masses. This *fact* confirms with clear evidence, from the "practical" point of view, too, not only the absurdity but even the *politically reactionary nature* of the "pedagogics" to which we are so often treated in the discussion of our

6. I recall that once a comrade told me of a factory inspector who wanted to help the Social-Democrats, and actually did, but complained bitterly that he did not know whether his "information" reached the proper revolutionary centre, how much his help was really required, and what possibilities there were for utilising his small and petty services. Every practical worker can, of course, cite many similar instances in which our primitiveness deprived us of allies. These services, each "small" in itself, but invaluable when taken in the mass, could and would be rendered to us by office employees and officials, not only in factories, but in the postal service, on the railways, in the Customs, among the nobility, among the clergy, and in *every* other walk of life, including even the police and the Court! Had we a real party, a real militant organisation of revolutionaries, we would not make undue demands on every one of these "aides," we would not hasten always and invariably to bring them right into the very heart of our "illegality," but, on the contrary, we would husband them most carefully and would even train people especially for such functions, bearing in mind that many students could be of much greater service to the Party as "aides" holding some official post than as "short-term" revolutionaries. But, I repeat, only an organisation that is firmly established and has no lack of active forces would have the right to apply such tactics. [*Lenin*]

duties to the workers. This fact proves that our very first and most pressing duty is to help to train working-class revolutionaries who will be on the same level *in regard to party activity* as the revolutionaries from amongst the intellectuals (we emphasise the words "in regard to party activity," for, although necessary, it is neither so easy nor so pressingly necessary to bring the workers up to the level of intellectuals in other respects). Attention, therefore, must be devoted *principally* to *raising* the workers to the level of revolutionaries; it is not at all our task *to descend* to the level of the "working masses" as the Economists wish to do, or to the level of the "average worker," as *Svoboda* desires to do (and by this ascends to the second grade of Economist "pedagogics"). I am far from denying the necessity for popular literature for the workers, and especially popular (of course, not vulgar) literature for the especially backward workers. But what annoys me is this constant confusion of pedagogics with questions of politics and organisation. You, gentlemen, who are so much concerned about the "average worker," as a matter of fact, rather insult the workers by your desire to *talk down* to them when discussing working-class politics and working-class organisation. Talk about serious things in a serious manner; leave pedagogics to the pedagogues, and not to politicians and organisers! Are there not advanced people, "average people," and "masses" among the intelligentsia too? Does not everyone recognise that popular literature is also required for the intelligentsia, and is not such literature written? Imagine someone, in an article on organising college or high-school students, repeating over and over again, as if he had made a new discovery, that first of all we must have an organisation of "average students." The author of such an article would be ridiculed, and rightly so. Give us your ideas on organisation, if you have any, he would be told, and we ourselves will decide who is "average," who above average, and who below. But if you have no organisational ideas *of your own*, then all your exertions in behalf of the "masses" and "average people" will be simply boring. You must realise that these questions of "politics" and "organisation" are so serious in themselves that they cannot be dealt with in any other but a serious way. We can and must *educate* workers (and university and Gymnasium students) so that we *may be able to discuss* these questions with them. But once you do bring up these questions, you must give real replies to them; do not fall back on the "average," or on the "masses"; do not try to dispose of the matter with facetious remarks and mere phrases.[7]

To be fully prepared for his task, the worker-revolutionary must

7. *Svoboda*, No. 1, p. 66, in the article "Organisation": "The heavy tread of the army of workers will reinforce all the demands that will be advanced in behalf of Russian Labour"—Labour with a capital L, of course. And the author ex-

likewise become a professional revolutionary. Hence B——v is wrong in saying that since the worker spends eleven and a half hours in the factory, the brunt of all other revolutionary functions (apart from agitation) *"must necessarily* fall mainly upon the shoulders of an extremely small force of intellectuals." But this condition does not obtain out of sheer "necessity." It obtains because we are backward, because we do not recognise our duty to assist every capable worker to become a *professional* agitator, organiser, propagandist, literature distributor, etc., etc. In this respect, we waste our strength in a positively shameful manner; we lack the ability to husband that which should be tended and reared with special care. Look at the Germans: their forces are a hundredfold greater than ours. But they understand perfectly well that really capable agitators, etc., are not often promoted from the ranks of the "average." For this reason they immediately try to place every capable working man in conditions that will enable him to develop and apply his abilities to the fullest: he is made a professional agitator; he is encouraged to widen the field of his activity, to spread it from one factory to the whole of the industry, from a single locality to the whole country. He acquires experience and dexterity in his profession; he broadens his outlook and increases his knowledge; he observes at close quarters the prominent political leaders from other localities and of other parties; he strives to rise to their level and combine in himself the knowledge of the working-class environment and the freshness of socialist convictions with professional skill, without which the proletariat *cannot* wage a stubborn struggle against its excellently trained enemies. In this way alone do the working masses produce men of the stamp of Bebel and Auer. But what is to a great extent automatic in a politically free country must in Russia be done deliberately and systematically by our organisations. A worker-agitator who is at all gifted and "promising" *must not be left* to work eleven hours a day in a factory. We must arrange that he be maintained by the Party; that he may go underground in good time; that he change the place of his activity, if he is to enlarge his experience, widen his outlook, and be able to hold out for at least a few years in the struggle against the gendarmes. As the spontaneous rise of their movement becomes broader and deeper, the working-class masses promote from their ranks not only an increasing number of talented agitators, but also talented organisers, propagandists, and "practical workers" in the best sense of the term (of whom there are so few among our intellectuals who,

claims: "I am not in the least hostile towards the intelligentsia, but [*but*—the word that Shchedrin translated as meaning: The ears never grow higher than the forehead!]—but I always get frightfully annoyed when a man comes to me uttering beautiful and charming words and demands that they be accepted for their [his?] beauty and other virtues" (p. 62). Yes, I "always get frightfully annoyed," too. [*Lenin*] for the most part, in the Russian manner, are somewhat careless and sluggish in their habits). When we have forces of specially trained worker-revolutionaries who have gone through extensive preparation (and, of course, revolutionaries "of all arms of the service"), no political police in the world will then be able to contend with them, for these forces, boundlessly devoted to the revolution, will enjoy the boundless confidence of the widest masses of the workers. We are directly to *blame* for doing too little to "stimulate" the workers to take this path, common to them and to the "intellectuals," of professional revolutionary training, and for all too often dragging them back by our silly speeches about what is "accessible" to the masses of the workers, to the "average workers," etc.

In this, as in other respects, the narrow scope of our organisational work is without a doubt due directly to the fact (although the overwhelming majority of the "Economists" and the novices in practical work do not perceive it) that we restrict our theories and our political tasks to a narrow field. Subservience to spontaneity seems to inspire a fear of taking even one step away from what is "accessible" to the masses, a fear of rising too high above mere attendance on the immediate and direct requirements of the masses. Have no fear, gentlemen! Remember that we stand so low on the plane of organisation that the very idea that we *could* rise *too* high is absurd!

E. *"Conspiratorial" Organisation and "Democratism"*

Yet there are many people among us who are so sensitive to the "voice of life" that they fear it more than anything in the world and charge the adherents of the views here expounded with following a Narodnaya Volya line, with failing to understand "democratism," etc. These accusations, which, of course, have been echoed by *Rabocheye Dyelo,* need to be dealt with.

The writer of these lines knows very well that the St. Petersburg Economists levelled the charge of Narodnaya Volya tendencies also against *Rabochaya Gazeta* (which is quite understandable when one compares it with *Rabochaya Mysl*). We were not in the least surprised, therefore, when, soon after the appearance of *Iskra,* a comrade informed us that the Social-Democrats in the town of X describe *Iskra* as a Narodnaya Volya organ. We, of course, were flattered by this accusation; for what decent Social-Democrat has not been accused by the Economists of being a Narodnaya Volya sympathiser?

These accusations are the result of a twofold misunderstanding.

First, the history of the revolutionary movement is so little known among us that the name "Narodnaya Volya" is used to denote any idea of a militant centralised organisation which declares determined war upon tsarism. But the magnificent organisation that the revolutionaries had in the seventies, and that should serve us as a model, was not established by the Narodnaya Volya, but by the Zemlya i Volya,[8] which split up into the Chorny Peredel and the Narodnaya Volya. Consequently, to regard a militant revolutionary organisation as something specifically Narodnaya Volya in character is absurd both historically and logically; for *no* revolutionary trend, if it seriously thinks of struggle, can dispense with such an organization. The mistake the Narodnaya Volya committed was not in striving to enlist *all* the discontented in the organisation and to direct this organisation to resolute struggle against the autocracy; on the contrary, that was its great historical merit. The mistake was in relying on a theory which in substance was not a revolutionary theory at all, and the Narodnaya Volya members either did not know how, or were unable, to link their movement inseparably with the class struggle in the developing capitalist society. Only a gross failure to understand Marxism (or an "understanding" of it in the spirit of "Struve-ism") could prompt the opinion that the rise of a mass, spontaneous working-class movement *relieves* us of the duty of creating as good an organisation of revolutionaries as the Zemlya i Volya had, or, indeed, an incomparably better one. On the contrary, this movement *imposes* the duty upon us; for the spontaneous struggle of the proletariat will not become its genuine "class struggle" until this struggle is led by a strong organisation of revolutionaries.

Secondly, many people, including apparently B. Krichevsky (*Rabocheye Dyelo*, No. 10, p. 18), misunderstand the polemics that Social-Democrats have always waged against the "conspiratorial" view of the political struggle. We have always protested, and will, of course, continue to protest against *confining* the political struggle to conspiracy.[9] But this does not, of course, mean that we deny the need for a strong revolutionary organisation. Thus, in the pamphlet mentioned in the preceding footnote, after the polemics against reducing the political struggle to a conspiracy, a description is given (as a Social-Democratic ideal) of an organisation so strong as to be able to "resort to . . . rebellion" and to every "other form of attack," in order to "deliver a smashing blow against absolut-

8. Zemlya i Volya (Land and Freedom) was a secret organisation of revolutionary Narodniks formed in the autumn of 1876 in St. Petersburg. Its members included Mark and Olga Natanson, G. V. Plekhanov, O. V. Aptekman, S. M. Krav- chinsky, S. L. Perovskaya, and A. D. and A. F. Mikhailov.
9. Cf. *The Tasks of the Russian Social-Democrats*, p. 21, polemics against P. L. Lavrov. [*Lenin*]

ism."[1] In *form* such a strong revolutionary organisation in an autocratic country may also be described as a "conspiratorial" organisation, because the French word *conspiration* is the equivalent of the Russian word *zagovor* ("conspiracy"), and such an organisation must have the utmost secrecy. Secrecy is such a necessary condition for this kind of organisation that all the other conditions (number and selection of members, functions, etc.) must be made to conform to it. It would be extremely naïve indeed, therefore, to fear the charge that we Social-Democrats desire to create a conspiratorial organisation. Such a charge should be as flattering to every opponent of Economism as the charge of following a Narodnaya Volya line.

The objection may be raised that such a powerful and strictly secret organisation, which concentrates in its hands all the threads of secret activities, an organisation which of necessity is centralised, may too easily rush into a premature attack, may thoughtlessly intensify the movement before the growth of political discontent, the intensity of the ferment and anger of the working class, etc., have made such an attack possible and necessary. Our reply to this is: Speaking abstractly, it cannot be denied, of course, that a militant organisation *may* thoughtlessly engage in battle, which *may* end in a defeat entirely avoidable under other conditions. But we cannot confine ourselves to abstract reasoning on such a question, because every battle bears within itself the abstract possibility of defeat, and there is no way of *reducing* this possibility except by organised preparation for battle. If, however, we proceed from the concrete conditions at present obtaining in Russia, we must come to the positive conclusion that a strong revolutionary organisation is absolutely necessary precisely for the purpose of giving stability to the movement and of *safeguarding* it against the possibility of making thoughtless attacks. Precisely at the present time, when no such organisation yet exists, and when the revolutionary movement is rapidly and spontaneously growing, we *already observe* two opposite extremes (which, as is to be expected, "meet"). These are: the utterly unsound Economism and the preaching of moderation, and the equally unsound "excitative terror," which strives "artifi-

---

1. *The Tasks of the Russian Social-Democrats*, p. 23. Apropos, we shall give another illustration of the fact that *Rabocheye Dyelo* either does not understand what it is talking about or changes its views "with the wind." In No. 1 of *Rabocheye Dyelo*, we find the following passage in italics: *"The substance set forth in the pamphlet accords entirely with the editorial programme of 'Rabocheye Dyelo' "* (p. 142). Really? Does the view that the overthrow of the autoc- racy must not be set as the first task of the mass movement accord with the views expressed in *The Tasks of the Russian Social-Democrats*? Do the theory of "the economic struggle against the employers and the government" and the stages theory accord with the views expressed in that pamphlet? We leave it to the reader to judge whether a periodical that understands the meaning of "accordance in opinion" in this peculiar manner can have firm principles. [*Lenin*]

cially to call forth symptoms of the end of the movement, which is developing and strengthening itself, when this movement is as yet nearer to the start than to the end" (V. Zasulich, in *Zarya*, No. 2–3, p. 353). And the instance of *Rabocheye Dyelo* shows that *there exist* Social-Democrats who give way to both these extremes. This is not surprising, for, apart from other reasons, the "economic struggle against the employers and the government" can *never* satisfy revolutionaries, and opposite extremes will therefore always appear here and there. Only a centralised, militant organisation that consistently carries out a Social-Democratic policy, that satisfies, so to speak, all revolutionary instincts and strivings, can safeguard the movement against making thoughtless attacks and prepare attacks that hold out the promise of success.

A further objection may be raised, that the views on organisation here expounded contradict the "democratic principle." Now, while the earlier accusation was specifically Russian in origin, this one is *specifically foreign* in character. And only an organisation abroad (the Union of Russian Social-Democrats Abroad) was capable of giving its Editorial Board instructions like the following:

> *Organisational Principle.* In order to secure the successful development and unification of Social-Democracy, the broad democratic principle of party organisation must be emphasised, developed, and fought for; this is particularly necessary in view of the anti-democratic tendencies that have revealed themselves in the ranks of our party. [*Two Conferences*, p. 18.]

We shall see in the next chapter how *Rabocheye Dyelo* combats *Iskra*'s "anti-democratic tendencies." For the present, we shall examine more closely the "principle" that the Economists advance. Everyone will probably agree that "the broad democratic principle" presupposes the two following conditions: first, full publicity, and secondly, election to all offices. It would be absurd to speak of democracy without publicity, moreover, without a publicity that is not limited to the membership of the organisation. We call the German Socialist Party a democratic organisation because all its activities are carried out publicly; even its party congresses are held in public. But no one would call an organisation democratic that is hidden from every one but its members by a veil of secrecy. What is the use, then, of advancing "the *broad* democratic principle" when the fundamental condition for this principle *cannot be fulfilled* by a secret organisation? "The broad principle" proves itself simply to be a resounding but hollow phrase. Moreover, it reveals a total lack of understanding of the urgent tasks of the moment in regard to organisation. Everyone knows how great the lack of secrecy is among the "broad" masses of our revolutionaries. We have heard the bitter complaints of B—v on this score and his absolutely just demand for a "strict selection of members" (*Rabocheye Dyelo*, No. 6, p. 42). Yet, persons who boast a keen "sense of realities" *urge*, in a situation like this, not the strictest secrecy and the strictest (consequently, more restricted) selection of members, but "the *broad* democratic principle"! This is what you call being wide of the mark.

Nor is the situation any better with regard to the second attribute of democracy, the principle of election. In politically free countries, this condition is taken for granted. "They are members of the Party who accept the principles of the Party programme and render the Party all possible support," reads Clause 1 of the Rules of the German Social-Democratic Party. Since the entire political arena is as open to the public view as is a theatre stage to the audience, this acceptance or non-acceptance, support or opposition, is known to all from the press and from public meetings. Everyone knows that a certain political figure began in such and such a way, passed through such and such an evolution, behaved in a trying moment in such and such a manner, and possesses such and such qualities; consequently, *all* party members, knowing all the facts, can elect or refuse to elect this person to a particular party office. The general control (in the literal sense of the term) exercised over every act of a party man in the political field brings into existence an automatically operating mechanism which produces what in biology is called the "survival of the fittest." "Natural selection" by full publicity, election, and general control provides the assurance that, in the last analysis, every political figure will be "in his proper place," do the work for which he is best fitted by his powers and abilities, feel the effects of his mistakes on himself, and prove before all the world his ability to recognize mistakes and to avoid them.

Try to fit this picture into the frame of our autocracy! Is it conceivable in Russia for all "who accept the principles of the Party programme and render the Party all possible support" to control every action of the revolutionary working in secret? Is it possible for all to elect one of these revolutionaries to any particular office, when, in the very interests of the work, the revolutionary *must* conceal his identity from nine out of ten of these "all"? Reflect somewhat over the real meaning of the high-sounding phrases to which *Rabocheye Dyelo* gives utterance, and you will realise that "broad democracy" in Party organisation, amidst the gloom of the autocracy and the domination of gendarmerie, is nothing more than a *useless and harmful toy*. It is a useless toy because, in point of fact, no revolutionary organisation has ever practised, or could practise, *broad* democracy, however much it may have desired to do so. It is a harmful toy because any attempt to practise "the broad democratic principle" will simply facilitate the work of the police in carrying out large-scale raids, will perpetuate the prevailing primitiveness, and will divert the thoughts of the practical workers from the serious and pressing task of training themselves to become professional revolutionaries to that of drawing up detailed "paper" rules for election systems. Only abroad, where very often people with no opportunity for conducting really active work gather, could this "playing at democracy" develop here and there, especially in small groups.

To show the unseemliness of *Rabocheye Dyelo*'s favourite trick of advancing the plausible "principle" of democracy in revolutionary affairs, we shall again summon a witness. This witness, Y. Serebryakov, editor of the London magazine *Nakanune*, has a soft spot for *Rabocheye Dyelo* and is filled with a great hatred for Plekhanov and the "Plekhanovites." In its articles on the split in the Union of Russian Social-Democrats Abroad, *Nakanune* definitely sided with *Rabocheye Dyelo* and poured a stream of petty abuse upon Plekhanov. All the more valuable, therefore, is this witness in the question at issue. In *Nakanune* for July (No. 7) 1899, in an article entitled "Concerning the Manifesto of the Self-Emancipation of the Workers Group," Serebryakov argued that it was "indecent" to talk about such things as "self-deception, leadership, and the so-called Areopagus in a serious revolutionary movement" and, *inter alia*, wrote:

> Myshkin, Rogachov, Zhelyabov, Mikhailov, Perovskaya, Figner, and others never regarded themselves as leaders, and no one ever elected or appointed them as such, although in actuality, they were leaders, because, in the propaganda period, as well as in the period of the struggle against the government, they took the brunt of the work upon themselves, they went into the most dangerous places, and their activities were the most fruitful. They became leaders, not because they wished it, but because the comrades surrounding them had confidence in their wisdom, in their energy, in their loyalty. To be afraid of some kind of Areopagus [if it is not feared, why write about it?] that would arbitrarily govern the movement is far too naïve. Who would pay heed to it?

We ask the reader, in what way does the "Areopagus" differ from "anti-democratic tendencies"? And is it not evident that *Rabocheye Dyelo*'s "plausible" organisational principle is equally naïve and indecent; naïve, because no one would pay heed to the "Areopagus," or people with "anti-democratic tendencies," if "the comrades surrounding them had" no "confidence in their wisdom, energy, and loyalty"; indecent, because it is a demagogic sally calculated to play on the conceit of some, on the ignorance of others regarding the actual state of our movement, and on the lack of training and the ignorance of the history of the revolutionary movement on the part of still others. The only serious organisational principle for the active workers of our movement should be the strictest secrecy, the strictest selection of members, and the training of professional revolutionaries. Given these qualities, something even more than "democratism" would be guaranteed to us, namely, complete, comradely, mutual confidence among revolutionaries. This is absolutely essential for us, because there can be no question of replacing it by general democratic control in Russia. It would be a great mistake to believe that the impossibility of establishing real "democratic" control renders the members of the revolutionary organisation beyond control altogether. They have not the time to think about toy forms of democratism (democratism within a close and compact body of comrades in which complete, mutual confidence prevails), but they have a lively sense of their *responsibility*, knowing as they do from experience that an organisation of real revolutionaries will stop at nothing to rid itself of an unworthy member. Moreover, there is a fairly well-developed public opinion in Russian (and international) revolutionary circles which has a long history behind it, and which sternly and ruthlessly punishes every departure from the duties of comradeship (and "democratism," real and not toy democratism, certainly forms a component part of the conception of comradeship). Take all this into consideration and you will realise that this talk and these resolutions about "anti-democratic tendencies" have the musty odour of the playing at generals which is indulged in abroad.

It must be observed also that the other source of this talk, viz., naïveté, is likewise fostered by the confusion of ideas concerning the meaning of democracy. In Mr. and Mrs. Webb's book on the English trade unions there is an interesting chapter entitled "Primitive Democracy." In it the authors relate how the English workers, in the first period of existence of their unions, considered it an indispensable sign of democracy for all the members to do all the work of managing the unions; not only were all questions decided by the vote of all the members, but all official duties were fulfilled by all the members in turn. A long period of historical experience was required for workers to realise the absurdity of such a conception of democracy and to make them understand the necessity for representative institutions, on the one hand, and for full-time officials, on the other. Only after a number of cases of financial bankruptcy of trade union treasuries had occurred did the workers realise that the rates of contributions and benefits cannot be decided merely by a democratic vote, but that this requires also the advice of insurance experts. Let us take also Kautsky's book on parliamentarism and legislation by the people. There we find that the conclusions drawn by the Marxist theoretician coincide with the lessons learned from many years of practical experience by the workers who organised "spontaneously." Kautsky strongly protests against Rittinghausen's primitive conception of democracy; he ridicules those who in the name of democracy demand that "popular newspapers shall be edited directly by the people"; he shows the need for *professional* journalists, parliamentarians, etc., for the Social-Democratic leadership of the proletarian class struggle; he attacks the "socialism of anarchists and *littérateurs,*" who in their "striving for effect" extol direct legislation by the whole people, completely failing to understand that this idea can be applied only relatively in modern society.

Those who have performed practical work in our movement know how widespread the "primitive" conception of democracy is among the masses of the students and workers. It is not surprising that this conception penetrates also into rules of organisations and into literature. The Economists of the Bernsteinian persuasion included in their rules the following: "§ 10. All affairs affecting the interests of the whole of the union organisation shall be decided by a majority vote of all its members." The Economists of the terrorist persuasion repeat after them: "The decisions of the committee shall become effective only after they have been referred to all the circles" (*Svoboda*, No. 1, p. 67). Observe that this proposal for a widely applied referendum is advanced *in addition* to the demand that *the whole of* the organisation be built on an elective basis! We would not, of course, on this account condemn practical workers who have had too few opportunities for studying the theory and practice of real democratic organisations. But when *Rabocheye Dyelo*, which lays claim to leadership, confines itself, under such conditions, to a resolution on broad democratic principles, can this be described as anything but a mere "striving for effect"?

F. Local and All-Russia Work

The objections raised against the plan of organisation here outlined on the grounds that it is undemocratic and conspiratorial are totally unsound. Nevertheless, there remains a question which is frequently put and which deserves detailed examination. This is the question of the relations between local work and all-Russia work. Fears are expressed that the formation of a centralised organisation may shift the centre of gravity from the former to the latter, damage the movement through weakening our contacts with the working masses and the continuity of local agitation generally. To these fears we reply that our movement in the past few years has suffered precisely from the fact that local workers have been too absorbed in local work; that therefore it is absolutely necessary to shift the centre of gravity somewhat to national work; and that, far from weakening, this would strengthen our ties and the continuity of our local agitation. Let us take the question of central and local newspapers. I would ask the reader not to forget that we cite the publication of newspapers only as *an example* illustrating an immeasurably broader and more varied revolutionary activity in general.

In the first period of the mass movement (1896–98), an attempt was made by local revolutionary workers to publish an all-Russia paper—*Rabochaya Gazeta*. In the next period (1898–1900), the movement made an enormous stride forward, but the attention of the leaders was wholly absorbed by local publications. If we compute the total number of the local papers that were published, we shall find that on the average one issue per month was published.[2] Does this not clearly illustrate our amateurism? Does this not clearly show that our revolutionary organisation lags behind the spontaneous growth of the movement? If *the same number* of issues had been published, not by scattered local groups, but by a single organisation, we would not only have saved an enormous amount of effort, but we would have secured immeasurably greater stability and continuity in our work. This simple point is frequently lost sight of by those practical workers who work *actively* and almost exclusively on local publications (unfortunately this is true even now in the overwhelming majority of cases), as well as by the publicists who display an astonishing quixotism on this question. The practical workers usually rest content with the argument that "it is difficult"[3] for local workers to engage in the organisation of an all-Russia newspaper, and that local newspapers are better than no newspapers at all. This argument is, of course, perfectly just, and we, no less than any practical worker, appreciate the enormous importance and usefulness of local newspapers *in general*. But this is not the point. The point is, can we not overcome the fragmentation and primitiveness that are so glaringly expressed in the thirty issues of local newspapers that have been published throughout Russia in the course of two and a half years? Do not restrict yourselves to the indisputable, but too general, statement about the usefulness of local newspapers generally, have the courage frankly to admit their negative aspects revealed by the experience of two

2. See *Report to the Paris Congress*, p. 14. "From that time (1897) to the spring of 1900, thirty issues of various papers were published in various places. . . . On an average, over one issue per month was published." [*Lenin*]

3. This difficulty is more apparent than real. In fact, *there is not* a single local study circle that lacks the opportunity of taking up some function or other in connection with all-Russia work. "Don't say, I can't; say, I won't." [*Lenin*]

and a half years. This experience has shown that under the conditions in which we work, these local newspapers prove, in the majority of cases, to be unstable in their principles, devoid of political significance, extremely costly in regard to expenditure of revolutionary forces, and totally unsatisfactory from a technical point of view (I have in mind, of course, not the technique of printing, but the frequency and regularity of publication). These defects are not accidental; they are the inevitable outcome of the fragmentation which, on the one hand, explains the predominance of local newspapers in the period under review, and, on the other, is *fostered by* this predominance. It is positively *beyond the strength* of a separate local organisation to raise its newspaper to the level of a political organ maintaining stability of principles; it is *beyond its strength* to collect and utilise sufficient material to shed light on the whole of our political life. The argument usually advanced to support the need for numerous local newspapers in free countries that the cost of printing by local workers is low and that the people can be kept more fully and quickly informed—this *argument,* as experience has shown, speaks *against* local newspapers in Russia. They turn out to be excessively costly in regard to the expenditure of revolutionary forces, and appear *very* rarely, for the simple reason that the publication of an *illegal* newspaper, however small its size, requires an extensive secret apparatus, such as is possible with large-scale factory production; for this apparatus cannot be created in a small, handicraft workshop. Very frequently, the primitiveness of the secret apparatus (every practical worker can cite numerous cases) enables the police to take advantage of the publication and distribution of one or two issues to make *mass* arrests, which result in such a clean sweep that it becomes necessary to start all over again. A well-organised secret apparatus requires professionally well-trained revolutionaries and a division of labour applied with the greatest consistency, but both these requirements are beyond the strength of a separate local organisation, however strong it may be at any given moment. Not only the general interests of our movement as a whole (training of the workers in consistent socialist and political principles) but also specifically local interests are *better served by non-local newspapers.* This may seem paradoxical at first sight, but it has been proved to the hilt by the two and a half years of experience referred to. Everyone will agree that had all the local forces that were engaged in the publication of the thirty issues of newspapers worked on a single newspaper, sixty, if not a hundred, issues could easily have been published, with a fuller expression, in consequence, of all the specifically local features of the movement. True, it is no easy matter to attain such a degree of organisation, but we must realise the need for it. Every local study circle must think about it and *work actively* to achieve it, without waiting for an impetus from outside, without being tempted by the popularity and closer proximity of a local newspaper which, as our revolutionary experience has shown, proves to a large extent to be illusory.

* * *

The predominance of the local papers over a central press may be a sign of either poverty or luxury. Of poverty, when the movement has not yet developed the forces for large-scale production, continues to flounder in amateurism, and is all but swamped with "the petty details of factory life." Of luxury, when the movement *has fully mastered* the task of comprehensive exposure and comprehensive agitation, and it becomes necessary to publish numerous local newspapers in addition to the central organ. Let each decide for himself what the predominance of local newspapers implies in present-day Russia. I shall limit myself to a precise formulation of my own conclusion, to leave no grounds for misunderstanding. Hitherto, the majority of our local organisations have thought almost exclusively in terms of local newspapers, and have devoted almost all their activities to this work. This is abnormal; the very opposite should have been the case. The majority of the local organisations should think principally of the publication of an all-Russia newspaper and devote their activities chiefly to it. Until this is done, we shall *not* be able to establish a *single* newspaper capable, to any degree, of serving the movement with *comprehensive* press agitation. When this is done, however, normal relations between the necessary central newspaper and the necessary local newspapers will be established automatically.

It would seem at first glance that the conclusion on the necessity for shifting the centre of gravity from local to all-Russia work does not apply to the sphere of the specifically economic struggle. In this struggle, the immediate enemies of the workers are the individual employers or groups of employers, who are not bound by any organisation having even the remotest resemblance to the purely military, strictly centralised organisation of the Russian Government—our immediate enemy in the political struggle—which is led in all its minutest details by a single will.

But that is not the case. As we have repeatedly pointed out, the economic struggle is a trade struggle, and for that reason it requires that the workers be organized according to trades, not only according to place of employment. Organisation by trades becomes all the more urgently necessary, the more rapidly our employers organise in all sorts of companies and syndicates. Our fragmentation and our amateurism are an outright hindrance to this work of organisation which requires the existence of a single, all-Russia body of revolutionaries capable of giving leadership to the all-Russia trade unions. We have described above the type of organisation that is needed for this purpose; we shall now add but a few words on the question of our press in this connection.

Hardly anyone will doubt the necessity for every Social-Democratic newspaper to have *a special department* devoted to the trade union (economic) struggle. But the growth of the trade union movement compels us to think about the creation of a trade union press. It seems to us, however, that with rare exceptions, there can be no question of trade union newspapers in Russia at the present time; they would be a luxury, and many a time we lack even our daily bread. The form of trade union press that would suit the conditions of our illegal work and is already required at the present time is *trade union pamphlets*. In these pamphlets, legal[4] and illegal material should be gathered and grouped systematically, on the working conditions in a given trade, on the differences in this respect in the various parts of Russia; on the main demands advanced by the workers in the given trade; on the inadequacies of legislation affecting that trade; on outstanding instances of economic struggle by the workers in the trade; on the beginnings, the present state, and the requirements of their trade union organisation, etc. Such pamphlets would, in the first place, relieve our Social-Democratic press of a mass of trade details that are of interest only to workers in the given trade. Secondly, they would record the results of our experience in the trade union struggle, they would preserve the gathered material, which now literally gets lost in a mass of leaflets and fragmentary correspondence; and they would summarise this material. Thirdly, they could serve as guides for

4. Legal material is particularly important in this connection, and we are particularly behind in our ability to gather and utilise it systematically. It would not be an exaggeration to say that one could somehow compile a trade union pamphlet on the basis solely of legal material, but it could not be done on the basis of illegal material alone. In gathering illegal material from workers on questions like those dealt with in the publications of *Rabochaya Mysl*, we waste a great deal of the efforts of revolutionaries (whose place in this work could very easily be taken by legal workers), and yet we never obtain good material. The reason is that a worker who very often knows only a single department of a large factory and almost always the economic results, but not the general conditions and standards of his work, cannot acquire the knowledge which is possessed by the office staff of a factory, by inspectors, doctors, etc., and which is scattered in petty newspaper reports and in special industrial, medical, Zemstvo, and other publications.

I vividly recall my "first experiment," which I would never like to repeat. I spent many weeks "examining" a worker, who would often visit me, regarding every aspect of the conditions prevailing in the enormous factory at which he was employed. True, after great effort, I managed to obtain material for a description (of the one single factory!), but at the end of the interview the worker would wipe the sweat from his brow, and say to me smilingly: "I find it easier to work overtime than to answer your questions."

The more energetically we carry on our revolutionary struggle, the more the government will be compelled to legalise part of the "trade union" work, thereby relieving us of part of our burden. [*Lenin*]

agitators, because working conditions change relatively slowly and the main demands of the workers in a given trade are extremely stable (cf., for example, the demands advanced by the weavers in the Moscow district in 1885 and in the St. Petersburg district in 1896). A compilation of such demands and needs might serve for years as an excellent handbook for agitators on economic questions in backward localities or among the backward strata of the workers. Examples of successful strikes in a given region, information on higher living standards, on improved working conditions, in one locality, would encourage the workers in other localities to take up the fight again and again. Fourthly, having made a start in generalizing the trade union struggle and in this way strengthening the link between the Russian trade union movement and socialism, the Social-Democrats would at the time see to it that our trade union work occupied neither too small nor too large a place in our Social-Democratic work as a whole. A local organisation that is cut off from organisations in other towns finds it very difficult, sometimes almost impossible, to maintain a correct sense of proportion (the example of *Rabochaya Mysl* shows what a monstrous exaggeration can be made in the direction of trade-unionism). But an all-Russia organisation of revolutionaries that stands undeviatingly on the basis of Marxism, that leads the entire political struggle and possesses a staff of professional agitators, will never find it difficult to determine the proper proportion.

V. The "Plan" for an All-Russia Political Newspaper

"The most serious blunder *Iskra* committed in this connection," writes B. Krichevsky (*Rabocheye Dyelo*, No. 10, p. 30), charging us with a tendency to "convert theory into a lifeless doctrine by isolating it from practice," "was its 'plan' for a general party organisation" (viz., the article entitled "Where to Begin"). Martynov echoes this idea in declaring that "*Iskra*'s tendency to belittle the significance of the forward march of the drab everyday struggle in comparison with the propaganda of brilliant and completed ideas . . . was crowned with the plan for the organisation of a party which it sets forth in the article entitled 'Where to Begin' in issue No. 4" (*ibid.*, p. 61). Finally, L. Nadezhdin has of late joined in the chorus of indignation against this "plan" (the quotation marks were meant to express sarcasm). In his pamphlet, which we have just received, entitled *The Eve of the Revolution* (published by the "Revolutionary-Socialist Group" *Svoboda*, whose acquaintance we have made), he declares (p. 126): "To speak now of an organisation held together by an all-Russia newspaper means propagating armchair ideas and armchair work" and represents a manifestation of "bookishness," etc.

That our terrorist turns out to be in agreement with the champions of the "forward march of the drab everyday struggle" is not surprising, since we have traced the roots of this intimacy between them in the chapters on politics and organisation. But we must draw attention here to the fact that Nadezhdin is the only one who has conscientiously tried to grasp the train of thought in an article he disliked and has made an attempt to reply to the point, whereas *Rabocheye Dyelo* has said nothing that is material to the subject, but has tried merely to confuse the question by a series of unseemly, demagogic sallies. Unpleasant though the task may be, we must first spend some time in cleansing this Augean stable.

A. *Who Was Offended by the Article "Where to Begin"*

Let us present a small selection of the expletives and exclamations that *Rabocheye Dyelo* hurled at us. "It is not a newspaper that can create a party organisation, but vice versa. . . ." "A newspaper, standing *above* the party, *outside of its control*, and independent of it, thanks to its having its own staff of agents. . . ." "By what miracle has *Iskra* forgotten about the actually existing Social-Democratic organisations of the party to which it belongs? . . ." "Those who possess firm principles and a corresponding plan are the supreme regulators of the real struggle of the party and dictate to it their plan. . . ." "The plan drives our active and virile organisations into the kingdom of shadows and desires to call into being a fantastic network of agents. . . ." "Were *Iskra's* plan carried into effect, every trace of the Russian Social-Democratic Labour Party, which is taking shape, would be obliterated. . . ." "A propagandist organ becomes an uncontrolled autocratic law-maker for the entire practical revolutionary struggle. . . ." "How should our Party react to the suggestion that it be *completely* subordinated to an autonomous editorial board?," etc., etc.

As the reader can see from the contents and the tone of these above quotations, *Rabocheye Dyelo has taken offence.* Offence, not for its own sake, but for the sake of the organisations and committees of our Party which it alleges *Iskra* desires to drive into the kingdom of shadows and whose very traces it would obliterate. How terrible! But a curious thing should be noted. The article "Where to Begin" appeared in May 1901. The articles in *Rabocheye Dyelo* appeared in September 1901. Now we are in mid-January 1902. During these five months (prior to and after September), *not a single* committee and *not a single* organisation of the Party protested formally against this monster that seeks to drive them into the kingdom of shadows; and yet scores and hundreds of communications from all parts of Russia have appeared during this period in *Iskra*, as well as in numerous local and non-local publications. How could it happen that those who would be driven into the realm of shadows are not aware of it and have not taken offence, though a third party has?

The explanation is that the committees and other organisations are engaged in real work and are not playing at "democracy." The committees read the article "Where to Begin," saw that it represented an attempt "to elaborate a definite plan for an organisation, *so that its formation may be undertaken from all aspects*"; and since they knew and saw very well that *not one* of these "sides" would dream of "setting about to build it" until it was convinced of its necessity, and of the correctness of the architectural plan, it has naturally never occurred to them to take offence at the boldness of the people who said in *Iskra*: "In view of the pressing importance of the question, we, on our part, take the liberty of submitting to the comrades a skeleton plan to be developed in greater detail in a pamphlet now in preparation for the print." With a conscientious approach to the work, was it possible to view things otherwise than that if the comrades *accepted* the plan submitted to them, they would carry it out, not because they are "subordinate," but because they would be convinced of its necessity for our common cause, and that if they *did not accept it*, then the "skeleton" (a pretentious word, is it not?) would remain merely a skeleton? Is it not demagogy to fight against the skeleton of a plan, not only by "picking it to pieces" and advising comrades to reject it, but by *inciting* people inexperienced in revolutionary matters against its authors *merely on the grounds* that they *dare* to "legislate" and come out as the "supreme regulators," i.e., because they dare *to propose* an outline of a plan? Can our Party develop and make progress if an attempt *to raise* local functionaries to broader views, tasks, plans, etc., is objected to, not only with the claim that these views are erroneous, but on the grounds that the very "desire" *to* "*raise*" us gives "offence"? Nadezhdin, too, "picked" our plan "to pieces," but he did not sink to such demagogy as cannot be explained solely by naïveté or by primitiveness of political views. From the outset, he emphatically rejected the charge that we intended to establish an "inspectorship over the Party." That is why Nadezhdin's criticism of the plan can and should be answered on its merits, while *Rabocheye Dyelo* deserves only to be treated with contempt.

* * *

B. Can a Newspaper Be a Collective Organiser?

The quintessence of the article "Where to Begin" consists in the fact that it discusses *precisely* this question and gives an affirmative reply to it. As far as we know, the only attempt to examine this question on its merits and to prove that it must be answered in the negative was made by L. Nadezhdin, whose argument we reproduce in full:

> It pleased us greatly to see *Iskra* (No. 4) present the question of the need for an all-Russia newspaper; but we cannot agree that this presentation bears relevance to the title "Where to Begin." Undoubtedly this is an extremely important matter, but neither a newspaper, nor a series of popular leaflets, nor a mountain of manifestoes, can serve as the basis for a militant organisation in revolutionary times. We must set to work to build strong political organisations in the localities. We lack such organisations; we have been carrying on our work mainly among enlightened workers, while the masses have been engaged almost exclusively in the economic struggle. *If strong political organisations are not trained locally, what significance will even an excellently organised all-Russia newspaper have?* It will be a burning bush, burning without being consumed, but firing no one! *Iskra* thinks that around it and in the activities in its behalf people will gather and organise. *But they will find it far easier to gather and organise around activities that are more concrete.* This something more concrete must and should be the extensive organisation of local newspapers, the immediate preparation of the workers' forces for demonstrations, the constant activity of local organisations among the unemployed (indefatigable distribution of pamphlets and leaflets, convening of meetings, appeals to actions of protest against the government, etc.). We must begin live political work in the localities, and when the time comes to unite on this real basis, it will not be an artificial, paper unity; not by means of newspapers can such a unification of local work into an all-Russia cause be achieved! [*The Eve of the Revolution*, p. 54.]

We have emphasised the passages in this eloquent tirade that most clearly show the author's incorrect judgement of our plan, as well as the incorrectness of his point of view in general, which is here contraposed to that of *Iskra*. Unless we train strong political organisations in the localities, even an excellently organised all-Russia newspaper will be of no avail. This is incontrovertible. But the whole point is that *there is no other way of training* strong political organisations except through the medium of an all-Russia newspaper. The author missed the most important statement *Iskra* made *before it proceeded* to set forth its "plan": that it was necessary "to call for the formation of a revolutionary organisation, capable of uniting all forces and guiding the movement in actual practice and *not in name alone*, that is, *an organisation ready at any time to support every protest and every outbreak* and use it to build up and consolidate the fighting forces suitable for the decisive struggle." But now after the February and March events, everyone will agree with this in principle, continues *Iskra.* Yet what we need is not a solution of the question in principle, but its *practical solution*; we must immediately advance a definite constructive plan through which all may immediately set to work to build *from every side.* Now we are again being dragged away from the practical solution towards something which in principle is correct, indisputable, and great, but which is entirely inadequate and incomprehensible to the broad masses of workers, namely, "to rear strong political organisations"! This is not the point at issue, most worthy author. The point is *how* to go about the rearing and how to accomplish it.

It is not true to say that "we have been carrying on our work mainly among enlightened workers, while the masses have been engaged almost exclusively in the economic struggle." Presented in such a form, the thesis reduces itself to *Svoboda's* usual but fundamentally false contraposition of the enlightened workers to the "masses." In recent years, even the enlightened workers have been "engaged almost exclusively in the economic struggle." That is the first point. On the other hand, the masses will never learn to conduct the political struggle until we help *to train* leaders for this struggle, both from among the enlightened workers and from among the intellectuals. Such leaders can acquire training *solely* by systematically evaluating *all* the everyday aspects of our political life, *all attempts* at protest and struggle on the part of the various classes and on various grounds. Therefore, to talk of "rearing political organisations" and at the same time *to contrast* the "paper work" of a political newspaper to "live political work in the localities" is plainly ridiculous. *Iskra* has adapted its "plan" for a newspaper to the "plan" for creating a "militant preparedness" to support the unemployed movement, peasant revolts, discontent among the Zemstvo people, "popular indignation against some tsarist bashibazouk on the rampage," etc. Anyone who is at all acquainted with the movement knows full well that the vast majority of local organisations have *never even dreamed* of these things; that many of the prospects of "live political work" here indicated *have never* been realised by a single organisation; that the attempt, for example, to call attention to the growth of discontent and protest among the Zemstvo intelligentsia rouses feelings of consternation and perplexity in Nadezhdin ("Good Lord, is this newspaper intended for

Zemstvo people?"—*The Eve*, p. 129), among the Economists (letter to *Iskra*, No. 12), and among many practical workers. Under these circumstances, it is possible to "begin" *only* by inducing people *to think* about all these things, to summarise and generalise all the diverse signs of ferment and active struggle. In our time, when Social-Democratic tasks are being degraded, *the only way* "live political work" can be *begun* is with live political agitation, which is impossible unless we have an all-Russia newspaper, frequently issued and regularly distributed.

Those who regard the *Iskra* "plan" as a manifestation of "bookishness" have totally failed to understand its substance and take for the goal that which is suggested as the most suitable means for the present time. These people have not taken the trouble to study the two comparisons that were drawn to present a clear illustration of the plan. *Iskra* wrote: The publication of an all-Russia political newspaper must be *the main line* by which we may unswervingly develop, deepen, and expand the organisation (viz., the revolutionary organisation that is ever ready to support every protest and every outbreak). Pray tell me, when bricklayers lay bricks in various parts of an enormous, unprecedentedly large structure, is it "paper" work to use a line to help them find the correct place for the bricklaying; to indicate to them the ultimate goal of the common work; to enable them to use, not only every brick, but even every piece of brick which, cemented to the bricks laid before and after it, forms a finished, continuous line? And are we not now passing through precisely such a period in our Party life when we have bricks and bricklayers, but lack the guide line for all to see and follow? Let them shout that in stretching out the line, we want to command. Had we desired to command, gentlemen, we would have written on the title page, not "*Iskra*, No. 1," but "*Rabochaya Gazeta*, No. 3," as we were invited to do by certain comrades, and *as we would have had a perfect right to do* after the events described above. But we did not do that. We wished to have our hands free to wage an irreconcilable struggle against all pseudo-Social-Democrats; we wanted our line, if properly laid, to be respected because it was correct, and not because it had been laid by an official organ.

"The question of uniting local activity in central bodies runs in a vicious circle," Nadezhdin lectures us; "unification requires homogeneity of the elements, and the homogeneity can be created only by something that unites; but the unifying element may be the product of strong local organisations which at the present time are by no means distinguished for their homogeneity." This truth is as revered and as irrefutable as that we must train strong political organisations. And it is equally barren. *Every* question "runs in a vicious circle" because political life as a whole is an endless chain consisting of an infinite number of links. The whole art of politics lies in finding and taking as firm a grip as we can of the link that is least likely to be struck from our hands, the one that is most important at the given moment, the one that most of all guarantees its possessor the possession of the whole chain.[5] If we had a crew of experienced bricklayers who had learned to work so well together that they could lay their bricks exactly as required without a guide line (which, speaking abstractly, is by no means impossible), then perhaps we might take hold of some other link. But it is unfortunate that as yet we have no experienced bricklayers trained for teamwork, that bricks are often laid where they are not needed at all, that they are not laid according to the general line, but are so scattered that the enemy can shatter the structure as if it were made of sand and not of bricks.

Another comparison: "A newspaper is not only a collective propagandist and a collective agitator, it is also a collective organiser. In this respect *it may be compared to the scaffolding* erected round a building under construction; it marks the contours of the structure and facilitates communication between the builders, permitting them to distribute the work and to view the common results achieved by their organised labour."[6] Does this sound anything like the attempt of an armchair author to exaggerate his role? The scaffolding is not required at all for the dwelling; it is made of cheaper material, is put up only temporarily, and is scrapped for firewood as soon as the shell of the structure is completed. As for the building of revolutionary organisations, experience shows that sometimes they may be built without scaffolding, as the seventies showed. But at the present time we cannot even imagine the possibility of erecting the building we require without scaffolding.

Nadezhdin disagrees with this, saying: "*Iskra* thinks that around it and in the activities in its behalf people will gather and organise. *But they will find it far easier* to gather and organise around *activities that are more concrete*!" Indeed, "far easier around activities that are more concrete." A Russian proverbs holds: "Don't spit into a well, you may want to drink from it." But there are people who do not object to drinking from a well that has been spat into. What despicable things our magnificent, legal "Critics of Marxism" and

5. Comrade Krichevsky and Comrade Martynov! I call your attention to this outrageous manifestation of "autocracy," "uncontrolled authority," "supreme regulating," etc. Just think of it: a desire *to possess* the whole chain!! Send in a complaint at once. Here you have a ready-made topic for two leading articles for No. 12 of *Rabocheye Dyelo*! [*Lenin*]
6. Martynov, in quoting the first sentence of this passage in *Rabocheye Dyelo* (No. 10, p. 62), omitted the second, as if desiring to emphasise either his unwillingness to discuss the essentials of the question or his inability to understand them. [*Lenin*]

illegal admirers of *Rabochaya Mysl* have said in the name of this something more concrete! How restricted our movement is by our own narrowness, lack of initiative, and hesitation, which are justified with the traditional argument about finding it "far easier to gather around something more concrete"! And Nadezhdin—who regards himself as possessing a particularly keen sense of the "realities of life," who so severely condemns "armchair" authors and (with pretensions to wit) accuses *Iskra* of a weakness for seeing Economism everywhere, and who sees himself standing far above the division between the orthodox and the Critics—fails to see that with his arguments he contributes to the narrowness that arouses his indignation and that he is drinking from the most spat-in well! The sincerest indignation against narrowness, the most passionate desire to raise its worshippers from their knees, will not suffice if the indignant one is swept along without sail or rudder and, as "spontaneously" as the revolutionaries of the seventies, clutches at such things as "excitative terror," "agrarian terror," "sounding the tocsin," etc. * * *

All without exception now talk of the importance of unity, of the necessity for "gathering and organising"; but in the majority of cases what is lacking is a definite idea of where to begin and how to bring about this unity. Probably all will agree that if we "unite," say, the district circles in a given town, it will be necessary to have for this purpose *common institutions*, i.e., not merely the common title of "League," but genuinely *common* work, exchange of material, experience, and forces, distribution of functions, not only by districts, but through specialisation on a town-wide scale. All will agree that a big secret apparatus will not pay its way (to use a commercial expression) "with the resources" (in both money and manpower, of course) of a single district, and that this narrow field will not provide sufficient scope for a specialist to develop his talents. But the same thing applies to the co-ordination of activities of a number of towns, since even a specific locality *will be* and, in the history of our Social-Democratic movement, has proved to be, far too narrow a field; we have demonstrated this above in detail with regard to political agitation and organisational work. What we require foremost and imperatively is to broaden the field, establish *real* contacts between the towns on the basis of *regular, common* work; for fragmentation weighs down on the people and they are "stuck in a hole" (to use the expression employed by a correspondent to *Iskra*), not knowing what is happening in the world, from whom to learn, or how to acquire experience and satisfy their desire to engage in broad activities. I continue to insist that we can *start* establishing *real* contacts only with the aid of a common newspaper, as the only regular, all-Russia enterprise, one which will summarise the results of the most diverse forms of activity and thereby *stimulate* people to march forward untiringly along *all* the innumerable paths leading to revolution, in the same way as all roads lead to Rome. If we do not want unity in name only, we must arrange for all local study circles *immediately to assign*, say, a fourth of their forces to *active* work for the *common* cause, and the newspaper will immediately convey to them[7] the general design, scope, and character of the cause; it will give them a precise indication of the most keenly felt shortcomings in the all-Russia activity, where agitation is lacking and contacts are weak, and it will point out which little wheels in the vast general mechanism a given study circle might repair or replace with better ones. A study circle that has not yet begun to work, but which is only just seeking activity, could then start, not like a craftsman in an isolated little workshop unaware of the earlier development in "industry" or of the general level of production methods prevailing in industry, but as a participant in an extensive enterprise that *reflects* the whole general revolutionary attack on the autocracy. The more perfect the finish of each little wheel and the larger the number of detail workers engaged in the common cause, the closer will our network become and the less will be the disorder in the ranks consequent on inevitable police raids.

The mere function of distributing a newspaper would help to establish *actual* contacts (if it is a newspaper worthy of the name, i.e., if it is issued regularly, not once a month like a magazine, but at least four times a month). At the present time, communication between towns on revolutionary business is an extreme rarity, and, at all events, is the exception rather than the rule. If we had a newspaper, however, such communication would become the rule and would secure, not only the distribution of the newspaper, of course, but (what is more important) an exchange of experience, of material, of forces, and of resources. Organisational work would immediately acquire much greater scope, and the success of one locality would serve as a standing encouragement to further perfection; it would arouse the desire to utilise the experience gained by comrades working in other parts of the country. Local work would become far richer and more varied than it is at present. Political and economic exposures gathered from all over Russia would provide mental food for workers of all trades and *all stages of development*; they would provide material and occasion for talks and read-

---

7. *A reservation*: that is, if a given study circle sympathises with the policy of the newspaper and considers it useful to become a collaborator, meaning by that, not only for literary collaboration, but for revolutionary collaboration generally.

Note for Rabocheye Dyelo: Among revolutionaries who attach value to the cause and not to playing at democracy, who do not separate "sympathy" from the most active and lively participation, this reservation is taken for granted. [*Lenin*]

ings on the most diverse subjects, which would, in addition, be suggested by hints in the legal press, by talk among the people, and by "shamefaced" government statements. Every outbreak, every demonstration, would be weighed and discussed in its every aspect in all parts of Russia and would thus stimulate a desire to keep up with, and even surpass, the others (we socialists do not by any means flatly reject all emulation or all "competition"!) and consciously prepare that which at first, as it were, sprang up spontaneously, a desire to take advantage of the favourable conditions in a given district or at a given moment for modifying the plan of attack, etc. At the same time, this revival of local work would obviate that desperate, "convulsive" exertion of *all* efforts and risking of *all* forces which every single demonstration or the publication of every single issue of a local newspaper now frequently entails. On the one hand, the police would find it much more difficult to get at the "roots," if they did not know in what district to dig down for them. On the other hand, regular common work would train our people to adjust the force of a *given* attack to the strength of the given contingent of the common army (at the present time hardly anyone ever thinks of doing that, because in nine cases out of ten these attacks occur spontaneously); such regular common work would facilitate the "transportation" from one place to another, not only of literature, but also of revolutionary forces.

In a great many cases these forces are now being bled white on restricted local work, but under the circumstances we are discussing it would be possible to transfer a capable agitator or organiser from one end of the country to the other, and the occasion for doing this would constantly arise. Beginning with short journeys on Party business at the Party's expense, the comrades would become accustomed to being maintained by the Party, to becoming professional revolutionaries, and to training themselves as real political leaders.

And if indeed we succeeded in reaching the point when all, or at least a considerable majority, of the local committees, local groups, and study circles took up active work for the common cause, we could, in the not distant future, establish a weekly newspaper for regular distribution in tens of thousands of copies throughout Russia. This newspaper would become part of an enormous pair of smith's bellows that would fan every spark of the class struggle and of popular indignation into a general conflagration. Around what is in itself still a very innocuous and very small, but regular and *common*, effort, in the full sense of the word, a regular army of tried fighters would systematically gather and receive their training. On the ladders and scaffolding of this general organisational structure there would soon develop and come to the fore Social-Democratic Zhelyabovs from among our revolutionaries and Russian Bebels from among our workers, who would take their place at the head of the mobilised army and rouse the whole people to settle accounts with the shame and the curse of Russia.

That is what we should dream of!

"We should dream!" I wrote these words and became alarmed. I imagined myself sitting at a "unity conference" and opposite me were the *Rabocheye Dyelo* editors and contributors. Comrade Martynov rises and, turning to me, says sternly: "Permit me to ask you, has an autonomous editorial board the right to dream without first soliciting the opinion of the Party committees?" He is followed by Comrade Krichevsky, who (philosophically deepening Comrade Martynov, who long ago rendered Comrade Plekhanov more profound) continues even more sternly: "I go further. I ask, has a Marxist any right at all to dream, knowing that according to Marx mankind always sets itself the tasks it can solve and that tactics is a process of the growth of Party tasks which grow together with the Party?"

The very thought of these stern questions sends a cold shiver down my spine and makes me wish for nothing but a place to hide in. I shall try to hide behind the back of Pisarev.

"There are rifts and rifts," wrote Pisarev of the rift between dreams and reality.

My dream may run ahead of the natural march of events or may fly off at a tangent in a direction in which no natural march of events will ever proceed. In the first case my dream will not cause any harm; it may even support and augment the energy of the working men. . . . There is nothing in such dreams that would distort or paralyse labour-power. On the contrary, if man were completely deprived of the ability to dream in this way, if he could not from time to time run ahead and mentally conceive, in an entire and completed picture, the product to which his hands are only just beginning to lend shape, then I cannot at all imagine what stimulus there would be to induce man to undertake and complete extensive and strenuous work in the sphere of art, science, and practical endeavour. . . . The rift between dreams and reality causes no harm if only the person dreaming believes seriously in his dream, if he attentively observes life, compares his observations with his castles in the air, and if, generally speaking, he works conscientiously for the achievement of his fantasies. If there is some connection between dreams and life then all is well.[8]

8. Lenin cites D. I. Pisarev's article "Blunders of Immature Thinking." Pisarev (1840–68) was a prominent Russian publicist and literary critic of the 1860s.

Of this kind of dreaming there is unfortunately too little in our movement. And the people most responsible for this are those who boast of their sober views, their "closeness" to the "concrete," the representatives of legal criticism and of illegal "tail-ism."

C. What Type of Organisation Do We Require?

From what has been said the reader will see that our "tactics-as-plan" consists in rejecting an immediate *call* for assault; in demanding "to lay effective siege to the enemy fortress"; or, in other words, in demanding that all efforts be directed towards gathering, organising, and *mobilising* a permanent army. When we ridiculed *Rabocheye Dyelo* for its leap from Economism to shouting for an assault (for which it clamoured in *April* 1901, in *"Listok" Rabochego Dyela*, No. 6) it of course came down on us with accusations of being "doctrinaire," of failing to understand our revolutionary duty, of calling for caution, etc. Of course, we were not in the least surprised to hear these accusations from those who totally lack principles and who evade all arguments by references to a profound "tactics-as-process," any more than we were surprised by the fact that these charges were repeated by Nadezhdin, who in general has a supreme contempt for durable programmes and the fundamentals of tactics.

It is said that history does not repeat itself. But Nadezhdin exerts every effort to cause it to repeat itself and he zealously imitates Tkachov in strongly condemning "revolutionary culturism," in shouting about "sounding the tocsin" and about a special "eve-of-the-revolution point of view," etc. Apparently, he has forgotten the well-known maxim that while an original historical event represents a tragedy, its replica is merely a farce.[9] The attempt to seize power, which was prepared by the preaching of Tkachov and carried out by means of the "terrifying" terror that did really terrify, had grandeur, but the "excitative" terror of a Tkachov the Little is simply ludicrous, particularly so when it is supplemented with the idea of an organisation of average people.

"If *Iskra* would only emerge from its sphere of bookishness," wrote Nadezhdin, "it would realise that these [instances like the worker's letter to *Iskra*, No. 7, etc.] are symptoms of the fact that soon, very soon, the 'assault' will begin, and to speak now [sic!] of an organisation linked with an all-Russia newspaper means to propagate armchair ideas and armchair activity." What an unimaginable

---

9. Lenin refers to the following passage from Marx's *The Eighteenth Brumaire of Louis Bonaparte*: "Hegel remarks somewhere that all facts and personages of great importance in world history occur, as it were, twice. He forgot to add: the first time as tragedy, the second as farce."

muddle—on the one hand, excitative terror and an "organisation of average people," along with the opinion that it is far "easier" to gather around something "more concrete," like a local newspaper, and, on the other, the view that to talk "now" about an all-Russia organisation means to propagate armchair thoughts, or, bluntly put, "now" it is already too late! But what of the "extensive organisation of local newspapers"—is it not too late for that, my dear L. Nadezhdin? And compare with this *Iskra*'s point of view and tactical line: excitative terror is nonsense; to talk of an organisation of average people and of the *extensive* publication of local newspapers means to fling the door wide open to Economism. We must speak of a single all-Russia organisation of revolutionaries, and it will never be too late to talk of that until the real, not a paper, assault begins.

"Yes, as far as organisation is concerned the situation is anything but brilliant," continues Nadezhdin.

> Yes, *Iskra* is entirely right in saying that the mass of our fighting forces consists of volunteers and insurgents. . . . You do well to give such a sober picture of the state of our forces. But why, at the same time, do you forget that *the masses are not ours at all*, and consequently, *will not ask us* when to begin military operations; they will simply go and "rebel." . . . When the crowd itself breaks out with its elemental destructive force it *may* overwhelm and sweep aside the "regular troops" among whom we prepared all the time to introduce extremely systematic organisation, but never *managed* to do so. [Our italics.]

Astounding logic! *For the very reason* that the "masses are not ours" it is stupid and unseemly to shout about an immediate "assault," for assault means attack by regular troops and not a spontaneous mass upsurge. For the very reason that the masses *may* overwhelm and sweep aside the regular troops we must without fail "manage to keep up" with the spontaneous upsurge by our work of "introducing extremely systematic organisation" in the regular troops, for the more we "manage" to introduce such organisation the more probably will the regular troops not be overwhelmed by the masses, but will take their place at their head. Nadezhdin is confused because he imagines that troops in the course of systematic organisation are engaged in something that isolates them from the masses, when in actuality they are engaged exclusively in all-sided and all-embracing political agitation, i.e., precisely in work that *brings closer and merges into a single whole* the elemental destructive force of the masses and the conscious destructive force of the organisation of revolutionaries. You, gentlemen, wish to lay the blame where it does not belong. For it is precisely the *Svoboda* group that, by including terror *in its programme*, calls for an organisation of terrorists, and such an organisation would indeed prevent our troops from establishing closer contacts with the masses, which, unfortunately, are still not ours, and which, unfortunately, do not yet ask us, or rarely ask us, when and how to launch their military operations.

"We shall miss the revolution itself," continues Nadezhdin in his attempt to scare *Iskra*, "in the same way as we missed the recent events, which came upon us like a bolt from the blue." This sentence, taken in connection with what has been quoted above, clearly demonstrates the absurdity of the "eve-of-the-revolution point of view" invented by *Svoboda*.[1] Plainly put, this special "point of view" boils down to this: that it is too late "now" to discuss and prepare. If that is the case, most worthy opponent of "bookishness," what was the use of writing a pamphlet of 132 pages on "questions of theory[2] and tactics"? Don't you think it would have been more becoming for the "eve-of-the-revolution point of view" to have issued 132,000 leaflets containing the summary call, "Bang them—knock 'em down!"?

Those who make nation-wide political agitation the cornerstone of their programme, *their tactics, and their organisational work*, as *Iskra* does, stand the least risk of missing the revolution. The people who are now engaged throughout Russia in weaving the network of connections that spread from the all-Russia newspaper not only did not miss the spring events, but, on the contrary, gave us an opportunity to foretell them. Nor did they miss the demonstrations that were described in *Iskra*, Nos. 13 and 14;[3] on the contrary, they took part in them, clearly realising that it was their duty to come to the aid of the spontaneously rising masses and, at the same time, through the medium of the newspaper, help all the comrades in Russia to inform themselves of the demonstrations and to make use of their gathered experience. And if they live they will not miss the revolution, which, first and foremost, will demand of us experience in agitation, ability to support (in a Social-Democratic man-

1. *The Eve of the Revolution*, p. 62. [*Lenin*]
2. In his *Review of Questions of Theory*, Nadezhdin, by the way, made almost no contribution whatever to the discussion of questions of theory, apart, perhaps, from the following passage, a most peculiar one from the "eve-of-the-revolution point of view": "Bernsteinism, on the whole, is losing its acuteness for us at the present moment, as is the question whether Mr. Struve has already earned a lacing, or, on the contrary, whether Mr. Struve will refute Mr. Adamovich and will refuse to resign—it really makes no difference, because the hour of revolution has struck" (p. 110). One can hardly imagine a more glaring illustration of Nadezhdin's infinite disregard for theory. We have proclaimed "the eve of the revolution," *therefore* "it really makes no difference" whether or not the orthodox will succeed in finally driving the Critics from their positions! Our wiseacre fails to see that it is precisely during the revolution that we shall stand in need of the results of our theoretical battles with the Critics in order to be able resolutely to combat their *practical* positions! [*Lenin*]
3. A wave of student demonstrations spread over Russia in November and December 1901, supported by workers.

ner) every protest, as well as direct the spontaneous movement, while safeguarding it from the mistakes of friends and the traps of enemies.

We have thus come to the last reason that compels us so strongly to insist on the plan of an organisation centred round an all-Russia newspaper, through the common work for the common newspaper. Only such organisation will ensure the *flexibility* required of a militant Social-Democratic organisation, viz., the ability to adapt itself immediately to the most diverse and rapidly changing conditions of struggle, the ability, "on the one hand, to avoid an open battle against an overwhelming enemy, when the enemy has concentrated all his forces at one spot and yet, on the other, to take advantage of his unwieldiness and to attack him when and where he least expects it."[4] It would be a grievous error indeed to build the Party organisation in anticipation only of outbreaks and street fighting, or only upon the "forward march of the drab everyday struggle." We must *always* conduct our everyday work and always be prepared for every situation, because very frequently it is almost impossible to foresee when a period of outbreak will give way to a period of calm. In the instances, however, when it is possible to do so, we could not turn this foresight to account for the purpose of reconstructing our organisation; for in an autocratic country these changes take place with astonishing rapidity, being sometimes connected with a single night raid by the tsarist janizaries. And the revolution itself must not by any means be regarded as a single act (as the Nadezhdins apparently imagine), but as a series of more or less powerful outbreaks rapidly alternating with periods of more or less complete calm. For that reason, the principal content of the activity of our Party organisation, the focus of this activity, should be work that is both possible and essential in the period of a most powerful outbreak as well as in the period of complete calm, namely, work of political agitation, connected throughout Russia, illuminating all aspects of life, and conducted among the broadest possible strata of the masses. But this work is *unthinkable* in present-day Russia without an all-Russia newspaper, issued very frequently. The organisation, which will form round this newspaper,

4. *Iskra*, No. 4, "Where to Begin." "Revolutionary culturists, who do not accept the eve-of-the-revolution point of view, are not in the least perturbed by the prospect of working for a long period of time," writes Nadezhdin (p. 62). This brings us to observe: Unless we are able to devise political tactics and an organisational plan for *work over a long period*, while ensuring, in *the very process of this work*, our Party's readiness to be at its post and fulfil its duty in every contingency whenever the march of events is accelerated—unless we succeed in doing this, we shall prove to be but miserable political adventurers. Only Nadezhdin, who began but yesterday to describe himself as a Social-Democrat, can forget that the aim of Social-Democracy is to transform radically the conditions of life of the whole of mankind and that for this reason it is not permissible for a Social-Democrat to be "perturbed" by the question of the duration of the work. [*Lenin*]

the organisation of its *collaborators* (in the broad sense of the word, i.e., all those working for it), will be ready *for everything*, from upholding the honour, the prestige, and the continuity of the Party in periods of acute revolutionary "depression" to preparing for, appointing the time for, and carrying out the *nation-wide armed uprising*.

Indeed, picture to yourselves a very ordinary occurrence in Russia—the total round-up of our comrades in one or several localities. In the absence of a *single*, common, regular activity that combines all the local organisations, such round-ups frequently result in the interruption of the work for many months. If, however, all the local organisations had one common activity, then, even in the event of a very serious round-up, two or three energetic persons could in the course of a few weeks establish contact between the common centre and new youth circles, which, as we know, spring up very quickly even now. And when the common activity, hampered by the arrests, is apparent to all, new circles will be able to come into being and make connections with the centre even more rapidly.

On the other hand, picture to yourselves a popular uprising. Probably everyone will now agree that we must think of this and prepare for it. But *how*? Surely the Central Committee cannot appoint agents to all localities for the purpose of preparing the uprising. Even if we had a Central Committee, it could achieve absolutely nothing by such appointments under present-day Russian conditions. But a network of agents[5] that would form in the course of establishing and distributing the common newspaper would not have to "sit about and wait" for the call for an uprising, but could carry on the regular activity that would guarantee the highest probability of success in the event of an uprising. Such activity would strengthen our contacts with the broadest strata of the working masses and with all social strata that are discontented with the autocracy, which is of such importance for an uprising. Precisely such activity would serve to cultivate the ability to estimate correctly the general political situation and, consequently, the ability to select the proper moment for an uprising. Precisely such activity

---

5. Alas, alas! Again I have let slip that awful word "agents," which jars so much on the democratic ears of the Martynovs! I wonder why this word did not offend the heroes of the seventies and yet offends the amateurs of the nineties? I like the word, because it clearly and trenchantly indicates *the common cause* to which all the agents bend their thoughts and actions, and if I had to replace this word by another, the only word I might select would be the word "collaborator," if it did not suggest a certain bookishness and vagueness. The thing we need is a military organisation of agents. However, the numerous Martynovs (particularly abroad), whose favourite pastime is "mutual grants of generalships to one another," may instead of saying "passport agent" prefer to say, "Chief of the Special Department for Supplying Revolutionaries with Passports," etc. [*Lenin*]

would train *all* local organisations to respond simultaneously to the same political questions, incidents, and events that agitate the whole of Russia and to react to such "incidents" in the most vigorous, uniform, and expedient manner possible; for an uprising is in essence the most vigorous, most uniform, and most expedient "answer" of the entire people to the government. Lastly, it is precisely such activity that would train all revolutionary organisations throughout Russia to maintain the most continuous, and at the same time the most secret, contacts with one another, thus creating *real* Party unity; for without such contacts it will be impossible collectively to discuss the plan for the uprising and to take the necessary preparatory measures on the eve, measures that must be kept in the strictest secrecy.

In a word, the "plan for an all-Russia political newspaper," far from representing the fruits of the labour of armchair workers, infected with dogmatism and bookishness (as it seemed to those who gave but little thought to it), is the most practical plan for immediate and all-round preparation of the uprising, with, at the same time, no loss of sight for a moment of the pressing day-to-day work.

Conclusion

The history of Russian Social-Democracy can be distinctly divided into three periods:

The first period embraces about ten years, approximately from 1884 to 1894. This was the period of the rise and consolidation of the theory and programme of Social-Democracy. The adherents of the new trend in Russia were very few in number. Social-Democracy existed without a working-class movement, and as a political party it was at the embryonic stage of development.

The second period embraces three or four years—1894–98. In this period Social-Democracy appeared on the scene as a social movement, as the upsurge of the masses of the people, as a political party. This is the period of its childhood and adolescence. The intelligentsia was fired with a vast and general zeal for struggle against Narodism and for going among the workers; the workers displayed a general enthusiasm for strike action. The movement made enormous strides. The majority of the leaders were young people who had not reached "the age of thirty-five," which to Mr. N. Mikhailovsky appeared to be a sort of natural border-line. Owing to their youth, they proved to be untrained for practical work and they left the scene with astonishing rapidity. But in the majority of cases the scope of their activity was very wide. Many of them had begun their revolutionary thinking as adherents of Narodnaya Volya. Nearly all had in their early youth enthusiastically worshipped the terrorist heroes. It required a struggle to abandon the captivating impressions of those heroic traditions, and the struggle was accompanied by the breaking off of personal relations with people who were determined to remain loyal to the Narodnaya Volya and for whom the young Social-Democrats had profound respect. The struggle compelled the youthful leaders to educate themselves, to read illegal literature of every trend, and to study closely the questions of legal Narodism. Trained in this struggle, Social-Democrats went into the working-class movement without "for a moment" forgetting either the theory of Marxism, which brightly illumined their path, or the task of overthrowing the autocracy. The formation of the Party in the spring of 1898 was the most striking and at the same time the *last* act of the Social-Democrats of this period.

The third period, as we have seen, was prepared in 1897 and it definitely cut off the second period in 1898 (1898–?). This was a period of disunity, dissolution and vacillation. During adolescence a youth's voice breaks. And so, in this period, the voice of Russian Social-Democracy began to break, to strike a false note—on the one hand, in the writings of Messrs. Struve and Prokopovich, of Bulgakov and Berdyaev, and on the other, in those of V. I—n and R. M., of B. Krichevsky and Martynov. But it was only the leaders who wandered about separately and drew back; the movement itself continued to grow, and it advanced with enormous strides. The proletarian struggle spread to new strata of the workers and extended to the whole of Russia, at the same time indirectly stimulating the revival of the democratic spirit among the students and among other sections of the population. The political consciousness of the leaders, however, capitulated before the breadth and power of the spontaneous upsurge; among the Social-Democrats, another type had become dominant—the type of functionaries, trained almost exclusively on "legal Marxist" literature, which proved to be all the more inadequate the more the spontaneity of the masses demanded political consciousness on the part of the leaders. The leaders not only lagged behind in regard to theory ("freedom of criticism") and practice ("primitiveness"), but they sought to justify their backwardness by all manner of high-flown arguments. Social-Democracy was degraded to the level of trade-unionism by the Brentano adherents in legal literature, and by the tail-enders in illegal literature. The *Credo* programme began to be put into operation, especially when the "primitive methods" of the Social-Democrats caused a revival of revolutionary non-Social-Democratic tendencies.

If the reader should feel critical that I have dealt at too great length with a certain *Rabocheye Dyelo*, I can say only that *Rabocheye Dyelo* acquired "historical" significance because it most notably reflected the "spirit" of this third period.[6] It was not the consistent R. M., but the weathercock Krichevskys and Martynovs who were able properly to express the disunity and vacillation, the readiness to make concessions to "criticism," to "Economism," and to terrorism. Not the lofty contempt for practical work displayed by some worshipper of the "absolute" is characteristic of this period, but the combination of pettifogging practice and utter disregard for theory. It was not so much in the direct rejection of "grandiose phrases" that the heroes of this period engaged as in their vulgarisation. Scientific socialism ceased to be an integral revolutionary theory and became a hodgepodge "freely" diluted with the content of every new German textbook that appeared; the slogan "class struggle" did not impel to broader and more energetic activity but served as a balm, since "the economic struggle is inseparably linked with the political struggle"; the idea of a party did not serve as a call for the creation of a militant organisation of revolutionaries, but was used to justify some sort of "revolutionary bureaucracy" and infantile playing at "democratic" forms.

When the third period will come to an end and the fourth (now heralded by many portents) will begin we do not know. We are passing from the sphere of history to the sphere of the present and, partly, of the future. But we firmly believe that the fourth period will lead to the consolidation of militant Marxism, that Russian Social-Democracy will emerge from the crisis in the full flower of manhood, that the opportunist rearguard will be "replaced" by the genuine vanguard of the most revolutionary class.

In the sense of calling for such a "replacement" and by way of summing up what has been expounded above, we may meet the question, What is to be done? with the brief reply:

Put an End to the Third Period.

---

6. I could also reply with the German proverb: *Den Sack schlägt man, den Esel meint man* (you beat the sack, but you mean the donkey). Not *Rabocheye Dyelo* alone, but also *the broad mass* of practical workers *and theoreticians* was carried away by the "criticism" *à la mode*, becoming confused in regard to the question of spontaneity and lapsing from the Social-Democratic to the trade-unionist conception of our political and organisational tasks. [*Lenin*]

One Step Forward, Two Steps Back

This most purely polemical of all Lenin's major writings, written in the early months of 1904, was an outgrowth and continuation of the controversy that developed at the party's Second Congress over the clause of the draft rules that defined the meaning of party membership. Menshevik resistance to the party conception set forth in *What Is to Be Done?*, and implicit in the Bolshevik position on membership, Lenin ascribes to "intellectualist anarchism." The following excerpt, in which he summarizes the work's argument, is the concluding section of *One Step Forward*.

* * *

A Few Words on Dialectics. Two Revolutions

A general glance at the development of our Party crisis will readily show that in the main, with minor exceptions, the composition of the two contending sides remained unchanged throughout. It was a struggle between the revolutionary wing and the opportunist wing in our Party. But this struggle passed through the most varied stages, and anyone who wants to find his bearings in the vast amount of literature already accumulated, the mass of fragmentary evidence, passages torn from their context, isolated accusations, and so on and so forth, must thoroughly familiarise himself with the peculiarities of each of these stages.

Let us enumerate the principal and clearly distinct stages: 1) The controversy over Paragraph 1 of the Rules. A purely ideological struggle over the basic principles of organisation. Plekhanov and I are in the minority. Martov and Axelrod propose an opportunist formulation and find themselves in the arms of the opportunists. 2) The split in the *Iskra* organisation over the lists of candidates for the Central Committee: Fomin or Vasilyev in a committee of five, Trotsky or Travinsky in a committee of three. Plekhanov and I gain the majority (nine to seven), partly because of the very fact that we were in the minority on Paragraph 1. Martov's coalition with the opportunists confirmed my worst fears over the Organising Committee incident. 3) Continuation of the controversy over details of the Rules. Martov is again saved by the opportunists. We are again in the minority and fight for the rights of the minority on the central bodies. 4) The seven extreme opportunists withdraw from the Congress. We become the majority and defeat the coalition (the *Iskra*-ist minority, the "Marsh," and the anti-*Iskra*-ists) in the elections. Martov and Popov decline to accept seats in our trios. 5) The post-Congress squabble over co-optation. An orgy of anarchistic behaviour and anarchistic phrase-mongering. The least stable and steadfast elements among the "minority" gain the upper hand. 6) To avert a split, Plekhanov adopts the policy of "killing with kindness." The "minority" occupy the editorial board of the Central Organ and the Council and attack the Central Committee with all their might. The squabble continues to pervade everything. 7) First attack on the Central Committee repulsed. The squabble seems to be subsiding somewhat. It becomes possible to discuss in comparative calm two purely ideological questions which profoundly agitate the Party: a) what is the political significance and explanation of the division of our Party into "majority" and "minority" which took shape at the Second Congress and superseded all earlier divisions? b) what is the significance in principle of the new *Iskra*'s new position on the question of organisation?

In each of these stages the circumstances of the struggle and the immediate object of the attack are materially different; each stage is, as it were, a separate battle in one general military campaign. Our struggle cannot be understood at all unless the concrete circumstances of each battle are studied. But once that is done, we see clearly that development does indeed proceed dialectically, by way of contradictions: the minority becomes the majority, and the majority becomes the minority; each side passes from the defensive to the offensive, and from the offensive to the defensive; the starting-point of ideological struggle (Paragraph 1) is "negated" and gives place to an all-pervading squabble;[1] but then begins "the negation of the negation," and, having just about managed to "rub along" with our god-given wife on different central bodies, we return to the starting-point, the purely ideological struggle; but by now this "thesis" has been enriched by all the results of the "anti-thesis" and has

---

1. The difficult problem of drawing a line between squabbling and differences of principle now solves itself: all that relates to co-optation is squabbling; all that relates to analysis of the struggle at the Congress, to the controversy over Paragraph 1 and the swing towards opportunism and anarchism is a difference of principle. [*Lenin*]

become a higher synthesis, in which the isolated, random error over Paragraph 1 has grown into a quasi-system of opportunist views on matters of organisation, and in which the connection between this fact and the basic division of our Party into a revolutionary and an opportunist wing becomes increasingly apparent to all. In a word, not only do oats grow according to Hegel, but the Russian Social-Democrats war among themselves according to Hegel.

But the great Hegelian dialectics which Marxism made its own, having first turned it right side up, must never be confused with the vulgar trick of justifying the zigzags of politicians who swing over from the revolutionary to the opportunist wing of the Party, with the vulgar habit of lumping together particular statements, and particular developmental factors, belonging to different stages of a single process. Genuine dialectics does not justify the errors of individuals, but studies the inevitable turns, proving that they were inevitable by a detailed study of the process of development in all its concreteness. One of the basic principles of dialectics is that there is no such thing as abstract truth, truth is always concrete. . . . And, one thing more, the great Hegelian dialectics should never be confused with that vulgar worldly wisdom so well expressed by the Italian saying: *mettere la coda dove non va il capo* (sticking in the tail where the head will not go through).

The outcome of the dialectical development of our Party struggle has been two revolutions. The Party Congress was a real revolution, as Comrade Martov justly remarked in his *Once More in the Minority*. The wits of the minority are also right when they say: "The world moves through revolutions; well, we have made a revolution!" They did indeed make a revolution after the Congress; and it is true, too, that generally speaking the world does move through revolutions. But the concrete significance of each concrete revolution is not defined by this general aphorism; there are revolutions which are more like reaction, to paraphrase the unforgettable expression of the unforgettable Comrade Makhov. We must know whether it was the revolutionary or the opportunist wing of the Party that was the actual force that made the revolution, must know whether it was revolutionary or opportunist principle that inspired the fighters, before we can determine whether a particular concrete revolution moved the "world" (our Party) forward or backward.

Our Party Congress was unique and unprecedented in the entire history of the Russian revolutionary movement. For the first time a secret revolutionary party succeeded in emerging from the darkness of underground life into broad daylight, showing everyone the whole course and outcome of our internal Party struggle, the whole character of our Party and of each of its more or less noticeable components in matters of programme, tactics, and organisation. For the first time we succeeded in throwing off the traditions of circle looseness and revolutionary philistinism, in bringing together dozens of very different groups, many of which had been fiercely warring among themselves and had been linked solely by the force of an idea, and which were now prepared (in principle, that is) to sacrifice all their group aloofness and group independence for the sake of the great whole which we were for the first time actually creating—the *Party*. But in politics sacrifices are not obtained gratis, they have to be won in battle. The battle over the slaughter of organisations necessarily proved terribly fierce. The fresh breeze of free and open struggle blew into a gale. The gale swept away—and a very good thing that it did!—each and every remnant of all circle interests, sentiments, and traditions without exception, and for the first time created genuinely Party institutions.

But it is one thing to call oneself something, and another to be it. It is one thing to sacrifice the circle system in principle for the sake of the Party, and another to renounce one's own circle. The fresh breeze proved too fresh as yet for people used to musty philistinism. "The Party was unable to stand the strain of its first congress," as Comrade Martov rightly put it (inadvertently) in his *Once More in the Minority*. The sense of injury over the slaughter of organisations was too strong. The furious gale raised all the mud from the bottom of our Party stream; and the mud took its revenge. The old hidebound circle spirit overpowered the still young party spirit. The opportunist wing of the Party, routed though it had been, got the better—temporarily, of course—of the revolutionary wing, having been reinforced by Akimov's accidental gain.

The result is the new *Iskra*, which is compelled to develop and deepen the error its editors committed at the Party Congress. The old *Iskra* taught the truths of revolutionary struggle. The new *Iskra* teaches the worldly wisdom of yielding and getting on with everyone. The old *Iskra* was the organ of militant orthodoxy. The new *Iskra* treats us to a recrudescence of opportunism—chiefly on questions of organisation. The old *Iskra* earned the honour of being detested by the opportunists, both Russian and West-European. The new *Iskra* has "grown wise" and will soon cease to be ashamed of the praises lavished on it by the extreme opportunists. The old *Iskra* marched unswervingly towards its goal, and there was no discrepancy between its word and its deed. The inherent falsity of the new *Iskra*'s position inevitably leads—independently even of anyone's will or intention—to political hypocrisy. It inveighs against the circle spirit in order to conceal the victory of the circle spirit over the party spirit. It hypocritically condemns splits, as if one can imagine any way of avoiding splits in any at all organised party except by the subordination of the minority to the majority. It says that heed must be paid to revolutionary public opinion, yet, while concealing the praises of the Akimovs, indulges in petty scandal-mongering about the committees of the revolutionary wing of the Party.[2] How shameful! How they have disgraced our old *Iskra*!

One step forward, two steps back. . . . It happens in the lives of individuals, and it happens in the history of nations and in the development of parties. It would be the most criminal cowardice to doubt even for a moment the inevitable and complete triumph of the principles of revolutionary Social-Democracy, of proletarian organisation and Party discipline. We have already won a great deal, and we must go on fighting, undismayed by reverses, fighting steadfastly, scorning the philistine methods of circle wrangling, doing our very utmost to preserve the hard-won single Party tie linking all Russian Social-Democrats, and striving by dint of persistent and systematic work to give all Party members, and the workers in particular, a full and conscious understanding of the duties of Party members, of the struggle at the Second Party Congress, of all the causes and all the stages of our divergence, and of the utter disastrousness of opportunism, which, in the sphere of organisation as in the sphere of our programme and our tactics, helplessly surrenders to the bourgeois psychology, uncritically adopts the point of view of bourgeois democracy, and blunts the weapon of the class struggle of the proletariat.

In its struggle for power the proletariat has no other weapon but organisation. Disunited by the rule of anarchic competition in the bourgeois world, ground down by forced labour for capital, constantly thrust back to the "lower depths" of utter destitution, savagery, and degeneration, the proletariat can, and inevitably will, become an invincible force only through its ideological unification on the principles of Marxism being reinforced by the material unity of organisation, which welds millions of toilers into an army of the working class. Neither the senile rule of the Russian autocracy nor the senescent rule of international capital will be able to withstand this army. It will more and more firmly close its ranks, in spite of all zigzags and backward steps, in spite of the opportunist phrase-mongering of the Girondists of present-day Social-Democracy, in spite of the self-satisfied exaltation of the retrograde circle spirit, and in spite of the tinsel and fuss of *intellectualist* anarchism.

2. A stereotyped form has even been worked out for this charming pastime: our special correspondent X informs us that Committee Y of the majority has behaved badly to Comrade Z of the minority. [*Lenin*]

Two Tactics of Social-Democracy in the Democratic Revolution

Written in Geneva in June and July 1905, while the Revolution of 1905 was taking place in Russia, this work is one of Lenin's most important contributions to revolutionary theory. To the Menshevik tactic of supporting liberal leadership in the Russian Revolution on the assumption that a bourgeois democratic Russian republic was the maximum achievable goal at the present stage, Lenin counterposed a radical tactic of seeking to bring the popular insurrectionary movement under Marxist leadership with the aim of creating a "democratic dictatorship of the proletariat and peasantry." The upshot was to make Marxist revolutionary politics relevant to the situations of under-developed countries (like the Russia of 1905) which from a Marxist viewpoint have not yet undergone a bourgeois revolution and full-scale development of capitalism. Although the two men were then more conscious of their differences than their common ground, Lenin's position was not unlike that taken by Trotsky in his *Results and Prospects* of 1906, which espoused (under the heading of "permanent revolution") a similar revolutionary tactic with the proviso that the victorious Russian proletariat might, given help from socialist revolutions in Western Europe, proceed beyond the tasks of the "democratic revolution" to the building of socialism in Russia.

Preface

In a revolutionary period it is very difficult to keep abreast of events which provide an astonishing amount of new material for an appraisal of the tactical slogans of revolutionary parties. The present pamphlet was written before the Odessa events.[1] We have already pointed out in *Proletary* (No. 9—"Revolution Teaches") that these events have forced even those Social-Democrats who created the "uprising-as-process" theory and who rejected propaganda for a provisional revolutionary government actually to go over, or begin to go over, to their opponents' side. Revolution

1. The reference is to the mutiny on the armoured cruiser *Potemkin*. [*Lenin, 1907 edition*]

undoubtedly teaches with a rapidity and thoroughness which appear incredible in peaceful periods of political development. And, what is particularly important, it teaches not only the leaders, but the masses as well.

There is not the slightest doubt that the revolution will teach Social-Democratism to the masses of the workers in Russia. The revolution will confirm the programme and tactics of Social-Democracy in actual practice by demonstrating the true nature of the various classes of society, by demonstrating the bourgeois character of our democracy and the real aspirations of the peasantry, who, while being revolutionary in the bourgeois-democratic sense, carry within themselves not the idea of "socialisation," but the seeds of a new class struggle between the peasant bourgeoisie and the rural proletariat. The old illusions of the old Narodism,[2] so clearly-visible, for instance, in the draft programme of the "Socialist-Revolutionary Party"[3] on the question of the development of capitalism in Russia, the question of the democratic character of our "society," and the question of the significance of a complete victory of a peasant uprising—all these illusions will be completely and mercilessly dispelled by the revolution. For the first time, the various classes will be given their real political baptism. These classes will emerge from the revolution with a definite political physiognomy, for they will have revealed themselves not only in the programme and tactical slogans of their ideologists but also in open political action by the masses.

Undoubtedly, the revolution will teach us, and will teach the masses of the people. But the question that now confronts a militant political party is: shall we be able to teach the revolution anything? Shall we be able to make use of the correctness of our Social-Democratic doctrine, of our bond with the only thoroughly

2. From the word *narod* ("people"): a trend in the Russian revolutionary movement which began to manifest itself in the sixties and seventies of the nineteenth century. The Narodniks stood for the abolition of the autocracy and the transfer of the landed estates to the peasantry. They considered the peasantry, and not the proletariat, to be the main revolutionary force in Russia. They saw in the village commune the germ of socialism. 3. The programme of the Party of Socialist-Revolutionaries was adopted at its first congress held in Finland from December 29, 1905, to January 6, 1906. The Socialist-Revolutionaries (S.R.s) were a party formed in Russia at the end of 1901 and beginning of 1902 through the amalgamation of various Narodnik groups and circles, with the newspaper *Revolutsionnaya Rossiya* (*Revolutionary Russia;* 1900–1905) and the magazine *Vestnik Russkoi Revoliutsii* (*Herald of the Russian Revolution;* 1901–5) as its official organs. The Socialist-Revolutionaries' agrarian programme envisaged the abolition of private ownership of the land and its transfer to the village communes on the basis of equalised tenure, and also the development of co-operatives of all kinds. In the years of the first Russian revolution the Right wing of the party broke away and formed the legal Trudovik Popular-Socialist Party, close in its views to the Cadets; the Left wing took shape as the semi-anarchist Maximalist League. After the victory of the February Revolution in 1917, the Socialist-Revolutionaries, together with the Mensheviks and Cadets, were the mainstay of the Provisional Government, of which leaders of the party (Kerensky, Avksentyev, Chernov) were members. The Left wing of the party, influenced by the growing revolutionary spirit of the peasants, founded at the end of November 1917 an independent Left Socialist-Revolutionary Party.

revolutionary class, the proletariat, to put a proletarian imprint on the revolution, to carry the revolution to a real and decisive victory, not in word but in deed, and to paralyse the instability, half-heartedness, and treachery of the democratic bourgeoisie?

It is to this end that we must direct all our efforts, and the achievement of that end will depend, on the one hand, on the accuracy of our appraisal of the political situation and the correctness of our tactical slogans, and, on the other hand, on whether these slogans will be backed by the real fighting strength of the masses of the workers. All the usual, regular, and current work of all organisations and groups of our Party, the work of propaganda, agitation, and organisation, is directed towards strengthening and expanding the ties with the masses. Necessary as this work always is it cannot be considered adequate at a time of revolution. In such a contingency the working class feels an instinctive urge for open revolutionary action, and we must learn to set the aims of this action correctly, and then make these aims as widely known and understood as possible. It must not be forgotten that the current pessimism about our ties with the masses very often serves as a screen for bourgeois ideas regarding the proletariat's role in the revolution. Undoubtedly, we still have a great deal to do in educating and organising the working class; but now the gist of the matter is: where should we place the main political emphasis in this work of education and organisation? On the trade unions and legally existing associations, or on an insurrection, on the work of creating a revolutionary army and a revolutionary government? Both serve to educate and organise the working class. Both are, of course, necessary. But in the present revolution the problem amounts to this: which is to be emphasised in the work of educating and organising the working class, the former or the latter?

The outcome of the revolution depends on whether the working class will play the part of a subsidiary to the bourgeoisie, a subsidiary that is powerful in the force of its onslaught against the autocracy, but impotent politically, or whether it will play the part of leader of the people's revolution.

* * *

Whence Is the Proletariat Threatened with the Danger of Finding Itself with Its Hands Tied in the Struggle Against the Inconsistent Bourgeoisie?

Marxists are absolutely convinced of the bourgeois character of the Russian revolution. What does that mean? It means that the democratic reforms in the political system, and the social and economic reforms that have become a necessity for Russia, do not in themselves imply the undermining of capitalism, the undermining of bourgeois rule; on the contrary, they will, for the first time, really clear the ground for a wide and rapid, European, and not Asiatic, development of capitalism; they will, for the first time, make it possible for the bourgeoisie to rule as a class. The Socialist-Revolutionaries cannot grasp this idea, for they do not know the ABC of the laws of development of commodity and capitalist production; they fail to see that even the complete success of a peasant insurrection, even the redistribution of the whole of the land in favour of the peasants and in accordance with their desires ("general redistribution" or something of the kind) will not destroy capitalism at all, but will, on the contrary, give an impetus to its development and hasten the class disintegration of the peasantry itself. Failure to grasp this truth makes the Socialist-Revolutionaries unconscious ideologists of the petty bourgeoisie. Insistence on this truth is of enormous importance for Social-Democracy not only from the standpoint of theory but also from that of practical politics, for it follows therefrom that complete class independence of the party of the proletariat in the present "general democratic" movement is an indispensable condition.

But it does not by any means follow that a *democratic* revolution (bourgeois in its social and economic essence) would not be of *enormous* interest to the proletariat. It does not follow that the democratic revolution could not take place both in a form advantageous mainly to the big capitalist, the financial magnate, and the "enlightened" landlord, and in a form advantageous to the peasant and the worker.

The new-*Iskra* group completely misunderstands the meaning and significance of bourgeois revolution as a category. The idea that is constantly running through their arguments is that a bourgeois revolution is one that can be advantageous only to the bourgeoisie. And yet nothing can be more erroneous than such an idea. A bourgeois revolution is a revolution which does not depart from the framework of the bourgeois, i.e., capitalist, socio-economic system. A bourgeois revolution expresses the needs of capitalist development, and, far from destroying the foundations of capitalism, it effects the contrary—it broadens and deepens them. This revolution, therefore, expresses the interests not only of the working class but of the entire bourgeoisie as well. Since the rule of the bourgeoisie over the working class is inevitable under capitalism, it can well be said that a bourgeois revolution expresses the interests not so much of the proletariat as of the bourgeoisie. But it is quite absurd to think that a bourgeois revolution does not at all express proletarian interests. This absurd idea boils down either to the hoary Narodnik theory that a bourgeois revolution runs counter to the interests of the proletariat, and that, therefore, we do not need bourgeois political liberty; or to anarchism which denies any participation of the proletariat in bourgeois politics, in a bourgeois revolution and in bourgeois parliamentarism. From the standpoint of theory this idea disregards the elementary propositions of Marxism concerning the inevitability of capitalist development on the basis of commodity production. Marxism teaches us that at a certain stage of its development a society which is based on commodity production and has commercial intercourse with civilised capitalist nations must inevitably take the road of capitalism. Marxism has irrevocably broken with the Narodnik and anarchist gibberish that Russia, for instance, can bypass capitalist development, escape from capitalism, or skip it in some way other than that of the class struggle, on the basis and within the framework of this same capitalism.

All these principles of Marxism have been proved and explained in minute detail in general and with regard to Russia in particular. And from these principles it follows that the idea of seeking salvation for the working class in anything save the further development of capitalism is *reactionary*. In countries like Russia the working class suffers not so much from capitalism as from the insufficient development of capitalism. The working class is, therefore, *most certainly interested* in the broadest, freest, and most rapid development of capitalism. The removal of all the remnants of the old order which hamper the broad, free, and rapid development of capitalism is of absolute *advantage* to the working class. The bourgeois revolution is precisely an upheaval that most resolutely sweeps away survivals of the past, survivals of the serf-owning system (which include not only the autocracy but the monarchy as well), and most fully guarantees the broadest, freest, and most rapid development of capitalism.

That is why a *bourgeois* revolution is *in the highest degree advantageous to the proletariat*. A bourgeois revolution is *absolutely* necessary in the interests of the proletariat. The more complete, determined, and consistent the bourgeois revolution, the more assured will the proletariat's struggle be against the bourgeoisie and for socialism. Only those who are ignorant of the ABC of scientific socialism can regard this conclusion as new, strange, or paradoxical. And from this conclusion, among other things, follows the thesis that *in a certain sense* a bourgeois revolution is *more advantageous* to the proletariat than to the bourgeoisie. This thesis is unquestionably correct in the following sense: it is to the advantage of the bourgeoisie to rely on certain remnants of the past, as against the proletariat, for instance, on the monarchy, the standing army, etc. It is to the advantage of the bourgeoisie for the bourgeois revolution not to sweep away all remnants of the past too resolutely, but keep some of them, i.e., for this revolution not to be fully consistent, not to be complete, and not to be determined and relentless. Social-Democrats often express this idea somewhat differently by stating that the bourgeoisie betrays its own self, that the bourgeoisie betrays the cause of liberty, that the bourgeoisie is incapable of being consistently democratic. It is of greater advantage to the bourgeoisie for the necessary changes in the direction of bourgeois democracy to take place more slowly, more gradually, more cautiously, less resolutely, by means of reforms and not by means of revolution; for these changes to spare the "venerable" institutions of the serf-owning system (such as the monarchy) as much as possible; for these changes to develop as little as possible the independent revolutionary activity, initiative, and energy of the common people, i.e., the peasantry and especially the workers, for otherwise it will be easier for the workers, as the French say, "to change the rifle from one shoulder to the other," i.e., to turn against the bourgeoisie the weapon the bourgeois revolution will supply them with, the liberty the revolution will bring, and the democratic institutions that will spring up on the ground cleared of the serf-owning system.

On the other hand, it is more advantageous to the working class for the necessary changes in the direction of bourgeois democracy to take place by way of revolution and not by way of reform, because the way of reform is one of delay, procrastination, the painfully slow decomposition of the putrid parts of the national organism. It is the proletariat and the peasantry that suffer first of all and most of all from that putrefaction. The revolutionary path is one of rapid amputation, which is the least painful to the proletariat, the path of the immediate removal of what is putrescent, the path of least compliance with and consideration for the monarchy and the abominable, vile, rotten, and noxious institutions that go with it.

So it is not only because of the censorship, not only "for fear of the Jews," that our bourgeois-liberal press deplores the possibility of the revolutionary path, fears the revolution, tries to frighten the tsar with the bogey of revolution, seeks to avoid revolution, and grovels and toadies for the sake of miserable reforms as the foundation of the reformist path. This standpoint is shared not only by *Russkiye Vedomosti*, *Syn Otechestva*, *Nasha Zhizn*, and *Nashi Dni*, but also by the illegal, uncensored *Osvobozhdeniye*.[4] The very posi-

---

4. *Russkiye Vedomosti* (*Russian Recorder*) was a newspaper published in Moscow from 1863 onwards; it expressed the views of the moderate liberal intelligentsia. In 1918 it was closed down together with other newspapers.

Syn Otechestva (*Son of the Fatherland*) was a liberal daily published in St. Petersburg from 1856 to 1900, and after November 18 (December 1), 1904. Its

tion the bourgeoisie holds as a class in capitalist society inevitably leads to its inconsistency in a democratic revolution. The very position the proletariat holds as a class compels it to be consistently democratic. The bourgeoisie looks backward in fear of democratic progress which threatens to strengthen the proletariat. The proletariat has nothing to lose but its chains, but with the aid of democratism it has the whole world to win. That is why the more consistent the bourgeois revolution is in achieving its democratic transformations, the less will it limit itself to what is of advantage exclusively to the bourgeoisie. The more consistent the bourgeois revolution, the more does it guarantee the proletariat and the peasantry the benefits accruing from the democratic revolution.

Marxism teaches the proletarian not to keep aloof from the bourgeois revolution, not to be indifferent to it, not to allow the leadership of the revolution to be assumed by the bourgeoisie but, on the contrary, to take a most energetic part in it, to fight most resolutely for consistent proletarian democratism, for the revolution to be carried to its conclusion. We cannot get out of the bourgeois-democratic boundaries of the Russian revolution, but we can vastly extend these boundaries, and within these boundaries we can and must fight for the interests of the proletariat, for its immediate needs and for conditions that will make it possible to prepare its forces for the future complete victory. There is bourgeois democracy and bourgeois democracy. The Zemstvo monarchist who favours an upper chamber and "asks" for universal suffrage, while secretly, on the sly, striking a bargain with tsarism for a docked constitution, is a bourgeois democrat too. The peasant, who has taken up arms against the landlords and the government officials, and with a "naïve republicanism" proposes "to send the tsar packing,"[5] is also a bourgeois democrat. There are bourgeois-democratic regimes like the one in Germany, and also like the one in England; like the one in Austria and also like those in America and Switzerland. He would be a fine Marxist indeed who in a period of democratic revolution failed to see this difference between the de-

---

contributors represented various shades of Narodism. Following November 15 (28), 1905, it became the organ of the S.R.s. It was suppressed on December 2 (15), 1905.

Nasha Zhizn (*Our Life*): a daily newspaper close to the left wing of the Cadet Party; it appeared irregularly from November 6 (19), 1904, to July 11 (24), 1906, in St. Petersburg.

Nashi Dni (*Our Days*) was a liberal daily published in St. Petersburg from December 18 (31), 1904, to February 5 (18), 1905.

Osvobozhdeniye (*Emancipation*) was a fortnightly journal published abroad from June 1902 to October 1905 under the editorship of P. B. Struve. The journal was an organ of the Russian liberal-monarchist bourgeoisie. In 1903 there gathered around the journal (and in January 1904 took organisational shape) the liberal-monarchist Osvobozhdeniye League that existed until October 1905. The members of this League, together with the Zemstvo constitutionalists, made up the core of the Cadet Party.

5. See *Osvobozhdeniye*, No. 71, p. 337, footnote 2. [*Lenin*]

grees of democratism and the difference between its forms, and confined himself to "clever" remarks to the effect that, after all, this is "a bourgeois revolution," the fruit of "bourgeois revolution."

Our new-Iskrists are just such clever fellows, who actually flaunt their short-sightedness. They confine themselves to disquisitions on the bourgeois character of revolution, just when and where it is necessary to be able to draw a distinction between republican-revolutionary and monarchist-liberal bourgeois democracy, to say nothing of the distinction between inconsistent bourgeois democratism and consistent proletarian democratism. They are satisfied—as if they had really become like the "man in a shell"[6]—with doleful talk about a "process of mutual struggle of antagonistic classes," when the question is one of providing *democratic leadership* in the present revolution, of emphasising *progressive democratic* slogans, as distinct from the treacherous slogans of Mr. Struve and Co., of bluntly and straightforwardly stating the immediate aims of the really revolutionary struggle of the proletariat and the peasantry, as distinct from the liberal haggling of the landlords and manufacturers. Such now is the gist of the matter, which you, gentlemen, have missed, namely: will our revolution result in a real, immense victory, or merely in a wretched deal; will it go so far as the revolutionary-democratic dictatorship of the proletariat and the peasantry, or will it "peter out" in a liberal constitution *à la* Shipov?[7]

At first sight it may appear that in raising this question we are deviating entirely from our subject. However, that may appear so only at first sight. As a matter of fact, it is precisely this question that lies at the root of the difference in principle which has already become clearly marked between the Social-Democratic tactics of the Third Congress of the Russian Social-Democratic Labour Party and the tactics initiated by the Conference of the new-*Iskra* supporters. The latter have already taken not two but three steps back, resurrecting the mistakes of Economism in solving problems that are incomparably more complex, more important, and more vital to the workers' party, viz., questions of its tactics in time of revolution. That is why we must analyse the question we have raised with all due attention.

* * * [A] section of the new-Iskrists' resolution points to the danger of Social-Democracy tying its own hands in the struggle against the inconsistent policy of the bourgeoisie, of its becoming dissolved in bourgeois democracy. The thought of this danger pervades all specifically new-Iskrist literature; it lies at the very heart

6. The main character in Chekhov's story of the same name, a man typifying the narrow-minded philistine who abhors all innovations or initiative.

7. Lenin here refers to the constitutional platform of D. N. Shipov, one of the leaders of the liberal Zemstvo movement at the turn of the century. The platform envisaged a constitution "to be granted by the tsar."

of the principle involved in our Party split (ever since the bickering in the split was completely over-shadowed by the turn towards Economism). Without any equivocation we admit that this danger really exists, that just at the present time, at the height of the Russian revolution, this danger has become particularly grave. The pressing and extremely responsible duty that devolves on all of us theoreticians or—as I should prefer to say of myself—publicists of Social-Democracy is to find out *from what direction* this danger actually threatens. For the source of our disagreement is not a dispute as to whether such a danger exists, but the dispute as to whether it is caused by the so-called tail-ism of the "Minority" or the so-called revolutionism of the "Majority."

To remove all misinterpretations and misunderstandings let us first of all note that the danger to which we are referring lies not in the subjective, but in the objective aspect of the matter, not in the formal stand which Social-Democracy will take in the struggle, but in the material outcome of the entire present revolutionary struggle. The question is not whether this or that Social-Democratic group will want to dissolve in bourgeois democracy, or whether they realise that they are doing so. Nobody suggests that. We do not suspect any Social-Democrat of harbouring such a desire, and this is not at all a matter of desire. Nor is it a question of whether this or that Social-Democratic group will formally retain its separate identity, individuality, and independence of bourgeois democracy throughout the course of the revolution. They may not merely proclaim such "independence," but may even retain it formally, and yet *it may turn out* that their hands will nevertheless be tied in the struggle against the inconsistency of the bourgeoisie. The ultimate political outcome of the revolution may prove to be that, despite the formal "independence" of Social-Democracy, despite its complete organisational individuality as a separate party, it will in fact not be independent; it will not be able to place the imprint of its proletarian independence on the course of events; it will prove so weak that, on the whole and in the last analysis, its "dissolution" in bourgeois democracy will nevertheless be a historical fact.

That is what constitutes the real danger. Now let us see from what direction the danger threatens—from the deviation of Social-Democracy, as represented by the new *Iskra*, to the Right, as we believe; or from the deviation of Social-Democracy, as represented by the "Majority," *Vperyod*,[8] etc., to the Left—as the new-*Iskra* group believes.

8. The newspaper *Vperyod* [*Forward*], which was published in Geneva, began to appear in January 1905 as the organ of the Bolshevik section of the Party. From January to May eighteen issues appeared. In May, by virtue of the decision of the Third Congress of the Russian Social-Democratic Labour Party,

The answer to this question, as we have pointed out, is determined by the objective combination of the operation of the various social forces. The character of these forces has been defined theoretically by the Marxist analysis of Russian life; at present it is being determined in practice by open action by groups and classes in the course of the revolution. Now the entire theoretical analysis made by the Marxists long before the period we are now passing through, as well as all the practical observations of the development of revolutionary events, show that, from the standpoint of objective conditions, there are two possible courses and two possible outcomes of the revolution in Russia. The transformation of the economic and political system in Russia along bourgeois-democratic lines is inevitable and inescapable. No power on earth can prevent such a transformation, but the combined action of the existing forces which are effecting it may result in either of two things, may bring about either of two forms of that transformation. Either 1) matters will end in "the revolution's decisive victory over tsarism," or 2) the forces will be inadequate for a decisive victory, and matters will end in a deal between tsarism and the most "inconsistent" and most "self-seeking" elements of the bourgeoisie. By and large, all the infinite variety of details and combinations, which no one is able to foresee, lead to one outcome or the other.

Let us now consider these two possibilities, first, from the standpoint of their social significance and, secondly, from the standpoint of the position of Social-Democracy (its "dissolution" or "having its hands tied") in one outcome or the other.

What is meant by "the revolution's decisive victory over tsarism"? We have already seen that in using this expression the new-*Iskra* group fail to grasp even its immediate political significance. Still less do they seem to understand the class essence of this concept. Surely, we Marxists must not under any circumstances allow ourselves to be deluded by *words*, such as "revolution" or "the great Russian revolution," as do many revolutionary democrats (of the Gapon type). We must be perfectly certain in our minds as to what real social forces are opposed to "tsarism" (which is a real force perfectly intelligible to all) and are capable of gaining a "decisive victory" over it. The big bourgeoisie, the landlords, the factory owners, the "society" which follows the *Osvobozhdeniye* lead, cannot be such a force. We see that they do not even want a decisive victory. We know that owing to their class position they are incapable of waging a decisive struggle against tsarism; they are too heavily fettered by private property, by capital and land to enter

Proletary [*Proletarian*] replaced *Vperyod* as the Central Organ of the R.S.D.L.P. (The Congress took place in London, in May; the Mensheviks did not appear there but organised their own "Conference" in Geneva.) [*Lenin, 1907 edition*]

into a decisive struggle. They stand in too great need of tsarism, with its bureaucratic, police, and military forces for use against the proletariat and the peasantry, to want it to be destroyed. No, the only force capable of gaining "a decisive victory over tsarism" is the *people*, i.e., the proletariat and the peasantry, if we take the main, big forces, and distribute the rural and urban petty bourgeoisie (also part of "the people") between the two. "The revolution's decisive victory over tsarism" means the establishment of the *revolutionary-democratic dictatorship of the proletariat and the peasantry*. Our new-*Iskra* group cannot escape from this conclusion, which *Vperyod* indicated long ago. No other force is capable of gaining a decisive victory over tsarism.

And such a victory will be precisely a dictatorship, i.e., it must inevitably rely on military force, on the arming of the masses, on an insurrection, and not on institutions of one kind or another established in a "lawful" or peaceful" way. It can be only a dictatorship, for realisation of the changes urgently and absolutely indispensable to the proletariat and the peasantry will evoke desperate resistance from the landlords, the big bourgeoisie, and tsarism. Without a dictatorship it is impossible to break down that resistance and repel counter-revolutionary attempts. But of course it will be a democratic, not a socialist dictatorship. It will be unable (without a series of intermediary stages of revolutionary development) to affect the foundations of capitalism. At best, it may bring about a radical redistribution of landed property in favour of the peasantry, establish consistent and full democracy, including the formation of a republic, eradicate all the oppressive features of Asiatic bondage, not only in rural but also in factory life, lay the foundation for a thorough improvement in the conditions of the workers and for a rise in their standard of living, and—last but not least—carry the revolutionary conflagration into Europe. Such a victory will not yet by any means transform our bourgeois revolution into a socialist revolution; the democratic revolution will not immediately overstep the bounds of bourgeois social and economic relationships; nevertheless, the significance of such a victory for the future development of Russia and of the whole world will be immense. Nothing will raise the revolutionary energy of the world proletariat so much, nothing will shorten the path leading to its complete victory to such an extent as this decisive victory of the revolution that has now started in Russia.

How far such a victory is probable is another question. We are not in the least inclined to be unreasonably optimistic on that score; we do not for a moment forget the immense difficulties of this task, but, since we are out to fight, we must desire victory and be able to point out the right road to it. Trends capable of leading to such a victory undoubtedly exist. True, our influence on the masses of the proletariat—the Social-Democratic influence—is as yet very, very inadequate; the revolutionary influence on the mass of the peasantry is quite insignificant; the proletarians, and especially the peasants, are still frightfully disunited, backward, and ignorant. However, revolution unites rapidly and enlightens rapidly. Every step in its development rouses the masses and attracts them with irresistible force to the side of the revolutionary programme, as the only programme that fully and consistently expresses their real and vital interests.

According to a law of mechanics, action and reaction are always equal. In history too, the destructive force of a revolution is to a considerable degree dependent on how strong and protracted the suppression of the striving for liberty has been, and how profound is the contradiction between the outmoded "superstructure" and the living forces of our times. The international political situation, too, is in many respects taking shape in a way most advantageous to the Russian revolution. The workers' and peasants' insurrection has already begun; it is sporadic, spontaneous, and weak, but it unquestionably and undoubtedly proves the existence of forces capable of waging a decisive struggle and marching towards a decisive victory.

If these forces prove inadequate tsarism will have time to conclude a deal, which is already being prepared at the two extremes by the Bulygins and the Struves. Then the whole matter will end in a docked constitution, or, if the worst comes to the worst, even in a travesty of a constitution. This, too, will be a "bourgeois revolution," but it will be a miscarriage, a premature birth, an abortion. Social-Democracy entertains no illusions on that score; it knows the treacherous nature of the bourgeoisie; it will not lose heart or abandon its presistent, patient, and sustained work of giving the proletariat class training, even in the most drab, humdrum days of bourgeois-constitutional "Shipov" bliss. Such an outcome would be more or less similar to that of almost all the nineteenth-century democratic revolutions in Europe, and our Party development would then proceed along the arduous, long, but familiar and beaten track.

The question now arises: in which outcome of the two possible will Social-Democracy find its hands actually tied in the struggle against the inconsistent and self-seeking bourgeoisie, find itself actually "dissolved," or almost so, in bourgeois democracy?

It is sufficient to put this question clearly to have a reply without a moment's difficulty.

If the bourgeoisie succeeds in frustrating the Russian revolution by coming to terms with tsarism, Social-Democracy will find its hands actually tied in the struggle against the inconsistent bourgeoisie; Social-Democracy will find itself "dissolved" in bourgeois democracy in the sense that the proletariat will not succeed in placing its clear imprint on the revolution, will not succeed in settling accounts with tsarism in the proletarian or, as Marx once said, "in the plebeian manner."

If the revolution gains a decisive victory—then we shall settle accounts with tsarism in the Jacobin, or, if you like, in the plebeian way. "The whole French terrorism," wrote Marx in 1848 in the famous *Neue Rheinische Zeitung*, "was nothing but a plebeian manner of settling accounts with the enemies of the bourgeoisie, with absolutism, feudalism, and philistinism" (see Marx, *Nachlass*, Mehring's edition, Vol. III, p. 211).[9] Have those people who in a period of a democratic revolution try to frighten the Social-Democratic workers in Russia with the bogey of "Jacobinism" ever given thought to the significance of these words of Marx?

The new-*Iskra* group, the Girondists of contemporary Russian Social-Democracy, does not merge with the *Osvobozhdeniye* group, but actually, by reason of the nature of its slogans, it follows in the wake of the latter. And the *Osvobozhdeniye* group, i.e., the representatives of the liberal bourgeoisie, wishes to settle accounts with the autocracy in a reformist manner, gently and compliantly, so as not to offend the aristocracy, the nobles, or the Court—cautiously, without breaking anything—kindly and politely as befits gentlemen in white gloves (like the ones Mr. Petrunkevich borrowed from a bashi-bazouk to wear at the reception of "representatives of the people" [?] held by Nicholas the Bloodstained; see *Proletary*, No. 5).

The Jacobins of contemporary Social-Democracy—the Bolsheviks, the *Vperyod* supporters, the "Congress" group, *Proletary* supporters—or whatever else we may call them—wish by their slogans to raise the revolutionary and republican petty bourgeoisie, and especially the peasantry, to the level of the consistent democratism of the proletariat, which fully retains its individuality as a class. They want the people, i.e., the proletariat and the peasantry, to settle accounts with the monarchy and the aristocracy in the "plebeian way," ruthlessly destroying the enemies of liberty, crushing their resistance by force, making no concessions whatever to the accursed heritage of serf-ownership, Asiatic barbarism, and human degradation.

This, of course, does not mean that we necessarily propose to imitate the Jacobins of 1793, and borrow their views, programme,

---

9. Lenin is referring to the book *Aus dem literarischen Nachlass von Karl Marx, Friedrich Engels und Ferdinand Lassalle. Herausgegeben von Franz Mehring*, Band III (Stuttgart, 1902), S. 211.

slogans, and methods of action. Nothing of the kind. Our programme is not an old one but a new—the minimum programme of
the Russian Social-Democratic Labour Party. We have a new slogan: the revolutionary-democratic dictatorship of the proletariat
and the peasantry. If we live to see the real victory of the revolution
we shall also have new methods of action in keeping with the
nature and aims of the working-class party that is striving for a
complete socialist revolution. By our parallel we merely want to
explain that the representatives of the progressive class of the twentieth century, the proletariat, i.e., the Social-Democrats, are divided
into two wings (the opportunist and the revolutionary) similar to
those into which the representatives of the progressive class of the
eighteenth century, the bourgeoisie, were divided, i.e., the Girondists and the Jacobins.

Only in the event of a complete victory of the democratic revolution will the proletariat have its hands free in the struggle against
the inconsistent bourgeoisie; only in that event will it not become
"dissolved" in bourgeois democracy, but will leave its proletarian,
or rather proletarian-peasant, imprint on the whole revolution.

In a word, to avoid finding itself with its hands tied in the
struggle against the inconsistent bourgeois democracy the proletariat must be class-conscious and strong enough to rouse the peasantry to revolutionary consciousness, guide its assault, and thereby
independently pursue the line of consistent proletarian democratism.

That is how matters stand in the question—so ineptly dealt with
by the new-*Iskra* group—of the danger of our hands being tied in
the struggle against the inconsistent bourgeoisie. The bourgeoisie
will always be inconsistent. There is nothing more naïve and futile
than attempts to set forth conditions and points which, if satisfied,
would enable us to consider that the bourgeois democrat is a sincere friend of the people. Only the proletariat can be a consistent
fighter for democracy. It can become a victorious fighter for democracy only if the peasant masses join its revolutionary struggle.
If the proletariat is not strong enough for this the bourgeoisie will
be at the head of the democratic revolution and will impart an
inconsistent and self-seeking nature to it. Nothing but a revolutionary-democratic dictatorship of the proletariat and the peasantry
can prevent this.

Thus, we arrive at the indubitable conclusion that it is the new-
Iskra tactics which, by its objective significance, is *playing into the
hands of the bourgeois democrats*. The preaching of organisational
diffuseness which goes to the length of plebiscites, the principle of
compromise, and the divorcement of Party literature from the
Party; belittling of the aims of insurrection; confusing of the popu-

lar political slogans of the revolutionary proletariat with those of the monarchist bourgeoisie; distortion of the requisites for "revolutions's decisive victory over tsarism"—all these taken together produce that very policy of tail-ism in a revolutionary period, which bewilders the proletariat, disorganises it, confuses its understanding, and belittles the tactics of Social-Democracy instead of pointing out the only way to victory and getting all the revolutionary and republican elements of the people to adhere to the proletariat's slogan.

* * *

Vulgar revolutionism fails to see that words are action, too; this proposition is indisputable when applied to history in *general*, or to those periods of history when no open political mass action takes place. No putsches of any sort can replace or artificially evoke such action. Tail-ist revolutionaries fail to understand that when a revolutionary period has set in, when the old "superstructure" has cracked from top to bottom, when open political action by the classes and masses that are creating a new superstructure for themselves has become a fact, and when civil war has begun—it is apathy, lifelessness, pedantry, or else betrayal of the revolution and treachery to it to confine oneself to "words" *in the old way*, without advancing the *direct slogan* on the need to pass over to "action," and to try to avoid action by pleading the need for "psychological conditions" and "propaganda" in general. The democratic bourgeoisie's Frankfort windbags are a memorable historical example of just such treachery or of just such pedantic stupidity.

* * *

A Social-Democrat must never for a moment forget that the proletariat will inevitably have to wage a class struggle for socialism even against the most democratic and republican bourgeoisie and petty bourgeoisie. This is beyond doubt. Hence, the absolute necessity of a separate, independent, strictly class party of Social-Democracy. Hence, the temporary nature of our tactics of "striking a joint blow" with the bourgeoisie and the duty of keeping a strict watch "over our ally, as over an enemy," etc. All this also leaves no room for doubt. However, it would be ridiculous and reactionary to deduce from this that we must forget, ignore, or neglect tasks which, although transient and temporary, are vital at the present time. The struggle against the autocracy is a temporary and transient task for socialists, but to ignore or neglect this task in any way amounts to betrayal of socialism and service to reaction. The revolutionary-democratic dictatorship of the proletariat and the peasantry is unquestionably only a transient, temporary socialist aim, but to ignore this aim in the period of a democratic revolution would be downright reactionary.

Concrete political aims must be set in concrete circumstances. All things are relative, all things flow, and all things change. German Social-Democracy does not put into its programme the demand for a republic. The situation in Germany is such that this question can in practice hardly be separated from that of socialism (although with regard to Germany too, Engels in his comments on the draft of the Erfurt Programme in 1891 warned against belittling the importance of a republic and of the struggle for a republic!).[1] In Russian Social-Democracy the question of eliminating the demand for a republic from its programme and its agitation has never even arisen, for in our country there can be no talk of an indissoluble link between the question of a republic and that of socialism. It was quite natural for a German Social-Democrat of 1898 not to place special emphasis on the question of a republic, and this evokes neither surprise nor condemnation. But in 1848 a German Social-Democrat who would have relegated to the background the question of a republic would have been a downright traitor to the revolution. There is no such thing as abstract truth. Truth is always concrete.

The time will come when the struggle against the Russian autocracy will end, and the period of democratic revolution will have passed in Russia; it will then be ridiculous even to speak of "singleness of will" of the proletariat and the peasantry, about a democratic dictatorship, etc. When that time comes we shall deal directly with the question of the socialist dictatorship of the proletariat and speak of it in greater detail. At present the party of the advanced class cannot but strive most energetically for the democratic revolution's decisive victory over tsarism. And a decisive victory means nothing else than the revolutionary-democratic dictatorship of the proletariat and the peasantry.

Note[2]

1) We would remind the reader that in the polemic between *Iskra* and *Vperyod*, the former referred, among other things, to Engels's letter to Turati, in which Engels warned the (future) leader of the Italian reformists against confusing the democratic revolution with the socialist.[3] The impending revolution in Italy, Engels wrote about the political situation in Italy in 1894, would be a petty-bourgeois, democratic and not a socialist revolution. *Iskra* reproached *Vperyod* with having departed from the principle laid down by Engels. This reproach was unjustified, because, on the

1. The Erfurt Programme of the German Social-Democratic Party was adopted in October 1891 at the Congress in Erfurt. Lenin considered that the Erfurt Programme's silence on the dictatorship of the proletariat was its chief defect and a concession to opportunism.
2. In July 1905 Lenin wrote a note to

Chapter 10 of *Two Tactics of Social-Democracy in the Democratic Revolution*. This note, not published in the first edition of the book, first appeared in 1926, in *Lenin Miscellany V.*
3. See Marx and Engels, *Selected Correspondence* (Moscow, 1953), pp. 551–55.

whole, V*peryod* (No. 14) fully acknowledged the correctness of Marx's theory of the distinction between the three main forces in nineteenth-century revolutions. According to this theory, the following forces take a stand against the old order, against the autocracy, feudalism, and the serf-owning system: 1) the liberal big bourgeoisie, 2) the radical petty bourgeoisie, 3) the proletariat. The first fights for nothing more than a constitutional monarchy; the second, for a democratic republic; the third, for a socialist revolution. To confuse the petty bourgeoisie's struggle for a complete democratic revolution with the proletariat's struggle for a socialist revolution threatens the socialist with political bankruptcy. Marx's warning to this effect is quite justified. It is, however, precisely for this very reason that the slogan of "revolutionary communes" is erroneous, because the very mistake made by the communes known to history was that of confusing the democratic revolution with the socialist revolution. On the other hand, our slogan—a revolutionary democratic dictatorship of the proletariat and the peasantry—fully safeguards us against this mistake. While recognising the incontestably bourgeois nature of a revolution incapable of *directly* overstepping the bounds of a mere democratic revolution our slogan *advances* this particular revolution and strives to give it forms most advantageous to the proletariat; consequently, it strives to make the utmost of the democratic revolution in order to attain the greatest success in the proletariat's further struggle for socialism.

* * *

Conclusion. Dare We Win?

People who are superficially acquainted with the state of affairs in Russian Social-Democracy, or who judge as mere onlookers, with no knowledge of the whole history of our inner-Party struggle since the days of Economism, very often dismiss the disagreements on tactics which have now taken shape, especially after the Third Congress, with the simple argument that there are two natural, inevitable, and quite reconcilable trends in every Social-Democratic movement. One side, they say, lays special emphasis on the ordinary, current, and everyday work, on the necessity of developing propaganda and agitation, of preparing forces, deepening the movement, etc., while the other side lays emphasis on the militant, general political, revolutionary tasks of the movement, points to the necessity of insurrection, and advances the slogans of a revolutionary-democratic dictatorship and a provisional revolutionary government. Neither side should exaggerate, they say; extremes are bad in both cases (and, generally speaking, everywhere in the world), etc., etc.

The cheap truism of the pedestrian (and "political" in quotation marks) wisdom undoubtedly contained in such arguments too often conceals an inability to understand the urgent and acute needs of the Party. Take the present-day tactical differences among Russian Social-Democrats. Of course, the special emphasis on the everyday, routine aspect of the work, such as we see in the new-*Iskra* arguments about tactics, could not of itself present any danger or give rise to any divergence of opinion regarding tactical slogans. But it is sufficient to compare the resolutions of the Third Congress of the Russian Social-Democratic Labour Party with the Conference resolutions for this divergence to become striking.

What, then, is the trouble? In the first place, it is not enough to speak in the abstract of two currents in the movement, and of the harmfulness of extremes. One must know concretely what ails a given movement at a given time, and what constitutes the real political danger to the Party at the present time. Secondly, one must know what real political forces profit by the tactical slogans advanced—or perhaps by the absence of certain slogans. If one were to listen to the new-Iskrists one would arrive at the conclusion that the Social-Democratic Party is threatened with the danger of throwing overboard propaganda and agitation, the economic struggle, and criticism of bourgeois democracy, the danger of becoming inordinately absorbed in military preparations, armed attacks, the seizure of power, etc. Actually, however, real danger is threatening the Party from an entirely different quarter. Anyone who is at all familiar with the state of the movement, anyone who follows it carefully and thoughtfully, cannot fail to see the ridiculous aspect of the new-Iskrists' fears. The entire work of the Russian Social-Democratic Labour Party has already taken definite and unvarying shape, which absolutely guarantees that our main attention will be fixed on propaganda and agitation, extemporaneous and mass meetings, the distribution of leaflets and pamphlets, assisting in the economic struggle and championing the slogans of that struggle. There is not a single Party committee, not a single district committee, not a single central delegates' meeting or a single factory group where ninety-nine per cent of all the attention, energy, and time is not always and invariably devoted to these functions, which have become firmly established ever since the middle of the nineties. Only those who are entirely unfamiliar with the movement do not know that. Only very naïve or ill-informed people will accept new *Iskra*'s repetition of stale truths at their face value, when that is done with an air of great importance.

The fact is that, far from displaying excessive zeal with regard to the tasks of insurrection, to general political slogans and to giving leadership to the entire popular revolution, we, on the contrary, display a most striking *backwardness* in this very respect, a backwardness which constitutes our greatest weakness and is a real danger to the movement, which may degenerate, and in some places is degenerating, from one that is revolutionary in deed into one that is revolutionary in word. Among the many, many hundreds of organisations, groups, and circles that are conducting the work of the Party you will not find one which has not, since its very inception, conducted the kind of day-by-day work the new-*Iskra* wiseacres now talk of with the air of people who have discovered new truths. On the other hand, you will find only an insignificant percentage of groups and circles that have understood the tasks an insurrection entails, have begun to carry them out, and have realised the necessity of leading the entire popular revolution against tsarism, the necessity of advancing certain definite progressive slogans and no others, for that purpose.

We have incredibly fallen behind our progressive and genuinely revolutionary tasks; in very many instances we have not even become aware of them; here and there we have failed to notice that revolutionary-bourgeois democracy has gained strength owing to our backwardness in this respect. But, with their backs turned to the course of events and the requirements of the times, the new-*Iskra* writers keep insistently repeating: "Don't forget the old! Don't let yourselves be carried away by the new!" This is the unvarying *leit-motiv* in all the important resolutions of the Conference; whereas in the Congress resolutions you just as unvaryingly read: while confirming the old (but not stopping to masticate it over and over again precisely because it *is* old and has already been settled and recorded in literature, in resolutions and by experience), we bring forward a new task, draw attention to it, issue a new slogan, and demand that genuinely revolutionary Social-Democrats immediately set to work to put it into effect.

That is how matters really stand with regard to the question of the two trends in Social-Democratic tactics. The revolutionary period has presented new tasks, which only the totally blind can fail to see. Some Social-Democrats unhesitatingly recognise these tasks and place them on the order of the day, declaring: the armed uprising brooks no delay; prepare yourselves for it immediately and energetically; remember that it is indispensable for a decisive victory; bring forward slogans for a republic, for a provisional government, for a revolutionary-democratic dictatorship of the proletariat and the peasantry. Other Social-Democrats, however, draw back, mark time, write prefaces instead of giving slogans; instead of seeing what is new, while confirming what is old, they masticate the latter tediously and at great length, inventing pretexts to avoid the new, unable to determine the conditions for a decisive victory or to bring forward slogans which alone are in line with a striving to achieve full victory.

* * *

In its social and economic essence, the democratic revolution in Russia is a bourgeois revolution. It is, however, not enough merely to repeat this correct Marxist proposition. It has to be properly understood and properly applied to political slogans. In general, all political liberty founded on present-day, i.e., capitalist, relations of production is bourgeois liberty. The demand for liberty expresses primarily the interests of the bourgeoisie. Its representatives were the first to raise this demand. Its supporters have everywhere used like masters the liberty they acquired, reducing it to moderate and meticulous bourgeois doses, combining it with the most subtle suppression of the revolutionary proletariat in peaceful times, and with savage suppression in times of storm.

But only rebel Narodniks, anarchists, and Economists could conclude therefrom that the struggle for liberty should be negated or disparaged. These intellectualist-philistine doctrines could be foisted on the proletariat only for a time and against its will. The proletariat has always realised instinctively that it needs political liberty, needs it more than anyone else, although the immediate effect of that liberty will be to strengthen and organise the bourgeoisie. It is not by evading the class struggle that the proletariat expects to find its salvation, but by developing it, by extending its scope, its consciousness, organisation, and resoluteness. Whoever disparages the tasks of the political struggle transforms the Social-Democrat from a tribune of the people into a trade union secretary. Whoever disparages the proletarian tasks in a democratic bourgeois revolution transforms the Social-Democrat from a leader of the people's revolution into a leader of a free labour union.

Yes, the *people*'s revolution. Social-Democacy has fought, and is quite rightly fighting, against the bourgeois-democratic abuse of the word "people." It demands that this word shall not be used to cover up failure to understand class antagonisms within the people. It insists categorically on the need for complete class independence for the party of the proletariat. However, it does not divide the "people" into "classes" so that the advanced class will become locked up within itself, will confine itself within narrow limits, and emasculate its activity for fear that the economic rulers of the world will recoil; it does that so that the advanced class, which does not suffer from the halfheartedness, vacillation, and indecision of the intermediate classes, should fight with all the greater energy and enthusiasm for the cause of the whole people, at the head of the whole people.

That is what the present-day new-Iskrists so often fail to understand, people who substitute for active political slogans in the democratic revolution a mere pedantic repetition of the word "class," declined in all cases and genders!

The democratic revolution is bourgeois in nature. The slogan of a general redistribution, or "land and freedom"—that most widespread slogan of the peasant masses, downtrodden and ignorant, yet passionately yearning for light and happiness—is a bourgeois slogan. But we Marxists should know that there is not, nor can there be, any other path to real freedom for the proletariat and the peasantry, than the path of bourgeois freedom and bourgeois progress. We must not forget that there is not, nor can there be at the present time, any other means of bringing socialism nearer, than complete political liberty, than a democratic republic, than the revolutionary-democratic dictatorship of the proletariat and the peasantry. As representatives of the advanced and only revolutionary class, revolutionary without any reservations, doubts, or looking back, we must confront the whole of the people with the tasks of the democratic revolution as extensively and boldly as possible and with the utmost initiative. To disparage these tasks means making a travesty of theoretical Marxism, distorting it in philistine fashion, while in practical politics it means placing the cause of the revolution into the hands of the bourgeoisie, which will inevitably recoil from the task of consistently effecting the revolution. The difficulties that lie on the road to complete victory of the revolution are very great. No one will be able to blame the proletariat's representatives if, when they have done everything in their power, their efforts are defeated by the resistance of reaction, the treachery of the bourgeoisie, and the ignorance of the masses. But everybody, and, above all, the class-conscious proletariat, will condemn Social-Democracy if it curtails the revolutionary energy of the democratic revolution and dampens revolutionary ardour because it is afraid to win, because it is actuated by the consideration: lest the bourgeoisie recoil.

Revolutions are the locomotives of history, said Marx. Revolutions are festivals of the oppressed and the exploited. At no other time are the mass of the people in a position to come forward so actively as creators of a new social order, as at a time of revolution. At such times the people are capable of performing miracles, if judged by the limited, philistine yardstick of gradualist progress. But it is essential that leaders of the revolutionary parties, too, should advance their aims more comprehensively and boldly at such a time, so that their slogans shall always be in advance of the revolutionary initiative of the masses, serve as a beacon, reveal to them our democratic and socialist ideal in all its magnitude and splendour, and show them the shortest and most direct route to complete, absolute, and decisive victory. Let us leave to the opportunists of the *Osvobozhdeniye* bourgeoisie the task of inventing roundabout, circuitous paths of compromise, out of fear of the revolution and of the direct path. If we are forcibly compelled to drag ourselves along such paths we shall be able to fulfill our duty in petty, everyday work also. But first let the choice of path be decided in ruthless struggle. We shall be traitors, betrayers of the revolution, if we do not use this festive energy of the masses and their revolutionary ardour to wage a ruthless and self-sacrificing struggle for the direct and decisive path. Let the bourgeois opportunists contemplate the future reaction with craven fear. The workers will not be intimidated either by the thought that reaction intends to be terrible, or that the bourgeoisie proposes to recoil. The workers do not expect to make deals; they are not asking for petty concessions. What they are striving towards is ruthlessly to crush the reactionary forces, i.e., to set up a *revolutionary-democratic dictatorship of the proletariat and the peasantry*.

Of course, in stormy times greater dangers threaten the ship of our Party than in periods of the smooth "sailing" of liberal progress, which means the painfully steady sucking of the working class's life-blood by its exploiters. Of course, the tasks of the revolutionary-democratic dictatorship are infinitely more difficult and more complex than the tasks of an "extreme opposition," or of an exclusively parliamentary struggle. But whoever is consciously capable of preferring smooth sailing and the course of safe "opposition" in the present revolutionary situation had better abandon Social-Democratic work for a while, had better wait until the revolution is over, until the festive days have passed, when humdrum, everyday life starts again, and his narrow routine standards no longer strike such an abominably discordant note, or constitute such an ugly distortion of the tasks of the advanced class.

At the head of the whole people, and particularly of the peasantry—for complete freedom, for a consistent democratic revolution, for a republic! At the head of all the toilers and the exploited —for socialism! Such in practice must be the policy of the revolutionary proletariat, such is the class slogan which must permeate and determine the solution of every tactical problem, every practical step of the workers' party during the revolution.

Epilogue

* * *

The Vulgar Bourgeois and the Marxist Views on Dictatorship

In his notes to Marx's articles from the *Neue Rheinische Zeitung* of 1848, which he published, Mehring tells us that one of the reproaches levelled at this newspaper by bourgeois publications was that it had allegedly demanded "the immediate introduction of a dictatorship as the sole means of achieving democracy" (Marx, *Nachlass*, Vol. III, p. 53). From the vulgar bourgeois standpoint the terms dictatorship and democracy are mutually exclusive. Failing to understand the theory of class struggle and accustomed to seeing in the political arena the petty squabbling of the various bourgeois circles and coteries, the bourgeois understands by dictatorship the annulment of all liberties and guarantees of democracy, arbitrariness of every kind, and every sort of abuse of power in a dictator's personal interests. In fact, it is precisely this vulgar bourgeois view that is manifested in the writings of our Martynov, who winds up his "new campaign" in the new *Iskra* by attributing the partiality of *Vperyod* and *Proletary* for the slogan of dictatorship to Lenin's "passionate desire to try his luck" (*Iskra*, No. 103, p. 3, col. 2). This charming explanation is wholly on a level with the bourgeois charges against the *Neue Rheinische Zeitung* and against the preaching of dictatorship. Thus Marx too was accused (by bourgeois liberals, not Social-Democrats) of "supplanting" the concepts of revolution and dictatorship. In order to explain to Martynov the meaning of the term class dictatorship, as distinct from personal dictatorship, and the tasks of a democratic dictatorship, as distinct from those of a socialist dictatorship, it would not be amiss to dwell on the views of the *Neue Rheinische Zeitung*.

"After a revolution," wrote the *Neue Rheinische Zeitung* on September 14, 1848,

> every provisional organisation of the state requires a dictatorship and an energetic dictatorship at that. From the very beginning we have reproached Camphausen [the head of the Ministry after March 18, 1848] for not acting dictatorially, for not having immediately smashed up and eliminated the remnants of the old institutions. And while Herr Camphausen was lulling himself with constitutional illusions the defeated party (i.e., the party of reaction) strengthened its positions in the bureaucracy and in the army, and here and there even began to venture upon open struggle.

These words, Mehring justly remarks, sum up in a few propositions all that was propounded in detail in the *Neue Rheinische Zeitung* in long articles on the Camphausen Ministry. What do these words of Marx tell us? That a provisional revolutionary government *must* act dictatorially (a proposition which *Iskra* was totally unable to grasp since it was fighting shy of the slogan of dictatorship), and that the task of such a dictatorship is to destroy the remnants of the old institutions (which is precisely what was clearly stated in the resolution of the Third Congress of the Russian Social-Democratic Labour Party on the struggle against counter-revolution and was omitted in the resolution of the Conference, as shown above). Thirdly, and lastly, it follows from these words that Marx castigated the bourgeois democrats for entertaining "constitutional illusions" in a period of revolution and open civil war. The meaning of these words becomes particularly obvious from the article in the *Neue Rheinische Zeitung* of June 6, 1848. "A constituent national assembly," Marx wrote,

> must first of all be an active, revolutionary-active assembly. The Frankfort Assembly, however, is busying itself with school exercises in parliamentarism while allowing the government to act. Let us assume that this learned assembly succeeds, after mature consideration, in evolving the best possible agenda and the best constitution, but what is the use of the best possible agenda and of the best possible constitution, if the German governments have in the meantime placed the bayonet on the agenda?

That is the meaning of the slogan: dictatorship. We can judge from this what Marx's attitude would have been towards resolutions which call a "decision to organise a constituent assembly" a decisive victory, or which invite us to "remain the party of extreme revolutionary opposition"!

Major questions in the life of nations are settled only by force. The reactionary classes themselves are usually the first to resort to violence, to civil war; they are the first to "place the bayonet on the agenda," as the Russian autocracy has systematically and unswervingly been doing everywhere ever since January 9. And since such a situation has arisen, since the bayonet has really become the main point on the political agenda, since insurrection has proved imperative and urgent—constitutional illusions and school exercises in parliamentarism become merely a screen for the bourgeois betrayal of the revolution, a screen to conceal the fact that the bourgeoisie is "recoiling" from the revolution. It is precisely the slogan of dictatorship that the genuinely revolutionary class must advance in that case.

On the question of the tasks of this dictatorship Marx wrote in the *Neue Rheinische Zeitung*: "The National Assembly should have acted dictatorially against the reactionary attempts of the obsolete governments, and thus gained for itself the power of public opinion against which all bayonets and rifle butts would have been shattered. . . . But this Assembly bores the German people instead of carrying them with it or being carried away by them." In Marx's opinion, the National Assembly should have "eliminated from the regime actually existing in Germany everything that contradicted the principle of the sovereignty of the people," and then it should have "consolidated the revolutionary ground on which it stands in order to make the sovereignty of the people, won by the revolution, secure against all attacks."

Consequently, in their content, the tasks which Marx set a revolutionary government or dictatorship in 1848 amounted first and foremost to a *democratic* revolution: defence against counter-revolution and the actual elimination of everything that contradicted the sovereignty of the people. That is nothing else than a revolutionary-democratic dictatorship.

To proceed: which classes, in Marx's opinion, could and should have achieved this task (to fully exercise in deed the principle of the people's sovereignty and beat off the attacks of the counter-revolution)? Marx speaks of the "people." But we know that he always fought ruthlessly against petty-bourgeois illusions about the unity of the "people" and the absence of a class struggle within the people. In using the word "people" Marx did not thereby gloss over class distinctions, but united definite elements capable of bringing the revolution to completion.

After the victory of the Berlin proletariat on March 18, the *Neue Rheinische Zeitung* wrote, the results of the revolution proved twofold:

> On the one hand, the arming of the people, the right of association, the actual achievement of the sovereignty of the people; on the other hand, the retention of the monarchy and the Camphausen-Hansemann Ministry, i.e., the government of representatives of the big bourgeoisie. Thus, the revolution had two series of results, which had inevitably to diverge. The people had achieved victory; they had won liberties of a decisively democratic nature, but immediate power did not pass into their hands, but into the hands of the big bourgeoisie. In short, the revolution was not consummated. The people let representatives of the big bourgeoisie form a ministry, and these representatives of the big bourgeoisie at once showed what they were after by offering an alliance to the old Prussian nobility and bureaucracy. Arnim, Canitz, and Schwerin joined the ministry.
> *The upper bourgeoisie, ever anti-revolutionary, concluded a*

defensive and offensive alliance with the reactionaries for fear of the people, that is to say, the workers and the democratic bourgeoisie. [Italics ours.]

Thus, not only a "decision to organise a constituent assembly," but even its actual convocation is insufficient for a decisive victory of the revolution! Even after a partial victory in an armed struggle (the victory of the Berlin workers over the troops on March 18, 1848) an "incomplete" revolution, a revolution "that has not been carried to completion," is possible. On what, then, does its completion depend? It depends on whose hands immediate power passes into, into the hands of the Petrunkeviches and Rodichevs, that is to say, the Camphausens and the Hansemanns, or into the hands of the *people,* i.e., the workers and the democratic bourgeoisie. In the first instance, the bourgeoisie will possess power, and the proletariat —"freedom of criticism," freedom to "remain the party of extreme revolutionary opposition." Immediately after the victory the bourgeoisie will conclude an alliance with the reactionaries (this would inevitably happen in Russia too, if, for example, the St. Petersburg workers gained only a partial victory in street fighting with the troops and left it to Messrs. Petrunkeviches and Co. to form a government). In the second instance, a revolutionary-democratic dictatorship, i.e., the complete victory of the revolution, would be possible.

It now remains to define more precisely what Marx really meant by "democratic bourgeoisie" (*demokratische Bürgerschaft*), which, together with the workers, he called the people, in contradistinction to the big bourgeoisie.

A clear answer to this question is supplied by the following passage from an article in the *Neue Rheinische Zeitung* of July 29, 1848:

. . . The German Revolution of 1848 is only a parody of the French Revolution of 1789.

On August 4, 1789, three weeks after the storming of the Bastille, the French people in a single day prevailed over all feudal burdens.

On July 11, 1848, four months after the March barricades, the feudal burdens prevailed over the German people. *Teste Gierke cum Hansemanno.*[4]

---

4. "Witnesses: Herr Gierke together with Herr Hansemann." Hansemann was a minister who represented the party of the big bourgeoisie (Russian counterpart: Trubetskoi or Rodichev, and the like); Gierke was Minister of Agriculture in the Hansemann Cabinet, who drew up a plan, a "bold" plan for "abolishing feudal burdens," professedly "without compensation," but in fact for abolishing only the minor and unimportant burdens, while preserving or granting compensation for the more essential ones. Herr Gierke was something like the Russian Kablukovs, Manuilovs, Hertzensteins, and similar bourgeois liberal friends of the *muzhik,* who desire the "extension of peasant landownership" but do not wish to offend the landlords. [*Lenin*]

The French bourgeoisie of 1789 did not for a moment leave its allies, the peasants, in the lurch. It knew that its rule was grounded in the destruction of feudalism in the countryside, the creation of a free landowning [*grundbesitzenden*] peasant class.

The German bourgeoisie of 1848 is, without the least compunction, betraying the peasants, who are its most natural allies, the flesh of its flesh, and without whom it is powerless against the aristocracy.

The continuance of feudal rights, their sanction under the guise of (illusory) redemption—such is the result of the German revolution of 1848. The mountain brought forth a mouse.

This is a very instructive passage, which provides us with four important propositions: 1) The uncompleted German revolution differs from the completed French revolution in that the German bourgeoisie betrayed not only democracy in general, but also the peasantry in particular. 2) The creation of a free class of peasants is the foundation for the consummation of a democratic revolution. 3) The creation of such a class means the abolition of feudal services, the destruction of feudalism, but does not yet mean a socialist revolution. 4) The peasants are the "most natural" allies of the bourgeoisie, that is to say, of the democratic bourgeoisie, which without them is "powerless" against reaction.

With the proper allowances for concrete national peculiarities and with serfdom substituted for feudalism, all these propositions are fully applicable to the Russia of 1905. There is no doubt that by learning from the experience of Germany as elucidated by Marx, we can arrive at no other slogan for a decisive victory of the revolution than: a revolutionary-democratic dictatorship of the proletariat and the peasantry. There is no doubt that the proletariat and the peasantry are the chief components of the "people" as contrasted by Marx in 1848 to the resisting reactionaries and the treacherous bourgeoisie. There is no doubt that in Russia, too, the liberal bourgeoisie and the gentlemen of the *Osvobozhdeniye* League are betraying and will betray the peasantry, i.e., will confine themselves to a pseudo-reform and take the side of the landlords in the decisive battle between them and the peasantry. In this struggle only the proletariat is capable of supporting the peasantry to the end. There is no doubt, finally, that in Russia, too, the success of the peasants' struggle, i.e., the transfer of the whole of the land to the peasantry, will signify a complete democratic revolution, and constitute the social basis of the revolution carried through to its completion, but this will by no means be a socialist revolution, or the "socialisation" that the ideologists of the petty bourgeoisie, the Socialist-Revolutionaries, talk about. The success of the peasant insurrection, the victory of the democratic revolution will merely clear the way for a genuine and decisive struggle for socialism, on the basis of a democratic republic. In this struggle the peasantry, as a landowning class, will play the same treacherous, unstable part as is now being played by the bourgeoisie in the struggle for democracy. To forget this is to forget socialism, to deceive oneself and others regarding the real interests and tasks of the proletariat.

* * *

The Party Organisation
and Party Literature

This article of November 1905, in which Lenin responded to incipient
Russian press freedom with a demand that literature written under the
party's auspices be "party literature," may be seen as a portent of party
control of the press in Bolshevik-ruled Russia. Although it seems clear from
the article that Lenin was speaking primarily of *political* writings, and although some Soviet intellectuals made this point in their efforts to emancipate cultural life from censorship during the later nineteen-fifties and early
nineteen-sixties, official opinion has, on the basis of this article, claimed
Leninist authority for the established practice of party control and censorship of all cultural expression in Soviet Russia.

The new conditions for Social-Democratic work in Russia which
have arisen since the October revolution have brought the question
of Party literature to the fore. The distinction between the illegal
and the legal press, that melancholy heritage of the epoch of feudal,
autocratic Russia, is beginning to disappear. It is not yet dead, by a
long way. * * *

So long as there was a distinction between the illegal and the
legal press, the question of the Party and non-Party press was
decided extremely simply and in an extremely false and abnormal
way. The entire illegal press was a Party press, being published by
organisations and run by groups which in one way or another were
linked with groups of practical Party workers. The entire legal press
was non-Party—since parties were banned—but it "gravitated" towards one party or another. Unnatural alliances, strange "bed-
fellows" and false cover-devices were inevitable. The forced reserve
of those who wished to express Party views merged with the immature thinking or mental cowardice of those who had not risen to
these views and who were not, in effect, Party people.

An accursed period of Aesopian language,[1] literary bondage,

1. See Introduction, p. xxxiv, above.[*R. T.*]

148

slavish speech, and ideological serfdom! The proletariat has put an end to this foul atmosphere which stifled everything living and fresh in Russia. But so far the proletariat has won only half freedom for Russia.

* * *

* * * The half-way revolution compels all of us to set to work at once organising the whole thing on new lines. Today literature, even that published "legally," can be nine-tenths Party literature. It must become Party literature. In contradistinction to bourgeois customs, to the profit-making, commercialised bourgeois press, to bourgeois literary careerism and individualism, "aristocratic anarchism" and drive for profit, the socialist proletariat must put forward the principle of *Party literature*, must develop this principle and put it into practice as fully and completely as possible.

What is this principle of Party literature? It is not simply that, for the socialist proletariat, literature cannot be a means of enriching individuals or groups: it cannot, in fact, be an individual undertaking, independent of the common cause of the proletariat. Down with non-partisan writers! Down with literary supermen! Literature must become *part* of the common cause of the proletariat, "a cog and a screw" of one single great Social-Democratic mechanism set in motion by the entire politically-conscious vanguard of the entire working class. Literature must become a component of organised, planned and integrated Social-Democratic Party work.

"All comparisons are lame," says a German proverb. So is my comparison of literature with a cog, of a living movement with a mechanism. And I daresay there will ever be hysterical intellectuals to raise a howl about such a comparison, which degrades, deadens, "bureaucratises" the free battle of ideas, freedom of criticism, freedom of literary creation, etc., etc. Such outcries, in point of fact, would be nothing more than an expression of bourgeois-intellectual individualism. There is no question that literature is least of all subject to mechanical adjustment or levelling, to the rule of the majority over the minority. There is no question, either, that in this field greater scope must undoubtedly be allowed for personal initiative, individual inclination, thought and fantasy, form and content. All this is undeniable; but all this simply shows that the literary side of the proletarian party cause cannot be mechanically identified with its other sides. This, however, does not in the least refute the proposition, alien and strange to the bourgeoisie and bourgeois democracy, that literature must by all means and necessarily become an element of Social-Democratic Party work, inseparably bound up with the other elements. Newspapers must become the organs of the various Party organisations, and their writers must by all means become members of these organisations. Publishing and distributing centres, bookshops and reading-rooms, libraries and similar establishments—must all be under Party control. The organised socialist proletariat must keep an eye on all this work, supervise it in its entirety, and, from beginning to end, without any exception, infuse into it the life-stream of the living proletarian cause, thereby cutting the ground from under the old, semi-Oblomov,[2] semi-shopkeeper Russian principle: the writer does the writing, the reader does the reading.

We are not suggesting, of course, that this transformation of literary work, which has been defiled by the Asiatic censorship and the European bourgeoisie, can be accomplished all at once. Far be it from us to advocate any kind of standardised system, or a solution by means of a few decrees. Cut-and-dried schemes are least of all applicable here. What is needed is that the whole of our Party, and the entire politically-conscious Social-Democratic proletariat throughout Russia, should become aware of this new problem, specify it clearly and everywhere set about solving it. Emerging from the captivity of the feudal censorship, we have no desire to become, and shall not become, prisoners of bourgeois-shopkeeper literary relations. We want to establish, and we shall establish, a free press, free not simply from the police, but also from capital, from careerism, and what is more, free from bourgeois-anarchist individualism.

These last words may sound paradoxical, or an affront to the reader. What! some intellectual, an ardent champion of liberty, may shout. What, you want to impose collective control on such a delicate, individual matter as literary work! You want workmen to decide questions of science, philosophy, or aesthetics by a majority of votes! You deny the absolute freedom of absolutely individual ideological work!

Calm yourselves, gentlemen! First of all, we are discussing Party literature and its subordination to Party control. Everyone is free to write and say whatever he likes, without any restrictions. But every voluntary association (including a party) is also free to expel members who use the name of the party to advocate anti-party views. Freedom of speech and the press must be complete. But then freedom of association must be complete too. I am bound to accord you, in the name of free speech, the full right to shout, lie and write to your heart's content. But you are bound to grant me, in the name of freedom of association, the right to enter into, or withdraw from, association with people advocating this or that view. The Party is a voluntary association, which would inevitably break up,

---

2. The reference is to Goncharov's novel *Oblomov* (1859), whose nobleman hero of that name was a lazy dreamer.

first ideologically and then materially, if it did not purge itself of people advocating anti-Party views. And to define the border-line between Party and anti-Party there is the Party programme, the Party's resolutions on tactics and its rules and, lastly, the entire experience of international Social-Democracy, the voluntary international associations of the proletariat, which has constantly brought into its parties individual elements and trends not fully consistent, not completely Marxist and not altogether correct and which, on the other hand, has constantly conducted periodical "cleansings" of its ranks. So it will be with us too, supporters of bourgeois "freedom of criticism," *within* the Party. We are now becoming a mass party all at once, changing abruptly to an open organisation, and it is inevitable that we shall be joined by many who are inconsistent (from the Marxist standpoint), perhaps we shall be joined even by some Christian elements, and even by some mystics. We have sound stomachs and we are rock-hard Marxists. We shall digest those inconsistent elements. Freedom of thought and freedom of criticism within the Party will never make us forget about the freedom of organising people into those voluntary associations known as parties.

Secondly, we must say to you bourgeois individualists that your talk about absolute freedom is sheer hypocrisy. There can be no real and effective "freedom" in a society based on the power of money, in a society in which the masses of working people live in poverty and the handful of rich live like parasites. Are you free in relation to your bourgeois publisher, Mr. Writer, in relation to your bourgeois public, which demands that you provide it with pornography in frames[3] and paintings, and prostitution as a "supplement" to "sacred" scenic art? This absolute freedom is a bourgeois or an anarchist phrase (since, as a world outlook, anarchism is bourgeois philosophy turned inside out). One cannot live in society and be free from society. The freedom of the bourgeois writer, artist or actress is simply masked (or hypocritically masked) dependence on the money-bag, on corruption, on prostitution.

And we socialists expose this hypocrisy and rip off the false labels, not in order to arrive at a non-class literature and art (that will be possible only in a socialist classless society), but to contrast this hypocritically free literature, which is in reality linked to the bourgeoisie, with a really free one that will be *openly* linked to the proletariat.

It will be a free literature, because the idea of socialism and sympathy with the working people, and not greed or careerism, will bring ever new forces to its ranks. It will be a free literature,

---

3. There must be a misprint in the source, which says *ramkakh* (frames), while the context suggests *romanakh* (novels).

because it will serve, not some satiated heroine, not the bored "upper ten thousand" suffering from fatty degeneration, but the millions and tens of millions of working people—the flower of the country, its strength and its future. It will be a free literature, enriching the last word in the revolutionary thought of mankind with the experience and living work of the socialist proletariat, bringing about permanent interaction between the experience of the past (scientific socialism, the completion of the development of socialism from its primitive, utopian forms) and the experience of the present (the present struggle of the worker comrades).

To work, then, comrades! We are faced with a new and difficult task. But it is a noble and grateful one—to organise a broad, multiform and varied literature inseparably linked with the Social-Democratic working-class movement. All Social-Democratic literature must become Party literature. Every newspaper, journal, publishing house, etc., must immediately set about reorganising its work, leading up to a situation in which it will, in one form or another, be integrated into one Party organisation or another. Only then will "Social-Democratic" literature really become worthy of that name, only then will it be able to fulfil its duty and, even within the framework of bourgeois society, break out of bourgeois slavery and merge with the movement of the really advanced and thoroughly revolutionary class.

The Right of Nations to Self-Determination

The Russian Empire was a multi-national state with a total population of about 170 million in which people of Great Russian nationality numbered somewhat under 75 million. The outlying territories were heavily populated by Slavs of non–Great Russian ethnic stock (Poles, Ukrainians, and Belorussians) and by non-Slavs (Estonians, Latvians, Lithuanians, Finns, Jews, Georgians, Armenians, and Turkic peoples of Russian Central Asia, then known as Turkestan). Given these circumstances, a revolutionary party had to define its tactics in relation not only to classes but also to nationalities. In this treatise, written in the first half of 1914, Lenin championed a tactic of promoting the revolutionary disintegration of empires like the Russian and Austro-Hungarian by party espousal of the right of minority nations to self-determination, i.e., secession and formation of independent nation-states. In the event, the disintegration of the Russian Empire in the aftermath of the World War was held in check by Lenin's party. Although Finland, Poland, and the Baltic countries seceded, the Lenin regime, whose commissar for nationality affairs was Stalin, managed to retain the great bulk of the former Empire for the new Soviet multi-national state, in part by forcibly suppressing national separatism in the Ukraine, Georgia, Armenia, and elsewhere.

* * *

1. What Is Meant by the Self-Determination of Nations?

Naturally, this is the first question that arises when any attempt is made at a Marxist examination of what is known as self-determination. What should be understood by that term? Should the answer be sought in legal definitions deduced from all sorts of "general concepts" of law? Or is it rather to be sought in a historico-economic study of the national movements?

* * *

* * * This is not the first time that national movements have arisen in Russia, nor are they peculiar to that country alone. Throughout the world, the period of the final victory of capitalism over feudalism has been linked up with national movements. For the complete victory of commodity production, the bourgeoisie must capture the home market, and there must be politically united territories whose population speak a single language, with all obstacles to the development of that language and to its consolidation in literature eliminated. Therein is the economic foundation of national movements. Language is the most important means of human intercourse. Unity and unimpeded development of language are the most important conditions for genuinely free and extensive commerce on a scale commensurate with modern capitalism, for a free and broad grouping of the population in all its various classes and, lastly, for the establishment of a close connection between the market and each and every proprietor, big or little, and between seller and buyer.

Therefore, the tendency of every national movement is towards the formation of *national states*, under which these requirements of modern capitalism are best satisfied. The most profound economic factors drive towards this goal, and, therefore, for the whole of Western Europe, nay, for the entire civilised world, the national state is *typical* and normal for the capitalist period.

Consequently, if we want to grasp the meaning of self-determination of nations, not by juggling with legal definitions, or "inventing" abstract definitions, but by examining the historico-economic conditions of the national movements, we must inevitably reach the conclusion that the self-determination of nations means the political separation of these nations from alien national bodies, and the formation of an independent national state.

Later on we shall see still other reasons why it would be wrong to interpret the right to self-determination as meaning anything but the right to existence as a separate state. At present, we must deal with Rosa Luxemburg's efforts to "dismiss" the inescapable conclusion that profound economic factors underlie the urge towards a national state.

Rosa Luxemburg is quite familiar with Kautsky's pamphlet *Nationality and Internationality*. (Supplement to *Die Neue Zeit* No. 1, 1907–8; Russian translation in the journal *Nauchnaya Mysl*, Riga, 1908.) She is aware that, after carefully analysing the question of the national state in § 4 of that pamphlet, Kautsky arrived at the conclusion that Otto Bauer "*underestimates* the strength of the urge towards a national state" (p. 23 of the pamphlet). Rosa Luxemburg herself quotes the following words of Kautsky's: "The national state is the form *most suited* to present-day conditions, [i.e., capitalist, civilised, economically progressive conditions, as distinguished from medieval, pre-capitalist, etc.]; it is the form in which the state can best fulfil its tasks" (i.e., the tasks of securing the freest, widest and speediest development of capitalism). To this we must add Kautsky's still more precise concluding remark that states of mixed national composition (known as multinational states, as distinct from national states) are "always those whose internal constitution has for some reason or other remained abnormal or underdeveloped" (backward). Needless to say, Kautsky speaks of abnormality exclusively in the sense of lack of conformity with what is best adapted to the requirements of a developing capitalism.

The question now is: How did Rosa Luxemburg treat these historico-economic conclusions of Kautsky's? Are they right or wrong? Is Kautsky right in his historico-economic theory, or is Bauer, whose theory is basically psychological? What is the connection between Bauer's undoubted "national opportunism," his defence of cultural-national autonomy,[1] his nationalistic infatuation ("an occasional emphasis on the national aspect," as Kautsky put it), his "enormous exaggeration of the national aspect and complete neglect of the international aspect" (Kautsky)—and his underestimation of the strength of the urge to create a national state?

Rosa Luxemburg has not even raised this question. She has not noticed the connection. She has not considered the *sum total* of Bauer's theoretical views. She has not even drawn a line between the historico-economic and the psychological theories of the national question. She confines herself to the following remarks in criticism of Kautsky: "This 'best' national state is only an abstraction, which can easily be developed and defended theoretically, but which does not correspond to reality" (*Przeglad Socjaldemokratyczny*,[2] 1908, No. 6, p. 499). And in corroboration of this emphatic statement there follow arguments to the effect that the "right to self-determination" of small nations is made illusory by the development of the great capitalist powers and by imperialism. "Can one seriously speak," Rosa Luxemburg exclaims, "about the 'self-determination' of the formally independent Montenegrins, Bulgarians, Rumanians, Serbs, Greeks, partly even the Swiss, whose independence is itself a result of the political struggle and the diplomatic game of the 'concert of Europe'?!" (p. 500). The state that best suits these conditions is "not a national state, as Kautsky believes, but a predatory one." Some dozens of figures are quoted

1. For a discussion of the issue of "cultural-national autonomy" see Robert C. Tucker, *Stalin as Revolutionary, 1879–1929* (New York, 1973), pp. 150–56. [*R. T.*]

2. *Przeglad Socjaldemokratyczny* (*Social-Democratic Review*) was a journal published monthly from 1902 to 1904 and from 1908 to 1910 in Cracow by Polish Social-Democrats, with Rosa Luxemburg's close collaboration.

relating to the size of British, French and other colonial possessions.

After reading such arguments, one cannot help marvelling at the
author's ability to misunderstand *the how and the why of things.*
To teach Kautsky, with a serious mien, that small states are economically dependent on big ones, that a struggle is raging among
the bourgeois states for the predatory suppression of other nations,
and that imperialism and colonies exist—all this is a ridiculous and
puerile attempt to be clever, for none of this has the slightest
bearing on the subject. Not only small states, but even Russia, for
example, is entirely dependent, economically, on the power of the
imperialist finance capital of the "rich" bourgeois countries. Not
only the miniature Balkan states, but even nineteenth-century
America was, economically, a colony of Europe, as Marx pointed
out in *Capital.*[3] Kautsky, like any Marxist, is, of course, well aware
of this, but that has nothing whatever to do with the question of
national movements and the national state.

For the question of the political self-determination of nations
and their independence as states in bourgeois society, Rosa Luxemburg has substituted the question of their economic independence.
This is just as intelligent as if someone, in discussing the program-
matic demand for the supremacy of parliament, i.e., the assembly
of people's representatives, in a bourgeois state, were to expound
the perfectly correct conviction that big capital dominates in a
bourgeois country, whatever the regime in it.

There is no doubt that the greater part of Asia, the most densely
populated continent, consists either of colonies of the "Great Powers," or of states that are extremely dependent and oppressed as
nations. But does this commonly-known circumstance in any way
shake the undoubted fact that in Asia itself the conditions for the
most complete development of commodity production and the
freest, widest and speediest growth of capitalism have been created
only in Japan, i.e., only in an independent national state? The latter
is a bourgeois state, and for that reason has itself begun to oppress
other nations and to enslave colonies. We cannot say whether Asia
will have had time to develop into a system of independent national
states, like Europe, before the collapse of capitalism, but it remains
an undisputed fact that capitalism, having awakened Asia, has called
forth national movements everywhere in that continent, too; that
the tendency of these movements is towards the creation of national states in Asia; that it is such states that ensure the best
conditions for the development of capitalism. The example of Asia
speaks *in favour* of Kautsky and *against* Rosa Luxemburg.

3. See Marx, *Capital*, Vol. I (Moscow, 1958), p. 765.

The example of the Balkan states likewise contradicts her, for anyone can now see that the best conditions for the development of capitalism in the Balkans are created precisely in proportion to the creation of independent national states in that peninsula.

Therefore, Rosa Luxemburg notwithstanding, the example of the whole of progressive and civilised mankind, the example of the Balkans and that of Asia prove that Kautsky's proposition is absolutely correct: the national state is the rule and the "norm" of capitalism; the multinational state represents backwardness, or is an exception. From the standpoint of national relations, the best conditions for the development of capitalism are undoubtedly provided by the national state. This does not mean, of course, that such a state, which is based on bourgeois relations, can eliminate the exploitation and oppression of nations. It only means that Marxists cannot lose sight of the powerful *economic* factors that give rise to the urge to create national states. It means that "self-determination of nations" in the Marxists' Programme *cannot*, from a historico-economic point of view, have any other meaning than political self-determination, state independence, and the formation of a national state.

* * *

2. The Historically Concrete Presentation of the Question

The categorical requirement of Marxist theory in investigating any social question is that it be examined within *definite* historical limits, and, if it refers to a particular country (e.g., the national programme for a given country), that account be taken of the specific features distinguishing that country from others in the same historical epoch.

What does this categorical requirement of Marxism imply in its application to the question under discussion?

First of all, it implies that a clear distinction must be drawn between the two periods of capitalism, which differ radically from each other as far as the national movement is concerned. On the one hand, there is the period of the collapse of feudalism and absolutism, the period of the formation of the bourgeois-democratic society and state, when the national movements for the first time become mass movements and in one way or another draw *all* classes of the population into politics through the press, participation in representative institutions, etc. On the other hand, there is the period of fully formed capitalist states with a long-established constitutional regime and a highly developed antagonism between the proletariat and the bourgeoisie—a period that may be called the eve of capitalism's downfall.

The typical features of the first period are: the awakening of national movements and the drawing of the peasants, the most numerous and the most sluggish section of the population, into these movements, in connection with the struggle for political liberty in general, and for the rights of the nation in particular. Typical features of the second period are: the absence of mass bourgeois-democratic movements and the fact that developed capitalism, in bringing closer together nations that have already been fully drawn into commercial intercourse, and causing them to intermingle to an increasing degree, brings the antagonism between internationally united capital and the international working-class movement into the forefront.

Of course, the two periods are not walled off from each other; they are connected by numerous transitional links, the various countries differing from each other in the rapidity of their national development, in the national make-up and distribution of their population, and so on. There can be no question of the Marxists of any country drawing up their national programme without taking into account all these general historical and concrete state conditions.

It is here that we come up against the weakest point in Rosa Luxemburg's arguments. With extraordinary zeal, she embellishes her article with a collection of hard words directed against § 9 of our Programme, which she declares to be "sweeping," "a platitude," "a metaphysical phrase," and so on without end. It would be natural to expect an author who so admirably condemns metaphysics (in the Marxist sense, i.e., anti-dialectics) and empty abstractions to set us an example of how to make a concrete historical analysis of the question. The question at issue is the national programme of the Marxists of a definite country—Russia, in a definite period— the beginning of the twentieth century. But does Rosa Luxemburg raise the question as to *what historical* period Russia is passing through, or *what are the concrete* features of the national question and the national movements of that *particular* country in that *particular* period?

No, she does not! *She says absolutely nothing about it*! In her work you will not find even the shadow of an analysis of how the national question stands in *Russia* in the present historical period, or of the specific features of *Russia* in this particular respect!

We are told that the national question in the Balkans is presented differently from that in Ireland; that Marx appraised the Polish and Czech national movements in the concrete conditions of 1848 in such and such a way (a page of excerpts from Marx); that Engels appraised the struggle of the forest cantons of Switzerland against Austria and the Battle of Morgarten which took place in 1315 in such and such a way (a page of quotations from Engels with the appropriate comments from Kautsky); that Lassalle regarded the peasant war in Germany of the sixteenth century as reactionary, etc.

It cannot be said that these remarks and quotations have any novelty about them, but at all events it is interesting for the reader to be occasionally reminded just how Marx, Engels and Lassalle approached the analysis of concrete historical problems in individual countries. And a perusal of these instructive quotations from Marx and Engels reveals most strikingly the ridiculous position Rosa Luxemburg has placed herself in. She preaches eloquently and angrily the need for a concrete historical analysis of the national question in different countries at different times, but she *does not make the least* attempt to determine *what* historical stage in the development of capitalism *Russia* is passing through at the beginning of the twentieth century, or what the *specific features* of the national question in this country are. Rosa Luxemburg gives examples of how *others* have treated the question in a Marxist fashion, as if deliberately stressing how often the road to hell is paved with good intentions and how often good counsel covers up unwillingness or inability to follow such advice in practice.

Here is one of her edifying comparisons. In protesting against the demand for the independence of Poland, Rosa Luxemburg refers to a pamphlet she wrote in 1898, proving the rapid "industrial development of Poland," with the latter's manufactured goods being marketed in Russia. Needless to say, no conclusion whatever can be drawn from this on the question of the *right* to self-determination; it only proves the disappearance of the old Poland of the landed gentry, etc. But Rosa Luxemburg always passes on imperceptibly to the conclusion that among the factors that unite Russia and Poland, the purely economic factors of modern capitalist relations now predominate.

Then our Rosa proceeds to the question of autonomy, and though her article is entitled "The National Question and Autonomy" *in general*, she begins to argue that the Kingdom of Poland has an *exclusive* right to autonomy (see *Prosveshchenie*, 1913, No. 12). To support Poland's right to autonomy, Rosa Luxemburg evidently judges the state system of Russia by her economic, political and sociological characteristics and everyday life—a totality of features which, taken together, produce the concept of "Asiatic despotism" (*Przeglad*, No. 12, p. 137).

It is generally known that this kind of state system possesses great stability whenever completely patriarchal and pre-capitalist features predominate in the economic system and where commodity production and class differentiation are scarcely developed. However, if in a country whose state system is distinctly *pre*-capitalist in character there exists a nationally demarcated region where capitalism is *rapidly* developing, then the more rapidly that capitalism develops, the greater will be the antagonism between it and the *pre*-capitalist state system, and the more likely will be the separation of the progressive region from the whole—with which it is connected, not by "modern capitalistic," but by "Asiatically despotic" ties.

Thus, Rosa Luxemburg does not get her arguments to hang together even on the question of the social structure of the government in Russia with regard to bourgeois Poland; as for the concrete, historical, specific features of the national movements in Russia—she does not even raise that question.

That is a point we must now deal with.

3. The Concrete Features of the National Question in Russia, and Russia's Bourgeois-Democratic Reformation

"Despite the elasticity of the principle of 'the right of nations to self-determination,' which is a mere platitude, and, obviously, equally applicable, not only to the nations inhabiting Russia, but also to the nations inhabiting Germany and Austria, Switzerland and Sweden, America and Australia, we do not find it in the programmes of any of the present-day socialist parties . . ." (*Przeglad*, No. 6, p. 483). This is how Rosa Luxemburg opens her attack upon § 9 of the Marxist programme. In trying to foist on us the conception that this clause in the programme is a "mere platitude," Rosa Luxemburg herself falls victim to this error, alleging with amusing boldness that this point is, "obviously, equally applicable" to Russia, Germany, etc.

Obviously, we shall reply, Rosa Luxemburg has decided to make her article a collection of errors in logic that could be used for schoolboy exercises. For Rosa Luxemburg's tirade is sheer nonsense and a mockery of the historically concrete presentation of the question.

If one interprets the Marxist programme in Marxist fashion, not in a childish way, one will without difficulty grasp the fact that it refers to bourgeois-democratic national movements. That being the case, it is "obvious" that this programme "sweepingly," and as a "mere platitude," etc., covers *all* instances of bourgeois-democratic national movements. No less obvious to Rosa Luxemburg, if she

gave the slightest thought to it, is the conclusion that our programme refers *only* to cases where such a movement is actually in
existence.

Had she given thought to these obvious considerations, Rosa
Luxemburg would have easily perceived what nonsense she was
talking. In accusing *us* of uttering a "platitude" she has used *against*
us the argument that no mention is made of the right to self-
determination in the programmes of countries where there are *no*
bourgeois-democratic national movements. A remarkably clever
argument!

A comparison of the political and economic development of
various countries, as well as of their Marxist programmes, is of
tremendous importance from the standpoint of Marxism, for there
can be no doubt that all modern states are of a common capitalist
nature and are therefore subject to a common law of development.
But such a comparison must be drawn in a sensible way. The
elementary condition for comparison is to find out whether the
historical periods of development of the countries concerned are at
all *comparable*. For instance, only absolute ignoramuses (such as
Prince Y. Trubetskoi in *Russkaya Mysl*[4]) are capable of "comparing" the Russian Marxists' agrarian programme with the programmes of Western Europe, since our programme replies to questions that concern the *bourgeois-democratic* agrarian reform,
whereas in the Western countries no such question arises.

The same applies to the national question. In most Western
countries it was settled long ago. It is ridiculous to seek an answer
to non-existent questions in the programmes of Western Europe. In
this respect Rosa Luxemburg has lost sight of the most important
thing—the difference between countries where bourgeois-democratic reforms have long been completed, and those where they
have not.

The crux of the matter lies in this difference. Rosa Luxemburg's
complete disregard of it transforms her verbose article into a collection of empty and meaningless platitudes.

The epoch of bourgeois-democratic revolutions in Western, continental Europe embraces a fairly definite period, approximately
between 1789 and 1871. This was precisely the period of national
movements and the creation of national states. When this period
drew to a close, Western Europe had been transformed into a
settled system of bourgeois states, which, as a general rule, were
nationally uniform states. Therefore, to seek the right to self-determination in the programmes of West-European socialists at this
time of day is to betray one's ignorance of the ABC of Marxism.

4. *Russkaya Mysl* (*Russian Thought*) was a liberal monthly published in Moscow
from 1880.

In Eastern Europe and Asia the period of bourgeois-democratic revolutions did not begin until 1905. The revolutions in Russia, Persia, Turkey and China, the Balkan wars—such is the chain of world events of *our* period in our "Orient." And only a blind man could fail to see in this chain of events the awakening of a *whole series* of bourgeois-democratic national movements which strive to create nationally independent and nationally uniform states. It is precisely and solely because Russia and the neighbouring countries are passing through this period that we must have a clause in our programme on the right of nations to self-determination.

But let us continue the quotation from Rosa Luxemburg's article a little more. She writes: "In particular, the programme of a party which is operating in a state with an extremely varied national composition, and for which the national question is a matter of first-rate importance—the programme of the Austrian Social-Democratic Party—does not contain the principle of the right of nations to self-determination" (*ibid.*). Thus, an attempt is made to convince the reader by the example of Austria "in particular." Let us examine this example in the light of concrete historical facts and see just how sound it is.

In the first place, let us pose the fundamental question of the completion of the bourgeois-democratic revolution. In Austria, this revolution began in 1848 and was over in 1867. Since then, a more or less fully established bourgeois constitution has dominated for nearly half a century, and on its basis a legal workers' party is legally functioning.

Therefore, in the internal conditions of Austria's development (i.e., from the standpoint of the development of capitalism in Austria in general, and among its various nations in particular), there are *no* factors that produce leaps and bounds, a concomitant of which might be the formation of nationally independent states. In assuming, by her comparison, that Russia is in an analogous position in this respect, Rosa Luxemburg not only makes a fundamentally erroneous and anti-historical assumption, but also involuntarily slips into liquidationism.

Secondly, the profound difference in the relations between the nationalities in Austria and those in Russia is particularly important for the question we are concerned with. Not only was Austria for a long time a state in which the Germans preponderated, but the Austrian Germans laid claim to hegemony in the German nation as a whole. This "claim," as Rosa Luxemburg (who is seemingly so averse to commonplaces, platitudes, abstractions . . .) will perhaps be kind enough to remember, was shattered in the war of 1866. The German nation predominating in Austria found itself *outside the pale* of the independent German state which finally took shape in 1871. On the other hand, the Hungarians' attempt to create an independent national state collapsed under the blows of the Russian serf army as far back as 1849.

A very peculiar situation was thus created—a striving on the part of the Hungarians and then of the Czechs, not for separation from Austria, but, on the contrary, for the preservation of Austria's integrity, precisely in order to preserve national independence, which might have been completely crushed by more rapacious and powerful neighbours! Owing to this peculiar situation, Austria assumed the form of a dual state, and she is now being transformed into a triple state (Germans, Hungarians, Slavs).

Is there anything like this in Russia? Is there in our country a striving of the "subject peoples" for unity with the Great Russians in face of the danger of *worse* national oppression?

One need only pose this question in order to see that the comparison between Russia and Austria on the question of self-determination of nations is meaningless, platitudinous and ignorant.

The peculiar conditions in Russia with regard to the national question are just the reverse of those we see in Austria. Russia is a state with a single national centre—Great Russia. The Great Russians occupy a vast, unbroken stretch of territory, and number about seventy million. The specific features of this national state are: first, that "subject peoples" (which, on the whole, comprise the majority of the entire population—57 per cent) inhabit the border regions; secondly, the oppression of these subject peoples is much stronger here than in the neighbouring states (and not even in the European states alone); thirdly, in a number of cases the oppressed nationalities inhabiting the border regions have compatriots across the border, who enjoy greater national independence (suffice it to mention the Finns, the Swedes, the Poles, the Ukrainians and the Rumanians along the western and southern frontiers of the state); fourthly, the development of capitalism and the general level of culture are often higher in the non-Russian border regions than in the centre. Lastly, it is in the neighbouring Asian states that we see the beginning of a phase of bourgeois revolutions and national movements which are spreading to some of the kindred nationalities within the borders of Russia.

Thus, it is precisely the special concrete, historical features of the national question in Russia that make the recognition of the right of nations to self-determination in the present period a matter of special urgency in our country.

* * *

4. "Practicality" in the National Question

* * *

In Russia, the creation of an independent national state remains, for the time being, the privilege of the Great-Russian nation alone. We, the Great-Russian proletarians, who defend no privileges whatever, do not defend this privilege either. We are fighting on the ground of a definite state; we unite the workers of all nations living in this state; we cannot vouch for any particular path of national development, for we are marching to our class goal along *all* possible paths.

However, we cannot move towards that goal unless we combat all nationalism, and uphold the equality of the various nations. Whether the Ukraine, for example, is destined to form an independent state is a matter that will be determined by a thousand unpredictable factors. Without attempting idle *"guesses,"* we firmly uphold something that is beyond doubt: the right of the Ukraine to form such a state. We respect this right; we do not uphold the privileges of Great Russians with regard to Ukrainians; we *educate* the masses in the spirit of recognition of that right, in the spirit of rejecting *state* privileges for any nation.

In the leaps which all nations have made in the period of bourgeois revolutions, clashes and struggles over the right to a national state are possible and probable. We proletarians declare in advance that we are *opposed* to Great-Russian privileges, and this is what guides our entire propaganda and agitation.

In her quest for "practicality" Rosa Luxemburg has lost sight of the *principal* practical task both of the Great-Russian proletariat and of the proletariat of other nationalities: that of day-by-day agitation and propaganda against all state and national privileges, and for the right, the equal right of all nations, to their national state. This (at present) is our principal task in the national question, for only in this way can we defend the interests of democracy and the alliance of all proletarians of all nations on an equal footing.

This propaganda may be "unpractical" from the point of view of the Great-Russian oppressors, as well as from the point of view of the bourgeoisie of the oppressed nations (both demand a *definite* "yes" or "no," and accuse the Social-Democrats of being "vague"). In reality it is this propaganda, and this propaganda alone, that ensures the genuinely democratic, the genuinely socialist education of the masses. This is the only propaganda to ensure the greatest chances of national peace in Russia, should she remain a multinational state, and the most peaceful (and for the proletarian class struggle, harmless) division into separate national states, should the question of such a division arise.

To explain this policy—the only proletarian policy—in the national question more concretely, we shall examine the attitude of Great-Russian liberalism towards the "self-determination of nations," and the example of Norway's secession from Sweden.

5. The Liberal Bourgeoisie and the Socialist Opportunists in the National Question

We have seen that the following argument is one of Rosa Luxemburg's "trump cards" in her struggle against the programme of the Marxists in Russia: recognition of the right to self-determination is tantamount to supporting the bourgeois nationalism of the oppressed nations. On the other hand, she says, if we take this right to mean no more than combating all violence against other nations, there is no need for a special clause in the programme, for Social-Democrats are, in general, opposed to all national oppression and inequality.

The first argument, as Kautsky irrefutably proved nearly twenty years ago, is a case of blaming other people for one's own nationalism; in her fear of the nationalism of the bourgeoisie of oppressed nations, Rosa Luxemburg is *actually* playing into the hands of the Black-Hundred nationalism of the Great Russians! Her second argument is actually a timid evasion of the question whether or not recognition of national equality includes recognition of the right to secession. If it does, then Rosa Luxemburg admits that, in principle, § 9 of our Programme is correct. If it does not, then she does not recognise national equality. Shuffling and evasions will not help matters here!

* * *

To accuse those who support freedom of self-determination, i.e., freedom to secede, of encouraging separatism, is as foolish and hypocritical as accusing those who advocate freedom of divorce of encouraging the destruction of family ties. Just as in bourgeois society the defenders of privilege and corruption, on which bourgeois marriage rests, oppose freedom of divorce, so, in the capitalist state, repudiation of the right to self-determination, i.e., the right of nations to secede, means nothing more than defence of the privileges of the dominant nation and police methods of administration, to the detriment of democratic methods.

* * *

The liberals' hostility to the principle of political self-determination of nations can have one, and only one, real class meaning: national-liberalism, defence of the state privileges of the Great-Russian bourgeoisie. And the opportunists among the Marxists in Russia, who today, under the Third of June regime, are against the right of nations to self-determination—the liquidator Semkovsky, the Bundist Liebman, the Ukrainian petty-bourgeois Yurkevich—are *actually* following in the wake of the national-liberals, and corrupting the working class with national-liberal ideas.

The interests of the working class and of its struggle against capitalism demand complete solidarity and the closest unity of the workers of all nations; they demand resistance to the nationalist policy of the bourgeoisie of every nationality. Hence, Social-Democrats would be deviating from proletarian policy and subordinating the workers to the policy of the bourgeoisie if they were to repudiate the right of nations to self-determination, i.e., the right of an oppressed nation to secede, or if they were to support all the national demands of the bourgeoisie of oppressed nations. It makes no difference to the hired worker whether he is exploited chiefly by the Great-Russian bourgeoisie rather than the non-Russian bourgeoisie, or by the Polish bourgeoisie rather than the Jewish bourgeoisie, etc. The hired worker who has come to understand his class interests is equally indifferent to the state privileges of the Great-Russian capitalists and to the promises of the Polish or Ukrainian capitalists to set up an earthly paradise when they obtain state privileges. Capitalism is developing and will continue to develop, anyway, both in integral states with a mixed population and in separate national states.

In any case the hired worker will be an object of exploitation. Successful struggle against exploitation requires that the proletariat be free of nationalism, and be absolutely neutral, so to speak, in the fight for supremacy that is going on among the bourgeoisie of the various nations. If the proletariat of any one nation gives the slightest support to the privileges of its "own" national bourgeoisie, that will inevitably rouse distrust among the proletariat of another nation; it will weaken the international class solidarity of the workers and divide them, to the delight of the bourgeoisie. Repudiation of the right to self-determination or to secession inevitably means, in practice, support for the privileges of the dominant nation.

* * *

7. The Resolution of the London International Congress, 1896[5]

This resolution reads:

> This Congress declares that it stands for the full right of all nations to self-determination [*Selbstbestimmungsrecht*] and expresses its sympathy for the workers of every country now suffering under the yoke of military, national or other absolutism. This Congress calls upon the workers of all these countries to join the ranks of the class-conscious [*Klassenbewusste*—those who understand their class interests] workers of the whole world in order jointly to fight for the defeat of international capitalism and for the achievement of the aims of international Social-Democracy.

As we have already pointed out, our opportunists—Semkovsky, Liebman and Yurkevich—are simply unaware of this resolution. But Rosa Luxemburg knows it and quotes the full text, which contains the same expression as that contained in our programme, viz., "self-determination."

How does Rosa Luxemburg remove this obstacle from the path of her "original" theory?

Oh, quite simply . . . the whole emphasis lies in the second part of the resolution . . . its declarative character . . . one can refer to it only by mistake!

* * *

The International's resolution reproduces the most essential and fundamental propositions in this point of view: on the one hand, the absolutely direct, unequivocal recognition of the full right of all nations to self-determination; on the other hand, the equally unambiguous appeal to the workers for *international* unity in their class struggle.

We think that this resolution is absolutely correct, and that, to the countries of Eastern Europe and Asia at the beginning of the twentieth century, it is this resolution, with both its parts being taken as an integral whole, that gives the only correct lead to the proletarian class policy in the national question.

Let us deal with the three above-mentioned viewpoints in somewhat greater detail.

As is known, Karl Marx and Frederick Engels considered it the bounden duty of the whole of West-European democracy, and still more of Social-Democracy, to give active support to the demand for Polish independence. For the period of the 1840s and 1860s,

---

5. Section 6, "Norway's Secession from Sweden," has been omitted. The 1896 London Congress was a congress of the socialist Second International. [*R. T.*]

the period of the bourgeois revolutions in Austria and Germany, and the period of the "Peasant Reform" in Russia, this point of view was quite correct and the only one that was consistently democratic and proletarian. So long as the masses of the people in Russia and in most of the Slav countries were still sunk in torpor, so long as *there were no* independent, mass, democratic movements in those countries, the liberation movement of the *gentry* in Poland assumed an immense and paramount importance from the point of view, not only of Russian, not only of Slav, but of European democracy as a whole.[6]

But while Marx's standpoint was quite correct for the forties, fifties and sixties or for the third quarter of the nineteenth century, it has ceased to be correct by the twentieth century. Independent democratic movements, and even an independent proletarian movement, have arisen in most Slav countries, even in Russia, one of the most backward Slav countries. Aristocratic Poland has disappeared, yielding place to capitalist Poland. Under such circumstances Poland could not but lose her *exceptional* revolutionary importance.

The attempt of the P.S.P. (the Polish Socialist Party, the present-day "Fracy") in 1896 to "establish" for all time the point of view Marx had held in a *different epoch* was an attempt to use the *letter* of Marxism against the *spirit* of Marxism. The Polish Social-Democrats were therefore quite right in attacking the extreme nationalism of the Polish petty bourgeoisie and pointing out that the national question was of secondary importance to Polish workers, in creating for the first time a purely proletarian party in Poland and proclaiming the extremely important principle that the Polish and the Russian workers must maintain the closest alliance in their class struggle.

But did this mean that at the beginning of the twentieth century the International could regard the principle of political self-determination of nations, or the right to secede, as unnecessary to Eastern Europe and Asia? This would have been the height of absurdity, and (theoretically) tantamount to admitting that the bourgeois-democratic reform of the Turkish, Russian and Chinese states had been consummated; indeed it would have been tantamount (in practice) to opportunism towards absolutism.

No. At a time when bourgeois-democratic revolutions in Eastern

---

6. It would be a very interesting piece of historical research to compare the position of a noble Polish rebel in 1863 with that of the All-Russia revolutionary democrat, Chernyshevsky, who (like Marx), was able to appreciate the importance of the Polish movement, and with that of the Ukrainian petty bourgeois Dragomanov, who appeared much later and expressed the views of a peasant, so ignorant and sluggish, and so attached to his dung heap, that his legitimate hatred of the Polish gentry blinded him to the significance which their struggle had for All-Russia democracy. (Cf. Dragomanov, *Historical Poland and Great-Russian Democracy.*) Dragomanov richly deserved the fervent kisses which were subsequently bestowed on him by Mr. P. B. Struve, who by that time had become a national-liberal. [*Lenin*]

Europe and Asia have begun, in this period of the awakening and intensification of national movements and of the formation of independent proletarian parties, the task of these parties with regard to national policy must be twofold: recognition of the right of all nations to self-determination, since bourgeois-democratic reform is not yet completed and since working-class democracy consistently, seriously and sincerely (and not in a liberal, Kokoshkin[7] fashion) fights for equal rights for nations; then, a close, unbreakable alliance in the class struggle of the proletarians of all nations in a given state, throughout all the changes in its history, irrespective of any reshaping of the frontiers of the individual states by the bourgeoisie.

It is this twofold task of the proletariat that the 1896 resolution of the International formulates. That is the substance, the underlying principle, of the resolution adopted by the Conference of Russian Marxists held in the summer of 1913. Some people profess to see a "contradiction" in the fact that while point 4 of this resolution, which recognises the right to self-determination and secession, seems to "concede" the maximum to nationalism (in reality, the recognition of the *right of all* nations to self-determination implies the maximum of *democracy* and the minimum of nationalism), point 5 warns the workers against the nationalist slogans of the bourgeoisie of any nation and demands the unity and amalgamation of the workers of all nations in internationally united proletarian organisations. But this is a "contradiction" only for extremely shallow minds, which, for instance, cannot grasp why the unity and class solidarity of the Swedish and the Norwegian proletariat *gained* when the Swedish workers upheld Norway's freedom to secede and form an independent state.

8. The Utopian Karl Marx and the Practical Rosa Luxemburg

Calling Polish independence a "utopia" and repeating this *ad nauseam*, Rosa Luxemburg exclaims ironically: Why not raise the demand for the independence of Ireland?

The "practical" Rosa Luxemburg evidently does not know what Karl Marx's attitude to the question of Irish independence was. It is worth while dwelling upon this, so as to show how a *concrete* demand for national independence was analysed from a genuinely Marxist, not opportunist, standpoint.

It was Marx's custom to "sound out" his socialist acquaintances, as he expressed it, to test their intelligence and the strength of their

7. F. F. Kokoshkin was one of the founders of the centrist Russian Constitutional Democratic (Cadet) Party.

convictions.[8] After making the acquaintance of Lopatin, Marx wrote to Engels on July 5, 1870, expressing a highly flattering opinion of the young Russian socialist but adding at the same time: "*Poland* is his weak point. On this point he speaks quite like an Englishman—say, an English Chartist of the old school—about Ireland." Marx questions a socialist belonging to an oppressor nation about his attitude to the oppressed nation and at once reveals a defect *common* to the socialists of the dominant nations (the English and the Russian): failure to understand their socialist duties towards the downtrodden nations, their echoing of the prejudices acquired from the bourgeoisie of the "dominant nation."

Before passing on to Marx's positive declarations on Ireland, we must point out that in general the attitude of Marx and Engels to the national question was strictly critical, and that they recognised its historically conditioned importance. Thus, Engels wrote to Marx on May 23, 1851, that the study of history was leading him to pessimistic conclusions in regard to Poland, that the importance of Poland was temporary—only until the agrarian revolution in Russia. The role of the Poles in history was one of "bold (hotheaded) foolishness." "And one cannot point to a single instance in which Poland has successfully represented progress, even in relation to Russia, or done anything at all of historical importance." Russia contains more of civilisation, education, industry and the bourgeoisie than "the Poland of the indolent gentry." "What are Warsaw and Cracow compared to St. Petersburg, Moscow, Odessa!" Engels had no faith in the success of the Polish gentry's insurrections.

But all these thoughts, showing the deep insight of genius, by no means prevented Engels and Marx from treating the Polish movement with the most profound and ardent sympathy twelve years later, when Russia was still dormant and Poland was seething.

When drafting the Address of the International in 1864, Marx wrote to Engels (on November 4, 1864) that he had to combat Mazzini's nationalism, and went on to say: "Inasmuch as international politics occurred in the Address, I spoke of countries, not of nationalities, and denounced Russia, not the *minores gentium.*"[9] Marx had no doubt as to the subordinate position of the national question as compared with the "labour question." But his theory is as far from ignoring national movements as heaven is from earth.

Then came 1866. Marx wrote to Engels about the "Proudhonist clique" in Paris which "declares nationalities to be an absurdity, attacks Bismarck and Garibaldi. As polemics against chauvinism their doings are useful and explicable. But as believers in Proudhon

---

8. Lenin refers here to Wilhelm Liebknecht's "Reminiscences of Marx." See *Reminiscences of Marx and Engels* (Moscow, 1957), p. 98.
9. The lesser nations.

(Lafargue and Longuet, two very good friends of mine here, also belong to them), who think all Europe must and will sit quietly on their hind quarters until the gentlemen in France abolish poverty and ignorance—they are grotesque" (letter of June 7, 1866).

"Yesterday," Marx wrote on June 20, 1866,

> there was a discussion in the International Council on the present war. . . . The discussion wound up, as was to be foreseen, with "the question of nationality" in general and the attitude we take towards it. . . . The representatives of "Young France" (*non-workers*) came out with the announcement that all nationalities and even nations were "antiquated prejudices." Proudhonised Stirnerism. . . . the whole world waits until the French are ripe for a social revolution. . . . The English laughed very much when I began my speech by saying that our friend Lafargue and others, who had done away with nationalities, had spoken "French" to us, i.e., a language which nine-tenths of the audience did not understand. I also suggested that by the negation of nationalities he appeared, quite unconsciously, to understand their absorption by the model French nation.

The conclusion that follows from all these critical remarks of Marx's is clear: the working class should be the last to make a fetish of the national question, since the development of capitalism does not necessarily awaken *all* nations to independent life. But to brush aside the mass national movements once they have started, and to refuse to support what is progressive in them means, in effect, pandering to *nationalistic* prejudices, that is, recognising "one's own nation" as a model nation (or, we would add, one possessing the exclusive privilege of forming a state).[1]

But let us return to the question of Ireland.

Marx's position on this question is most clearly expressed in the following extracts from his letters:

> I have done my best to bring about this demonstration of the English workers in favour of Fenianism.[2] . . . I used to think the separation of Ireland from England impossible. I now think it inevitable, although after the separation there may come federation.

This is what Marx wrote to Engels on November 2, 1867. In his letter of November 30 of the same year he added:

> . . . what shall we advise the *English* workers? In my opinion they must make the *Repeal of the Union*" [Ireland with England,

1. Cf. also Marx's letter to Engels of June 3, 1867: ". . . I have learned with real pleasure from the Paris letters to *The Times* about the pro-Polish exclamations of the Parisians against Russia. . . .

Mr. Proudhon and his little doctrinaire clique are not the French people. [*Lenin*]
2. An Irish revolutionary movement that developed in the eighteen-fifties.

i.e., the separation of Ireland from England] (in short, the affair of 1783, only democratised and adapted to the conditions of the time) an article of their *pronunziamento*. This is the only legal and therefore only possible form of Irish emancipation which can be admitted in the programme of an *English* party. Experience must show later whether a mere personal union can continue to subsist between the two countries. . . .

. . . What the Irish need is:
1) Self-government and independence from England;
2) An agrarian revolution. . . .

Marx attached great importance to the Irish question and delivered hour-and-a-half lectures on this subject at the German Workers' Union (letter of December 17, 1867).

In a letter dated November 20, 1868, Engels spoke of "the hatred towards the Irish found among the English workers," and almost a year later (October 24, 1869), returning to this subject, he wrote:

> *Il n'y a qu'un pas* [it is only one step] from Ireland to Russia. . . . Irish history shows what a misfortune it is for one nation to have subjugated another. All the abominations of the English have their origin in the Irish Pale. I have still to plough my way through the Cromwellian period, but this much seems certain to me, that things would have taken another turn in England, too, but for the necessity of military rule in Ireland and the creation of a new aristocracy there.

Let us note, in passing, Marx's letter to Engels of August 18, 1869:

> The Polish workers in Posen have brought a strike to a victorious end with the help of their colleagues in Berlin. This struggle against Monsieur le Capital—even in the lower form of the strike —is a more serious way of getting rid of national prejudices than peace declamations from the lips of bourgeois gentlemen.

The policy on the Irish question pursued by Marx in the International may be seen from the following:

On November 18, 1869, Marx wrote to Engels that he had spoken for an hour and a quarter at the Council of the International on the question of the attitude of the British Ministry to the Irish Amnesty, and had proposed the following resolution:

> Resolved,
> that in his reply to the Irish demands for the release of the imprisoned Irish patriots Mr. Gladstone deliberately insults the Irish nation;
> that he clogs political amnesty with conditions alike degrading to the victims of misgovernment and the people they belong to;
> that having, in the teeth of his responsible position, publicly

and enthusiastically cheered on the American slaveholders' rebellion, he now steps in to preach to the Irish people the doctrine of passive obedience;

that his whole proceedings with reference to the Irish Amnesty question are the true and genuine offspring of that *"policy of conquest,"* by the fiery denunciation of which Mr. Gladstone ousted his Tory rivals from office;

that the General Council of the International Workingmen's Association express their admiration of the spirited, firm and high-souled manner in which the Irish people carry on their Amnesty movement;

that this resolution be communicated to all branches of, and workingmen's bodies connected with, the International Workingmen's Association in Europe and America.

On December 10, 1869, Marx wrote that his paper on the Irish question to be read at the Council of the International would be couched as follows:

Quite apart from all phrases about "international" and "humane" justice for Ireland—which are taken for granted in the International Council—*it is in the direct and absolute interest of the English working class to get rid of their present connexion with Ireland.* And this is my fullest conviction, and for reasons which in part I can *not* tell the English workers themselves. For a long time I believed that it would be possible to overthrow the Irish regime by English working-class ascendancy. I always expressed this point of view in the *New York Tribune* [an American paper to which Marx contributed for a long time]. Deeper study has now convinced me of the opposite. The English working class will *never accomplish anything* until it has got rid of Ireland. . . . The English reaction in England had its roots in the subjugation of Ireland. [Marx's italics.]

Marx's policy on the Irish question should now be quite clear to our readers.

Marx, the "utopian," was so "unpractical" that he stood for the separation of Ireland, which half a century later has not yet been achieved.

What gave rise to Marx's policy, and was it not mistaken?

At first Marx thought that Ireland would not be liberated by the national movement of the oppressed nation, but by the working-class movement of the oppressor nation. Marx did not make an absolute of the national movement, knowing, as he did, that only the victory of the working class can bring about the complete liberation of all nationalities. It is impossible to estimate beforehand all the possible relations between the bourgeois liberation movements of the oppressed nations and the proletarian emancipation movement of the oppressor nation (the very problem which today makes the national question in Russia so difficult).

However, it so happened that the English working class fell under the influence of the liberals for a fairly long time, became an appendage to the liberals, and by adopting a liberal-labour policy left itself leaderless. The bourgeois liberation movement in Ireland grew stronger and assumed revolutionary forms. Marx reconsidered his view and corrected it. "What a misfortune it is for a nation to have subjugated another." The English working class will never be free until Ireland is freed from the English yoke. Reaction in England is strengthened and fostered by the enslavement of Ireland (just as reaction in Russia is fostered by her enslavement of a number of nations!).

And, in proposing in the International a resolution of sympathy with "the Irish nation," "the Irish people" (the clever L. Vl. would probably have berated poor Marx for forgetting about the class struggle!), Marx advocated the *separation* of Ireland from England, "although after the separation there may come federation."

What were the theoretical grounds for Marx's conclusion? In England the bourgeois revolution had been consummated long ago. But it had not yet been consummated in Ireland; it is being consummated only now, after the lapse of half a century, by the reforms of the English Liberals. If capitalism had been overthrown in England as quickly as Marx had at first expected, there would have been no room for a bourgeois-democratic and general national movement in Ireland. But since it had arisen, Marx advised the English workers to support it, give it a revolutionary impetus and see it through in the interests of *their own* liberty.

The economic ties between Ireland and England in the 1860s were, of course, even closer than Russia's present ties with Poland, the Ukraine, etc. The "unpracticality" and "impracticability" of the separation of Ireland (if only owing to geographical conditions and England's immense colonial power) were quite obvious. Though, in principle, an enemy of federalism, Marx in this instance granted the possibility of federation as well,[3] if *only* the emancipation of Ireland was achieved in a revolutionary, not reformist way, through a movement of the mass of the people of Ireland supported by the

---

3. By the way, it is not difficult to see why, from a Social-Democratic point of view, the right to "self-determination" means *neither* federation *nor* autonomy (although, speaking in the abstract, both come under the category of "self-determination"). The right to federation is simply meaningless, since federation implies a bilateral contract. It goes without saying that Marxists cannot include the defence of federalism in general in their programme. As far as autonomy is concerned, Marxists defend, not the "right to autonomy," but autonomy *itself*, as a general universal principle of a democratic state with a mixed national composition, and a great variety of geographical and other conditions. Consequently, the recognition of the "right of nations to autonomy" is as absurd as that of the "right of nations to federation." [*Lenin*]

working class of England. There can be no doubt that only such a solution of the historical problem would have been in the best interests of the proletariat and most conducive to rapid social progress.

Things turned out differently. Both the Irish people and the English proletariat proved weak. Only now, through the sordid deals between the English Liberals and the Irish bourgeoisie, is the Irish problem *being solved* (the example of Ulster shows with what difficulty) through the land reform (with compensation) and Home Rule (not yet introduced). Well then? Does it follow that Marx and Engels were "utopians," that they put forward "impracticable" national demands, or that they allowed themselves to be influenced by the Irish petty bourgeois nationalists (for there is no doubt about the petty-bourgeois nature of the Fenian movement), etc.?

No. In the Irish question, too, Marx and Engels pursued a consistently proletarian policy, which really educated the masses in a spirit of democracy and socialism. Only such a policy could have saved both Ireland and England half a century of delay in introducing the necessary reforms, and prevented these reforms from being mutilated by the Liberals to please the reactionaries.

The policy of Marx and Engels on the Irish question serves as a splendid example of the attitude the proletariat of the oppressor nations should adopt towards national movements, an example which has lost none of its immense *practical* importance. It serves as a warning against that "servile haste" with which the philistines of all countries, colours and languages hurry to label as "utopian" the idea of altering the frontiers of states that were established by the violence and privileges of the landlords and bourgeoisie of one nation.

If the Irish and English proletariat had not accepted Marx's policy and had not made the secession of Ireland their slogan, this would have been the worst sort of opportunism, a neglect of their duties as democrats and socialists, and a concession to *English* reaction and the *English* bourgeoisie.

9. The 1903 Programme and Its Liquidators

The Minutes of the 1903 Congress, at which the Programme of the Russian Marxists was adopted, have become a great rarity, and the vast majority of the active members of the working-class movement today are unacquainted with the motives underlying the various points (the more so since not all the literature relating to it enjoys the blessings of legality . . .). It is therefore necessary to analyse the debate that took place at the 1903 Congress on the question under discussion.

Let us state first of all that however meagre the Russian Social-Democratic literature on the "right of nations to self-determination" may be, it nevertheless shows clearly that this right has always been understood to mean the right to secession. The Semkovskys, Liebmans and Yurkeviches who doubt this and declare that § 9 is "vague," etc., do so only because of their sheer ignorance or carelessness. As far back as 1902, Plekhanov, in *Zarya*, defended "the right to self-determination" in the draft programme, and wrote that this demand, while not obligatory upon bourgeois democrats, was "obligatory upon Social-Democrats." "If we were to forget it or hesitate to advance it," Plekhanov wrote, "for fear of offending the national prejudices of our fellow-countrymen of Great-Russian nationality, the call . . . 'workers of all countries, unite!' would be a shameful lie on our lips. . . ."[4]

This is a very apt description of the fundamental argument in favour of the point under consideration; so apt that it is not surprising that the "anythingarian" critics of our programme have been timidly avoiding it. The abandonment of this point, no matter for what motives, is *actually* a "shameful" concession to *Great-Russian* nationalism. But why Great-Russian, when it is a question of the right of *all* nations to self-determination? Because it refers to secession *from* the Great Russians. The interests of the *unity of the proletarians*, the interests of their class solidarity call for recognition of the right of *nations to secede*—that is what Plekhanov admitted twelve years ago in the words quoted above. Had our opportunists given thought to this they would probably not have talked so much nonsense about self-determination.

At the 1903 Congress, which adopted the draft programme that Plekhanov advocated, the main work was done by the *Programme Commission*. Unfortunately no Minutes of its proceedings were kept; they would have been particularly interesting on this point, for it was *only* in the Commission that the representatives of the Polish Social-Democrats, Warszawski and Hanecki, tried to defend their views and to dispute "recognition of the right to self-determination." Any reader who goes to the trouble of comparing their arguments (set forth in the speech by Warszawski and the statement by him and Hanecki, pp. 134–36 and 388–90 of the Congress Minutes) with those which Rosa Luxemburg advanced in her Polish article, which we have analysed, will find them identical.

How were these arguments treated by the Programme Commission of the Second Congress, where Plekhanov, more than anyone

4. Quoted from Plekhanov's article "The Draft Programme of the Russian Social- Democratic Party" published in *Zarya*, No. 4, 1902.

else, spoke against the Polish Marxists? They were mercilessly ridiculed! The absurdity of proposing to the Marxists of *Russia* that they should reject the recognition of the right of nations to self-determination was demonstrated so plainly and clearly that the Polish Marxists *did not even venture to repeat their arguments at the plenary meeting of the Congress!* They left the Congress, convinced of the hopelessness of their case at the supreme assembly of Marxists—Great-Russian, Jewish, Georgian, and Armenian.

Needless to say, this historic episode is of very great importance to everyone seriously interested in *his own* programme. The fact that the Polish Marxists' arguments were completely defeated at the Programme Commission of the Congress, and that the Polish Marxists gave up the attempt to defend their views at the plenary meeting of the Congress is very significant. No wonder Rosa Luxemburg maintained a "modest" silence about it in her article in 1908—the recollection of the Congress must have been too unpleasant! She also kept quiet about the ridiculously inept proposal made by Warszawski and Hanecki in 1903, on behalf of all Polish Marxists, to "amend" § 9 of the Programme, a proposal which neither Rosa Luxemburg nor the other Polish Social-Democrats have ventured (or will ever venture) to repeat.

But although Rosa Luxemburg, concealing her defeat in 1903, has maintained silence over these facts, those who take an interest in the history of their Party will make it their business to ascertain them and give thought to their significance.

* * *

10. Conclusion

To sum up.

As far as the theory of Marxism in general is concerned, the question of the right to self-determination presents no difficulty. No one can seriously question the London resolution of 1896, or the fact that self-determination implies only the right to secede, or that the formation of independent national states is the tendency in all bourgeois-democratic revolutions.

A difficulty is to some extent created by the fact that in Russia the proletariat of both the oppressed and oppressor nations are fighting, and must fight, side by side. The task is to preserve the unity of the proletariat's class struggle for socialism, and to resist all bourgeois and Black-Hundred nationalist influences. Where the oppressed nations are concerned, the separate organisation of the proletariat as an independent party sometimes leads to such a bitter struggle against local nationalism that the perspective becomes distorted and the nationalism of the oppressor nation is lost sight of.

But this distortion of perspective cannot last long. The experience of the joint struggle waged by the proletarians of various nations has demonstrated all too clearly that we must formulate political issues from the all-Russia, not the "Cracow" point of view. And in all-Russia politics it is the Purishkeviches[5] and the Kokoshkins who are in the saddle. Their ideas predominate, and their persecution of non-Russians for "separatism," for *thinking* about secession, is being preached and practised in the Duma, in the schools, in the churches, in the barracks, and in hundreds and thousands of newspapers. It is this Great-Russian nationalist poison that is polluting the entire all-Russia political atmosphere. This is the misfortune of one nation, which, by subjugating other nations, is strengthening reaction throughout Russia. The memories of 1849 and 1863 form a living political tradition, which, unless great storms arise, threatens to hamper every democratic and *especially* every Social-Democratic movement for decades to come.

There can be no doubt that however natural the point of view of certain Marxists belonging to the oppressed nations (whose "misfortune" is sometimes that the masses of the population are blinded by the idea of their "own" national liberation) may appear at times, *in reality* the objective alignment of class forces in Russia makes refusal to advocate the right to self-determination tantamount to the worst opportunism, to the infection of the proletariat with the ideas of the Kokoshkins. And these ideas are, essentially, the ideas and the policy of the Purishkeviches.

Therefore, although Rosa Luxemburg's point of view could at first have been excused as being specifically Polish, "Cracow" narrow-mindedness,[6] it is inexcusable today, when nationalism and, above all, governmental Great-Russian nationalism, has everywhere gained ground, and when policy is being shaped by this *Great-Russian nationalism*. In actual fact, it is being seized upon by the opportunists of all nations, who fight shy of the idea of "storms" and "leaps," believe that the bourgeois-democratic revolution is over, and follow in the wake of the liberalism of the Kokoshkins.

Like any other nationalism, Great-Russian nationalism passes through various phases, according to the classes that are dominant in the bourgeois country at any given time. Up to 1905, we almost

---

5. V. M. Purishkevich (1870–1920), a Russian monarchist, founded the terrorist Black Hundred movement in 1905–7. Its sympathies were reactionary and anti-Semitic.

6. It is not difficult to understand that the recognition by the Marxists of the *whole of Russia*, and first and foremost by the Great Russians, of the *right* of nations to secede in no way precludes *agitation* against secession by Marxists of a particular *oppressed* nation, just as the recognition of the right to divorce does not preclude agitation against divorce in a particular case. We think, therefore, that there will be an inevitable increase in the number of Polish Marxists who laugh at the non-existent "contradiction" now being "encouraged" by Semkovsky and Trotsky. [*Lenin*]

exclusively knew national-reactionaries. After the revolution, *national-liberals* arose in our country.

In our country this is virtually the stand adopted both by the Octobrists and by the Cadets (Kokoshkin), i.e., by the whole of the present-day bourgeoisie.

Great-Russian national-democrats will *inevitably* appear later on. Mr. Peshekhonov, one of the founders of the "Popular Socialist" Party, already expressed this point of view (in the issue of *Russkoye Bogatstvo* for August 1906) when he called for caution in regard to the peasants' nationalist prejudices. However much others may slander us Bolsheviks and accuse us of "idealising" the peasant, we always have made and always will make a clear distinction between peasant intelligence and peasant prejudice, between peasant strivings for democracy and opposition to Purishkevich, and the peasant desire to make peace with the priest and the landlord.

Even now, and probably for a fairly long time to come, proletarian democracy must reckon with the nationalism of the Great-Russian peasants (not with the object of making concessions to it, but in order to combat it).[7] The awakening of nationalism among the oppressed nations, which became so pronounced after 1905 (let us recall, say, the group of "Federalist-Autonomists" in the First Duma, the growth of the Ukrainian movement, of the Moslem movement, etc.), will inevitably lead to greater nationalism among the Great-Russian petty bourgeoisie in town and countryside. The slower the democratisation of Russia, the more persistent, brutal and bitter will be the national persecution and bickering among the bourgeoisie of the various nations. The particularly reactionary nature of the Russian Purishkeviches will simultaneously give rise to (and strengthen) "separatist" tendencies among the various oppressed nationalities, which sometimes enjoy far greater freedom in neighbouring states.

In this situation, the proletariat of Russia is faced with a two-fold or, rather, a two-sided task: to combat nationalism of every kind, above all, Great-Russian nationalism; to recognise, not only fully equal rights for all nations in general, but also equality of

7. It would be interesting to trace the changes that take place in Polish nationalism, for example, in the process of its transformation from gentry nationalism into bourgeois nationalism, and then into peasant nationalism. In his book *Das polnische Gemeinwesen im preussischen Staat* (*The Polish Community in the Prussian State*; there is a Russian translation), Ludwig Bernhard, who shares the view of a German Kokoshkin, describes a very typical phenomenon: the formation of a sort of "peasant republic" by the Poles in Germany in the form of a close alliance of the various co-operatives and other associations of *Polish* peasants in their struggle for nationality, religion, and "Polish" land. German oppression has welded the Poles together and segregated them, after first awakening the nationalism of the gentry, then of the bourgeoisie, and finally of the peasant masses (especially after the campaign the Germans launched in 1873 against the use of the Polish language in schools). Things are moving in the same direction in Russia, and not only with regard to Poland. [*Lenin*]

rights as regards polity, i.e., the right of nations to self-determination, to secession. And at the same time, it is their task, in the interests of a successful struggle against all and every kind of nationalism among all nations, to preserve the unity of the proletarian struggle and the proletarian organisations, amalgamating these organisations into a close-knit international association, despite bourgeois strivings for national exclusiveness.

Complete equality of rights for all nations; the right of nations to self-determination; the unity of the workers of all nations—such is the national programme that Marxism, the experience of the whole world, and the experience of Russia, teach the workers.

* * *

PART II

Revolutionary Politics in a World at War

Socialism and War

Although the Social-Democratic parties of the Second International had passed anti-war resolutions before 1914, most supported their respective belligerent governments when the World War broke out. For Lenin the war was imperialist in nature; thus such support was "social-chauvinism" and treason to the socialist cause. Revolutionary Marxists should seek to transform the war into a series of civil wars in which worker-soldiers would turn their rifles against their own rulers. The Second International was finished and must be replaced by a truly revolutionary Third International. These ideas underlay *Socialism and War*, which he wrote in the summer of 1915 with the help of his associate Gregory Zinoviev, in preparation for a conference of anti-war socialist internationalists which was to be held at the village of Zimmerwald in neutral Switzerland in September. The majority of the thirty-eight delegates from eleven European countries who met at Zimmerwald, as well as the majority of those who attended a subsequent meeting held at Kienthal, Switzerland, in April 1916, rejected Lenin's revolutionary anti-war program in favor of a simple stress upon the ending of the war. Lenin adhered to his position, however, and the schism between Social-Democracy and Communism as well as the rise of the Third International in 1919 could be said to have originated at this early date.

Chapter I. The Principles of Socialism and the War of 1914–15

The Attitude of Socialists Towards Wars

Socialists have always condemned wars between nations as barbarous and brutal. Our attitude towards war, however, is fundamentally different from that of the bourgeois pacifists (supporters and advocates of peace) and of the anarchists. We differ from the former in that we understand the inevitable connection between wars and the class struggle within a country; we understand that wars cannot be abolished unless classes are abolished and socialism is created; we also differ in that we regard civil wars, i.e., wars

183

waged by an oppressed class against the oppressor class, by slaves against slaveholders, by serfs against landowners, and by wage-workers against the bourgeoisie, as fully legitimate, progressive and necessary. We Marxists differ from both pacifists and anarchists in that we deem it necessary to study each war historically (from the standpoint of Marx's dialectical materialism) and separately. There have been in the past numerous wars which, despite all the horrors, atrocities, distress and suffering that inevitably accompany all wars, were progressive, i.e., benefited the development of mankind by helping to destroy most harmful and reactionary institutions (e.g., an autocracy or serfdom) and the most barbarous despotisms in Europe (the Turkish and the Russian). That is why the features historically specific to the present war must come up for examination.

The Historical Types of Wars in Modern Times

The Great French Revolution ushered in a new epoch in the history of mankind. From that time down to the Paris Commune, i.e., between 1789 and 1871, one type of war was of a bourgeois progressive character, waged for national liberation. In other words, the overthrow of absolutism and feudalism, the undermining of these institutions, and the overthrow of alien oppression, formed the chief content and historical significance of such wars. These were therefore progressive wars; during *such* wars, all honest and revolutionary democrats, as well as all socialists, always wished success to that country (i.e., that bourgeoisie) which had helped to overthrow or undermine the most baneful foundations of feudalism, absolutism and the oppression of other nations. For example, the revolutionary wars waged by France contained an element of plunder and the conquest of foreign territory by the French, but this does not in the least alter the fundamental historical significance of those wars, which destroyed and shattered feudalism and absolutism in the whole of the old, serf-owning Europe. In the Franco-Prussian war, Germany plundered France but this does not alter the fundamental historical significance of that war, which liberated tens of millions of German people from feudal disunity and from the oppression of two despots, the Russian tsar and Napoleon III.

The Difference Between Wars of Aggression and of Defence

The period of 1789–1871 left behind it deep marks and revolutionary memories. There could be no development of the proletarian struggle for socialism prior to the overthrow of feudalism, absolutism and alien oppression. When, in speaking of the wars of *such* periods, socialists stressed the legitimacy of "defensive" wars, they always had these aims in mind, namely revolution against medievalism and serfdom. By a "defensive" war socialists have always understood a *"just"* war in this particular sense (Wilhelm Liebknecht once expressed himself precisely in this way). It is only in this sense that socialists have always regarded wars "for the defence of the fatherland," or "defensive" wars, as legitimate, progressive and just. For example, if tomorrow, Morocco were to declare war on France, or India on Britain, or Persia or China on Russia, and so on, these would be "just," and "defensive" wars, *irrespective* of who would be the first to attack; any socialist would wish the oppressed, dependent and unequal states victory over the oppressor, slaveholding and predatory "Great" Powers.

But imagine a slave-holder who owns a hundred slaves warring against another who owns two hundred slaves, for a more "just" redistribution of slaves. The use of the term of a "defensive" war, or a war "for the defence of the fatherland," would clearly be historically false in such a case and would in practice be sheer deception of the common people, philistines, and the ignorant, by the astute slave-holders. It is in this way that the peoples are being deceived with "national" ideology and the term of "defence of the fatherland," by the present-day imperialist bourgeoisie, in the war now being waged between slave-holders with the purpose of consolidating slavery.

The War of Today Is an Imperialist War

It is almost universally admitted that this war is an imperialist war. In most cases, however, this term is distorted, or applied to one side, or else a loophole is left for the assertion that this war may, after all, be bourgeois-progressive, and of significance to the national-liberation movement. Imperialism is the highest stage in the development of capitalism, reached only in the twentieth century. Capitalism now finds that the old national states, without whose formation it could not have overthrown feudalism, are too cramped for it. Capitalism has developed concentration to such a degree that entire branches of industry are controlled by syndicates, trusts and associations of capitalist multimillionaires and almost the entire globe has been divided up among the "lords of capital" either in the form of colonies, or by entangling other countries in thousands of threads of financial exploitation. Free trade and competition have been superseded by a striving towards monopolies, the seizure of territory for the investment of capital and as sources of raw materials, and so on. From the liberator of nations, which it was in the struggle against feudalism, capitalism in its imperialist stage has turned into the greatest oppressor of nations. Formerly progressive, capitalism has become reactionary; it has developed the forces of production to such a degree that mankind is faced with the alternative of adopting socialism or of experiencing years and even decades of armed struggle between the "Great" Powers for the artificial preservation of capitalism by means of colonies, monopolies, privileges and national oppression of every kind.

A War Between the Biggest Slave-Holders for the Maintenance and Consolidation of Slavery

To make the significance of imperialism clear, we will quote precise figures showing the partition of the world among the so-called "Great" Powers (i.e., those successful in great plunder).

Hence it will be seen that, since 1876, most of the nations which were foremost fighters for freedom in 1789–1871, have, on the basis of a highly developed and "over-mature" capitalism, become oppressors and enslavers of most of the population and the nations of the globe. From 1876 to 1914, six "Great" Powers grabbed twenty-five million square kilometres, i.e., an area two and a half times that of Europe! Six Powers have enslaved 523 *million* people in the colonies. For every four inhabitants in the "Great" Powers there are five in "their" colonies. It is common knowledge that colonies are conquered with fire and sword, that the population of the colonies are brutally treated, and that they are exploited in a thousand ways (by exporting capital, through concessions, etc., cheating in the sale of goods, submission to the authorities of the "ruling" nation, and so on and so forth). The Anglo-French bourgeoisie are deceiving the people when they say that they are waging a war for the freedom of nations and of Belgium; in fact they are waging a war for the purpose of retaining the colonies they have grabbed and robbed. The German imperialists would free Belgium, etc., at once if the British and French would agree to "fairly" share their colonies with them. A feature of the situation is that in this war the fate of the colonies is being decided by a war on the Continent. From the standpoint of bourgeois justice and national freedom (or the right of nations to existence), Germany might be considered absolutely in the right as against Britain and France, for she has been "done out" of colonies, her enemies are oppressing an immeasurably far larger number of nations than she is, and the Slavs that are being oppressed by her ally, Austria, undoubtedly enjoy far more freedom than those of tsarist Russia, that veritable

Partition of the World Among the "Great" Slave-holding Powers

"Great" Powers	Colonies 1876		Colonies 1914		Metropolis 1914		Total	
	Square kilometres	Population	Square kilometres	Population	Square kilometres	Population	Square kilometres	Population
	millions		millions		millions		millions	
Britain	22.5	251.9	33.5	393.5	0.3	46.5	33.8	440.0
Russia	17.0	15.9	17.4	33.2	5.4	136.2	22.8	169.4
France	0.9	6.0	10.6	55.5	0.5	39.6	11.1	95.1
Germany	—	—	2.9	12.3	0.5	64.9	3.4	77.2
Japan	—	—	0.3	19.2	0.4	53.0	0.7	72.2
United States of America	—	—	0.3	9.7	9.4	97.0	9.7	106.7
Total for the six "Great" Powers	40.4	273.8	65.0	523.4	16.5	437.2	81.5	960.6
Colonies belonging to *other* than Great Powers (Belgium, Holland and other states)			9.9	45.3			9.9	45.3
Three "semi-colonial" countries (Turkey, China and Persia)							14.5	361.2
Total							105.9	1,367.1
Other states and countries							28.0	289.9
Entire globe (exclusive of Arctic and Antarctic regions) *Grand Total*							133.9	1,657.0

"prison of nations." Germany, however, is fighting, not for the liberation of nations, but for their oppression. It is not the business of socialists to help the younger and stronger robber (Germany) to plunder the older and overgorged robbers. Socialists must take advantage of the struggle between the robbers to overthrow all of them. To be able to do this, socialists must first of all tell the people the truth, namely, that this war is, in three respects, a war between slave-holders with the aim of consolidating slavery. This is a war, firstly, to increase the enslavement of the colonies by means of a "more equitable" distribution and subsequent more concerted exploitation of them; secondly, to increase the oppression of other nations within the "Great" Powers, since *both* Austria *and* Russia (Russia in greater degree and with results far worse than Austria) maintain their rule only by such oppression, intensifying it by means of war; and thirdly, to increase and prolong wage slavery, since the proletariat is split up and suppressed, while the capitalists are the gainers, making fortunes out of the war, fanning national prejudices and intensifying reaction, which has raised its head in all countries, even in the freest and most republican.

"War Is the Continuation of Politics by Other" (i.e., Violent) "Means"

This famous dictum was uttered by Clausewitz, one of the profoundest writers on the problems of war. Marxists have always rightly regarded this thesis as the theoretical basis of views on the significance of any war. It was from this viewpoint that Marx and Engels always regarded the various wars.

Apply this view to the present war. You will see that for decades, for almost half a century, the governments and the ruling classes of Britain and France, Germany and Italy, Austria and Russia have pursued a policy of plundering colonies, oppressing other nations, and suppressing the working-class movement. It is this, and only this, policy that is being continued in the present war. In particular, the policy of both Austria and Russia, in peacetime as well as in wartime, is a policy of enslaving nations, not of liberating them. In China, Persia, India and other dependent countries, on the contrary, we have seen during the past decades a policy of rousing tens and hundreds of millions of people to a national life, of their liberation from the reactionary "Great" Powers' oppression. A war waged on such a historical basis can even today be a bourgeois-progessive war of national liberation.

If the present war is regarded as a continuation of the politics of the "Great" Powers and of the principal classes within them, a glance will immediately reveal the glaring anti-historicity, falseness and hypocrisy of the view that the "defence-of-the-fatherland" idea can be justified in the present war.

The Case of Belgium

The favourite plea of the social-chauvinists of the Triple (now Quadruple) Entente (in Russia, Plekhanov and Co.) is the case of Belgium. This instance, however, speaks against them. The German imperialists have brazenly violated the neutrality of Belgium, as belligerent states have done always and everywhere, trampling upon *all* treaties and obligations if necessary. Let us suppose that all states interested in the observance of international treaties should declare war on Germany with the demand that Belgium be liberated and indemnified. In that case, the sympathies of socialists would, of course, be with Germany's enemies. But the whole point is that the Triple (and Quadruple) Entente is waging war, *not* over Belgium: this is common knowledge and only hypocrites will disguise the fact. Britain is grabbing at Germany's colonies and Turkey; Russia is grabbing at Galicia and Turkey, France wants Alsace-Lorraine and even the left bank of the Rhine; a treaty has been concluded with Italy for the division of the spoils (Albania and Asia Minor); bargaining is going on with Bulgaria and Rumania, also for the division of the spoils. In the present war waged by the governments of today, it is *impossible* to help Belgium *otherwise* than by helping to throttle Austria or Turkey, etc.! Where does "defence of the fatherland" come in here? Herein lies the specific feature of imperialist war, a war between reactionary-bourgeois and historically outmoded governments, waged for the purpose of oppressing other nations. Whoever justifies participation in the present war is perpetuating the imperialist oppression of nations. Whoever advocates taking advantage of the present embarrassments of the governments so as to fight for the social revolution is championing the real freedom of really all nations, which is possible only under socialism.

What Russia Is Fighting For

In Russia, capitalist imperialism of the latest type has fully revealed itself in the policy of tsarism towards Persia, Manchuria and Mongolia, but, in general, military and feudal imperialism is predominant in Russia. In no country in the world are the majority of the population oppressed so much as in Russia; Great Russians constitute only 43 per cent of the population, i.e., less than half; the non-Russians are denied all rights. Of the 170 million inhabitants of Russia, *about 100 million* are oppressed and denied their rights. Tsarism is waging a war to seize Galicia and finally crush the liberties of the Ukrainians, and to obtain possession of Armenia, Constantinople, etc. Tsarism regards the war as a means of diverting attention from the mounting discontent within the country and of suppressing the growing revolutionary movement. To every two Great Russians in Russia today there are two or three non-Russians without even elementary rights: tsarism is striving, by means of the war, to increase the number of nations oppressed by Russia, to perpetuate this oppression, and thereby undermine the struggle for freedom which the Great Russians themselves are waging. The possibility of oppressing and robbing other nations perpetuates economic stagnation, because the source of income is frequently, not the development of productive forces, but the semi-feudal exploitation of non-Russians. Thus on the part of Russia, the war is marked by its profoundly reactionary character, its hostility to national liberation.

What Social-Chauvinism Is

Social-chauvinism is advocacy of the idea of "defence of the fatherland" in the present war. This idea logically leads to the abandonment of the class struggle during the war, to voting for war credits, etc. In fact, the social-chauvinists are pursuing an anti-proletarian bourgeois policy, for they are actually championing, not "defence of the fatherland" in the sense of combating foreign oppression, but the "right" of one or other of the "Great" Powers to plunder colonies and to oppress other nations. The social-chauvinists reiterate the bourgeois deception of the people that the war is being waged to protect the freedom and existence of nations, thereby taking sides with the bourgeoisie against the proletariat. Among the social-chauvinists are those who justify and varnish the governments and bourgeoisie of *one* of the belligerent groups of powers, as well as those who, like Kautsky, argue that the socialists of *all* the belligerent powers are equally entitled to "defend the fatherland." Social-chauvinism, which is, in effect, defence of the privileges, the advantages, the right to pillage and plunder, of one's "own" (or any) imperialist bourgeoisie, is the utter betrayal of all socialist convictions and of the decision of the Basle International Socialist Congress.

The Basle Manifesto

The Manifesto on war unanimously adopted in Basle in 1912 has in view the very kind of war between Britain and Germany and their present allies, which broke out in 1914. The Manifesto openly declares that no interests of the people can serve to justify such a war waged "for the sake of the profits of the capitalists and the ambitions of dynasties," on the basis of the imperialist, predatory policy of the Great Powers. The Manifesto openly declares that war is dangerous to "governments" (all of them without exception), notes their fear of "a proletarian revolution," and very definitely points to the example set by the Commune of 1871, and by October–December 1905, i.e., *to the examples of revolution and civil war*. Thus, the Basle Manifesto lays down, precisely for the present war, the tactics of the workers' revolutionary struggle on an international scale against their governments, the tactics of proletarian revolution. The Basle Manifesto repeats the words in the Stuttgart resolution that, in the event of war, socialists must take advantage of the "economic and political crisis" it will cause so as to "hasten the downfall of capitalism," i.e., take advantage of the governments' wartime difficulties and the indignation of the masses, to advance the socialist revolution.

The social-chauvinists' policy, their justification of the war from the bourgeois-liberation standpoint, their sanctioning of "defence of the fatherland," their voting for credits, membership in governments, and so on and so forth, are downright treachery to socialism, which can be explained only, as we will soon show, by the victory of opportunism and of the national liberal-labour policy in the majority of European parties.

False References to Marx and Engels

The Russian social-chauvinists (headed by Plekhanov) make references to Marx's tactics in the war of 1870; the German (of the type of Lensch, David and Co.)—to Engels's statement in 1891 that, in the event of war against Russia and France combined, it would be the duty of the German socialists to defend their fatherland; finally, the social-chauvinists of the Kautsky type, who want to reconcile and legitimatise international chauvinism, refer to the fact that Marx and Engels, while condemning war, nevertheless, from 1854–55 to 1870–71 and 1876–77, always took the side of one belligerent state or another, once war had broken out.

All these references are outrageous distortions of the views of Marx and Engels, in the interest of the bourgeoisie and the opportunists, in just the same way as the writings of the anarchists Guillaume and Co. distort the views of Marx and Engels so as to justify anarchism. The war of 1870–71 was historically progressive on the part of Germany, until Napoleon III was defeated: the latter, together with the tsar, had oppressed Germany for years, keeping her in a state of feudal disunity. But as soon as the war developed into the plundering of France (the annexation of Alsace and Lorraine), Marx and Engels emphatically condemned the Germans. Even at the beginning of the war, Marx and Engels approved of the refusal of Bebel and Liebknecht to vote for war credits, and advised Social-Democrats not to merge with the bourgeoisie, but to uphold the independent class interests of the proletariat. To apply to the present imperialist war the appraisal of this bourgeois-progressive war of national liberation is a mockery of the truth. The same applies with still greater force to the war of 1854–55, and to all the wars of the nineteenth century, when there existed *no* modern imperialism, *no* mature objective conditions for socialism, and *no* mass socialist parties *in any* of the belligerent countries, i.e., none of the conditions from which the Basle Manifesto deduced the tactics of a "proletarian revolution" *in connection* with a war between Great Powers.

Anyone who today refers to Marx's attitude towards the wars of the epoch of the *progressive* bourgeoisie, and forgets Marx's statement that "the workingmen have no country"—a statement that applies *precisely* to the period of the reactionary and outmoded bourgeoisie, to the epoch of the socialist revolution, is shamelessly distorting Marx, and is substituting the bourgeois point of view for the socialist.

The Collapse of the Second International

Socialists of all the world solemnly declared in Basle, in 1912, that they regarded the impending war in Europe as the "criminal" and most reactionary deed of *all* the governments, which must hasten the downfall of capitalism by inevitably engendering a revolution against it. The war came, the crisis was there. Instead of revolutionary tactics, most of the Social-Democratic parties launched reactionary tactics, and went over to the side of their respective governments and bourgeoisie. This betrayal of socialism signifies the collapse of the Second (1889–1914) International, and we must realise what caused this collapse, what brought social-chauvinism into being and gave it strength.

Social-Chauvinism Is the Acme of Opportunism

Throughout the existence of the Second International, a struggle was raging within all the Social-Democratic parties, between their revolutionary and their opportunist wings. In a number of countries a split took place along this line (Britain, Italy, Holland, Bulgaria). Not one Marxist has ever doubted that opportunism expresses bourgeois policies within the working-class movement, expresses the interests of the petty bourgeoisie and the alliance of a tiny section of bourgeoisified workers with their "*own*" bourgeoisie, against the interests of the proletarian masses, the oppressed masses.

The objective conditions at the close of the nineteenth century greatly intensified opportunism, converted the utilisation of bourgeois legality into subservience to the latter, created a thin crust of a working-class officialdom and aristocracy and attracted numerous petty-bourgeois "fellow travellers" to the Social-Democratic parties.

The war has speeded up this development and transformed opportunism into social-chauvinism, transformed the secret alliance between the opportunists and the bourgeoisie into an open one. Simultaneously, the military authorities have everywhere instituted martial law and have muzzled the mass of the workers, whose old leaders have nearly all gone over to the bourgeoisie.

Opportunism and social-chauvinism stand on a common economic basis—the interests of a thin crust of privileged workers and of the petty bourgeoisie, who are defending their privileged position, their "right" to some modicum of the profits that their "own" national bourgeoisie obtain from robbing other nations, from the advantages of their Great-Power status, etc.

Opportunism and social-chauvinism have the same politico-ideological content—class collaboration instead of the class struggle, renunciation of revolutionary methods of struggle, helping one's "own" government in its embarrassed situation, instead of taking advantage of these embarrassments so as to advance the revolution. If we take Europe as a whole and if we pay attention, not to individuals (even the most authoritative), we will find that it is the opportunist *trend* that has become the bulwark of social-chauvinism, whereas from the camp of the revolutionaries, more or less consistent protests against it are heard from almost all sides. And if we take, for example, the grouping of trends at the Stuttgart International Socialist Congress in 1907, we shall find that international Marxism was opposed to imperialism, while international opportunism was already in favour of it at the time.

Unity with the Opportunists Means an Alliance Between the Workers and Their "Own" National Bourgeoisie, and Splitting the International Revolutionary Working Class

In the past, before the war, opportunism was often looked upon as a legitimate, though "deviationist" and "extremist," component of the Social-Democratic Party. The war has shown the impossibility of this in the future. Opportunism has "matured," and is now playing to the full its role as emissary of the bourgeoisie in the working-class movement. Unity with the opportunists has become sheer hypocrisy, exemplified by the German Social-Democratic Party. On every important occasion (e.g., the August 4 vote), the opportunists present an ultimatum, to which they give effect through their numerous links with the bourgeoisie, their majority on the executives of the trade unions, etc. Today *unity* with the opportunists *actually* means subordinating the working class to their "own" national bourgeoisie, and an alliance with the latter for the purpose of oppressing other nations and of fighting for dominant-nation privileges; it means *splitting* the revolutionary proletariat of all countries.

No matter how hard, in individual instances, the struggle may be against the opportunists, who predominate in many organisations, whatever the specific nature of the purging of the workers' parties of opportunists in individual countries, this process is inevitable and fruitful. Reformist socialism is dying; regenerated socialism "will be revolutionary, uncompromising and insurrectionary," to use the apt expression of the French Socialist Paul Golay.

"Kautskyism"

Kautsky, the leading authority in the Second International, is a most typical and striking example of how a verbal recognition of Marxism has led in practice to its conversion into "Struvism" or into "Brentanoism."[1] Another example is Plekhanov. By means of patent sophistry, Marxism is stripped of its revolutionary living spirit; *everything* is recognised in Marxism *except* the revolutionary methods of struggle, the propaganda and preparation of those methods, and the education of the masses in this direction. Kautsky "reconciles" in an unprincipled way the fundamental idea of social-chauvinism, recognition of defence of the fatherland in the present war, with a diplomatic sham concession to the Lefts—his abstention from voting for war credits, his verbal claim to be in the opposition, etc. Kautsky, who in 1909 wrote a book on the approaching epoch of revolutions and on the connection between war and revolution, Kautsky, who in 1912 signed the Basle Manifesto on taking revolutionary advantage of the impending war, is outdoing himself in justifying and embellishing social-chauvinism and, like Plekhanov, joins the bourgeoisie in ridiculing any thought of revolution and all steps towards the immediate revolutionary struggle.

The working class cannot play its world-revolutionary role unless it wages a ruthless struggle against this backsliding, spinelessness, subservience to opportunism, and unparalleled vulgarisation of the theories of Marxism. Kautskyism is not fortuitous; it is the social product of the contradictions within the Second International, a blend of loyalty to Marxism in word, and subordination to opportunism in deed.

This fundamental falseness of "Kautskyism" manifests itself in different ways in different countries. In Holland, Roland-Holst,

---

1. Revisionist Marxist positions associated with the names of Peter Struve in Russia and the economist Lujo Brentano in Germany. [*R. T.*]

while rejecting the idea of defending the fatherland, defends unity with the opportunists' party. In Russia, Trotsky, while rejecting this idea, also defends unity with the opportunist and chauvinist *Nasha Zarya* group. In Rumania, Rakovsky, while declaring war on opportunism as being responsible for the collapse of the International, is at the same time ready to recognise the legitimacy of the idea of defending the fatherland. All this is a manifestation of the evil which the Dutch Marxists (Gorter and Pannekoek) have called "passive radicalism," and which amounts to replacing revolutionary Marxism with eclecticism in theory, and servility to or impotence towards opportunism, in practice.

The Marxists' Slogan Is a Slogan of
Revolutionary Social-Democracy

The war has undoubtedly created a most acute crisis and has immeasurably increased the distress of the masses. The reactionary nature of this war, and the unblushing lies told by the bourgeoisie of *all* countries to conceal their predatory aims with "national" ideology are, on the basis of an objectively revolutionary situation, inevitably creating revolutionary moods among the masses. It is our duty to help the masses become conscious of these moods, deepen them and give them shape. This task finds correct expression only in the slogan: convert the imperialist war into a civil war; *all* consistently waged class struggles in wartime and all seriously conducted "mass-action" tactics inevitably lead to this. It is impossible to foretell whether a powerful revolutionary movement will flare up in connection with, during or after the first or the second imperialist war of the Great Powers; in any case it is our bounden duty to work systematically and unswervingly in this direction.

The Basle Manifesto makes direct reference to the example set by the Paris Commune, i.e., the conversion of a war between governments into a civil war. Half a century ago, the proletariat was too weak; the objective conditions for socialism had not yet matured, there could be no co-ordination and co-operation between the revolutionary movements in all the belligerent countries; the "national ideology" (the traditions of 1792), with which a section of the Parisian workers were imbued, was a petty-bourgeois weakness, which Marx noted at the time, and was one of the causes of the downfall of the Commune. Half a century since that time, the conditions that then weakened the revolution have ceased to operate, and today it is unpardonable for a socialist to resign himself to a renunciation of activities in the spirit of the Paris Communards.

* * *

On the National Pride
of the Great Russians

The outbreak of the World War caused a wave of patriotic publicity and chauvinist feeling in the belligerent countries, Russia included. Lenin's revolutionary defeatism, his view expressed in an article of September 1914 ("The War and Russian Social-Democracy") that the defeat of the tsarist monarchy would be the "lesser evil" because it was the most reactionary and barbarous of the warring governments, went against this current. "On the National Pride of the Great Russians," published in December 1914 in the Geneva-based party paper *Sotsial-Demokrat,* does not deal directly with the war issue. But it may be interpreted as the apologia of an anti-war Russian radical for his position, an attempt to show how such a position could itself be patriotic insofar as Russia's revolutionary tradition was a legitimate basis for national pride.

What a lot of talk, argument and vociferation there is nowadays about nationality and the fatherland! Liberal and radical cabinet ministers in Britain, a host of "forward-looking" journalists in France (who have proved in full agreement with their reactionary colleagues), and a swarm of official Cadet and progressive scribblers in Russia (including several Narodniks and "Marxists")—all have effusive praise for the liberty and independence of their respective countries, the grandeur of the principle of national independence. Here one cannot tell where the venal eulogist of the butcher Nicholas Romanov or of the brutal oppressors of Negroes and Indians ends, and where the common philistine, who from sheer stupidity or spinelessness drifts with the stream, begins. Nor is that distinction important. We see before us an extensive and very deep ideological trend, whose origins are closely interwoven with the interests of the landowners and the capitalists of the dominant nations. Scores and hundreds of millions are being spent every year for the propaganda of ideas advantageous to those classes: it is a pretty big mill-race that takes its waters from all sources—from Menshikov, a chauvinist by conviction, to chauvinists for reason of opportunism or spinelessness, such as Plekhanov and Maslov, Rubanovich and Smirnov, Kropotkin and Burtsev.

Let us, Great-Russian Social-Democrats, also try to define our attitude to this ideological trend. It would be unseemly for us, representatives of a dominant nation in the far east of Europe and a goodly part of Asia, to forget the immense significance of the national question—especially in a country which has been rightly called the "prison of the peoples," and particularly at a time when, in the far east of Europe and in Asia, capitalism is awakening to life and self-consciousness a number of "new" nations, large and small; at a moment when the tsarist monarchy has called up millions of Great Russians and non-Russians, so as to "solve" a number of national problems in accordance with the interests of the Council of the United Nobility and of the Guchkovs, Krestovnikovs, Dolgorukovs, Kutlers and Rodichevs.

Is a sense of national pride alien to us, Great-Russian class-conscious proletarians? Certainly not! We love our language and our country, and we are doing our very utmost to raise *her* toiling masses (i.e., nine-tenths of *her* population) to the level of a democratic and socialist consciousness. To us it is most painful to see and feel the outrages, the oppression and the humiliation our fair country suffers at the hands of the tsar's butchers, the nobles and the capitalists. We take pride in the resistance to these outrages put up from our midst, from the Great Russians; in *that* midst having produced Radishchev, the Decembrists and the revolutionary commoners of the seventies; in the Great-Russian working class having created, in 1905, a mighty revolutionary party of the masses; and in the Great-Russian peasantry having begun to turn towards democracy and set about overthrowing the clergy and the landed proprietors.

We remember that Chernyshevksy, the Great-Russian democrat, who dedicated his life to the cause of revolution, said half a century ago: "A wretched nation, a nation of slaves, from top to bottom—all slaves."[1] The overt and covert Great-Russian slaves (slaves with regard to the tsarist monarchy) do not like to recall these words. Yet, in our opinion, these were words of genuine love for our country, a love distressed by the absence of a revolutionary spirit in the masses of the Great-Russian people. There was none of that spirit at the time. There is little of it now, but it already exists. We are full of national pride because the Great-Russian nation, *too*, has created a revolutionary class, because it, *too*, has proved capable of providing mankind with great models of the struggle for

---

1. The quotation is from Chernyshevsky's novel *The Prologue*.

freedom and socialism, and not only with great pogroms, rows of gallows, dungeons, great famines and great servility to priests, tsars, landowners and capitalists.

We are full of a sense of national pride, and for that very reason we *particularly* hate *our* slavish past (when the landed nobility led the peasants into war to stifle the freedom of Hungary, Poland, Persia and China), and our slavish present, when these selfsame landed proprietors, aided by the capitalists, are leading us into a war in order to throttle Poland and the Ukraine, crush the democratic movement in Persia and China, and strengthen the gang of Romanovs, Bobrinskys and Purishkeviches, who are a disgrace to our Great-Russian national dignity. Nobody is to be blamed for being born a slave; but a slave who not only eschews a striving for freedom but justifies and eulogises his slavery (e.g., calls the throttling of Poland and the Ukraine, etc., a "defence of the fatherland" of the Great Russians)—such a slave is a lickspittle and a boor, who arouses a legitimate feeling of indignation, contempt, and loathing.

"No nation can be free if it oppresses other nations,"[2] said Marx and Engels, the greatest representatives of consistent nineteenth-century democracy, who became the teachers of the revolutionary proletariat. And, full of a sense of national pride, we Great-Russian workers want, come what may, a free and independent, a democratic, republican and proud Great Russia, one that will base its relations with its neighbours on the human principle of equality, and not on the feudalist principle of privilege, which is so degrading to a great nation. Just because we want that, we say: it is impossible, in the twentieth century and in Europe (even in the far east of Europe), to "defend the fatherland" otherwise than by using every revolutionary means to combat the monarchy, the landowners and the capitalists of one's *own* fatherland, i.e., the *worst* enemies of our country. We say that the Great Russians cannot "defend the fatherland" otherwise than by desiring the defeat of tsarism in any war, this as the lesser evil to nine-tenths of the inhabitants of Great Russia. For tsarism not only oppresses those nine-tenths economically and politically, but also demoralises, degrades, dishonours and prostitutes them by teaching them to oppress other nations and to cover up this shame with hypocritical and quasi-patriotic phrases.

The objection may be advanced that, besides tsarism and under its wing, another historical force has arisen and become strong, viz., Great-Russian capitalism, which is carrying on progressive work by economically centralising and welding together vast re-

2. See Friedrich Engels, *Emigré Litera-*   *Volksstaat*, No. 73, 1874.)
ture. I. The Polish Proclamation. (*Der*

gions. This objection, however, does not excuse, but on the contrary still more condemns our socialist-chauvinists, who should be called tsarist-Purishkevich socialists (just as Marx called the Lassalleans Royal-Prussian socialists). Let us even assume that history will decide in favour of Great-Russian dominant-nation capitalism, and against the hundred and one small nations. That is not impossible, for the entire history of capital is one of violence and plunder, blood and corruption. We do not advocate preserving small nations at all costs; *other conditions being equal*, we are decidedly for centralisation and are opposed to the petty-bourgeois ideal of federal relationships. Even if our assumption were true, however, it is, firstly, not our business, or that of democrats (let alone of socialists), to help Romanov-Bobrinsky-Purishkevich throttle the Ukraine, etc. In his own Junker fashion, Bismarck accomplished a progressive historical task, but he would be a fine "Marxist" indeed who, on such grounds, thought of justifying socialist support for Bismarck! Moreover, Bismarck promoted economic development by bringing together the disunited Germans, who were being oppressed by other nations. The economic prosperity and rapid development of Great Russia, however, require that the country be liberated from Great-Russian oppression of other nations—that is the difference that our admirers of the true-Russian would-be Bismarcks overlook.

Secondly, if history were to decide in favour of Great-Russian dominant-nation capitalism, it follows hence that the *socialist* role of the Great-Russian proletariat, as the principal driving force of the communist revolution engendered by capitalism, will be all the greater. The proletarian revolution calls for a prolonged education of the workers in the spirit of the *fullest* national equality and brotherhood. Consequently, the interests of the Great-Russian proletariat require that the masses be systematically educated to champion—most resolutely, consistently, boldly and in a revolutionary manner—complete equality and the right to self-determination for all the nations oppressed by the Great Russians. The interests of the Great Russians' national pride (understood, not in the slavish sense) coincide with the *socialist* interests of the Great-Russian (and all other) proletarians. Our model will always be Marx, who, after living in Britain for decades and becoming half-English, demanded freedom and national independence for Ireland in the interests of the socialist movement of the British workers.

In the second hypothetical case we have considered, our homegrown socialist-chauvinists, Plekhanov, etc., etc., will prove traitors, not only to their own country—a free and democratic Great Russia, but also to the proletarian brotherhood of all the nations of Russia, i.e., to the cause of socialism.

On the Slogan for a
United States of Europe

In the manifesto of September 1914 on "The War and Russian Social-Democracy," Lenin had espoused the formation of a republican United States of Europe, via revolutionary overthrow of the German, Austrian, and Russian monarchies, as a political slogan for Europe's Social-Democrats. However, further thought and discussion among the editors of the party's central organ (*Sotsial-Demokrat*) led to the rejection of this slogan for the reasons given in this article published in *Sotsial-Demokrat* in August 1915. Notable among these reasons is the argument that "uneven economic and political development is an absolute law of capitalism," from which Lenin deduces that "the victory of socialism is possible in several or even in one capitalist country alone." In the party controversies of the mid-twenties Stalin would repeatedly cite this statement to prove that Lenin originated the concept of "socialism in one country." Lenin's point, however, was only that a socialist revolution might *originate* in one country.

In No. 40 of *Sotsial-Demokrat* we reported that a conference of our Party's groups abroad[1] had decided to defer the question of the "United States of Europe" slogan pending a discussion, in the press, on the *economic* aspect of the matter.

At our conference the debate on this question assumed a purely political character. Perhaps this was partly caused by the Central Committee's Manifesto having formulated this slogan as a forthright political one ("the immediate *political* slogan . . . ," as it says there); not only did it advance the slogan of a republican United States of Europe, but expressly emphasised that this slogan is meaningless and false "without the revolutionary overthrow of the German, Austrian and Russian monarchies."

It would be quite wrong to object to such a presentation of the question *within the limits* of a political appraisal of this slogan—

1. The Conference of R.S.D.L.P. groups abroad, February 27–March 4, 1915, was held in Berne, Switzerland. The conference was called on Lenin's initia-tive and had the significance of a general Bolshevik Party conference, since an all-Russia conference could not be called owing to the war.

e.g., to argue that it obscures or weakens, etc., the slogan of a socialist revolution. Political changes of a truly democratic nature, and especially political revolutions, can under no circumstances whatsoever either obscure or weaken the slogan of a socialist revolution. On the contrary, they always bring it closer, extend its basis, and draw new sections of the petty bourgeoisie and the semi-proletarian masses into the socialist struggle. On the other hand, political revolutions are inevitable in the course of the socialist revolution, which should not be regarded as a single act, but as a period of turbulent political and economic upheavals, the most intense class struggle, civil war, revolutions, and counter-revolutions.

But while the slogan of a republican United States of Europe—if accompanied by the revolutionary overthrow of the three most reactionary monarchies in Europe, headed by the Russian—is quite invulnerable as a political slogan, there still remains the highly important question of its economic content and significance. From the standpoint of the economic conditions of imperialism—i.e., the export of capital and the division of the world by the "advanced" and "civilised" colonial powers—a United States of Europe, under capitalism, is either impossible or reactionary.

Capital has become international and monopolist. The world has been carved up by a handful of Great Powers, i.e., powers successful in the great plunder and oppression of nations. The four Great Powers of Europe—Britain, France, Russia and Germany, with an aggregate population of between 250,000,000 and 300,000,000, and an area of about 7,000,000 square kilometres—possess colonies with a population of *almost 500 million* (494,500,000) and an area of 64,600,000 square kilometres, i.e., almost half the surface of the globe (133,000,000 square kilometres, exclusive of Arctic and Antarctic regions). Add to this the three Asian states—China, Turkey and Persia, now being rent piecemeal by thugs that are waging a war of "liberation," namely, Japan, Russia, Britain and France. Those three Asian states, which may be called semi-colonies (in reality they are now 90 per cent colonies), have a total population of 360,000,000 and an area of 14,500,000 square kilometres (almost one and a half times the area of all Europe).

Furthermore, Britain, France and Germany have invested capital abroad to the value of no less than 70,000 million rubles. The business of securing "legitimate" profits from this tidy sum—these exceed 3,000 million rubles annually—is carried out by the national committees of the millionaires, known as governments, which are equipped with armies and navies and which provide the sons and brothers of the millionaires with jobs in the colonies and semi-colonies as viceroys, consuls, ambassadors, officials of all kinds, clergymen, and other leeches.

That is how the plunder of about a thousand million of the

earth's population by a handful of Great Powers is organised in the epoch of the highest development of capitalism. No other organisation is possible under capitalism. Renounce colonies, "spheres of influence," and the export of capital? To think that it is possible means coming down to the level of some snivelling parson who every Sunday preaches to the rich on the lofty principles of Christianity and advises them to give the poor, well, if not millions, at least several hundred rubles yearly.

A United States of Europe under capitalism is tantamount to an agreement on the partition of colonies. Under capitalism, however, no other basis and no other principle of division are possible except force. A multi-millionaire cannot share the "national income" of a capitalist country with anyone otherwise than "in proportion to the capital invested" (with a bonus thrown in, so that the biggest capital may receive more than its share). Capitalism is private ownership of the means of production, and anarchy in production. To advocate a "just" division of income on such a basis is sheer Proudhonism, stupid philistinism. No division can be effected otherwise than in "proportion to strength," and strength changes with the course of economic development. Following 1871, the rate of Germany's accession of strength was three or four times as rapid as that of Britain and France, and of Japan about ten times as rapid as Russia's. There is and there can be no other way of testing the real might of a capitalist state than by war. War does not contradict the fundamentals of private property—on the contrary, it is a direct and inevitable outcome of those fundamentals. Under capitalism the smooth economic growth of individual enterprises or individual states is impossible. Under capitalism, there are no other means of restoring the periodically disturbed equilibrium than crises in industry and wars in politics.

Of course, *temporary* agreements are possible between capitalists and between states. In this sense a United States of Europe is possible as an agreement between the *European* capitalists . . . but to what end? Only for the purpose of jointly suppressing socialism in Europe, of jointly protecting colonial booty *against* Japan and America, who have been badly done out of their share by the present partition of colonies, and the increase of whose might during the last fifty years has been immeasurably more rapid than that of backward and monarchist Europe, now turning senile. Compared with the United States of America, Europe as a whole denotes economic stagnation. On the present economic basis, i.e., under capitalism, a United States of Europe would signify an organisation of reaction to retard America's more rapid development. The times when the cause of democracy and socialism was associated only with Europe alone have gone for ever.

A United States of the World (not of Europe alone) is the state form of the unification and freedom of nations which we associate with socialism—until the time when the complete victory of communism brings about the total disappearance of the state, including the democratic. As a separate slogan, however, the slogan of a United States of the World would hardly be a correct one, first, because it merges with socialism; second, because it may be wrongly interpreted to mean that the victory of socialism in a single country is impossible, and it may also create misconceptions as to the relations of such a country to the others.

Uneven economic and political development is an absolute law of capitalism. Hence, the victory of socialism is possible first in several or even in one capitalist country alone. After expropriating the capitalists and organising their own socialist production, the victorious proletariat of that country will arise *against* the rest of the world—the capitalist world—attracting to its cause the oppressed classes of other countries, stirring uprisings in those countries against the capitalists, and in case of need using even armed force against the exploiting classes and their states. The political form of a society wherein the proletariat is victorious in overthrowing the bourgeoisie will be a democratic republic, which will more and more concentrate the forces of the proletariat of a given nation or nations, in the struggle against states that have not yet gone over to socialism. The abolition of classes is impossible without a dictatorship of the oppressed class, of the proletariat. A free union of nations in socialism is impossible without a more or less prolonged and stubborn struggle of the socialist republics against the backward states.

It is for these reasons and after repeated discussions at the conference of R.S.D.L.P. groups abroad, and following that conference, that the central organ's editors have come to the conclusion that the slogan for a United States of Europe is an erroneous one.

Imperialism, the Highest Stage of Capitalism

A POPULAR OUTLINE

Imperialism, first published early in 1917 in Petrograd, was to become one of the most influential of all Lenin's writings, and on the face of it was one of the most theoretical. It must be seen, however, as a theoretical study which was highly political in its origin and aim. By demonstrating that the World War was an imperialist one in essence—for which purpose a general discussion of imperialism was necessary—he would justify in theoretical terms his anti-war political position and revolutionary defeatism. The consequence, whether or not intended, was to supply Marxist thought with something that it had lacked up to this point—a cogent theory of international relations in the early twentieth century. In preparing the study in 1915–16, Lenin made use of earlier Marxist as well as non-Marxist writings about imperialism, materials first published in 1939 in his voluminous *Notebooks on Imperialism*.

Preface

The pamphlet here presented to the reader was written in the spring of 1916, in Zurich. In the conditions in which I was obliged to work there I naturally suffered somewhat from a shortage of French and English literature and from a serious dearth of Russian literature. However, I made use of the principal English work on imperialism, the book by J. A. Hobson, with all the care that, in my opinion, that work deserves.

This pamphlet was written with an eye to the tsarist censorship. Hence, I was not only forced to confine myself strictly to an exclusively theoretical, specifically economic analysis of facts, but to formulate the few necessary observations on politics with extreme caution, by hints, in an allegorical language—in that accursed Aesopian language—to which tsarism compelled all revolutionaries to have recourse whenever they took up the pen to write a "legal" work.

It is painful, in these days of liberty, to re-read the passages of the pamphlet which have been distorted, cramped, compressed in an iron vise on account of the censor. That the period of imperialism is the eve of the socialist revolution; that social-chauvinism (socialism in words, chauvinism in deeds) is the utter betrayal of socialism, complete desertion to the side of the bourgeoisie; that this split in the working-class movement is bound up with the objective conditions of imperialism, etc.—on these matters I had to speak in a "slavish" tongue, and I must refer the reader who is interested in the subject to the articles I wrote abroad in 1914–17, a new edition of which is soon to appear. Special attention should be drawn to a passage on pages 119–20.[1] In order to show the reader, in a guise acceptable to the censors, how shamelessly untruthful the capitalists and the social-chauvinists who have deserted to their side (and whom Kautsky opposes so inconsistently) are on the question of annexations; in order to show how shamelessly they *screen* the annexations of *their* capitalists, I was forced to quote as an example—Japan! The careful reader will easily substitute Russia for Japan, and Finland, Poland, Courland, the Ukraine, Khiva, Bokhara, Estonia or other regions peopled by non-Great Russians, for Korea.

I trust that this pamphlet will help the reader to understand the fundamental economic question, that of the economic essence of imperialism, for unless this is studied, it will be impossible to understand and appraise modern war and modern politics.

Petrograd Author
April 26, 1917

Preface to the French and German Editions

I

As was indicated in the preface to the Russian edition, this pamphlet was written in 1916, with an eye to the tsarist censorship. I am unable to revise the whole text at the present time, nor, perhaps, would this be advisable, since the main purpose of the book was, and remains, to present, on the basis of the summarised returns of irrefutable bourgeois statistics, and the admissions of bourgeois scholars of all countries, a *composite picture* of the world capitalist system in its international relationships at the beginning

1. See p. 269, below. [*R. T.*]

of the twentieth century—on the eve of the first world imperialist war.

To a certain extent it will even be useful for many Communists in advanced capitalist countries to convince themselves by the example of this pamphlet, *legal from the standpoint of the tsarist censor*, of the possibility, and necessity, of making use of even the slight remnants of legality which still remain at the disposal of the Communists, say, in contemporary America or France, after the recent almost wholesale arrests of Communists, in order to explain the utter falsity of social-pacifist views and hopes for "world democracy." The most essential of what should be added to this censored pamphlet I shall try to present in this preface.

II

It is proved in the pamphlet that the war of 1914–18 was imperialist (that is, an annexationist, predatory, war of plunder) on the part of both sides; it was a war for the division of the world, for the partition and repartition of colonies and spheres of influence of finance capital, etc.

Proof of what was the true social, or rather, the true class character of the war is naturally to be found, not in the diplomatic history of the war, but in an analysis of the *objective* position of the ruling *classes* in *all* the belligerent countries. In order to depict this objective position one must not take examples or isolated data (in view of the extreme complexity of the phenomena of social life it is always possible to select any number of examples or separate data to prove any proposition), but *all* the data on the *basis* of economic life in *all* the belligerent countries and the *whole* world.

It is precisely irrefutable summarised data of this kind that I quoted in describing the *partition of the world* in 1876 and 1914 (in Chapter VI) and the division of the world's *railways* in 1890 and 1913 (in Chapter VII). Railways are a summation of the basic capitalist industries, coal, iron and steel; a summation and the most striking index of the development of world trade and bourgeois-democratic civilisation. How the railways are linked up with large-scale industry, with monopolies, syndicates, cartels, trusts, banks and the financial oligarchy is shown in the preceding chapters of the book. The uneven distribution of the railways, their uneven development—sums up, as it were, modern monopolist capitalism on a world-wide scale. And this summary proves that imperialist wars are absolutely inevitable under *such* an economic system, *as long as* private property in the means of production exists.

The building of railways seems to be a simple, natural, democratic, cultural and civilising enterprise; that is what it is in the opinion of the bourgeois professors who are paid to depict capitalist slavery in bright colours, and in the opinion of petty-bourgeois philistines. But as a matter of fact the capitalist threads, which in thousands of different intercrossings bind these enterprises with private property in the means of production in general, have converted this railway construction into an instrument for oppressing *a thousand million* people (in the colonies and semi-colonies), that is, more than half the population of the globe that inhabits the dependent countries, as well as the wage-slaves of capital in the "civilised" countries.

Private property based on the labour of the small proprietor, free competition, democracy, all the catchwords with which the capitalists and their press deceive the workers and the peasants—are things of the distant past. Capitalism has grown into a world system of colonial oppression and of the financial strangulation of the overwhelming majority of the population of the world by a handful of "advanced" countries. And this "booty" is shared between two or three powerful world plunderers armed to the teeth (America, Great Britain, Japan), who are drawing the whole world into *their* war over the division of *their* booty.

III

The Treaty of Brest-Litovsk dictated by monarchist Germany, and the subsequent much more brutal and despicable Treaty of Versailles dictated by the "democratic" republics of America and France and also by "free" Britain, have rendered a most useful service to humanity by exposing both imperialism's hired coolies of the pen and petty-bourgeois reactionaries who, although they call themselves pacifists and socialists, sang praises to "Wilsonism," and insisted that peace and reforms were possible under imperialism.

The tens of millions of dead and maimed left by the war—a war to decide whether the British or German group of financial plunderers is to receive the most booty—and those two "peace treaties," are with unprecedented rapidity opening the eyes of the millions and tens of millions of people who are downtrodden, oppressed, deceived and duped by the bourgeoisie. Thus, out of the universal ruin caused by the war a world-wide revolutionary crisis is arising which, however prolonged and arduous its stages may be, cannot end otherwise than in a proletarian revolution and in its victory.

The Basle Manifesto of the Second International, which in 1912 gave an appraisal of the very war that broke out in 1914 and not of war in general (there are different kinds of wars, including revolutionary wars)—this Manifesto is now a monument exposing to the full the shameful bankruptcy and treachery of the heroes of the Second International.

That is why I reproduce this Manifesto as a supplement to the present edition, and again and again I urge the reader to note that the heroes of the Second International are as assiduously avoiding the passages of this Manifesto which speak precisely, clearly and definitely of the connection between that impending war and the proletarian revolution, as a thief avoids the scene of his crime.

IV

Special attention has been devoted in this pamphlet to a criticism of Kautskyism, the international ideological trend represented in all countries of the world by the "most prominent theoreticians," the leaders of the Second International (Otto Bauer and Co. in Austria, Ramsay MacDonald and others in Britain, Albert Thomas in France, etc., etc.) and a multitude of socialists, reformists, pacifists, bourgeois democrats and parsons.

This ideological trend is, on the one hand, a product of the disintegration and decay of the Second International, and, on the other hand, the inevitable fruit of the ideology of the petty bourgeoisie, whose entire way of life holds them captive to bourgeois and democratic prejudices.

The views held by Kautsky and his like are a complete renunciation of those same revolutionary principles of Marxism that he has championed for decades, especially, by the way, in his struggle against socialist opportunism (of Bernstein, Millerand, Hyndman, Gompers, etc.). It is not a mere accident, therefore, that Kautsky's followers all over the world have now united in practical politics with the extreme opportunists (through the Second, or Yellow International) and with the bourgeois governments (through bourgeois coalition governments in which socialists take part).

The growing world proletarian revolutionary movement in general, and the communist movement in particular, cannot dispense with an analysis and exposure of the theoretical errors of Kautskyism. The more so since pacifism and "democracy" in general, which lay no claim to Marxism whatever, but which, like Kautsky and Co., are obscuring the profundity of the contradictions of imperialism and the inevitable revolutionary crisis to which it gives rise, are still very widespread all over the world. To combat these tendencies is the bounden duty of the party of the proletariat, which must win away from the bourgeoisie the small proprietors who are duped by them, and the millions of working people who enjoy more or less petty-bourgeois conditions of life.

V

A few words must be said about Chapter VIII, "Parasitism and Decay of Capitalism." As already pointed out in the text, Hilferding, ex-"Marxist," and now a comrade-in-arms of Kautsky and one of the chief exponents of bourgeois, reformist policy in the Independent Social-Democratic Party of Germany, has taken a step backward on this question compared with the *frankly* pacifist and reformist Englishman, Hobson. The international split of the entire working-class movement is now quite evident (the Second and the Third Internationals). The fact that armed struggle and civil war is now raging between the two trends is also evident—the support given to Kolchak and Denikin in Russia by the Mensheviks and Socialist-Revolutionaries against the Bolsheviks; the fight the Scheidemanns and Noskes have conducted in conjunction with the bourgeoisie against the Spartacists[1] in Germany; the same thing in Finland, Poland, Hungary, etc. What is the economic basis of this world-historical phenomenon?

It is precisely the parasitism and decay of capitalism, characteristic of its highest historical stage of development, i.e., imperialism. As this pamphlet shows, capitalism has now singled out a *handful* (less than one-tenth of the inhabitants of the globe; less than one-fifth at a most "generous" and liberal calculation) of exceptionally rich and powerful states which plunder the whole world simply by "clipping coupons." Capital exports yield an income of eight to ten thousand million francs per annum, at pre-war prices and according to pre-war bourgeois statistics. Now, of course, they yield much more.

Obviously, out of such enormous *superprofits* (since they are obtained over and above the profits which capitalists squeeze out of the workers of their "own" country) it is *possible to bribe* the labour leaders and the upper stratum of the labour aristocracy. And that is just what the capitalists of the "advanced" countries are doing: they are bribing them in a thousand different ways, direct and indirect, overt and covert.

This stratum of workers-turned-bourgeois, or the labour aristocracy, who are quite philistine in their mode of life, in the size of their earnings and in their entire outlook, is the principal prop of the Second International, and in our days, the principal *social* (not military) *prop of the bourgeoisie*. For they are the real *agents of the bourgeoisie in the working-class* movement, the labour lieutenants of the capitalist class, real vehicles of reformism and chauvin-

---

1. Members of the Spartakusbund (Spartacus League) formed during the First World War. At the beginning of the war the Internationale group of German Left Social-Democrats was formed, headed by Rosa Luxemburg, Karl Liebknecht, Franz Mehring, Clara Zetkin and others. This was the group that later took the name of "Spartakusbund." It played an important role in the history of the German working-class movement. In 1917 the Spartacus League entered the Centrist Independent Social-Democratic Party of Germany but retained its organisational independence. After the November revolution in Germany in 1918, the Spartacists formed the Communist Party of Germany. In January 1919, after an unsuccessful Spartacist uprising, Luxemburg and Liebknecht were murdered while being taken to prison.

ism. In the civil war between the proletariat and the bourgeoisie they inevitably, and in no small numbers, take the side of the bourgeoisie, the "Versaillese" against the "Communards."

Unless the economic roots of this phenomenon are understood and its political and social significance is appreciated, not a step can be taken toward the solution of the practical problems of the communist movement and of the impending social revolution.

Imperialism is the eve of the social revolution of the proletariat. This has been confirmed since 1917 on a world-wide scale.

July 6, 1920   *N. Lenin*

IMPERIALISM, THE HIGHEST STAGE OF CAPITALISM

During the last fifteen to twenty years, especially since the Spanish-American War (1898) and the Anglo-Boer War (1899–1902), the economic and also the political literature of the two hemispheres has more and more often adopted the term "imperialism" in order to describe the present era. In 1902, a book by the English economist J. A. Hobson, *Imperialism*, was published in London and New York. This author, whose point of view is that of bourgeois social-reformism and pacifism which, in essence, is identical with the present point of view of the ex-Marxist, Karl Kautsky, gives a very good and comprehensive description of the principal specific economic and political features of imperialism. In 1910, there appeared in Vienna the work of the Austrian Marxist, Rudolf Hilferding, *Finance Capital* (Russian edition, Moscow, 1912). In spite of the mistake the author makes on the theory of money, and in spite of a certain inclination on his part to reconcile Marxism with opportunism, this work gives a very valuable theoretical analysis of "the latest phase of capitalist development," as the subtitle runs. Indeed, what has been said of imperialism during the last few years, especially in an enormous number of magazine and newspaper articles, and also in the resolutions, for example, of the Chemnitz[1] and Basle congresses which took place in the autumn of 1912, has scarcely gone beyond the ideas expounded, or more exactly, summed up by the two writers mentioned above. . . .

1. The Chemnitz Congress of the German Social-Democratic Party, September 15–21, 1912; the Congress adopted a resolution on imperialism that described the policy of the imperialist states as "a shameless policy of plunder and annexation" and called upon the Party to "struggle against imperialism with redoubled energy."

Later on, I shall try to show briefly, and as simply as possible, the connection and relationships between the *principal* economic features of imperialism. I shall not be able to deal with the non-economic aspects of the question, however much they deserve to be dealt with. References to literature and other notes which, perhaps, would not interest all readers, are to be found at the end of this pamphlet.

I. Concentration of Production and Monopolies

The enormous growth of industry and the remarkably rapid concentration of production in ever-larger enterprises are one of the most characteristic features of capitalism. Modern production censuses give most complete and most exact data on this process.

In Germany, for example, out of every thousand industrial enterprises, large enterprises, i.e., those employing more than fifty workers, numbered three in 1882, six in 1895 and nine in 1907; and out of every one hundred workers employed, this group of enterprises employed twenty-two, thirty and thirty-seven, respectively. Concentration of production, however, is much more intense than the concentration of workers, since labour in the large enterprises is much more productive. * * *

* * *

In another advanced country of modern capitalism, the United States of America, the growth of the concentration of production is still greater. Here statistics single out industry in the narrow sense of the word and classify enterprises according to the value of their annual output. In 1904 large-scale enterprises with an output valued at one million dollars and over numbered 1,900 (out of 216,180, i.e., 0.9 per cent). These employed 1,400,000 workers (out of 5,500,000, i.e., 25.6 per cent) and the value of their output amounted to $5,600,000,000 (out of $14,800,000,000, i.e., 38 per cent). Five years later, in 1909, the corresponding figures were: 3,060 enterprises (out of 268,491, i.e., 1.1 per cent) employing 2,000,000 workers (out of 6,600,000, i.e., 3.5 per cent) with an output valued at $9,000,000,000 (out of $20,700,000,000, i.e., 43.8 per cent).[2]

Almost half the total production of all the enterprises of the country was carried on by *one-hundredth part* of these enterprises! These 3,000 giant enterprises embrace 258 branches of industry. From this it can be seen that at a certain stage of its development

2. *Statistical Abstract of the United States 1912*, p. 202. [Lenin]

concentration itself, as it were, leads straight to monopoly, for a score or so of giant enterprises can easily arrive at an agreement, and on the other hand, the hindrance to competition, the tendency towards monopoly, arises from the huge size of the enterprises. This transformation of competition into monopoly is one of the most important—if not the most important—phenomena of modern capitalist economy, and we must deal with it in greater detail. But first we must clear up one possible misunderstanding.

American statistics speak of 3,000 giant enterprises in 250 branches of industry, as if there were only a dozen enterprises of the largest scale for each branch of industry.

But this is not the case. Not in every branch of industry are there large-scale enterprises; and moreover, a very important feature of capitalism in its highest stage of development is so-called *combination* of production, that is to say, the grouping in a single enterprise of different branches of industry, which either represent the consecutive stages in the processing of raw materials (for example, the smelting of iron ore into pig-iron, the conversion of pig-iron into steel, and then, perhaps, the manufacture of steel goods)—or are auxiliary to one another (for example, the utilisation of scrap, or of by-products, the manufacture of packing materials, etc.).

* * *

Half a century ago, when Marx was writing *Capital*, free competition appeared to the overwhelming majority of economists to be a "natural law." Official science tried, by a conspiracy of silence, to kill the works of Marx, who by a theoretical and historical analysis of capitalism had proved that free competition gives rise to the concentration of production, which, in turn, at a certain stage of development, leads to monopoly. Today, monopoly has become a fact. Economists are writing mountains of books in which they describe the diverse manifestations of monopoly, and continue to declare in chorus that "Marxism is refuted." But facts are stubborn things, as the English proverb says, and they have to be reckoned with, whether we like it or not. The facts show that differences between capitalist countries, e.g., in the matter of protection or free trade, only give rise to insignificant variations in the form of monopolies or in the moment of their appearance; and that the rise of monopolies, as the result of the concentration of production, is a general and fundamental law of the present stage of development of capitalism.

For Europe, the time when the new capitalism *definitely* superseded the old can be established with fair precision; it was the beginning of the twentieth century. * * *

* * *

[T]he principal stages in the history of monopolies are the following: (1) 1860–70, the highest stage, the apex of development of free competition; monopoly is in the barely discernible, embryonic stage. (2) After the crisis of 1873, a lengthy period of development of cartels; but they are still the exception. They are not yet durable. They are still a transitory phenomenon. (3) The boom at the end of the nineteenth century and the crisis of 1900–1903. Cartels become one of the foundations of the whole of economic life. Capitalism has been transformed into imperialism.

Cartels come to an agreement on the terms of sale, dates of payment, etc. They divide the markets among themselves. They fix the quantity of goods to be produced. They fix prices. They divide the profits among the various enterprises, etc.

The number of cartels in Germany was estimated at about 250 in 1896 and at 385 in 1905, with about 12,000 firms participating.[3] But it is generally recognised that these figures are underestimations. * * *

* * *

Competition becomes transformed into monopoly. The result is immense progress in the socialisation of production. In particular, the process of technical invention and improvement becomes socialised.

This is something quite different from the old free competition between manufacturers, scattered and out of touch with one another, and producing for an unknown market. Concentration has reached the point at which it is possible to make an approximate estimate of all sources of raw materials (for example, the iron ore deposits) of a country and even, as we shall see, of several countries, or of the whole world. Not only are such estimates made, but these sources are captured by gigantic monopolist associations. An approximate estimate of the capacity of markets is also made, and the associations "divide" them up amongst themselves by agreement. Skilled labour is monopolised, the best engineers are engaged; the means of transport are captured—railways in America, shipping companies in Europe and America. Capitalism in its imperialist stage leads directly to the most comprehensive socialisation of production; it, so to speak, drags the capitalists, against their will and consciousness, into some sort of a new social order, a transitional one from complete free competition to complete socialisation.

Production becomes social, but appropriation remains private.

---

3. Dr. Riesser, *Die deutschen Gross-banken und ihre Konzentration im Zusammenhange mit der Entwicklung der Gesamtwirtschaft in Deutschland*, 4. Aufl. (1912), S. 149; Robert Liefmann, *Kartelle und Trusts und die Weiterbildung der volkswirtschaftlichen Organisation*, 2. Aufl. (1910), S. 25. [*Lenin*]

The social means of production remain the private property of a few. The general framework of formally recognised free competition remains, and the yoke of a few monopolists on the rest of the population becomes a hundred times heavier, more burdensome and intolerable.

* * *

Monopoly! This is the last word in the "latest phase of capitalist development." But we shall only have a very insufficient, incomplete, and poor notion of the real power and the significance of modern monopolies if we do not take into consideration the part played by the banks.

II. Banks and Their New Role

The principal and primary function of banks is to serve as middlemen in the making of payments. In so doing they transform inactive money capital into active, that is, into capital yielding a profit; they collect all kinds of money revenues and place them at the disposal of the capitalist class.

As banking develops and becomes concentrated in a small number of establishments, the banks grow from modest middlemen into powerful monopolies having at their command almost the whole of the money capital of all the capitalists and small businessmen and also the larger part of the means of production and sources of raw materials in any one country and in a number of countries. This transformation of numerous modest middlemen into a handful of monopolists is one of the fundamental processes in the growth of capitalism into capitalist imperialism; for this reason we must first of all examine the concentration of banking.

* * *

At the end of 1913, Schulze-Gaevernitz estimated the deposits in the nine big Berlin banks at 5,100 million marks, out of a total of about 10,000 million marks. Taking into account not only the deposits, but the total bank capital, this author wrote: "At the end of 1909, the nine big Berlin banks, *together with their affiliated banks*, controlled 11,300 million marks, that is, about 83 per cent of the total German bank capital. The Deutsche Bank, which *together with its affiliated banks* controls nearly 3,000 million marks, represents, parallel to the Prussian State Railway Administration, the biggest and also the most decentralised accumulation of capital in the Old World."[4]

4. Schulze-Gaevernitz, "Die deutsche Kreditbank," in *Grundriss der Sozial-* *ökonomik* (Tübingen, 1915), S. 12, 137. [Lenin]

I have emphasised the reference to the "affiliated" banks because it is one of the most important distinguishing features of modern capitalist concentration. The big enterprises, and the banks in particular, not only completely absorb the small ones, but also "annex" them, subordinate them, bring them into their "own" group or "concern" (to use the technical term) by acquiring "holdings" in their capital, by purchasing or exchanging shares, by a system of credits, etc., etc. * * *

* * *

In the older capitalist countries this "banking network" is still more close. In Great Britain and Ireland, in 1910, there were in all 7,151 branches of banks. Four big banks had more than 400 branches each (from 447 to 689); four had more than 200 branches each, and eleven more than 100 each.

* * *

The change from the old type of capitalism, in which free competition predominated, to the new capitalism, in which monopoly reigns, is expressed, among other things, by a decline in the importance of the Stock Exchange. The review, *Die Bank*, writes: "The Stock Exchange has long ceased to be the indispensable medium of circulation that it formerly was when the banks were not yet able to place the bulk of new issues with their clients."[5]

" 'Every bank is a Stock Exchange,' and the bigger the bank, and the more successful the concentration of banking, the truer does this modern aphorism ring."[6]

While formerly, in the seventies, the Stock Exchange, flushed with the exuberance of youth [a "subtle" allusion to the Stock Exchange crash of 1873, the company promotion scandals, etc.], opened the era of the industrialisation of Germany, nowadays the banks and industry are able to "manage it alone." The domination of our big banks over the Stock Exchange . . . is nothing else than the expression of the completely organised German industrial state. If the domain of the automatically functioning economic laws is thus restricted, and if the domain of conscious regulation by the banks is considerably enlarged, the national economic responsibility of a few guiding heads is immensely increased.

So writes the German Professor Schulze-Gaevernitz,[7] an apologist of German imperialism, who is regarded as an authority by the imperialists of all countries, and who tries to gloss over the "mere detail" that the "conscious regulation" of economic life by the

5. *Die Bank*, 1914, 1, S. 316. [*Lenin*]
6. Dr. Oscar Stillich, *Geld- und Bank-wesen* (Berlin, 1907), S. 169. [*Lenin*]

7. Schulze-Gaevernitz, *op. cit.*, S. 101. [*Lenin*]

banks consists in the fleecing of the public by a handful of "completely organised" monopolists. The task of a bourgeois professor is not to lay bare the entire mechanism, or to expose all the machinations of the bank monopolists, but rather to present them in a favourable light.

* * *

In other words, the old capitalism, the capitalism of free competition with its indispensable regulator, the Stock Exchange, is passing away. A new capitalism has come to take its place, bearing obvious features of something transient, a mixture of free competition and monopoly. The question naturally arises: *into what* is this new capitalism "developing"? But the bourgeois scholars are afraid to raise this question.

"Thirty years ago, businessmen, freely competing against one another, performed nine-tenths of the work connected with their business other than manual labour. At the present time, nine-tenths of this 'brain work' is performed by *employees*. Banking is in the forefront of this evolution."[8] This admission by Schulze-Gaevernitz brings us once again to the question: into what is this new capitalism, capitalism in its imperialist stage, developing?

Among the few banks which remain at the head of all capitalist economy as a result of the process of concentration, there is naturally to be observed an increasingly marked tendency towards monopolist agreements, towards a *bank trust*. In America, not nine, but *two* very big banks, those of the multimillionaires Rockefeller and Morgan, control a capital of eleven thousand million marks.[9] * * *

* * *

Again and again, the final word in the development of banking is monopoly.

As regards the close connection between the banks and industry, it is precisely in this sphere that the new role of the banks is, perhaps, most strikingly felt. When a bank discounts a bill for a firm, opens a current account for it, etc., these operations, taken separately, do not in the least diminish its independence, and the bank plays no other part than that of a modest middleman. But when such operations are multiplied and become an established practice, when the bank "collects" in its own hands enormous amounts of capital, when the running of a current account for a given firm enables the bank—and this is what happens—to obtain fuller and more detailed information about the economic position

8. Schulze-Gaevernitz, *op. cit.*, S. 151.   9. *Die Bank*, 1912, 1, S. 435. [*Lenin*] [*Lenin*]

of its client, the result is that the industrial capitalist becomes more completely dependent on the bank.

At the same time a personal link-up, so to speak, is established between the banks and the biggest industrial and commercial enterprises, the merging of one with another through the acquisition of shares, through the appointment of bank directors to the Supervisory Boards (or Boards of Directors) of industrial and commercial enterprises, and vice versa. * * *

* * *

The building and development, so to speak, of the big capitalist monopolies is therefore going on full steam ahead in all "natural" and "supernatural" ways. A sort of division of labour is being systematically developed amongst the several hundred kings of finance who reign over modern capitalist society.

* * *

The result is, on the one hand, the ever-growing merger, or, as N. I. Bukharin aptly calls it, coalescence, of bank and industrial capital and, on the other hand, the growth of the banks into institutions of a truly "universal character." * * *

* * *

The old capitalism has had its day. The new capitalism represents a transition towards something. It is hopeless, of course, to seek for "firm principles and a concrete aim" for the purpose of "reconciling" monopoly with free competition. The admission of the practical men has quite a different ring from the official praises of the charms of "organised" capitalism sung by its apologists, Schulze-Gaevernitz, Liefmann and similar "theoreticians."

At precisely what period were the "new activities" of the big banks finally established? Jeidels gives us a fairly exact answer to this important question:

> The connections between the banks and industrial enterprises, with their new content, their new forms and their new organs, namely, the big banks which are organised on both a centralised and a decentralised basis, were scarcely a characteristic economic phenomenon before the nineties; in one sense, indeed, this initial date may be advanced to the year 1897, when the important "mergers" took place and when, for the first time, the new form of decentralised organisation was introduced to suit the industrial policy of the banks. This starting-point could perhaps be placed at an even later date, for it was the crisis of 1900 that enormously accelerated and intensified the process of concentration of industry and of banking, consolidated that process, for the first time

transformed the connection with industry into the actual monopoly of the big banks, and made this connection much closer and more active.[1]

Thus, the twentieth century marks the turning-point from the old capitalism to the new, from the domination of capital in general to the domination of finance capital.

III. Finance Capital and the Financial Oligarchy

"A steadily increasing proportion of capital in industry," writes Hilferding, "ceases to belong to the industrialists who employ it. They obtain the use of it only through the medium of the banks which, in relation to them, represent the owners of the capital. On the other hand, the bank is forced to sink an increasing share of its funds in industry. Thus, to an ever greater degree the banker is being transformed into an industrial capitalist. This bank capital, i.e., capital in money form, which is thus actually transformed into industrial capital, I call 'finance capital.' . . . Finance capital is capital controlled by banks and employed by industrialists."[2]

This definition is incomplete insofar as it is silent on one extremely important fact—on the increase of concentration of production and of capital to such an extent that concentration is leading, and has led, to monopoly. But throughout the whole of his work, and particularly in the two chapters preceding the one from which this definition is taken, Hilferding stresses the part played by *capitalist monopolies*.

The concentration of production; the monopolies arising therefrom; the merging or coalescence of the banks with industry—such is the history of the rise of finance capital and such is the content of that concept.

We now have to describe how, under the general conditions of commodity production and private property, the "business operations" of capitalist monopolies inevitably lead to the domination of a financial oligarchy. It should be noted that German—and not only German—bourgeois scholars, like Riesser, Schulze-Gaevernitz, Liefmann and others, are all apologists of imperialism and of finance capital. Instead of revealing the "mechanics" of the formation of an oligarchy, its methods, the size of its revenues "impeccable and peccable," its connections with parliaments, etc., etc., they obscure or gloss over them. They evade these "vexed questions" by

1. Jeidels, *Das Verhältnis der deutschen Grossbanken zur Industrie mit besonderer Berücksichtigung der Eisenindustrie* (Leipzig, 1905), S. 181. [*Lenin*]

2. R. Hilferding, *Finance Capital* (Moscow, 1912 [in Russian]), pp. 338–39. [*Lenin*]

pompous and vague phrases, appeals to the "sense of responsibility" of bank directors, by praising "the sense of duty" of Prussian officials, giving serious study to the petty details of absolutely ridiculous parliamentary bills for the "supervision" and "regulation" of monopolies, playing spillikins with theories, like, for example, the following "scholarly" definition, arrived at by Professor Liefmann: **"Commerce is an occupation having for its object the collection, storage and supply of goods."**[3] (The Professor's bold-face italics.) . . . From this it would follow that commerce existed in the time of primitive man, who knew nothing about exchange, and that it will exist under socialism!

But the monstrous facts concerning the monstrous rule of the financial oligarchy are so glaring that in all capitalist countries, in America, France and Germany, a whole literature has sprung up, written from the *bourgeois* point of view, but which, nevertheless, gives a fairly truthful picture and criticism—petty-bourgeois, naturally—of this oligarchy.

Paramount importance attaches to the "holding system." * * * The German economist, Heymann, probably the first to call attention to this matter, describes the essence of it in this way:

> The head of the concern controls the principal company [literally: the "mother company"]; the latter reigns over the subsidiary companies ["daughter companies"] which in their turn control still other subsidiaries ["grandchild companies"] etc. In this way, it is possible with a comparatively small capital to dominate immense spheres of production. Indeed, if holding 50 per cent of the capital is always sufficient to control a company, the head of the concern needs only one million to control eight million in the second subsidiaries. And if this "interlocking" is extended, it is possible with one millon to control sixteen million, thirty-two million, etc.[4]

As a matter of fact, experience shows that it is sufficient to own 40 per cent of the shares of a company in order to direct its affairs,[5] since in practice a certain number of small, scattered shareholders find it impossible to attend general meetings, etc. The "democratisation" of the ownership of shares, from which the bourgeois sophists and opportunist so-called "Social-Democrats" expect (or say that they expect) the "democratisation of capital," the strengthening of the role and significance of small-scale produc-

3. R. Liefmann, *Beteiligungs- und Finanzierungsgesellschaften. Eine Studie über den modernen Kapitalismus und das Effektenwesen*, 1., Aufl. (Jena, 1909), S. 476.

4. Hans Gideon Heymann, *Die gemisch-* *ten Werke im deutschen Grosseisengewerbe* (Stuttgart, 1904), S. 268–69. [*Lenin*]

5. Liefmann, *Beteiligungsgesellschaften*, etc., S. 258 of the first edition. [*Lenin*]

tion, etc., is, in fact, one of the ways of increasing the power of the financial oligarchy. Incidentally, this is why, in the more advanced, or in the older and more "experienced" capitalist countries, the law allows the issue of shares of smaller denomination. In Germany, the law does not permit the issue of shares of less than one thousand marks denomination, and the magnates of German finance look with an envious eye at Britain, where the issue of one-pound shares (= 20 marks, about 10 rubles) is permitted. Siemens, one of the biggest industrialists and "financial kings" in Germany, told the Reichstag on June 7, 1900, that "the one-pound share is the basis of British imperialism."[6] This merchant has a much deeper and more "Marxist" understanding of imperialism than a certain disreputable writer who is held to be one of the founders of Russian Marxism[7] and believes that imperialism is a bad habit of a certain nation. . . .

But the "holding system" not only serves enormously to increase the power of the monopolists; it also enables them to resort with impunity to all sorts of shady and dirty tricks to cheat the public, because formally the directors of the "mother company" are not legally responsible for the "daughter company," which is supposed to be "independent," and *through the medium* of which they can "pull off" *anything.* * * *

* * *

Finance capital, concentrated in a few hands and exercising a virtual monopoly, exacts enormous and ever-increasing profits from the floating of companies, issue of stock, state loans, etc., strengthens the domination of the financial oligarchy and levies tribute upon the whole of society for the benefit of monopolists. Here is an example, taken from a multitude of others, of the "business" methods of the American trusts, quoted by Hilferding. In 1887, Havemeyer founded the Sugar Trust by amalgamating fifteen small firms, whose total capital amounted to 6,500,000 dollars. Suitably "watered," as the Americans say, the capital of the trust was declared to be 50 million dollars. This "over-capitalisation" anticipated the monopoly profits, in the same way as the United States Steel Corporation anticipates its monopoly profits in buying up as many iron ore fields as possible. In fact, the Sugar Trust set up monopoly prices, which secured it such profits that it could pay 10 per cent dividend on capital "watered" *sevenfold, or about 70 per cent on the capital actually invested at the time the trust was formed!* In 1909, the capital of the Sugar Trust amounted to 90 million dollars. In twenty-two years, it had increased its capital more than tenfold.

In France the domination of the "financial oligarchy" (*Against*

---

6. Schulze-Gaevernitz in *Grundriss der Sozialökonomik*, V, 2, S. 110. [*Lenin*]   7. Lenin is referring to G. V. Plekhanov.

the Financial Oligarchy in France, the title of the well-known book by Lysis, the fifth edition of which was published in 1908) assumed a form that was only slightly different. Four of the most powerful banks enjoy, not a relative, but an "absolute monopoly" in the issue of bonds. In reality, this is a "trust of big banks." And monopoly ensures monopoly profits from bond issues. Usually a borrowing country does not get more than 90 per cent of the sum of the loan, the remaining 10 per cent goes to the banks and other middlemen. The profit made by the banks out of the Russo-Chinese loan of 400 million francs amounted to 8 per cent; out of the Russian (1904) loan of 800 million francs the profit amounted to 10 per cent; and out of the Moroccan (1904) loan of 62,500,000 francs it amounted to 18.75 per cent. Capitalism, which began its development with petty usury capital, is ending its development with gigantic usury capital. "The French," says Lysis, "are the usurers of Europe." All the conditions of economic life are being profoundly modified by this transformation of capitalism. With a stationary population, and stagnant industry, commerce and shipping, the "country" can grow rich by usury. "Fifty persons, representing a capital of eight million francs, can control 2,000 *million* francs deposited in four banks." The "holding system," with which we are already familiar, leads to the same result. One of the biggest banks, the Société Générale, for instance, issues 64,000 bonds for its "daughter company," the Egyptian Sugar Refineries. The bonds are issued at 150 per cent, i.e., the bank gains 50 centimes on the franc. The dividends of the new company were found to be fictitious, the "public" lost from 90 to 100 million francs. "One of the directors of the Société Générale was a member of the board of directors of the Sugar Refineries." It is not surprising that the author is driven to the conclusion that "the French Republic is a financial monarchy"; "it is the complete domination of the financial oligarchy; the latter dominates over the press and the government."[8]

The extraordinarily high rate of profit obtained from the issue of bonds, which is one of the principal functions of finance capital, plays a very important part in the development and consolidation of the financial oligarchy. "There is not a single business of this type within the country that brings in profits even approximately equal to those obtained from the floatation of foreign loans," says *Die Bank*.[9]

"No banking operation brings in profits comparable with those obtained from the issue of securities!" According to the *German Economist*, the average annual profits made on the issue of industrial stock were as follows:

8. Lysis, *Contre l'oligarchie financière en France*, 5 éd. (Paris, 1908), pp. 11, 12, 26, 39, 40, 48. [Lenin]

9. *Die Bank*, 1913, No. 7, S. 630. [Lenin]

Per cent

1895	38.6
1896	36.1
1897	66.7
1898	67.7
1899	66.9
1900	55.2

"In the ten years from 1891 to 1900, *more than a thousand million* marks were 'earned' by issuing German industrial stock."[1]

During periods of industrial boom, the profits of finance capital are immense, but during periods of depression, small and unsound businesses go out of existence, and the big banks acquire "holdings" in them by buying them up for a mere song, or participate in profitable schemes for their "reconstruction" and "reorganisation." In the "reconstruction" of undertakings which have been running at a loss, "the share capital is written down, that is, profits are distributed on a smaller capital and continue to be calculated on this smaller basis. Or, if the income has fallen to zero, new capital is called in, which, combined with the old and less remunerative capital, will bring in an adequate return." "Incidentally," adds Hilferding, "all these reorganisations and reconstructions have a twofold significance for the banks: first, as profitable transactions; and secondly, as opportunities for securing control of the companies in difficulties."[2]

* * *

A monopoly, once it is formed and controls thousands of millions, inevitably penetrates into *every* sphere of public life, regardless of the form of government and all other "details." In German economic literature one usually comes across obsequious praise of the integrity of the Prussian bureaucracy, and allusions to the French Panama scandal[3] and to political corruption in America. But the fact is that *even* bourgeois literature devoted to German banking matters constantly has to go far beyond the field of purely banking operations; it speaks, for instance, about "the attraction of the banks" in reference to the increasing frequency with which public officials take employment with the banks, as follows: "How about the integrity of a state official who in his innermost heart is aspiring to a soft job in the Behrenstrasse?"[4] (The Berlin street where the head office of the Deutsche Bank is situated.) In 1909,

1. Stillich, *op. cit.*, S. 143, also W. Sombart, *Die deutsche Volkswirtschaft im 19. Jahrhundert*, 2, Aufl. (1909), S. 526, Anlage 8. [*Lenin*]
2. *Finance Capital*, p. 172. [*Lenin*]
3. A scandal, exposed in 1892–93, involving fraud and corruption among politicians, officials and newspapers bribed by the French Panama Canal company.
4. "Der Zug zur Bank" in *Die Bank*, 1909, 1, S. 79. [*Lenin*]

the publisher of *Die Bank*, Alfred Lansburgh, wrote an article entitled "The Economic Significance of Byzantinism," in which he incidentally referred to Wilhelm II's tour of Palestine, and to "the immediate result of this journey, the construction of the Baghdad railway, that fatal 'great product of German enterprise,' which is more responsible for the 'encirclement' than all our political blunders put together."[5] (By encirclement is meant the policy of Edward VII to isolate Germany and surround her with an imperialist anti-German alliance.) In 1911, Eschwege, the contributor to this same magazine to whom I have already referred, wrote an article entitled "Plutocracy and Bureaucracy," in which he exposed, for example, the case of a German official named Völker, who was a zealous member of the Cartel Committee and who, it turned out some time later, obtained a lucrative post in the biggest cartel, the Steel Syndicate. Similar cases, by no means casual, forced this bourgeois author to admit that "the economic liberty guaranteed by the German Constitution has become, in many departments of economic life, a meaningless phrase" and that under the existing rule of the plutocracy, "even the widest political liberty cannot save us from being converted into a nation of unfree people."[6]

As for Russia, I shall confine myself to one example. Some years ago, all the newspapers announced that Davydov, the director of the Credit Department of the Treasury, had resigned his post to take employment with a certain big bank at a salary which, according to the contract, would total over one million rubles in the course of several years. The Credit Department is an institution, the function of which is to "co-ordinate the activities of all the credit institutions of the country" and which grants subsidies to banks in St. Petersburg and Moscow amounting to between 800 and 1,000 million rubles.

It is characteristic of capitalism in general that the ownership of capital is separated from the application of capital to production, that money capital is separated from industrial or productive capital, and that the rentier who lives entirely on income obtained from money capital is separated from the entrepreneur and from all who are directly concerned in the management of capital. Imperialism, or the domination of finance capital, is that highest stage of capitalism in which this separation reaches vast proportions. The supremacy of finance capital over all other forms of capital means the predominance of the rentier and of the financial oligarchy; it means that a small number of financially "powerful" states stand out among all the rest. The extent to which this process is going on

5. *Ibid.*, S. 301. [*Lenin*]
6. *Ibid.*, 1911, 2, S. 825; 1913, 2, S. 962. [*Lenin*]

may be judged from the statistics on emissions, i.e., the issue of all kinds of securities.

In the *Bulletin of the International Statistical Institute*, A. Neymarck[7] has published very comprehensive, complete and comparative figures covering the issue of securities all over the world, which have been repeatedly quoted in part in economic literature. The following are the totals he gives for four decades:

Total Issues in Francs per Decade
(billions)

1871–80	76.1
1881–90	64.5
1891–1900	100.4
1901–10	197.8

In the 1870s the total amount of issues for the whole world was high, owing particularly to the loans floated in connection with the Franco-Prussian War, and the company-promotion boom which set in in Germany after the war. On the whole, the increase was relatively not very rapid during the three last decades of the nineteenth century, and only in the first ten years of the twentieth century is an enormous increase of almost 100 per cent to be observed. Thus the beginning of the twentieth century marks the turning-point, not only in the growth of monopolies (cartels, syndicates, trusts), of which we have already spoken, but also in the growth of finance capital.

Neymarck estimates the total amount of issued securities current in the world in 1910 at about 815,000 million francs. Deducting from this sum amounts which might have been duplicated, he reduces the total to 575,000–600,000 million, which is distributed among the various countries as follows (I take 600,000 million):

Financial Securities Current in 1910
(billion francs)

Great Britain	142	Holland	12.5
United States	132	Belgium	7.5
France	110 } 479	Spain	7.5
Germany	95	Switzerland	6.25
Russia	31	Denmark	3.75
Austria-Hungary	24	Sweden, Norway,	
Italy	14	Rumania, etc.	2.5
Japan	12		
		Total	600

From these figures we at once see standing out in sharp relief four of the richest capitalist countries, each of which holds securi-

7. *Bulletin de l'institut international de statistique*, t. XIX, livr. II (La Haye, 1912). Data concerning small states, second column, are estimated by adding 20 per cent to the 1902 figures. [*Lenin*]

ties to amounts ranging approximately from 100,000 to 150,000 million francs. Of these four countries, two, Britain and France, are the oldest capitalist countries, and, as we shall see, possess the most colonies; the other two, the United States and Germany, are capitalist countries leading in the rapidity of development and the degree of extension of capitalist monopolies in industry. Together, these four countries own 479,000 million francs, that is, nearly 80 per cent of the world's finance capital. In one way or another, nearly the whole of the rest of the world is more or less the debtor to and tributary of these international banker countries, these four "pillars" of world finance capital.

It is particularly important to examine the part which the export of capital plays in creating the international network of dependence on and connections of finance capital.

IV. Export of Capital

Typical of the old capitalism, when free competition held undivided sway, was the export of *goods*. Typical of the latest stage of capitalism, when monopolies rule, is the export of *capital*.

Capitalism is commodity production at its highest stage of development, when labour-power itself becomes a commodity. The growth of internal exchange, and, particularly, of international exchange, is a characteristic feature of capitalism. The uneven and spasmodic development of individual enterprises, individual branches of industry and individual countries is inevitable under the capitalist system. England became a capitalist country before any other, and by the middle of the nineteenth century, having adopted free trade, claimed to be the "workshop of the world," the supplier of manufactured goods to all countries, which in exchange were to keep her provided with raw materials. But in the last quarter of the nineteenth century, *this* monopoly was already undermined; for other countries, sheltering themselves with "protective" tariffs, developed into independent capitalist states. On the threshold of the twentieth century we see the formation of a new type of monopoly: firstly, monopolist associations of capitalists in all capitalistically developed countries; secondly, the monopolist position of a few very rich countries, in which the accumulation of capital has reached gigantic proportions. An enormous "surplus of capital" has arisen in the advanced countries.

It goes without saying that if capitalism could develop agriculture, which today is everywhere lagging terribly behind industry, if it could raise the living standards of the masses, who in spite of the amazing technical progress are everywhere still half-starved and poverty-stricken, there could be no question of a surplus of capital. This "argument" is very often advanced by the petty-bourgeois critics of capitalism. But if capitalism did these things it would not be capitalism; for both uneven development and a semi-starvation level of existence of the masses are fundamental and inevitable conditions and constitute premises of this mode of production. As long as capitalism remains what it is, surplus capital will be utilised not for the purpose of raising the standard of living of the masses in a given country, for this would mean a decline in profits for the capitalists, but for the purpose of increasing profits by exporting capital abroad to the backward countries. In these backward countries profits are usually high, for capital is scarce, the price of land is relatively low, wages are low, raw materials are cheap. The export of capital is made possible by a number of backward countries having already been drawn into world capitalist intercourse; main railways have either been or are being built in those countries, elementary conditions for industrial development have been created, etc. The need to export capital arises from the fact that in a few countries capitalism has become "overripe" and (owing to the backward state of agriculture and the poverty of the masses) capital cannot find a field for "profitable" investment.

Here are approximate figures showing the amount of capital invested abroad by the three principal countries:[8]

Capital Invested Abroad
(billion francs)

Year	Great Britain	France	Germany
1862	3.6	—	—
1872	15.0	10(1869)	—
1882	22.0	15(1880)	?
1893	42.0	20(1890)	?
1902	62.0	27–37	12.5
1914	75–100.0	60	44.0

This table shows that the export of capital reached enormous dimensions only at the beginning of the twentieth century. Before the war the capital invested abroad by the three principal countries amounted to between 175,000 million and 200,000 million francs.

8. Hobson, *Imperialism* (London, 1902), p. 58; Riesser, *op. cit.*, S. 395 und 404; P. Arndt in *Weltwirtschaftliches Archiv*, Bd. 7 (1916), S. 35; Neymarck in *Bulletin*; Hilferding, *Finance Capital*, p. 492; Lloyd George, Speech in the House of Commons, May 4, 1915, reported in the *Daily Telegraph*, May 5, 1915; B. Harms, *Probleme der Weltwirtschaft* (Jena, 1912), S. 235 *et seq.*; Dr. Siegmund Schilder, *Entwicklungstendenzen der Weltwirtschaft* (Berlin, 1912), Band I, S. 150; George Paish, "Great Britain's Capital Investments, etc.," in *Journal of the Royal Statistical Society*, LXXIV (1910–11), p. 167 *et seq.*; Georges Diouritch, *L'Expansion des banques allemandes à l'étranger, ses rapports avec le développement économique de l'Allemagne* (Paris, 1909), p. 84. [*Lenin*]

At the modest rate of 5 per cent, the income from this sum should reach from 80,000 to 10,000 million francs a year—a sound basis for the imperialist oppression and exploitation of most of the countries and nations of the world, for the capitalist parasitism of a handful of wealthy states!

How is this capital invested abroad distributed among the various countries? *Where* is it invested? Only an approximate answer can be given to these questions, but it is one sufficient to throw light on certain general relations and connections of modern imperialism.

Distribution (Approximate) of Foreign Capital in Different Parts of the Globe
(circa 1910)

	Great Britain	France	Germany	Total
		(billion marks)		
Europe	4	23	18	45
America	37	4	10	51
Asia, Africa and Australia	29	8	7	44
Total	70	35	35	140

The principal spheres of investment of British capital are the British colonies, which are very large also in America (for example, Canada), not to mention Asia, etc. In this case, enormous exports of capital are bound up most closely with vast colonies, of the importance of which for imperialism I shall speak later. In the case of France the situation is different. French capital exports are invested mainly in Europe, primarily in Russia (at least ten thousand million francs). This is mainly *loan* capital, government loans, and not capital invested in industrial undertakings. Unlike British colonial imperialism, French imperialism might be termed usury imperialism. In the case of Germany, we have a third type; colonies are inconsiderable, and German capital invested abroad is divided most evenly between Europe and America.

The export of capital influences and greatly accelerates the development of capitalism in those countries to which it is exported. While, therefore, the export of capital may tend to a certain extent to arrest development in the capital-exporting countries, it can only do so by expanding and deepening the further development of capitalism throughout the world.

The capital-exporting countries are nearly always able to obtain certain "advantages," the character of which throws light on the peculiarity of the epoch of finance capital and monopoly. The following passage, for instance, appeared in the Berlin review, *Die Bank*, for October 1913:

A comedy worthy of the pen of Aristophanes is lately being played on the international capital market. Numerous foreign countries, from Spain to the Balkan states, from Russia to Argentina, Brazil and China, are openly or secretly coming into the big money market with demands, sometimes very persistent, for loans. The money markets are not very bright at the moment and the political outlook is not promising. But not a single money market dares to refuse a loan for fear that its neighbour may forestall it, consent to grant a loan and so secure some reciprocal service. In these international transactions the creditor nearly always manages to secure some extra benefit: a favourable clause in a commercial treaty, a coaling station, a contract to construct a harbour, a fat concession, or an order for guns.[9]

Finance capital has created the epoch of monopolies, and monopolies introduce everywhere monopolist principles: the utilisation of "connections" for profitable transactions takes the place of competition on the open market. The most usual thing is to stipulate that part of the loan granted shall be spent on purchases in the creditor country, particularly on orders for war materials, or for ships, etc. In the course of the last two decades (1890–1910), France has very often resorted to this method. The export of capital thus becomes a means of encouraging the export of commodities. In this connection, transactions between particularly big firms assume a form which, as Schilder[1] "mildly" puts it, "borders on corruption." Krupp in Germany, Schneider in France, Armstrong in Britain are instances of firms which have close connections with powerful banks and governments and which cannot easily be "ignored" when a loan is being arranged.

France, when granting loans to Russia, "squeezed" her in the commercial treaty of September 16, 1905, stipulating for certain concessions to run till 1917. She did the same in the commercial treaty with Japan of August 19, 1911. The tariff war between Austria and Serbia, which lasted, with a seven months' interval, from 1906 to 1911, was partly caused by Austria and France competing to supply Serbia with war materials. In January 1912, Paul Deschanel stated in the Chamber of Deputies that from 1908 to 1911 French firms had supplied war materials to Serbia to the value of 45 million francs.

A report from the Austro-Hungarian Consul at São-Paulo (Brazil) states: "The Brazilian railways are being built chiefly by French, Belgian, British and German capital. In these financial operations connected with the construction of these railways the

9. *Die Bank*, 1913, 2, S. 1024–25. [*Lenin*]
1. Schilder, *op. cit.*, S. 346, 350, 371. [*Lenin*]

countries involved stipulate for orders for the necessary railway materials."

Thus finance capital, literally, one might say, spreads its net over all countries of the world. An important role in this is played by banks founded in the colonies and by their branches. German imperialists look with envy at the "old" colonial countries which have been particularly "successful" in providing for themselves in this respect. In 1904, Great Britain had 50 colonial banks with 2,279 branches (in 1910 there were 72 banks with 5,449 branches); France had 20 with 136 branches; Holland, 16 with 68 branches; and Germany had "only" 13 with 70 branches.[2] The American capitalists, in their turn, are jealous of the English and German: "In South America," they complained in 1915, "five German banks have forty branches and five British banks have seventy branches.... Britain and Germany have invested in Argentina, Brazil, and Uruguay in the last twenty-five years approximately four thousand million dollars, and as a result together enjoy 46 per cent of the total trade of these three countries."[3]

The capital-exporting countries have divided the world among themselves in the figurative sense of the term. But finance capital has led to the *actual* division of the world.

V. Division of the World Among Capitalist Associations

Monopolist capitalist associations, cartels, syndicates and trusts first divided the home market among themselves and obtained more or less complete possession of the industry of their own country. But under capitalism the home market is inevitably bound up with the foreign market. Capitalism long ago created a world market. As the export of capital increased, and as the foreign and colonial connections and "spheres of influence" of the big monopolist associations expanded in all ways, things "naturally" gravitated towards an international agreement among these associations, and towards the formation of international cartels.

This is a new stage of world concentration of capital and production, incomparably higher than the preceding stages. Let us see how this supermonopoly develops.

The electrical industry is highly typical of the latest technical achievements and is most typical of capitalism at the *end* of the

2. Riesser, *op. cit.*, 4th ed., S. 375; Diouritch, p. 283. [*Lenin*]
3. *The Annals of the American Academy of Political and Social Science*, Vol. LIX (May 1915), p. 301. In the same volume on p. 331, we read that the well-known statistician Paish, in the last issue of the financial magazine *The Statist*, estimated the amount of capital exported by Britain, Germany, France, Belgium and Holland at $40,000 million, i.e., 200,000 million francs. [*Lenin*]

nineteenth and the beginning of the twentieth centuries. This industry has developed most in the two leaders of the new capitalist countries, the United States and Germany. In Germany, the crisis of 1900 gave a particularly strong impetus to its concentration. During the crisis, the banks, which by that time had become fairly well merged with industry, enormously accelerated and intensified the ruin of relatively small firms and their absorption by the large ones. "The banks," writes Jeidels, "refused a helping hand to the very firms in greatest need of capital, and brought on first a frenzied boom and then the hopeless failure of the companies which had not been connected with them closely enough."[4]

As a result, after 1900, concentration in Germany progressed with giant strides. Up to 1900 there had been seven or eight "groups" in the electrical industry. Each consisted of several companies (altogether there were twenty-eight) and each was backed by from two to eleven banks. Between 1908 and 1912 all these groups were merged into two, or one. * * *

The famous A.E.G. (General Electric Company), which grew up in this way, controls 175 to 200 companies (through the "holding" system), and a total of approximately 15,000 *million* marks. * * *

[I]n 1907, the German and American trusts concluded an agreement by which they divided the world between them. Competition between them ceased. The American General Electric Company (G.E.C.) "got" the United States and Canada. The German General Electric Company (A.E.G.) "got" Germany, Austria, Russia, Holland, Denmark, Switzerland, Turkey and the Balkans. Special agreements, naturally secret, were concluded regarding the penetration of "daughter companies" into new branches of industry, into "new" countries formally not yet allotted. The two trusts were to exchange inventions and experiments.[5]

The difficulty of competing against this trust, actually a single world-wide trust controlling a capital of several thousand million, with "branches," agencies, representatives, connections, etc., in every corner of the world, is self-evident. But the division of the world between two powerful trusts does not preclude *redivision* if the relation of forces changes as a result of uneven development, war, bankruptcy, etc.

An instructive example of an attempt at such a redivision, of the struggle for redivision, is provided by the oil industry.

"The world oil market," wrote Jeidels in 1905, "is even today still divided between two great financial groups—Rockefeller's

4. Jeidels, *op. cit.*, S. 232. [*Lenin*]
5. Riesser, *op. cit.*; Diouritch, *op. cit.*, p. 239; Kurt Heinig, "Der Weg des

Elektrotrusts" in *Die Neue Zeit*, 1912, 30. Jahrg., 2, S. 484.

American Standard Oil Co., and Rothschild and Nobel, the control-ling interests of the Russian oilfields in Baku. The two groups are closely connected. But for several years five enemies have been threatening their monopoly"[6]: (1) the exhaustion of the American oilfields; (2) the competition of the firm of Mantashev of Baku; (3) the Austrian oilfields; (4) the Rumanian oilfields; (5) the overseas oilfields, particularly in the Dutch colonies (the extremely rich firms, Samuel, and Shell, also connected with British capital). The three last groups are connected with the big German banks, headed by the huge Deutsche Bank. These banks independently and systematically developed the oil industry in Rumania, for example, in order to have a foothold of their "own." In 1907, the foreign capital invested in the Rumanian oil industry was estimated at 185 million francs, of which 74 million was German capital.[7]

A struggle began for the "division of the world," as, in fact, it is called in economic literature. On the one hand, the Rockefeller "oil trust" wanted to lay its hands on *everything*; it formed a "daughter company" *right in* Holland, and bought up oilfields in the Dutch Indies, in order to strike at its principal enemy, the Anglo-Dutch Shell trust. On the other hand, the Deutsche Bank and the other German banks aimed at "retaining" Rumania "for themselves" and at uniting her with Russia against Rockefeller. The latter possessed far more capital and an excellent system of oil transportation and distribution. The struggle had to end, and did end in 1907, with the utter defeat of the Deutsche Bank, which was confronted with the alternative: either to liquidate its "oil interests" and lose millions, or submit. It chose to submit, and concluded a very disadvanta-geous agreement with the "oil trust." The Deutsche Bank agreed "not to attempt anything which might injure American interests." Provision was made, however, for the annulment of the agreement in the event of Germany establishing a state oil monopoly.

Then the "comedy of oil" began. One of the German finance kings, von Gwinner, a director of the Deutsche Bank, through his private secretary, Stauss, launched a campaign *for* a state oil mo-nopoly. The gigantic machine of the huge German bank and all its wide "connections" were set in motion. The press bubbled over with "patriotic" indignation against the "yoke" of the American trust, and, on March 15, 1911, the Reichstag, by an almost unani-mous vote, adopted a motion asking the government to introduce a bill for the establishment of an oil monopoly. The government seized upon this "popular" idea, and the game of the Deutsche Bank, which hoped to cheat its American counterpart and improve its business by a state monopoly, appeared to have been won. The

---

6. Jeidels, *op. cit.*, S. 192–93. [*Lenin*]   7. Diouritch, *op. cit.*, pp. 245–46. [*Lenin*]

German oil magnates already saw visions of enormous profits, which would not be less than those of the Russian sugar refiners. . . . But, firstly, the big German banks quarrelled among themselves over the division of the spoils. The Disconto-Gesellschaft exposed the covetous aims of the Deutsche Bank; secondly, the government took fright at the prospect of a struggle with Rockefeller, for it was very doubtful whether Germany could be sure of obtaining oil from other sources (the Rumanian output was small); thirdly, just at that time the 1913 credits of a thousand million marks were voted for Germany's war preparations. The oil monopoly project was postponed. The Rockefeller "oil trust" came out of the struggle, for the time being, victorious.

The Berlin review, *Die Bank*, wrote in this connection that Germany could fight the oil trust only by establishing an electricity monopoly and by converting water-power into cheap electricity. "But," the author added,

> the electricity monopoly will come when the producers need it, that is to say, when the next great crash in the electrical industry is imminent, and when the gigantic, expensive power stations now being put up at great cost everywhere by private electrical concerns, which are already obtaining certain franchises from towns, from states, etc., can no longer work at a profit. Water-power will then have to be used. But it will be impossible to convert it into cheap electricity at state expense; it will also have to be handed over to a "private monopoly controlled by the state," because private industry has already concluded a number of contracts and has stipulated for heavy compensation. . . . So it was with the nitrate monopoly, so it is with the oil monopoly, so it will be with the electric power monopoly. It is time our state socialists, who allow themselves to be blinded by a beautiful principle, understood, at last, that in Germany the monopolies have never pursued the aim, nor have they had the result, of benefiting the consumer, or even of handing over to the state part of the promoter's profits; they have served only to facilitate, at the expense of the state, the recovery of private industries which were on the verge of bankruptcy.[8]

Such are the valuable admissions which the German bourgeois economists are forced to make. We see plainly here how private and state monopolies are interwoven in the epoch of finance capital; how both are but separate links in the imperialist struggle between the big monopolists for the division of the world.

* * *

8. *Die Bank*, 1912, 1, S. 1036; 1912, 2, S. 629; 1913, 1, S. 388. [*Lenin*]

Certain bourgeois writers (now joined by Karl Kautsky, who has completely abandoned the Marxist position he had held, for example, in 1909) have expressed the opinion that international cartels, being one of the most striking expressions of the internationalisation of capital, give the hope of peace among nations under capitalism. Theoretically, this opinion is absolutely absurd, while in practice it is sophistry and a dishonest defence of the worst opportunism. International cartels show to what point capitalist monopolies have developed, and *the object* of the struggle between the various capitalist associations. This last circumstance is the most important; it alone shows us the historico-economic meaning of what is taking place; for the *forms* of the struggle may and do constantly change in accordance with varying, relatively specific and temporary causes, but the *substance* of the struggle, its class *content*, positively *cannot* change while classes exist. Naturally, it is in the interests of, for example, the German bourgeoisie, to whose side Kautsky has in effect gone over in his theoretical arguments (I shall deal with this later), to obscure the *substance* of the present economic struggle (the division of the world) and to emphasise now this and now another *form* of the struggle. Kautsky makes the same mistake. Of course, we have in mind not only the German bourgeoisie, but the bourgeoisie all over the world. The capitalists divide the world, not out of any particular malice, but because the degree of concentration which has been reached forces them to adopt this method in order to obtain profits. And they divide it "in proportion to capital," "in proportion to strength," because there cannot be any other method of division under commodity production and capitalism. But strength varies with the degree of economic and political development. In order to understand what is taking place, it is necessary to know what questions are settled by the changes in strength. The question as to whether these changes are "purely" economic or *non*-economic (e.g., military) is a secondary one, which cannot in the least affect fundamental views on the latest epoch of capitalism. To substitute the question of the form of the struggle and agreements (today peaceful, tomorrow warlike, the next day warlike again) for the question of the *substance* of the struggle and agreements between capitalist associations is to sink to the role of a sophist.

The epoch of the latest stage of capitalism shows us that certain relations between capitalist associations grow up, *based on* the economic division of the world; while parallel to and in connection with it, certain relations grow up between political alliances, between states, on the basis of the territorial division of the world, of the struggle for colonies, of the "struggle for spheres of influence."

VI. Division of the World Among the Great Powers

In his book, on "the territorial development of the European colonies," A. Supan,[9] the geographer, gives the following brief summary of this development at the end of the nineteenth century:

Percentage of Territory Belonging to the European Colonial Powers
(Including the United States)

	1876	1900	Increase or decrease
Africa	10.8	90.4	+79.6
Polynesia	56.8	98.9	+42.1
Asia	51.5	56.6	+ 5.1
Australia	100.0	100.0	—
America	27.5	27.2	− 0.3

"The characteristic feature of this period," he concludes, "is, therefore, the division of Africa and Polynesia." As there are no unoccupied territories—that is, territories that do not belong to any state—in Asia and America, it is necessary to amplify Supan's conclusion and say that the characteristic feature of the period under review is the final partitioning of the globe—final, not in the sense that *repartition* is impossible; on the contrary, repartitions are possible and inevitable—but in the sense that the colonial policy of the capitalist countries has *completed* the seizure of the unoccupied territories on our planet. For the first time the world is completely divided up, so that in the future *only* redivision is possible, i.e., territories can only pass from one "owner" to another, instead of passing as ownerless territory to an "owner."

Hence, we are living in a peculiar epoch of world colonial policy, which is most closely connected with the "latest stage in the development of capitalism," with finance capital. For this reason, it is essential first of all to deal in greater detail with the facts, in order to ascertain as exactly as possible what distinguishes this epoch from those preceding it, and what the present situation is. In the first place, two questions of fact arise here: is an intensification of colonial policy, a sharpening of the struggle for colonies, observed precisely in the epoch of finance capital? And how, in this respect, is the world divided at the present time?

The American writer, Morris, in his book on the history of colonisation,[1] made an attempt to sum up the data on the colonial possessions of Great Britain, France and Germany during different

---

9. A. Supan, *Die territoriale Entwicklung der europäischen Kolonien* (1906), S. 254. [*Lenin*]
1. Henry C. Morris, *The History of Colonisation* (New York, 1900), Vol. II, p. 88; Vol. I, p. 419; Vol. II, p. 304. [*Lenin*]

periods of the nineteenth century. The following is a brief summary of the results he has obtained:

Colonial Possessions

Year	Great Britain		France		Germany	
	Area (million sq. mi.)	Pop. (million)	Area (million sq. mi.)	Pop. (million)	Area (million sq. mi.)	Pop. (million)
1815–30	?	126.4	0.02	0.5	—	—
1860	2.5	145.1	0.2	3.4	—	—
1880	7.7	267.9	0.7	7.5	—	—
1899	9.3	309.0	3.7	56.4	1.0	14.7

For Great Britain, the period of the enormous expansion of colonial conquests was that between 1860 and 1880, and it was also very considerable in the last twenty years of the nineteenth century. For France and Germany this period falls precisely in these twenty years. We saw above that the development of pre-monopoly capitalism, of capitalism in which free competition was predominant, reached its limit in the 1860s and 1870s. We now see that it is *precisely after that period* that the tremendous "boom" in colonial conquests begins, and that the struggle for the territorial division of the world becomes extraordinarily sharp. It is beyond doubt, therefore, that capitalism's transition to the stage of monopoly capitalism, to finance capital, *is connected* with the intensification of the struggle for the partitioning of the world.

Hobson, in his work on imperialism, marks the years 1884–1900 as the epoch of intensified "expansion" of the chief European states. According to his estimate, Great Britain during these years acquired 3,700,000 square miles of territory with 57,000,000 inhabitants; France, 3,600,000 square miles with 36,500,000; Germany, 1,000,000 square miles with 14,700,000; Belgium 900,000 square miles with 30,000,000; Portugal, 800,000 square miles with 9,000,000 inhabitants. The scramble for colonies by all the capitalist states at the end of the nineteenth century and particularly since the 1880s is a commonly known fact in the history of diplomacy and of foreign policy.

In the most flourishing period of free competition in Great Britain, i.e., between 1840 and 1860, the leading British bourgeois politicians were *opposed* to colonial policy and were of the opinion that the liberation of the colonies, their complete separation from Britain, was inevitable and desirable. M. Beer, in an article, "Modern British Imperialism,"[2] published in 1898, shows that in 1852, Disraeli, a statesman who was generally inclined towards imperial-

2. *Die Neue Zeit*, XVI, I, 1898, S. 302. [*Lenin*]

ism, declared: "The colonies are millstones round our necks." But at the end of the nineteenth century the British heroes of the hour were Cecil Rhodes and Joseph Chamberlain, who openly advocated imperialism and applied the imperialist policy in the most cynical manner!

It is not without interest to observe that even then these leading British bourgeois politicians saw the connection between what might be called the purely economic and the socio-political roots of modern imperialism. Chamberlain advocated imperialism as a "true, wise and economical policy," and pointed particularly to the German, American and Belgian competition which Great Britain was encountering in the world market. Salvation lies in monopoly, said the capitalists as they formed cartels, syndicates and trusts. Salvation lies in monopoly, echoed the political leaders of the bourgeoisie, hastening to appropriate the parts of the world not yet shared out. And Cecil Rhodes, we are informed by his intimate friend, the journalist Stead, expressed his imperialist views to him in 1895 in the following terms:

> I was in the East End of London [a working-class quarter] yesterday and attended a meeting of the unemployed. I listened to the wild speeches, which were just a cry for "bread! bread!" and on my way home I pondered over the scene and I became more than ever convinced of the importance of imperialism. . . . My cherished idea is a solution for the social problem, i.e., in order to save the 40,000,000 inhabitants of the United Kingdom from a bloody civil war, we colonial statesmen must acquire new lands to settle the surplus population, to provide new markets for the goods produced in the factories and mines. The Empire, as I have always said, is a bread and butter question. If you want to avoid civil war, you must become imperialists.[3]

That was said in 1895 by Cecil Rhodes, millionaire, a king of finance, the man who was mainly responsible for the Anglo-Boer War. True, his defence of imperialism is crude and cynical, but in substance it does not differ from the "theory" advocated by Messrs. Maslov, Südekum, Potresov, David, the founder of Russian Marxism and others. Cecil Rhodes was a somewhat more honest social-chauvinist. . . .

To present as precise a picture as possible of the territorial division of the world and of the changes which have occurred during the last decades in this respect, I shall utilise the data furnished by Supan in the work already quoted on the colonial possessions of all the powers of the world. Supan takes the years 1876 and 1900; I shall take the year 1876—a year very aptly selected, for it is pre-

3. *Ibid.*, S. 304. [*Lenin*]

cisely by that time that the pre-monopolist stage of development of West-European capitalism can be said to have been, in the main, completed—and the year 1914, and instead of Supan's figures I shall quote the more recent statistics of Hübner's *Geographical and Statistical Tables*. Supan gives figures only for colonies; I think it useful, in order to present a complete picture of the division of the world, to add brief data on non-colonial and semi-colonial countries, in which category I place Persia, China and Turkey: the first of these countries is already almost completely a colony, the second and third are becoming such.

We thus get the following result:

Colonial Possessions of the Great Powers
(million square kilometres and million inhabitants)

	Colonies				Metropolitan Countries		Total	
	1876		1914		1914		1914	
	Area	Pop.	Area	Pop.	Area	Pop.	Area	Pop.
Great Britain .	22.5	251.9	33.5	393.5	0.3	46.5	33.8	440.0
Russia	17.0	15.9	17.4	33.2	5.4	136.2	22.8	169.4
France	0.9	6.0	10.6	55.5	0.5	39.6	11.1	95.1
Germany	—	—	2.9	12.3	0.5	64.9	3.4	77.2
United States .	—	—	0.3	9.7	9.4	97.0	9.7	106.7
Japan	—	—	0.3	19.2	0.4	53.0	0.7	72.2
Total for Six Great Powers	40.4	273.8	65.0	523.4	16.5	437.2	81.5	960.6
Colonies of other powers (Belgium, Holland, etc.)							9.9	45.3
Semi-colonial countries (Persia, China, Turkey)							14.5	361.2
Other countries							28.0	289.9
Total for the world							133.9	1,657.0

We clearly see from these figures how "complete" was the partition of the world at the turn of the twentieth century. After 1876 colonial possessions increased to enormous dimensions, by more than fifty per cent, from 40,000,000 to 65,000,000 square kilometres for the six biggest powers; the increase amounts to 25,000,-000 square kilometres, fifty per cent more than the area of the metropolitan countries (16,500,000 square kilometres). In 1876 three powers had no colonies, and a fourth, France, had scarcely any. By 1914 these four powers had acquired colonies with an area of 14,100,000 square kilometres, i.e., about half as much again as the area of Europe, with a population of nearly 100,000,000. The unevenness in the rate of expansion of colonial possessions is very great. If, for instance, we compare France, Germany and Japan, which do not differ very much in area and population, we see that the first has acquired almost three times as much colonial territory as the other two combined. In regard to finance capital, France, at the beginning of the period we are considering, was also, perhaps, several times richer than Germany and Japan put together. In addition to, and on the basis of, purely economic conditions, geographical and other conditions also affect the dimensions of colonial possessions. However strong the process of levelling the world, of levelling the economic and living conditions in different countries, may have been in the past decades as a result of the pressure of large-scale industry, exchange and finance capital, considerable differences still remain; and among the six countries mentioned we see, firstly, young capitalist countries (America, Germany, Japan) whose progress has been extraordinarily rapid; secondly, countries with an old capitalist development (France and Great Britain), whose progress lately has been much slower than that of the previously mentioned countries, and thirdly, a country most backward economically (Russia), where modern capitalist imperialism is enmeshed, so to speak, in a particularly close network of pre-capitalist relations.

Alongside the colonial possessions of the Great Powers, we have placed the small colonies of the small states, which are, so to speak, the next objects of a possible and probable "redivision" of colonies. These small states mostly retain their colonies only because the big powers are torn by conflicting interests, friction, etc., which prevent them from coming to an agreement on the division of the spoils. As to the "semi-colonial" states, they provide an example of the transitional forms which are to be found in all spheres of nature and society. Finance capital is such a great, such a decisive, you might say, force in all economic and in all international relations, that it is capable of subjecting, and actually does subject, to itself even states enjoying the fullest political independence; we shall shortly see examples of this. Of course, finance capital finds most "convenient," and derives the greatest profit from, a *form* of subjection which involves the loss of the political independence of the subjected countries and peoples. In this respect, the semi-colonial countries provide a typical example of the "middle stage." It is natural that the struggle for these semi-dependent countries should have become particularly bitter in the epoch of finance capital, when the rest of the world has already been divided up.

Colonial policy and imperialism existed before the latest stage of capitalism, and even before capitalism. Rome, founded on slavery, pursued a colonial policy and practised imperialism. But "general" disquisitions on imperialism, which ignore, or put into the background, the fundamental difference between socio-economic formations, inevitably turn into the most vapid banality or bragging, like the comparison: "Greater Rome and Greater Britain."[4] Even the capitalist colonial policy of *previous* stages of capitalism is essentially different from the colonial policy of finance capital.

The principal feature of the latest stage of capitalism is the domination of monopolist associations of big employers. These monopolies are most firmly established when *all* the sources of raw materials are captured by one group, and we have seen with what zeal the international capitalist associations exert every effort to deprive their rivals of all opportunity of competing, to buy up, for example, ironfields, oilfields, etc. Colonial possession alone gives the monopolies complete guarantee against all contingencies in the struggle against competitors, including the case of the adversary wanting to be protected by a law establishing a state monopoly. The more capitalism is developed, the more strongly the shortage of raw materials is felt, the more intense the competition and the hunt for sources of raw materials throughout the whole world, the more desperate the struggle for the acquisition of colonies.

"It may be asserted," writes Schilder, "although it may sound paradoxical to some, that in the more or less foreseeable future the growth of the urban and industrial population is more likely to be hindered by a shortage of raw materials for industry than by a shortage of food." For example, there is a growing shortage of timber—the price of which is steadily rising—of leather, and of raw materials for the textile industry. "Associations of manufacturers are making efforts to create an equilibrium between agriculture and industry in the whole of world economy; as an example of this we might mention the International Federation of Cotton Spinners' Associations in several of the most important industrial countries, founded in 1904, and the European Federation of Flax Spinners' Associations, founded on the same model in 1910."[5]

Of course, the bourgeois reformists, and among them particularly the present-day adherents of Kautsky, try to belittle the importance of facts of this kind by arguing that raw materials "could be" obtained in the open market without a "costly and dangerous" colonial policy; and that the supply of raw materials "could be" increased enormously by "simply" improving conditions in agriculture in general. But such arguments become an apology for imperialism, an attempt to paint it in bright colours, because they ignore the principal feature of the latest stage of capitalism: monopolies. The free market is becoming more and more a thing of the past; monopolist syndicates and trusts are restricting it with every passing day, and "simply" improving conditions in agriculture means

4. C. P. Lucas, *Greater Rome and Greater Britain* (Oxford, 1912); or the Earl of Cromer's *Ancient and Modern Imperialism* (London, 1910). [*Lenin*]
5. Schilder, *op. cit.*, S. 38–42. [*Lenin*]

improving the conditions of the masses, raising wages and reducing profits. Where, except in the imagination of sentimental reformists, are there any trusts capable of concerning themselves with the condition of the masses instead of the conquest of colonies?

Finance capital is interested not only in the already discovered sources of raw materials but also in potential sources, because present-day technical development is extremely rapid, and land which is useless today may be improved tomorrow if new methods are devised (to this end a big bank can equip a special expedition of engineers, agricultural experts, etc.), and if large amounts of capital are invested. This also applies to prospecting for minerals, to new methods of processing up and utilising raw materials, etc., etc. Hence, the inevitable striving of finance capital to enlarge its spheres of influence and even its actual territory. In the same way that the trusts capitalise their property at two or three times its value, taking into account its "potential" (and not actual) profits and the further results of monopoly, so finance capital in general strives to seize the largest possible amount of land of all kinds in all places, and by every means, taking into account potential sources of raw materials and fearing to be left behind in the fierce struggle for the last remnants of independent territory, or for the repartition of those territories that have been already divided.

The British capitalists are exerting every effort to develop cotton growing in *their* colony, Egypt (in 1904, out of 2,300,000 hectares of land under cultivation, 600,000, or more than one-fourth, were under cotton); the Russians are doing the same in *their* colony, Turkestan, because in this way they will be in a better position to defeat their foreign competitors, to monopolise the sources of raw materials and form a more economical and profitable textile trust in which *all* the processes of cotton production and manufacturing will be "combined" and concentrated in the hands of one set of owners.

The interests pursued in exporting capital also give an impetus to the conquest of colonies, for in the colonial market it is easier to employ monopoly methods (and sometimes they are the only methods that can be employed) to eliminate competition, to ensure supplies, to secure the necessary "connections," etc.

The non-economic superstructure which grows up on the basis of finance capital, its politics and its ideology, stimulates the striving for colonial conquest. "Finance capital does not want liberty, it wants domination," as Hilferding very truly says. And a French bourgeois writer, developing and supplementing, as it were, the ideas of Cecil Rhodes quoted above,[6] writes that social causes

6. See p. 236, above. [*R. T.*]

should be added to the economic causes of modern colonial policy: "Owing to the growing complexities of life and the difficulties which weigh not only on the masses of the workers, but also on the middle classes, 'impatience, irritation and hatred are accumulating in all the countries of the old civilisation and are becoming a menace to public order; the energy which is being hurled out of the definite class channel must be given employment abroad in order to avert an explosion at home.' "[7]

Since we are speaking of colonial policy in the epoch of capitalist imperialism, it must be observed that finance capital and its foreign policy, which is the struggle of the great powers for the economic and political division of the world, give rise to a number of *transitional* forms of state dependence. Not only are the two main groups of countries, those owning colonies, and the colonies themselves, but also the diverse forms of dependent countries which, politically, are formally independent, but in fact, are enmeshed in the net of financial and diplomatic dependence, typical of this epoch. We have already referred to one form of dependence—the semi-colony. An example of another is provided by Argentina.

"South America, and especially Argentina," writes Schulze-Gaevernitz in his work on British imperialism, "is so dependent financially on London that it ought to be described as almost a British commercial colony."[8] Basing himself on the reports of the Austro-Hungarian Consul at Buenos Aires for 1909, Schilder estimated the amount of British capital invested in Argentina at 8,750 million francs. It is not difficult to imagine what strong connections British finance capital (and its faithful "friend," diplomacy) thereby acquires with the Argentine bourgeoisie, with the circles that control the whole of that country's economic and political life.

A somewhat different form of financial and diplomatic dependence, accompanied by political independence, is presented by Portugal. Portugal is an independent sovereign state, but actually, for more than two hundred years, since the war of the Spanish Succession (1701–14), it has been a British protectorate. Great Britain has protected Portugal and her colonies in order to fortify her own positions in the fight against her rivals, Spain and France. In return Great Britain has received commercial privileges, preferential conditions for importing goods and especially capital into Portugal and the Portuguese colonies, the right to use the ports and islands of Portugal, her telegraph cables, etc., etc.[9] Relations of this kind

7. Wahl, *La France aux colonies*, quoted by Henri Russier, *Le Partage de l'Océanie* (Paris, 1905), p. 165. [*Lenin*]
8. Schulze-Gaevernitz, *Britischer Imperialismus und englischer Freihandel zu Beginn des 20-ten Jahrhunderts* (Leipzig, 1906), S. 318. Sartorius v. Waltershausen says the same in *Das volkswirtschaftliche System der Kapitalanlage im Auslande* (Berlin, 1907), S, 46. [*Lenin*]
9. Schilder, *op. cit.*, Vol. I, S. 160–61. [*Lenin*]

have always existed between big and little states, but in the epoch of capitalist imperialism they become a general system, they form part of the sum total of "divide the world" relations and become links in the chain of operations of world finance capital.

In order to finish with the question of the division of the world, I must make the following additional observation. This question was raised quite openly and definitely not only in American literature after the Spanish-American War, and in English literature after the Anglo-Boer War, at the very end of the nineteenth century and the beginning of the twentieth; not only has German literature, which has "most jealously" watched "British imperialism," systematically given its appraisal of this fact. This question has also been raised in French bourgeois literature as definitely and broadly as is thinkable from the bourgeois point of view. Let me quote Driault, the historian, who, in his book, *Political and Social Problems at the End of the Nineteenth Century*, in the chapter "The Great Powers and the Division of the World," wrote the following:

> During the past few years, all the free territory of the globe, with the exception of China, has been occupied by the powers of Europe and North America. This has already brought about several conflicts and shifts of spheres of influence, and these foreshadow more terrible upheavals in the near future. For it is necessary to make haste. The nations which have not yet made provision for themselves run the risk of never receiving their share and never participating in the tremendous exploitation of the globe which will be one of the most essential features of the next century [i.e., the twentieth]. That is why all Europe and America have lately been afflicted with the fever of colonial expansion, of "imperialism," that most noteworthy feature of the end of the nineteenth century.

And the author added:

> In this partition of the world, in this furious hunt for the treasures and the big markets of the globe, the relative strength of the empires founded in this nineteenth century is totally out of proportion to the place occupied in Europe by the nations which founded them. The dominant powers in Europe, the arbiters of her destiny, are *not* equally preponderant in the whole world. And, as colonial might, the hope of controlling as yet unassessed wealth, will evidently react upon the relative strength of the European powers, the colonial question—"imperialism," if you will —which has already modified the political conditions of Europe itself, will modify them more and more.[1]

---

1. J.-E. Driault, *Problèmes politiques et sociaux* (Paris, 1900), p. 299. [*Lenin*]

VII. Imperialism, as a Special Stage of Capitalism

We must now try to sum up, to draw together the threads of what has been said above on the subject of imperialism. Imperialism emerged as the development and direct continuation of the fundamental characteristics of capitalism in general. But capitalism only became capitalist imperialism at a definite and very high stage of its development, when certain of its fundamental characteristics began to change into their opposites, when the features of the epoch of transition from capitalism to a higher social and economic system had taken shape and revealed themselves in all spheres. Economically, the main thing in this process is the displacement of capitalist free competition by capitalist monopoly. Free competition is the basic feature of capitalism, and of commodity production generally; monopoly is the exact opposite of free competition, but we have seen the latter being transformed into monopoly before our eyes, creating large-scale industry and forcing out small industry, replacing large-scale by still larger-scale industry, and carrying concentration of production and capital to the point where out of it has grown and is growing monopoly: cartels, syndicates and trusts, and merging with them, the capital of a dozen or so banks, which manipulate thousands of millions. At the same time the monopolies, which have grown out of free competition, do not eliminate the latter, but exist above it and alongside it, and thereby give rise to a number of very acute, intense antagonisms, frictions and conflicts. Monopoly is the transition from capitalism to a higher system.

If it were necessary to give the briefest possible definition of imperialism we should have to say that imperialism is the monopoly stage of capitalism. Such a definition would include what is most important, for, on the one hand, finance capital is the bank capital of a few very big monopolist banks, merged with the capital of the monopolist associations of industrialists; and, on the other hand, the division of the world is the transition from a colonial policy which has extended without hindrance to territories unseized by any capitalist power, to a colonial policy of monopolist possession of the territory of the world, which has been completely divided up.

But very brief definitions, although convenient, for they sum up the main points, are nevertheless inadequate, since we have to deduce from them some especially important features of the phenomenon that has to be defined. And so, without forgetting the conditional and relative value of all definitions in general, which can never embrace all the concatenations of a phenomenon in its full development, we must give a definition of imperialism that will include the following five of its basic features:

(1) the concentration of production and capital has developed to such a high stage that it has created monopolies which play a decisive role in economic life; (2) the merging of bank capital with industrial capital, and the creation, on the basis of this "finance capital," of a financial oligarchy; (3) the export of capital as distinguished from the export of commodities acquires exceptional importance; (4) the formation of international monopolist capitalist associations which share the world among themselves, and (5) the territorial division of the whole world among the biggest capitalist powers is completed. Imperialism is capitalism at that stage of development at which the dominance of monopolies and finance capital is established; in which the export of capital has acquired pronounced importance; in which the division of the world among the international trusts has begun, in which the division of all territories of the globe among the biggest capitalist powers has been completed.

We shall see later that imperialism can and must be defined differently if we bear in mind not only the basic, purely economic concepts—to which the above definition is limited—but also the historical place of this stage of capitalism in relation to capitalism in general, or the relation between imperialism and the two main trends in the working-class movement. The thing to be noted at this point is that imperialism, as interpreted above, undoubtedly represents a special stage in the development of capitalism. To enable the reader to obtain the most well-grounded idea of imperialism, I deliberately tried to quote as extensively as possible *bourgeois* economists who have to admit the particularly incontrovertible facts concerning the latest stage of capitalist economy. With the same object in view, I have quoted detailed statistics which enable one to see to what degree bank capital, etc., has grown, in what precisely the transformation of quantity into quality, of developed capitalism into imperialism, was expressed. Needless to say, of course, all boundaries in nature and in society are conventional and changeable, and it would be absurd to argue, for example, about the particular year or decade in which imperialism "definitely" became established.

In the matter of defining imperialism, however, we have to enter into controversy, primarily, with Karl Kautsky, the principal Marxist theoretician of the epoch of the so-called Second International—that is, of the twenty-five years between 1889 and 1914. The fundamental ideas expressed in our definition of imperialism were very resolutely attacked by Kautsky in 1915, and even in November 1914, when he said that imperialism must not be regarded as a "phase" or stage of economy, but as a policy, a definite policy "preferred" by finance capital; that imperialism must not be "identified" with "present-day capitalism"; that if imperialism is to be understood to mean "all the phenomena of present-day capitalism" —cartels, protection, the domination of the financiers, and colonial policy—then the question as to whether imperialism is necessary to capitalism becomes reduced to the "flattest tautology," because, in that case, "imperialism is naturally a vital necessity for capitalism," and so on. The best way to present Kautsky's ideas is to quote his own definition of imperialism, which is diametrically opposed to the substance of the ideas which I have set forth (for the objections coming from the camp of the German Marxists, who have been advocating similar ideas for many years already, have been long known to Kautsky as the objections of a definite trend in Marxism).

Kautsky's definition is as follows: "Imperialism is a product of highly developed industrial capitalism. It consists in the striving of every industrial capitalist nation to bring under its control or to annex all large areas of *agrarian* [Kautsky's italics] territory, irrespective of what nations inhabit it."[2]

This definition is of no use at all because it one-sidedly, i.e., arbitrarily, singles out only the national question (although the latter is extremely important in itself as well as in its relation to imperialism), it arbitrarily and *inaccurately* connects this question *only* with industrial capital in the countries which annex other nations, and in an equally arbitrary and inaccurate manner pushes into the forefront the annexation of agrarian regions.

Imperialism is a striving for annexations—this is what the *political* part of Kautsky's definition amounts to. It is correct, but very incomplete, for politically, imperialism is, in general, a striving towards violence and·reaction. For the moment, however, we are interested in the *economic* aspect of the question, which Kautsky *himself* introduced into *his* definition. The inaccuracies in Kautsky's definition are glaring. The characteristic feature of imperialism is *not* industrial *but* finance capital. It is not an accident that in France it was precisely the extraordinarily rapid development of *finance* capital, and the weakening of industrial capital, that from the eighties onwards gave rise to the extreme intensification of annexationist (colonial) policy. The characteristic feature of imperialism is precisely that it strives to annex *not only* agrarian territories, but even most highly industrialized regions (German appetite for Belgium; French appetite for Lorraine), because (1) the fact that the world is already partitioned obliges those contem-

2. *Die Neue Zeit*, 1914, 2 (B. 32), S. 909, Sept. 11, 1914; *cf.* 1915, 2, S. 107 *et seq.* [*Lenin*]

plating a *redivision* to reach out for *every kind* of territory, and (2) an essential feature of imperialism is the rivalry between several great powers in the striving for hegemony, i.e., for the conquest of territory, not so much directly for themselves as to weaken the adversary and undermine *his* hegemony. (Belgium is particularly important for Germany as a base for operations against Britain; Britain needs Baghdad as a base for operations against Germany, etc.)

Kautsky refers especially—and repeatedly—to English writers who, he alleges, have given a purely political meaning to the word "imperialism" in the sense that he, Kautsky, understands it. We take up the work by the English writer Hobson, *Imperialism*, which appeared in 1902, and there we read: "The new imperialism differs from the older, first, in substituting for the ambition of a single growing empire the theory and the practice of competing empires, each motivated by similar lusts of political aggrandisement and commercial gain; secondly, in the dominance of financial or investing over mercantile interests."[3]

We see that Kautsky is absolutely wrong in referring to English writers generally (unless he meant the vulgar English imperialists, or the avowed apologists for imperialism). We see that Kautsky, while claiming that he continues to advocate Marxism, as a matter of fact takes a step backward compared with the *social-liberal* Hobson, who *more correctly* takes into account two "historically concrete" (Kautsky's definition is a mockery of historical concreteness!) features of modern imperialism: (1) the competition between *several* imperialisms, and (2) the predominance of the financier over the merchant. If it is chiefly a question of the annexation of agrarian countries by industrial countries, then the role of the merchant is put in the forefront.

Kautsky's definition is not only wrong and un-Marxist. It serves as a basis for a whole system of views which signify a rupture with Marxist theory and Marxist practice all along the line. I shall refer to this later. The argument about words which Kautsky raises as to whether the latest stage of capitalism should be called imperialism or the stage of finance capital is not worth serious attention. Call it what you will, it makes no difference. The essence of the matter is that Kautsky detaches the politics of imperialism from its economics, speaks of annexations as being a policy "preferred" by finance capital, and opposes to it another bourgeois policy which, he alleges, is possible on this very same basis of finance capital. It follows, then, that monopolies in the economy are compatible with non-monopolistic, non-violent, non-annexationist methods in poli-

3. *Op. cit.*, p. 324. [*Lenin*]

tics. It follows, then, that the territorial division of the world, which was completed during this very epoch of finance capital, and which constitutes the basis of the present peculiar forms of rivalry between the biggest capitalist states, is compatible with a non-imperialist policy. The result is a slurring-over and a blunting of the most profound contradictions of the latest stage of capitalism, instead of an exposure of their depth; the result is bourgeois reformism instead of Marxism.

Kautsky enters into controversy with the German apologist of imperialism and annexations, Cunow, who clumsily and cynically argues that imperialism is present-day capitalism; the development of capitalism is inevitable and progressive; therefore imperialism is progressive; therefore, we should grovel before it and glorify it! This is something like the caricature of the Russian Marxists which the Narodniks drew in 1894–95. They argued: if the Marxists believe that capitalism is inevitable in Russia, that it is progressive, then they ought to open a tavern and begin to implant capitalism! Kautsky's reply to Cunow is as follows: imperialism is not present-day capitalism; it is only one of the forms of the policy of present-day capitalism. This policy we can and should fight, fight imperialism, annexations, etc.

The reply seems quite plausible, but in effect it is a more subtle and more disguised (and therefore more dangerous) advocacy of conciliation with imperialism, because a "fight" against the policy of the trusts and banks that does not affect the economic basis of the trusts and banks is mere bourgeois reformism and pacifism, the benevolent and innocent expression of pious wishes. Evasion of existing contradictions, forgetting the most important of them, instead of revealing their full depth—such is Kautsky's theory, which has nothing in common with Marxism. Naturally, such a "theory" can only serve the purpose of advocating unity with the Cunows!

"From the purely economic point of view," writes Kautsky, "it is not impossible that capitalism will yet go through a new phase, that of the extension of the policy of the cartels to foreign policy, the phase of ultra-imperialism,"[4] i.e., of a superimperialism, of a union of the imperialisms of the whole world and not struggles among them, a phase when wars shall cease under capitalism, a phase of "the joint exploitation of the world by internationally united finance capital."[5]

We shall have to deal with this "theory of ultra-imperialism" later on in order to show in detail how decisively and completely it breaks with Marxism. At present, in keeping with the general plan of the present work, we must examine the exact economic data on

4. *Die Neue Zeit*, 1914, 2 (B. 32), S. 921, Sept. 11, 1914. Cf. 1915, 2, S. 107 *et seq.*   [*Lenin*]
5. *Ibid.*, 1915, 1, S. 144, April 30, 1915.

this question. "From the purely economic point of view," is "ultra-imperialism" possible, or is it ultra-nonsense?

If the purely economic point of view is meant to be a "pure" abstraction, then all that can be said reduces itself to the following proposition: development is proceeding towards monopolies, hence, towards a single world monopoly, towards a single world trust. This is indisputable, but it is also as completely meaningless as is the statement that "development is proceeding" towards the manufacture of foodstuffs in laboratories. In this sense the "theory" of ultra-imperialism is no less absurd than a "theory of ultra-agriculture" would be.

If, however, we are discussing the "purely economic" conditions of the epoch of finance capital as a historically concrete epoch which began at the turn of the twentieth century, then the best reply that one can make to the lifeless abstractions of "ultra-imperialism" (which serve exclusively a most reactionary aim: that of diverting attention from the depth of *existing* antagonisms) is to contrast them with the concrete economic realities of the present-day world economy. Kautsky's utterly meaningless talk about ultra-imperialism encourages, among other things, that profoundly mistaken idea which only brings grist to the mill of the apologists of imperialism, i.e., that the rule of finance capital *lessens* the unevenness and contradictions inherent in the world economy, whereas in reality it *increases* them.

R. Calwer, in his little book, *An Introduction to the World Economy*,[6] made an attempt to summarise the main, purely economic, data that enable one to obtain a concrete picture of the internal relations of the world economy at the turn of the twentieth century. He divides the world into five "main economic areas," as follows: (1) Central Europe (the whole of Europe with the exception of Russia and Great Britain); (2) Great Britain; (3) Russia; (4) Eastern Asia; (5) America; he includes the colonies in the "areas" of the states to which they belong and "leaves aside" a few countries not distributed according to areas, such as Persia, Afghanistan, and Arabia in Asia, Morocco and Abyssinia in Africa, etc.

[On the following page] is a brief summary of the economic data he quotes on these regions.

We see three areas of highly developed capitalism (high development of means of transport, of trade and of industry): the Central European, the British and the American areas. Among these are three states which dominate the world: Germany, Great Britain, and the United States. Imperialist rivalry and the struggle between these countries have become extremely keen because Ger-

---

6. R. Calwer, *Einführung in die Weltwirtschaft* (Berlin, 1906). [*Lenin*]

Principal Economic Areas	Area Million sq. km.	Population Millions	Transport		Trade	Industry		
			Railways (thousand km.)	Mercantile fleet (million tons)	Imports, exports (thousand million marks)	Of coal (million tons)	Of pig iron (million tons)	Number of cotton spindles (millions)
						Output		
1) Central Europe	27.6 (23.6)*	388 (146)	204	8	41	251	15	26
2) Britain	28.9 (28.6)*	398 (355)	140	11	25	249	9	51
3) Russia	22	131	63	1	3	16	3	7
4) Eastern Asia	12	389	8	1	2	8	0.02	2
5) America	30	148	379	6	14	245	14	19

* The figures in parentheses show the area and population of the colonies.

many has only an insignificant area and few colonies; the creation of "Central Europe" is still a matter for the future, it is being born in the midst of a desperate struggle. For the moment the distinctive feature of the whole of Europe is political disunity. In the British and American areas, on the other hand, political concentration is very highly developed, but there is a vast disparity between the immense colonies of the one and the insignificant colonies of the other. In the colonies, however, capitalism is only beginning to develop. The struggle for South America is becoming more and more acute.

There are two areas where capitalism is little developed: Russia and Eastern Asia. In the former, the population is extremely sparse, in the latter it is extremely dense; in the former political concentration is high, in the latter it does not exist. The partitioning of China is only just beginning, and the struggle for it between Japan, the U.S., etc., is continually gaining in intensity.

Compare this reality—the vast diversity of economic and political conditions, the extreme disparity in the rate of development of the various countries, etc., and the violent struggles among the imperialist states—with Kautsky's silly little fable about "peaceful" ultra-imperialism. Is this not the reactionary attempt of a frightened philistine to hide from stern reality? Are not the international cartels which Kautsky imagines are the embryos of "ultra-imperialism" (in the same way as one "can" describe the manufacture of tablets in a laboratory as ultra-agriculture in embryo) an example of the division *and the redivision* of the world, the transition from peaceful division to non-peaceful division and vice versa? Is not American and other finance capital, which divided the whole world peacefully with Germany's participation in, for example, the international rail syndicate, or in the international mercantile shipping trust, now engaged in *redividing* the world on the basis of a new relation of forces that is being changed by methods *anything but* peaceful?

Finance capital and the trusts do not diminish but increase the differences in the rate of growth of the various parts of the world economy. Once the relation of forces is changed, what other solution of the contradictions can be found *under capitalism* than that of *force*? Railway statistics[7] provide remarkably exact data on the different rates of growth of capitalism and finance capital in world economy. In the last decades of imperialist development, the total length of railways has changed as follows:

	Railways (thousand kilometres)		
	1890	1913	+
Europe	224	346	+122
U.S.	268	411	+143
All colonies	82 ⎫	210 ⎫	+128 ⎫
Independent and semi-independent states of Asia and America	125	347	+222
	43 ⎭	137 ⎭	+ 94 ⎭
Total	617	1,104	

Thus, the development of railways has been most rapid in the colonies and in the independent (and semi-independent) states of Asia and America. Here, as we know, the finance capital of the four or five biggest capitalist states holds undisputed sway. Two hundred thousand kilometres of new railways in the colonies and in the other countries of Asia and America represent a capital of more than 40,000 million marks newly invested on particularly advantageous terms, with special guarantees of a good return and with profitable orders for steel works, etc., etc.

Capitalism is growing with the greatest rapidity in the colonies and in overseas countries. Among the latter, *new* imperialist powers are emerging (e.g., Japan). The struggle among the world imperialisms is becoming more acute. The tribute levied by finance capital on the most profitable colonial and overseas enterprises is increasing. In the division of this "booty," an exceptionally large part goes to countries which do not always stand at the top of the list in the rapidity of the development of their productive forces. In the case of the biggest countries, together with their colonies, the total length of railways was as [shown on the following page].

Thus, about 80 per cent of the total existing railways are concentrated in the hands of the five biggest powers. But the concentration of the *ownership* of these railways, the concentration of finance capital, is immeasurably greater since the French and British millionaires, for example, own an enormous amount of shares and bonds in American, Russian and other railways.

7. *Statistisches Jahrbuch für das deutsche Reich, 1915; Archiv für Eisenbahnwesen, 1892.* Minor details for the distribution of railways among the colonies of the various countries in 1890 had to be estimated approximately. [*Lenin*]

	(thousand kilometres)		
	1890	1913	
U.S.	268	413	+145
British Empire	107	208	+101
Russia	32	78	+ 46
Germany	43	68	+ 25
France	41	63	+ 22
Total for five powers	491	830	+339

Thanks to her colonies, Great Britain has increased the length of "her" railways by 100,000 kilometres, four times as much as Germany. And yet, it is well known that the development of productive forces in Germany, and especially the development of the coal and iron industries, has been incomparably more rapid during this period than in Britain—not to speak of France and Russia. In 1892, Germany produced 4,900,000 tons of pig-iron and Great Britain produced 6,800,000 tons; in 1912, Germany produced 17,600,000 tons and Great Britain, 9,000,000 tons. Germany, therefore, had an overwhelming superiority over Britain in this respect.[8] The question is: what means other than war could there be *under capitalism* to overcome the disparity between the development of productive forces and the accumulation of capital on the one side, and the division of colonies and spheres of influence for finance capital on the other?

VIII. Parasitism and Decay of Capitalism

We now have to examine yet another significant aspect of imperialism to which most of the discussions on the subject usually attach insufficient importance. One of the shortcomings of the Marxist Hilferding is that on this point he has taken a step backward compared with the non-Marxist Hobson. I refer to parasitism, which is characteristic of imperialism.

As we have seen, the deepest economic foundation of imperialism is monopoly. This is capitalist monopoly, i.e., monopoly which has grown out of capitalism and which exists in the general environment of capitalism, commodity production and competition, in permanent and insoluble contradiction to this general environment. Nevertheless, like all monopoly, it inevitably engenders a tendency of stagnation and decay. Since monopoly prices are established, even temporarily, the motive cause of technical and, consequently,

8. *Cf.* also Edgar Crammond, "The Economic Relations of the British and German Empires," in *The Journal of the* *Royal Statistical Society*, July 1914, p. 777 *et seq.* [*Lenin*]

of all other progress disappears to a certain extent and, further, the *economic* possibility arises of deliberately retarding technical progress. For instance, in America, a certain Owens invented a machine which revolutionised the manufacture of bottles. The German bottle-manufacturing cartel purchased Owens's patent, but pigeonholed it, refrained from utilising it. Certainly, monopoly under capitalism can never completely, and for a very long period of time, eliminate competition in the world market (and this, by the by, is one of the reasons why the theory of ultra-imperialism is so absurd). Certainly, the possibility of reducing the cost of production and increasing profits by introducing technical improvements operates in the direction of change. But the *tendency* to stagnation and decay, which is characteristic of monopoly, continues to operate, and in some branches of industry, in some countries, for certain periods of time, it gains the upper hand.

The monopoly ownership of very extensive, rich or well-situated colonies operates in the same direction.

Further, imperialism is an immense accumulation of money capital in a few countries, amounting, as we have seen, to 100,000–150,000 million francs in securities. Hence the extraordinary growth of a class, or rather, of a stratum of rentiers, i.e., people who live by "clipping coupons," who take no part in any enterprise whatever, whose profession is idleness. The export of capital, one of the most essential economic bases of imperialism, still more completely isolates the rentiers from production and sets the seal of parasitism on the whole country that lives by exploiting the labour of several overseas countries and colonies.

"In 1893," writes Hobson, "the British capital invested abroad represented about 15 per cent of the total wealth of the United Kingdom."[9] Let me remind the reader that by 1915 this capital had increased about two and a half times. "Aggressive imperialism," says Hobson further on, "which costs the tax-payer so dear, which is of so little value to the manufacturer and trader . . . is a source of great gain to the investor. . . . The annual income Great Britain derives from commissions in her whole foreign and colonial trade, import and export, is estimated by Sir. R. Giffen at £18,000,000 [nearly 170 million rubles] for 1899, taken at 2½ per cent, upon a turnover of £800,000,000." Great as this sum is, it cannot explain the aggressive imperialism of Great Britain, which is explained by the income of £90 million to £100 million from "invested" capital, the income of the rentiers.

The income from the rentiers is *five times greater* than the income obtained from the foreign trade of the biggest "trading" coun-

9. Hobson, *op. cit.*, pp. 59, 62. [*Lenin*]

try in the world! This is the essence of imperialism and imperialist parasitism.

For that reason the term "rentier state" (*Rentnerstaat*), or usurer state, is coming into common use in the economic literature that deals with imperialism. The world has become divided into a handful of usurer states and a vast majority of debtor states. "At the top of the list of foreign investments," says Schulze-Gaevernitz, "are those placed in politically dependent or allied countries: Great Britain grants loans to Egypt, Japan, China and South America. Her navy plays here the part of bailiff in case of necessity. Great Britain's political power protects her from the indignation of her debtors."[1] Sartorius von Waltershausen in his book, *The National Economic System of Capital Investments Abroad*, cites Holland as the model "rentier state" and points out that Great Britain and France are now becoming such.[2] Schilder is of the opinion that five industrial states have become "definitely pronounced creditor countries": Great Britain, France, Germany, Belgium and Switzerland. He does not include Holland in this list simply because she is "industrially little developed."[3] The United States is a creditor only of the American countries.

"Great Britain," says Schulze-Gaevernitz,

is gradually becoming transformed from an industrial into a creditor state. Notwithstanding the absolute increase in industrial output and the export of manufactured goods, there is an increase in the relative importance of income from interest and dividends, issues of securities, commissions and speculation in the whole of the national economy. In my opinion it is precisely this that forms the economic basis of imperialist ascendancy. The creditor is more firmly attached to the debtor than the seller is to the buyer.[4]

In regard to Germany, A. Lansburgh, the publisher of the Berlin *Die Bank*, in 1911, in an article entitled "Germany—a Rentier State," wrote the following: "People in Germany are ready to sneer at the yearning to become rentiers that is observed in France. But they forget that as far as the bourgeoisie is concerned the situation in Germany is becoming more and more like that in France."[5]

The rentier state is a state of parasitic, decaying capitalism, and this circumstance cannot fail to influence all the socio-political conditions of the countries concerned, in general, and the two fundamental trends in the working-class movement, in particular. To

1. Schulze-Gaevernitz, *Britischer Imperialismus*, S. 320 *et seq.* [*Lenin*]
2. Sartorius von Waltershausen, *Das volkswirtschaftliche System, etc.* (Berlin, 1907), Buch IV. [*Lenin*]
3. Schilder, *op. cit.*, S. 393. [*Lenin*]
4. Schulze-Gaevernitz, *op. cit.*, S. 122. [*Lenin*]
5. *Die Bank*, 1911, 1, S. 10–11. [*Lenin*]

demonstrate this in the clearest possible manner let me quote Hobson, who is a most reliable witness, since he cannot be suspected of leaning towards Marxist orthodoxy; on the other hand, he is an Englishman who is very well acquainted with the situation in the country which is richest in colonies, in finance capital, and in imperialist experience.

With the Anglo-Boer War fresh in his mind, Hobson describes the connection between imperialism and the interests of the "financiers," their growing profits from contracts, supplies, etc., and writes: "While the directors of this definitely parasitic policy are capitalists, the same motives appeal to special classes of the workers. In many towns most important trades are dependent upon government employment or contracts; the imperialism of the metal and shipbuilding centres is attributable in no small degree to this fact." Two sets of circumstances, in this writer's opinion, have weakened the old empires: (1) "economic parasitism," and (2) the formation of armies recruited from subject peoples. "There is first the habit of economic parasitism, by which the ruling state has used its provinces, colonies, and dependencies in order to enrich its ruling class and to bribe its lower classes into acquiescence." And I shall add that the economic possibility of such bribery, whatever its form may be, requires high monopolist profits.

As for the second circumstance, Hobson writes:

> One of the strangest symptoms of the blindness of imperialism is the reckless indifference with which Great Britain, France and other imperial nations are embarking on this perilous dependence. Great Britain has gone farthest. Most of the fighting by which we have won our Indian Empire has been done by natives; in India, as more recently in Egypt, great standing armies are placed under British commanders; almost all the fighting associated with our African dominions, except in the southern part, has been done for us by natives.

Hobson gives the following economic appraisal of the prospect of the partitioning of China:

> The greater part of Western Europe might then assume the appearance and character already exhibited by tracts of country in the South of England, in the Riviera and in the tourist-ridden or residential parts of Italy and Switzerland, little clusters of wealthy aristocrats drawing dividends and pensions from the Far East, with a somewhat larger group of professional retainers and tradesmen and a larger body of personal servants and workers in the transport trade and in the final stages of production of the more perishable goods; all the main arterial industries would have disappeared, the staple foods and manufactures flowing in as

tribute from Asia and Africa. . . . We have foreshadowed the possibility of even a larger alliance of Western states, a European federation of great powers which, so far from forwarding the cause of world civilisation, might introduce the gigantic peril of a Western parasitism, a group of advanced industrial nations, whose upper classes drew vast tribute from Asia and Africa, with which they supported great tame masses of retainers, no longer engaged in the staple industries of agriculture and manufacture, but kept in the performance of personal or minor industrial services under the control of a new financial aristocracy. Let those who would scout such a theory [it would be better to say: prospect] as undeserving of consideration examine the economic and social condition of districts in Southern England today which are already reduced to this condition, and reflect upon the vast extension of such a system which might be rendered feasible by the subjection of China to the economic control of similar groups of financiers, investors, and political and business officials, draining the greatest potential reservoir of profit the world has ever known, in order to consume it in Europe. The situation is far too complex, the play of world forces far too incalculable, to render this or any other single interpretation of the future very probable; but the influences which govern the imperialism of Western Europe today are moving in this direction, and, unless counteracted or diverted, make towards some such consummation.[6]

The author is quite right: *if* the forces of imperialism had not been counteracted they would have led precisely to what he has described. The significance of a "United States of Europe" in the present imperialist situation is correctly appraised. He should have added, however, that, also *within* the working-class movement, the opportunists, who are for the moment victorious in most countries, are "working" systematically and undeviatingly in this very direction. Imperialism, which means the partitioning of the world, and the exploitation of other countries besides China, which means high monopoly profits for a handful of very rich countries, makes it economically possible to bribe the upper strata of the proletariat, and thereby fosters, gives shape to, and strengthens opportunism. We must not, however, lose sight of the forces which counteract imperialism in general, and opportunism in particular, and which naturally, the social-liberal Hobson is unable to perceive.

The German opportunist, Gerhard Hildebrand, who was once expelled from the Party for defending imperialism, and who could today be a leader of the so-called "Social-Democratic" Party of Germany, supplements Hobson well by his advocacy of a "United States of Western Europe" (without Russia) for the purpose of "joint" action . . . against the African Negroes, against the "great

6. Hobson, *op. cit.*, pp. 103, 205, 144, 335, 386. [*Lenin*]

Islamic movement," for the maintenance of a "powerful army and navy," against a "Sino-Japanese coalition,"[7] etc.

The description of "British imperialism" in Schulze-Gaevernitz's book reveals the same parasitical traits. The national income of Great Britain approximately doubled from 1865 to 1898, while the income "from abroad" increased *ninefold* in the same period. While the "merit" of imperialism is that it "trains the Negro to habits of industry" (you cannot manage without coercion . . .), the "danger" of imperialism lies in that "Europe will shift the burden of physical toil—first agricultural and mining, then the rougher work in industry—on to the coloured races, and itself be content with the role of rentier, and in this way, perhaps, pave the way for the economic, and later, the political emancipation of the coloured races."

An increasing proportion of land in England is being taken out of cultivation and used for sport, for the diversion of the rich. As far as Scotland—the most aristocratic place for hunting and other sports—is concerned, it is said that "it lives on its past and on Mr. Carnegie" (the American multimillionaire). On horse racing and fox hunting alone England annually spends £14,000,000 (nearly 130 million rubles). The number of rentiers in England is about one million. The percentage of the productively employed population to the total population is declining:

	Population of England and Wales (millions)	Workers in basic industries (millions)	Per cent of total population
1851	17.9	4.1	23
1901	32.5	4.9	15

And in speaking of the British working class the bourgeois student of "British imperialism at the beginning of the twentieth century" is obliged to distinguish systematically between the *"upper stratum"* of the workers and the *"lower stratum of the proletariat proper."* The upper stratum furnishes the bulk of the membership of co-operatives, of trade unions, of sporting clubs and of numerous religious sects. To this level is adapted the electoral system, which in Great Britain is still *"sufficiently restricted to exclude the lower stratum of the proletariat proper"*! In order to present the condition of the British working class in a rosy light, only this upper stratum—which constitutes a *minority* of the proletariat—is usually spoken of. For instance, "the problem of unemployment is mainly a London problem and that of the lower proletarian stratum,

7. Gerhard Hildebrand, *Die Erschütterung der Industrieherrschaft und des Industriesozialismus* (1910), S. 229 *et seq.* [Lenin]

to which the politicians attach little importance. . . ."[8] He should have said: to which the bourgeois politicians and the "socialist" opportunists attach little importance.

One of the special features of imperialism connected with the facts I am describing, is the decline in emigration from imperialist countries and the increase in immigration into these countries from the more backward countries where lower wages are paid. As Hobson observes, emigration from Great Britain has been declining since 1884. In that year the number of emigrants was 242,000, while in 1900, the number was 169,000. Emigration from Germany reached the highest point between 1881 and 1890, with a total of 1,453,000 emigrants. In the course of the following two decades, it fell to 544,000 and to 341,000. On the other hand, there was an increase in the number of workers entering Germany from Austria, Italy, Russia and other countries. According to the 1907 census, there were 1,342,294 foreigners in Germany, of whom 440,800 were industrial workers and 257,329 agricultural workers.[9] In France, the workers employed in the mining industry are, "in great part," foreigners: Poles, Italians and Spaniards.[1] In the United States, immigrants from Eastern and Southern Europe are engaged in the most poorly paid jobs, while American workers provide the highest percentage of overseers or of the better-paid workers.[2] Imperialism has the tendency to create privileged sections also among the workers, and to detach them from the broad masses of the proletariat.

It must be observed that in Great Britain the tendency of imperialism to split the workers, to strengthen opportunism among them and to cause temporary decay in the working-class movement, revealed itself much earlier than the end of the nineteenth and the beginning of the twentieth centuries; for two important distinguishing features of imperialism were already observed in Great Britain in the middle of the nineteenth century—vast colonial possessions and a monopolist position in the world market. Marx and Engels traced this connection between opportunism in the working–class movement, and the imperialist features of British capitalism systematically, during the course of several decades. For example, on October 7, 1858, Engels wrote to Marx: "The English proletariat is actually becoming more and more bourgeois, so that this most bourgeois of all nations is apparently aiming ultimately at the possession of a bourgeois aristocracy and a bourgeois proletariat *alongside* the bourgeoisie. For a nation which exploits the whole

8. Schulze-Gaevernitz, *Britischer Imperialismus*, S. 301. [*Lenin*]
9. *Statistik des Deutschen Reichs*, Bd. 211. [*Lenin*]

1. Henger, *Die Kapitalsanlage der Franzosen* (Stuttgart, 1913). [*Lenin*]
2. Hourwich, *Immigration and Labour* (New York, 1913). [*Lenin*]

world this is of course to a certain extent justifiable." Almost a quarter of a century later, in a letter dated August 11, 1881, Engels speaks of the "worst English trade unions which allow themselves to be led by men sold to, or at least paid by, the middle class." In a letter to Kautsky, dated September 12, 1882, Engels wrote: "You ask me what the English workers think about colonial policy. Well, exactly the same as they think about politics in general. There is no workers' party here, there are only Conservatives and Liberal-Radicals, and the workers gaily share the feast of England's monopoly of the world market and the colonies."[3] (Engels expressed similar ideas in the press in his preface to the second edition of *The Condition of the Working Class in England*, which appeared in 1892.)

This clearly shows the causes and effects. The causes are: (1) exploitation of the whole world by this country; (2) its monopolist position in the world market; (3) its colonial monopoly. The effects are: (1) a section of the British proletariat becomes bourgeois; (2) a section of the proletariat allows itself to be led by men bought by, or at least paid by, the bourgeoisie. The imperialism of the beginning of the twentieth century completed the division of the world among a handful of states, each of which today exploits (in the sense of drawing superprofits from) a part of the "whole world" only a little smaller than that which England exploited in 1858; each of them occupies a monopolist position in the world market thanks to trusts, cartels, finance capital and creditor and debtor relations; each of them enjoys to some degree a colonial monopoly (we have seen that out of the total of 75,000,000 sq. km., which comprise the *whole* colonial world, 65,000,000 sq. km., or 86 per cent, belong to six powers; 61,000,000 sq. km., or 81 per cent, belong to three powers).

The distinctive feature of the present situation is the prevalence of such economic and political conditions that are bound to increase the irreconcilability between opportunism and the general and vital interests of the working-class movement: imperialism has grown from an embryo into the predominant system; capitalist monopolies occupy first place in economics and politics; the division of the world has been completed; on the other hand, instead of the undivided monopoly of Great Britain, we see a few imperialist powers contending for the right to share in this monopoly, and this struggle is characteristic of the whole period of the early twentieth century. Opportunism cannot now be completely triumphant in the working-class movement of one country for decades as it was in

---

3. *Briefwechsel von Marx und Engels*, Bd. II, S. 290; IV, 433.—Karl Kautsky, *Sozialismus und Kolonialpolitik* (Berlin, 1907), S. 79; this pamphlet was written by Kautsky in those infinitely distant days when he was still a Marxist. [*Lenin*]

Britain in the second half of the nineteenth century; but in a number of countries it has grown ripe, overripe, and rotten, and has become completely merged with bourgeois policy in the form of "social-chauvinism."[4]

IX. Critique of Imperialism

By the critique of imperialism, in the broad sense of the term, we mean the attitude of the different classes of society towards imperialist policy in connection with their general ideology.

The enormous dimensions of finance capital concentrated in a few hands and creating an extraordinarily dense and widespread network of relationships and connections which subordinates not only the small and medium, but also the very small capitalists and small masters, on the one hand, and the increasingly intense struggle waged against other national state groups of financiers for the division of the world and domination over other countries, on the other hand, cause the propertied classes to go over entirely to the side of imperialism. "General" enthusiasm over the prospects of imperialism, furious defence of it and painting it in the brightest colours—such are the signs of the times. Imperialist ideology also penetrates the working class. No Chinese Wall separates it from the other classes. The leaders of the present-day, so-called, "Social-Democratic" Party of Germany are justly called "social-imperialists," that is, socialists in words and imperialists in deeds; but as early as 1902, Hobson noted the existence in Britain of "Fabian imperialists" who belonged to the opportunist Fabian Society.

Bourgeois scholars and publicists usually come out in defence of imperialism in a somewhat veiled form; they obscure its complete domination and its deep-going roots, strive to push specific and secondary details into the forefront and do their very best to distract attention from essentials by means of absolutely ridiculous schemes for "reform," such as police supervision of the trusts or banks, etc. Cynical and frank imperialists who are bold enough to admit the absurdity of the idea of reforming the fundamental characteristics of imperialism are a rarer phenomenon.

Here is an example. The German imperialists attempt, in the magazine *Archives of World Economy*, to follow the national emancipation movements in the colonies, particularly, of course, in colonies other than those belonging to Germany. They note the unrest and the protest movements in India, the movement in Natal

---

4. Russian social-chauvinism in its overt form, represented by the Potresovs, Chkhenkelis, Maslovs, etc., and in its covert form (Chkheidze, Skobelev, Axel-rod, Martov, etc.), also emerged from the Russian variety of opportunism, namely, liquidationism. [*Lenin*]

(South Africa), in the Dutch East Indies, etc. One of them, commenting on an English report of a conference held on June 28–30, 1910, of representatives of various subject nations and races, of peoples of Asia, Africa and Europe who are under foreign rule, writes as follows in appraising the speeches delivered at this conference:

> We are told that we must fight imperialism; that the ruling states should recognise the right of subject peoples to independence; that an international tribunal should supervise the fulfilment of treaties concluded between the great powers and weak peoples. Further than the expression of these pious wishes they do not go. We see no trace of understanding of the fact that imperialism is inseparably bound up with capitalism in its present form and that, therefore [!!], an open struggle against imperialism would be hopeless, unless, perhaps, the fight were to be confined to protests against certain of its especially abhorrent excesses.[5]

Since the reform of the basis of imperialism is a deception, a "pious wish," since the bourgeois representatives of the oppressed nations go no "further" forward, the bourgeois representative of an oppressing nation goes "further" *backward*, to servility towards imperialism under cover of the claim to be "scientific." That is also "logic"!

The questions as to whether it is possible to reform the basis of imperialism, whether to go forward to the further intensification and deepening of the antagonisms which it engenders, or backward, towards allaying these antagonisms, are fundamental questions in the critique of imperialism. Since the specific political features of imperialism are reaction everywhere and increased national oppression due to the oppression of the financial oligarchy and the elimination of free competition, a petty-bourgeois-democratic opposition to imperialism arose at the beginning of the twentieth century in nearly all imperialist countries. Kautsky not only did not trouble to oppose, was not only unable to oppose this petty-bourgeois reformist opposition, which is really reactionary in its economic basis, but became merged with it in practice, and this is precisely where Kautsky and the broad international Kautskian trend deserted Marxism.

In the United States, the imperialist war waged against Spain in 1898 stirred up the opposition of the "anti-imperialists," the last of the Mohicans of bourgeois democracy who declared this war to be "criminal," regarded the annexation of foreign territories as a violation of the Constitution, declared that the treatment of Aguinaldo, leader of the Filipinos (the Americans promised him the independence of his country, but later landed troops and annexed it), was

5. *Weltwirtschaftliches Archiv*, Bd. II, S. 193. [*Lenin*]

"Jingo treachery," and quoted the words of Lincoln: "When the white man governs himself, that is self-government; but when he governs himself and also governs others, it is no longer self-government; it is despotism."[6] But as long as all this criticism shrank from recognising the inseverable bond between imperialism and the trusts, and, therefore, between imperialism and the foundations of capitalism, while it shrank from joining the forces engendered by large-scale capitalism and its development—it remained a "pious wish."

This is also the main attitude taken by Hobson in his critique of imperialism. Hobson anticipated Kautsky in protesting against the "inevitability of imperialism" argument, and in urging the necessity of "increasing the consuming capacity" of the people (under capitalism!). The petty-bourgeois point of view in the critique of imperialism, the omnipotence of the banks, the financial oligarchy, etc., is adopted by the authors I have often quoted, such as Agahd, A. Lansburgh, L. Eschwege, and among the French writers Victor Berard, author of a superficial book entitled *England and Imperialism* which appeared in 1900. All these authors, who make no claim to be Marxists, contrast imperialism with free competition and democracy, condemn the Baghdad railway scheme, which is leading to conflicts and war, utter "pious wishes" for peace, etc. This applies also to the compiler of international stock and share issue statistics, A. Neymarck, who, after calculating the thousands of millions of francs representing "international" securities, exclaimed in 1912: "Is it possible to believe that peace may be disturbed . . . that, in the face of these enormous figures, anyone would risk starting a war?"[7]

Such simple-mindedness on the part of the bourgeois economists is not surprising; moreover, *it is in their interest* to pretend to be so naïve and to talk "seriously" about peace under imperialism. But what remains of Kautsky's Marxism, when, in 1914, 1915 and 1916, he takes up the same bourgeois-reformist point of view and affirms that "everybody is agreed" (imperialists, pseudo-socialists and social-pacifists) on the matter of peace? Instead of an analysis of imperialism and an exposure of the depths of its contradictions, we have nothing but a reformist "pious wish" to wave them aside, to evade them.

Here is a sample of Kautsky's economic criticism of imperialism. He takes the statistics of the British export and import trade with Egypt for 1872 and 1912; it seems that this export and import trade has grown more slowly than British foreign trade as a whole. From

6. J. Patouillet, *L'impérialisme américain* (Dijon, 1904), p. 272. [*Lenin*]
7. *Bulletin de l'Institut International de* *Statistique*, T. XIX, livr. II, p. 225. [*Lenin*]

this Kautsky concludes that "we have no reason to suppose that without military occupation the growth of British trade with Egypt would have been less, simply as a result of the mere operation of economic factors." "The urge of capital to expand . . . can be best promoted, not by the violent methods of imperialism, but by peaceful democracy."[8]

This argument of Kautsky's which is repeated in every key by his Russian armour-bearer (and Russian shielder of the social-chauvinists), Mr. Spectator, constitutes the basis of Kautskian critique of imperialism, and that is why we must deal with it in greater detail. We will begin with a quotation from Hilferding, whose conclusions Kautsky on many occasions, and notably in April 1915, has declared to have been "unanimously adopted by all socialist theoreticians."

> It is not the business of the proletariat [writes Hilferding] to contrast the more progressive capitalist policy with that of the now bygone era of free trade and of hostility towards the state. The reply of the proletariat to the economic policy of finance capital, to imperialism, cannot be free trade, but socialism. The aim of proletarian policy cannot today be the ideal of restoring free competition—which has now become a reactionary ideal—but the complete elimination of competition by the abolition of capitalism.[9]

Kautsky broke with Marxism by advocating in the epoch of finance capital a "reactionary ideal," "peaceful democracy," "the mere operation of economic factors," for *objectively* this ideal drags us back from monopoly to non-monopoly capitalism, and is a reformist swindle.

Trade with Egypt (or with any other colony or semi-colony) "would have grown more" *without* military occupation, without imperialism, and without finance capital. What does this mean? That capitalism would have developed more rapidly if free competition had not been restricted by monopolies in general, or by the "connections," yoke (i.e., also the monopoly) of finance capital, or by the monopolist possession of colonies by certain countries?

Kautsky's argument can have no other meaning; and *this* "meaning" is meaningless. Let us assume that free competition, without any sort of monopoly, *would* have developed capitalism and trade more rapidly. But the more rapidly trade and capitalism develop, the greater is the concentration of production and capital which *gives rise* to monopoly. And monopolies have *already* arisen—precisely *out of* free competition! Even if monopolies have now

8. Kautsky, *Nationalstaat, imperialistischer Staat und Staatenbund* (Nürnberg, 1915), S. 72, 70. [*Lenin*]
9. *Finance Capital*, p. 567. [*Lenin*]

begun to retard progress, it is not an argument in favour of free competition, which has become impossible after it has given rise to monopoly.

Whichever way one turns Kautsky's argument, one will find nothing in it except reaction and bourgeois reformism.

Even if we correct this argument and say, as Spectator says, that the trade of the colonies with Britain is now developing more slowly than their trade with other countries, it does not save Kautsky; for it is *also* monopoly, *also* imperialism that is beating Great Britain, only it is the monopoly and imperialism of another country (America, Germany). It is known that the cartels have given rise to a new and peculiar form of protective tariffs, i.e., goods suitable for export are protected (Engels noted this in Vol. III of *Capital*).[1] It is known too, that the cartels and finance capital have a system peculiar to themselves, that of "exporting goods at cut-rate prices," or "dumping," as the English call it: within a given country the cartel sells its goods at high monopoly prices, but sells them abroad at a much lower price to undercut the competitor, to enlarge its own production to the utmost, etc. If Germany's trade with the British colonies is developing more rapidly than Great Britain's, it only proves that German imperialism is younger, stronger and better organised than British imperialism, is superior to it; but it by no means proves the "superiority" of free trade, for it is not a fight between free trade and protection and colonial dependence, but between two rival imperialisms, two monopolies, two groups of finance capital. The superiority of German imperialism over British imperialism is more potent than the wall of colonial frontiers or of protective tariffs: to use this as an "argument" *in favour of* free trade and "peaceful democracy" is banal, it means forgetting the essential features and characteristics of imperialism, substituting petty-bourgeois reformism for Marxism.

It is interesting to note that even the bourgeois economist, A. Lansburgh, whose criticism of imperialism is as petty-bourgeois as Kautsky's, nevertheless got closer to a more scientific study of trade statistics. He did not compare one single country, chosen at random, and one single colony with the other countries: he examined the export trade of an imperialist country: (1) with countries which are financially dependent upon it, and borrow money from it; and (2) with countries which are financially independent. He obtained [the results shown on the following page].

Lansburgh did not draw *conclusions* and therefore, strangely enough, failed to observe that *if* the figures prove anything at all, they prove that *he is wrong*, for the exports to countries financially

1. Karl Marx, *Capital*, Vol. III (Moscow, 1962), p. 118.

Export Trade of Germany
(million marks)

	1889	1908	Per cent increase
To countries financially dependent on Germany			
Rumania	48.2	70.8	47
Portugal	19.0	32.8	73
Argentina	60.7	147.0	143
Brazil	48.7	84.5	73
Chile	28.3	52.4	85
Turkey	29.9	64.0	114
Total	234.8	415.5	92
To countries financially independent of Germany			
Great Britain	651.8	997.4	53
France	210.2	437.9	108
Belgium	137.2	322.8	135
Switzerland	177.4	401.1	127
Australia	21.2	64.5	205
Dutch East Indies	8.8	40.7	363
Total	1,206.6	2,264.4	87

dependent on Germany have grown *more rapidly*, if only slightly, than exports to the countries which are financially independent. (I emphasise the "if," for Lansburgh's figures are far from complete.)

Tracing the connection between exports and loans, Lansburgh writes:

> In 1890–91, a Rumanian loan was floated through the German banks, which had already in previous years made advances on this loan. It was used chiefly to purchase railway materials in Germany. In 1891, German exports to Rumania amounted to 55 million marks. The following year they dropped to 39.4 million marks and, with fluctuations, to 25.4 million in 1900. Only in very recent years have they regained the level of 1891, thanks to two new loans.
>
> German exports to Portugal rose, following the loans of 1888–89, to 21,100,000 (1890); then, in the two following years, they dropped to 16,200,000 and 7,400,000, and regained their former level only in 1903.
>
> The figures of German trade with Argentina are still more striking. Loans were floated in 1888 and 1890; German exports to Argentina reached 60,700,000 marks (1889). Two years later they amounted to only 18,600,000 marks, less than one-third of the previous figure. It was not until 1901 that they regained and surpassed the level of 1889, and then only as a result of new loans floated by the state and by municipalities, with advances to build power stations, and with other credit operations.

Exports to Chile, as a consequence of the loan of 1889, rose to 45,200,000 marks (in 1892), and a year later dropped to 22,-500,000 marks. A new Chilean loan floated by the German banks in 1906 was followed by a rise of exports to 84,700,000 marks in 1907, only to fall again to 52,400,000 marks in 1908.[2]

From these facts Lansburgh draws the amusing petty-bourgeois moral of how unstable and irregular export trade is when it is bound up with loans, how bad it is to invest capital abroad instead of "naturally" and "harmoniously" developing home industry, how "costly" are the millions in bakshish that Krupp has to pay in floating foreign loans, etc. But the facts tell us clearly: the increase in exports is connected with *just these* swindling tricks of finance capital, which is not concerned with bourgeois morality, but with skinning the ox twice—first, it pockets the profits from the loan; then it pockets other profits from the *same* loan which the borrower uses to make purchases from Krupp, or to purchase railway material from the Steel Syndicate, etc.

I repeat that I do not by any means consider Lansburgh's figures to be perfect; but I had to quote them because they are more scientific than Kautsky's and Spectator's and because Lansburgh showed the correct way to approach the question. In discussing the significance of finance capital in regard to exports, etc., one must be able to single out the connection of exports especially and solely with the tricks of the financiers, especially and solely with the sale of goods by cartels, etc. Simply to compare colonies with non-colonies, one imperialism with another imperialism, one semi-colony or colony (Egypt) with all other countries, is to evade and to obscure the very *essence* of the question.

Kautsky's theoretical critique of imperialism has nothing in common with Marxism and serves only as a preamble to propaganda for peace and unity with the opportunists and the social-chauvinists, precisely for the reason that it evades and obscures the very profound and fundamental contradictions of imperialism: the contradictions between monopoly and free competition which exists side by side with it, between the gigantic "operations" (and gigantic profits) of finance capital and "honest" trade in the free market, the contradiction between cartels and trusts, on the one hand, and non-cartelised industry, on the other, etc.

The notorious theory of "ultra-imperialism," invented by Kautsky, is just as reactionary. Compare his arguments on this subject in 1915, with Hobson's arguments in 1902.

Kautsky: ". . . Cannot the present imperialist policy be supplanted by a new, ultra-imperialist policy, which will introduce the

2. *Die Bank*, 1909, 2, S. 819 *et seq.* [Lenin]

joint exploitation of the world by internationally united finance capital in place of the mutual rivalries of national finance capitals? Such a new phase of capitalism is at any rate conceivable. Can it be achieved? Sufficient premises are still lacking to enable us to answer this question."[3]

Hobson: "Christendom thus laid out in a few great federal empires, each with a retinue of uncivilised dependencies, seems to many the most legitimate development of present tendencies, and one which would offer the best hope of permanent peace on an assured basis of inter-Imperialism."

Kautsky called ultra-imperialism or super-imperialism what Hobson, thirteen years earlier, described as inter-imperialism. Except for coining a new and clever catchword, replacing one Latin prefix by another, the only progress Kautsky has made in the sphere of "scientific" thought is that he gave out as Marxism what Hobson, in effect, described as the cant of English parsons. After the Anglo-Boer War it was quite natural for this highly honourable caste to exert their main efforts to *console* the British middle class and the workers who had lost many of their relatives on the battle-fields of South Africa and who were obliged to pay higher taxes in order to guarantee still higher profits for the British financiers. And what better consolation could there be than the theory that imperialism is not so bad; that it stands close to inter- (or ultra-) imperialism, which can ensure permanent peace? No matter what the good intentions of the English parsons, or of sentimental Kautsky, may have been, the only objective, i.e., real, social significance of Kautsky's "theory" is this: it is a most reactionary method of consoling the masses with hopes of permanent peace being possible under capitalism, by distracting their attention from the sharp antagonisms and acute problems of the present times, and directing it towards illusory prospects of an imaginary "ultra-imperialism" of the future. Deception of the masses—that is all there is in Kautsky's "Marxist" theory.

Indeed, it is enough to compare well-known and indisputable facts to become convinced of the utter falsity of the prospects which Kautsky tries to conjure up before the German workers (and the workers of all lands). Let us consider India, Indo-China and China. It is known that these three colonial and semi-colonial countries, with a population of six to seven hundred million, are subjected to the exploitation of the finance capital of several imperialist powers; Great Britain, France, Japan, the U.S.A., etc. Let us assume that these imperialist countries form alliances against one another in order to protect or enlarge their possessions, their inter-

3. *Die Neue Zeit*, April 30, 1915, S. 144. [*Lenin*]

ests and their spheres of influence in these Asiatic states; these alliances will be "inter-imperialist," or "ultra-imperialist" alliances. Let us assume that *all* the imperialist countries conclude an alliance for the "peaceful" division of these parts of Asia; this alliance would be an alliance of "internationally united finance capital." There are actual examples of alliances of this kind in the history of the twentieth century—the attitude of the powers to China, for instance. We ask, is it "conceivable," assuming that the capitalist system remains intact—and this is precisely the assumption that Kautsky does make—that such alliances would be more than temporary, that they would eliminate friction, conflicts and struggle in every possible form?

The question has only to be presented clearly for any other than a negative answer to be impossible. This is because the only conceivable basis under capitalism for the division of spheres of influence, interests, colonies, etc., is a calculation of the *strength* of those participating, their general economic, financial, military strength, etc. And the strength of these participants in the division does not change to an equal degree, for the *even* development of different undertakings, trusts, branches of industry, or countries is impossible under capitalism. Half a century ago Germany was a miserable, insignificant country, if her capitalist strength is compared with that of the Britain of that time; Japan compared with Russia in the same way. Is it "conceivable" that in ten or twenty years' time the relative strength of the imperialist powers will have remained *un*changed? It is out of the question.

Therefore, in the realities of the capitalist system, and not in the banal philistine fantasies of English parsons, or of the German "Marxist," Kautsky, "inter-imperialist" or "ultra-imperialist" alliances, no matter what form they may assume, whether of one imperialist coalition against another, or of a general alliance embracing *all* the imperialist powers, are *inevitably* nothing more than a "truce" in periods between wars. Peaceful alliances prepare the ground for wars, and in their turn grow out of wars; the one conditions the other, producing alternating forms of peaceful and non-peaceful struggle on *one and the same* basis of imperialist connections and relations within world economics and world politics. But in order to pacify the workers and reconcile them with the social-chauvinists who have deserted to the side of the bourgeoisie, over-wise Kautsky *separates* one link of a single chain from another, separates the present peaceful (and ultra-imperialist, nay, ultra-ultra-imperialist) alliance of *all* the powers for the "pacification" of China (remember the suppression of the Boxer Rebellion) from the non-peaceful conflict of tomorrow, which will prepare the ground for another "peaceful" general alliance for the partition, say, of Turkey, on the day after tomorrow, *etc., etc.* Instead of showing the living connection between periods of imperialist peace and periods of imperialist war, Kautsky presents the workers with a lifeless abstraction in order to reconcile them to their lifeless leaders.

An American writer, Hill, in his *A History of the Diplomacy in the International Development of Europe* refers in his preface to the following periods in the recent history of diplomacy: (1) the era of revolution; (2) the constitutional movement; (3) the present era of "commercial imperialism."[4] Another writer divides the history of Great Britain's "world policy" since 1870 into four periods: (1) the first Asiatic period (that of the struggle against Russia's advance in Central Asia towards India); (2) the African period (approximately 1885–1902): that of the struggle against France for the partition of Africa (the "Fashoda incident" of 1898 which brought her within a hair's breadth of war with France); (3) the second Asiatic period (alliance with Japan against Russia); and (4) the "European" period, chiefly anti-German.[5] "The political patrol clashes take place on the financial field," wrote the banker, Riesser, in 1905, in showing how French finance capital operating in Italy was preparing the way for a political alliance of these countries, and how a conflict was developing between Germany and Great Britain over Persia, between all the European capitalists over Chinese loans, etc. Behold, the living reality of peaceful "ultra-imperialist" alliances in their inseverable connection with ordinary imperialist conflicts!

Kautsky's obscuring of the deepest contradictions of imperialism, which inevitably boils down to painting imperialism in bright colours, leaves its traces in this writer's criticism of the political features of imperialism. Imperialism is the epoch of finance capital and of monopolies, which introduce everywhere the striving for domination, not for freedom. Whatever the political system, the result of these tendencies is everywhere reaction and an extreme intensification of antagonisms in this field. Particularly intensified become the yoke of national oppression and the striving for annexations, i.e., the violation of national independence (for annexation is nothing but the violation of the right of nations to self-determination). Hilferding rightly notes the connection between imperialism and the intensification of national oppression. "In the newly opened-up countries," he writes,

the capital imported into them intensifies antagonisms and excites against the intruders the constantly growing resistance of the

---

4. David Jayne Hill, *A History of the Diplomacy in the International Develop-* *ment of Europe*, Vol. I, p. X. [Lenin]
5. Schilder, *op. cit.*, S. 178. [Lenin]

peoples who are awakening to national consciousness; this resistance can easily develop into dangerous measures against foreign capital. The old social relations become completely revolutionised, the age-long agrarian isolation of "nations without history" is destroyed and they are drawn into the capitalist whirlpool. Capitalism itself gradually provides the subjugated with the means and resources for their emancipation and they set out to achieve the goal which once seemed highest to the European nations: the creation of a united national state as a means to economic and cultural freedom. This movement for national independence threatens European capital in its most valuable and most promising fields of exploitation, and European capital can maintain its domination only by continually increasing its military forces.[6]

To this must be added that it is not only in newly opened-up countries, but also in the old, that imperialism is leading to annexation, to increased national oppression, and, consequently, also to increasing resistance. While objecting to the intensification of political reaction by imperialism, Kautsky leaves in the shade a question that has become particularly urgent, viz., the impossibility of unity with the opportunists in the epoch of imperialism. While objecting to annexations, he presents his objections in a form that is most acceptable and least offensive to the opportunists. He addresses himself to a German audience, yet he obscures the most topical and important point, for instance, the annexation of Alsace-Lorraine by Germany. In order to appraise this "mental aberration" of Kautsky's I shall take the following example. Let us suppose that a Japanese condemns the annexation of the Philippines by the Americans. The question is: will many believe that he does so because he has a horror of annexations as such, and not because he himself has a desire to annex the Philippines? And shall we not be constrained to admit that the "fight" the Japanese is waging against annexations can be regarded as being sincere and politically honest only if he fights against the annexation of Korea by Japan, and urges freedom for Korea to secede from Japan?

Kautsky's theoretical analysis of imperialism, as well as his economic and political critique of imperialism, are permeated *through and through* with a spirit, absolutely irreconcilable with Marxism, of obscuring and glossing over the fundamental contradictions of imperialism and with a striving to preserve at all costs the crumbling unity with opportunism in the European working-class movement.

6. *Finance Capital*, p. 487. [*Lenin*]

X. The Place of Imperialism in History

We have seen that in its economic essence imperialism is monopoly capitalism. This in itself determines its place in history, for monopoly that grows out of the soil of free competition, and precisely out of free competition, is the transition from the capitalist system to a higher socio-economic order. We must take special note of the four principal types of monopoly, or principal manifestations of monopoly capitalism, which are characteristic of the epoch we are examining.

Firstly, monopoly arose out of the concentration of production at a very high stage. This refers to the monopolist capitalist associations, cartels, syndicates and trusts. We have seen the important part these play in present-day economic life. At the beginning of the twentieth century, monopolies had acquired complete supremacy in the advanced countries, and although the first steps towards the formation of the cartels were taken by countries enjoying the protection of high tariffs (Germany, America), Great Britain, with her system of free trade, revealed the same basic phenomenon, only a little later, namely, the birth of monopoly out of the concentration of production.

Secondly, monopolies have stimulated the seizure of the most important sources of raw materials, especially for the basic and most highly cartelised industries in capitalist society: the coal and iron industries. The monopoly of the most important sources of raw materials has enormously increased the power of big capital, and has sharpened the antagonism between cartelised and non-cartelised industry.

Thirdly, monopoly has sprung from the banks. The banks have developed from modest middleman enterprises into the monopolists of finance capital. Some three to five of the biggest banks in each of the foremost capitalist countries have achieved the "personal link-up" between industrial and bank capital, and have concentrated in their hands the control of thousands upon thousands of millions which form the greater part of the capital and income of entire countries. A financial oligarchy, which throws a close network of dependence relationships over all the economic and political institutions of present-day bourgeois society without exception—such is the most striking manifestation of this monopoly.

Fourthly, monopoly has grown out of colonial policy. To the numerous "old" motives of colonial policy, finance capital has added the struggle for the sources of raw materials, for the export of capital, for spheres of influence, i.e., for spheres for profitable deals, concessions, monopoly profits and so on, economic territory in general. When the colonies of the European powers, for instance, comprised only one-tenth of the territory of Africa (as was the case in 1876), colonial policy was able to develop by methods other than those of monopoly—by the "free grabbing" of territories, so to speak. But when nine-tenths of Africa had been seized (by 1900), when the whole world had been divided up, there was inevitably ushered in the era of monopoly possession of colonies and, consequently, of particularly intense struggle for the division and the redivision of the world.

The extent to which monopolist capital has intensified all the contradictions of capitalism is generally known. It is sufficient to mention the high cost of living and the tyranny of the cartels. This intensification of contradictions constitutes the most powerful driving force of the transitional period of history, which began from the time of the final victory of world finance capital.

Monopolies, oligarchy, the striving for domination and not for freedom, the exploitation of an increasing number of small or weak nations by a handful of the richest or most powerful nations—all these have given birth to those distinctive characteristics of imperialism which compel us to define it as parasitic or decaying capitalism. More and more prominently there emerges, as one of the tendencies of imperialism, the creation of the "rentier state," the usurer state, in which the bourgeoisie to an ever-increasing degree lives on the proceeds of capital exports and by "clipping coupons." It would be a mistake to believe that this tendency to decay precludes the rapid growth of capitalism. It does not. In the epoch of imperialism, certain branches of industry, certain strata of the bourgeoisie and certain countries betray, to a greater or lesser degree, now one and now another of these tendencies. On the whole, capitalism is growing far more rapidly than before; but this growth is not only becoming more and more uneven in general, its unevenness also manifests itself, in particular, in the decay of the countries which are richest in capital (Britain).

In regard to the rapidity of Germany's economic development, Riesser, the author of the book on the big German banks, states:

> The progress of the preceding period (1848–70), which had not been exactly slow, compares with the rapidity with which the whole of Germany's national economy, and with it German banking, progressed during this period (1870–1905) in about the same way as the speed of the mail coach in the good old days compares with the speed of the present-day automobile . . . which is whizzing past so fast that it endangers not only innocent pedestrians in its path, but also the occupants of the car.

In its turn, this finance capital which has grown with such extraordinary rapidity is not unwilling, precisely because it has grown so quickly, to pass on to a more "tranquil" possession of colonies which have to be seized—and not only by peaceful methods—from richer nations. In the United States, economic development in the last decades has been even more rapid than in Germany, *and for this very reason*, the parasitic features of modern American capitalism have stood out with particular prominence. On the other hand, a comparison of, say, the republican American bourgeoisie with the monarchist Japanese or German bourgeoisie shows that the most pronounced political distinction diminishes to an extreme degree in the epoch of imperialism—not because it is unimportant in general, but because in all these cases we are talking about a bourgeoisie which has definite features of parasitism.

The receipt of high monopoly profits by the capitalists in one of the numerous branches of industry, in one of the numerous countries, etc., makes it economically possible for them to bribe certain sections of the workers, and for a time a fairly considerable minority of them, and win them to the side of the bourgeoisie of a given industry or given nation against all the others. The intensification of antagonisms between imperialist nations for the division of the world increases this urge. And so there is created that bond between imperialism and opportunism, which revealed itself first and most clearly in Great Britain, owing to the fact that certain features of imperialist development were observable there much earlier than in other countries. Some writers, L. Martov, for example, are prone to wave aside the connection between imperialism and opportunism in the working-class movement—a particularly glaring fact at the present time—by resorting to "official optimism" (*à la* Kautsky and Huysmans) like the following: the cause of the opponents of capitalism would be hopeless if it were progressive capitalism that led to the increase of opportunism, or, if it were the best-paid workers who were inclined towards opportunism, etc. We must have no illusions about "optimism" of this kind. It is optimism in respect of opportunism; it is optimism which serves to conceal opportunism. As a matter of fact the extraordinary rapidity and the particularly revolting character of the development of opportunism is by no means a guarantee that its victory will be durable: the rapid growth of a painful abscess on a healthy body can only cause it to burst more quickly and thus relieve the body of it. The most dangerous of all in this respect are those who do not wish to understand that the fight against imperialism is a sham and humbug unless it is inseparably bound up with the fight against opportunism.

From all that has been said in this book on the economic essence of imperialism, it follows that we must define it as capitalism in transition, or, more precisely, as moribund capitalism. It is very instructive in this respect to note that bourgeois economists, in describing modern capitalism, frequently employ catchwords and phrases like "interlocking," "absence of isolation," etc.; "in conformity with their functions and course of development," banks are "not purely private business enterprises; they are more and more outgrowing the sphere of purely private business regulation." And this very Riesser, whose words I have just quoted, declares with all seriousness that the "prophecy" of the Marxists concerning "socialisation" has "not come true"!

What then does this catchword "interlocking" express? It merely expresses the most striking feature of the process going on before our eyes. It shows that the observer counts the separate trees, but cannot see the wood. It slavishly copies the superficial, the fortuitous, the chaotic. It reveals the observer as one who is overwhelmed by the mass of raw material and is utterly incapable of appreciating its meaning and importance. Ownership of shares, the relations between owners of private property "interlock in a haphazard way." But underlying this interlocking, its very base, are the changing social relations of production. When a big enterprise assumes gigantic proportions, and, on the basis of an exact computation of mass data, organises according to plan the supply of primary raw materials to the extent of two-thirds, or three-fourths, of all that is necessary for tens of millions of people; when the raw materials are transported in a systematic and organised manner to the most suitable places of production, sometimes situated hundreds or thousands of miles from each other; when a single centre directs all the consecutive stages of processing the material right up to the manufacture of numerous varieties of finished articles; when these products are distributed according to a single plan among tens and hundreds of millions of consumers (the marketing of oil in America and Germany by the American oil trust)—then it becomes evident that we have socialisation of production, and not mere "interlocking"; that private economic and private property relations constitute a shell which no longer fits its contents, a shell which must inevitably decay if its removal is artificially delayed, a shell which may remain in a state of decay for a fairly long period (if, at the worst, the cure of the opportunist abscess is protracted), but which will inevitably be removed.

The enthusiastic admirer of German imperialism, Schulze-Gaevernitz, exclaims:

> Once the supreme management of the German banks has been entrusted to the hands of a dozen persons, their activity is even today more significant for the public good than that of the majority of the Ministers of State. . . . [The "interlocking" of bankers, ministers, magnates of industry and rentiers is here conveniently forgotten.] If we imagine the development of those tendencies we have noted carried to their logical conclusion we will have: the

money capital of the nation united in the banks; the banks themselves combined into cartels; the investment capital of the nation cast in the shape of securities. Then the forecast of that genius Saint-Simon will be fulfilled: "The present anarchy of production, which corresponds to the fact that economic relations are developing without uniform regulation, must make way for organisation in production. Production will no longer be directed by isolated manufacturers, independent of each other and ignorant of man's economic needs; that will be done by a certain public institution. A central committee of management, being able to survey the large field of social economy from a more elevated point of view, will regulate it for the benefit of the whole of society, will put the means of production into suitable hands, and above all will take care that there be constant harmony between production and consumption. Institutions already exist which have assumed as part of their functions a certain organisation of economic labour, the banks." We are still a long way from the fulfilment of Saint-Simon's forecast, but we are on the way towards it: Marxism, different from what Marx imagined, but different only in form.[7]

A crushing "refutation" of Marx, indeed, which retreats a step from Marx's precise, scientific analysis to Saint-Simon's guesswork, the guess-work of a genius, but guess-work all the same.

7. *Grundriss der Sozialökonomik*, S. 146. [*Lenin*]

The Symptoms of a
Revolutionary Situation

From the beginning of the World War Lenin envisaged revolution in the warring countries, Russia included, as the best way to end it. In a long article on "The Downfall of the Second International," written in the summer of 1915 and published in Geneva in September in the party's theoretical journal *Kommunist*, he set forth in the passage here presented a conception of the meaning of a "revolutionary situation." His assumptions were that the war was generating revolutionary situations in a number of the belligerent countries, and that out of such situations might come revolutions.

For a Marxist it is indubitable that a revolution is impossible without a revolutionary situation, likewise that not every revolutionary situation leads to a revolution. What in general are the symptoms of a revolutionary situation? We shall not likely err if we cite the following three principal symptoms: (1) the impossibility for the ruling classes to preserve their domination in unaltered form; this or that crisis "up above," a crisis of the ruling class's policy, creating a fissure into which pour the discontent and indignation of the oppressed classes. For a revolution to come about it is normally insufficient that "those down below did not desire" to go on in the old way; it is also requisite that "those up above were unable" to; (2) a more than normal aggravation of the want and tribulations of the oppressed classes; (3) a considerable rise, for the aforementioned reasons, in the level of activity of the masses, which in times of "peace" calmly allow themselves to be robbed but in turbulent times are drawn into independent historical action both by the crisis situation as a whole *and by those "up above" themselves.*

Without these objective changes, which take place independently of the will not only of particular groups and parties but of various classes, revolution, as a general rule, is impossible. These objective changes, in the aggregate, amount to what is called a revolutionary situation. Such situations came about in 1905 in Russia and in all the revolutionary epochs in the West; but also in the sixties of the past century in Germany, and in 1859–61 and 1879–80 in Russia, although in these instances no revolution occurred. Why? Because a revolution comes not out of every revolutionary situation, but only out of those situations in which the above-catalogued objective changes are accompanied by a subjective one, namely: the capacity of the revolutionary *class* to take mass revolutionary actions that are *strong enough* to smash (or break up) the old government, which, not even in time of crises, will "fall" unless it is "dropped."

Such are the Marxist views on revolution, which many, many times have been set forth and accepted as axiomatic by all Marxists and which for us Russians were confirmed in an especially vivid way by the experience of 1905. * * *

That a European war would be difficult beyond all precedent is something that everyone realized, saw and accepted. The experience of the war is more and more confirming it. The war is expanding. The political foundations of Europe are more and more starting to waver. The tribulations of the masses are awful, and the efforts of the governments, the bourgeoisie and the opportunists to hush up these tribulations are failing more and more often. The war profits of certain capitalist groups are unprecedentedly huge, scandalously huge. An inchoate indignation among the masses, a dim desire among the dark and downtrodden strata for a nice ("democratic") peace, an incipient muttering "down below"—all this is evident. And the longer the war goes on and the worse it becomes, the more the governments intensify and must intensify the activities of the masses by appealing to them for supreme feats of effort and self-sacrifice. The war experience, like the experience of every crisis in history, every great calamity and every turning-point in a man's life, dulls the minds and breaks the spirit of some *but enlightens and tempers others*; and by and large in world history the number and strength of the latter have proved greater than that of the former except in certain instances of the decline and fall of this or that state.

In a word, a revolutionary situation is at hand in the majority of leading countries and great powers of Europe. * * *

Will this situation last long and to what extent will it be further aggravated? Will it lead to revolution? This we do not know and no one can know. Only the *experience* of the development of revolutionary attitudes and transition of the leading class, the proletariat, to revolutionary action will show it. There cannot be any question here either of "illusions" or of their being punctured, for nowhere and never has any socialist given guarantees that this very war (and not the next one), this existing (and not tomorrow's) revolutionary situation will give rise to a revolution. It is a question of the most indubitable and fundamental obligation of all socialists: the obligation to make plain to the masses the existence of a revolutionary situation, to clarify its breadth and depth, to awaken the proletariat's revolutionary consciousness and revolutionary resolve, to help it go over to revolutionary actions and to create organizations corresponding to the revolutionary situation for work in that direction. * * *

Lecture on the 1905 Revolution

Lenin's lecture on 1905 is significant as evidence both of the huge importance he attached to that event and of the degree to which the experience of the 1905 revolution informed his whole way of conceiving the process of social revolution. He delivered the lecture in German to a meeting of Swiss working youth in the People's House in Zurich in January 1914. It is interesting that though he spoke of "the coming European revolution," he concluded that "we of the older generation may not live to see the decisive battles of this coming revolution." The Russian Revolution broke out about a month later.

My young friends and comrades.

Today is the twelfth anniversary of "Bloody Sunday," which is rightly regarded as the beginning of the Russian revolution.

Thousands of workers—not Social-Democrats, but loyal God-fearing subjects—led by the priest Gapon, streamed from all parts of the capital to its centre, to the square in front of the Winter Palace, to submit a petition to the tsar. The workers carried icons. In a letter to the tsar, their then leader, Gapon, had guaranteed his personal safety and asked him to appear before the people.

Troops were called out. Uhlans and Cossacks attacked the crowd with drawn swords. They fired on the unarmed workers, who on their bended knees implored the Cossacks to allow them to go to the tsar. Over one thousand were killed and over two thousand wounded on that day, according to police reports. The indignation of the workers was indescribable.

Such is the general picture of January 22, 1905—"Bloody Sunday."

That you may understand more clearly the historic significance of this event, I shall quote a few passages from the workers' petition. It begins with the following words:

> We workers, inhabitants of St. Petersburg, have come to Thee.
> We are unfortunate, reviled slaves, weighed down by despotism

and tyranny. Our patience exhausted, we ceased work and begged our masters to give us only that without which life is a torment. But this was refused; to the employers everything seemed unlawful. We are here, many thousands of us. Like the whole of the Russian people, we have no human rights whatever. Owing to the deeds of Thy officials we have become slaves.

The petition contains the following demands: amnesty, civil liberties, fair wages, gradual transfer of the land to the people, convocation of a constituent assembly on the basis of universal and equal suffrage. It ends with the following words:

> Sire, do not refuse aid to Thy people! Demolish the wall that separates Thee from Thy people. Order and promise that our requests will be granted, and Thou wilt make Russia happy; if not, we are ready to die on this very spot. We have only two roads: freedom and happiness, or the grave.

Reading it *now*, this petition of uneducated, illiterate workers, led by a patriarchal priest, creates a strange impression. Involuntarily one compares this naïve petition with the present peace resolutions of the social-pacifists, the would-be socialists who in reality are bourgeois phrase-mongers. The unenlightened workers of pre-revolutionary Russia did not know that the tsar was the head of the *ruling class*, the class, namely, of big landowners, already bound by a thousand ties with the big bourgeoisie and prepared to defend their monopoly, privileges and profits by every means of violence. The social-pacifists of today, who pretend to be "highly educated" people—no joking—do not realise that it is just as foolish to expect a "democratic" peace from bourgeois governments that are waging an imperialist predatory war, as it was to believe that peaceful petitions would induce the bloody tsar to grant democratic reforms.

Nevertheless, there is a great difference between the two—the present-day social-pacifists are, to a large extent, hypocrites, who strive by gentle admonitions to divert the people from the revolutionary struggle, whereas the uneducated workers in pre-revolutionary Russia proved by their deeds that they were straightforward people awakened to political consciousness for the first time.

It is in this awakening of tremendous masses of the people to political consciousness and revolutionary struggle that the historic significance of January 22, 1905, lies.

"There is not yet a revolutionary people in Russia," wrote Mr. Pyotr Struve, then leader of the Russian liberals and publisher abroad of an illegal, uncensored organ, *two days* before "Bloody Sunday." The idea that an illiterate peasant country could produce a revolutionary people seemed utterly absurd to this "highly educated," supercilious and extremely stupid leader of the bourgeois reformists. So deep was the conviction of the reformists of those days—as of the reformists of today—that a real revolution was impossible!

Prior to January 22 (or January 9, old style), 1905, the revolutionary party of Russia consisted of a small group of people, and the reformists of those days (exactly like the reformists of today) derisively called us a "sect." Several hundred revolutionary organisers, several thousand members of local organisations, half a dozen revolutionary papers appearing not more frequently than once a month, published mainly abroad and smuggled into Russia with incredible difficulty and at the cost of many sacrifices—such were the revolutionary parties in Russia, and the revolutionary Social-Democracy in particular, prior to January 22, 1905. This circumstance gave the narrow-minded and overbearing reformists formal justification for their claim that there was not yet a revolutionary people in Russia.

Within a few months, however, the picture changed completely. The hundreds of revolutionary Social-Democrats "suddenly" grew into thousands; the thousands became the leaders of between two and three million proletarians. The proletarian struggle produced widespread ferment, often revolutionary movements among the peasant masses, fifty to a hundred million strong; the peasant movement had its reverberations in the army and led to soldiers' revolts, to armed clashes between one section of the army and another. In this manner a colossal country, with a population of 130,000,000, went into the revolution; in this way, dormant Russia was transformed into a Russia of a revolutionary proletariat and a revolutionary people.

It is necessary to study this transformation, understand why it was possible, its methods and ways, so to speak.

The principal factor in this transformation was the *mass strike*. The peculiarity of the Russian revolution is that it was a *bourgeois-democratic* revolution in its social content, but a *proletarian* revolution in its methods of struggle. It was a bourgeois-democratic revolution since its immediate aim, which it could achieve directly and with its own forces, was a democratic republic, the eight-hour day and confiscation of the immense estates of the nobility—all the measures the French bourgeois revolution in 1792–93 had almost completely achieved.

At the same time, the Russian revolution was also a proletarian revolution, not only in the sense that the proletariat was the leading force, the vanguard of the movement, but also in the sense that a specifically proletarian weapon of struggle—the strike—was the principal means of bringing the masses into motion and the most characteristic phenomenon in the wave-like rise of decisive events.

The Russian revolution was the *first*, though certainly not the last, great revolution in history in which the mass political strike played an extraordinarily important part. It may even be said that the events of the Russian revolution and the sequence of its political forms cannot be understood without a study of the *strike statistics* to disclose the *basis* of these events and this sequence of forms.

I know perfectly well that dry statistics are hardly suitable in a lecture and are likely to bore the hearer. Nevertheless, I cannot refrain from quoting a few figures, in order that you may be able to appreciate the real objective basis of the whole movement. The average annual number of strikers in Russia during the ten years preceding the revolution was 43,000, which means 430,000 for the decade. In January 1905, the first month of the revolution, the number of strikers was 440,000. In other words, there were *more* strikers *in one month* than in the whole of the preceding decade!

In no capitalist country in the world, not even in the most advanced countries like England, the United States of America, or Germany, has there been anything to match the tremendous Russian strike movement of 1905. The total number of strikers was 2,800,000, more than two times the number of factory workers in the country! This, of course, does not prove that the urban factory workers of Russia were more educated, or stronger, or more adapted to the struggle than their brothers in Western Europe. The very opposite is true.

But it does show how great the dormant energy of the proletariat can be. It shows that in a revolutionary epoch—I say this without the slightest exaggeration, on the basis of the most accurate data of Russian history—the proletariat *can* generate fighting energy *a hundred times greater* than in ordinary, peaceful times. It shows that up to 1905 mankind did not yet know what a great, what a tremendous exertion of effort the proletariat is, and will be, capable of in a fight for really great aims, and one waged in a really revolutionary manner!

The history of the Russian revolution shows that it was the vanguard, the finest elements of the wage-workers, that fought with the greatest tenacity and the greatest devotion. The larger the mills and factories involved, the more stubborn were the strikes, and the more often did they recur during the year. The bigger the city, the more important was the part the proletariat played in the struggle. Three big cities, St. Petersburg, Riga and Warsaw, which have the largest and most class-conscious working-class element, show an immeasurably greater number of strikers, in relation to all workers, than any other city, and, of course, much greater than the rural districts.

In Russia—as probably in other capitalist countries—the metalworkers represent the vanguard of the proletariat. In this connection we note the following instructive fact: taking all industries, the number of persons involved in strikes in 1905 was 160 per hundred workers employed, but in the *metal industry* the number was 320 per hundred! It is estimated that in consequence of the 1905 strikes every Russian factory worker lost an average of ten rubles in wages —approximately 26 francs at the pre-war rate of exchange—sacrificing this money, as it were, for the sake of the struggle. But if we take the metal workers, we find that the loss in wages was *three times as great!* The finest elements of the working class marched in the forefront, giving leadership to the hesitant, rousing the dormant and encouraging the weak.

A distinctive feature was the manner in which economic strikes were interwoven with political strikes during the revolution. There can be no doubt that only this very close link-up of the two forms of strike gave the movement its great power. The broad masses of the exploited could not have been drawn into the revolutionary movement had they not been given daily examples of how the wage-workers in the various industries were forcing the capitalists to grant immediate, direct improvements in their conditions. This struggle imbued the masses of the Russian people with a new spirit. Only then did the old serf-ridden, sluggish, patriarchal, pious and obedient Russia cast out the old Adam; only then did the Russian people obtain a really democratic and really revolutionary education.

When the bourgeois gentry and their uncritical echoers, the social-reformists, talk priggishly about the "education" of the masses, they usually mean something schoolmasterly, pedantic, something that demoralises the masses and instils in them bourgeois prejudices.

The real education of the masses can never be separated from their independent political, and especially revolutionary, struggle. Only struggle educates the exploited class. Only struggle discloses to it the magnitude of its own power, widens its horizon, enhances its abilities, clarifies its mind, forges its will. That is why even reactionaries had to admit that the year 1905, the year of struggle, the "mad year," definitely buried patriarchal Russia.

Let us examine more closely the relation, in the 1905 strike struggles, between the metalworkers and the textile workers. The metalworkers are the best paid, the most class-conscious and best educated proletarians. The textile workers, who in 1905 were two and a half times more numerous than the metalworkers, are the most backward and the worst paid body of workers in Russia, and in very many cases have not yet definitely severed connections with their peasant kinsmen in the village. This brings us to a very important circumstance.

Throughout the whole of 1905, the metalworkers' strikes show a preponderance of political over economic strikes, though this preponderance was far greater toward the end of the year than at the beginning. Among the textile workers, on the other hand, we observe an overwhelming preponderance of economic strikes at the beginning of 1905, and it is only at the end of the year that we get a preponderance of political strikes. From this it follows quite obviously that the economic struggle, the struggle for immediate and direct improvement of conditions, is alone capable of rousing the most backward strata of the exploited masses, gives them a real education and transforms them—during a revolutionary period—into an army of political fighters within the space of a few months.

Of course, for this to happen, it was necessary for the vanguard of the workers not to regard the class struggle as a struggle in the interests of a thin upper stratum—a conception the reformists all too often try to instil—but for the proletariat to come forward as the real vanguard of the majority of the exploited and draw that majority into the struggle, as was the case in Russia in 1905, and as must be, and certainly will be, the case in the impending proletarian revolution in Europe.

The beginning of 1905 brought the first great wave of strikes that swept the entire country. As early as the spring of that year we see the rise of the first big, not only economic, but also political *peasant movement* in Russia. The importance of this historical turning-point will be appreciated if it is borne in mind that the Russian peasantry was liberated from the severest form of serfdom only in 1861, that the majority of the peasants are illiterate, that they live in indescribable poverty, oppressed by the landlords, deluded by the priests and isolated from each other by vast distances and an almost complete absence of roads.

Russia witnessed the first revolutionary movement against tsarism in 1825, a movement represented almost exclusively by noblemen. Thereafter and up to 1881, when Alexander II was assassinated by the terrorists, the movement was led by middle-class intellectuals. They displayed supreme self-sacrifice and astonished the whole world by the heroism of their terrorist methods of struggle. Their sacrifices were certainly not in vain. They doubtlessly contributed—directly or indirectly—to the subsequent revolutionary education of the Russian people. But they did not, and could not, achieve their immediate aim of generating a people's revolution.

That was achieved only by the revolutionary struggle of the proletariat. Only the waves of mass strikes that swept over the whole country, strikes connected with the severe lessons of the imperialist Russo-Japanese War, roused the broad masses of peasants from their lethargy. The word "striker" acquired an entirely new meaning among the peasants: it signified a rebel, a revolutionary, a term previously expressed by the word "student." But the "student" belonged to the middle class, to the "learned," to the "gentry," and was therefore alien to the people. The "striker," on the other hand, was of the people; he belonged to the exploited class. Deported from St. Petersburg, he often returned to the village where he told his fellow-villagers of the conflagration which was spreading to all the cities and would destroy both the capitalists and the nobility. A new type appeared in the Russian village—the class-conscious young peasant. He associated with "strikers," he read newspapers, he told the peasants about events in the cities, explained to his fellow-villagers the meaning of political demands, and urged them to fight the landowning nobility, the priests and the government officials.

The peasants would gather in groups to discuss their conditions, and gradually they were drawn into the struggle. Large crowds attacked the big estates, set fire to the manor-houses and appropriated supplies, seized grain and other foodstuffs, killed policemen and demanded transfer to the people of the huge estates.

In the spring of 1905, the peasant movement was only just beginning, involving only a minority, approximately one-seventh, of the districts.

But the combination of the proletarian mass strikes in the cities with the peasant movement in the rural areas was sufficient to shake the "firmest" and last prop of tsarism. I refer to the *army*.

There began a series of *mutinies* in the navy and the army. During the revolution, every fresh wave of strikes and of the peasant movement was accompanied by mutinies in all parts of Russia. The most well-known of these is the mutiny on the Black Sea cruiser *Prince Potemkin*, which was seized by the mutineers and took part in the revolution in Odessa. After the defeat of the revolution and unsuccessful attempts to seize other ports (Feodosia in the Crimea, for instance), it surrendered to the Rumanian authorities in Constantsa.

Permit me to relate in detail one small episode of the Black Sea mutiny in order to give you a concrete picture of events at the peak of the movement:

Gatherings of revolutionary workers and sailors were being organised more and more frequently. Since servicemen were not allowed to attend workers' meetings, large crowds of workers came to military meetings. They came in thousands. The idea of joint action found a lively response. Delegates were elected from the companies where political understanding among the men was higher.

The military authorities thereupon decided to take action. Some of the officers tried to deliver "patriotic" speeches at the meetings but failed dismally: the sailors, who were accustomed to debating, put their officers to shameful flight. In view of this, it was decided to prohibit meetings altogether. On the morning of November 24, 1905, a company of sailors, in full combat kit, was posted at the gates of the naval barracks. Rear-Admiral Pisarevksy gave the order in a loud voice: "No one is to leave the barracks! Shoot anyone who disobeys!" A sailor named Petrov, of the company that had been given that order, stepped forth from the ranks, loaded his rifle in the view of all, and with one shot killed Captain Stein of the Belostok Regiment, and with another wounded Rear-Admiral Pisarevsky. "Arrest him!" one of the officers shouted. No one budged. Petrov threw down his rifle, exclaiming: "Why don't you move? Take me!" He was arrested. The sailors, who rushed from every side, angrily demanded his release, declaring that they vouched for him. Excitement ran high.

"Petrov, the shot was an accident, wasn't it?" asked one of the officers, trying to find a way out of the situation.

"What do you mean, an accident? I stepped forward, loaded and took aim. Is that an accident?"

"They demand your release. . . ."

And Petrov was released. The sailors, however, were not content with that; all officers on duty were arrested, disarmed, and locked up at headquarters. . . . Sailor delegates, about forty in number, conferred the whole night. The decision was to release the officers, but not to permit them to enter the barracks again.

This small incident clearly shows you how events developed in most of the mutinies. The revolutionary ferment among the people could not but spread to the armed forces. It is indicative that the leaders of the movement came from *those elements* in the army and the navy who had been recruited mainly from among the industrial workers and of whom more technical training was required, for instance, the sappers. The broad masses, however, were still too naïve, their mood was too passive, too good-natured, too Christian. They flared up rather quickly; any instance of injustice, excessively harsh treatment by the officers, bad food, etc., could lead to revolt. But what they lacked was persistence, a clear perception of aim, a clear understanding that only the most vigorous continuation of the armed struggle, only a victory over all the military and civil authorities, only the overthrow of the government and the seizure of power throughout the country could guarantee the success of the revolution.

The broad masses of sailors and soldiers were easily roused to revolt. But with equal light-heartedness they foolishly released arrested officers. They allowed the officers to pacify them by promises and persuasion; in this way the officers gained precious time, brought in reinforcements, broke the strength of the rebels, and then followed the most brutal suppression of the movement and the execution of its leaders.

A comparison of these 1905 mutinies with the Decembrist uprising of 1825 is particularly interesting. In 1825 the leaders of the political movement were almost exclusively officers, and officers drawn from the nobility. They had become infected, through contact, with the democratic ideas of Europe during the Napoleonic wars. The mass of the soldiers, who at that time were still serfs, remained passive.

The history of 1905 presents a totally different picture. With few exceptions, the mood of the officers was either bourgeois-liberal, reformist, or frankly counter-revolutionary. The workers and peasants in military uniform were the soul of the mutinies. The movement spread to all sections of the people, and for the first time in Russia's history involved the majority of the exploited. But what it lacked was, on the one hand, persistence and determination among the masses—they were too much afflicted with the malady of trustfulness—and, on the other, organisation of revolutionary Social-Democratic workers in military uniform—they lacked the ability to take the leadership into their own hands, march at the head of the revolutionary army and launch an offensive against the government.

I might remark, incidentally, that these two shortcomings will—more slowly, perhaps, than we would like, but surely—be eliminated not only by the general development of capitalism, but also by the present war. . . .

At any rate, the history of the Russian revolution, like the history of the Paris Commune of 1871, teaches us the incontrovertible lesson that militarism can never and under no circumstances be defeated and destroyed, except by a victorious struggle of one section of the national army against the other section. It is not sufficient simply to denounce, revile and "repudiate" militarism, to criticise and prove that it is harmful; it is foolish peacefully to refuse to perform military service. The task is to keep the revolutionary consciousness of the proletariat tense and train its best elements, not only in a general way, but concretely, so that when popular ferment reaches the highest pitch, they will put themselves at the head of the revolutionary army.

The day-to-day experience of any capitalist country teaches us the same lesson. Every "minor" crisis that such a country experiences discloses to us in miniature the elements, the rudiments, of the battles that will inevitably take place on a large scale during a big crisis. What else, for instance, is a strike if not a minor crisis of capitalist society? Was not the Prussian Minister for Internal Affairs, Herr von Puttkammer, right when he coined the famous phrase: "In every strike there lurks the hydra of revolution"? Does not the calling out of troops during strikes in all, even the most peaceful, the most "democratic"—save the mark—capitalist countries show *how* things will turn out in a really *big* crisis?

But to return to the history of the Russian revolution.

I have tried to show you how the workers' strikes stirred up the whole country and the broadest, most backward strata of the exploited, how the peasant movement began, and how it was accompanied by mutiny in the armed forces.

The movement reached its zenith in the autumn of 1905. On August 19 (6), the tsar issued a manifesto on the introduction of popular representation. The so-called Bulygin Duma was to be created on the basis of a suffrage embracing a ridiculously small number of voters, and this peculiar "parliament" was to have no legislative powers whatever, only *advisory*, consultative powers!

The bourgeoisie, the liberals, the opportunists were ready to grasp with both hands this "gift" of the frightened tsar. Like all reformists, our reformists of 1905 could not understand that historic situations arise when reforms, and particularly promises of reforms, pursue only one aim: to allay the unrest of the people, force the revolutionary class to cease, or at least slacken, its struggle.

The Russian revolutionary Social-Democracy was well aware of the real nature of this grant of an illusory constitution in August 1905. That is why, without a moment's hesitation, it issued the slogans: "Down with the advisory Duma! Boycott the Duma! Down with the tsarist government! Continue the revolutionary struggle to overthrow it! Not the tsar, but a provisional revolutionary government must convene Russia's first real, popular representative assembly!"

History proved that the revolutionary Social-Democrats were right, for the *Bulygin Duma* was never convened. It was swept away by the revolutionary storm before it could be convened. And this storm forced the tsar to promulgate a new electoral law, which provided for a considerable increase in the number of voters, and to recognise the legislative character of the Duma.

October and December 1905 marked the highest point in the rising tide of the Russian revolution. All the wellsprings of the people's revolutionary strength flowed in a wider stream than ever before. The number of strikers—which in January 1905, as I have already told you, was 440,000—reached over half a million in October 1905 (in a single month!). To this number, which applies *only* to factory workers, must be added several hundred thousand railway workers, postal and telegraph employees, etc.

The general railway strike stopped all rail traffic and paralysed the power of the government in the most effective manner. The doors of the universities were flung wide open, and the lecture halls, which in peacetime were used solely to befuddle youthful minds with pedantic professorial wisdom and to turn the students into docile servants of the bourgeoisie and tsarism, now became the scene of public meetings at which thousands of workers, artisans and office workers openly and freely discussed political issues.

Freedom of the press was won. The censorship was simply ignored. No publisher dared send the obligatory censor-copy to the authorities, and the authorities did not dare take any measure against this. For the first time in Russian history, revolutionary newspapers appeared freely in St. Petersburg and other towns. In St. Petersburg alone, three Social-Democratic daily papers were published, with circulations ranging from 50,000 to 100,000.

The proletariat marched at the head of the movement. It set out to win the eight-hour day by revolutionary action. *"An Eight-Hour Day and Arms!"* was the fighting slogan of the St. Petersburg proletariat. That the fate of the revolution could, and would, be decided only by armed struggle was becoming obvious to an ever-increasing mass of workers.

In the fire of battle, a peculiar mass organisation was formed, the famous *Soviets of Workers' Deputies*, comprising delegates from all factories. In several cities these *Soviets of Workers' Deputies* began more and more to play the part of a provisional revolutionary government, the part of organs and leaders of the uprising. Attempts were made to organise Soviets of Soldiers' and Sailors' Deputies and to combine them with the Soviets of Workers' Deputies.

For a time several cities in Russia became something in the nature of small local "republics." The government authorities were deposed and the Soviet of Workers' Deputies actually functioned as the new government. Unfortunately, these periods were all too brief, the "victories" were too weak, too isolated.

The peasant movement in the autumn of 1905 reached still greater dimensions. *Over one-third* of all the *uyezds*[1] were affected by the so-called "peasant disorders" and regular peasant uprisings. The peasants burned down no less than two thousand estates and distributed among themselves the food stocks of which the predatory nobility had robbed the people.

Unfortunately, this work was not thorough enough! Unfortunately, the peasants destroyed only one-fifteenth of the total number of landed estates, only one-fifteenth part of what they *should have* destroyed in order to wipe the shame of large feudal land-

---

1. Counties. [*R. T.*]

ownership from the face of the Russian earth. Unfortunately, the peasants were too scattered, too isolated from each other in their actions; they were not organised enough, not aggressive enough, and therein lies one of the fundamental reasons for the defeat of the revolution.

A movement for national liberation flared up among the oppressed peoples of Russia. *Over one-half, almost three-fifths* (*to be exact, 57 per cent*) of the population of Russia is subject to national oppression; they are not even free to use their native language, they are forcibly Russified. The Moslems, for instance, who number tens of millions, were quick to organise a Moslem League —this was a time of rapid growth of all manner of organisations.

The following instance will give the audience, particularly the youth, an example of how at that time the movement for national liberation in Russia rose in conjunction with the labour movement.

In December 1905, Polish children in hundreds of schools burned all Russian books, pictures and portraits of the tsar, and attacked and drove out the Russian teachers and their Russian schoolfellows, shouting: "Get out! Go back to Russia!" The Polish secondary school pupils put forward, among others, the following demands: (1) all secondary schools must be under the control of a Soviet of Workers' Deputies; (2) joint pupils' and workers' meetings to be held in school premises; (3) secondary school pupils to be allowed to wear red blouses as a token of adherence to the future proletarian republic.

The higher the tide of the movement rose, the more vigorously and decisively did the reaction arm itself to fight the revolution. The Russian Revolution of 1905 confirmed the truth of what Karl Kautsky wrote in 1902 in his book *Social Revolution* (he was still, incidentally, a revolutionary Marxist and not, as at present, a champion of social-patriotism and opportunism). This is what he wrote: ". . . The impending revolution . . . will be less like a spontaneous uprising against the government and more like a protracted *civil war*."

That is how it was, and undoubtedly that is how it will be in the coming European revolution!

Tsarism vented its hatred particularly upon the Jews. On the one hand, the Jews furnished a particularly high percentage (compared with the total Jewish population) of leaders of the revolutionary movement. And now, too, it should be noted to the credit of the Jews, they furnish a relatively high percentage of internationalists, compared with other nations. On the other hand, tsarism adroitly exploited the basest anti-Jewish prejudices of the most ignorant strata of the population in order to organise, if not to lead directly, *pogroms*—over 4,000 were killed and more than 10,000 mutilated in 100 towns. These atrocious massacres of peaceful Jews, their wives and children roused disgust throughout the civilised world. I have in mind, of course, the disgust of the truly democratic elements of the civilised world, and these are *exclusively* the socialist workers, the proletarians.

Even in the freest, even in the republican countries of Western Europe, the bourgeoisie manages very well to combine its hypocritical phrases about "Russian atrocities" with the most shameless financial transactions, particularly with financial support of tsarism and imperialist exploitation of Russia through export of capital, etc.

The climax of the 1905 Revolution came in the December uprising in Moscow. For nine days a small number of rebels, of organised and armed workers—there were not more than *eight thousand*—fought against the tsar's government, which dared not trust the Moscow garrison. In fact, it had to keep it locked up, and was able to quell the rebellion only by bringing in the Semenovsky Regiment from St. Petersburg.

The bourgeoisie likes to describe the Moscow uprising as something artificial, and to treat it with ridicule. For instance, in German so-called "scientific" literature, Herr Professor Max Weber, in his lengthy survey of Russia's political development, refers to the Moscow uprising as a "putsch." "The Lenin group," says this "highly learned" Herr Professor, "and a section of the Socialist-Revolutionaries had long prepared for this *senseless* uprising."

To properly assess this piece of professional wisdom of the cowardly bourgeoisie, one need only recall the strike statistics. In January 1905, only 123,000 were involved in purely political strikes, in October the figure was 330,000, and *in December the maximum was reached*—370,000 taking part in purely political strikes in a single month! Let us recall, too, the progress of the revolution, the peasant and soldier uprisings, and we shall see that the bourgeois "scientific" view of the December uprising is not only absurd. It is a subterfuge resorted to by the representatives of the cowardly bourgeoisie, which sees in the proletariat its most dangerous class enemy.

In reality, the inexorable trend of the Russian revolution was towards an armed, decisive battle between the tsarist government and the vanguard of the class-conscious proletariat.

I have already pointed out, in my previous remarks, wherein lay the weakness of the Russian revolution that led to its temporary defeat.

The suppression of the December uprising marked the beginning of the ebb of the revolution. But in this period, too, extremely interesting moments are to be observed. Suffice it to recall that twice the foremost militant elements of the working class tried to check the retreat of the revolution and to prepare a new offensive.

But my time has nearly expired, and I do not want to abuse the patience of my audience. I think, however, that I have outlined the most important aspects of the revolution—its class character, its driving forces and its methods of struggle—as fully as so big a subject can be dealt with in a brief lecture.

A few brief remarks concerning the world significance of the Russian revolution.

Geographically, economically and historically, Russia belongs not only to Europe, but also to Asia. That is why the Russian revolution succeeded not only in finally awakening Europe's biggest and most backward country and in creating a revolutionary people led by a revolutionary proletariat.

It achieved more than that. The Russian revolution engendered a movement throughout the whole of Asia. The revolutions in Turkey, Persia and China prove that the mighty uprising of 1905 left a deep imprint, and that its influence, expressed in the forward movement of *hundreds and hundreds* of millions, is ineradicable.

In an indirect way, the Russian revolution influenced also the countries of the West. One must not forget that news of the tsar's constitutional manifesto, on reaching Vienna on October 30, 1905, played a decisive part in the final victory of universal suffrage in Austria.

A telegram bearing the news was placed on the speaker's rostrum at the Congress of the Austrian Social-Democratic Party just as Comrade Ellenbogen—at that time he was not yet a social-patriot, but a comrade—was delivering his report on the political strike. The discussion was immediately adjourned. "Our place is in the streets!"—was the cry that resounded through the hall where the delegates of the Austrian Social-Democracy were assembled. And the following days witnessed the biggest street demonstrations in Vienna and barricades in Prague. The battle for universal suffrage in Austria was won.

We very often meet West-Europeans who talk of the Russian revolution as if events, the course and methods of struggle in that backward country have very little resemblance to West-European patterns, and, therefore, can hardly have any practical significance.

Nothing could be more erroneous.

The forms and occasions for the impending battles in the coming European revolution will doubtlessly differ in many respects from the forms of the Russian revolution.

Nevertheless, the Russian revolution—precisely because of its proletarian character, in that particular sense of which I have spoken—is the *prologue* to the coming European revolution. Undoubtedly, this coming revolution can only be a proletarian revolution, and in an even more profound sense of the word: a proletarian, socialist revolution also in its content. This coming revolution will show to an even greater degree, on the one hand, that only stern battles, only civil wars, can free humanity from the yoke of capital, and, on the other hand, that only class-conscious proletarians can and will give leadership to the vast majority of the exploited.

We must not be deceived by the present grave-like stillness in Europe. Europe is pregnant with revolution. The monstrous horror of the imperialist war, the suffering caused by the high cost of living everywhere engender a revolutionary mood; and the ruling classes, the bourgeoisie, and its servitors, the governments, are more and more moving into a blind alley from which they can never extricate themselves without tremendous upheavals.

Just as in Russia in 1905, a popular uprising against the tsarist government began under the leadership of the proletariat with the aim of achieving a democratic republic, so, in Europe, the coming years, precisely because of this predatory war, will lead to popular uprisings under the leadership of the proletariat against the power of finance capital, against the big banks, against the capitalists; and these upheavals cannot end otherwise than with the expropriation of the bourgeoisie, with the victory of socialism.

We of the older generation may not live to see the decisive battles of this coming revolution. But I can, I believe, express the confident hope that the youth which is working so splendidly in the socialist movement of Switzerland, and of the whole world, will be fortunate enough not only to fight, but also to win, in the coming proletarian revolution.

PART III

The Revolutionary Taking of Power

The Tasks of the Proletariat in the Present Revolution ("April Theses")

Lenin arrived in Petrograd on the night of April 3 (old style), a little over a month after the February Revolution, which deposed the tsar and set up a Provisional Government accountable to the State Duma. The next day he presented before two party meetings a set of theses on the situation, and these were published in *Pravda* on April 7 in the article that appears here in full. Those who had preceded him to Petrograd and were in charge of party policy during March, Kamenev and Stalin in particular, had followed a line of conditional support for the Provisional Government combined with pressure on it to end Russia's participation in the war. This was predicated on the assumption that a substantial interval would have to separate the bourgeois political revolution embodied in the Provisional Government and a future socialist revolution. In September 1914 (in "The War and Social-Democracy") Lenin himself had said that while socialist revolution was on the agenda of all the advanced countries, "since Russia is most backward and has not yet completed its bourgeois revolution, it still remains the task of Social Democrats in that country to achieve the three fundamental conditions for consistent democratic reform, viz., a democratic republic . . . , confiscation of the landed estates, and an eight-hour working day." But now, to the initial dismay of many of his party comrades, he proclaimed the imminence of the second, proletarian stage of the Russian Revolution, a policy of no support for the Provisional Government, and the aim of creating a "commune state" modeled on the Paris Commune of 1871 and based on the revolutionary councils (soviets) which were springing up spontaneously in Russia in early 1917. His position was soon adopted as Bolshevik party policy.

I did not arrive in Petrograd until the night of April 3, and therefore at the meeting on April 4 I could, of course, deliver the report on the tasks of the revolutionary proletariat only on my own behalf, and with reservations as to insufficient preparation.

The only thing I could do to make things easier for myself—and for *honest* opponents—was to prepare the theses *in writing*. I read them out, and gave the text to Comrade Tsereteli. I read them *twice* very slowly: first at a meeting of Bolsheviks and then at a meeting of both Bolsheviks and Mensheviks.

I publish these personal theses of mine with only the briefest explanatory notes, which were developed in far greater detail in the report.

Theses

1) In our attitude towards the war, which under the new government of Lvov and Co. unquestionably remains on Russia's part a predatory imperialist war owing to the capitalist nature of that government, not the slightest concession to "revolutionary defencism" is permissible.

The class-conscious proletariat can give its consent to a revolutionary war, which would really justify revolutionary defencism, only on condition: (a) that the power pass to the proletariat and the poorest sections of the peasants aligned with the proletariat; (b) that all annexations be renounced in deed and not in word; (c) that a complete break be effected in actual fact with all capitalist interests.

In view of the undoubted honesty of those broad sections of the mass believers in revolutionary defencism who accept the war only as a necessity, and not as a means of conquest, in view of the fact that they are being deceived by the bourgeoisie, it is necessary with particular thoroughness, persistence and patience to explain their error to them, to explain the inseparable connection existing between capital and the imperialist war, and to prove that without overthrowing capital *it is impossible* to end the war by a truly democratic peace, a peace not imposed by violence.

The most widespread campaign for this view must be organised in the army at the front.

Fraternisation.

2) The specific feature of the present situation in Russia is that the country is *passing* from the first stage of the revolution—which, owing to the insufficient class-consciousness and organisation of the proletariat, placed power in the hands of the bourgeoisie—to its *second* stage, which must place power in the hands of the proletariat and the poorest sections of the peasants.

This transition is characterised, on the one hand, by a maximum of legally recognised rights (Russia is *now* the freest of all the belligerent countries in the world); on the other, by the absence of violence towards the masses, and, finally, by their unreasoning trust in the government of capitalists, those worst enemies of peace and socialism.

This peculiar situation demands of us an ability to adapt ourselves to the *special* conditions of Party work among unprecedentedly large masses of proletarians who have just awakened to political life.

3) No support for the Provisional Government; the utter falsity of all its promises should be made clear, particularly of those relating to the renunciation of annexations. Exposure in place of the impermissible, illusion-breeding "demand" that *this* government, a government of capitalists, should *cease* to be an imperialist government.

4) Recognition of the fact that in most of the Soviets of Workers' Deputies our Party is in a minority, so far a small minority, as against *a bloc of all* the petty-bourgeois opportunist elements, from the Popular Socialists and the Socialist-Revolutionaries[1] down to the Organising Committee (Chkheidze, Tsereteli, etc.), Steklov, etc., etc., who have yielded to the influence of the bourgeoisie and spread that influence among the proletariat.

The masses must be made to see that the Soviets of Workers' Deputies are the *only possible* form of revolutionary government, and that therefore our task is, as long as *this* government yields to the influence of the bourgeoisie, to present a patient, systematic, and persistent *explanation* of the errors of their tactics, an explanation especially adapted to the practical needs of the masses.

As long as we are in the minority we carry on the work of criticising and exposing errors and at the same time we preach the necessity of transferring the entire state power to the Soviets of Workers' Deputies, so that the people may overcome their mistakes by experience.

5) Not a parliamentary republic—to return to a parliamentary republic from the Soviets of Workers' Deputies would be a retrograde step—but a Republic of Soviets of Workers', Agricultural Labourers' and Peasants' Deputies throughout the country, from top to bottom.

Abolition of the police, the army and the bureaucracy.[2]

The salaries of all officials, all of whom are elective and displaceable at any time, not to exceed the average wage of a competent worker.

1. The Popular Socialists split off from the Right Socialist-Revolutionaries in 1906; their demands were moderately democratic and did not go beyond a constitutional monarchy. The Popular Socialists rejected the Socialist-Revolutionaries' programme for the socialisation of the land and recognised the payment of compensation for socialised lands. After the February Revolution the Popular Socialists gave the Provisional Government their active support.

The Socialist Revolutionaries, (S.R.s) emerged in late 1901–early 1902 when a number of Narodnik groups and circles joined forces (the Union of Socialist-Revolutionaries, the Party of Socialist-Revolutionaries and others). Their official publications were the newspaper *Revoliutsionnaya Rossiya* (*Revolutionary Russia*) (1900–1905) and the journal *Herald of the Russian Revolution* (1901–1905).

2. I.e., the standing army to be replaced by the arming of the whole people. [*Lenin*]

6) The weight of emphasis in the agrarian programme to be shifted to the Soviets of Agricultural Labourers' Deputies.

Confiscation of all landed estates.

Nationalisation of *all* lands in the country, the land to be disposed of by the local Soviets of Agricultural Labourers' and Peasants' Deputies. The organisation of separate Soviets of Deputies of Poor Peasants. The setting up of a model farm on each of the large estates (ranging in size from 100 to 300 dessiatines, according to local and other conditions, and to the decisions of the local bodies) under the control of the Soviets of Agricultural Labourers' Deputies and for the public account.

7) The immediate amalgamation of all banks in the country into a single national bank, and the institution of control over it by the Soviets of Workers' Deputies.

8) It is not our *immediate* task to "introduce" socialism, but only to bring social production and the distribution of products at once under the *control* of the Soviets of Workers' Deputies.

9) Party tasks:

(a) Immediate convocation of a Party congress;

(b) Alteration of the Party Programme, mainly:

(1) On the question of imperialism and the imperialist war;

(2) On our attitude towards the state and *our* demand for a "commune state";[3]

(3) Amendment of our out-of-date minimum programme.

(c) Change of the Party's name.[4]

10) A new International.

We must take the initiative in creating a revolutionary International, an International against the *social-chauvinists* and against the "Centre."[5]

In order that the reader may understand why I had especially to emphasise as a rare exception the "case" of honest opponents, I invite him to compare the above theses with the following objection by Mr. Goldenberg: Lenin, he said, "has planted the banner of civil war in the midst of revolutionary democracy" (quoted in No. 5 of Mr. Plekhanov's *Yedinstvo*[6]).

---

3. I.e., a state of which the Paris Commune was the prototype. [*Lenin*]

4. Instead of "Social-Democracy," whose official leaders *throughout* the world have betrayed socialism and deserted to the bourgeoisie (the "defencists" and the vacillating "Kautskyites"), we must call ourselves the *Communist Party*. [*Lenin*]

5. The "Centre" in the international Social-Democratic movement is the trend which vacillates between the chauvinists (="defencists") and internationalists, i.e., Kautsky and Co. in Germany, Longuet and Co. in France, Chkheidze and Co. in Russia, Turati and Co. in Italy, MacDonald and Co. in Britain, etc. [*Lenin*]

6. *Yedinstvo* (*Unity*) was a daily newspaper published in Petrograd from March to November 1917 and again, under the name of *Nashe Yedinstvo* (*Our Unity*), from December 1917 to January 1918. Its editor from issue No. 5 of April 5 (18) was G. V. Plekhanov.

Isn't it a gem?

I write, announce and elaborately explain: "In view of the undoubted honesty of those *broad* sections of the *mass* believers in revolutionary defencism . . . in view of the fact that they are being deceived by the bourgeoisie, it is necessary with *particular* thoroughness, persistence and *patience* to explain their error to them. . . ."

Yet the bourgeois gentlemen who call themselves Social-Democrats, who *do not* belong either to the *broad* sections or to the *mass* believers in defencism, with serene brow present my views thus: "The banner [!] of civil war" (of which there is not a word in the theses and not a word in my speech!) has been planted (!) "in the midst [!!] of revolutionary democracy. . . ."

What does this mean? In what way does this differ from riot-inciting agitation, from *Russkaya Volya*?[7]

I write, announce and elaborately explain: "The Soviets of Workers' Deputies are the *only possible* form of revolutionary government, and therefore our task is to present a patient, systematic, and persistent *explanation* of the errors of their tactics, an explanation especially adapted to the practical needs of the masses."

Yet opponents of a certain brand present my views as a call to "civil war in the midst of revolutionary democracy"!

I attacked the Provisional Government for *not* having appointed an early date, or any date at all, for the convocation of the Constituent Assembly, and for confining itself to promises. I argued that *without* the Soviets of Workers' and Soldiers' Deputies the convocation of the Constituent Assembly is not guaranteed and its success is impossible.

And the view is attributed to me that I am opposed to the speedy convocation of the Constituent Assembly!

I would call this "raving," had not decades of political struggle taught me to regard honesty in opponents as a rare exception.

Mr. Plekhanov in his paper called my speech "raving." Very good, Mr. Plekhanov! But look how awkward, uncouth, and slowwitted you are in your polemics. If I delivered a raving speech for two hours, how is it that an audience of hundreds tolerated this "raving"? Further, why does your paper devote a whole column to an account of the "raving"? Inconsistent, highly inconsistent!

It is, of course, much easier to shout, abuse, and howl than to attempt to relate, to explain, to recall *what* Marx and Engels said in

7. *Russkaya Volya* (*Russian Will*), was a daily paper published in Petrograd from December 1916. Following the February Revolution it actively supported the domestic and foreign policy of the Provisional Government and agitated for the destruction of the Bolshevik Party. Lenin called it one of the rottenest bourgeois newspapers. The Revolutionary Military Committee of the Petrograd Soviet suppressed it on October 25 (November 7), 1917.

1871, 1872 and 1875 about the experience of the Paris Commune and about the *kind* of state the proletariat needs.

Ex-Marxist Mr. Plekhanov evidently does not care to recall Marxism.

I quoted the words of Rosa Luxemburg, who on August 4, 1914,[8] called *German* Social-Democracy a "stinking corpse." And the Plekhanovs, Goldenbergs and Co. feel "offended." On whose behalf? On behalf of the *German* chauvinists, because they were called chauvinists!

They have got themselves in a mess, these poor Russian social-chauvinists—socialists in word and chauvinists in deed.

8. On that date, the Social-Democratic group in the German Reichstag voted in favour of granting war credits to the government of Kaiser Wilhelm II.

The Dual Power

This brief article, published in *Pravda* on April 9, 1917, continues the argument of the "April Theses" and illuminates Lenin's underlying assumption that an early, more radical Russian revolution was possible because a "second *government*" already existed in the form of the Soviets of Workers' and Soldiers' Deputies. As he defined Russia's revolutionary situation, there already existed two alternative and antagonistic systems of political authority—an official government and an unofficial one. Here, then, was the foundation of the Bolshevik slogan, "All Power to the Soviets."

The basic question of every revolution is that of state power. Unless this question is understood, there can be no intelligent participation in the revolution, not to speak of guidance of the revolution.

The highly remarkable feature of our revolution is that it has brought about a *dual power*. This fact must be grasped first and foremost: unless it is understood, we cannot advance. We must know how to supplement and amend old "formulas," for example, those of Bolshevism, for while they have been found to be correct on the whole, their concrete realisation *has turned out to be* different. *Nobody* previously thought, or could have thought, of a dual power.

What is this dual power? Alongside the Provisional Government, the government of the *bourgeoisie, another government* has arisen, so far weak and incipient, but undoubtedly a government that actually exists and is growing—the Soviets of Workers' and Soldiers' Deputies.

What is the class composition of this other government? It consists of the proletariat and the peasants (in soldiers' uniforms). What is the political nature of this government? It is a revolutionary dictatorship, i.e., a power directly based on revolutionary seizure, on the direct initiative of the people from below, and *not on a law* enacted by a centralised state power. It is an entirely different kind of power from the one that generally exists in the parliamentary bourgeois-democratic republics of the usual type still prevailing in the advanced countries of Europe and America. This circumstance is often overlooked, often not given enough thought, yet it is the crux of the matter. *This* power is of *the same type* as the Paris Commune of 1871. The fundamental characteristics of this type are: (1) the source of power is not a law previously discussed and enacted by parliament, but the direct initiative of the people from below, in their local areas—direct "seizure," to use a current expression; (2) the replacement of the police and the army, which are institutions divorced from the people and set against the people, by the direct arming of the whole people; order in the state under such a power is maintained by the armed workers and peasants *themselves*, by the armed people *themselves*; (3) officialdom, the bureaucracy, is either similarly replaced by the direct rule of the people themselves or at least placed under special control; they not only become elected officials, but are also *subject to recall* at the people's first demand; they are reduced to the position of simple agents; from a privileged group holding "jobs" remunerated on a high, bourgeois scale, they become workers of a special "arm of the service," whose remuneration *does not exceed* the ordinary pay of a competent worker.

This, and this *alone*, constitutes the *essence* of the Paris Commune as a special type of state. This essence has been forgotten or perverted by the Plekhanovs (downright chauvinists who have betrayed Marxism), the Kautskys (the men of the "Centre," i.e., those who vacillate between chauvinism and Marxism), and generally by all those Social-Democrats, Socialist-Revolutionaries, etc., etc., who now rule the roost.

They are trying to get away with empty phrases, evasions, subterfuges; they congratulate each other a thousand times upon the revolution, but refuse to *consider what* the Soviets of Workers' and Soldiers' Deputies *are*. They refuse to recognise the obvious truth that inasmuch as these Soviets exist, *inasmuch as* they are a power, we have in Russia a state of the *type* of the Paris Commune.

I have emphasised the words "inasmuch as," for it is only an incipient power. By direct agreement with the bourgeois Provisional Government and by a series of actual concessions, it has itself *surrendered and is surrendering* its positions to the bourgeoisie.

Why? Is it because Chkheidze, Tsereteli, Steklov and Co. are making a "mistake"? Nonsense. Only a philistine can think so—not a Marxist. The reason is *insufficient class-consciousness* and organisation of the proletarians and peasants. The "mistake" of the leaders I have named lies in their petty-bourgeois position, in the fact that instead of clarifying the minds of the workers, they are *befog-*

ging them; instead of dispelling petty-bourgeois illusions, they are *instilling* them; instead of freeing the people from bourgeois influence, they are *strengthening* that influence.

It should be clear from this why our comrades, too, make so many mistakes when putting the question "simply": Should the Provisional Government be overthrown immediately?

My answer is: (1) it should be overthrown, for it is an oligarchic, bourgeois, and not a people's government, and *is unable* to provide peace, bread, or full freedom; (2) it cannot be overthrown just now, for it is being kept in power by a direct and indirect, a formal and actual *agreement* with the Soviets of Workers' Deputies, and primarily with the chief Soviet, the Petrograd Soviet; (3) generally, it cannot be "overthrown" in the ordinary way, for it rests on the "*support*" given to the bourgeoisie by the *second* government—the Soviet of Workers' Deputies, and that government is the only possible revolutionary government, which directly expresses the mind and will of the majority of the workers and peasants. Humanity has not yet evolved and we do not as yet know a type of government superior to and better than the Soviets of Workers', Agricultural Labourers', Peasants', and Soldiers' Deputies.

To become a power the class-conscious workers must win the majority to their side. *As long as* no violence is used against the people there is no other road to power. We are not Blanquists,[1] we do not stand for the seizure of power by a minority. We are Marxists, we stand for proletarian class struggle against petty-bourgeois intoxication, against chauvinism-defencism, phrasemongering and dependence on the bourgeoisie.

Let us create a proletarian Communist Party; its elements have already been created by the best adherents of Bolshevism; let us rally our ranks for proletarian class work; and larger and larger numbers from among the proletarians, from among the *poorest* peasants will range themselves on our side. For *actual experience* will from day to day shatter the petty-bourgeois illusions of those "Social-Democrats," the Chkheidzes, Tseretelis, Steklovs and others, the "Socialist-Revolutionaries," the petty bourgeois of an even purer water, and so on and so forth.

The bourgeoisie stands for the undivided power of the bourgeoisie

The class-conscious workers stand for the undivided power of the Soviets of Workers', Agricultural Labourers', Peasants', and Soldiers' Deputies—for undivided power made possible not by adven-

---

1. Louis-Auguste Blanqui (1805–81) was a prominent French revolutionary who advocated the seizure of power by a small, disciplined group operating conspiratorially. [*R. T.*]

turist acts, but by *clarifying* proletarian minds, by *emancipating* them from the influence of the bourgeoisie.

The petty bourgeoisie—"Social-Democrats," Socialist-Revolutionaries, etc., etc.—vacillate and, thereby, *hinder* this clarification and emancipation.

This is the actual, the *class* alignment of forces that determines our tasks.

Enemies of the People

Written and published in *Pravda* in June 1917, this article well conveys Lenin's sense of Bolshevism as the Jacobinism of twentieth-century Russia. In an article for *Pravda* about two weeks later ("Can 'Jacobinism' Frighten the Working Class?"), he wrote: "'Jacobinism' in Europe or on the boundary line between Europe and Asia in the twentieth century would be the rule of the revolutionary class, of the proletariat, which, supported by the peasant poor and taking advantage of the existing material basis for advancing to socialism, could not only provide all the great, ineradicable, unforgettable things provided by the Jacobins in the eighteenth century, but bring about a lasting world-wide victory for the working people."

The phrase "enemies of the people," which Lenin found applicable in revolutionary Russia against class enemies, was destined to be applied to party enemies en masse by Stalin in the nineteen-thirties.

Plekhanov's *Yedinstvo* (which even the Socialist-Revolutionary *Dyelo Naroda* justly calls a newspaper at one with the liberal bourgeoisie) has recently recalled the law of the French Republic of 1793 relating to enemies of the people.

A very timely recollection.

The Jacobins of 1793 belonged to the most revolutionary class of the eighteenth century, the town and country poor. It was against this class, which had in fact (and not just in words) done away with its monarch, its landowners and its moderate bourgeoisie by the most revolutionary measures, including the guillotine—against this truly revolutionary class of the eighteenth century—that the monarchs of Europe combined to wage war.

The Jacobins proclaimed enemies of the people those "promoting the schemes of the allied tyrants directed against the Republic."

The Jacobins' example is instructive. It has not become obsolete to this day, except that it must be applied to the revolutionary class of the twentieth century, to the workers and semi-proletarians. To this class, the enemies of the people in the twentieth century are not the monarchs, but the landowners and capitalists as a class.

If the "Jacobins" of the twentieth century, the workers and semi-proletarians, assumed power, they would proclaim enemies of the people the capitalists who are making thousands of millions in profits from the imperialist war, *that is*, a war for the division of capitalist spoils and profits.

The "Jacobins" of the twentieth century would not guillotine the capitalists—to follow a good example does not mean copying it. It would be enough to arrest fifty to a hundred financial magnates and bigwigs, the chief knights of embezzlement and of robbery by the banks. It would be enough to arrest them for a few weeks *to expose their frauds* and show all exploited people "who needs the war." Upon exposing the frauds of the banking barons, we could release them, placing the banks, the capitalist syndicates, and all the contractors "working" for the government under workers' control.

The Jacobins of 1793 have gone down in history for their great example of a truly revolutionary struggle against *the class of the exploiters by the class of the working people and the oppressed* who had taken *all* state power into their own hands.

The miserable *Yedinstvo* (with which the Menshevik defencists were ashamed to form a bloc) wants to borrow Jacobinism in letter and not in spirit, its exterior trappings and not the content of its policy. This amounts in effect to a betrayal of the revolution of the twentieth century, a betrayal disguised by spurious reference to the revolutionaries of the eighteenth century.

The Beginning of Bonapartism

Lenin wrote this article at the end of July 1917 while in hiding. It reflects his belief that the choice for Russia was not between liberal democracy and a Bolshevik regime of "proletarian dictatorship," but between the latter and a regime of disguised military dictatorship—"Bonapartism." In later years of exile, e.g., in his book of 1937, *The Revolution Betrayed*, Trotsky would characterize Stalin's regime as "Bonapartism" in a Soviet form.

Now that the Cabinet of Kerensky, Nekrasov, Avksentyev and Co.[1] has been formed, the gravest and most disastrous error Marxists could make would be to mistake words for deeds, deceptive appearances for reality or generally for something serious.

Let's leave this pastime to the Mensheviks and Socialist-Revolutionaries who have already gone as far as to play the part of clowns around the Bonapartist Kerensky. * * *

* * *

Just as the Cadets in 1906 prostituted the first assembly of popular representatives in Russia by reducing it to a miserable talking shop in face of the growing tsarist counter-revolution, so the S.R.s and Mensheviks in 1917 have prostituted the Soviets by reducing them to a miserable talking-shop in face of the growing Bonapartist counter-revolution.

Kerensky's Cabinet is undoubtedly a cabinet taking the first steps towards Bonapartism.

We see the chief historical symptom of Bonapartism: the manoeuvring of a state power dependent on the military (on the worst

---

1. Lenin means the coalition Provisional Government formed on July 24 (August 6), 1917. It included A. F. Kerensky, premier and war and naval minister (S. R.), N. V. Nekrasov, deputy premier and minister of finance (Cadet), and N. D. Avksentyev, minister of the interior (S. R.). The cabinet was composed of Cadets, Socialist-Revolutionaries, Mensheviks, Popular Socialists, and non-party people who were close to the Cadets.

elements of the army) for support, between two hostile classes and forces which more or less balance each other out.

The class struggle between the bourgeoisie and the proletariat has reached the limit and on April 20 and 21, as well as on July 3–5, the country was within a hair's breadth of civil war. This socio-economic condition certainly forms the classical basis for Bonapartism. And then, this condition is combined with others that are quite akin to it; the bourgeoisie are ranting and raving against the Soviets, but are *as yet* powerless to disperse them, while the Soviets, prostituted by Tsereteli, Chernov and Co., are *now* powerless to put up serious resistance to the bourgeoisie.

The landowners and peasants, too, live as on the eve of civil war: the peasants demand land and freedom, they can be kept in check, if at all, only by a Bonapartist government capable of making the most unscrupulous promises to all classes without keeping any of them.

Add to this the situation created by a foolhardy offensive and military reverses, in which fancy phrases about saving the country are particularly fashionable (concealing the desire to save the imperialist programme of the bourgeoisie), and you have a perfect picture of the socio-political setting for Bonapartism.

Don't let us be deluded by phrases. Don't let us be misled by the idea that all we have is the first steps of Bonapartism. It is the first steps we must be able to discern unless we want to find ourselves in the ridiculous predicament of the stupid philistine who laments the second step although he himself helped to take the first.

It would now be nothing short of stupid philistinism to entertain constitutional illusions, such as, for instance, that the present Cabinet is probably more Left than all the preceding ones (see *Izvestia*), that well-meaning criticism by the Soviets could rectify the errors of the government, that the arbitrary arrests and suppression of newspapers were isolated incidents which, it is to be hoped, will never recur, or that Zarudny is an honest man and that in republican and democratic Russia a fair trial is possible and everyone should appear at it, and so on, and so forth.

The stupidity of these constitutional philistine illusions is too obvious to require special refutation.

The struggle against the bourgeois counter-revolution demands soberness and the ability to see and speak of things as they are.

Bonapartism in Russia is no accident but a natural product of the evolution of the class struggle in a petty-bourgeois country with a considerably developed capitalism and a revolutionary proletariat. Historical stages like April 20 and 21, May 6, June 9 and 10, June 18 and 19, and July 3–5 are landmarks which show clearly how preparations for Bonapartism proceeded. It would be a very big mistake to think that a democratic situation rules out Bonapartism. On the contrary, it is exactly in a situation like this (the history of France has confirmed it twice) that Bonapartism emerges, given a certain relationship between classes and their struggle.

However, to recognise the inevitability of Bonapartism does not at all mean forgetting the inevitability of its downfall.

If we *only* said the counter-revolution had temporarily gained the upper hand here in Russia we should be dodging the issue.

If we analysed the origin of Bonapartism and, fearlessly facing the truth, told the working class and the whole people that the beginning of Bonapartism is a fact, we should thereby start a real and stubborn struggle to overthrow Bonapartism, a struggle waged on a large political scale and based on far-reaching class interests.

The Russian Bonapartism of 1917 differs from the beginnings of French Bonapartism in 1799 and 1849 in several respects, such as the fact that not a single important task of the revolution has been accomplished here. The struggle to settle the agrarian and the national questions is only just gathering momentum.

Kerensky and the counter-revolutionary Cadets who use him as a pawn can neither convoke the Constituent Assembly on the appointed date, nor postpone it, without in both cases promoting the revolution. And the catastrophe engendered by the prolongation of the imperialist war keeps on approaching with even greater force and speed than ever.

The advance contingents of the Russian proletariat succeeded in emerging from our June and July days without losing too much blood. The proletarian party has every opportunity to choose the tactics and form, or forms, of organisation that will in any circumstances prevent unexpected (seemingly unexpected) Bonapartist persecutions from cutting short its existence and its regular messages to the people.

Let the Party loudly and clearly tell the people the whole truth that Bonapartism is beginning; that the "new" government of Kerensky, Avksentyev and Co. is merely a screen for the counter-revolutionary Cadets and the military clique which is in power at present; that the people can get no peace, the peasants no land, the workers no eight-hour day, and the hungry no bread unless the counter-revolution is completely stamped out. Let the Party say so, and every step in the march of events will bear it out.

With remarkable speed Russia has gone through a whole epoch in which the majority of the people put their faith in the petty-bourgeois Socialist-Revolutionary and Menshevik parties. And now the majority of the working people are beginning to pay heavily for their credulity.

All indications are that the march of events is continuing at a very fast pace and that the country is approaching the next epoch, when the majority of the working people will have to entrust their fate to the revolutionary proletariat. The revolutionary proletariat will take power and begin a socialist revolution; despite all the difficulties and possible zigzags of development, it will draw the workers of all the advanced countries into the revolution, and will defeat both war and capitalism.

The State and Revolution

THE MARXIST THEORY OF THE STATE AND THE TASKS OF THE PROLETARIAT IN THE REVOLUTION

While still in Switzerland in 1916, Lenin decided that a book on the Marxist theory of the state was needed, and gathered material in a notebook which he entitled "Marxism on the State" and left behind in Stockholm when he returned to Russia in April 1917. Except for a short section (Section 3 of Chapter II) which he added later, he wrote the study—for which he used the notebook—during his interlude of forced hiding in August–September 1917 and left it unfinished when he took personal command of the revolutionary regime in October. As he explained in the November 30 postscript, he had not had time to write the planned Chapter VII, on the experience of the Russian revolutions of 1905 and 1917. The work, his most important contribution to Marxist political theory, is here presented in unabridged form.

Like virtually all Lenin's theoretical writings, *The State and Revolution* had a practical purpose connected with the politics of revolution. As indicated by the work's subtitle, referring to the revolutionary tasks impending, this purpose was to substantiate, in terms of authoritative statements by Marx and Engels, the Marxist propriety of seizing power and setting up a regime of "proletarian dictatorship" which would rule by force and by the suppression of hostile class elements.

Preface to the First Edition

The question of the state is now acquiring particular importance both in theory and in practical politics. The imperialist war has immensely accelerated and intensified the process of transformation of monopoly capitalism into state-monopoly capitalism. The monstrous oppression of the working people by the state, which is merging more and more with the all-powerful capitalist associations, is becoming increasingly monstrous. The advanced countries —we mean their hinterland—are becoming military convict prisons for the workers.

The unprecedented horrors and miseries of the protracted war are making the people's position unbearable and increasing their anger. The world proletarian revolution is clearly maturing. The question of its relation to the state is acquiring practical importance.

The elements of opportunism that accumulated over the decades of comparatively peaceful development have given rise to the trend of social-chauvinism which dominates the official socialist parties throughout the world. This trend—socialism in words and chauvinism in deeds (Plekhanov, Potresov, Breshkovskaya, Rubanovich, and, in a slightly veiled form, Tsereteli, Chernov and Co. in Russia; Scheidemann, Legien, David and others in Germany; Renaudel, Guesde and Vandervelde in France and Belgium; Hyndman and the Fabians in England, etc., etc.)—is conspicuous for the base, servile adaptation of the "leaders of socialism" to the interests not only of "their" national bourgeoisie, but of "their" state, for the majority of the so-called Great Powers have long been exploiting and enslaving a whole number of small and weak nations. And the imperialist war is a war for the division and redivision of this kind of booty. The struggle to free the working people from the influence of the bourgeoisie in general, and of the imperialist bourgeoisie in particular, is impossible without a struggle against opportunist prejudices concerning the "state."

First of all we examine the theory of Marx and Engels on the state, and dwell in particular detail on those aspects of this theory which are ignored or have been distorted by the opportunists. Then we deal specially with the one who is chiefly responsible for these distortions, Karl Kautsky, the best-known leader of the Second International (1889–1914), which has met with such miserable bankruptcy in the present war. Lastly, we sum up the main results of the experience of the Russian revolutions of 1905 and particularly of 1917. Apparently, the latter is now (early August 1917) completing the first stage of its development; but this revolution as a whole can only be understood as a link in a chain of socialist proletarian revolutions being caused by the imperialist war. The question of the relation of the socialist proletarian revolution to the state, therefore, is acquiring not only practical political importance, but also the significance of a most urgent problem of the day, the problem of explaining to the masses what they will have to do before long to free themselves from capitalist tyranny.

August 1917   *The Author*

Preface to the Second Edition

The present, second edition is published virtually unaltered, except that section 3 has been added to Chapter II.

Moscow   *The Author*
December 17, 1918

Chapter I. Class Society and the State

1. *The State—A Product of the Irreconcilability of Class Antagonisms*

What is now happening to Marx's theory has, in the course of history, happened repeatedly to the theories of revolutionary thinkers and leaders of oppressed classes fighting for emancipation. During the lifetime of great revolutionaries, the oppressing classes constantly hounded them, received their theories with the most savage malice, the most furious hatred and the most unscrupulous campaigns of lies and slander. After their death, attempts are made to convert them into harmless icons, to canonise them, so to say, and to hallow their *names* to a certain extent for the "consolation" of the oppressed classes and with the object of duping the latter, while at the same time robbing the revolutionary theory of its *substance*, blunting its revolutionary edge and vulgarising it. Today, the bourgeoisie and the opportunists within the labour movement concur in this doctoring of Marxism. They omit, obscure or distort the revolutionary side of this theory, its revolutionary soul. They push to the foreground and extol what is or seems acceptable to the bourgeoisie. All the social-chauvinists are now "Marxists" (don't laugh!). And more and more frequently German bourgeois scholars, only yesterday specialists in the annihilation of Marxism, are speaking of the "national-German" Marx, who, they claim, educated the labour unions which are so splendidly organised for the purpose of waging a predatory war!

In these circumstances, in view of the unprecedentedly widespread distortion of Marxism, our prime task is to *re-establish* what Marx really taught on the subject of the state. This will necessitate a number of long quotations from the works of Marx and Engels themselves. Of course, long quotations will render the text cumbersome and not help at all to make it popular reading, but we cannot possibly dispense with them. All, or at any rate all the most essential passages in the works of Marx and Engels on the subject of the state must by all means be quoted as fully as possible so that the reader may form an independent opinion of the totality of the views of the founders of scientific socialism, and of the evolution of those views, and so that their distortion by the "Kautskyism" now prevailing may be documentarily proved and clearly demonstrated.

Let us begin with the most popular of Engels's works, *The Origin of the Family, Private Property and the State*, the sixth edition of which was published in Stuttgart as far back as 1894. We shall have to translate the quotations from the German originals, as the Russian translations, while very numerous, are for the most part either incomplete or very unsatisfactory.

Summing up his historical analysis, Engels says:

> The state is, therefore, by no means a power forced on society from without; just as little is it "the reality of the ethical idea," "the image and reality of reason," as Hegel maintains. Rather, it is a product of society at a certain stage of development; it is the admission that this society has become entangled in an insoluble contradiction with itself, that it has split into irreconcilable antagonisms which it is powerless to dispel. But in order that these antagonisms, these classes with conflicting economic interests might not consume themselves and society in fruitless struggle, it became necessary to have a power, seemingly standing above society, that would alleviate the conflict and keep it within the bounds of "order"; and this power, arisen out of society but placing itself above it, and alienating itself more and more from it, is the state. [Pp. 177–78, sixth German edition.]

This expresses with perfect clarity the basic idea of Marxism with regard to the historical role and the meaning of the state. The state is a product and a manifestation of the *irreconcilability* of class antagonisms. The state arises where, when and insofar as class antagonisms objectively *cannot* be reconciled. And, conversely, the existence of the state proves that the class antagonisms are irreconcilable.

It is on this most important and fundamental point that the distortion of Marxism, proceeding along two main lines, begins.

On the one hand, the bourgeois, and particularly the petty-bourgeois, ideologists, compelled under the weight of indisputable historical facts to admit that the state only exists where there are class antagonisms and a class struggle, "correct" Marx in such a way as to make it appear that the state is an organ for the *reconciliation* of classes. According to Marx, the state could neither have arisen nor maintained itself had it been possible to reconcile classes. From what the petty-bourgeois and philistine professors and publicists say, with quite frequent and benevolent references to Marx, it appears that the state does reconcile classes. According to Marx, the state is an organ of class *rule,* an organ for the *oppression* of one class by another; it is the creation of "order," which legalises and perpetuates this oppression by moderating the conflict between the classes. In the opinion of the petty-bourgeois politicians, however, order means the reconciliation of classes, and not the oppression of one class by another; to alleviate the conflict means reconciling classes and not depriving the oppressed classes of definite means and methods of struggle to overthrow the oppressors.

For instance, when, in the revolution of 1917, the question of the significance and role of the state arose in all its magnitude as a practical question demanding immediate action, and moreover, action on a mass scale, all the Socialist-Revolutionaries and Mensheviks descended at once to the petty-bourgeois theory that the "state" "reconciles" classes. Innumerable resolutions and articles by politicians of both these parties are thoroughly saturated with this petty-bourgeois and philistine "reconciliation" theory. That the state is an organ of the rule of a definite class which *cannot* be reconciled with its antipode (the class opposite to it) is something the petty-bourgeois democrats will never be able to understand. Their attitude to the state is one of the most striking manifestations of the fact that our Socialist-Revolutionaries and Mensheviks are not socialists at all (a point that we Bolsheviks have always maintained), but petty-bourgeois democrats using near-socialist phraseology.

On the other hand, the "Kautskyite" distortion of Marxism is far more subtle. "Theoretically," it is not denied that the state is an organ of class rule, or that class antagonisms are irreconcilable. But what is overlooked or glossed over is this: if the state is the product of the irreconcilability of class antagonisms, if it is a power standing *above* society and *"alienating* itself *more and more* from it," it is clear that the liberation of the oppressed class is impossible not only without a violent revolution, *but also without the destruction* of the apparatus of state power which was created by the ruling class and which is the embodiment of this "alienation." As we shall see later, Marx very explicitly drew this theoretically self-evident conclusion on the strength of a concrete historical analysis of the tasks of the revolution. And—as we shall show in detail further on—it is this conclusion which Kautsky has "forgotten" and distorted.

2. Special Bodies of Armed Men, Prisons, Etc.

Engels continues: "As distinct from the old gentile [tribal or clan] order, the state, first, divides its subjects *according to territory.* . . ." This division seems "natural" to us, but it cost a prolonged struggle against the old organisation according to generations or tribes.

> The second distinguishing feature is the establishment of a *public power* which no longer directly coincides with the population organising itself as an armed force. This special, public power is necessary because a self-acting armed organisation of the population has become impossible since the split into classes. . . . This public power exists in every state; it consists not merely of armed men but also of material adjuncts, prisons, and institutions of coercion of all kinds, of which gentile [clan] society knew nothing. . . .

Engels elucidates the concept of the "power" which is called the state, a power which arose from society but places itself above it and alienates itself more and more from it. What does this power mainly consist of? It consists of special bodies of armed men having prisons, etc., at their command.

We are justified in speaking of special bodies of armed men, because the public power which is an attribute of every state "does not directly coincide" with the armed population, with its "self-acting armed organisation."

Like all great revolutionary thinkers, Engels tries to draw the attention of the class-conscious workers to what prevailing philistinism regards as least worthy of attention, as the most habitual thing, hallowed by prejudices that are not only deep-rooted but, one might say, petrified. A standing army and police are the chief instruments of state power. But how can it be otherwise?

From the viewpoint of the vast majority of Europeans of the end of the nineteenth century whom Engels was addressing, and who had not gone through or closely observed a single great revolution, it could not have been otherwise. They could not understand at all what a "self-acting armed organisation of the population" was. When asked why it became necessary to have special bodies of armed men placed above society and alienating themselves from it (police and a standing army), the West-European and Russian philistines are inclined to utter a few phrases borrowed from Spencer or Mikhailovsky, to refer to the growing complexity of social life, the differentiation of functions, and so on.

Such a reference seems "scientific," and effectively lulls the ordinary person to sleep by obscuring the important and basic fact, namely, the split of society into irreconcilably antagonistic classes.

Were it not for this split, the "self-acting armed organisation of the population" would differ from the primitive organisation of a stick-wielding herd of monkeys, or of primitive men, or of men united in clans, by its complexity, its high technical level, and so on. But such an organisation would still be possible.

It is impossible because civilised society is split into antagonistic, and, moreover, irreconcilably antagonistic, classes, whose "self-acting" arming would lead to an armed struggle between them. A state arises, a special power is created, special bodies of armed men, and every revolution, by destroying the state apparatus, shows us the naked class struggle, clearly shows us how the ruling class strives to restore the special bodies of armed men which serve *it*, and how the oppressed class strives to create a new organisation of this kind, capable of serving the exploited instead of the exploiters.

In the above argument, Engels raises theoretically the very same question which every great revolution raises before us in practice, palpably and, what is more, on a scale of mass action, namely, the question of the relationship between "special" bodies of armed men and the "self-acting armed organisation of the population." We shall see how this question is specifically illustrated by the experience of the European and Russian revolutions.

But to return to Engels's exposition.

He points out that sometimes—in certain parts of North America, for example—this public power is weak (he has in mind a rare exception in capitalist society, and those parts of North America in its pre-imperialist days where the free colonist predominated), but that, generally speaking, it grows stronger: "It [the public power] grows stronger, however, in proportion as class antagonisms within the state become more acute, and as adjacent states become larger and more populous. We have only to look at our present-day Europe, where class struggle and rivalry in conquest have tuned up the public power to such a pitch that it threatens to swallow the whole of society and even the state."

This was written not later than the early nineties of the last century, Engels's last preface being dated June 16, 1891. The turn towards imperialism—meaning the complete domination of the trusts, the omnipotence of the big banks, a grand-scale colonial policy, and so forth—was only just beginning in France, and was even weaker in North America and in Germany. Since then "rivalry in conquest" has taken a gigantic stride, all the more because by the beginning of the second decade of the twentieth century the world had been completely divided up among these "rivals in conquest," i.e., among the predatory Great Powers. Since then, military and naval armaments have grown fantastically and the predatory war of 1914–17 for the domination of the world by Britain or Germany, for the division of the spoils, has brought the "swallowing" of all the forces of society by the rapacious state power close to complete catastrophe.

Engels could, as early as 1891, point to "rivalry in conquest" as one of the most important distinguishing features of the foreign policy of the Great Powers, while the social-chauvinist scoundrels have ever since 1914, when this rivalry, many times intensified, gave rise to an imperialist war, been covering up the defence of the predatory interests of "their own" bourgeoisie with phrases about "defence of the fatherland," "defence of the republic and the revolution," etc.!

3. The State—An Instrument for the Exploitation of the Oppressed Class

The maintenance of the special public power standing above society requires taxes and state loans. "Having public power and the right to levy taxes," Engels writes, "the officials now stand, as organs of society, *above* society. The free, voluntary respect that was accorded to the organs of the gentile [clan] constitution does not satisfy them, even if they could gain it. . . ." Special laws are enacted proclaiming the sanctity and immunity of the officials. "The shabbiest police servant" has more "authority" than the representatives of the clan, but even the head of the military power of a civilised state may well envy the elder of a clan the "unstrained respect" of society.

The question of the privileged position of the officials as organs of state power is raised here. The main point indicated is: what is it that places them *above* society? We shall see how this theoretical question was answered in practice by the Paris Commune in 1871 and how it was obscured from a reactionary standpoint by Kautsky in 1912. "Because the state arose from the need to hold class antagonisms in check, but because it arose, at the same time, in the midst of the conflict of these classes, it is, as a rule, the state of the most powerful, economically dominant class, which, through the medium of the state, becomes also the politically dominant class, and thus acquires new means of holding down and exploiting the oppressed class. . . ." The ancient and feudal states were organs for the exploitation of the slaves and serfs; likewise, "the modern representative state is an instrument of exploitation of wage labour by capital. By way of exception, however, periods occur in which the warring classes balance each other so nearly that the state power as ostensible mediator acquires, for the moment, a certain degree of independence of both. . . ." Such were the absolute monarchies of the seventeenth and eighteenth centuries, the Bonapartism of the First and Second Empires in France, and the Bismarck regime in Germany.[1]

Such, we may add, is the Kerensky government in republican

---

1. Lenin is still citing Engel's *The Origin of the Family, Private Property, and the State*. [R. T.]

Russia since it began to persecute the revolutionary proletariat, at a moment when, owing to the leadership of the petty-bourgeois democrats, the Soviets have *already* become impotent, while the bourgeoisie are not *yet* strong enough simply to disperse them.

In a democratic republic, Engels continues, "wealth exercises its power indirectly, but all the more surely," first, by means of the "direct corruption of officials" (America); secondly, by means of an "alliance of the government and the Stock Exchange" (France and America). At present, imperialism and the domination of the banks have "developed" into an exceptional art both these methods of upholding and giving effect to the omnipotence of wealth in democratic republics of all descriptions. Since, for instance, in the very first months of the Russian democratic republic, one might say during the honeymoon of the "socialist" S.R.s and Mensheviks joined in wedlock to the bourgeoisie, in the coalition government, Mr. Palchinsky obstructed every measure intended for curbing the capitalists and their marauding practices, their plundering of the state by means of war contracts; and since later on Mr. Palchinsky, upon resigning from the Cabinet (and being, of course, replaced by another quite similar Palchinsky), was "rewarded" by the capitalists with a lucrative job with a salary of 120,000 rubles per annum —what would you call that? Direct or indirect bribery? An alliance of the government and the syndicates, or "merely" friendly relations? What role do the Chernovs, Tseretelis, Avksentyevs and Skobelevs play? Are they the "direct" or only the indirect allies of the millionaire treasury-looters?

Another reason why the omnipotence of "wealth" is more *certain* in a democratic republic is that it does not depend on defects in the political machinery or on the faulty political shell of capitalism. A democratic republic is the best possible political shell for capitalism, and, therefore, once capital has gained possession of this very best shell (through the Palchinskys, Chernovs, Tseretelis and Co.), it establishes its power so securely, so firmly, that *no* change of persons, institutions or parties in the bourgeois-democratic republic can shake it.

We must also note that Engels is most explicit in calling universal suffrage as well an instrument of bourgeois rule. Universal suffrage, he says, obviously taking account of the long experience of German Social-Democracy, is "the gauge of the maturity of the working class. It cannot and never will be anything more in the present-day state." The petty-bourgeois democrats, such as our Socialist-Revolutionaries and Mensheviks, and also their twin brothers, all the social-chauvinists and opportunists of Western Europe, expect just this "more" from universal suffrage. They themselves share, and instil into the minds of the people, the false notion that universal suffrage "in the *present-day* state" is really capable of revealing the will of the majority of the working people and of securing its realisation.

Here we can only indicate this false notion, only point out that Engels's perfectly clear, precise and concrete statement is distorted at every step in the propaganda and agitation of the "official" (i.e., opportunist) socialist parties. A detailed exposure of the utter falsity of this notion which Engels brushes aside here is given in our further account of the views of Marx and Engels on the "*present-day*" state.

Engels gives a general summary of his views in the most popular of his works in the following words:

> The state, then, has not existed from all eternity. There have been societies that did without it, that had no idea of the state and state power. At a certain stage of economic development, which was necessarily bound up with the split of society into classes, the state became a necessity owing to this split. We are now rapidly approaching a stage in the development of production at which the existence of these classes not only will have ceased to be a necessity, but will become a positive hindrance to production. They will fall as inevitably as they arose at an earlier stage. Along with them the state will inevitably fall. Society, which will reorganise production on the basis of a free and equal association of the producers, will put the whole machinery of state where it will then belong: into a museum of antiquities, by the side of the spinning-wheel and the bronze axe.

We do not often come across this passage in the propaganda and agitation literature of the present-day Social-Democrats. Even when we do come across it, it is mostly quoted in the same manner as one bows before an icon, i.e., it is done to show official respect for Engels, and no attempt is made to gauge the breadth and depth of the revolution that this relegating of "the whole machinery of state to a museum of antiquities" implies. In most cases we do not even find an understanding of what Engels calls the state machine.

4. The "Withering Away" of the State, and Violent Revolution

Engels's words regarding the "withering away" of the state are so widely known, they are so often quoted, and so clearly reveal the essence of the customary adaptation of Marxism to opportunism that we must deal with them in detail. We shall quote the whole argument from which they are taken.

> *The proletariat seizes state power and turns the means of production into state property to begin with.* But thereby it abolishes

itself as the proletariat, abolishes all class distinctions and class antagonisms, and abolishes also the state as state. Society thus far, operating amid class antagonisms, needed the state, that is, an organisation of the particular exploiting class, for the maintenance of its external conditions of production, and, therefore, especially, for the purpose of forcibly keeping the exploited class in the conditions of oppression determined by the given mode of production (slavery, serfdom or bondage, wage-labour). The state was the official representative of society as a whole, its concentration in a visible corporation. But it was this only insofar as it was the state of that class which itself represented, for its own time, society as a whole: in ancient times, the state of slave-owning citizens; in the Middle Ages, of the feudal nobility; in our own time, of the bourgeoisie. When at last it becomes the real representative of the whole of society, it renders itself unnecessary. As soon as there is no longer any social class to be held in subjection, as soon as class rule, and the individual struggle for existence based upon the present anarchy in production, with the collisions and excesses arising from this struggle, are removed, nothing more remains to be held in subjection—nothing necessitating a special coercive force, a state. The first act by which the state really comes forward as the representative of the whole of society—the taking possession of the means of production in the name of society—is also its last independent act as a state. State interference in social relations becomes, in one domain after another, superfluous, and then dies down of itself. The government of persons is replaced by the administration of things, and by the conduct of processes of production. The state is not "abolished." *It withers away*. This gives the measure of the value of the phrase "a free people's state," both as to its justifiable use for a time from an agitational point of view, and as to its ultimate scientific insufficiency; and also of the so-called anarchists' demand that the state be abolished overnight. [*Herr Eugen Dühring's Revolution in Science* (*Anti-Dühring*), pp. 301–3, third German edition.]

It is safe to say that of this argument of Engels's, which is so remarkably rich in ideas, only one point has become an integral part of socialist thought among modern socialist parties, namely, that according to Marx the state "withers away"—as distinct from the anarchist doctrine of the "abolition" of the state. To prune Marxism to such an extent means reducing it to opportunism, for this "interpretation" only leaves a vague notion of a slow, even, gradual change, of absence of leaps and storms, of absence of revolution. The current, widespread, popular, if one may say so, conception of the "withering away" of the state undoubtedly means obscuring, if not repudiating, revolution.

Such an "interpretation," however, is the crudest distortion of Marxism, advantageous only to the bourgeoisie. In point of theory, it is based on disregard for the most important circumstances and considerations indicated in, say, Engels's "summary" argument we have just quoted in full.

In the first place, at the very outset of his argument, Engels says that, in seizing state power, the proletariat thereby "abolishes the state as state." It is not "good form" to ponder over the meaning of this. Generally, it is either ignored altogether, or is considered to be something in the nature of a "Hegelian weakness" on Engels's part. As a matter of fact, however, these words briefly express the experience of one of the greatest proletarian revolutions, the Paris Commune of 1871; of which we shall speak in greater detail in its proper place. As a matter of fact, Engels speaks here of the proletarian revolution "abolishing" the *bourgeois* state, while the words about the state withering away refer to the remnants of the *proletarian* state *after* the socialist revolution. According to Engels, the bourgeois state does not "wither away," but is *"abolished"* by the proletariat in the course of the revolution. What withers away after this revolution is the proletarian state or semi-state.

Secondly, the state is a "special coercive force." Engels gives this splendid and extremely profound definition here with the utmost lucidity. And it follows from it that the "special coercive force" for the suppression of the proletariat by the bourgeoisie, of millions of working people by handfuls of the rich, must be replaced by a "special coercive force" for the suppression of the bourgeoisie by the proletariat (the dictatorship of the proletariat). This is precisely what is meant by "abolition of the state as state." This is precisely the "act" of taking possession of the means of production in the name of society. And it is self-evident that *such* a replacement of one (bourgeois) "special force" by another (proletarian) "special force" cannot possibly take place in the form of "withering away."

Thirdly, in speaking of the state "withering away," and the even more graphic and colourful "dying down of itself," Engels refers quite clearly and definitely to the period *after* "the state has taken possession of the means of production in the name of the whole of society," that is, *after* the socialist revolution. We all know that the political form of the "state" at that time is the most complete democracy. But it never enters the head of any of the opportunists, who shamelessly distort Marxism, that Engels is consequently speaking here of *democracy* "dying down of itself," or "withering away." This seems very strange at first sight. But it is "incomprehensible" only to those who have not thought about democracy *also* being a state and, consequently, also disappearing when the state disappears. Revolution alone can "abolish" the bourgeois state. The state in general, i.e., the most complete democracy, can only "wither away."

Fourthly, after formulating his famous proposition that "the state withers away," Engels at once explains specifically that this proposition is directed against both the opportunists and the anarchists. In doing this, Engels puts in the forefront that conclusion, drawn from the proposition that "the state withers away," which is directed against the opportunists.

One can wager that out of every 10,000 persons who have read or heard about the "withering away" of the state, 9,990 are completely unaware, or do not remember, that Engels directed his conclusions from that proposition *not* against the anarchists *alone*. And of the remaining ten, probably nine do not know the meaning of a "free people's state" or why an attack on this slogan means an attack on the opportunists. This is how history is written! This is how a great revolutionary teaching is imperceptibly falsified and adapted to prevailing philistinism. The conclusion directed against the anarchists has been repeated thousands of times; it has been vulgarised, and rammed into people's heads in the shallowest form, and has acquired the strength of a prejudice, whereas the conclusion directed against the opportunists has been obscured and "forgotten!"

The "free people's state" was a programme demand and a catchword current among the German Social-Democrats in the seventies. This catchword is devoid of all political content except that it describes the concept of democracy in a pompous philistine fashion. Insofar as it hinted in a legally permissible manner at a democratic republic, Engels was prepared to "justify" its use "for a time" from an agitational point of view. But it was an opportunist catchword, for it amounted to something more than prettifying bourgeois democracy, and was also a failure to understand the socialist criticism of the state in general. We are in favour of a democratic republic as the best form of state for the proletariat under capitalism. But we have no right to forget that wage slavery is the lot of the people even in the most democratic bourgeois republic. Furthermore, every state is a "special force" for the suppression of the oppressed class. Consequently, *every* state is *not* "free" and *not* a "people's state." Marx and Engels explained this repeatedly to their party comrades in the seventies.

Fifthly, the same work of Engels's, whose argument about the withering away of the state everyone remembers, also contains an argument on the significance of violent revolution. Engels's historical analysis of its role becomes a veritable panegyric on violent revolution. This "no one remembers." It is not customary in modern socialist parties to talk or even think about the significance of this idea, and these thoughts play no part whatever in their daily propaganda and agitation among the people. And yet they are inseparably linked with the "withering away" of the state in one harmonious whole.

Here is Engels's argument:

> . . . That force, however, plays yet another role [other than that of a diabolical power] in history, a revolutionary role; that, in the words of Marx, it is the midwife of every old society which is pregnant with a new one, that it is the instrument with which social movement forces its way through and shatters the dead, fossilised political forms—of this there is not a word in Herr Dühring. It is only with sighs and groans that he admits the possibility that force will perhaps be necessary for the overthrow of an economy based on exploitation—unfortunately, because all use of force demoralises, he says, the person who uses it. And this in spite of the immense moral and spiritual impetus which has been given by every victorious revolution! And this in Germany, where a violent collision—which may, after all, be forced on the people—would at least have the advantage of wiping out the servility which has penetrated the nation's mentality following the humiliation of the Thirty Years' War. And this parson's mode of thought—dull, insipid and impotent—presumes to impose itself on the most revolutionary party that history has known!" [P. 193, third German edition, Part II, end of Chap. IV.]

How can this panegyric on violent revolution, which Engels insistently brought to the attention of the German Social-Democrats between 1878 and 1894, i.e., right up to the time of his death, be combined with the theory of the "withering away" of the state to form a single theory?

Usually the two are combined by means of eclecticism, by an unprincipled or sophistic selection made arbitrarily (or to please the powers that be) of first one, then another argument, and in ninety-nine cases out of a hundred, if not more, it is the idea of the "withering away" that is placed in the forefront. Dialectics are replaced by eclecticism—this is the most usual, the most widespread practice to be met with in present-day official Social-Democratic literature in relation to Marxism. This sort of substitution is, of course, nothing new; it was observed even in the history of classical Greek philosophy. In falsifying Marxism in opportunist fashion, the substitution of eclecticism for dialectics is the easiest way of deceiving the people. It gives an illusory satisfaction; it seems to take into account all sides of the process, all trends of development, all the conflicting influences, and so forth, whereas in reality it provides no integral and revolutionary conception of the process of social development at all.

We have already said above, and shall show more fully later, that the theory of Marx and Engels of the inevitability of a violent revolution refers to the bourgeois state. The latter *cannot* be superseded by the proletarian state (the dictatorship of the proletariat) through the process of "withering away," but, as a general rule, only through a violent revolution. The panegyric Engels sang in its honour, and which fully corresponds to Marx's repeated statements (see the concluding passages of *The Poverty of Philosophy* and the *Communist Manifesto*, with their proud and open proclamation of the inevitability of a violent revolution; see what Marx wrote nearly thirty years later, in criticising the Gotha Programme of 1875, when he mercilessly castigated the opportunist character of that programme)—this panegyric is by no means a mere "impulse," a mere declamation or a polemical sally. The necessity of systematically imbuing the masses with *this* and precisely this view of violent revolution lies at the root of the *entire* theory of Marx and Engels. The betrayal of their theory by the now prevailing social-chauvinist and Kautskyite trends expresses itself strikingly in both these trends ignoring *such* propaganda and agitation.

The supersession of the bourgeois state by the proletarian state is impossible without a violent revolution. The abolition of the proletarian state, i.e., of the state in general, is impossible except through the process of "withering away."

A detailed and concrete elaboration of these views was given by Marx and Engels when they studied each particular revolutionary situation, when they analysed the lessons of the experience of each particular revolution. We shall now pass to this, undoubtedly the most important, part of their theory.

Chapter II. The State and Revolution. The Experience of 1848–51

1. The Eve of the Revolution

The first works of mature Marxism—*The Poverty of Philosophy* and the *Communist Manifesto*—appeared just on the eve of the revolution of 1848. For this reason, in addition to presenting the general principles of Marxism, they reflect to a certain degree the concrete revolutionary situation of the time. It will, therefore, be more expedient, perhaps, to examine what the authors of these works said about the state immediately before they drew conclusions from the experience of the years 1848–51.

In *The Poverty of Philosophy*, Marx wrote: "The working class, in the course of development, will substitute for the old bourgeois society an association which will preclude classes and their antagonism, and there will be no more political power proper, since political power is precisely the official expression of class antagonism in bourgeois society." (P. 182, German edition, 1885.)

It is instructive to compare this general exposition of the idea of the state disappearing after the abolition of classes with the exposition contained in the *Communist Manifesto*, written by Marx and Engels a few months later—in November 1847, to be exact:

> . . . In depicting the most general phases of the development of the proletariat, we traced the more or less veiled civil war, raging within existing society up to the point where that war breaks out into open revolution, and where the violent overthrow of the bourgeoisie lays the foundation for the sway of the proletariat. . . .
>
> . . . We have seen above that the first step in the revolution by the working class is to raise the proletariat to the position of ruling class, to win the battle of democracy.
>
> The proletariat will use its political supremacy to wrest, by degrees, all capital from the bourgeoisie, to centralise all instruments of production in the hands of the state, i.e., of the proletariat organised as the ruling class; and to increase the total of productive forces as rapidly as possible. [Pp. 31 and 37, seventh German edition, 1906.]

Here we have a formulation of one of the most remarkable and most important ideas of Marxism on the subject of the state, namely, the idea of the "dictatorship of the proletariat" (as Marx and Engels began to call it after the Paris Commune); and also, a highly interesting definition of the state, which is also one of the "forgotten words" of Marxism: *"the state, i.e., the proletariat organised as the ruling class."*

This definition of the state has never been explained in the prevailing propaganda and agitation literature of the official Social-Democratic parties. More than that, it has been deliberately ignored, for it is absolutely irreconcilable with reformism, and is a slap in the face for the common opportunist prejudices and philistine illusions about the "peaceful development of democracy."

The proletariat needs the state—this is repeated by all the opportunists, social-chauvinists and Kautskyites, who assure us that this is what Marx taught. But they *"forget"* to add that, in the first place, according to Marx, the proletariat needs only a state which is withering away, i.e., a state so constituted that it begins to wither away immediately, and cannot but wither away. And, secondly, the working people need a "state, i.e., the proletariat organised as the ruling class."

The state is a special organisation of force: it is an organisation of violence for the suppression of some class. What class must the proletariat suppress? Naturally, only the exploiting class, i.e., the bourgeoisie. The working people need the state only to suppress the resistance of the exploiters, and only the proletariat can direct this suppression, can carry it out. For the proletariat is the only class that is consistently revolutionary, the only class that can unite all the working and exploited people in the struggle against the bourgeoisie, in completely removing it.

The exploiting classes need political rule to maintain exploitation, i.e., in the selfish interests of an insignificant minority against the vast majority of the people. The exploited classes need political rule in order to completely abolish all exploitation, i.e., in the interests of the vast majority of the people, and against the insignificant minority consisting of the modern slave-owners—the landowners and capitalists.

The petty-bourgeois democrats, those sham socialists who replaced the class struggle by dreams of class harmony, even pictured the socialist transformation in a dreamy fashion—not as the overthrow of the rule of the exploiting class, but as the peaceful submission of the minority to the majority which has become aware of its aims. This petty-bourgeois utopia, which is inseparable from the idea of the state being above classes, led in practice to the betrayal of the interests of the working classes, as was shown, for example, by the history of the French revolutions of 1848 and 1871, and by the experience of "socialist" participation in bourgeois cabinets in Britain, France, Italy and other countries at the turn of the century.

All his life Marx fought against this petty-bourgeois socialism, now revived in Russia by the Socialist-Revolutionary and Menshevik parties. He developed his theory of the class struggle consistently, down to the theory of political power, of the state.

The overthrow of bourgeois rule can be accomplished only by the proletariat, the particular class whose economic conditions of existence prepare it for this task and provide it with the possibility and the power to perform it. While the bourgeoisie break up and disintegrate the peasantry and all the petty-bourgeois groups, they weld together, unite and organise the proletariat. Only the proletariat—by virtue of the economic role it plays in large-scale production—is capable of being the leader of *all* the working and exploited people, whom the bourgeoisie exploit, oppress and crush, often not less but more than they do the proletarians, but who are incapable of waging an *independent* struggle for their emancipation.

The theory of the class struggle, applied by Marx to the question of the state and the socialist revolution, leads as a matter of course to the recognition of the *political rule* of the proletariat, of its dictatorship, i.e., of undivided power directly backed by the armed force of the people. The overthrow of the bourgeoisie can be achieved only by the proletariat becoming the *ruling class,* capable of crushing the inevitable and desperate resistance of the bourgeoisie, and of organising *all* the working and exploited people for the new economic system.

The proletariat needs state power, a centralised organisation of force, an organisation of violence, both to crush the resistance of the exploiters and to *lead* the enormous mass of the population—the peasants, the petty bourgeoisie, and semi-proletarians—in the work of organising a socialist economy.

By educating the workers' party, Marxism educates the vanguard of the proletariat, capable of assuming power and *leading the whole people* to socialism, of directing and organising the new system, of being the teacher, the guide, the leader of all the working and exploited people in organising their social life without the bourgeoisie and against the bourgeoisie. By contrast, the opportunism now prevailing trains the members of the workers' party to be the representatives of the better-paid workers, who lose touch with the masses, "get along" fairly well under capitalism, and sell their birthright for a mess of pottage, i.e., renounce their role as revolutionary leaders of the people against the bourgeoisie.

Marx's theory of "the state, i.e., the proletariat organised as the ruling class," is inseparably bound up with the whole of his doctrine of the revolutionary role of the proletariat in history. The culmination of this role is the proletarian dictatorship, the political rule of the proletariat.

But since the proletariat needs the state as a *special* form of organisation of violence *against* the bourgeoisie, the following conclusion suggests itself: is it conceivable that such an organisation can be created without first abolishing, destroying the state machine created by the bourgeoisie *for themselves?* The *Communist Manifesto* leads straight to this conclusion, and it is of this conclusion that Marx speaks when summing up the experience of the revolution of 1848–51.

2. The Revolution Summed Up

Marx sums up his conclusions from the revolution of 1848–51, on the subject of the state we are concerned with, in the following argument contained in *The Eighteenth Brumaire of Louis Bonaparte:*

> But the revolution is thoroughgoing. It is still journeying through purgatory. It does its work methodically. By December 2, 1851 [the day of Louis Bonaparte's *coup d'état*], it had com-

pleted one half of its preparatory work. It is now completing the other half. First it perfected the parliamentary power, in order to be able to overthrow it. Now that it has attained this, it is perfecting the *executive power*, reducing it to its purest expression, isolating it, setting it up against itself as the sole object, *in order to concentrate all its forces of destruction against it* [italics ours]. And when it has done this second half of its preliminary work, Europe will leap from its seat and exultantly exclaim: well grubbed, old mole!

This executive power with its enormous bureaucratic and military organisation, with its vast and ingenious state machinery, with a host of officials numbering half a million, besides an army of another half million, this appalling parasitic body, which enmeshes the body of French society and chokes all its pores, sprang up in the days of the absolute monarchy, with the decay of the feudal system, which it helped to hasten.

The first French Revolution developed centralisation, "but at the same time" it increased "the extent, the attributes and the number of agents of governmental power. Napoleon completed this state machinery." The legitimate monarchy and the July monarchy "added nothing but a greater division of labour." . . .

. . . Finally, in its struggle against the revolution, the parliamentary republic found itself compelled to strengthen, along with repressive measures, the resources and centralisation of governmental power. *All revolutions perfected this machine instead of smashing it* [italics ours]. The parties that contended in turn for domination regarded the possession of this huge state edifice as the principal spoils of the victor. [*The Eighteenth Brumaire of Louis Bonaparte*, pp. 98–99, fourth edition, Hamburg, 1907.]

In this remarkable argument Marxism takes a tremendous step forward compared with the *Communist Manifesto*. In the latter the question of the state is still treated in an extremely abstract manner, in the most general terms and expressions. In the above-quoted passage, the question is treated in a concrete manner, and the conclusion is extremely precise, definite, practical and palpable: all previous revolutions perfected the state machine, whereas it must be broken, smashed.

This conclusion is the chief and fundamental point in the Marxist theory of the state. And it is precisely this fundamental point which has been completely *ignored* by the dominant official Social-Democratic parties and, indeed, *distorted* (as we shall see later) by the foremost theoretician of the Second International, Karl Kautsky.

The *Communist Manifesto* gives a general summary of history, which compels us to regard the state as the organ of class rule and leads us to the inevitable conclusion that the proletariat cannot overthrow the bourgeoisie without first winning political power, without attaining political supremacy, without transforming the state into the "proletariat organised as the ruling class"; and that this proletarian state will begin to wither away immediately after its victory because the state is unnecessary and cannot exist in a society in which there are no class antagonisms. The question as to how, from the point of view of historical development, the replacement of the bourgeois by the proletarian state is to take place is not raised here.

This is the question Marx raises and answers in 1852. True to his philosophy of dialectical materialism, Marx takes as his basis the historical experience of the great years of revolution, 1848 to 1851. Here, as everywhere else, his theory is a *summing up of experience*, illuminated by a profound philosophical conception of the world and a rich knowledge of history.

The problem of the state is put specifically: How did the bourgeois state, the state machine necessary for the rule of the bourgeoisie, come into being historically? What changes did it undergo, what evolution did it perform in the course of bourgeois revolutions and in the face of the independent actions of the oppressed classes? What are the tasks of the proletariat in relation to this state machine?

The centralised state power that is peculiar to bourgeois society came into being in the period of the fall of absolutism. Two institutions most characteristic of this state machine are the bureaucracy and the standing army. In their works, Marx and Engels repeatedly show that the bourgeoisie are connected with these institutions by thousands of threads. Every worker's experience illustrates this connection in an extremely graphic and impressive manner. From its own bitter experience, the working class learns to recognise this connection. That is why it so easily grasps and so firmly learns the doctrine which shows the inevitability of this connection, a doctrine which the petty-bourgeois democrats either ignorantly and flippantly deny, or still more flippantly admit "in general," while forgetting to draw appropriate practical conclusions.

The bureaucracy and the standing army are a "parasite" on the body of bourgeois society—a parasite created by the internal antagonisms which rend that society, but a parasite which "chokes" all its vital pores. The Kautskyite opportunism now prevailing in official Social-Democracy considers the view that the state is a *parasitic organism* to be the peculiar and exclusive attribute of anarchism. It goes without saying that this distortion of Marxism is of vast advantage to those philistines who have reduced socialism to the unheard-of disgrace of justifying and prettifying the imperialist war by applying to it the concept of "defence of the fatherland"; but it is unquestionably a distortion, nevertheless.

The development, perfection and strengthening of the bureaucratic and military apparatus proceeded during all the numerous bourgeois revolutions which Europe has witnessed since the fall of feudalism. In particular, it is the petty bourgeoisie who are attracted to the side of the big bourgeoisie and are largely subordinated to them through this apparatus, which provides the upper sections of the peasants, small artisans, tradesmen and the like with comparatively comfortable, quiet and respectable jobs raising their holders *above* the people. Consider what happened in Russia during the six months following February 27, 1917. The official posts which formerly were given by preference to the Black Hundreds have now become the spoils of the Cadets, Mensheviks and Socialist-Revolutionaries. Nobody has really thought of introducing any serious reforms. Every effort has been made to put them off "until the Constituent Assembly meets," and to steadily put off its convocation until after the war! But there has been no delay, no waiting for the Constituent Assembly, in the matter of dividing the spoils, of getting the lucrative jobs of ministers, deputy ministers, governors-general, etc., etc.! The game of combinations that has been played in forming the government has been, in essence, only an expression of this division and redivision of the "spoils," which has been going on above and below, throughout the country, in every department of central and local government. The six months between February 27 and August 27, 1917, can be summed up, objectively summed up beyond all dispute, as follows: reforms shelved, distribution of official jobs accomplished and "mistakes" in the distribution corrected by a few redistributions.

But the more the bureaucratic apparatus is "redistributed" among the various bourgeois and petty-bourgeois parties (among the Cadets, Socialist-Revolutionaries and Mensheviks in the case of Russia), the more keenly aware the oppressed classes, and the proletariat at their head, become of their irreconcilable hostility to the *whole* of bourgeois society. Hence the need for all bourgeois parties, even for the most democratic and "revolutionary-democratic" among them, to intensify repressive measures against the revolutionary proletariat, to strengthen the apparatus of coercion, i.e., the state machine. This course of events compels the revolution *"to concentrate all its forces of destruction"* against the state power, and to set itself the aim, not of improving the state machine, but of *smashing and destroying* it.

It was not logical reasoning, but actual developments, the actual experience of 1848–51, that led to the matter being presented in this way. The extent to which Marx held strictly to the solid ground of historical experience can be seen from the fact that, in 1852, he did not yet specifically raise the question of *what* was to take the place of the state machine to be destroyed. Experience had not yet provided material for dealing with this question, which history placed on the agenda later on, in 1871. In 1852, all that could be established with the accuracy of scientific observation was that the proletarian revolution *had approached* the task of "concentrating all its forces of destruction" against the state power, of "smashing" the state machine.

Here the question may arise: is it correct to generalise the experience, observations and conclusions of Marx, to apply them to a field that is wider than the history of France during the three years 1848–51? Before proceeding to deal with this question, let us recall a remark made by Engels and then examine the facts. In his introduction to the third edition of *The Eighteenth Brumaire*, Engels wrote:

> France is the country where, more than anywhere else, the historical class struggles were each time fought out to a finish, and where, consequently, the changing political forms within which they move and in which their results are summarised have been stamped in the sharpest outlines. The centre of feudalism in the Middle Ages, the model country, since the Renaissance, of a unified monarchy based on social estates, France demolished feudalism in the Great Revolution and established the rule of the bourgeoisie in a classical purity unequalled by any other European land. And the struggle of the upward striving proletariat against the ruling bourgeoisie appeared here in an acute form unknown elsewhere. [P. 4, 1907 edition.]

The last remark is out of date inasmuch as since 1871 there has been a lull in the revolutionary struggle of the French proletariat, although, long as this lull may be, it does not at all preclude the possibility that in the coming proletarian revolution France may show herself to be the classic country of the class struggle to a finish.

Let us, however, cast a general glance over the history of the advanced countries at the turn of the century. We shall see that the same process went on more slowly, in more varied forms, in a much wider field: on the one hand, the development of "parliamentary power" both in the republican countries (France, America, Switzerland), and in the monarchies (Britain, Germany to a certain extent, Italy, the Scandinavian countries, etc.); on the other hand, a struggle for power among the various bourgeois and petty-bourgeois parties which distributed and redistributed the "spoils" of office, with the foundations of bourgeois society unchanged; and, lastly, the perfection and consolidation of the "executive power," of its bureaucratic and military apparatus.

There is not the slightest doubt that these features are common to the whole of the modern evolution of all capitalist states in general. In the three years 1848–51 France displayed, in a swift, sharp, concentrated form, the very same processes of development which are peculiar to the whole capitalist world.

Imperialism—the era of bank capital, the era of gigantic capitalist monopolies, of the development of monopoly capitalism into state-monopoly capitalism—has clearly shown an extraordinary strengthening of the "state machine" and an unprecedented growth in its bureaucratic and military apparatus in connection with the intensification of repressive measures against the proletariat both in the monarchical and in the freest, republican countries.

World history is now undoubtedly leading, on an incomparably larger scale than in 1852, to the "concentration of all the forces" of the proletarian revolution on the "destruction" of the state machine.

What the proletariat will put in its place is suggested by the highly instructive material furnished by the Paris Commune.

3. The Presentation of the Question by Marx in 1852[2]

In 1907, Mehring, in the magazine *Neue Zeit*[3] (Vol. XXV, 2, p. 164), published extracts from Marx's letter to Weydemeyer dated March 5, 1852. This letter, among other things, contains the following remarkable observation:

> And now as to myself, no credit is due to me for discovering the existence of classes in modern society or the struggle between them. Long before me bourgeois historians had described the historical development of this class struggle and bourgeois economists the economic anatomy of the classes. What I did that was new was to prove: (1) that the *existence of classes* is only bound up with *particular, historical phases in the development of production* [*historische Entwicklungsphasen der Produktion*], (2) that the class struggle necessarily leads to the *dictatorship of the proletariat*, (3) that this dictatorship itself only constitutes the transition to the *abolition of all classes* and to a *classless society*.[4]

In these words, Marx succeeded in expressing with striking clarity, first, the chief and radical difference between his theory and

---

2. Added in the second edition. [*Lenin*]
3. *Die Neue Zeit* (*New Times*) was the theoretical journal of the Social-Democratic Party of Germany, published in Stuttgart from 1883 to 1923. Up to October 1917 it was edited by Karl Kautsky, after 1917 by H. Cunow.
4. Marx and Engels, *Selected Correspondence* (Moscow, 1965), pp. 69–70.

that of the foremost and most profound thinkers of the bourgeoisie; and, secondly, the essence of his theory of the state.

It is often said and written that the main point in Marx's theory is the class struggle. But this is wrong. And this wrong notion very often results in an opportunist distortion of Marxism and its falsification in a spirit acceptable to the bourgeoisie. For the theory of the class struggle was created *not* by Marx, *but* by the bourgeoisie *before* Marx, and, generally speaking, it is *acceptable* to the bourgeoisie. Those who recognize *only* the class struggle are not yet Marxists; they may be found to be still within the bounds of bourgeois thinking and bourgeois politics. To confine Marxism to the theory of the class struggle means curtailing Marxism, distorting it, reducing it to something acceptable to the bourgeoisie. Only he is a Marxist who *extends* the recognition of the class struggle to the recognition of the *dictatorship of the proletariat*. This is what constitutes the most profound distinction between the Marxist and the ordinary petty (as well as big) bourgeois. This is the touchstone on which the *real* understanding and recognition of Marxism should be tested. And it is not surprising that when the history of Europe brought the working class face to face with this question as a *practical* issue, not only all the opportunists and reformists, but all the Kautskyites (people who vacillate between reformism and Marxism) proved to be miserable philistines and petty-bourgeois democrats *repudiating* the dictatorship of the proletariat. Kautsky's pamphlet, *The Dictatorship of the Proletariat*, published in August 1918, i.e., long after the first edition of the present book, is a perfect example of petty-bourgeois distortion of Marxism and base renunciation of it *in deeds*, while hypocritically recognising it *in words* (see my pamphlet, *The Proletarian Revolution and the Renegade Kautsky*, Petrograd and Moscow, 1918).

Opportunism today, as represented by its principal spokesman, the ex-Marxist Karl Kautsky, fits in completely with Marx's characterization of the *bourgeois* position quoted above, for this opportunism limits recognition of the class struggle to the sphere of bourgeois relations. (Within this sphere, within its framework, not a single educated liberal will refuse to recognise the class struggle "in principle"!) Opportunism *does not extend* recognition of the class struggle to the cardinal point, to the period of *transition* from capitalism to communism, of the *overthrow* and the complete *abolition* of the bourgeoisie. In reality, this period inevitably is a period of an unprecedentedly violent class struggle in unprecedentedly acute forms, and, consequently, during this period the state must inevitably be a state that is democratic *in a new way* (for the proletariat and the propertyless in general) and dictatorial *in a new way* (against the bourgeoisie).

Further. The essence of Marx's theory of the state has been

mastered only by those who realise that the dictatorship of a *single* class is necessary not only for every class society in general, not only for the *proletariat* which has overthrown the bourgeoisie, but also for the entire *historical period* which separates capitalism from "classless society," from communism. Bourgeois states are most varied in form, but their essence is the same: all these states, whatever their form, in the final analysis are inevitably the *dictatorship of the bourgeoisie*. The transition from capitalism to communism is certainly bound to yield a tremendous abundance and variety of political forms, but the essence will inevitably be the same: *the dictatorship of the proletariat*.

Chapter III. The State and Revolution. Experience of the Paris Commune of 1871. Marx's Analysis

1. What Made the Communards' Attempt Heroic?

It is well known that in the autumn of 1870, a few months before the Commune, Marx warned the Paris workers that any attempt to overthrow the government would be the folly of despair. But when, in March 1871, a decisive battle was *forced* upon the workers and they accepted it, when the uprising had become a fact, Marx greeted the proletarian revolution with the greatest enthusiasm, in spite of unfavourable auguries. Marx did not persist in the pedantic attitude of condemning an "untimely" movement as did the ill-famed Russian renegade from Marxism, Plekhanov, who in November 1905 wrote encouragingly about the workers' and peasants' struggle, but after December 1905 cried, liberal fashion: "They should not have taken up arms."

Marx, however, was not only enthusiastic about the heroism of the Communards, who, as he expressed it, "stormed heaven." Although the mass revolutionary movement did not achieve its aim, he regarded it as a historic experience of enormous importance, as a certain advance of the world proletarian revolution, as a practical step that was more important than hundreds of programmes and arguments. Marx endeavoured to analyse this experiment, to draw tactical lessons from it and re-examine his theory in the light of it.

The only "correction" Marx thought it necessary to make to the *Communist Manifesto* he made on the basis of the revolutionary experience of the Paris Communards.

The last preface to the new German edition of the *Communist Manifesto*, signed by both its authors, is dated June 24, 1872. In this preface the authors, Karl Marx and Frederick Engels, say that the programme of the *Communist Manifesto* "has in some details become out-of-date," and they go on to say: ". . . *One thing especially was proved by the Commune, viz., that 'the working class cannot simply lay hold of the ready-made state machinery and wield it for its own purposes.'* . . ." The authors took the words that are in single quotation marks in this passage from Marx's book, *The Civil War in France*.

Thus, Marx and Engels regarded one principal and fundamental lesson of the Paris Commune as being of such enormous importance that they introduced it as an important correction into the *Communist Manifesto*.

Most characteristically, it is this important correction that has been distorted by the opportunists, and its meaning probably is not known to nine-tenths, if not ninety-nine-hundredths, of the readers of the *Communist Manifesto*. We shall deal with this distortion more fully farther on, in a chapter devoted specially to distortions. Here it will be sufficient to note that the current, vulgar "interpretation" of Marx's famous statement just quoted is that Marx here allegedly emphasises the idea of slow development in contradistinction to the seizure of power, and so on.

As a matter of fact, *the exact opposite is the case*. Marx's idea is that the working class must *break up*, *smash* the "ready-made state machinery," and not confine itself merely to laying hold of it.

On April 12, 1871, i.e., just at the time of the Commune, Marx wrote to Kugelmann: "If you look up the last chapter of my *Eighteenth Brumaire*, you will find that I declare that the next attempt of the French Revolution will be no longer, as before, to transfer the bureaucratic-military machine from one hand to another, but to *smash* it [Marx's italics—the original is *zerbrechen*], and this is the precondition for every real people's revolution on the Continent. And this is what our heroic Party comrades in Paris are attempting." (*Neue Zeit*, Vol. XX, 1, 1901–2, p. 709.)[5] (The letters of Marx to Kugelmann have appeared in Russian in no less than two editions, one of which I edited and supplied with a preface.)

The words, "to smash the bureaucratic-military machine," briefly express the principal lesson of Marxism regarding the tasks of the proletariat during a revolution in relation to the state. And it is this lesson that has been not only completely ignored, but positively distorted by the prevailing, Kautskyite, "interpretation" of Marxism!

As for Marx's reference to *The Eighteenth Brumaire*, we have quoted the relevant passage in full above.

It is interesting to note, in particular, two points in the above-quoted argument of Marx. First, he restricts his conclusion to the

5. Marx and Engels, *Selected Correspondence* (Moscow, 1965), pp. 262–63.

Continent. This was understandable in 1871, when Britain was still the model of a purely capitalist country, but without a militarist clique and, to a considerable degree, without a bureaucracy. Marx therefore excluded Britain, where a revolution, even a people's revolution, then seemed possible, and indeed was possible, *without* the precondition of destroying the "ready-made state machinery."

Today, in 1917, at the time of the first great imperialist war, this restriction made by Marx is no longer valid. Both Britain and America, the biggest and the last representatives—in the whole world—of Anglo-Saxon "liberty," in the sense that they had no militarist cliques and bureaucracy, have completely sunk into the all-European filthy, bloody morass of bureaucratic-military institutions which subordinate everything to themselves, and suppress everything. Today, in Britain and America, too, "the precondition for every real people's revolution" is the *smashing*, the *destruction* of the "ready-made state machinery" (made and brought up to "European," general imperialist, perfection in those countries in the years 1914–17).

Secondly, particular attention should be paid to Marx's extremely profound remark that the destruction of the bureaucratic-military state machine is "the precondition for every real *people's* revolution." This idea of a "people's" revolution seems strange coming from Marx, so that the Russian Plekhanovites and Mensheviks, those followers of Struve who wish to be regarded as Marxists, might possibly declare such an expression to be a "slip of the pen" on Marx's part. They have reduced Marxism to such a state of wretchedly liberal distortion that nothing exists for them beyond the antithesis between bourgeois revolution and proletarian revolution, and even this antithesis they interpret in an utterly lifeless way.

If we take the revolutions of the twentieth century as examples we shall, of course, have to admit that the Portuguese and the Turkish revolutions are both bourgeois revolutions. Neither of them, however, is a "people's" revolution, since in neither does the mass of the people, their vast majority, come out actively, independently, with their own economic and political demands to any noticeable degree. By contrast, although the Russian bourgeois revolution of 1905–7 displayed no such "brilliant" successes as at times fell to the Portuguese and Turkish revolutions, it was undoubtedly a "real people's" revolution, since the mass of the people, their majority, the very lowest social groups, crushed by oppression and exploitation, rose independently and stamped on the entire course of the revolution the imprint of *their* own demands, *their* attempts to build in their own way a new society in place of the old society that was being destroyed.

In Europe, in 1871, the proletariat did not constitute the majority of the people in any country on the Continent. A "people's" revolution, one actually sweeping the majority into its stream, could be such only if it embraced both the proletariat and the peasants. These two classes then constituted the "people." These two classes are united by the fact that the "bureaucratic-military state machine" oppresses, crushes, exploits them. To *smash* this machine, *to break it up*, is truly in the interest of the "people," of their majority, of the workers and most of the peasants, is "the precondition" for a free alliance of the poor peasants and the proletarians, whereas without such an alliance democracy is unstable and socialist transformation is impossible.

As is well known, the Paris Commune was actually working its way toward such an alliance, although it did not reach its goal owing to a number of circumstances, internal and external.

Consequently, in speaking of a "real people's revolution," Marx, without in the least discounting the special features of the petty bourgeosie (he spoke a great deal about them and often), took strict account of the actual balance of class forces in most of the continental countries of Europe in 1871. On the other hand, he stated that the "smashing" of the state machine was required by the interests of both the workers and the peasants, that it united them, that it placed before them the common task of removing the "parasite" and of replacing it by something new.

By what exactly?

2. What Is to Replace the Smashed State Machine?

In 1847, in the *Communist Manifesto*, Marx's answer to this question was as yet a purely abstract one; to be exact, it was an answer that indicated the tasks, but not the ways of accomplishing them. The answer given in the *Communist Manifesto* was that this machine was to be replaced by "the proletariat organised as the ruling class," by the "winning of the battle of democracy."

Marx did not indulge in utopias; he expected the *experience* of the mass movement to provide the reply to the question as to the specific forms this organisation of the proletariat as the ruling class would assume and as to the exact manner in which this organisation would be combined with the most complete, most consistent "winning of the battle of democracy."

Marx subjected the experience of the Commune, meagre as it was, to the most careful analysis in *The Civil War in France*. Let us quote the most important passages of this work. Originating from the Middle Ages, there developed in the nineteenth century "the centralised state power, with its ubiquitous organs of standing army, police, bureaucracy, clergy, and judicature." With the development of class antagonisms between capital and labour, "state power assumed more and more the character of a public force for the suppression of the working class, of a machine of class rule. After every revolution, which marks an advance in the class struggle, the purely coercive character of the state power stands out in bolder and bolder relief." After the revolution of 1848–49, state power became "the national war instrument of capital against labour." The Second Empire consolidated this. "The direct antithesis to the empire was the Commune." It was the "specific form" of "a republic that was not only to remove the monarchical form of class rule, but class rule itself. . . ."

What was this "specific" form of the proletarian, socialist republic? What was the state it began to create? ". . . The first decree of the Commune . . . was the suppression of the standing army, and its replacement by the armed people. . . ." This demand now figures in the programme of every party calling itself socialist. The real worth of their programmes, however, is best shown by the behaviour of our Socialist-Revolutionaries and Mensheviks, who, right after the revolution of February 27, actually refused to carry out this demand!

> The Commune was formed of the municipal councillors, chosen by universal suffrage in the various wards of Paris, responsible and revocable at any time. The majority of its members were naturally working men, or acknowledged representatives of the working class. . . . The police, which until then had been the instrument of the Government, was at once stripped of its political attributes, and turned into the responsible and at all times revocable instrument of the Commune. So were the officials of all other branches of the administration. From the members of the Commune downwards, public service had to be done at *workmen's wages*. The privileges and the representation allowances of the high dignitaries of state disappeared along with the dignitaries themselves. . . . Having once got rid of the standing army and the police, the instruments of the physical force of the old Government, the Commune proceeded at once to break the instrument of spiritual suppression, the power of the priests. . . . The judicial functionaries lost that sham independence . . . they were thenceforward to be elective, responsible, and revocable. . . .

The Commune, therefore, appears to have replaced the smashed state machine "only" by fuller democracy: abolition of the standing army; all officials to be elected and subject to recall. But as a matter of fact this "only" signifies a gigantic replacement of certain institutions by other institutions of a fundamentally different type. This is exactly a case of "quantity being transformed into quality": democracy, introduced as fully and consistently as is at all conceivable, is transformed from bourgeois into proletarian democracy; from the state (= a special force for the suppression of a particular class) into something which is no longer the state proper.

It is still necessary to suppress the bourgeoisie and crush their resistance. This was particularly necessary for the Commune; and one of the reasons for its defeat was that it did not do this with sufficient determination. The organ of suppression, however, is here the majority of the population, and not a minority, as was always the case under slavery, serfdom and wage slavery. And since the majority of the people *itself* suppresses its oppressors, a "special force" for suppression *is no longer necessary*! In this sense, the state *begins to wither away*. Instead of the special institutions of a privileged minority (privileged officialdom, the chiefs of the standing army), the majority itself can directly fulfil all these functions, and the more the functions of state power are performed by the people as a whole, the less need there is for the existence of this power.

In this connection, the following measures of the Commune, emphasised by Marx, are particularly noteworthy: the abolition of all representation allowances, and of all monetary privileges to officials, the reduction of the remuneration of *all* servants of the state to the level of *"workmen's wages."* This shows more clearly than anything else the *turn* from bourgeois to proletarian democracy, from the democracy of the oppressors to that of the oppressed classes, from the state as a *"special force"* for the suppression of a particular class to the suppression of the oppressors by the *general force* of the majority of the people—the workers and the peasants. And it is on this particularly striking point, perhaps the most important as far as the problem of the state is concerned, that the ideas of Marx have been most completely ignored! In popular commentaries, the number of which is legion, this is not mentioned. The thing done is to keep silent about it as if it were a piece of old-fashioned "naïveté," just as Christians, after their religion had been given the status of a state religion, "forgot" the "naïveté" of primitive Christianity with its democratic revolutionary spirit.

The reduction of the remuneration of high state officials seems to be "simply" a demand of naïve, primitive democracy. One of the "founders" of modern opportunism, the ex-Social-Democrat Eduard Bernstein, has more than once repeated the vulgar bourgeois jeers at "primitive" democracy. Like all opportunists, and like the present Kautskyites, he did not understand at all that, first of all, the transition from capitalism to socialism is *impossible* without a certain "reversion" to "primitive" democracy (for how else can the majority, and then the whole population without exception, proceed to discharge state functions?); and that, secondly, "primitive democracy" based on capitalism and capitalist culture is not the same as primitive democracy in prehistoric or precapitalist times. Capitalist culture has *created* large-scale production, factories, railways, the postal service, telephones, etc., and *on this basis* the great majority of the functions of the old "state power" have become so simplified and can be reduced to such exceedingly simple operations of registration, filing and checking that they can be easily performed by every literate person, can quite easily be performed for ordinary "workmen's wages," and that these functions can (and must) be stripped of every shadow of privilege, of every semblance of "official grandeur."

All officials, without exception, elected and subject to recall *at any time*, their salaries reduced to the level of ordinary "workmen's wages"—these simple and "self-evident" democratic measures, while completely uniting the interests of the workers and the majority of the peasants, at the same time serve as a bridge leading from capitalism to socialism. These measures concern the reorganisation of the state, the purely political reorganisation of society; but, of course, they acquire their full meaning and significance only in connection with the "expropriation of the expropriators" either being accomplished or in preparation, i.e., with the transformation of capitalist private ownership of the means of production into social ownership. "The Commune," Marx wrote, "made that catchword of all bourgeois revolutions, cheap government, a reality, by abolishing the two greatest sources of expenditure—the army and the officialdom."

From the peasants, as from other sections of the petty bourgeoisie, only an insignificant few "rise to the top," "get on in the world" in the bourgeois sense, i.e., become either well-do-do, bourgeois, or officials in secure and privileged positions. In every capitalist country where there are peasants (as there are in most capitalist countries), the vast majority of them are oppressed by the government and long for its overthrow, long for "cheap" government. This can be achieved *only* by the proletariat; and by achieving it, the proletariat at the same time takes a step towards the socialist reorganisation of the state.

3. Abolition of Parliamentarism

"The Commune," Marx wrote, "was to be a working, not a parliamentary, body, executive and legislative at the same time. . . . Instead of deciding once in three or six years which member of the ruling class was to represent and repress [*ver- und zertreten*] the people in parliament, universal suffrage was to serve the people constituted in communes, as individual suffrage serves every other employer in the search for workers, foremen and accountants for his business."

Owing to the prevalence of social-chauvinism and opportunism, this remarkable criticism of parliamentarism, made in 1871, also belongs now to the "forgotten words" of Marxism. The professional Cabinet Ministers and parliamentarians, the traitors to the proletariat and the "practical" socialists of our day, have left all criticism of parliamentarism to the anarchists, and, on this wonderfully reasonable ground, they denounce *all* criticism of parliamentarism as "anarchism"! It is not surprising that the proletariat of the "advanced" parliamentary countries, disgusted with such "socialists" as the Scheidemanns, Davids, Legiens, Sembats, Renaudels, Hendersons, Vanderveldes, Staunings, Brantings, Bissolatis and Co., has been with increasing frequency giving its sympathies to anarcho-syndicalism, in spite of the fact that the latter is merely the twin brother of opportunism.

For Marx, however, revolutionary dialectics was never the empty fashionable phrase, the toy rattle, which Plekhanov, Kautsky and others have made of it. Marx knew how to break with anarchism ruthlessly for its inability to make use even of the "pigsty" of bourgeois parliamentarism, especially when the situation was obviously not revolutionary; but at the same time he knew how to subject parliamentarism to genuinely revolutionary proletarian criticism.

To decide once every few years which member of the ruling class is to repress and crush the people through parliament—this is the real essence of bourgeois parliamentarism, not only in parliamentary-constitutional monarchies, but also in the most democratic republics.

But if we deal with the question of the state, and if we consider parliamentarism as one of the institutions of the state, from the point of view of the tasks of the proletariat in *this* field, what is the way out of parliamentarism? How can it be dispensed with?

Once again we must say: the lessons of Marx, based on the study of the Commune, have been so completely forgotten that the present-day "Social-Democrat" (i.e., present-day traitor to socialism) really cannot understand any criticism of parliamentarism other than anarchist or reactionary criticism.

The way out of parliamentarism is not, of course, the abolition of representative institutions and the elective principle, but the conversion of the representative institutions from talking shops into "working" bodies. "The Commune was to be a working, not a parliamentary, body, executive and legislative at the same time."

"A working, not a parliamentary, body"—this is a blow straight from the shoulder at the present-day parliamentarians and parliamentary "lap dogs" of Social-Democracy! Take any parliamentary country, from America to Switzerland, from France to Britain, Norway and so forth—in these countries the real business of "state" is performed behind the scenes and is carried on by the departments, chancelleries and General Staffs. Parliament is given up to talk for the special purpose of fooling the "common people." This is so true that even in the Russian republic, a bourgeois-democratic republic, all these sins of parliamentarism came out at once, even before it managed to set up a real parliament. The heroes of rotten philistinism, such as the Skobelevs and Tseretelis, the Chernovs and Avksentyevs, have even succeeded in polluting the Soviets after the fashion of the most disgusting bourgeois parliamentarism, in converting them into mere talking shops. In the Soviets, the "socialist" Ministers are fooling the credulous rustics with phrase-mongering and resolutions. In the government itself a sort of permanent shuffle is going on in order that, on the one hand, as many Socialist-Revolutionaries and Mensheviks as possible may in turn get near the "pie," the lucrative and honourable posts, and that, on the other hand, the "attention" of the people may be "engaged." Meanwhile the chancelleries and army staffs "do" the business of "state."

Dyelo Naroda, the organ of the ruling Socialist-Revolutionary Party, recently admitted in a leading article—with the matchless frankness of people of "good society," in which "all" are engaged in political prostitution—that even in the ministries headed by the "socialists" (save the mark!), the whole bureaucratic apparatus is in fact unchanged, is working in the old way and quite "freely" sabotaging revolutionary measures! Even without this admission, does not the actual history of the participation of the Socialist-Revolutionaries and Mensheviks in the government prove this? It is noteworthy, however, that in the ministerial company of the Cadets, the Chernovs, Rusanovs, Zenzinovs and the other editors of *Dyelo Naroda* have so completely lost all sense of shame as to brazenly assert, as if it were a mere bagatelle, that in "their" ministries everything is unchanged!! Revolutionary-democratic phrases to gull the rural Simple Simons, and bureaucracy and red tape to "gladden the hearts" of the capitalists—that is the *essence* of the "honest" coalition.

The Commune substitutes for the venal and rotten parliamentarism of bourgeois society institutions in which freedom of opinion and discussion does not degenerate into deception, for the parliamentarians themselves have to work, have to execute their own laws, have themselves to test the results achieved in reality, and to account directly to their constituents. Representative institutions remain, but there is *no* parliamentarism here as a special system, as the division of labour between the legislative and the executive, as a privileged position for the deputies. We cannot imagine democracy, even proletarian democracy, without representative institutions, but we can and *must* imagine democracy without parliamentarism, if criticism of bourgeois society is not mere words for us, if the desire to overthrow the rule of the bourgeoisie is our earnest and sincere desire, and not a mere "election" cry for catching workers' votes, as it is with the Mensheviks and Socialist-Revolutionaries, and also the Scheidemanns and Legiens, the Sembats and Vanderveldes.

It is extremely instructive to note that, in speaking of the functions of *those* officials who are necessary for the Commune and for proletarian democracy, Marx compares them to the workers of "every other employer," that is, of the ordinary capitalist enterprise, with its "workers, foremen and accountants."

There is no trace of utopianism in Marx, in the sense that he made up or invented a "new" society. No, he studied the *birth* of the new society *out of* the old, and the forms of transition from the latter to the former, as a natural-historical process. He examined the actual experience of a mass proletarian movement and tried to draw practical lessons from it. He "learned" from the Commune, just as all the great revolutionary thinkers learned unhesitatingly from the experience of great movements of the oppressed classes, and never addressed them with pedantic "homilies" (such as Plekhanov's "They should not have taken up arms" or Tsereteli's "A class must limit itself").

Abolishing the bureaucracy at once, everywhere and completely, is out of the question. It is a utopia. But to *smash* the old bureaucratic machine at once and to begin immediately to construct a new one that will make possible the gradual abolition of all bureaucracy —this is *not* a utopia, it is the experience of the Commune, the direct and immediate task of the revolutionary proletariat.

Capitalism simplifies the functions of "state" administration; it makes it possible to cast "bossing" aside and to confine the whole matter to the organisation of the proletarians (as the ruling class), which will hire "workers, foremen and accountants" in the name of the whole of society.

We are not utopians, we do not "dream" of dispensing *at once* with all administration, with all subordination. These anarchist dreams, based upon incomprehension of the tasks of the proletarian dictatorship, are totally alien to Marxism, and, as a matter of fact, serve only to postpone the socialist revolution until people are different. No, we want the socialist revolution with people as they are now, with people who cannot dispense with subordination, control and "foremen and accounts."

The subordination, however, must be to the armed vanguard of all the exploited and working people, i.e., to the proletariat. A beginning can and must be made at once, overnight, to replace the specific "bossing" of state officials by the simple functions of "foremen and accountants," functions which are already fully within the ability of the average town dweller and can well be performed for "workmen's wages."

We, the workers, shall organise large-scale production on the basis of what capitalism has already created, relying on our own experience as workers, establishing strict, iron discipline backed up by the state power of the armed workers. We shall reduce the role of state officials to that of simply carrying out our instructions as responsible, revocable, modestly paid "foremen and accountants" (of course, with the aid of technicians of all sorts, types and degrees). This is *our* proletarian task, this is what we can and must *start* with in accomplishing the proletarian revolution. Such a beginning, on the basis of large-scale production, will of itself lead to the gradual "withering away" of all bureaucracy, to the gradual creation of an order—an order without inverted commas, an order bearing no similarity to wage slavery—an order under which the functions of control and accounting, becoming more and more simple, will be performed by each in turn, will then become a habit and will finally die out as the *special* functions of a special section of the population.

A witty German Social-Democrat of the seventies of the last century called the *postal service* an example of the socialist economic system. This is very true. At present the postal service is a business organised on the lines of a state-*capitalist* monopoly. Imperialism is gradually transforming all trusts into organisations of a similar type, in which, standing over the "common" people, who are overworked and starved, one has the same bourgeois bureaucracy. But the mechanism of social management is here already to hand. Once we have overthrown the capitalists, crushed the resistance of these exploiters with the iron hand of the armed workers, and smashed the bureaucratic machine of the modern state, we shall have a splendidly-equipped mechanism, freed from the "parasite," a mechanism which can very well be set going by the united workers themselves, who will hire technicians, foremen and accountants, and pay them *all,* as indeed *all* "state" officials in general, workmen's wages. Here is a concrete, practical task which can immediately be fulfilled in relation to all trusts, a task whose fulfilment will rid the working people of exploitation, a task which takes account of what the Commune had already begun to practice (particularly in building up the state).

To organise the *whole* economy on the lines of the postal service so that the technicians, foremen and accountants, as well as *all* officials, shall receive salaries no higher than "a workman's wage," all under the control and leadership of the armed proletariat—this is our immediate aim. This is the state and this is the economic foundation we need. This is what will bring about the abolition of parliamentarism and the preservation of representative institutions. This is what will rid the labouring classes of the bourgeoisie's prostitution of these institutions.

4. Organisation of National Unity

"In a brief sketch of national organisation which the Commune had no time to develop, it states explicitly that the Commune was to be the political form of even the smallest village. . . ." The communes were to elect the "National Delegation" in Paris.

. . . The few but important functions which would still remain for a central government were not to be suppressed, as has been deliberately mis-stated, but were to be transferred to communal, i.e., strictly responsible, officials.
. . . National unity was not to be broken, but, on the contrary, organised by the communal constitution; it was to become a reality by the destruction of state power which posed as the embodiment of that unity yet wanted to be independent of, and superior to, the nation, on whose body it was but a parasitic excrescence. While the merely repressive organs of the old governmental power were to be amputated, its legitimate functions were to be wrested from an authority claiming the right to stand above society, and restored to the responsible servants of society.[6]

The extent to which the opportunists of present-day Social-Democracy have failed—perhaps it would be more true to say, have refused—to understand these observations of Marx is best shown by that book of Herostratean fame of the renegade Bernstein, *The Premises of Socialism and the Tasks of the Social-Democrats.* It is in connection with the above passage from Marx that Bernstein wrote that "as far as its political content is concerned," this programme "displays, in all its essential features, the greatest similarity to the federalism of Proudhon. . . . In spite of all the other points of difference between Marx and the 'petty-bourgeois' Proudhon [Bernstein places the word "petty-bourgeois" in inverted commas to make it sound ironical] on these points, their lines of reasoning run as close as could be." Of course, Bernstein continues, the importance of the municipalities is growing, but "it seems doubt-

6. Lenin is quoting from Marx, *The Civil War in France.* [R. T.]

ful to me whether the first job of democracy would be such a dissolution [*Auflösung*] of the modern states and such a complete transformation [*Umwandlung*] of their organisation as is visualised by Marx and Proudhon (the formation of a National Assembly from delegates of the provincial or district assemblies, which, in their turn, would consist of delegates from the communes), so that consequently the previous mode of national representation would disappear." (Bernstein, *Premises*, German edition, 1899, pp. 134 and 136.)

To confuse Marx's views on the "destruction of state power, a parasitic excrescence," with Proudhon's federalism is positively monstrous! But it is no accident, for it never occurs to the opportunist that Marx does not speak here at all about federalism as opposed to centralism, but about smashing the old bourgeois state machine which exists in all bourgeois countries.

The only thing that does occur to the opportunist is what he sees around him, in an environment of petty-bourgeois philistinism and "reformist" stagnation, namely, only "municipalities"! The opportunist has even grown out of the habit of thinking about proletarian revolution.

It is ridiculous. But the remarkable thing is that nobody argued with Bernstein on this point. Bernstein has been refuted by many, especially by Plekhanov in Russian literature and by Kautsky in European literature, but neither of them has said *anything* about *this* distortion of Marx by Bernstein.

The opportunist has so much forgotten how to think in a revolutionary way and to dwell on revolution that he attributes "federalism" to Marx, whom he confuses with the founder of anarchism, Proudhon. As for Kautsky and Plekhanov, who claim to be orthodox Marxists and defenders of the theory of revolutionary Marxism, they are silent on this point! Here is one of the roots of the extreme vulgarisation of the views on the difference between Marxism and anarchism, which is characteristic of both the Kautskyites and the opportunists, and which we shall discuss again later.

There is not a trace of federalism in Marx's above-quoted observations on the experience of the Commune. Marx agreed with Proudhon on the very point that the opportunist Bernstein did not see. Marx disagreed with Proudhon on the very point on which Bernstein found a similarity between them.

Marx agreed with Proudhon in that they both stood for the "smashing" of the modern state machine. Neither the opportunists nor the Kautskyites wish to see the similarity of views on this point between Marxism and anarchism (both Proudhon and Bakunin) because this is where they have departed from Marxism.

Marx disagreed both with Proudhon and Bakunin precisely on

the question of federalism (not to mention the dictatorship of the proletariat). Federalism as a principle follows logically from the petty-bourgeois views of anarchism. Marx was a centralist. There is no departure whatever from centralism in his observations just quoted. Only those who are imbued with the philistine "superstitious belief" in the state can mistake the destruction of the bourgeois state machine for the destruction of centralism!

Now if the proletariat and the poor peasants take state power into their own hands, organise themselves quite freely in communes, and *unite* the action of all the communes in striking at capital, in crushing the resistance of the capitalists, and in transferring the privately-owned railways, factories, land and so on to the *entire* nation, to the whole of society, won't that be centralism? Won't that be the most consistent democratic centralism and, moreover, proletarian centralism?

Bernstein simply cannot conceive of the possibility of voluntary centralism, of the voluntary amalgamation of the communes into a nation, of the voluntary fusion of the proletarian communes, for the purpose of destroying bourgeois rule and the bourgeois state machine. Like all philistines, Bernstein pictures centralism as something which can be imposed and maintained solely from above, and solely by the bureaucracy and the military clique.

As though foreseeing that his views might be distorted, Marx expressly emphasised that the charge that the Commune had wanted to destroy national unity, to abolish the central authority, was a deliberate fraud. Marx purposely used the words: "National unity was . . . to be organised," so as to oppose conscious, democratic, proletarian centralism to bourgeois, military, bureaucratic centralism.

But there are none so deaf as those who will not hear. And the very thing the opportunists of present-day Social-Democracy do not want to hear about is the destruction of state power, the amputation of the parasitic excrescence.

5. Abolition of the Parasite State

We have already quoted Marx's words on this subject, and we must now supplement them.

. . . It is generally the fate of new historical creation [he wrote] to be mistaken for the counterpart of older and even defunct forms of social life, to which they may bear a certain likeness. Thus, this new Commune, which breaks [*bricht*, smashes] the modern state power, has been regarded as a revival of the medieval communes . . . as a federation of small states (as

Montesquieu and the Girondins visualised it) . . . as an exaggerated form of the old struggle against over-centralisation. . . .

. . . The Communal Constitution would have restored to the social body all the forces hitherto absorbed by that parasitic excrescence, the "state," feeding upon and hampering the free movement of society. By this one act it would have initiated the regeneration of France. . . .

. . . The Communal Constitution would have brought the rural producers under the intellectual lead of the central towns of their districts, and there secured to them, in the town working men, the natural trustees of their interests. The very existence of the Commune involved, as a matter of course, local self-government, but no longer as a counterpoise to state power, now become superfluous.[7]

"Breaking state power," which was a "parasitic excrescence"; its "amputation," its "smashing"; "state power, now become superfluous"—these are the expressions Marx used in regard to the state when appraising and analysing the experience of the Commune.

All this was written a little less than half a century ago; and now one has to engage in excavations, as it were, in order to bring undistorted Marxism to the knowledge of the mass of the people. The conclusions drawn from the observation of the last great revolution which Marx lived through were forgotten just when the time for the next great proletarian revolutions had arrived.

. . . The multiplicity of interpretations to which the Commune has been subjected, and the multiplicity of interests which expressed themselves in it show that it was a thoroughly flexible political form, while all previous forms of government had been essentially repressive. Its true secret was this: it was essentially *a working-class government*, the result of the struggle of the producing against the appropriating class, the political form at last discovered under which the economic emancipation of labour could be accomplished. . . .

Except on this last condition, the Communal Constitution would have been an impossibility and a delusion. . . .

The utopians busied themselves with "discovering" political forms under which the socialist transformation of society was to take place. The anarchists dismissed the question of political forms altogether. The opportunists of present-day Social-Democracy accepted the bourgeois political forms of the parliamentary democratic state as the limit which should not be overstepped; they battered their foreheads praying before this "model," and denounced as anarchism every desire to *break* these forms.

Marx deduced from the whole history of socialism and the polit-

7. All quotations from Marx in this section are from *The Civil War in France*. [R. T.]

ical struggle that the state was bound to disappear, and that the transitional form of its disappearance (the transition from state to non-state) would be the "proletariat organised as the ruling class." Marx, however, did not set out to *discover* the political *forms* of this future stage. He limited himself to carefully observing French history, to analysing it, and to drawing the conclusion to which the year 1851 had led, namely, that matters were moving towards the *destruction* of the bourgeois state machine.

And when the mass revolutionary movement of the proletariat burst forth, Marx, in spite of its failure, in spite of its short life and patent weakness, began to study the forms it had *discovered*.

The Commune is the form "at last discovered" by the proletarian revolution, under which the economic emancipation of labour can take place.

The Commune is the first attempt by a proletarian revolution to *smash* the bourgeois state machine; and it is the political form "at last discovered," by which the smashed state machine can and must be *replaced*.

We shall see further on that the Russian revolutions of 1905 and 1917, in different circumstances and under different conditions, continue the work of the Commune and confirm Marx's brilliant historical analysis.

Chapter IV. Continuation. Supplementary Explanations by Engels

Marx gave the fundamentals concerning the significance of the experience of the Commune. Engels returned to the same subject time and again, and explained Marx's analysis and conclusions, sometimes elucidating *other* aspects of the question with such power and vividness that it is necessary to deal with his explanations specially.

1. The Housing Question

In his work, *The Housing Question* (1872), Engels already took into account the experience of the Commune, and dealt several times with the tasks of the revolution in relation to the state. It is interesting to note that the testament of this specific subject clearly revealed, on the one hand, points of similarity between the proletarian state and the present state—points that warrant speaking of the state in both cases—and, on the other hand, points of difference between them, or the transition to the destruction of the state.

How is the housing question to be settled, then? In present-day society, it is settled just as any other social question: by the gradual economic levelling of demand and supply, a settlement which reproduces the question itself again and again and therefore is no settlement. How a social revolution would settle this question not only depends on the circumstances in each particular case, but is also connected with much more far-reaching questions, one of the most fundamental of which is the abolition of the antithesis between town and country. As it is not our task to create utopian systems for the organisation of the future society, it would be more than idle to go into the question here. But one thing is certain: there is already a sufficient quantity of houses in the big cities to remedy immediately all real "housing *shortage*," provided they are used judiciously. This can naturally only occur through the expropriation of the present owners and by quartering in their houses homeless workers or workers overcrowded in their present homes. As soon as the proletariat has won political power, such a measure prompted by concern for the common good will be just as easy to carry out as are other expropriations and billetings by the present-day state. [German edition, 1887, p. 22.]

The change in the form of state power is not examined here, but only the content of its activity. Expropriations and billetings take place by order even of the present state. From the formal point of view, the proletarian state will also "order" the occupation of dwellings and expropriation of houses. But it is clear that the old executive apparatus, the bureaucracy, which is connected with the bourgeoisie, would simply be unfit to carry out the orders of the proletarian state.

. . . It must be pointed out that the "actual seizure" of all the instruments of labour, the taking possession of industry as a whole by the working people, is the exact opposite of the Proudhonist "redemption." In the latter case the individual worker becomes the owner of the dwelling, the peasant farm, the instruments of labour; in the former case, the "working people" remain the collective owners of the houses, factories and instruments of labour, and will hardly permit their use, at least during a transitional period, by individuals or associations without compensation for the cost. In the same way, the abolition of property in land is not the abolition of ground rent but its transfer, if in a modified form, to society. The actual seizure of all the instruments of labour by the working people, therefore, does not at all preclude the retention of rent relations. [P. 68.]

We shall examine the question touched upon in this passage, namely, the economic basis for the withering away of the state, in the next chapter. Engels expresses himself most cautiously, saying that the proletarian state would "hardly" permit the use of houses without payment, "at least during a transitional period." The letting of houses owned by the whole people to individual families presupposes the collection of rent, a certain amount of control, and the employment of some standard in allotting the housing. All this calls for a certain form of state, but it does not at all call for a special military and bureaucratic apparatus, with officials occupying especially privileged positions. The transition to a situation in which it will be possible to supply dwellings rent-free depends on the complete "withering away" of the state.

Speaking of the Blanquists' adoption of the fundamental position of Marxism after the Commune and under the influence of its experience, Engels, in passing, formulates this position as follows: ". . . Necessity of political action by the proletariat and of its dictatorship as the transition to the abolition of classes and, with them, of the state. . . ." (P. 55.) Addicts to hair-splitting criticism, or bourgeois "exterminators of Marxism," will perhaps see a contradiction between this *recognition* of the "abolition of the state" and repudiation of this formula as an anarchist one in the above passage from *Anti-Dühring*. It would not be surprising if the opportunists classed Engels, too, as an "anarchist," for it is becoming increasingly common with the social-chauvinists to accuse the internationalists of anarchism.

Marxism has always taught that with the abolition of classes the state will also be abolished. The well-known passage on the "withering away of the state" in *Anti-Dühring* accuses the anarchists not simply of favouring the abolition of the state, but of preaching that the state can be abolished "overnight."

As the now prevailing "Social-Democratic" doctrine completely distorts the relation of Marxism to anarchism on the question of the abolition of the state, it will be particularly useful to recall a certain controversy in which Marx and Engels came out against the anarchists.

2. Controversy with the Anarchists

This controversy took place in 1873. Marx and Engels contributed articles against the Proudhonists, "autonomists" or "anti-authoritarians," to an Italian socialist annual, and it was not until 1913 that these articles appeared in German in *Neue Zeit*.[8] "If the political struggle of the working class assumes revolutionary forms,"

---

8. The articles referred to are "Political Indifferentism" by Marx and "On Authority" by Engels. On pp. 353–55, below, Lenin again refers to these articles. [R. T.]

wrote Marx, ridiculing the anarchists for their repudiation of politics, "and if the workers set up their revolutionary dictatorship in place of the dictatorship of the bourgeoisie, they commit the terrible crime of violating principles, for in order to satisfy their wretched, vulgar everyday needs and to crush the resistance of the bourgeoisie, they give the state a revolutionary and transient form, instead of laying down their arms and abolishing the state. . . ." (*New Zeit*, Vol. XXII, 1, 1913–14, p. 40.)

It was solely against this kind of "abolition" of the state that Marx fought in refuting the anarchists! He did not at all oppose the view that the state would disappear when classes disappeared, or that it would be abolished when classes were abolished. What he did oppose was the proposition that the workers should renounce the use of arms, organised violence, *that is, the state*, which is to serve to "crush the resistance of the bourgeoisie."

To prevent the true meaning of his struggle against anarchism from being distorted, Marx expressly emphasised the "revolutionary and *transient* form" of the state which the proletariat needs. The proletariat needs the state only temporarily. We do not at all differ with the anarchists on the question of the abolition of the state as the *aim*. We maintain that, to achieve this aim, we must temporarily make use of the instruments, resources and methods of state power *against* the exploiters, just as the temporary dictatorship of the oppressed class is necessary for the abolition of classes. Marx chooses the sharpest and clearest way of stating his case against the anarchists: After overthrowing the yoke of the capitalists, should the workers "lay down their arms," or use them against the capitalists in order to crush their resistance? But what is the systematic use of arms by one class against another if not a "transient form" of state?

Let every Social-Democrat ask himself: Is *that* how he has been posing the question of the state in controversy with the anarchists? Is *that* how it has been posed by the vast majority of the official socialist parties of the Second International?

Engels expounds the same ideas in much greater detail and still more popularly. First of all he ridicules the muddled ideas of the Proudhonists, who called themselves "anti-authoritarians," i.e., repudiated all authority, all subordination, all power. Take a factory, a railway, a ship on the high seas, said Engels: is it not clear that not one of these complex technical establishments, based on the use of machinery and the systematic co-operation of many people, could function without a certain amount of subordination and, consequently, without a certain amount of authority or power? ". . . When I counter the most rabid anti-authoritarians with these arguments, the only answer they can give me is the following: Oh, that's true, except that here it is not a question of authority with which we vest our delegates, *but of a commission!* These people imagine they can change a thing by changing its name. . . ."

Having thus shown that authority and autonomy are relative terms, that the sphere of their application varies with the various phases of social development, that it is absurd to take them as absolutes, and adding that the sphere of application of machinery and large-scale production is steadily expanding, Engels passes from the general discussion of authority to the question of the state.

> Had the autonomists [he wrote] contented themselves with saying that the social organisation of the future would allow authority only within the bounds which the conditions of production make inevitable, one could have come to terms with them. But they are blind to all facts that make authority necessary and they passionately fight the word.
> Why do the anti-authoritarians not confine themselves to crying out against political authority, the state? All socialists are agreed that the state, and with it political authority, will disappear as a result of the coming social revolution, that is, that public functions will lose their political character and become mere administrative functions of watching over social interests. But the anti-authoritarians demand that the political state be abolished at one stroke, even before the social relations that gave birth to it have been destroyed. They demand that the first act of the social revolution shall be the abolition of authority.
> Have these gentlemen ever seen a revolution? A revolution is certainly the most authoritarian thing there is; it is an act whereby one part of the population imposes its will upon the other part by means of rifles, bayonets and cannon, all of which are highly authoritarian means. And the victorious party must maintain its rule by means of the terror which its arms inspire in the reactionaries. Would the Paris Commune have lasted more than a day if it had not used the authority of the armed people against the bourgeoisie? Cannot we, on the contrary, blame it for having made too little use of that authority? Therefore, one of two things: either the anti-authoritarians don't know what they are talking about, in which case they are creating nothing but confusion. Or they do know, and in that case they are betraying the cause of the proletariat. In either case they serve only reaction. [P. 39.]

This argument touches upon questions which should be examined in connection with the relationship between politics and economics during the withering away of the state (the next chapter is devoted to this). These questions are: the transformation of public functions from political into simple functions of administration, and the "political state." This last term, one particularly liable to cause misunderstanding, indicates the process of the withering away of the state: at a certain stage of this process, the state which is withering away may be called a non-political state.

Again, the most remarkable thing in this argument of Engels is the way he states his case against the anarchists. Social-Democrats, claiming to be disciples of Engels, have argued on this subject against the anarchists millions of times since 1873, but they have *not* argued as Marxists could and should. The anarchist idea of the abolition of the state is muddled and *non-revolutionary*—that is how Engels put it. It is precisely the revolution in its rise and development, with its specific tasks in relation to violence, authority, power, the state, that the anarchists refuse to see.

The usual criticism of anarchism by present-day Social-Democrats has boiled down to the purest philistine banality: "We recognise the state, whereas the anarchists do not!" Naturally, such banality cannot but repel workers who are at all capable of thinking and revolutionary-minded. What Engels says is different. He stresses that all socialists recognise that the state will disappear as a result of the socialist revolution. He then deals specifically with the question of the revolution—the very question which, as a rule, the Social-Democrats evade out of opportunism, leaving it, so to speak, exclusively for the anarchists "to work out." And when dealing with this question, Engels takes the bull by the horns; he asks: should not the Commune have made *more* use of the *revolutionary* power of the *state*, that is, of the proletariat armed and organised as the ruling class?

Prevailing official Social-Democracy usually dismissed the question of the concrete tasks of the proletariat in the revolution either with a philistine sneer, or, at best, with the sophistic evasion: "The future will show." And the anarchists were justified in saying about such Social-Democrats that they were failing in their task of giving the workers a revolutionary education. Engels draws upon the experience of the last proletarian revolution precisely for the purpose of making a most concrete study of what should be done by the proletariat, and in what manner, in relation to both the banks and the state.

3. Letter to Bebel

One of the most, if not *the* most, remarkable observation on the state in the works of Marx and Engels is contained in the following passage in Engels's letter to Bebel dated March 18–28, 1875. This letter, we may observe in parenthesis, was, as far as we know, first published by Bebel in the second volume of his memoirs (*Aus meinem Leben*), which appeared in 1911, i.e., thirty-six years after the letter had been written and sent.

Engels wrote to Bebel criticising that same draft of the Gotha Programme which Marx criticised in his famous letter to Bracke. Referring specially to the question of the state, Engels said:

> The free people's state has been transformed into the free state. Taken in its grammatical sense, a free state is one where the state is free in relation to its citizens, hence a state with a despotic government. The whole talk about the state should be dropped, especially since the Commune, which was no longer a state in the proper sense of the word. The "people's state" has been thrown in our faces by the anarchists to the point of disgust, although already Marx's book against Proudhon and later the *Communist Manifesto* say plainly that with the introduction of the socialist order of society the state dissolves of itself [*sich auflöst*] and disappears. As the state is only a transitional institution which is used in the struggle, in the revolution, to hold down one's adversaries by force, it is sheer nonsense to talk of a "free people's state"; so long as the proletariat still *needs* the state, it does not need it in the interests of freedom but in order to hold down its adversaries, and as soon as it becomes possible to speak of freedom the state as such ceases to exist. We would therefore propose replacing *state* everywhere by *Gemeinwesen*, a good old German word which can very well take the place of the French word *commune*. [Pp. 321–22 of the German original.][9]

It should be borne in mind that this letter refers to the party programme which Marx criticised in a letter dated only a few weeks later than the above (Marx's letter is dated May 5, 1875), and that at the time Engels was living with Marx in London. Consequently, when he says "we" in the last sentence, Engels undoubtedly, in his own as well as in Marx's name, suggests to the leader of the German workers' party that the word "state" *be struck out of the programme* and replaced by the word "*community.*"

What a howl about "anarchism" would be raised by the leading lights of present-day "Marxism," which has been falsified for the convenience of the opportunists, if such an amendment of the programme were suggested to them!

Let them howl. This will earn them the praises of the bourgeoisie.

And we shall go on with our work. In revising the programme of our Party, we must by all means take the advice of Engels and Marx into consideration in order to come nearer the truth, to restore Marxism by ridding it of distortions, to guide the struggle of the working class for its emancipation more correctly. Certainly no

9. Marx and Engels, *Selected Correspondence* (Moscow, 1965), pp. 293–94.

one opposed to the advice of Engels and Marx will be found among the Bolsheviks. The only difficulty that may perhaps arise will be in regard to the term. In German there are two words meaning "community," of which Engels used the one which does *not* denote a single community, but their totality, a system of communities. In Russian there is no such word, and we may have to choose the French word *commune*, although this also has its drawbacks.

"The Commune was no longer a state in the proper sense of the word"—this is the most theoretically important statement Engels makes. After what has been said above, this statement is perfectly clear. The Commune *was ceasing* to be a state since it had to suppress, not the majority of the population, but a minority (the exploiters). It had smashed the bourgeois state machine. In place of a *special* coercive force the population itself came on the scene. All this was a departure from the state in the proper sense of the word. And had the Commune become firmly established, all traces of the state in it would have "withered away" of themselves; it would not have had to "abolish" the institutions of the state—they would have ceased to function as they ceased to have anything to do.

"The 'people's state' has been thrown in our faces by the anarchists." In saying this, Engels above all has in mind Bakunin and his attacks on the German Social-Democrats. Engels admits that these attacks were justified *insofar* as the "people's state" was as much an absurdity and as much a departure from socialism as the "free people's state." Engels tried to put the struggle of the German Social-Democrats against the anarchists on the right lines, to make this struggle correst in principle, to rid it of opportunist prejudices concerning the "state." Unfortunately, Engels's letter was pigeon-holed for thirty-six years. We shall see farther on that, even after this letter was published, Kautsky persisted in virtually the same mistakes against which Engels had warned.

Bebel replied to Engels in a letter dated September 21, 1875, in which he wrote, among other things, that he "fully agreed" with Engels's opinion of the draft programme, and that he had reproached Liebknecht with readiness to make concessions (p. 334 of the German edition of Bebel's memoirs, Vol. II). But if we take Bebel's pamphlet, *Our Aims*, we find there views on the state that are absolutely wrong. "The state must . . . be transformed from one based on *class rule* into a *people's state*" (*Unsere Ziele*, German edition, 1886, p. 14). This was printed in the *ninth* (the ninth!) edition of Bebel's pamphlet! It is not surprising that opportunist views on the state, so persistently repeated, were absorbed by the German Social-Democrats, especially as Engels's revolutionary interpretations had been safely pigeon-holed, and all the conditions of life were such as to "wean" them from revolution for a long time.

4. Criticism of the Draft of the Erfurt Programme

In analysing Marxist teachings on the state, the criticism of the draft of the Erfurt Programme,[1] sent by Engels to Kautsky on June 29, 1891, and only published ten years later in *Neue Zeit*, cannot be ignored; for it is with the *opportunist* views of the Social-Democrats on questions of *state* organisation that this criticism is mainly concerned.

We shall note in passing that Engels also makes an exceedingly valuable observation on economic questions, which shows how attentively and thoughtfully he watched the various changes occurring in modern capitalism, and how for this reason he was able to foresee to a certain extent the tasks of our present, the imperialist, epoch. Here is that observation: referring to the word "planlessness" (*Planlosigkeit*), used in the draft programme, as characteristic of capitalism, Engels wrote: "When we pass from joint-stock companies to trusts which assume control over, and monopolise, whole industries, it is not only private production that ceases, but also planlessness" (*Neue Zeit*, Vol. XX, 1, 1901–2, p. 8).

Here we have what is most essential in the theoretical appraisal of the latest phase of capitalism, i.e., imperialism, namely, that capitalism becomes monopoly *capitalism*. The latter must be emphasised because the erroneous bourgeois reformist assertion that monopoly capitalism or state-monopoly capitalism is *no longer* capitalism, but can now be called "state socialism" and so on, is very common. The trusts, of course, never provided, do not now provide, and cannot provide complete planning. But however much they do plan, however much the capitalist magnates calculate in advance the volume of production on a national and even on an international scale, and however much they systematically regulate it, we still remain under *capitalism*—at its new stage, it is true, but still capitalism, without a doubt. The "proximity" of *such* capitalism to socialism should serve genuine representatives of the proletariat as an argument proving the proximity, facility, feasibility and urgency of the socialist revolution, and not at all as an argument for tolerating the repudiation of such a revolution and the efforts to make capitalism look more attractive, something which all reformists are trying to do.

But to return to the question of the state. In his letter Engels makes three particularly valuable suggestions: first, in regard to the republic; second, in regard to the connection between the national

---

1. Engels criticised the errors in the Erfurt Programme in his article "Criticism and the Draft Social-Democratic Programme of 1891." On pp. 359–63, below, Lenin quotes from the same work.

question and state organisation, and, third, in regard to local self-government.

In regard to the republic, Engels made this the focal point of his criticism of the draft of the Erfurt Programme. And when we recall the importance which the Erfurt Programme acquired for all the Social-Democrats of the world, and that it became the model for the whole Second International, we may say without exaggeration that Engels thereby criticised the opportunism of the whole Second International. "The political demands of the draft," Engels wrote, "have one great fault. *It lacks* [Engels's italics] precisely what should have been said." And, later on, he makes it clear that the German Constitution is, strictly speaking, a copy of the extremely reactionary Constitution of 1850, that the Reichstag is only, as Wilhelm Liebknecht put it, "the fig leaf of absolutism" and that to wish "to transform all the instruments of labour into common property" on the basis of a constitution which legalises the existence of petty states and the federation of petty German states is an "obvious absurdity." "To touch on that is dangerous, however," Engels added, knowing only too well that it was impossible legally to include in the programme the demand for a republic in Germany. But he refused to merely accept this obvious consideration which satisfied "everybody." He continued:

> Nevertheless, somehow or other, the thing has to be attacked. How necessary this is is shown precisely at the present time by opportunism, which is gaining ground [*einreissende*] in a large section of the Social-Democratic press. Fearing a renewal of the Anti-Socialist Law,[2] or recalling all manner of overhasty pronouncements made during the reign of that law, they now want the Party to find the present legal order in Germany adequate for putting through all Party demands by peaceful means. . . .

Engels particularly stressed the fundamental fact that the German Social-Democrats were prompted by fear of a renewal of the Anti-Socialist Law, and explicitly described it as opportunism; he declared that precisely because there was no republic and no freedom in Germany, the dreams of a "peaceful" path were perfectly absurd. Engels was careful not to tie his hands. He admitted that in republican or very free countries "one can conceive" (only "conceive"!) of a peaceful development towards socialism, but in Ger-

2. The Anti-Socialist Law was promulgated in Germany in 1878 by the Bismarck government in the struggle against the working-class and socialist movement. The law prohibited all organisations of the Social-Democratic Party, mass workers' organisations and the working-class press; socialist literature was confiscated; during the years in which the law was operative about 350 Social-Democratic organisations were broken up, some 900 Social-Democrats were banished from Germany, 1,500 were imprisoned, and hundreds of newspapers, magazines and non-periodical publications were banned. The Anti-Socialist Law as annulled in 1890.

many, he repeated, ". . . in Germany, where the government is almost omnipotent and the Reichstag and all other representative bodies have no real power, to advocate such a thing in Germany, where, moreover, there is no need to do so, means removing the fig leaf from absolutism and becoming oneself a screen for its nakedness."

The great majority of the official leaders of the German Social-Democratic Party, which pigeon-holed this advice, have really proved to be a screen for absolutism.

> . . . In the long run such a policy can only lead one's own party astray. They push general, abstract political questions into the foreground, thereby concealing the immediate concrete questions, which at the moment of the first great events, the first political crisis, automatically pose themselves. What can result from this except that at the decisive moment the party suddenly proves helpless and that uncertainty and discord on the most decisive issues reign in it because these issues have never been discussed? . . .
>
> This forgetting of the great, the principal considerations for the momentary interests of the day, this struggling and striving for the success of the moment regardless of later consequences, this sacrifice of the future of the movement for its present may be "honestly" meant, but it is and remains opportunism, and "honest" opportunism is perhaps the most dangerous of all. . . .
>
> If one thing is certain it is that our party and the working class can only come to power in the form of the democratic republic. This is even the specific form for the dictatorship of the proletariat, as the Great French Revolution has already shown. . . .

Engels repeated here in a particularly striking form the fundamental idea which runs through all of Marx's works, namely, that the democratic republic is the nearest approach to the dictatorship of the proletariat. For such a republic, without in the least abolishing the rule of capital, and, therefore, the oppression of the masses and the class struggle, inevitably leads to such an extension, development, unfolding and intensification of this struggle that, as soon as it becomes possible to meet the fundamental interests of the oppressed masses, this possibility is realised inevitably and solely through the dictatorship of the proletariat, through the leadership of those masses by the proletariat. These, too, are "forgotten words" of Marxism for the whole of the Second International, and the fact that they have been forgotten was demonstrated with particular vividness by the history of the Menshevik Party during the first six months of the Russian revolution of 1917.

On the subject of a federal republic, in connection with the national composition of the population, Engels wrote:

What should take the place of present-day Germany [with its reactionary monarchical Constitution and its equally reactionary division into petty states, a division which perpetuates all the specific features of "Prussianism" instead of dissolving them in Germany as a whole]? In my view, the proletariat can only use the form of the one and indivisible republic. In the gigantic territory of the United States, a federal republic is still, on the whole, a necessity, although in the Eastern states it is already becoming a hindrance. It would be a step forward in Britain where the two islands are peopled by four nations and in spite of a single Parliament three different systems of legislation already exist side by side. In little Switzerland, it has long been a hindrance, tolerable only because Switzerland is content to be a purely passive member of the European state system. For Germany, federalisation on the Swiss model would be an enormous step backward. Two points distinguish a union state from a completely unified state: first, that each member state, each canton, has its own civil and criminal legislative and judicial system, and, second, that alongside a popular chamber there is also a federal chamber in which each canton, whether large or small, votes as such. In Germany, the union state is the transition to the completely unified state, and the "revolution from above" of 1866 and 1870[3] must not be reversed but supplemented by a "movement from below."

Far from being indifferent to the forms of state, Engels, on the contrary, tried to analyse the transitional forms with the utmost thoroughness in order to establish, in accordance with the concrete historical peculiarities of each particular case, *from what and to what* the given transitional form is passing.

Approaching the matter from the standpoint of the proletariat and the proletarian revolution, Engels, like Marx, upheld democratic centralism, the republic—one and indivisible. He regarded the federal republic either as an exception and a hindrance to development, or as a transition from a monarchy to a centralised republic, as a "step forward" under certain special conditions. And among these special conditions, he puts the national question to the fore.

Although mercilessly criticising the reactionary nature of small states, and the screening of this by the national question in certain concrete cases, Engels, like Marx, never betrayed the slightest desire to brush aside the national question—a desire of which the Dutch and Polish Marxists, who proceed from their perfectly justi-

---

3. This refers to the unification of Germany carried out by the Prussian ruling classes "from above" by means of the "blood and iron" policy, by diplomatic intrigues and wars. The war between Prussia and Austria in 1866 resulted in the foundation of the North-German Union, and the Franco-Prussian war of 1870–71 led to the foundation of the German Empire.

fied opposition to the narrow philistine nationalism of "their" little states, are often guilty.

Even in regard to Britain, where geographical conditions, a common language and the history of many centuries would seem to have "put an end" to the national question in the various small divisions of the country—even in regard to that country, Engels reckoned with the plain fact that the national question was not yet a thing of the past, and recognised in consequence that the establishment of a federal republic would be a "step forward." Of course, there is not the slightest hint here of Engels abandoning the criticism of the shortcomings of a federal republic or renouncing the most determined advocacy of, and struggle for, a unified and centralised democratic republic.

But Engels did not at all mean democratic centralism in the bureaucratic sense in which this term is used by bourgeois and petty-bourgeois ideologists, the anarchists among the latter. His idea of centralism did not in the least preclude such broad local self-government as would combine the voluntary defence of the unity of the state by the "communes" and districts, and the complete elimination of all bureaucratic practices and all "ordering" from above. Carrying forward the programme views of Marxism on the state, Engels wrote:

So, then, a unified republic—but not in the sense of the present French Republic, which is nothing but the Empire established in 1798 without the Emperor. From 1792 to 1798 each French department, each commune [*Gemeinde*], enjoyed complete self-government on the American model, and this is what we too must have. How self-government is to be organised and how we can manage without a bureaucracy has been shown to us by America and the first French Republic, and is being shown even today by Australia, Canada and the other English colonies. And a provincial [regional] and communal self-government of this type is far freer than, for instance, Swiss federalism, under which, it is true, the canton is very independent in relation to the Bund [i.e., the federated state as a whole], but is also independent in relation to the district [*Bezirk*] and the commune. The cantonal governments appoint the district governors [*Bezirksstatthalter*] and prefects—which is unknown in English-speaking countries and which we want to abolish here as resolutely in the future as the Prussian *Landräte* and *Regierungsräte* [commissioners, district police chiefs, governors, and in general all officials appointed from above].

Accordingly, Engels proposes the following wording for the self-government clause in the programme: "Complete self-government for the provinces [gubernias or regions], districts and communes through officials elected by universal suffrage. The abolition of all local and provincial authorities appointed by the state."

I have already had occasion to point out—in *Pravda* (No. 68, May 28, 1917), which was suppressed by the government of Kerensky and other "socialist" Ministers—how on this point (of course, not on this point alone by any means) our pseudo-socialist representatives of pseudo-revolutionary pseudo-democracy have made glaring departures *from democracy*. Naturally, people who have bound themselves by a "coalition" to the imperialist bourgeoisie have remained deaf to this criticism.

It is extremely important to note that Engels, armed with facts, disproved by a most precise example the prejudice which is very widespread, particularly among petty-bourgeois democrats, that a federal republic necessarily means a greater amount of freedom than a centralised republic. This is wrong. It is disproved by the facts cited by Engels regarding the centralised French Republic of 1792–98 and the federal Swiss Republic. The really democratic centralised republic gave *more* freedom than the federal republic. In other words, the *greatest* amount of local, regional and other freedom known in history was accorded by a *centralized* and not by a federal republic.

Insufficient attention has been and is being paid in our Party propaganda and agitation to this fact, as, indeed, to the whole question of the federal and the centralised republic and local self-government.

5. The 1891 Preface to Marx's The Civil War in France

In his preface to the third edition of *The Civil War in France* (this preface is dated March 18, 1891, and was originally published in *Neue Zeit*), Engels, in addition to some interesting incidental remarks on questions concerning the attitude towards the state, gave a remarkably vivid summary of the lessons of the Commune. This summary, made more profound by the entire experience of the twenty years that separated the author from the Commune, and directed expressly against the "superstitious belief in the state" so widespread in Germany, may justly be called the *last word* of Marxism on the question under consideration.

In France, Engels observed, the workers emerged with arms from every revolution; "therefore the disarming of the workers was the first commandment for the bourgeois, who were at the helm of the state. Hence, after every revolution won by the workers, a new struggle, ending with the defeat of the workers." This summary of the experience of bourgeois revolutions is as concise as it is expressive. The essence of the matter—among other things, on the question of the state (*has the oppressed class arms?*)—is here remarkably well grasped. It is precisely this essence that is most often evaded both by professors influenced by bourgeois ideology, and by petty-bourgeois democrats. In the Russian revolution of 1917, the honour (Cavaignac honour) of blabbing this secret of bourgeois revolutions fell to the Menshevik, would-be Marxist, Tsereteli. In his "historic" speech of June 11, Tsereteli blurted out that the bourgeoisie were determined to disarm the Petrograd workers—presenting, of course, this decision as his own, and as a necessity for the "state" in general!

Tsereteli's historic speech of June 11 will, of course, serve every historian of the revolution of 1917 as a graphic illustration of how the Socialist-Revolutionary and Menshevik bloc, led by Mr. Tsereteli, deserted to the bourgeoisie *against* the revolutionary proletariat.

Another incidental remark of Engels's, also connected with the question of the state, deals with religion. It is well known that the German Social-Democrats, as they degenerated and became increasingly opportunist, slipped more and more frequently into the philistine misinterpretation of the celebrated formula: "Religion is to be declared a private matter." That is, this formula was twisted to mean that religion was a private matter *even for the party* of the revolutionary proletariat!! It was against this complete betrayal of the revolutionary programme of the proletariat that Engels vigorously protested. In 1891 he saw only the *very feeble* beginnings of opportunism in his party, and, therefore, he expressed himself with extreme caution:

> As almost only workers, or recognised representatives of the workers, sat in the Commune, its decisions bore a decidedly proletarian character. Either they decreed reforms which the republican bourgeoisie had failed to pass solely out of cowardice, but which provided a necessary basis for the free activity of the working class—such as the realisation of the principle that in *relation to the state* religion is a purely private matter—or the Commune promulgated decrees which were in the direct interest of the working class and in part cut deeply into the old order of society.

Engels deliberately emphasised the words "in relation to the state," as a straight thrust at German opportunism, which had declared religion to be a private matter *in relation to the party*, thus degrading the party of the revolutionary proletariat to the level of the most vulgar "free-thinking" philistinism, which is prepared to allow a non-denominational status, but which renounces the *party* struggle against the opium of religion which stupefies the people.

The future historian of the German Social-Democrats, in tracing the roots of their shameful bankruptcy in 1914, will find a fair amount of interesting material on this question, beginning with the evasive declarations in the articles of the party's ideological leader, Kautsky, which throw the door wide open to opportunism, and ending with the attitude of the party towards the "Los-von-Kirche-Bewegung" (the "Leave-the-Church" movement) in 1913.

But let us see how, twenty years after the Commune, Engels summed up its lessons for the fighting proletariat.

Here are the lessons to which Engels attached prime importance:

> . . . It was precisely the oppressing power of the former central-ised government, army, political police, bureaucracy, which Napoleon had created in 1798 and which every new government had since then taken over as a welcome instrument and used against its opponents—it was this power which was to fall everywhere, just as it had fallen in Paris.
>
> From the very outset the Commune had to recognise that the working class, once in power, could not go on managing with the old state machine; that in order not to lose again its only just gained supremacy, this working class must, on the one hand, do away with all the old machinery of oppression previously used against it itself, and, on the other, safeguard itself against its own deputies and officials, by declaring them all, without exception, subject to recall at any time. . . .

Engels emphasised once again that not only under a monarchy, but *also in a democratic republic* the state remains a state, i.e., it retains its fundamental distinguishing feature of transforming the officials, the "servants of society," its organs, into the *masters* of society.

> Against this transformation of the state and the organs of the state from servants of society into masters of society—an inevitable transformation in all previous states—the Commune used two infallible means. In the first place, it filled all posts—administrative, judicial and educational—by election on the basis of universal suffrage of all concerned, subject to recall at any time by the electors. And, in the second place, it paid all officials, high or low, only the wages received by other workers. The highest salary paid by the Commune to anyone was 6,000 francs.[4] In this way a dependable barrier to place-hunting and careerism was set up, even apart from the binding mandates to delegates to representative bodies, which were added besides. . . .

---

4. Nominally about 2,400 rubles or, according to the present rate of exchange, about 6,000 rubles. The action of those Bolsheviks who propose that a salary of 9,000 rubles be paid to members of municipal councils, for instance, instead of a maximum salary of 6,000 rubles—quite an adequate sum—*throughout the state*, is inexcusable. [*Lenin*]

Engels here approached the interesting boundary line at which consistent democracy, on the one hand, is *transformed* into socialism and, on the other, *demands* socialism. For, in order to abolish the state, it is necessary to convert the functions of the civil service into the simple operations of control and accounting that are within the scope and ability of the vast majority of the population, and, subsequently, of every single individual. And if careerism is to be abolished completely, it must be made *impossible* for "honourable" though profitless posts in the Civil Service to be used as a springboard to highly lucrative posts in banks or joint-stock companies, as *constantly* happens in all the freest capitalist countries.

Engels, however, did not make the mistake some Marxists make in dealing, for example, with the question of the right of nations to self-determination, when they argue that it is impossible under capitalism and will be superfluous under socialism. This seemingly clever but actually incorrect statement might be made in regard to *any* democratic institution, including moderate salaries for officials, because fully consistent democracy is impossible under capitalism, and under socialism all democracy *will wither away*.

This is a sophism like the old joke about a man becoming bald by losing one more hair.

To develop democracy *to the utmost*, to find the *forms* for this development, to test them *by practice*, and so forth—all this is one of the component tasks of the struggle for the social revolution. Taken separately, no kind of democracy will bring socialism. But in actual life democracy will never be "taken separately"; it will be "taken together" with other things, it will exert its influence on economic life as well, will stimulate *its* transformation; and in its turn it will be influenced by economic development, and so on. This is the dialectics of living history.

Engels continued:

. . . This shattering [*Sprengung*] of the former state power and its replacement by a new and truly democratic one is described in detail in the third section of *The Civil War*. But it was necessary to touch briefly here once more on some of its features, because in Germany particularly the superstitious belief in the state has passed from philosophy into the general consciousness of the bourgeoisie and even of many workers. According to the philosophical conception, the state is the "realisation of the idea," or the Kingdom of God on earth, translated into philosophical terms, the sphere in which eternal truth and justice are, or should be, realised. And from this follows a superstitious reverence for the state and everything connected with it, which takes root the more readily since people are accustomed from childhood to imagine that the affairs and interests common to the whole of society could not be looked after other than as they have been looked after in the past, that is, through the state and its lucratively positioned officials. And people think they have taken quite an extraordinarily bold step forward when they have rid themselves of belief in hereditary monarchy and swear by the democratic republic. In reality, however, the state is nothing but a machine for the oppression of one class by another, and indeed in the democratic republic no less than in the monarchy. And at best it is an evil inherited by the proletariat after its victorious struggle for class supremacy, whose worst sides the victorious proletariat will have to lop off as speedily as possible, just as the Commune had to, until a generation reared in new, free social conditions is able to discard the entire lumber of the state.

Engels warned the Germans not to forget the principles of socialism with regard to the state in general in connection with the substitution of a republic for the monarchy. His warnings now read like a veritable lesson to the Tseretelis and Chernovs, who in their "coalition" practice have revealed a superstitious belief in, and a superstitious reverence for, the state!

Two more remarks:

1. Engels's statement that in a democratic republic, "no less" than in a monarchy, the state remains a "machine for the oppression of one class by another" by no means signifies that the *form* of oppression makes no difference to the proletariat, as some anarchists "teach." A wider, freer and more open *form* of the class struggle and of class oppression vastly assists the proletariat in its struggle for the abolition of classes in general.

2. Why will only a new generation be able to discard the entire lumber of the state? This question is bound up with that of overcoming democracy, with which we shall deal now.

6. *Engels on the Overcoming of Democracy*

Engels came to express his views on this subject when establishing that the term "Social-Democrat" was *scientifically* wrong.

In a preface to an edition of his articles of the seventies on various subjects, mostly on "international" questions (*Internationales aus dem Volksstaat*[5]), dated January 3, 1894, i.e., written a year and a half before his death, Engels wrote that in all his articles he used the word "Communist," and *not* "Social-Democrat," because at that time the Proudhonists in France and the Lassalleans in Germany called themselves Social-Democrats.

5. *On International Topics from "The People's State."*

. . . For Marx and myself [continued Engels], it was therefore absolutely impossible to use such a loose term to characterise our special point of view. Today things are different, and the word ["Social-Democrat"] may perhaps pass muster [*mag passieren*], inexact [*unpassend*, unsuitable] though it still is for a party whose economic programme is not merely socialist in general, but downright communist, and whose ultimate political aim is to overcome the whole state and, consequently, democracy as well. The names of *real* [Engels's italics] political parties, however, are never wholly appropriate; the party develops while the name stays.

The dialectician Engels remained true to dialectics to the end of his days. Marx and I, he said, had a splendid, scientifically exact name for the party, but there was no real party, i.e., no mass proletarian party. Now (at the end of the nineteenth century) there was a real party, but its name was scientifically wrong. Never mind, it would "pass muster," so long as the party *developed*, so long as the scientific inaccuracy of its name was not hidden from it and did not hinder its development in the right direction!

Perhaps some wit would console us Bolsheviks in the manner of Engels: we have a real party, it is developing splendidly; even such a meaningless and ugly term as "Bolshevik" will "pass muster," although it expresses nothing whatever but the purely accidental fact that at the Brussels-London Congress of 1903 we were in the majority.[6] Perhaps now that the persecution of our Party by republicans and "revolutionary" petty-bourgeois democrats in July and August has earned the name "Bolshevik" such universal respect, now that, in addition, this persecution marks the tremendous historical progress our Party has made in its *real* development—perhaps now even I might hesitate to insist on the suggestion I made in April to change the name of our Party. Perhaps I would propose a "compromise" to my comrades, namely, to call ourselves the Communist Party, but to retain the word "Bolsheviks" in brackets.

But the question of the name of the Party is incomparably less important than the question of the attitude of the revolutionary proletariat to the state.

In the usual arguments about the state, the mistake is constantly made against which Engels warned and which we have in passing indicated above, namely, it is constantly forgotten that the abolition of the state means also the abolition of democracy: that the withering away of the state means the withering away of democracy.

At first sight this assertion seems exceedingly strange and incom-

---

6. "Majority" in Russian is *bol'shinstvo*; hence the name *Bolshevik*.

prehensible; indeed, someone may even suspect us of expecting the advent of a system of society in which the principle of subordination of the minority to the majority will not be observed—for democracy means the recognition of this very principle.

No, democracy is *not* identical with the subordination of the minority to the majority. Democracy is a *state* which recognises the subordination of the minority to the majority, i.e., an organisation for the systematic use of *force* by one class against another, by one section of the population against another.

We set ourselves the ultimate aim of abolishing the state, i.e., all organised and systematic violence, all use of violence against people in general. We do not expect the advent of a system of society in which the principle of subordination of the minority to the majority will not be observed. In striving for socialism, however, we are convinced that it will develop into communism and, therefore, that the need for violence against people in general, for the *subordination* of one man to another, and of one section of the population to another, will vanish altogether since people will *become accustomed* to observing the elementary conditions of social life *without violence* and *without subordination*.

In order to emphasise this element of habit, Engels speaks of a new *generation*, "reared in new, free social conditions," which will "be able to discard the entire lumber of the state"—of any state, including the democratic-republican state.

In order to explain this, it is necessary to analyse the economic basis of the withering away of the state.

Chapter V. The Economic Basis of the Withering Away of the State

Marx explains this question most thoroughly in his *Critique of the Gotha Programme* (letter to Bracke, May 5, 1875, which was not published until 1891 when it was printed in *Neue Zeit*, Vol. IX, 1, and which has appeared in Russian in a special edition). The polemical part of this remarkable work, which contains a criticism of Lassalleanism, has, so to speak, overshadowed its positive part, namely, the analysis of the connection between the development of communism and the withering away of the state.

1. Presentation of the Question by Marx

From a superficial comparison of Marx's letter to Bracke of May 5, 1875, with Engels's letter to Bebel of March 28, 1875, which we examined above, it might appear that Marx was much more of a "champion of the state" than Engels, and that the difference of opinion between the two writers on the question of the state was very considerable.

Engels suggested to Bebel that all chatter about the state be dropped altogether, that the word "state" be eliminated from the programme altogether and the word "community" substituted for it. Engels even declared that the Commune was no longer a state in the proper sense of the word. Yet Marx even spoke of the "future state in communist society," i.e., he would seem to recognise the need for the state even under communism.

But such a view would be fundamentally wrong. A closer examination shows that Marx's and Engels's views on the state and its withering away were completely identical, and that Marx's expression quoted above refers to the state in the process of *withering away*.

Clearly there can be no question of specifying the moment of the *future* "withering away," the more so since it will obviously be a lengthy process. The apparent difference between Marx and Engels is due to the fact that they dealt with different subjects and pursued different aims. Engels set out to show Bebel graphically, sharply and in broad outline the utter absurdity of the current prejudices concerning the state (shared to no small degree by Lassalle). Marx only touched upon *this* question in passing, being interested in another subject, namely, the *development* of communist society.

The whole theory of Marx is the application of the theory of development—in its most consistent, complete, considered and pithy form—to modern capitalism. Naturally, Marx was faced with the problem of applying this theory both to the *forthcoming* collapse of capitalism and to the *future* development of *future* communism.

On the basis of what *facts*, then, can the question of the future development of future communism be dealt with?

On the basis of the fact that it *has its origin* in capitalism, that it develops historically from capitalism, that it is the result of the action of a social force to which capitalism *gave birth*. There is no trace of an attempt on Marx's part to make up a utopia, to indulge in idle guess-work about what cannot be known. Marx treated the question of communism in the same way as a naturalist would treat the question of the development of, say, a new biological variety, once he knew that it had originated in such and such a way and was changing in such and such a definite direction.

To begin with, Marx brushed aside the confusion the Gotha Programme brought into the question of the relationship between state and society. He wrote:

"Present-day society" is capitalist society, which exists in all civilised countries, being more or less free from medieval admixture, more or less modified by the particular historical development of each country, more or less developed. On the other hand, the "present-day state" changes with a country's frontier. It is different in the Prusso-German Empire from what it is in Switzerland, and different in England from what it is in the United States. "*The* present-day state" is, therefore, a fiction.

Nevertheless, the different states of the different civilised countries, in spite of their motley diversity of form, all have this in common, that they are based on modern bourgeois society, only one more or less capitalistically developed. They have, therefore, also certain essential characteristics in common. In this sense it is possible to speak of the "present-day state," in contrast with the future, in which its present root, bourgeois society, will have died off.

The question then arises: what transformation will the state undergo in communist society? In other words, what social functions will remain in existence there that are analogous to present state functions? This question can only be answered scientifically, and one does not get a flea-hop nearer to the problem by a thousandfold combination of the word "people" with the word "state."[7]

After thus ridiculing all talk about a "people's state," Marx formulated the question and gave warning, as it were, that those seeking a scientific answer to it should use only firmly-established scientific data.

The first fact that has been established most accurately by the whole theory of development, by science as a whole—a fact that was ignored by the utopians, and is ignored by the present-day opportunists, who are afraid of the socialist revolution—is that, historically, there must undoubtedly be a special stage, or a special phase, of *transition* from capitalism to communism.

2. The Transition from Capitalism to Communism

Marx continued: "Between capitalist and communist society lies the period of the revolutionary transformation of the one into the other. Corresponding to this is also a political transition period in which the state can be nothing but *the revolutionary dictatorship of the proletariat*." Marx bases this conclusion on an analysis of the role played by the proletariat in modern capitalist society, on the data concerning the development of this society, and on the ir-

---

7. Marx, *Critique of the Gotha Programme*.

reconcilability of the antagonistic interests of the proletariat and the bourgeoisie.

Previously the question was put as follows: to achieve its emancipation, the proletariat must overthrow the bourgeoisie, win political power and establish its revolutionary dictatorship.

Now the question is put somewhat differently: the transition from capitalist society—which is developing towards communism—to communist society is impossible without a "political transition period," and the state in this period can only be the revolutionary dictatorship of the proletariat.

What, then, is the relation of this dictatorship to democracy?

We have seen that the *Communist Manifesto* simply places side by side the two concepts: "to raise the proletariat to the position of the ruling class" and "to win the battle of democracy." On the basis of all that has been said above, it is possible to determine more precisely how democracy changes in the transition from capitalism to communism.

In capitalist society, providing it develops under the most favourable conditions, we have a more or less complete democracy in the democratic republic. But this democracy is always hemmed in by the narrow limits set by capitalist exploitation, and consequently always remains, in effect, a democracy for the minority, only for the propertied classes, only for the rich. Freedom in capitalist society always remains about the same as it was in the ancient Greek republics: freedom for the slave-owners. Owing to the conditions of capitalist exploitation, the modern wage slaves are so crushed by want and poverty that "they cannot be bothered with democracy," "cannot be bothered with politics"; in the ordinary, peaceful course of events, the majority of the population is debarred from participation in public and political life.

The correctness of this statement is perhaps most clearly confirmed by Germany, because constitutional legality steadily endured there for a remarkably long time—nearly half a century (1871–1914)—and during this period the Social-Democrats were able to achieve far more than in other countries in the way of "utilising legality," and organised a larger proportion of the workers into a political party than anywhere else in the world.

What is this largest proportion of politically conscious and active wage slaves that has so far been recorded in capitalist society? One million members of the Social-Democratic Party—out of fifteen million wage-workers! Three million organised in trade unions—out of fifteen million!

Democracy for an insignificant minority, democracy for the rich—that is the democracy of capitalist society. If we look more closely into the machinery of capitalist democracy, we see everywhere, in the "petty"—supposedly petty—details of the suffrage (residential qualification, exclusion of women, etc.), in the technique of the representative institutions, in the actual obstacles to the right of assembly (public buildings are not for "paupers"!), in the purely capitalist organisation of the daily press, etc., etc.—we see restriction after restriction upon democracy. These restrictions, exceptions, exclusions, obstacles for the poor seem slight, especially in the eyes of one who has never known want himself and has never been in close contact with the oppressed classes in their mass life (and nine out of ten, if not ninety-nine out of a hundred, bourgeois publicists and politicians come under this category); but in their sum total these restrictions exclude and squeeze out the poor from politics, from active participation in democracy.

Marx grasped this *essence* of capitalist democracy splendidly when, in analysing the experience of the Commune, he said that the oppressed are allowed once every few years to decide which particular representatives of the oppressing class shall represent and repress them in parliament!

But from this capitalist democracy—that is inevitably narrow and stealthily pushes aside the poor, and is therefore hypocritical and false through and through—forward development does not proceed simply, directly and smoothly, towards "greater and greater democracy," as the liberal professors and petty-bourgeois opportunists would have us believe. No, forward development, i.e., development towards communism, proceeds through the dictatorship of the proletariat, and cannot do otherwise, for the *resistance* of the capitalist exploiters cannot be *broken* by anyone else or in any other way.

And the dictatorship of the proletariat, i.e., the organisation of the vanguard of the oppressed as the ruling class for the purpose of suppressing the oppressors, cannot result merely in an expansion of democracy. *Simultaneously* with an immense expansion of democracy, which *for the first time* becomes democracy for the poor, democracy for the people, and not democracy for the money-bags, the dictatorship of the proletariat imposes a series of restrictions on the freedom of the oppressors, the exploiters, the capitalists. We must suppress them in order to free humanity from wage slavery, their resistance must be crushed by force; it is clear that there is no freedom and no democracy where there is suppression and where there is violence.

Engels expressed this splendidly in his letter to Bebel when he said, as the reader will remember, that "the proletariat needs the state, not in the interests of freedom but in order to hold down its adversaries, and as soon as it becomes possible to speak of freedom the state as such ceases to exist."

Democracy for the vast majority of the people, and suppression by force, i.e., exclusion from democracy, of the exploiters and oppressors of the people—this is the change democracy undergoes during the *transition* from capitalism to communism.

Only in communist society, when the resistance of the capitalists has been completely crushed, when the capitalists have disappeared, when there are no classes (i.e., when there is no distinction between the members of society as regards their relation to the social means of production), *only* then "the state . . . ceases to exist," and "*it becomes possible to speak of freedom.*" Only then will a truly complete democracy become possible and be realised, a democracy without any exceptions whatever. And only then will democracy begin to *wither away*, owing to the simple fact that, freed from capitalist slavery, from the untold horrors, savagery, absurdities and infamies of capitalist exploitation, people will gradually *become accustomed* to observing the elementary rules of social intercourse that have been known for centuries and repeated for thousands of years in all copy-book maxims. They will become accustomed to observing them without force, without coercion, without subordination, *without the special apparatus* for coercion called the state.

The expression "the state *withers away*" is very well chosen, for it indicates both the gradual and the spontaneous nature of the process. Only habit can, and undoubtedly will, have such an effect; for we see around us on millions of occasions how readily people become accustomed to observing the necessary rules of social intercourse when there is no exploitation, when there is nothing that arouses indignation, evokes protest and revolts, and creates the need for *suppression*.

And so in capitalist society we have a democracy that is curtailed, wretched, false, a democracy only for the rich, for the minority. The dictatorship of the proletariat, the period of transition to communism, will for the first time create democracy for the people, for the majority, along with the necessary suppression of the exploiters, of the minority. Communism alone is capable of providing really complete democracy, and the more complete it is, the sooner it will become unnecessary and wither away of its own accord.

In other words, under capitalism we have the state in the proper sense of the word, that is, a special machine for the suppression of one class by another, and, what is more, of the majority by the minority. Naturally, to be successful, such an undertaking as the systematic suppression of the exploited majority by the exploiting minority calls for the utmost ferocity and savagery in the matter of suppressing, it calls for seas of blood, through which mankind is actually wading its way in slavery, serfdom and wage labour.

Furthermore, during the *transition* from capitalism to communism suppression is *still* necessary, but it is now the suppression of the exploiting minority by the exploited majority. A special apparatus, a special machine for suppression, the "state," is *still* necessary, but this is now a transitional state. It is no longer a state in the proper sense of the word; for the suppression of the minority of exploiters by the majority of the wage slaves of *yesterday* is comparatively so easy, simple and natural a task that it will entail far less bloodshed than the suppression of the risings of slaves, serfs or wage-labourers, and it will cost mankind far less. And it is compatible with the extension of democracy to such an overwhelming majority of the population that the need for a *special machine* of suppression will begin to disappear. Naturally, the exploiters are unable to suppress the people without a highly complex machine for performing this task, but *the people* can suppress the exploiters even with a very simple "machine," almost without a "machine," without a special apparatus, by the simple *organisation of the armed people* (such as the Soviets of Workers' and Soldiers' Deputies, we would remark, running ahead).

Lastly, only communism makes the state absolutely unnecessary, for there is *nobody* to be suppressed—"nobody" in the sense of a *class*, of a systematic struggle against a definite section of the population. We are not utopians, and do not in the least deny the possibility and inevitability of excesses on the part of *individual persons*, or the need to stop *such* excesses. In the first place, however, no special machine, no special apparatus of suppression, is needed for this; this will be done by the armed people themselves, as simply and as readily as any crowd of civilised people, even in modern society, interferes to put a stop to a scuffle or to prevent a woman from being assaulted. And, secondly, we know that the fundamental social cause of excesses, which consist in the violation of the rules of social intercourse, is the exploitation of the people, their want and their poverty. With the removal of this chief cause, excesses will inevitably begin to *"wither away."* We do not know how quickly and in what succession, but we do know they will wither away. With their withering away the state will also *wither away*.

Without building utopias, Marx defined more fully what can be defined *now* regarding this future, namely, the difference between the lower and higher places (levels, stages) of communist society.

3. *The First Phase of Communist Society*

In the *Critique of the Gotha Programme*, Marx goes into detail to disprove Lassalle's idea that under socialism the worker will receive the "undiminished" or "full product of his labour." Marx shows that from the whole of the social labour of society there must be deducted a reserve fund, a fund for the expansion of production, a fund for the replacement of the "wear and tear" of machinery, and so on. Then, from the means of consumption must be deducted a fund for administrative expenses, for schools, hospitals, old people's homes, and so on.

Instead of Lassalle's hazy, obscure, general phrase ("the full product of his labour to the worker"), Marx makes a sober estimate of exactly how socialist society will have to manage its affairs. Marx proceeds to make a *concrete* analysis of the conditions of life of a society in which there will be no capitalism, and says: "What we have to deal with here [in analysing the programme of the workers' party] is a communist society, not as it has *developed* on its own foundations, but, on the contrary, just as it *emerges* from capitalist society; which is, therefore, in every respect, economically, morally and intellectually, still stamped with the birthmarks of the old society from whose womb it comes." It is this communist society, which has just emerged into the light of day out of the womb of capitalism and which is in every respect stamped with the birthmarks of the old society, that Marx terms the "first," or lower, phase of communist society.

The means of production are no longer the private property of individuals. The means of production belong to the whole of society. Every member of society, performing a certain part of the socially-necessary work, receives a certificate from society to the effect that he has done a certain amount of work. And with this certificate he receives from the public store of consumer goods a corresponding quantity of products. After a deduction is made of the amount of labour which goes to the public fund, every worker, therefore, receives from society as much as he has given to it.

"Equality" apparently reigns supreme.

But when Lassalle, having in view such a social order (usually called socialism, but termed by Marx the first phase of communism), says that this is "equitable distribution," that this is "the equal right of all to an equal product of labour," Lassalle is mistaken and Marx exposes the mistake.

"Equal right," says Marx, we certainly do have here; but it is still a "bourgeois right," which, like every right, *implies inequality*. Every right is an application of an *equal* measure to *different* people who in fact are not alike, are not equal to one another. That is why "equal right" is a violation of equality and an injustice. In fact, everyone, having performed as much social labour as another, receives an equal share of the social product (after the above-mentioned deductions).

But people are not alike: one is strong, another is weak; one is married, another is not; one has more children, another has less, and so on. And the conclusion Marx draws is: "With an equal performance of labour, and hence an equal share in the social consumption fund, one will in fact receive more than another, one will be richer than another, and so on. To avoid all these defects, right would have to be unequal rather than equal."[8]

The first phase of communism, therefore, cannot yet provide justice and equality: differences, and unjust differences, in wealth will still persist, but the *exploitation* of man by man will have become impossible because it will be impossible to seize the *means of production*—the factories, machines, land, etc.—and make them private property. In smashing Lassalle's petty-bourgeois, vague phrases about "equality" and "justice" *in general*, Marx shows the *course of development* of communist society, which is *compelled* to abolish at first *only* the "injustice" of the means of production seized by individuals, and which is *unable* at once to eliminate the other injustice, which consists in the distribution of consumer goods "according to the amount of labour performed" (and not according to needs).

The vulgar economists, including the bourgeois professors and "our" Tugan, constantly reproach the socialists with forgetting the inequality of people and with "dreaming" of eliminating this inequality. Such a reproach, as we see, only proves the extreme ignorance of the bourgeois ideologists.

Marx not only most scrupulously takes account of the inevitable inequality of men, but he also takes into account the fact that the mere conversion of the means of production into the common property of the whole of society (commonly called "socialism") *does not remove* the defects of distribution and the inequality of "bourgeois right," which *continues to prevail* so long as products are divided "according to the amount of labour performed." Continuing, Marx says: "But these defects are inevitable in the first phase of communist society as it is when it has just emerged, after prolonged birth pangs, from capitalist society. Right can never be higher than the economic structure of society and its cultural development conditioned thereby." And so, in the first phase of communist society (usually called socialism) "bourgeois right" is *not* abolished in its entirety, but only in part, only in proportion to the economic revolution so far attained, i.e., only in respect of the means of production. "Bourgeois right" recognises them as the private property of individuals. Socialism converts them into *common* property. *To that extent*—and to that extent alone—"bourgeois right" disappears.

However, it persists as far as its other part is concerned; it

---

8. All citations in this section are from Marx's *Critique of the Gotha Program*. [R. T.]

persists in the capacity of regulator (determining factor) in the distribution of products and the allotment of labour among the members of society. The socialist principle, "He who does not work shall not eat," is *already* realised; the other socialist principle, "An equal amount of products for an equal amount of labour," is also *already* realised. But this is not yet communism, and it does not yet abolish "bourgeois right," which gives unequal individuals, in return for unequal (really unequal) amounts of labour, equal amounts of products.

This is a "defect," says Marx, but it is unavoidable in the first phase of communism; for if we are not to indulge in utopianism, we must not think that having overthrown capitalism people will at once learn to work for society *without any standard of right*. Besides, the abolition of capitalism *does not immediately create* the economic prerequisites for *such* a change.

Now, there is no other standard than that of "bourgeois right." To this extent, therefore, there still remains the need for a state, which, while safeguarding the common ownership of the means of production, would safeguard equality in labour and in the distribution of products.

The state withers away insofar as there are no longer any capitalists, any classes, and, consequently, no *class* can be *suppressed*.

But the state has not yet completely withered away, since there still remains the safeguarding of "bourgeois right," which sanctifies actual inequality. For the state to wither away completely, complete communism is necessary.

4. The Higher Phase of Communist Society

Marx continues:

> In a higher phase of communist society, after the enslaving subordination of the individual to the division of labour and with it also the antithesis between mental and physical labour has vanished, after labour has become not only a livelihood but life's prime want, after the productive forces have increased with the all-round development of the individual, and all the springs of co-operative wealth flow more abundantly—only then can the narrow horizon of bourgeois right be crossed in its entirety and society inscribe on its banners: From each according to his ability, to each according to his needs!

Only now can we fully appreciate the correctness of Engels's remarks mercilessly ridiculing the absurdity of combining the words "freedom" and "state." So long as the state exists there is no freedom. When there is freedom, there will be no state.

The economic basis for the complete withering away of the state is such a high stage of development of communism at which the antithesis between mental and physical labour disappears, at which there consequently disappears one of the principal sources of modern *social* inequality—a source, moreover, which cannot on any account be removed immediately by the mere conversion of the means of production into public property, by the mere expropriation of the capitalists.

This expropriation will make it *possible* for the productive forces to develop to a tremendous extent. And when we see how incredibly capitalism is already *retarding* this development, when we see how much progress could be achieved on the basis of the level of technique already attained, we are entitled to say with the fullest confidence that the expropriation of the capitalists will inevitably result in an enormous development of the productive forces of human society. But how rapidly this development will proceed, how soon it will reach the point of breaking away from the division of labour, of doing away with the antithesis between mental and physical labour, of transforming labour into "life's prime want"—we do not and *cannot* know.

That is why we are entitled to speak only of the inevitable withering away of the state, emphasising the protracted nature of this process and its dependence upon the rapidity of development of the *higher phase* of communism, and leaving the question of the time required for, or the concrete forms of, the withering away quite open, because there is *no* material for answering these questions.

The state will be able to wither away completely when society adopts the rule: "From each according to his ability, to each according to his needs," i.e., when people have become so accustomed to observing the fundamental rules of social intercourse and when their labour has become so productive that they will voluntarily work *according to their ability*. "The narrow horizon of bourgeois right," which compels one to calculate with the heartlessness of a Shylock whether one has not worked half an hour more than somebody else, whether one is not getting less pay than somebody else— this narrow horizon will then be crossed. There will then be no need for society, in distributing products, to regulate the quantity to be received by each; each will take freely "according to his needs."

From the bourgeois point of view, it is easy to declare that such a social order is "sheer utopia" and to sneer at the socialists for promising everyone the right to receive from society, without any control over the labour of the individual citizen, any quantity of truffles, cars, pianos, etc. Even to this day, most bourgeois 'savants" confine themselves to sneering in this way, thereby betraying both their ignorance and their selfish defence of capitalism.

Ignorance—for it has never entered the head of any socialist to "promise" that the higher phase of the development of communism will arrive; as for the great socialists' *forecast* that it will arrive, it presupposes not the present productivity of labour and *not the present* ordinary run of people, who, like the seminary students in Pomyalovsky's stories, are capable of damaging the stocks of public wealth "just for fun," and of demanding the impossible.

Until the "higher" phase of communism arrives, the socialists demand the *strictest* control by society *and by the state* over the measure of labour and the measure of consumption; but this control must *start* with the expropriation of the capitalists, with the establishment of workers' control over the capitalists, and must be exercised not by a state of bureaucrats, but by a state of *armed workers*.

The selfish defence of capitalism by the bourgeois ideologists (and their hangers-on, like the Tseretelis, Chernovs and Co.) consists in that they *substitute* arguing and talk about the distant future for the vital and burning question of *present-day* politics, namely, the expropriation of the capitalists, the conversion of *all* citizens into workers and other employees of *one* huge "syndicate"—the whole state—and the complete subordination of the entire work of this syndicate to a genuinely democratic state, *the state of the Soviets of Workers' and Soldiers' Deputies*.

In fact, when a learned professor, followed by the philistine, followed in turn by the Tseretelis and Chernovs, talks of wild utopias, of the demagogic promises of the Bolsheviks, of the impossibility of "introducing" socialism, it is the higher stage, or phase, of communism he has in mind, which no one has ever promised or even thought to "introduce," because, generally speaking, it cannot be "introduced."

And this brings us to the question of the scientific distinction between socialism and communism which Engels touched on in his above-quoted argument about the incorrectness of the name "Social-Democrat." Politically, the distinction between the first, or lower, and the higher phase of communism will in time, probably, be tremendous. But it would be ridiculous to recognise this distinction now, under capitalism, and only individual anarchists, perhaps, could invest it with primary importance (if there still are people among the anarchists who have learned nothing from the "Plekhanov" conversion of the Kropotkins, of Grave, Cornelissen and other "stars" of anarchism into social-chauvinists or "anarcho-trenchists," as Ghe, one of the few anarchists who have still preserved a sense of honour and a conscience, has put it).

But the scientific distinction between socialism and communism is clear. What is usually called socialism was termed by Marx the "first," or lower, phase of communist society. Insofar as the means of production become *common* property, the word "communism" is also applicable here, providing we do not forget that this is *not* complete communism. The great significance of Marx's explanations is that here, too, he consistently applies materialist dialectics, the theory of development, and regards communism as something which develops *out of* capitalism. Instead of scholastically invented, "concocted" definitions and fruitless disputes over words (What is socialism? What is communism?), Marx gives an analysis of what might be called the stages of the economic maturity of communism.

In its first phase, or first stage, communism *cannot* as yet be fully mature economically and entirely free from traditions or vestiges of capitalism. Hence the interesting phenomenon that communism in its first phase retains "the narrow horizon of *bourgeois* right." Of course, bourgeois right in regard to the distribution of *consumer* goods inevitably presupposes the existence of the *bourgeois state*, for right is nothing without an apparatus capable of *enforcing* the observance of the standards of right.

It follows that under communism there remains for a time not only bourgeois right, but even the bourgeois state, without the bourgeoisie!

This may sound like a paradox or simply a dialectical conundrum of which Marxism is often accused by people who have not taken the slightest trouble to study its extraordinarily profound content.

But in fact, remnants of the old, surviving in the new, confront us in life at every step, both in nature and in society. And Marx did not arbitrarily insert a scrap of "bourgeois" right into communism, but indicated what is economically and politically inevitable in a society emerging *out of the womb* of capitalism.

Democracy is of enormous importance to the working class in its struggle against the capitalists for its emancipation. But democracy is by no means a boundary not to be overstepped; it is only one of the stages on the road from feudalism to capitalism, and from capitalism to communism.

Democracy means equality. The great significance of the proletariat's struggle for equality and of equality as a slogan will be clear if we correctly interpret it as meaning the abolition of *classes*. But democracy means only *formal* equality. And as soon as equality is achieved for all members of society *in relation* to ownership of the means of production, that is, equality of labour and wages, humanity will inevitably be confronted with the question of advancing farther, from formal equality to actual equality, i.e., to the operation of the rule "from each according to his ability, to each according to his needs." By what stages, by means of what practical measures humanity will proceed to this supreme aim we do not and cannot know. But it is important to realise how infinitely mendacious is the ordinary bourgeois conception of socialism as something lifeless, rigid, fixed once and for all, whereas in reality *only* socialism will be the beginning of a rapid, genuine, truly mass forward movement, embracing first the *majority* and then the whole of the population, in all spheres of public and private life.

Democracy is a form of the state, one of its varieties. Consequently, it, like every state, represents, on the one hand, the organised, systematic use of force against persons; but, on the other hand, it signifies the formal recognition of equality of citizens, the equal right of all to determine the structure of, and to administer, the state. This, in turn, results in the fact that, at a certain stage in the development of democracy, it first welds together the class that wages a revolutionary struggle against capitalism—the proletariat, and enables it to crush, smash to atoms, wipe off the face of the earth the bourgeois, even the republican-bourgeois, state machine, the standing army, the police and the bureaucracy and to substitute for them a *more* democratic state machine, but a state machine nevertheless, in the shape of armed workers who proceed to form a militia involving the entire population.

Here "quantity turns into quality": *such* a degree of democracy implies overstepping the boundaries of bourgeois society and beginning its socialist reorganisation. If really *all* take part in the administration of the state, capitalism cannot retain its hold. The development of capitalism, in turn, creates the *preconditions* that *enable* really "all" to take part in the administration of the state. Some of these preconditions are: universal literacy, which has already been achieved in a number of the most advanced capitalist countries, then the "training and disciplining" of millions of workers by the huge, complex, socialised apparatus of the postal service, railways, big factories, large-scale commerce, banking, etc., etc.

Given these *economic* preconditions, it is quite possible, after the overthrow of the capitalists and the bureaucrats, to proceed immediately, overnight, to replace them in the *control* over production and distribution, in the work of *keeping account* of labour and products, by the armed workers, by the whole of the armed population. (The question of control and accounting should not be confused with the question of the scientifically trained staff of engineers, agronomists and so on. These gentlemen are working today in obedience to the wishes of the capitalists, and will work even better tomorrow in obedience to the wishes of the armed workers.)

Accounting and control—that is *mainly* what is needed for the "smooth working," for the proper functioning, of the *first phase* of communist society. *All* citizens are transformed into hired employees of the state, which consists of the armed workers. *All* citizens become employees and workers of a *single* country-wide state "syndicate." All that is required is that they should work equally, do their proper share of work, and get equal pay. The accounting and control necessary for this have been *simplified* by capitalism to the utmost and reduced to the extraordinarily simple operations—which any literate person can perform—of supervising and recording, knowledge of the four rules of arithmetic, and issuing appropriate receipts.[9]

When the *majority* of the people begin independently and everywhere to keep such accounts and exercise such control over the capitalists (now coverted into employees) and over the intellectual gentry who preserve their capitalist habits, this control will really become universal, general and popular; and there will be no getting away from it, there will be "nowhere to go."

The whole of society will have become a single office and a single factory, with equality of labour and pay.

But this "factory" discipline, which the proletariat, after defeating the capitalists, after overthrowing the exploiters, will extend to the whole of society, is by no means our ideal, or our ultimate goal. It is only a necessary *step* for thoroughly cleaning society of all the infamies and abominations of capitalist exploitation, *and for further* progress.

From the moment all members of society, or at least the vast majority, have learned to administer the state *themselves*, have taken this work into their own hands, have organised control over the insignificant capitalist minority, over the gentry who wish to preserve their capitalist habits and over the workers who have been thoroughly corrupted by capitalism—from this moment the need for government of any kind begins to disappear altogether. The more complete the democracy, the nearer the moment when it becomes unnecessary. The more democratic the "state" which consists of the armed workers, and which is "no longer a state in the proper sense of the word," the more rapidly *every form* of state begins to wither away.

For when *all* have learned to administer and actually do independently administer social production, independently keep accounts and exercise control over the parasites, the sons of the wealthy, the swindlers and other "guardians of capitalist traditions," the escape from this popular accounting and control will inevitably become so incredibly difficult, such a rare exception, and

9. When the more important functions of the state are reduced to such accounting and control by the workers themselves, it will cease to be a "political state" and "public functions will lose their political character and become mere administrative functions" (*cf.* above, Chapter IV, 2, Engels's controversy with the anarchists). [*Lenin*]

will probably be accompanied by such swift and severe punishment (for the armed workers are practical men and not sentimental intellectuals, and they will scarcely allow anyone to trifle with them), that the *necessity* of observing the simple, fundamental rules of the community will very soon become a *habit*.

Then the door will be thrown wide open for the transition from the first phase of communist society to its higher phase, and with it to the complete withering away of the state.

Chapter VI. The Vulgarisation of Marxism by the Opportunists

The question of the relation of the state to the social revolution, and of the social revolution to the state, like the question of revolution generally, was given very little attention by the leading theoreticians and publicists of the Second International (1889–1914). But the most characteristic thing about the process of the gradual growth of opportunism that led to the collapse of the Second International in 1914 is the fact that even when these people were squarely faced with this question they *tried to evade* it or ignored it.

In general, it may be said that *evasiveness* over the question of the relation of the proletarian revolution to the state—an evasiveness which benefited and fostered opportunism—resulted in the *distortion* of Marxism and in its complete vulgarisation.

To characterise this lamentable process, if only briefly, we shall take the most prominent theoreticians of Marxism: Plekhanov and Kautsky.

1. Plekhanov's Controversy with the Anarchists

Plekhanov wrote a special pamphlet on the relation of anarchism to socialism, entitled *Anarchism and Socialism*, which was published in German in 1894.

In treating this subject, Plekhanov contrived completely to evade the most urgent, burning, and most politically essential issue in the struggle against anarchism, namely, the relation of the revolution to the state, and the question of the state in general! His pamphlet falls into two distinct parts: one of them is historical and literary, and contains valuable material on the history of the ideas of Stirner, Proudhon and others; the other is philistine, and contains a clumsy dissertation on the theme that an anarchist cannot be distinguished from a bandit.

It is a most amusing combination of subjects and most characteristic of Plekhanov's whole activity on the eve of the revolution and during the revolutionary period in Russia. In fact, in the years 1905 to 1917, Plekhanov revealed himself as a semi-doctrinaire and semi-philistine who, in politics, trailed in the wake of the bourgeoisie.

We have seen how, in their controversy with the anarchists, Marx and Engels with the utmost thoroughness explained their views on the relation of revolution to the state. In 1891, in his foreword to Marx's *Critique of the Gotha Programme*, Engels wrote that "we"—that is, Engels and Marx—"were at that time, hardly two years after the Hague Congress of the [First] International, engaged in the most violent struggle against Bakunin and his anarchists."

The anarchists had tried to claim the Paris Commune as their "own," so to say, as a corroboration of their doctrine; and they completely misunderstood its lessons and Marx's analysis of these lessons. Anarchism has given nothing even approximating true answers to the concrete political questions: Must the old state machine be *smashed*? And *what* should be put in its place?

But to speak of "anarchism and socialism" while completely evading the question of the state, and *disregarding* the whole development of Marxism before and after the Commune, meant inevitably slipping into opportunism. For what opportunism needs most of all is that the two questions just mentioned should *not* be raised at all. That *in itself* is a victory for opportunism.

2. Kautsky's Controversy with the Opportunists

Undoubtedly, an immeasurably larger number of Kautsky's works have been translated into Russian than into any other language. It is not without reason that some German Social-Democrats say in jest that Kautsky is read more in Russia than in Germany (let us say, in parenthesis, that this jest has a far deeper historical meaning than those who first made it suspect. The Russian workers, by making in 1905 an unusually great and unprecedented demand for the best works of the best Social-Democratic literature in the world, and by receiving translations and editions of these works in quantities unheard of in other countries, rapidly transplanted, so to speak, the enormous experience of a neighbouring, more advanced country to the young soil of our proletarian movement).

Besides his popularisation of Marxism, Kautsky is particularly known in our country for his controversy with the opportunists, with Bernstein at their head. One fact, however, is almost unknown, one which cannot be ignored if we set out to investigate how Kautsky drifted into the morass of unbelievably disgraceful confusion and defence of social-chauvinism during the supreme crisis of 1914–15. This fact is as follows: shortly before he came out against the most prominent representatives of opportunism in France (Millerand and Juarès) and in Germany (Bernstein), Kautsky betrayed very considerable vacillation. The Marxist *Zarya*,[1] which was published in Stuttgart in 1901–2, and advocated revolutionary proletarian views, was forced to *enter into controversy* with Kautsky and describe as "elastic" the half-hearted, evasive resolution, conciliatory towards the opportunists, that he proposed at the International Socialist Congress in Paris in 1900. Kautsky's letters published in Germany reveal no less hesitancy on his part before he took the field against Bernstein.

Of immeasurably greater significance, however, is the fact that, in his very controversy with the opportunists, in his formulation of the question and his manner of treating it, we can now see, as we study the *history* of Kautsky's latest betrayal of Marxism, his systematic deviation towards opportunism precisely on the question of the state.

Let us take Kautsky's first important work against opportunism, *Bernstein and the Social-Democratic Programme*. Kautsky refutes Bernstein in detail, but here is a characteristic thing:

Bernstein, in his *Premises of Socialism*, of Herostratean fame, accuses Marxism of "*Blanquism*" (an accusation since repeated thousands of times by the opportunists and liberal bourgeoisie in Russia against the revolutionary Marxists, the Bolsheviks). In this connection Bernstein dwells particularly on Marx's *The Civil War in France*, and tries, quite unsuccessfully, as we have seen, to identify Marx's views on the lessons of the Commune with those of Proudhon. Bernstein pays particular attention to the conclusion which Marx emphasised in his 1872 preface to the *Communist Manifesto*, namely, that "the working class cannot simply lay hold of the ready-made state machinery and wield it for its own purposes."

This statement "pleased" Bernstein so much that he used it no less than three times in his book, interpreting it in the most distorted, opportunist way.

As we have seen, Marx meant that the working class must *smash, break, shatter* (*Sprengung*, explosion—the expression used by Engels) the whole state machine. But according to Bernstein it would appear as though Marx in these words warned the working class *against* excessive revolutionary zeal when seizing power.

1. *Zarya* (*The Dawn*) was a Marxist scientific and political journal published in Stuttgart in 1901 and 1902 by the editors of *Iskra* (*The Spark*).

A cruder and more hideous distortion of Marx's idea cannot be imagined.

How, then, did Kautsky proceed in his most detailed refutation of Bernsteinism?

He refrained from analysing the utter distortion of Marxism by opportunism on this point. He cited the above-quoted passage from Engels's preface to Marx's *Civil War* and said that according to Marx the working class cannot *simply* take over the *ready-made* state machinery, but that, generally speaking, it *can* take it over—and that was all. Kautsky did not say a word about the fact that Bernstein attributed to Marx the *very opposite* of Marx's real idea, that since 1852 Marx had formulated the task of the proletarian revolution as being to "smash" the state machine.

The result was that the most essential distinction between Marxism and opportunism on the subject of the tasks of the proletarian revolution was slurred over by Kautsky!

"We can quite safely leave the solution of the problem of the proletarian dictatorship to the future," said Kautsky, writing "*against*" Bernstein (p. 172, German edition). This is not a polemic *against* Bernstein, but, in essence, a *concession* to him, a surrender to opportunism; for at present the opportunists ask nothing better than to "quite safely leave to the future" all fundamental questions of the tasks of the proletarian revolution.

From 1852 to 1891, or for forty years, Marx and Engels taught the proletariat that it must smash the state machine. Yet, in 1899, Kautsky, confronted with the complete betrayal of Marxism by the opportunists on this point, fraudulently *substituted* for the question whether it is necessary to smash this machine the question of the concrete forms in which it is to be smashed, and then sought refuge behind the "indisputable" (and barren) philistine truth that concrete forms cannot be known in advance!!

A gulf separates Marx and Kautsky over their attitudes towards the proletarian party's task of training the working class for revolution.

Let us take the next, more mature, work by Kautsky, which was also largely devoted to a refutation of opportunist errors. It is his pamphlet, *The Social Revolution*. In this pamphlet, the author chose as his special theme the question of "the proletarian revolution" and "the proletarian regime." He gave much that was exceedingly valuable, but he *avoided* the question of the state. Throughout the pamphlet the author speaks of the winning of state power—and no more; that is, he has chosen a formula which makes a concession to the opportunists, inasmuch as it *admits* the possibility of seizing power *without* destroying the state machine. The very thing which Marx in 1872 declared to be "obsolete" in the programme of the *Communist Manifesto, is revived* by Kautsky in 1902.

A special section in the pamphlet is devoted to the "forms and weapons of the social revolution." Here Kautsky speaks of the mass political strike, of civil war, and of the "instruments of the might of the modern large state, its bureaucracy and the army"; but he does not say a word about what the Commune has already taught the workers. Evidently, it was not without reason that Engels issued a warning, particularly to the German socialists, against "superstitious reverence" for the state.

Kautsky treats the matter as follows: the victorious proletariat "will carry out the democratic programme," and he goes on to formulate its clauses. But he does not say a word about the new material provided by 1871 on the subject of the replacement of bourgeois democracy by proletarian democracy. Kautsky disposes of the question of using such "impressive-sounding" banalities as: "Still, it goes without saying that we shall not achieve supremacy under the present conditions. Revolution itself presupposes long and deep-going struggles, which, in themselves, will change our present political and social structure." Undoubtedly, this "goes without saying," just as the fact that horses eat oats or the Volga flows into the Caspian. Only it is a pity that an empty and bombastic phrase about "deep-going" struggles is used to *avoid* a question of vital importance to the revolutionary proletariat, namely, *what* makes *its* revolution "deep-going" in relation to the state, to democracy, as distinct from previous, non-proletarian revolutions.

By avoiding this question, Kautsky *in practice* makes a concession to opportunism on this most essential point, although *in words* he declares stern war against it and stresses the importance of the "idea of revolution" (how much is this "idea" worth when one is afraid to teach the workers the concrete lessons of revolution?), or says, "revolutionary idealism before everything else," or announces that the English workers are now "hardly more than petty bourgeois."

> The most varied forms of enterprises—bureaucratic [??], trade unionist, co-operative, private . . . can exist side by side in socialist society [Kautsky writes]. . . . There are, for example, enterprises which cannot do without a bureaucratic [??] organisation, such as the railways. Here the democratic organisation may take the following shape: the workers elect delegates who form a sort of parliament, which establishes the working regulations and supervises the management of the bureaucratic apparatus. The management of other enterprises may be transferred to the trade unions, and still others may become co-operative enterprises.

This argument is erroneous; it is a step backward compared with the explanations Marx and Engels gave in the seventies, using the lessons of the Commune as an example.

As far as the supposedly necessary "bureaucratic" organisation is concerned, there is no difference whatever between a railway and any other enterprise in large-scale machine industry, any factory, large shop, or large-scale capitalist agricultural enterprise. The technique of all these enterprises makes absolutely imperative the strictest discipline, the utmost precision on the part of everyone in carrying out his allotted task, for otherwise the whole enterprise may come to a stop, or machinery or the finished product may be damaged. In all these enterprises the workers will, of course, "elect delegates who will form *a sort of parliament*."

The whole point, however, is that this "sort of parliament" will *not* be a parliament in the sense of a bourgeois parliamentary institution. The whole point is that this "sort of parliament" will *not* merely "establish the working regulations and supervise the management of the bureaucratic apparatus," as Kautsky, whose thinking does not go beyond the bounds of bourgeois parliamentarism, imagines. In socialist society, the "sort of parliament" consisting of workers' deputies will, of course, "establish the working regulations and supervise the management" of the "apparatus," *but* this apparatus will *not* be "bureaucratic." The workers, after winning political power, will smash the old bureaucratic apparatus, shatter it to its very foundations, and raze it to the ground; they will replace it by a new one, consisting of the very same workers and other employees, *against* whose transformation into bureaucrats the measures will at once be taken which were specified in detail by Marx and Engels: (1) not only election, but also recall at any time; (2) pay not to exceed that of a workman; (3) immediate introduction of control and supervision by *all*, so that *all* may become "bureaucrats" for a time and that, therefore, *nobody* may be able to become a "bureaucrat."

Kautsky has not reflected at all on Marx's words: "The Commune was a working, not a parliamentary, body, executive and legislative at the same time."

Kautsky has not understood at all the difference between bourgeois parliamentarism, which combines democracy (*not for the people*) with bureaucracy (*against the people*), and proletarian democracy, which will take immediate steps to cut bureaucracy down to the roots, and which will be able to carry these measures through to the end, to the complete abolition of bureaucracy, to the introduction of complete democracy for the people.

Kautsky here displays the same old "superstitious reverence" for the state, and "superstitious belief" in bureaucracy.

Let us now pass to the last and best of Kautsky's works against the opportunists, his pamphlet *The Road to Power* (which, I believe, has not been published in Russian, for it appeared in 1909, when reaction was its height in our country). This pamphlet is a big step forward, since it does not deal with the revolutionary programme in general, as the pamphlet of 1899 against Bernstein, or with the tasks of the social revolution irrespective of the time of its occurrence, as the 1902 pamphlet, *The Social Revolution*; it deals with the concrete conditions which compel us to recognise that the "era of revolutions" is *setting in*.

The author explicitly points to the aggravation of class antagonisms in general and to imperialism, which plays a particularly important part in this respect. After the "revolutionary period of 1789–1871" in Western Europe, he says, a similar period began in the East in 1905. A world war is approaching with menacing rapidity. "It [the proletariat] can no longer talk of premature revolution." "We have entered a revolutionary period." The "revolutionary era is beginning."

These statements are perfectly clear. This pamphlet of Kautsky's should serve as a measure of comparison of what the German Social-Democrats *promised to be* before the imperialist war and the depth of degradation to which they, including Kautsky himself, sank when the war broke out. "The present situation," Kautsky wrote in the pamphlet under survey, "is fraught with the danger that we [i.e., the German Social-Democrats] may easily appear to be more 'moderate' than we really are." It turned out that in reality the German Social-Democratic Party was much more moderate and opportunist than it appeared to be!

It is all the more characteristic, therefore, that although Kautsky so explicitly declared that the era of revolutions had already begun, in the pamphlet which he himself said was devoted to an analysis of the "*political* revolution," he again completely avoided the question of the state.

These evasions of the question, these omissions and equivocations, inevitably added up to that complete swing-over to opportunism with which we shall now have to deal.

Kautsky, the German Social-Democrats' spokesman, seems to have declared: I abide by revolutionary views (1899), I recognise, above all, the inevitability of the social revolution of the proletariat (1902), I recognise the advent of a new era of revolutions (1909). Still, I am going back on what Marx said as early as 1852, since the question of the tasks of the proletarian revolution in relation to the state is being raised (1912).

It was in this point-blank form that the question was put in Kautsky's controversy with Pannekoek.

3. *Kautsky's Controversy with Pannekoek*

In opposing Kautsky, Pannekoek came out as one of the representatives of the "Left radical" trend which included Rosa Luxemburg, Karl Radek and others. Advocating revolutionary tactics, they were united in the conviction that Kautsky was going over to the "Centre," which wavered in an unprincipled manner between Marxism and opportunism. This view was proved perfectly correct by the war, when this "Centrist" (wrongly called Marxist) trend, or Kautskyism, revealed itself in all its repulsive wretchedness.

In an article touching on the question of the state, entitled "Mass Action and Revolution" (*Neue Zeit*, 1912, Vol. XXX, 2), Pannekoek described Kautsky's attitude as one of "passive radicalism," as "a theory of inactive expectancy." "Kautsky refuses to see the process of revolution," wrote Pannekoek (p. 616). In presenting the matter in this way, Pannekoek approached the subject which interests us, namely, the tasks of the proletarian revolution in relation to the state.

> The struggle of the proletariat [he wrote] is not merely a struggle against the bourgeoisie *for* state power, but a struggle *against* state power. . . . The content of this [the proletarian] revolution is the destruction and dissolution [*Auflösung*] of the instruments of power of the state with the aid of the instruments of power of the proletariat [p. 544]. The struggle will cease only when, as the result of it, the state organisation is completely destroyed. The organisation of the majority will then have demonstrated its superiority by destroying the organisation of the ruling minority. [P. 548.]

The formulation in which Pannekoek presented his ideas suffers from serious defects. But its meaning is clear nonetheless, and it is interesting to note *how* Kautsky combated it. "Up to now," he wrote, "the antithesis between the Social-Democrats and the anarchists has been that the former wished to win state power while the latter wished to destroy it. Pannekoek wants to do both." (P. 724.) Although Pannekoek's exposition lacks precision and concreteness—not to speak of other shortcomings of his article which have no bearing on the present subject—Kautsky seized precisely on the point of *principle* raised by Pannekoek; and *on this fundamental* point of *principle* Kautsky completely abandoned the Marxist position and went over wholly to opportunism. His definition of the distinction between the Social-Democrats and the anarchists is absolutely wrong; he completely vulgarises and distorts Marxism.

The distinction between the Marxists and the anarchists is this:

(1) The former, while aiming at the complete abolition of the state, recognise that this aim can only be achieved after classes have been abolished by the socialist revolution, as the result of the establishment of socialism, which leads to the withering away of the state. The latter want to abolish the state completely overnight, not understanding the conditions under which the state can be abolished. (2) The former recognise that after the proletariat has won political power it must completely destroy the old state machine and replace it by a new one consisting of an organisation of the armed workers, after the type of the Commune. The latter, while insisting on the destruction of the state machine, have a very vague idea of *what* the proletariat will put in its place and *how* it will use its revolutionary power. The anarchists even deny that the revolutionary proletariat should use the state power, they reject its revolutionary dictatorship. (3) The former demand that the proletariat be trained for revolution by utilising the present state. The anarchists reject this.

In this controversy, it is not Kautsky but Pannekoek who represents Marxism, for it was Marx who taught that the proletariat cannot simply win state power in the sense that the old state apparatus passes into new hands, but must smash this apparatus, must break it and replace it by a new one.

Kautsky abandons Marxism for the opportunist camp, for this destruction of the state machine, which is utterly unacceptable to the opportunists, completely disappears from his argument, and he leaves a loophole for them in that "conquest" may be interpreted as the simple acquisition of a majority.

To cover up his distortion of Marxism, Kautsky behaves like a doctrinaire: he puts forward a "quotation" from Marx himself. In 1850 Marx wrote that a "resolute centralisation of power in the hands of the state authority" was necessary, and Kautsky triumphantly asks: does Pannekoek want to destroy "centralism"?

This is simply a trick, like Bernstein's identification of the views of Marxism and Proudhonism on the subject of federalism as against centralism.

Kautsky's "quotation" is neither here nor there. Centralism is possible with both the old and the new state machine. If the workers voluntarily unite their armed forces, this will be centralism, but it will be based on the "complete destruction" of the centralised state apparatus—the standing army, the police and the bureaucracy. Kautsky acts like an outright swindler by evading the perfectly well-known arguments of Marx and Engels on the Commune and plucking out a quotation which has nothing to do with the point at issue.

Perhaps he [Pannekoek] [Kautsky continues] wants to abolish the state functions of the officials? But we cannot do without officials even in the party and the trade unions, let alone in the state administration. And our programme does not demand the abolition of state officials, but that they be elected by the people. . . . We are discussing here not the form the administrative apparatus of the "future state" will assume, but whether our political struggle abolishes [literally *dissolves—auflöst*] the state power *before we have captured it* [Kautsky's italics]. Which ministry with its officials could be abolished? [Then follows an enumeration of the ministries of education, justice, finance and war.] No, not one of the present ministries will be removed by our political struggle against the government. . . . I repeat, in order to prevent misunderstanding: we are not discussing here the form the 'future state' will be given by the victorious Social-Democrats, but how the present state is changed by our opposition. [P. 725.]

This is an obvious trick. Pannekoek raised the question of *revolution*. Both the title of his article and the passages quoted above clearly indicate this. By skipping to the question of "opposition," Kautsky substitutes the opportunist for the revolutionary point of view. What he says means: at present we are an opposition; what we shall be *after* we have captured power, that we shall see. *Revolution has vanished*! And that is exactly what the opportunists wanted.

The point at issue is neither opposition nor political struggle in general, but *revolution*. Revolution consists in the proletariat *destroying* the "administrative apparatus" and the *whole* state machine, replacing it by a new one, made up of the armed workers. Kautsky displays a "superstitious reverence" for "ministries"; but why can they not be replaced, say, by committees of specialists working under sovereign, all-powerful Soviets of Workers' and Soldiers' Deputies?

The point is not at all whether the "ministries" will remain, or whether "committees of specialists" or some other bodies will be set up; that is quite immaterial. The point is whether the old state machine (bound by thousands of threads to the bourgeoisie and permeated through and through with routine and inertia) shall remain, or be *destroyed* and replaced by a *new* one. Revolution consists not in the new class commanding, governing with the aid of the *old* state machine, but in this class *smashing* this machine and commanding, governing with the aid of a *new* machine. Kautsky slurs over this *basic* idea of Marxism, or he does not understand it at all.

His question about officials clearly shows that he does not understand the lessons of the Commune or the teachings of Marx.

"We cannot do without officials even in the party and the trade unions. . . ."

We cannot do without officials *under capitalism*, under *the rule of the bourgeoisie*. The proletariat is oppressed, the working people are enslaved by capitalism. Under capitalism, democracy is restricted, cramped, curtailed, mutilated by all the conditions of wage slavery, and the poverty and misery of the people. This and this alone is the reason why the functionaries of our political organisations and trade unions are corrupted—or rather tend to be corrupted—by the conditions of capitalism and betray a tendency to become bureaucrats, i.e., privileged persons divorced from the people and standing *above* the people.

That is the *essence* of bureaucracy; and until the capitalists have been expropriated and the bourgeoisie overthrown, *even* proletarian functionaries will inevitably be "bureaucratised" to a certain extent.

According to Kautsky, since elected functionaries will remain under socialism, so will officials, so will the bureaucracy! This is exactly where he is wrong. Marx, referring to the example of the Commune, showed that under socialism functionaries will cease to be "bureaucrats," to be "officials," they will cease to be so *in proportion as*—in addition to the principle of election of officials—the principle of recall at any time is *also* introduced, as salaries are reduced to the level of the wages of the average workman, *and* as parliamentary institutions are replaced by "working bodies, executive and legislative at the same time."

As a matter of fact, the whole of Kautsky's argument against Pannekoek, and particularly the former's wonderful point that we cannot do without officials even in our party and trade union organisations, is merely a repetition of Bernstein's old "arguments" against Marxism in general. In his renegade book, *The Premises of Socialism*, Bernstein combats the ideas of "primitive" democracy, combats what he calls "doctrinaire democracy": binding mandates, unpaid officials, impotent central representative bodies, etc. To prove that this "primitive" democracy is unsound, Bernstein refers to the experience of the British trade unions, as interpreted by the Webbs. Seventy years of development "in absolute freedom," he says (p. 137, German edition), convinced the trade unions that primitive democracy was useless, and they replaced it by ordinary democracy, i.e., parliamentarism combined with bureaucracy.

In reality, the trade unions did not develop "in absolute freedom" *but in absolute capitalist slavery*, under which, it goes without saying, a number of concessions to the prevailing evil, violence, falsehood, exclusion of the poor from the affairs of "higher" administration, "cannot be done without." Under socialism much of "primitive" democracy will inevitably be revived, since, for the first time in the history of civilised society, the *mass* of the population will rise to taking an *independent* part, not only in voting and elections, *but also in the everyday administration of the state*. Under socialism *all* will govern in turn and will soon become accustomed to no one governing.

Marx's critico-analytical genius saw in the practical measures of the Commune the *turning-point* which the opportunists fear and do not want to recognise because of their cowardice, because they do not want to break irrevocably with the bourgeoisie, and which the anarchists do not want to see, either because they are in a hurry or because they do not understand at all the conditions of great social changes. "We must not even think of destroying the old state machine; how can we do without ministries and officials?" argues the opportunist, who is completely saturated with philistinism and who, at bottom, not only does not believe in revolution, in the creative power of revolution, but lives in mortal dread of it (like our Mensheviks and Socialist-Revolutionaries).

"We must think *only* of destroying the old state machine; it is no use probing into the *concrete* lessons of earlier proletarian revolutions and analysing *what* to put in the place of what has been destroyed, and *how*," argues the anarchist (the best of the anarchists, of course, and not those who, following the Kropotkins and Co., trail behind the bourgeoisie). Consequently, the tactics of the anarchist become the tactics of *despair* instead of a ruthlessly bold revolutionary effort to solve concrete problems while taking into account the practical conditions of the mass movement.

Marx teaches us to avoid both errors; he teaches us to act with supreme boldness in destroying the entire old state machine, and at the same time he teaches us to put the question concretely: the Commune was able in the space of a few weeks to *start* building a *new*, proletarian state machine by introducing such-and-such measures to provide wider democracy and to uproot bureaucracy. Let us learn revolutionary boldness from the Communards; let us see in their practical measures the *outline* of really urgent and immediately possible measures, and then, *following this road*, we shall achieve the complete destruction of bureaucracy.

The possibility of this destruction is guaranteed by the fact that socialism will shorten the working day, will raise the *people* to a new life, will create such conditions for the *majority* of the population as will enable *everybody*, without exception, to perform "state functions," and this will lead to the *complete withering away* of every form of state in general.

Kautsky continues:

Its object [the object of the mass strike] cannot be to *destroy* the state power; its only object can be to make the government compliant on some specific question, or to replace a government hostile to the proletariat by one willing to meet it half-way [*entgegenkommende*]. . . . But never, under any circumstances, can it [that is, the proletarian victory over a hostile government] lead to the *destruction* of the state power; it can lead only to a certain *shifting* [*Verschiebung*] of the balance of forces *within the state power*. . . . The aim of our political struggle remains, as in the past, the conquest of state power by winning a majority in parliament and by raising parliament to the rank of master of the government. [Pp. 726, 727, 732.]

This is nothing but the purest and most vulgar opportunism: repudiating revolution in deeds, while accepting it in words. Kautsky's thoughts go no further than a "government . . . willing to meet the proletariat half-way"—a step backward to philistinism compared with 1847, when the *Communist Manifesto* proclaimed "the organisation of the proletariat as the ruling class."

Kautsky will have to achieve his beloved "unity" with the Scheidemanns, Plekhanovs and Vanderveldes, all of whom agree to fight for a government "willing to meet the proletariat half-way."

We, however, shall break with these traitors to socialism, and we shall fight for the complete destruction of the old state machine, in order that the armed proletariat itself *may become the government.* These are two vastly different things.

Kautsky will have to enjoy the pleasant company of the Legiens and Davids, Plekhanovs, Potresovs, Tseretelis and Chernovs, who are quite willing to work for the "shifting of the balance of forces within the state power," for "winning a majority in parliament," and "raising parliament to the rank of master of the government." A most worthy object, which is wholly acceptable to the opportunists and which keeps everything within the bounds of the bourgeois parliamentary republic.

We, however, shall break with the opportunists; and the entire class-conscious proletariat will be with us in the fight—not to "shift the balance of forces," but *to overthrow the bourgeoisie, to destroy* bourgeois parliamentarism, for a democratic republic after the type of the Commune, or a republic of Soviets of Workers' and Soldiers' Deputies, for the revolutionary dictatorship of the proletariat.

To the right of Kautsky in international socialism there are trends such as *Socialist Monthly* in Germany (Legien, David, Kolb and many others, including the Scandinavians Stauning and Branting); Jaurès's followers and Vandervelde in France and Belgium; Turati, Trèves and other Right-wingers of the Italian Party; the Fabians and "Independents" (the Independent Labour Party, which, in fact, has always been dependent on the Liberals) in Britain; and the like. All these gentry, who play a tremendous, very often a predominant role in the parliamentary work and the press of their parties, repudiate outright the dictatorship of the proletariat and pursue a policy of undisguised opportunism. In the eyes of these gentry, the "dictatorship" of the proletariat "contradicts" democracy!! There is really no essential distinction between them and the petty-bourgeois democrats.

Taking this circumstance into consideration, we are justified in drawing the conclusion that the Second International, that is, the overwhelming majority of its official representatives, has completely sunk into opportunism. The experience of the Commune has been not only ignored, but distorted. Far from inculcating in the workers' minds the idea that the time is nearing when they must act to smash the old state machine, replace it by a new one, and in this way make their political rule the foundation for the socialist reorganisation of society, they have actually preached to the masses the very opposite and have depicted the "conquest of power" in a way that has left thousands of loopholes for opportunism.

The distortion and hushing up of the question of the relation of the proletarian revolution to the state could not but play an immense role at a time when states, which possess a military apparatus expanded as a consequence of imperialist rivalry, have become military monsters which are exterminating millions of people in order to settle the issue as to whether Britain or Germany—this or that finance capital—is to rule the world.

Chapter VII. The Experience of the Russian Revolutions of 1905 and 1917

The subject indicated in the title of this chapter is so vast that volumes could and should be written about it. In the present pamphlet we shall have to confine ourselves, naturally, to the most important lessons provided by experience, those bearing directly upon the tasks of the proletariat in the revolution with regard to state power.[3]

Postscript to the First Edition

This pamphlet was written in August and September 1917. I had already drawn up the plan for the next, the seventh, chapter, "The Experience of the Russian Revolutions of 1905 and 1917." Apart from the title, however, I had no time to write a single line of the chapter; I was "interrupted" by a political crisis—the eve of the October revolution of 1917. Such an "interruption" can only be

---

3. Here the manuscript breaks off.

welcomed; but the writing of the second part of the pamphlet ("The Experience of the Russian Revolutions of 1905 and 1917") will probably have to be put off for a long time. It is more pleasant and useful to go through the "experience of the revolution" than to write about it.

Petrograd   *The Author*
November 30, 1917

Can the Bolsheviks Retain State Power?

Despite tactical shifts in his position, Lenin's writings of 1917 were dominated by the main aim of persuading his party to prepare for and finally launch the decisive revolutionary action. Written at the end of September and published during October in the party journal *Prosveshchenie,* this article was ostensibly an attempt to refute non-Bolshevik disbelievers in this party's prospects. But it is rightly seen as a brief addressed to the Bolshevik leadership itself, a message of confidence in their ability to take power by revolutionary means and hold onto it by such measures as Lenin here sketches.

* * *

The Soviets are a new state apparatus which, in the first place, provides an armed force of workers and peasants; and this force is not divorced from the people, as was the old standing army, but is very closely bound up with the people. From the military point of view this force is incomparably more powerful than previous forces; from the revolutionary point of view, it cannot be replaced by anything else. Secondly, this apparatus provides a bond with the people, with the majority of the people, so intimate, so indissoluble, so easily verifiable and renewable, that nothing even remotely like it existed in the previous state apparatus. Thirdly, this apparatus, by virtue of the fact that its personnel is elected and subject to recall at the people's will without any bureaucratic formalities, is far more democratic than any previous apparatus. Fourthly, it provides a close contact with the most varied professions, thereby facilitating the adoption of the most varied and most radical reforms without red tape. Fifthly, it provides an organisational form for the vanguard, i.e., for the most class-conscious, most energetic and most progressive section of the *oppressed* classes, the workers and peasants, and so constitutes an apparatus by means of which the vanguard of the oppressed classes can elevate, train, educate, and lead *the entire vast mass* of these classes, which has up to now stood completely outside of political life and history. Sixthly, it makes it possible to combine the advantages of the parliamentary system with those of immediate and direct democracy, i.e., to vest in the people's elected representatives both legislative *and executive* functions. Compared with the bourgeois parliamentary system, this is an advance in democracy's development which is of world-wide, historic significance.

In 1905, our Soviets existed only in embryo, so to speak, as they lived altogether only a few weeks. Clearly, under the conditions of that time, their comprehensive development was out of the question. It is still out of the question in the 1917 Revolution, for a few months is an extremely short period and—this is most important—the Socialist-Revolutionary and Menshevik leaders have *prostituted* the Soviets, have reduced their role to that of a talking-shop, of an accomplice in the compromising policy of the leaders. The Soviets have been rotting and decaying alive under the leadership of the Liebers, Dans, Tseretelis and Chernovs. The Soviets will be able to develop properly, to display their potentialities and capabilities to the full only by taking over *full* state power; for otherwise they have *nothing to do*, otherwise they are either simply embryos (and to remain an embryo too long is fatal), or playthings. "Dual power" means paralysis for the Soviets.

If the creative enthusiasm of the revolutionary classes had not given rise to the Soviets, the proletarian revolution in Russia would have been a hopeless cause, for the proletariat could certainly not retain power with the old state apparatus, and it is impossible to create a new apparatus immediately. The sad history of the prostitution of the Soviets by the Tseretelis and Chernovs, the history of the "coalition," is also the history of the liberation of the Soviets from petty-bourgeois illusions, of their passage through the "purgatory" of the practical experience of the utter abomination and filth of *all* and *sundry* bourgeois coalitions. Let us hope that this "purgatory" has steeled rather than weakened the Soviets.

The chief difficulty facing the proletarian revolution is the establishment on a country-wide scale of the most precise and most conscientious accounting and control, of *workers' control* of the production and distribution of goods.

When the writers of *Novaya Zhizn* argued that in advancing the slogan "workers' control" we were slipping into syndicalism, this argument was an example of the stupid schoolboy method of applying "Marxism" without studying it, just *learning it by rote* in the Struve manner. Syndicalism either repudiates the revolutionary dictatorship of the proletariat, or else relegates it, as it does political power in general, to a back seat. We, however, put it in the forefront. * * *

* * *

This brings us to another aspect of the question of the state apparatus. In addition to the chiefly "oppressive" apparatus—the standing army, the police and the bureaucracy—the modern state possesses an apparatus which has extremely close connections with the banks and syndicates, an apparatus which performs an enormous amount of accounting and registration work, if it may be expressed this way. This apparatus must not, and should not, be smashed. It must be wrested from the control of the capitalists; the capitalists and the wires they pull must be *cut off, lopped off, chopped away from* this apparatus; it must be *subordinated* to the proletarian Soviets; it must be expanded, made more comprehensive, and nation-wide. And this *can* be done by utilising the achievements already made by large-scale capitalism (in the same way as the proletarian revolution can, in general, reach its goal only by utilising these achievements).

Capitalism has created an accounting *apparatus* in the shape of the banks, syndicates, postal service, consumers' societies, and office employees' unions. *Without big banks socialism would be impossible.*

The big banks *are* the "state apparatus" which we *need* to bring about socialism, and which we *take ready-made* from capitalism; our task here is merely to *lop off* what *capitalistically mutilates* this excellent apparatus, to make it *even bigger*, even more democratic, even more comprehensive. Quantity will be transformed into quality. A single State Bank, the biggest of the big, with branches in every rural district, in every factory, will constitute as much as ninetenths of the *socialist* apparatus. This will be country-wide *bookkeeping*, country-wide *accounting* of the production and distribution of goods, this will be, so to speak, something in the nature of the *skeleton* of socialist society.

We can "lay hold of" and "set in motion" this "state apparatus" (which is not fully a state apparatus under capitalism, but which will be so with us, under socialism) at one stroke, by a single decree, because the actual work of book-keeping, control, registering, accounting and counting is performed by *employees*, the majority of whom themselves lead a proletarian or semi-proletarian existence.

By a single decree of the proletarian government these employees can and must be transferred to the status of state employees, in the same way as the watchdogs of capitalism like Briand and other bourgeois ministers, by a single decree, transfer railwaymen on strike to the status of state employees. We shall need many more state employees of this kind, and more *can* be obtained, because capitalism has simplified the work of accounting and control, has reduced it to a comparatively simple system of *book-keeping*, which any literate person can do.

The conversion of the bank, syndicate, commercial, etc., etc., rank-and-file employees into state employees is quite feasible both technically (thanks to the preliminary work performed for us by capitalism, including finance capitalism) and politically provided the *Soviets* exercise control and supervision.

As for the higher officials, of whom there are very few, but who gravitate towards the capitalists, they will have to be dealt with in the same way as the capitalists, i.e., "severely." Like the capitalists, they will offer *resistance*. This resistance will have to be *broken*. * * *

We can do this, for it is merely a question of breaking the resistance of an insignificant minority of the population, literally a handful of people, over each of whom the employee's unions, the trade unions, the consumers' societies and the Soviets will institute such *supervision* that every Tit Titych[1] will be *surrounded* as the French were at Sedan. We know these Tit Tityches by name: we only have to consult the lists of directors, board members, large shareholders, etc. There are several hundred, at most several thousand of them in the *whole* of Russia, and the proletarian state, with the apparatus of the Soviets, of the employees' unions, etc., will be able to appoint ten or even a hundred supervisors to each of them, so that instead of "breaking resistance" it may even be possible, by means of *workers' control* (over the capitalists), to make all resistance *impossible*.

The important thing will not be even the confiscation of the capitalists' property, but country-wide, all-embracing workers' control over the capitalists and their possible supporters. Confiscation alone leads nowhere, as it does not contain the element of organisation, of accounting for proper distribution. Instead of confiscation, we could easily impose a *fair* tax (even on the Shingyarov[2] scale, for instance), taking care, of course, to preclude the possibility of anyone evading assessment, concealing the truth, evading the law. And this possibility can be *eliminated only* by the workers' control of the *workers' state*.

Compulsory syndication i.e., compulsory amalgamation in associations under state control—this is what capitalism has prepared the way for, this is what has been carried out in Germany by the Junkers' state, this is what can be easily carried out in Russia by the Soviets, by the proletarian dictatorship, and this is what will *provide us with a state apparatus* that will be universal, up-to-date, and non-bureaucratic.

* * *

1. A rich, tyrannical merchant in A. N. Ostrovsky's play *Shouldering Another's Troubles*.

2. A. I. Shingyarov (1869–1918) was minister of finance in the Provisional Government.

The proletariat, we are told, will not be able to set the state apparatus in motion.

Since the 1905 revolution, Russia has been governed by 130,000 landowners, who have perpetrated endless violence against 150,-000,000 people, heaped unconstrained abuse upon them, and condemned the vast majority to inhuman toil and semi-starvation.

Yet we are told that the 240,000 members of the Bolshevik Party will not be able to govern Russia, govern her in the interests of the poor and against the rich. These 240,000 are already backed by no less than a million votes of the adult population, for this is precisely the proportion between the number of Party members and the number of votes cast for the Party that has been established by the experience of Europe and the experience of Russia as shown, for example, by the elections to the Petrograd City Council last August. We therefore already have a "state apparatus" of *one million* people devoted to the socialist state for the sake of high ideals and not for the sake of a fat sum received on the 20th of every month.

In addition to that we have a "magic way" to enlarge our state apparatus *tenfold* at once, at one stroke, a way which no capitalist state ever possessed or could possess. This magic way is to draw the working people, to draw the poor, into the daily work of state administration.

To explain how easy it will be to employ this magic way and how faultlessly it will operate, let us take the simplest and most striking example possible.

The state is to forcibly evict a certain family from a flat and move another in. This often happens in the capitalist state, and it will also happen in our proletarian or socialist state.

The capitalist state evicts a working-class family which has lost its breadwinner and cannot pay the rent. The bailiff appears with police, or militia, a whole squad of them. To effect an eviction in a working-class district a whole detachment of Cossacks is required. Why? Because the bailiff and the militiaman refuse to go without a very strong military guard. They know that the scene of an eviction arouses such fury among the neighbours, among thousands and thousands of people who have been driven to the verge of desperation, arouses such hatred towards the capitalists and the capitalist state, that the bailiff and the squad of militiamen run the risk of being torn to pieces at any minute. Large military forces are required, several regiments must be brought into a big city, and the troops must come from some distant, outlying region so that the soldiers will not be familiar with the life of the urban poor, so that the soldiers will not be "infected" with socialism.

The proletarian state has to forcibly move a very poor family into a rich man's flat. Let us suppose that our squad of workers' militia is fifteen strong; two sailors, two soldiers, two class-conscious workers (of whom, let us suppose, only one is a member of our Party, or a sympathiser), one intellectual, and eight from the poor working people, of whom at least five must be women, domestic servants, unskilled labourers, and so forth. The squad arrives at the rich man's flat, inspects it and finds that it consists of five rooms occupied by two men and two women—"You must squeeze up a bit into two rooms this winter, citizens, and prepare two rooms for two families now living in cellars. Until the time, with the aid of engineers (you are an engineer, aren't you?), we have built good dwellings for everybody, you will have to squeeze up a little. Your telephone will serve ten families. This will save a hundred hours of work wasted on shopping, and so forth. Now in your family there are two unemployed persons who can perform light work: a citizeness fifty-five years of age and a citizen fourteen years of age. They will be on duty for three hours a day supervising the proper distribution of provisions for ten families and keeping the necessary account of this. The student citizen in our squad will now write out this state order in two copies and you will be kind enough to give us a signed declaration that you will faithfully carry it out."

This, in my opinion, can illustrate how the distinction between the old bourgeois and the new socialist state apparatus and state administration could be illustrated.

We are not utopians. We know that an unskilled labourer or a cook cannot immediately get on with the job of state administration. In this we agree with the Cadets, with Breshkovskaya, and with Tsereteli. We differ, however, from these citizens in that we demand an immediate break with the prejudiced view that only the rich, or officials chosen from rich families, are capable of *administering* the state, of performing the ordinary, everyday work of administration. We demand that *training* in the work of state administration be conducted by class-conscious workers and soldiers and that this training be begun at once, i.e., that a *beginning* be made at once in training all the working people, all the poor, for this work.

We know that the Cadets are also willing to teach the people democracy. Cadet ladies are willing to deliver lectures to domestic servants on equal rights for women in accordance with the best English and French sources. And also, at the very next concert-meeting, before an audience of thousands, an exchange of kisses will be arranged on the platform: the Cadet lady lecturer will kiss Breshkovskaya, Breshkovskaya will kiss ex-Minister Tsereteli, and the grateful people will therefore receive an object-lesson in republican equality, liberty and fraternity. . . .

Yes, we agree that the Cadets, Breshkovskaya, and Tsereteli are in their own way devoted to democracy and are propagating it among the people. But what is to be done if our conception of democracy is somewhat different from theirs?

In our opinion, to ease the incredible burdens and miseries of the war and also to heal the terrible wounds the war has inflicted on the people, *revolutionary* democracy is needed, *revolutionary* measures of the kind described in the example of the distribution of housing accommodation in the interests of the poor. *Exactly the same* procedure must be adopted in both town and country for the distribution of provisions, clothing, footwear, etc., in respect of the land in the rural districts, and so forth. For the administration of the state in *this* spirit we can *at once set in motion a state* apparatus consisting of ten if not twenty million people, an apparatus such as no capitalist state has ever known. We alone can create such an apparatus, for we are sure of the fullest and devoted sympathy of the vast majority of the population. We alone can create such an apparatus, because we have class-conscious workers disciplined by long capitalist "schooling" (it was not for nothing that we went to learn in the school of capitalism), workers who are *capable* of forming a workers' militia and of *gradually* expanding it (beginning to expand it at once) into a militia *embracing the whole people.* The class-conscious workers must lead, but for the work of administration they can enlist the vast mass of the working and oppressed people.

It goes without saying that this new apparatus is bound to make mistakes in taking its first steps. But did not the peasants make mistakes when they emerged from serfdom and began to manage their own affairs? Is there any way other than practice by which the people can learn to govern themselves and to avoid mistakes? Is there any way other than by proceeding immediately to genuine self-government by the people? The chief thing now is to abandon the prejudiced bourgeois-intellectualist view that only special officials, who by their very social position are entirely dependent upon capital, can administer the state. The chief thing is to put an end to the state of affairs in which bourgeois officials and "socialist" ministers are trying to govern in the old way, but are incapable of doing so and, after seven months, are faced with a peasant revolt in a peasant country! The chief thing is to imbue the oppressed and the working people with confidence in their own strength, to prove to them in practice that they can and must themselves ensure the *proper,* most strictly regulated and organised distribution of bread, all kinds of food, milk, clothing, housing, etc., *in the interests of the poor.* Unless this is done, Russia *cannot* be saved from collapse and ruin. The conscientious, bold, universal move to hand over administrative work to proletarians and semi-proletarians will, however, rouse such unprecedented revolutionary enthusiasm among the people, will so multiply the people's forces in combating distress, that much that seemed impossible to our narrow, old, bureaucratic forces will become possible for the millions, who will *begin to work for themselves* and not for the capitalists, the gentry, the bureaucrats, and not out of fear of punishment.

* * *

Ideas become a power when they grip the people. And precisely at the present time the Bolsheviks, i.e., the representatives of revolutionary proletarian internationalism, have embodied in their policy the idea that is motivating countless working people all over the world.

Justice alone, the mere anger of the people against exploitation, would never have brought them on to the true path of socialism. But now that, thanks to capitalism, the material apparatus of the big banks, syndicates, railways, and so forth, has grown, now that the immense experience of the advanced countries has accumulated a stock of engineering marvels, the employment of which is being *hindered* by capitalism, now that the class-conscious workers have built up a party of a quarter of a million members to systematically lay hold of this apparatus and set it in motion with the support of all the working and exploited people—now that these conditions *exist*, no power on earth can prevent the Bolsheviks, *if they do not allow themselves to be scared* and if they succeed in taking power, from retaining it until the triumph of the world socialist revolution.

Marxism and Insurrection

A LETTER TO THE CENTRAL COMMITTEE OF THE R.S.D.L.P.(B.)

Lenin wrote this document while in hiding in September 1917 as a secret letter to the Bolshevik Central Committee; it was first published in 1921. At the time of writing it was one of the salvoes in the barrage of arguments he was making to the effect that the Bolsheviks should proceed forthwith to the forcible seizure of power. It is of enduring theoretical interest as a statement of Leninist Marxism's views on the conditions for insurrectionary action and on the distinction between the Marxist approach to insurrection and that of "Blanquism."

One of the most vicious and probably most widespread distortions of Marxism resorted to by the dominant "socialist" parties is the opportunist lie that preparation for insurrection, and generally the treatment of insurrection as an art, is "Blanquism."

Bernstein, the leader of opportunism, has already earned himself unfortunate fame by accusing Marxism of Blanquism, and when our present-day opportunists cry Blanquism they do not improve on or "enrich" the meagre "ideas" of Bernstein one little bit.

Marxists are accused of Blanquism for treating insurrection as an art! Can there be a more flagrant perversion of the truth, when not a single Marxist will deny that it was Marx who expressed himself on this score in the most definite, precise and categorical manner, referring to insurrection specifically as an *art*, saying that it must be treated as an art, that you must *win* the first success and then proceed from success to success, never ceasing the *offensive* against the enemy, taking advantage of his confusion, etc., etc.?

To be successful, insurrection must rely not upon conspiracy and not upon a party, but upon the advanced class. That is the first point. Insurrection must rely upon a *revolutionary upsurge of the people*. That is the second point. Insurrection must rely upon that *turning-point* in the history of the growing revolution when the activity of the advanced ranks of the people is at its height, and when the *vacillations* in the ranks of the enemy and *in the ranks of the weak, half-hearted and irresolute friends of the revolution* are strongest. That is the third point. And these three conditions for raising the question of insurrection distinguish *Marxism from Blanquism*.

Once these conditions exist, however, to refuse to treat insurrection as an *art* is a betrayal of Marxism and a betrayal of the revolution.

To show that it is precisely the present moment that the Party *must* recognise as the one in which the entire course of events has objectively placed *insurrection* on the order of the day and that insurrection must be treated as an art, it will perhaps be best to use the method of comparison, and to draw a parallel between July 3–4 and the September days.

On July 3–4 it could have been argued, without violating the truth, that the correct thing to do was to take power, for our enemies would in any case have accused us of insurrection and ruthlessly treated us as rebels. However, to have decided on this account in favour of taking power at that time would have been wrong, because the objective conditions for the victory of the insurrection did not exist.

(1) We still lacked the support of the class which is the vanguard of the revolution.

We still did not have a majority among the workers and soldiers of Petrograd and Moscow. Now we have a majority in both Soviets. It was created *solely* by the history of July and August, by the experience of the "ruthless treatment" meted out to the Bolsheviks, and by the experience of the Kornilov revolt.[1]

(2) There was no country-wide revolutionary upsurge at that time. There is now, after the Kornilov revolt; the situation in the provinces and assumption of power by the Soviets in many localities prove this.

(3) At that time there was no *vacillation* on any serious political scale among our enemies and among the irresolute petty bourgeoisie. Now the vacillation is enormous. Our main enemy, Allied and world imperialism (for world imperialism is headed by the "Allies"), *has begun to waver* between a war to a victorious finish and a separate peace directed against Russia. Our petty-bourgeois democrats, having clearly lost their majority among the people, have begun to vacillate enormously, and have rejected a bloc, i.e., a coalition, with the Cadets.

(4) Therefore, an insurrection on July 3–4 would have been a

---

1. An unsuccessful counter-revolutionary action led by a tsarist general, Kornilov, in August 1917. [*R. T.*]

mistake; we could not have retained power either physically or politically. We could not have retained it physically even though Petrograd was at times in our hands, because at that time our workers and soldiers would not have *fought and died* for Petrograd. There was not at the time that "savageness," or fierce hatred *both of* the Kerenskys *and of* the Tseretelis and Chernovs. Our people had still not been tempered by the experience of the persecution of the Bolsheviks in which the Socialist-Revolutionaries and Mensheviks participated.

We could not have retained power politically on July 3–4 because, *before the Kornilov revolt*, the army and the provinces could and would have marched against Petrograd.

Now the picture is entirely different.

We have the following of the majority of a *class*, the vanguard of the revolution, the vanguard of the people, which is capable of carrying the masses with it.

We have the following of the *majority* of the people, because Chernov's resignation, while by no means the only symptom, is the most striking and obvious symptom that the peasants *will not receive land* from the Socialist-Revolutionaries' bloc (or from the Socialist-Revolutionaries themselves). And that is the chief reason for the popular character of the revolution.

We are in the advantageous position of a party that knows for certain which way to go at a time when *imperialism as a whole* and the Menshevik and Socialist-Revolutionary bloc as a whole are vacillating in an incredible fashion.

Our victory is assured, for the people are close to desperation, and we are showing the entire people a sure way out; we demonstrated to the entire people during the "Kornilov days" the value of our leadership, and then *proposed* to the politicians of the bloc a compromise, *which they rejected*, although there is no let-up in their vacillations.

It would be a great mistake to think that our offer of a compromise had not *yet* been rejected, and that the Democratic Conference may *still* accept it. The compromise was proposed *by a party to parties*; it could not have been proposed in any other way. It was rejected by *parties*. The Democratic Conference is a *conference*, and nothing more. One thing must not be forgotten, namely, that the *majority* of the revolutionary people, the poor, embittered peasants, are not represented in it. It is a conference of *a minority of the people*—this obvious truth must not be forgotten. It would be a big mistake, sheer parliamentary cretinism on our part, if we were to regard the Democratic Conference as a parliament; for even *if it were* to proclaim itself a permanent and sovereign parliament of the revolution, it would nevertheless *decide nothing*. The power of decision lies *outside it* in the working-class quarters of Petrograd and Moscow.

All the objective conditions exist for a successful insurrection. We have the exceptional advantage of a situation in which *only* our victory in the insurrection can put an end to that most painful thing on earth, vacillation, which has worn the people out; in which only our victory in the insurrection will give the peasants land immediately; a situation in which *only our* victory in the insurrection can *foil* the game of a separate peace directed against the revolution— foil it by publicly proposing a fuller, juster and earlier peace, a peace that will *benefit* the revolution.

Finally, our Party alone *can*, by a victorious insurrection, save Petrograd; for if our proposal for peace is rejected, if we do not secure even an armistice, then *we* shall become "defencists," we shall place ourselves *at the head of the war parties*, we shall be the *war party par excellence*, and we shall conduct the war in a truly revolutionary manner. We shall take away all the bread and boots from the capitalists. We shall leave them only crusts and dress them in bast shoes. We shall send all the bread and footwear to the front.

And then we shall save Petrograd.

The resources, both material and spiritual, for a truly revolutionary war in Russia are still immense; the chances are a hundred to one that the Germans will grant us at least an armistice. And to secure an armistice now would in itself mean to win the *whole world*.

Having recognised the absolute necessity for an insurrection of the workers of Petrograd and Moscow in order to save the revolution and to save Russia from a "separate" partition by the imperialists of both groups, we must first adapt our political tactics at the Conference to the conditions of the growing insurrection; secondly, we must show that it is not only in words that we accept Marx's idea that insurrection must be treated as an art.

At the Conference we must immediately cement the Bolshevik group, without striving after numbers, and without fearing to leave the waverers in the waverers' camp. They are more useful to the cause of the revolution *there* than in the camp of the resolute and devoted fighters.

We must draw up a brief declaration from the Bolsheviks, emphasising in no uncertain manner the irrelevance of long speeches and of "speeches" in general, the necessity for immediate action to save the revolution, the absolute necessity for a complete break with the bourgeoisie, for the removal of the present government, in its entirety, for a complete rupture with the Anglo-French imperialists, who are preparing a "separate" partition of Russia, and for the immediate transfer of all power to *revolutionary democrats, headed by the revolutionary proletariat.*

Our declaration must give the briefest and most trenchant formulation of *this* conclusion in connection with the programme proposals of peace for the peoples, land for the peasants, confiscation of scandalous profits, and a check on the scandalous sabotage of production by the capitalists.

The briefer and more trenchant the declaration, the better. Only two other highly important points must be clearly indicated in it, namely, that the people are worn out by the vacillations, that they are fed up with the irresolution of the Socialist-Revolutionaries and Mensheviks; and that we are definitely breaking with these *parties* because they have betrayed the revolution.

And another thing. By immediately proposing a peace without annexations, by immediately breaking with the Allied imperialists and with all imperialists, either we shall at once obtain an armistice, or the entire revolutionary proletariat will rally to the defence of the country, and a really just, really revolutionary war will then be waged by revolutionary democrats under the leadership of the proletariat.

Having read this declaration, and having appealed for *decisions* and not talk, for *action* and not resolution-writing, we must *dispatch* our entire group to the *factories and the barracks.* Their place is there, the pulse of life is there, there is the source of salvation for our revolution, and there is the motive force of the Democratic Conference.

There, in ardent and impassioned speeches, we must explain our programme and put the alternative: either the Conference adopts it *in its entirety*, or else insurrection. There is no middle course. Delay is impossible. The revolution is dying.

By putting the question in this way, by concentrating our entire group in the factories and barracks, *we shall be able to determine the right moment to start the insurrection.*

In order to treat insurrection in a Marxist way, i.e., as an art, we must at the same time, without losing a single moment, organise a *headquarters* of the insurgent detachments, distribute our forces, move the reliable regiments to the most important points, surround the Alexandrinsky Theatre, occupy the Peter and Paul Fortress,[2] arrest the General Staff and the government, and move against the officer cadets and the Savage Division those detachments which

2. Meetings of the Democratic Conference were held at the Alexandrinsky Theatre, in Petrograd. The Peter and Paul Fortress, on the River Neva, opposite the tsar's Winter Palace, was used as a prison for political offenders; it contained a huge arsenal and was an important strategic point in Petrograd.

would rather die than allow the enemy to approach the strategic points of the city. We must mobilise the armed workers and call them to fight the last desperate fight, occupy the telegraph and the telephone exchange at once, move *our* insurrection headquarters to the central telephone exchange and connect it by telephone with all the factories, all the regiments, all the points of armed fighting, etc.

Of course, this is all by way of example, only to *illustrate* the fact that at the present moment it is impossible to remain loyal to Marxism, to remain loyal to the revolution *unless insurrection is treated as an art.*

Advice of an Onlooker

Written on October 8, 1917, but first published in 1920, this document was one of Lenin's secret messages from hiding to the Bolshevik Central Committee, designed to nerve the party leadership into determined, violent action to seize power. It restates in greater detail the Marxian position on insurrectionary action as Lenin understood it.

* * *

It is clear that all power must pass to the Soviets. It should be equally indisputable for every Bolshevik that proletarian revolutionary power (or Bolshevik power—which is now one and the same thing) is assured of the utmost sympathy and unreserved support of all the working and exploited people all over the world in general, in the belligerent countries in particular, and among the Russian peasants especially. There is no need to dwell on these all too well known and long established truths.

What must be dealt with is something that is probably not quite clear to all comrades, namely, that in practice the transfer of power to the Soviets now means armed uprising. This would seem obvious, but not everyone was or is giving thought to the point. To repudiate armed uprising now would mean to repudiate the key slogan of Bolshevism (All Power to the Soviets) and proletarian revolutionary internationalism in general.

But armed uprising is a *special* form of political struggle, one subject to special laws to which attentive thought must be given. Karl Marx expressed this truth with remarkable clarity when he wrote that *"insurrection is an art quite as much as war."*

Of the principal rules of this art, Marx noted the following:

(1) *Never play* with insurrection, but when beginning it realise firmly that you must *go all the way*.

(2) Concentrate a *great superiority of forces* at the decisive point and at the decisive moment, otherwise the enemy, who has the advantage of better preparation and organisation, will destroy the insurgents.

(3) Once the insurrection has begun, you must act with the greatest *determination*, and by all means, without fail, take the *offensive*. "The defensive is the death of every armed rising."

(4) You must try to take the enemy by surprise and seize the moment when his forces are scattered.

(5) You must strive for *daily* successes, however small (one might say hourly, if it is the case of one town), and at all costs retain *"moral superiority."*

Marx summed up the lessons of all revolutions in respect to armed uprising in the words of "Danton, the greatest master of revolutionary tactics yet known: *de l'audace, de l'audace, encore de l'audace.*"[1]

Applied to Russia and to October 1917, this means: a simultaneous offensive on Petrograd, as sudden and as rapid as possible, which must without fail be carried out from within and from without, from the working-class quarters and from Finland, from Revel and from Kronstadt, an offensive of the *entire* navy, the concentration of a *gigantic superiority* of forces over the 15,000 or 20,000 (perhaps more) of our "bourgeois guard" (the officers' schools), our "Vendée troops" (part of the Cossacks), etc.

Our *three* main forces—the fleet, the workers, and the army units—must be so combined as to occupy without fail and to hold *at any cost*: (a) the telephone exchange; (b) the telegraph office; (c) the railway stations; (d) and above all, the bridges.

The *most determined* elements (our "shock forces" and *young workers*, as well as the best of the sailors) must be formed into small detachments to occupy all the more important points and to *take part* everywhere in all important operations, for example:

to encircle and cut off Petrograd; to seize it by a combined attack of the sailors, the workers, and the troops—a task which requires *art and triple audacity*;

to form detachments from the best workers, armed with rifles and bombs, for the purpose of attacking and surrounding the enemy's "centres" (the officers' schools, the telegraph office, the telephone exchange, etc.). Their watchword must be: *"Better die to a man than let the enemy pass!"*

Let us hope that if action is decided on, the leaders will successfully apply the great precepts of Danton and Marx.

The success of both the Russian and the world revolution depends on two or three days' fighting.

---

1. Friedrich Engels, *Revolution and Counter-Revolution in Germany*, Section XVII.

PART IV

The Revolutionary State and Its Policies

To the Citizens of Russia

The Bolsheviks overthrew the Provisional Government and took power on the night of October 24–25 old style (November 6–7), 1917, whence the name "October Revolution." The operation was directed by the Petrograd Soviet's Revolutionary Military Committee, headed by Trotsky. Lenin arrived at revolutionary headquarters in the Smolny Institute while the operation was in progress. This proclamation to the people of Russia, which he drafted, was issued on the morning of November 7 in the name of the Revolutionary Military Committee. The Second All-Russian Congress of Soviets, then meeting in Petrograd, approved the new government formed by Lenin under the title "Council of People's Commissars." Lenin was chairman of the council. Trotsky was initially commissar for foreign affairs, but soon relinquished that post in order to become war commissar and take direct charge of organizing and directing the Red Army in the Civil War of 1918–21.

The Provisional Government has been deposed. State power has passed into the hands of the organ of the Petrograd Soviet of Workers' and Soldiers' Deputies—the Revolutionary Military Committee, which heads the Petrograd proletariat and the garrison.

The cause for which the people have fought, namely, the immediate offer of a democratic peace, the abolition of landed proprietorship, workers' control over production, and the establishment of Soviet power—this cause has been secured.

Long live the revolution of workers, soldiers and peasants!

Revolutionary Military Committee
of the Petrograd Soviet
of Workers' and Soldiers' Deputies

10 A.M., October 25, 1917

Theses on the Constituent Assembly

The demand for convocation of a Constituent Assembly to form a Russian democratic republic figured in the programs of all the liberal and radical parties, Bolsheviks included, from early 1917. The Provisional Government set November 25 as the date for the election of delegates to the Assembly. By then the Bolsheviks were in power. Having criticized the Provisional Government for postponing the election, the Bolsheviks felt compelled to go through with it, and the election took place on November 25 and the following days. The Bolsheviks received about a quarter of the votes, the conservative and liberal parties about 13 percent, and the moderate socialists about 62 percent. The bulk of the latter votes went to the Socialist-Revolutionary (peasant socialist) Party, and a leading figure of this party, Chernov, was elected president of the Constituent Assembly when it met in Petrograd on January 18 for what proved its first and last meeting; the Assembly was forcibly dispersed by Bolshevik forces. Lenin's argument foreshadowing this action, and attempting to justify it, is contained in these "Theses," which were published in *Pravda* on December 26, 1917. The election for the Constituent Assembly was the first and (so far) the last free Russian parliamentary election based on universal suffrage.*

---

1. The demand for the convocation of a Constituent Assembly was a perfectly legitimate part of the programme of revolutionary Social-Democracy, because in a bourgeois republic the Constituent Assembly represents the highest form of democracy and because, in setting up a Pre-parliament, the imperialist republic headed by Kerensky was preparing to rig the elections and violate democracy in a number of ways.

2. While demanding the convocation of a Constituent Assembly, revolutionary Social-Democracy has ever since the beginning of the Revolution of 1917 repeatedly emphasised that a republic of Soviets is a higher form of democracy than the usual bourgeois republic with a Constituent Assembly.

* For a detailed factual account of these events, see William Henry Chamberlin, *The Russian Revolution* (New York, 1965), Vol. I, pp. 364–371. [R. T.]

3. For the transition from the bourgeois to the socialist system, for the dictatorship of the proletariat, the Republic of Soviets (of Workers', Soldiers' and Peasants' Deputies) is not only a higher type of democratic institution (as compared with the usual bourgeois republic crowned by a Constituent Assembly), but is the only form capable of securing the most painless transition to socialism.

4. The convocation of the Constituent Assembly in our revolution on the basis of lists submitted in the middle of October 1917 is taking place under conditions which preclude the possibility of the elections to this Constituent Assembly faithfully expressing the will of the people in general and of the working people in particular.

5. Firstly, proportional representation results in a faithful expression of the will of the people only when the party lists correspond to the real division of the people according to the party groupings reflected in those lists. In our case, however, as is well known, the party which from May to October had the largest number of followers among the people, and especially among the peasants—the Socialist-Revolutionary Party—came out with united election lists for the Constituent Assembly in the middle of October 1917, but split in November 1917, after the elections and before the Assembly met.

For this reason, there is not, nor can there be, even a formal correspondence between the will of the mass of the electors and the composition of the elected Constituent Assembly.

6. Secondly, a still more important, not a formal nor legal, but a socio-economic, class source of the discrepancy between the will of the people, and especially the will of the working classes, on the one hand, and the composition of the Constituent Assembly, on the other, is due to the elections to the Constituent Assembly having taken place at a time when the overwhelming majority of the people could not yet know the full scope and significance of the October, Soviet, proletarian-peasant revolution, which began on October 25, 1917, i.e., after the lists of candidates for the Constituent Assembly had been submitted.

7. The October Revolution is passing through successive stages of development before our very eyes, winning power for the Soviets and wresting political rule from the bourgeoisie and transferring it to the proletariat and poor peasantry.

8. It began with the victory of October 24–25 in the capital, when the Second All-Russia Congress of Soviets of Workers' and Soldiers' Deputies, the vanguard of the proletarians and of the most politically active section of the peasants, gave a majority to the Bolshevik Party and put it in power.

9. Then, in the course of November and December, the revolution spread to the entire army and peasants, this being expressed

first of all in the deposition of the old leading bodies (army committees, *gubernia*[1] peasant committees, the Central Executive Committee of the All-Russia Soviet of Peasants' Deputies, etc.)—which expressed the superseded, compromising phase of the revolution, its bourgeois, and not proletarian, phase, and which were therefore inevitably bound to disappear under the pressure of the deeper and broader masses of the people—and in the election of new leading bodies in their place.

10. This mighty movement of the exploited people for the reconstruction of the leading bodies of their organisations has not ended even now, in the middle of December 1917, and the Railwaymen's Congress, which is still in session, represents one of its stages.

11. Consequently, the grouping of the class forces in Russia in the course of their class struggle is in fact assuming, in November and December 1917, a form differing in principle from the one that the party lists of candidates for the Constituent Assembly compiled in the middle of October 1917 could have reflected.

12. Recent events in the Ukraine (partly also in Finland and Byelorussia, as well as in the Caucasus) point similarly to a regrouping of class forces which is taking place in the process of the struggle between the bourgeois nationalism of the Ukrainian Rada,[2] the Finnish Diet, etc., on the one hand, and Soviet power, the proletarian-peasant revolution in each of these national republics, on the other.

13. Lastly, the civil war which was started by the Cadet-Kaledin[3] counter-revolutionary revolt against the Soviet authorities, against the workers' and peasants' government, has finally brought the class struggle to a head and has destroyed every chance of settling in a formally democratic way the very acute problems with which history has confronted the peoples of Russia, and in the first place her working class and peasants.

14. Only the complete victory of the workers and peasants over the bourgeois and landowner revolt (as expressed in the Cadet-Kaledin movement), only the ruthless military suppression of this revolt of the slave-owners can really safeguard the proletarian-peasant revolution. The course of events and the development of the class struggle in the revolution have resulted in the slogan "All Power to the Constituent Assembly!"—which disregards the gains

1. *Gubernia*: province. [R. T.]
2. The Ukrainian Central Rada was a council established at Kiev in April 1917 at a congress of Ukrainian nationalist groups and parties. After the October Revolution, it proclaimed itself the supreme organ of the "Ukrainian People's Republic." In January 1918 Soviet forces occupied Kiev, ending the rule of the Rada. [R. T.]
3. A. M. Kaledin, a tsarist general, headed a counter-revolutionary revolt in the Don area.

of the workers' and peasants' revolution, which disregards Soviet power, which disregards the decisions of the Second All-Russia Congress of Soviets of Workers' and Soldiers' Deputies, of the Second All-Russia Congress of Peasants' Deputies, etc.—*becoming in fact* the slogan of the Cadets and the Kaledinites and of their helpers. The entire people are now fully aware that the Constituent Assembly, if it parted ways with Soviet power, would inevitably be doomed to political extinction.

15. One of the particularly acute problems of national life is the problem of peace. A really revolutionary struggle for peace began in Russia only after the victory of the October 25 Revolution, and the first fruits of this victory were the publication of the secret treaties, the conclusion of an armistice, and the beginning of open negotiations for a general peace without annexations and indemnities.

Only now are the broad sections of the people actually receiving a chance fully and openly to observe the policy of revolutionary struggle for peace and to study its results.

At the time of the elections to the Constituent Assembly the mass of the people had no such chance.

It is clear that the discrepancy between the composition of the elected Constituent Assembly and the actual will of the people on the question of terminating the war is inevitable from this point of view too.

16. The result of all the above-mentioned circumstances taken together is that the Constituent Assembly, summoned on the basis of the election lists of the parties existing prior to the proletarian-peasant revolution under the rule of the bourgeoisie, must inevitably clash with the will and interests of the working and exploited classes which on October 25 began the socialist revolution against the bourgeoisie. Naturally, the interests of this revolution stand higher than the formal rights of the Constituent Assembly, even if those formal rights were not undermined by the absence in the law on the Constituent Assembly of a provision recognising the right of the people to recall their deputies and hold new elections at any moment.

17. Every direct or indirect attempt to consider the question of the Constituent Assembly from a formal, legal point of view, within the framework of ordinary bourgeois democracy and disregarding the class struggle and civil war, would be a betrayal of the proletariat's cause, and the adoption of the bourgeois standpoint. The revolutionary Social-Democrats are duty bound to warn all and sundry against this error, into which a few Bolshevik leaders, who have been unable to appreciate the significance of the October uprising and the tasks of the dictatorship of the proletariat, have strayed.

18. The only chance of securing a painless solution to the crisis which has arisen owing to the divergence between the elections to the Constituent Assembly, on the one hand, and the will of the people and the interests of the working and exploited classes, on the other, is for the people to exercise as broadly and as rapidly as possible the right to elect the members of the Constituent Assembly anew, and for the Constituent Assembly to accept the law of the Central Executive Committee on these new elections, to proclaim that it unreservedly recognises Soviet power, the Soviet revolution, and its policy on the questions of peace, the land and workers' control, and to resolutely join the camp of the enemies of the Cadet-Kaledin counter-revolution.

19. Unless these conditions are fulfilled, the crisis in connection with the Constituent Assembly can be settled only in a revolutionary way, by Soviet power adopting the most energetic, speedy, firm and determined revolutionary measures against the Cadet-Kaledin counter-revolution, no matter behind what slogans and institutions (even participation in the Constituent Assembly) this counter-revolution may hide. Any attempt to tie the hands of Soviet power in this struggle would be tantamount to aiding counter-revolution.

On Revolutionary Violence and Terror

In early January 1918, after the Bolsheviks had been in power for two months, Lenin went on a four-day vacation to Finland. While there he jotted down some themes for future elaboration ("From a Publicist's Notebook") and drafted a decree issued in April 1918. He also drafted two articles: "Fright at the Fall of the Old and the Fight for the New" and "How to Organize Competition." The first was a general defense of the necessity and legitimacy of proletarian violence and terror against bourgeois resistance to the revolution, and the second spelled out this general position in terms of more specific prescriptions for Draconian Bolshevik punitive actions. The first follows in unabridged form, the second in somewhat abridged form.

Lenin withheld these two articles from publication. They were first published in January 1929, when they appeared in *Pravda* on the occasion of the fifth anniversary of his death. In her memoirs (*Vospominaniia o Lenine* [Moscow, 1957], p. 344), Krupskaya explains his withholding of them from publication by saying that he considered them "not fully worked up" ("*nedodelannym*"). Since, however, they are as worked up as many other articles that Lenin did publish, his decision remains unexplained. Perhaps he had second thoughts about issuing such a frank public defense of terroristic policies on the part of the revolutionary regime. But other statements and actions of his make it quite clear that these two articles did represent, at the time of writing, his considered position.

In *The Gulag Archipelago*, the exiled Russian writer Alexander Solzhenitsyn has quoted several passages from "How to Organize Competition" (without noting its actual date of publication) to show that Lenin himself furnished the original inspiration for the practices which were to evolve under Stalin in the nineteen-thirties into a monstrous slave-labor empire operating by systematic cruelty and inhumanity on a huge scale. While Lenin was indeed a principled advocate of revolutionary terror, forced labor for opponents of the regime, etc., it may be questioned whether the terror of the Civil War period (1917–21) was either quantitatively or qualitatively the same phenomenon as the Stalinist terror of 1929–39 and later.

Fright at the Fall of the Old and the Fight for the New

The capitalists and their supporters, witting and unwitting, are thinking, saying and writing: "The Bolsheviks have now been in power for two months, but instead of a socialist paradise we find the hell of chaos, civil war and even greater dislocation."

We reply: the Bolsheviks have been in power for only two months, but a tremendous step towards socialism has already been made. This is not evident only to those who do not wish to see or are unable to analyse the chain of historical events. They refuse to see that in a matter of weeks the undemocratic institutions in the army, the countryside and industry have been almost completely destroyed. There is no other way—there can be no other way—to socialism save through such destruction. They refuse to see that in a few weeks, the lying imperialist foreign policy, which dragged out the war and covered up plunder and seizure through secret treaties, has been replaced by a truly revolutionary-democratic policy working for a really democratic peace, a policy which has already produced such a great practical success as the armistice and has increased the propaganda power of our revolution a hundredfold. They refuse to see that workers' control and the nationalisation of the banks are being put into practice, and these are the first steps towards socialism.

Those tyrannised by capitalist routine, shocked by the thundering crash of the old world, and the blast, rumble, and "chaos" (apparent chaos) as the age-old structures of tsarism and the bourgeoisie break up and cave in cannot see the historical prospects; nor can those who are scared by the class struggle at its highest pitch when it turns into civil war, the only war that is legitimate, just and sacred—not in the clerical but in the human sense—the sacred war of the oppressed to overthrow the oppressors and liberate the working people from all oppression. Actually all these tyrannised, shocked and scared bourgeois, petty bourgeois and "those in the service of the bourgeoisie" are frequently guided, without realising it, by that old, absurd, sentimental and vulgar intellectualist idea of "introducing socialism," which they have acquired from hearsay and scraps of socialist theory, repeating the distortions of this theory produced by ignoramuses and half-scholars, and attributing to us Marxists the idea, and even the plan, to "introduce" socialism.

To us Marxists these notions, to say nothing of the plans, are alien. We have always known, said and emphasised that socialism cannot be "introduced," that it takes shape in the course of the most intense, the most acute class struggle—which reaches heights of frenzy and desperation—and civil war; we have always said that a long period of "birth-pangs" lies between capitalism and social-ism; that violence is always the midwife of the old society; that a special state (that is, a special system of organised coercion of a definite class) corresponds to the transitional period between the bourgeois and the socialist society, namely, the dictatorship of the proletariat. What dictatorship implies and means is a state of sim-mering war, a state of military measures of struggle against the enemies of the proletarian power. The Commune was a dictatorship of the proletariat, and Marx and Engels reproached it for what they considered to be one of the causes of its downfall, namely, that the Commune had not used its armed force with *sufficient* vigour to suppress the resistance of the exploiters.

These intellectualist howls about the suppression of capitalist resistance are actually nothing but an echo of the old "concilia-tion," to put it in a "genteel" manner. Putting it with proletarian bluntness, this means: continued kowtowing to the money-bags is what lies behind the howls against the present working-class coer-cion now being applied (unfortunately, with insufficient pressure or vigour) against the bourgeoisie, the saboteurs and counter-revolu-tionaries. The kind Peshekhonov, one of the conciliating ministers, proclaimed in June 1917: "The resistance of the capitalists has been broken." This kind soul had no inkling of the fact that their resistance must really be *broken*, and it *will* be broken, and that the scientific name for this breaking-up operation is dictatorship of the proletariat; that an entire historical period is marked by the sup-pression of capitalist resistance, and, consequently, by systematic application of *coercion* to an entire class (the bourgeoisie) and its accomplices.

The grasping, malicious, frenzied filthy avidity of the money-bags, the cowed servility of their hangers-on is the true social source of the present wail raised by the spineless intellectuals— from those of *Rech* to those of *Novaya Zhizn*—against violence on the part of the proletariat and the revolutionary peasants. Such is the objective meaning of their howls, their pathetic speeches, their clownish cries of "freedom" (freedom for the capitalists to oppress the people), etc. They would be "prepared" to recognise socialism, if mankind could jump straight into it in one spectacular leap, without any of the friction, the struggles, the exploiters' gnashing of teeth, or their diverse attempts to preserve the old order, or smuggle it back through the window, without the revolutionary proletariat responding to each attempt in a violent manner. These spineless hangers-on of the bourgeoisie with intellectualist pretensions are quite "prepared" to wade into the water provided they do not get their feet wet.

The drooping intellectuals are terrified when the bourgeoisie and the civil servants, employees, doctors, engineers, etc., who have grown accustomed to serving the bourgeoisie, go to extremes in their resistance. They tremble and utter even shriller cries about the need for a return to "conciliation." Like all true friends of the oppressed class, we can only derive satisfaction from the exploiters' extreme measures of resistance, because we do not expect the proletariat to mature for power in an atmosphere of cajoling and persuasion, in a school of mealy sermons or didactic declamations, but in the school of life and struggle. To become the ruling class and defeat the bourgeoisie for good the proletariat must be *schooled*, because the skill this implies does not come ready-made. The proletariat must do its learning in the struggle, and stubborn, desperate struggle in earnest is the only real teacher. The greater the extremes of the exploiters' resistance, the more vigorously, firmly, ruthlessly and successfully will they be suppressed by the exploited. The more varied the exploiters' attempts to uphold the old, the sooner will the proletariat learn to ferret out its enemies from their last nook and corner, to pull up the roots of their domination, and cut the very ground which could (and had to) breed wage-slavery, mass poverty and the profiteering and effrontery of the moneybags.

The strength of the proletariat and the peasantry allied to it grows with the resistance of the bourgeoisie and its retainers. As their enemies, the exploiters, step up their resistance, the exploited mature and gain in strength; they grow and learn and they cast out the "old Adam" of wage-slavery. Victory will be on the side of the exploited, for on their side is life, numerical strength, the strength of the mass, the strength of the inexhaustible sources of all that is selfless, dedicated and honest, all that is surging forward and awakening to the building of the new, all the vast reserves of energy and talent latent in the so-called "common people," the workers and peasants. Victory will be theirs.

How to Organise Competition

Bourgeois authors have been filling mountains of paper with praises of competition, private enterprise, and all the other magnificent virtues and blessings of the capitalists and of the capitalist system. Socialists have been accused of refusing to understand the importance of these virtues, and of ignoring "human nature." As a matter of fact, however, capitalism long ago replaced small, independent commodity production, under which competition could develop enterprise, energy and bold initiative to any *considerable* extent, with large and very large-scale factory production, joint-stock companies, syndicates and other monopolies. Under *such* capitalism, competition means the incredibly brutal suppression of the enterprise, energy and bold initiative of the *masses* of the population, of its overwhelming majority, of ninety-nine out of every hundred toilers; it also means that competition is replaced by financial fraud, despotism, servility on the upper rungs of the social ladder.

Far from extinguishing competition, socialism, on the contrary, for the first time creates the opportunity for employing it on a really *wide* and on a really *mass* scale, for actually drawing the majority of toilers into an arena of such labour in which they can display their abilities, develop their capacities, reveal their talents, of which there is an untapped spring among the people, and which capitalism crushed, suppressed and strangled in thousands and millions.

Now that a socialist government is in power our task is to organise competition.

The hangers-on and spongers on the bourgeoisie described socialism as a uniform, routine, monotonous and drab barrack system. The lackeys of the moneybags, the lickspittles of the exploiters— Messieurs the bourgeois intellectuals—used socialism as a bogey to "frighten" the people, who, precisely under capitalism, were doomed to penal servitude and the barracks, to arduous, monotonous toil, to a life of dire poverty and semi-starvation. The first step towards the emancipation of the people from this penal servitude is the confiscation of the landed estates, the introduction of workers' control and the nationalisation of the factories and works, the compulsory organisation of the whole population in consumers' cooperative societies, which are at the same time societies for the sale of products, and the state monopoly of the trade in grain and other necessities.

* * *

The great change from working in subjection to working for oneself, to labour planned and organised on a gigantic, national (and to a certain extent international, world) scale also requires— in addition to "*military*" measures for the suppression of the resistance of the exploiters—tremendous *organizational*, organizing effort on the part of the proletariat and the poor peasants. The organizational task is interwoven to form a single whole with the task of ruthlessly suppressing by military methods yesterday's slaveowners (capitalists) and their packs of lackeys—Messieurs the bourgeois intellectuals. Yesterday's slaveowners and their stooges, the intellectuals, say and think, "We have always been organizers and chiefs. We have commanded, and we want to continue doing so. We shall refuse to obey the 'common people,' the workers and peasants. We shall not submit to them. We shall convert knowledge into a weapon for the defence of the privileges of the moneybags and of the rule of capital over the people."

That is what the bourgeoisie and the bourgeois intellectuals say, think, and do. From the point of view of *self-interest* their behaviour is comprehensible. The hangers-on and spongers on the feudal landlords—the priests, the scribes, the bureaucrats as Gogol depicted them, and the "intellectuals" who hated Belinsky—also found it "hard" to part with serfdom. But the cause of the exploiters and of their intellectual menials is hopeless. The workers and peasants are breaking their resistance—unfortunately, not yet firmly, resolutely and ruthlessly enough—*and will break it.*

The workers and peasants are still "shy," they have not yet become accustomed to the idea that *they* are the *ruling* class now; they are not yet sufficiently resolute. The revolution could not *at one stroke* instil these qualities in millions and millions of people who all their lives had been compelled by hunger and want to work under the threat of the stick. But the strength, the virility, the invincibility of the Revolution of October 1917 lie exactly in the fact that it *awakens* these qualities, breaks down the old impediments, tears the obsolete shackles, and leads the toilers on to the road of *independent* creation of a new life.

Accounting and control—this is the *main* economic task of every Soviet of Workers', Soldiers' and Peasants' Deputies, of every consumers' society, of every union or committee of supplies, of every factory committee or organ of workers' control in general.

* * *

Accounting and control, *if* carried on by the Soviets of Workers', Soldiers' and Peasants' Deputies as the supreme state power, or on the instructions, on the authority, of *this* power—widespread, general, universal accounting and control, the accounting and control of the amount of labour performed and of the distribution of products—is the *essence* of the socialist transformation, once the political rule of the proletariat has been established and secured.

The accounting and control that is essential for the transition to socialism can be exercised only by the masses. The voluntary and conscientious cooperation, marked by revolutionary enthusiasm, of the masses of the workers and peasants in accounting and controlling *the rich, the crooks, the idlers and hooligans* can alone conquer these survivals of accursed capitalist society, these dregs of humanity, these hopelessly decayed and atrophied limbs, this contagion, this plague, this ulcer that socialism has inherited from capitalism.

Workers and peasants, toilers and exploited! The land, the banks, the factories and works have now become the possession of the whole of the people! You *yourselves* must set to work to take account of and control the production and the distribution of products—this, and this *alone* is the road to the victory of socialism, the only guarantee of its victory, the guarantee of victory over all exploitation, over all poverty and want! For there is enough bread, iron, timber, wool, cotton and flax in Russia to satisfy the needs of all, provided only labour and its products are properly distributed, provided only the *businesslike, practical* control over this distribution by the whole of the people is established, provided only we can defeat the enemies of the people: the rich and their hangers-on, and the rogues, the idlers and the hooligans, *not only* in politics, but also in *everyday economic* life.

No mercy to these enemies of the people, the enemies of socialism, the enemies of the toilers! War to the bitter end on the rich and their hangers-on, the bourgeois intellectuals; war on the rogues, the idlers and hooligans! Both, the former and the latter, are of the same brood—the spawn of capitalism, the offspring of aristocratic and bourgeois society; the society in which a handful of men robbed and insulted the people; the society in which poverty and want forced thousands and thousands into the path of hooliganism, corruption and roguery, and caused them to lose all semblance of human beings; the society which inevitably cultivated in the toiler the desire to escape exploitation even by means of deception, to manoeuvre out of it, to escape, if only for a moment, from loathsome toil, to procure at least a crust of bread by any possible means, at any cost, so as not to starve, so as to subdue the pangs of hunger suffered by himself and by his near ones.

The rich and the crooks are two sides of the same medal, they are the two principal categories of *parasites* which capitalism fostered; they are the principal enemies of socialism. These enemies must be placed under the special surveillance of the whole people; they must be ruthlessly punished for the slightest violation of the laws and regulations of socialist society. Any display of weakness, hesitation or sentimentality in this respect would be an immense crime against socialism.

In order to render these parasites harmless to socialist society we must organise the accounting and control of the amount of labour performed, of production and distribution, to be exercised by the whole of the people, by millions and millions of workers and peasants, voluntarily, energetically and with revolutionary enthusiasm. And in order to organize this accounting and control, which is *fully within the ability* of every honest, intelligent and efficient worker and peasant, we must rouse their own organising talent, the talent which comes from their midst; we must rouse among them—and organise on a national scale—*competition* in the sphere of organisational successes; the workers and peasants must be brought to see clearly the difference between the necessary advice of an educated man and the necessary control by the "common" worker and peasant of the *slovenliness* that is so usual among the "educated."

This slovenliness, this carelessness, untidiness, unpunctuality, nervous haste, the inclination to substitute discussion for action, talk for work, the inclination to undertake everything under the sun without finishing anything, is one of the characteristics of the "educated"; and this is not due to the fact that they are bad by nature, still less is it due to their evil will; it is due to all their habits of life, the conditions of their work, to fatigue, to the abnormal separation of mental from manual labour, and so on, and so forth.

Among the mistakes, shortcomings and omissions of our revolution a by no means unimportant place is occupied by the mistakes, etc., which are due to these deplorable—but at present inevitable— characteristics of the intellectuals in our midst, and to the *lack* of sufficient supervision by the *workers* over the *organizational* work of the intellectuals.

The workers and peasants are still "shy"; they must get rid of this shyness, and they *certainly* will get rid of it. We cannot·dispense with the advice, the instruction of educated people, of intellectuals and specialists. Every sensible worker and peasant understands this perfectly well, and the intellectuals in our midst cannot complain of a lack of attention and comradely respect on the part of the workers and peasants. But advice and instruction is one thing, and the organization of *practical* accounting and control is another thing. Very often the intellectuals give excellent advice and instruction, but they prove to be ridiculously, *absurdly*, shamefully "unhandy" and incapable of *carrying out* this advice and instruction, of exercising *practical control* over the translation of words into deeds.

And in this very respect it is utterly impossible to dispense with the help and the *leading role* of the practical workers-organisers from among the "people," from among the workers and toiling peasants. "It is not the gods who make pots"—this is the truth that the workers and peasants should get well drilled into their minds. They must understand that the whole thing now is *practical work*; that the historical moment has arrived when theory is being transformed into practice, is vitalised by practice, corrected by practice, tested by practice; when the words of Marx, "Every step of real movement is more important than a dozen programmes," become particularly true—every step in really curbing in practice, restricting, fully registering and supervising the rich and the rogues is worth more than a dozen excellent arguments about socialism. For "theory, my friend, is grey, but green is the eternal tree of life."[1]

Competition must be organised among the practical workers-organisers from the workers and peasants. Every attempt to establish stereotyped forms and to impose uniformity from above, as intellectuals are so inclined to do, must be combated. Stereotyped forms and uniformity imposed from above have nothing in common with democratic and socialist centralism. The unity of essentials, of fundamentals, of the substance, is not disturbed but ensured by *variety* in details, in specific local features, in methods of *approach*, in *methods* of exercising control, in *ways* of exterminating and rendering harmless the parasites (the rich and the crooks, slovenly and hysterical intellectuals, etc., etc.).

The Paris Commune gave a great example of how to combine initiative, independence, freedom of action and vigour from below with voluntary centralism free from stereotyped forms. Our Soviets are following the same road. But they are still "shy," they have not yet got into their stride, have not yet "bitten into" their new, great, creative task of building the socialist system. The Soviets must set to work more boldly and display greater initiative. Every "commune," every factory, every village, every consumers' society, every committee of supply, must *compete* with its neighbours as a practical organiser of accounting and control of labour and distribution of products. The programme of this accounting and control is simple, clear and intelligible to all; it is: everyone to have bread; everyone to have sound footwear and whole clothing; everyone to have warm dwellings; everyone to work conscientiously; not a single rogue (including those who shirk their work) should be allowed to be at liberty, but kept in prison, or serve his sentence of compulsory labour of the hardest kind; not a single rich man who violates the laws and regulations of socialism to be allowed to escape the fate of the crook, which should, in justice, be the fate of the rich man. "He who does not work, neither shall he eat"—this is the *practical* commandment of socialism. This is how things should be organised *practically*. These are the *practical* successes our "communes" and our worker- and peasant-organisers should be proud of. And this applies *particularly* to the organisers among the intellectuals (*particularly*, because they are *too much, far too much* in the habit of being proud of their general instructions and resolutions).

Thousands of practical forms and methods of accounting and controlling the rich, the rogues and the idlers should be devised and put to a practical test by the communes themselves, by small units in town and country. Variety is a guarantee of vitality here, a pledge of success in achieving the single common aim—to cleanse

---

1. Said by Mephistopheles in Goethe's *Faust*, Part I, Scene 4.

the land of Russia of all sorts of harmful insects, of crook-fleas, of bedbugs—the rich, and so on and so forth. In one place half a score of rich, a dozen crooks, half a dozen workers who shirk their work (in the hooligan manner in which many compositors in Petrograd, particularly in the Party printing shops, shirk their work) will be put in prison. In another place they will be put to cleaning latrines. In a third place they will be provided with "yellow tickets" after they have served their time, so that all the people shall have them under surveillance, as *harmful* persons, until they reform. In a fourth place, one out of every ten idlers will be shot on the spot. In a fifth place mixed methods may be adopted, and by probational release, for example, the rich, the bourgeois intellectuals, the crooks and hooligans who are corrigible will be given an opportunity to reform quickly. The more variety there will be, the better and richer will be our general experience, the more certain and rapid will be the success of socialism, and the easier will it be for practice to devise—for only practice can devise—the *best* methods and means of struggle.

In what commune, in what district of a large town, in what factory and in what village are there *no* starving people, *no* unemployed, *no* idle rich, *no* scoundrelly lackeys of the bourgeoisie, saboteurs who call themselves intellectuals? Where has most been done to raise the productivity of labour, to build good new houses for the poor, to put the poor in the houses of the rich, to regularly provide a bottle of milk for every child of every poor family? It is on these points that *competition* should unfold itself between the communes, communities, producers-consumers' societies and associations, and Soviets of Workers', Soldiers' and Peasants' Deputies. This is the work in which *organising talent* should reveal itself *in practice* and be promoted to work in the administration of the state. There is a great deal of this talent among the people. It is merely suppressed. It must be given an opportunity to display itself. *It, and it alone*, with the support of the masses, can save Russia and save the cause of socialism.

The Chief Task of Our Day

The Bolsheviks owed their revolutionary success in part to popular approval of their commitment to lead the country out of a seemingly endless war which had cost it countless casualties and hardships. But the representatives of the Imperial German Government with whom Trotsky negotiated at Brest-Litovsk offered terms so onerous that many Bolsheviks supported a Left Communist faction, headed by Bukharin, in its proposal to wage "revolutionary war" against the Germans rather than submit to such terms. By threatening his resignation, Lenin won a bare majority of the party Central Committee for his position that acceptance of this "Tilsit peace" (a reference to the harsh peace imposed by Napoleon upon Prussia in 1807) was necessary to save the Revolution from certain destruction, and the terms were signed on March 3, 1918. In this article, published March 12, Lenin looked beyond the Tilsit peace to the prospect of building a socialist society—in part by learning the ways of those very Germans whose "brutal imperialism" coexisted with a culture of organization, discipline, and cooperation that was needed in Mother Russia.

> Thou art wretched, thou art abundant.
> Thou art mighty, thou art impotent—Mother Russia![1]

Human history these days is making a momentous and most difficult turn, a turn, one might say without the least exaggeration, of immense significance for the emancipation of the world. A turn from war to peace; a turn from a war between plunderers who are sending to the shambles millions of the working and exploited people for the sake of establishing a new system of dividing the spoils looted by the strongest of them, to a war of the oppressed against the oppressors for liberation from the yoke of capital; a turn from an abyss of suffering, anguish, starvation and degradation to the bright future of communist society, universal prosperity and enduring peace. No wonder that at the sharpest points of this sharp turn, when all around the old order is breaking down and collapsing with a terrible grinding crash, and the new order is being born amid indescribable suffering, there are some whose heads

1. Lenin's epigraph comes from Nekrasov's poem "Who Lives Well in Russia?"

433

grow dizzy, some who are seized by despair, some who seek salvation from the at times too bitter reality in fine-sounding and alluring phrases.

It has been Russia's lot to see most clearly, and experience most keenly and painfully the sharpest of sharp turning-points in history as it swings round from imperialism towards the communist revolution. In the space of a few days we destroyed one of the oldest, most powerful, barbarous and brutal of monarchies. In the space of a few months we passed through a number of stages of collaboration with the bourgeoisie and of shaking off petty-bourgeois illusions, for which other countries have required decades. In the course of a few weeks, having overthrown the bourgeoisie, we crushed its open resistance in civil war. We passed in a victorious triumphal march of Bolshevism from one end of a vast country to the other. We raised the lowest strata of the working people oppressed by tsarism and the bourgeoisie to liberty and independent life. We established and consolidated a Soviet Republic, a new type of state, which is infinitely superior to, and more democratic than, the best of the bourgeois-parliamentary republics. We established the dictatorship of the proletariat supported by the poor peasantry, and began a broadly conceived system of socialist reforms. We awakened the faith of the millions upon millions of workers of all countries in their own strength and kindled the fires of enthusiasm in them. Everywhere we issued the call for a world workers' revolution. We flung a challenge to the imperialist plunderers of all countries.

Then in a few days we were thrown to the ground by an imperialist plunderer, who fell upon the unarmed. He compelled us to sign an incredibly burdensome and humiliating peace—as tribute for having dared to tear ourselves, even for the shortest space of time, from the iron clutches of an imperialist war. The more ominously the shadow of a workers' revolution in his own country rises before the plunderer, the greater his ferocity in crushing and stifling Russia and tearing her to pieces.

We were compelled to sign a "Tilsit" peace. We need no self-deception. We must courageously look the bitter, unadorned truth straight in the face. We must measure fully, to the very bottom, that abyss of defeat, dismemberment, enslavement, and humiliation into which we have now been pushed. The more clearly we understand this, the firmer, the more steeled and tempered will be our will to liberation, our aspiration to rise again from enslavement to independence, and our unbending determination to ensure that at any price Russia ceases to be wretched and impotent and becomes mighty and abundant in the full meaning of these words.

And mighty and abundant she can become, for, after all, we still have sufficient territory and natural wealth left to us to supply each and all, if not with abundant, at least with adequate means of life. Our natural wealth, our man-power and the splendid impetus which the great revolution has given to the creative powers of the people are ample material to build a truly mighty and abundant Russia.

Russia will become mighty and abundant if she abandons all dejection and all phrase-making, if, with clenched teeth, she musters all her forces and strains every nerve and muscle, if she realises that salvation lies *only* along that road of world socialist revolution upon which we have set out. March forward along that road, undismayed by defeats, lay the firm foundation of socialist society stone by stone, work with might and main to establish discipline and self-discipline, consolidate everywhere organisation, order, efficiency, and the harmonious co-operation of all the forces of the people, introduce comprehensive accounting of and control over production and distribution—such is the way to build up military might and socialist might.

It would be unworthy of a genuine socialist who has suffered grave defeat either to bluster or to give way to despair. It is not true that our position is hopeless and that all that remains for us is to choose between an "inglorious" death (inglorious from the point of view of the *szlachcic*[2]), such as this harsh peace represents, and a "gallant" death in a hopeless fight. It is not true that by signing a "Tilsit" peace we have betrayed our ideals or our friends. We have betrayed nothing and nobody, we have not sanctified or covered up any lie, we have not refused to help a single friend or comrade in misfortune in every way we could and with everything at our disposal. A general who withdraws the remnants of his army into the heart of the country when it has been beaten or is in panic-stricken flight, or who, in extremity, shields this retreat by a harsh and humiliating peace, is not guilty of treachery towards that part of his army which he is powerless to help and which has been cut off by the enemy. Such a general performs his duty by choosing the only way of saving what can still be saved, by refusing to gamble recklessly, by not embellishing the bitter truth for the people, by "surrendering space in order to gain time," by taking advantage of *any and every* respite, even the briefest, in which to muster his forces and to allow his army to rest or recover, if it is affected by disintegration and demoralisation.

We have signed a "Tilsit" peace. When Napoleon I, in 1807, compelled Prussia to sign the Peace of Tilsit, the conqueror smashed the Germans' entire army, occupied their capital and all their big cities, brought in his own police, compelled the vanquished to sup-

---

2. Polish for "landowners." [*R. T.*]

ply him, the conqueror, with auxiliary corps for fresh predatory wars, and partitioned Germany, concluding alliances with some German states against others. Nevertheless, the German people survived even *such* a peace, proved able to muster their forces, to rise and to win the right to liberty and independence.

To all those who are able and willing to think, the example of the Peace of Tilsit (which was only one of many harsh and humiliating treaties forced upon the Germans at that period) clearly shows how childishly naïve is the idea that under all conditions a harsh peace means the bottomless pit of ruin, while war is the path of valour and salvation. Periods of war teach us that peace has not infrequently in history served as a respite and a means of mustering forces for new battles. The Peace of Tilsit was a supreme humiliation for Germany, but at the same time it marked a turn towards a supreme national resurgence. At that time historical conditions were such that this resurgence could be channelled only in the direction of a *bourgeois* state. At that time, more than a hundred years ago, history was made by handfuls of nobles and a sprinkling of bourgeois intellectuals, while the worker and peasant masses were somnolent and dormant. As a result history at that time could only crawl along at a terribly slow pace.

But now capitalism has raised culture in general, and the culture of the masses in particular, to a much higher level. War has shaken up the masses, its untold horrors and suffering have awakened them. War has given history momentum and it is now flying with locomotive speed. History is now being independently made by millions and tens of millions of people. Capitalism has now matured for socialism.

Consequently, if Russia is now passing—as she undeniably is—from a "Tilsit" peace to a national resurgence, to a great patriotic war, the outlet for it is not in the direction of a bourgeois state, but in the direction of a world socialist revolution. Since October 25, 1917, we have been defencists. We are for "defence of the fatherland"; but that patriotic war towards which we are moving is a war for a socialist fatherland, for socialism as a fatherland, for the Soviet Republic as a *contingent* of the world army of socialism.

"Hate the Germans, kill the Germans"—such was, and is, the slogan of common, i.e., bourgeois, patriotism. But we will say, "Hate the imperialist plunderers, hate capitalism, death to capitalism" and at the same time "Learn from the Germans! Remain true to the brotherly alliance with the German workers. They are late in coming to our aid. We shall gain time, we shall live to see them coming, and they *will come,* to our aid."

Yes, learn from the Germans! History is moving in zigzags and by roundabout ways. It so happens that it is the Germans who now personify, besides a brutal imperialism, the principle of discipline, organisation, harmonious co-operation on the basis of modern machine industry, and strict accounting and control.

And that is just what we are lacking. That is just what we must learn. That is just what our great revolution needs in order to pass from a triumphant beginning, through a succession of severe trials, to its triumphant goal. That is just what the Russian Soviet Socialist Republic requires in order to cease being wretched and impotent and become mighty and abundant for all time.

The Immediate Tasks of the Soviet Government

Having won a "breathing spell" for the revolutionary regime by acceptance of the Brest-Litovsk peace, Lenin was able to concentrate attention upon the internal situation and tasks in a way that had not been possible hitherto; and this major article, written in the second half of April 1918, resulted. In its emphasis on the theme that "dictatorship is iron rule . . . ," and on the necessity of coercion for the transition from capitalism to socialism, it is illustrative of one significant tendency of Bolshevik thought that characterized the period of War Communism.

The International Position of the Russian Soviet Republic and the Fundamental Tasks of the Socialist Revolution

Thanks to the peace which has been achieved—despite its extremely onerous character and extreme instability—the Russian Soviet Republic has gained an opportunity to concentrate its efforts for a while on the most important and most difficult aspect of the socialist revolution, namely, the task of organisation.

This task was clearly and definitely set before all the working and oppressed people in the fourth paragraph (Part 4) of the resolution adopted at the Extraordinary Congress of Soviets in Moscow on March 15, 1918, in that paragraph (or part) which speaks of the self-discipline of the working people and of the ruthless struggle against chaos and disorganisation.

Of course, the peace achieved by the Russian Soviet Republic is unstable not because she is now thinking of resuming military operations; apart from bourgeois counter-revolutionaries and their henchmen (the Mensheviks and others), no sane politician thinks of doing that. The instability of the peace is due to the fact that in the imperialist states bordering on Russia to the West and the East, which command enormous military forces, the war party, tempted by Russia's momentary weakness and egged on by capitalists, who hate socialism and are eager for plunder, may gain the upper hand at any moment.

Under these circumstances the only real, not paper, guarantee of peace we have is the antagonism among the imperialist powers, which has reached extreme limits, and which is apparent on the one hand in the resumption of the imperialist butchery of the peoples in the West, and on the other hand in the extreme intensification of imperialist rivalry between Japan and America for supremacy in the Pacific and on the Pacific coast.

It goes without saying that with such an unreliable guard for protection, our Soviet Socialist Republic is in an extremely unstable and certainly critical international position. All our efforts must be exerted to the very utmost to make use of the respite given us by the combination of circumstances so that we can heal the very severe wounds inflicted by the war upon the entire social organism of Russia and bring about an economic revival, without which a real increase in our country's defence potential is inconceivable.

It also goes without saying that we shall be able to render effective assistance to the socialist revolution in the West, which has been delayed for a number of reasons, only to the extent that we are able to fulfil the task of organisation confronting us.

A fundamental condition for the successful accomplishment of the primary task of organisation confronting us is that the people's political leaders, i.e., the members of the Russian Communist Party (Bolsheviks), and following them all the class-conscious representatives of the mass of the working people, shall fully appreciate the radical distinction in this respect between previous bourgeois revolutions and the present socialist revolution.

In bourgeois revolutions, the principal task of the mass of working people was to fulfil the negative or destructive work of abolishing feudalism, monarchy and medievalism. The positive or constructive work of organising the new society was carried out by the property-owning bourgeois minority of the population. And the latter carried out this task with relative ease, despite the resistance of the workers and the poor peasants, not only because the resistance of the people exploited by capital was then extremely weak, since they were scattered and uneducated, but also because the chief organising force of anarchically built capitalist society is the spontaneously growing and expanding national and international market.

In every socialist revolution, however—and consequently in the socialist revolution in Russia which we began on October 25, 1917 —the principal task of the proletariat, and of the poor peasants which it leads, is the positive or constructive work of setting up an

extremely intricate and delicate system of new organisational relationships extending to the planned production and distribution of
the goods required for the existence of tens of millions of people.
Such a revolution can be successfully carried out only if the majority of the population, and primarily the majority of the working
people, engage in independent creative work as makers of history.
Only if the proletariat and the poor peasants display sufficient class-
consciousness, devotion to principle, self-sacrifice and perseverance,
will the victory of the socialist revolution be assured. By creating a
new, Soviet type of state, which gives the working and oppressed
people the chance to take an active part in the independent building
up of a new society, we solved only a small part of this difficult
problem. The principal difficulty lies in the economic sphere,
namely, the introduction of the strictest and universal accounting
and control of the production and distribution of goods, raising the
productivity of labour and *socialising* production *in practice*.

The development of the Bolshevik Party, which today is the
governing party in Russia, very strikingly indicates the nature of
the turning-point in history we have now reached, which is the
peculiar feature of the present political situation, and which calls
for a new orientation of Soviet power, i.e., for a new presentation
of new tasks.

The first task of every party of the future is to convince the
majority of the people that its programme and tactics are correct.
This task stood in the forefront both in tsarist times and in the
period of the Chernovs' and Tseretelis' policy of compromise with
the Kerenskys and Kishkins. This task has now been fulfilled in the
main, for, as the recent Congress of Soviets in Moscow incontro-
vertibly proved, the majority of the workers and peasants of Russia
are obviously on the side of the Bolsheviks; but of course, it is far
from being completely fulfilled (and it can never be completely
fulfilled).

The second task that confronted our Party was to capture political power and to suppress the resistance of the exploiters. This task
has not been completely fulfilled either, and it cannot be ignored
because the monarchists and Constitutional-Democrats on the one
hand, and their henchmen and hangers-on, the Mensheviks and
Right Socialist-Revolutionaries, on the other, are continuing their
efforts to unite for the purpose of overthrowing Soviet power. In
the main, however, the task of suppressing the resistance of the
exploiters was fulfilled in the period from October 25, 1917, to
(approximately) February 1918, or to the surrender of Bogayev-
sky.

A third task is now coming to the fore as the immediate task and one which constitutes the peculiar feature of the present situation, namely, the task of organising *administration* of Russia. Of course, we advanced and tackled this task on the very day following October 25, 1917. Up to now, however, since the resistance of the exploiters still took the form of open civil war, up to now the task of administration *could not* become the *main*, the *central* task.

Now it has become the main and central task. We, the Bolshevik Party, have *convinced* Russia. We have *won* Russia from the rich for the poor, from the exploiters for the working people. Now we must *administer* Russia. And the whole peculiarity of the present situation, the whole difficulty, lies in understanding *the specific features of the transition* from the principal task of convincing the people and of suppressing the exploiters by armed force to the principal task of *administration*.

For the first time in human history a socialist party has managed to complete in the main the conquest of power and the suppression of the exploiters, and has managed to *approach directly* the task of *administration*. We must prove worthy executors of this most difficult (and most gratifying) task of the socialist revolution. We must *fully realise* that in order to administer successfully, *besides* being able to convince people, besides being able to win a civil war, we must be able to do *practical organisational work*. This is the most difficult task, because it is a matter of organising in a new way the most deep-rooted, the economic, foundations of life of scores of millions of people. And it is the most gratifying task, because only *after* it has been fulfilled (in the principal and main outlines) will it be possible to say that Russia *has become* not only a Soviet, but also a socialist, republic.

* * *

The New Phase of the Struggle Against the Bourgeoisie

The bourgeoisie in our country has been conquered, but it has not yet been uprooted, not yet destroyed, and not even utterly broken. That is why we are faced with a new and higher form of struggle against the bourgeoisie, the transition from the very simple task of further expropriating the capitalists to the much more complicated and difficult task of creating conditions in which it will be impossible for the bourgeoisie to exist, or for a new bourgeoisie to arise. Clearly, this task is immeasurably more significant than the previous one; and until it is fulfilled there will be no socialism.

If we measure our revolution by the scale of West-European revolutions we shall find that at the present moment we are approximately at the level reached in 1793 and 1871. We can be legitimately proud of having risen to this level, and of having certainly, in one respect, advanced somewhat further, namely: we have decreed and introduced throughout Russia the highest *type* of state—Soviet power. Under no circumstances, however, can we rest content with what we have achieved, because we have only just started the transition to socialism, we have *not yet* done the decisive thing in *this* respect.

The decisive thing is the organisation of the strictest and country-wide accounting and control of production and distribution of goods. And yet, we have *not yet* introduced accounting and control in those enterprises and in those branches and fields of economy which we have taken away from the bourgeoisie; and without this there can be no thought of achieving the second and equally essential material condition for introducing socialism, namely, raising the productivity of labour on a national scale.

That is why the present task could not be defined by the simple formula: continue the offensive against capital. Although we have certainly not finished off capital and although it is certainly necessary to continue the offensive against this enemy of the working people, such a formula would be inexact, would not be concrete, would not take into account the *peculiarity* of the present situation in which, in order to go on advancing successfully *in the future*, we must "suspend" our offensive *now*.

This can be explained by comparing our position in the war against capital with the position of a victorious army that has captured, say, a half or two-thirds of the enemy's territory and is compelled to halt in order to muster its forces, to replenish its supplies of munitions, repair and reinforce the lines of communication, build new storehouses, bring up new reserves, etc. To suspend the offensive of a victorious army under such conditions is necessary precisely in order to gain the rest of the enemy's territory, i.e., in order to achieve complete victory. Those who have failed to understand that the objective state of affairs at the present moment dictates to us precisely such a "suspension" of the offensive against capital have failed to understand anything at all about the present political situation.

It goes without saying that we can speak about the "suspension" of the offensive against capital only in quotation marks, i.e., only metaphorically. In ordinary war, a general order can be issued to stop the offensive, the advance can actually be stopped. In the war against capital, however, the advance cannot be stopped, and there can be no thought of our abandoning the further expropriation of capital. What we are discussing is the shifting of the *centre of gravity* of our economic and political work. Up to now measures for the direct expropriation of the expropriators were *in the fore-front*. Now the organisation of accounting and control in those enterprises in which the capitalists have already been expropriated, and in all other enterprises, advances *to the forefront*.

If we decided to continue to expropriate capital at the same rate at which we have been doing it up to now, we should certainly suffer defeat, because our work of organising proletarian accounting and control has obviously—obviously to every thinking person —*fallen behind* the work of *directly* "expropriating the expropriators." If we now concentrate all our efforts on the organisation of accounting and control, we shall be able to solve this problem, we shall be able to make up for lost time, we shall *completely* win our "campaign" against capital.

But is not the admission that we must make up for lost time tantamount to admission of some kind of an error? Not in the least. Take another military example. If it is possible to defeat and push back the enemy merely with detachments of light cavalry, it should be done. But if this can be done successfully only up to a certain point, then it is quite conceivable that when this point has been reached, it will be necessary to bring up heavy artillery. By admitting that it is now necessary to make up for lost time in bringing up heavy artillery, we do not admit that the successful cavalry attack was a mistake.

* * *

This is a peculiar epoch, or rather stage of development, and in order to defeat capital completely, we must be able to adapt the forms of our struggle to the peculiar conditions of this stage. Without the guidance of experts in the various fields of knowledge, technology and experience, the transition to socialism will be impossible, because socialism calls for a conscious mass advance to greater productivity of labour compared with capitalism, and on the basis achieved by capitalism. Socialism must achieve this advance *in its own way*, by its own methods—or, to put it more concretely, by *Soviet* methods. And the specialists, because of the whole social environment which made them specialists, are, in the main, inevitably bourgeois. Had our proletariat, after capturing power, quickly solved the problem of accounting, control and organisation on a national scale (which was impossible owing to the war and Russia's backwardness), then we, after breaking the sabotage, would also have completely subordinated these bourgeois experts to ourselves by means of universal accounting and control. Owing to the considerable "delay" in introducing accounting and control generally, we, although we have managed to conquer sabotage, have *not yet* created the conditions which would place the bourgeois specialists at our disposal. The mass of saboteurs are "going to work," but the best organisers and the top experts can be utilised by the state either in the old way, in the bourgeois way (i.e., for high salaries), or in the new way, in the proletarian way (i.e., creating the conditions of national accounting and control from below, which would inevitably and of themselves subordinate the experts and enlist them for our work).

Now we have to resort to the old bourgeois method and to agree to pay a very high price for the "services" of the top bourgeois experts. All those who are familiar with the subject appreciate this, but not all ponder over the significance of this measure being adopted by the proletarian state. Clearly, this measure is a compromise, a departure from the principles of the Paris Commune and of every proletarian power, which call for the reduction of all salaries to the level of the wages of the average worker, which urge that careerism be fought not merely in words, but in deeds.

Moreover, it is clear that this measure not only implies the cessation—in a certain field and to a certain degree—of the offensive against capital (for capital is not a sum of money, but a definite social relation); it is also *a step backward* on the part of our socialist Soviet state power, which from the very outset proclaimed and pursued the policy of reducing high salaries to the level of the wages of the average worker.[1]

* * *

Our work of organising country-wide accounting and control of production and distribution under the supervision of the proletariat has lagged very much behind our work of directly expropriating the expropriators. This proposition is of fundamental importance for understanding the specific features of the present situation and the tasks of the Soviet government that follow from it. The centre of gravity of our struggle against the bourgeoisie is shifting to the organisation of such accounting and control. Only with this as our starting-point will it be possible to determine correctly the immediate tasks of economic and financial policy in the sphere of nationalisation of the banks, monopolisation of foreign trade, the state control of money circulation, the introduction of a property and income tax satisfactory from the proletarian point of view, and the introduction of compulsory labour service.

We have been lagging very far behind in introducing socialist

1. An order by the Council of People's Commissars, published on November 18 (December 1), 1917, placed the maximum monthly salary of People's Commissars at 500 rubles. At the request of the People's Commissariat of Labour, the Council of People's Commissars shortly after this issued another order permitting higher salaries for highly qualified scientists and engineers.

reforms in these spheres (very, very important spheres), and this is because accounting and control are insufficiently organised in general. It goes without saying that this is one of the most difficult tasks, and in view of the ruin caused by the war, it can be fulfilled only over a long period of time; but we must not forget that it is precisely here that the bourgeoisie—and particularly the numerous petty and peasant bourgeoisie—are putting up the most serious fight, disrupting the control that is already being organised, disrupting the grain monopoly, for example, and gaining positions for profiteering and speculative trade. We have far from adequately carried out the things we have decreed, and the principal task of the moment is to concentrate all efforts on the businesslike, practical *realisation* of the principles of the reforms which have already become law (but not yet reality).

In order to proceed with the nationalisation of the banks and to go on steadfastly towards transforming the banks into nodal points of public accounting under socialism, we must first of all, and above all, achieve real success in increasing the number of branches of the People's Bank, in attracting deposits, in simplifying the paying in and withdrawal of deposits by the public, in abolishing queues, in catching and *shooting* bribe-takers and crooks, etc. At first we must really carry out the simplest things, properly organise what is available, and then prepare for the more intricate things.

Consolidate and improve the state monopolies (in grain, leather, etc.) which have already been introduced, and by doing so prepare for the state monopoly of foreign trade. Without this monopoly we shall not be able to "free ourselves" from foreign capital by paying "tribute." And the possibility of building up socialism depends entirely upon whether we shall be able, by paying a certain tribute to foreign capital during a certain transitional period, to safeguard our internal economic independence.

We are also lagging very far behind in regard to the collection of taxes generally, and of the property and income tax in particular. The imposing of indemnities upon the bourgeoisie—a measure which in principle is absolutely permissible and deserves proletarian approval—shows that in this respect we are still nearer to the methods of warfare (to win Russia from the rich for the poor) than to the methods of administration. In order to become stronger, however, and in order to be able to stand firmer on our feet, we must adopt the latter methods, we must substitute for the indemnities imposed upon the bourgeoisie the constant and regular collection of a property and income tax, which will bring a *greater* return to the proletarian state, and which calls for better organisation on our part and better accounting and control.

The fact that we are late in introducing compulsory labour service also shows that the work that is coming to the fore at the present time is precisely the preparatory organisational work that, on the one hand, will finally consolidate our gains and that, on the other, is necessary in order to prepare for the operation of "surrounding" capital and compelling it to "surrender." We ought to begin introducing compulsory labour service immediately, but we must do so very gradually and circumspectly, testing every step by practical experience, and, of course, taking the first step by introducing compulsory labour service *for the rich*. The introduction of work and consumers' budget books for every bourgeois, including every rural bourgeois, would be an important step towards completely "surrounding" the enemy and towards the creation of a truly popular accounting and control of the production and distribution of goods.

The Significance of the Struggle for Country-wide Accounting and Control

The state, which for centuries has been an organ for oppression and robbery of the people, has left us a legacy of the people's supreme hatred and suspicion of everything that is connected with the state. It is very difficult to overcome this, and only a Soviet government can do it. Even a Soviet government, however, will require plenty of time and enormous perseverance to accomplish it. This "legacy" is especially apparent in the problem of accounting and control—the fundamental problem facing the socialist revolution on the morrow of the overthrow of the bourgeoisie. A certain amount of time will inevitably pass before the people, who feel free for the first time now that the landowners and the bourgeoisie have been overthrown, will understand—not from books, but from their own, *Soviet* experience—will understand and *feel* that without comprehensive state accounting and control of the production and distribution of goods, the power of the working people, the freedom of the working people, *cannot* be maintained, and that a return to the yoke of capitalism is *inevitable*.

* * *

The socialist state can arise only as a network of producers' and consumers' communes, which conscientiously keep account of their production and consumption, economise on labour, and steadily raise the productivity of labour, thus making it possible to reduce the working day to seven, six and even fewer hours. Nothing will be achieved unless the strictest, country-wide, comprehensive accounting and control of *grain* and the *production of grain* (and later of all other essentials goods) are set going. Capitalism left us a legacy of mass organisations which can facilitate our transition to the mass accounting and control of the distribution of goods, namely, the consumers' co-operative societies. In Russia these societies are not so well developed as in the advanced countries, nevertheless, they have over ten million members. * * *

* * *

Raising the Productivity of Labour

In every socialist revolution, after the proletariat has solved the problem of capturing power, and to the extent that the task of expropriating the expropriators and suppressing their resistance has been carried out in the main, there necessarily comes to the fore-front the fundamental task of creating a social system superior to capitalism, namely, raising the productivity of labour, and in this connection (and for this purpose) securing better organisation of labour. Our Soviet state is precisely in the position where, thanks to the victories over the exploiters—from Kerensky to Kornilov—it is able to approach this task directly, to tackle it in earnest. And here it becomes immediately clear that while it is possible to take over the central government in a few days, while it is possible to sup-press the military resistance (and sabotage) of the exploiters even in different parts of a great country in a few weeks, the capital solution of the problem of raising the productivity of labour re-quires, at all events (particularly after a most terrible and devastat-ing war), several years. The protracted nature of the work is certainly dictated by objective circumstances.

The raising of the productivity of labour first of all requires that the material basis of large-scale industry shall be assured, namely, the development of the production of fuel, iron, the engineering and chemical industries. The Russian Soviet Republic enjoys the favour-able position of having at its command, even after the Brest peace, enormous reserves of ore (in the Urals), fuel in Western Siberia (coal), in the Caucasus and the South-East (oil), in Central Russia (peat), enormous timber reserves, water power, raw materials for the chemical industry (Karabugaz), etc. The development of these natu-ral resources by methods of modern technology will provide the basis for the unprecedented progress of the productive forces.

Another condition for raising the productivity of labour is, firstly, the raising of the educational and cultural level of the mass of the population. This is now taking place extremely rapidly, a fact which those who are blinded by bourgeois routine are unable to see; they are unable to understand what an urge towards enlightenment and initiative is now developing among the "lower ranks" of the people thanks to the Soviet form of organisation. Secondly, a condition for economic revival is the raising of the working people's discipline, their skill, the effectiveness, the intensity of labour and its better organisation.

In this respect the situation is particularly bad and even hopeless if we are to believe those who have allowed themselves to be intimidated by the bourgeoisie or by those who are serving the bourgeoisie for their own ends. These people do not understand that there has not been, nor could there be, a revolution in which the supporters of the old system did not raise a howl about chaos, anarchy, etc. Naturally, among the people who have only just thrown off an unprecedentedly savage yoke there is deep and widespread seething and ferment; the working out of new principles of labour discipline by the people is a very protracted process, and this process could not even start until complete victory had been achieved over the landowners and the bourgeoisie.

We, however, without in the least yielding to the despair (it is often false despair) which is spread by the bourgeoisie and the bourgeois intellectuals (who have despaired of retaining their old privileges), must under no circumstances conceal an obvious evil. On the contrary, we shall expose it and intensify the Soviet methods of combating it, because the victory of socialism is inconceivable without the victory of proletarian conscious discipline over spontaneous petty-bourgeois anarchy, this real guarantee of a possible restoration of Kerenskyism and Kornilovism.

The more class-conscious vanguard of the Russian proletariat has already set itself the task of raising labour discipline. For example, both the Central Committee of the Metalworkers' Union and the Central Council of Trade Unions have begun to draft the necessary measures and decrees. This work must be supported and pushed ahead with all speed. We must raise the question of piecework and apply and test it in practice; we must raise the question of applying much of what is scientific and progressive in the Taylor system; we must make wages correspond to the total amount of goods turned out, or to the amount of work done by the railways, the water transport system, etc., etc.

The Russian is a bad worker compared with people in advanced countries. It could not be otherwise under the tsarist regime and in view of the persistence of the hangover from serfdom. The task that the Soviet government must set the people in all its scope is—learn to work. The Taylor system, the last word of capitalism in this respect, like all capitalist progress, is a combination of the refined brutality of bourgeois exploitation and a number of the greatest scientific achievements in the field of analysing mechanical motions during work, the elimination of superfluous and awkward motions, the elaboration of correct methods of work, the introduction of the best system of accounting and control, etc. The Soviet Republic must at all costs adopt all that is valuable in the achievements of science and technology in this field. The possibility of building socialism depends exactly upon our success in combining the Soviet power and the Soviet organisation of administration with the up-to-date achievements of capitalism. We must organise in Russia the study and teaching of the Taylor system and systematically try it out and adapt it to our own ends. At the same time, in working to raise the productivity of labour, we must take into account the specific features of the transition period from capitalism to socialism, which, on the one hand, require that the foundations be laid of the socialist organisation of competition, and, on the other hand, require the use of compulsion, so that the slogan of the dictatorship of the proletariat shall not be desecrated by the practice of a jelly-like form of proletarian state authority.

The Organisation of Competition

Among the absurdities which the bourgeoisie are fond of spreading about socialism is the allegation that socialists deny the importance of competition. In fact, it is only socialism which, by abolishing classes, and, consequently, by abolishing the enslavement of the people, for the first time opens the way for competition on a really mass scale. And it is precisely the Soviet form of organisation, by ensuring transition from the formal democracy of the bourgeois republic to real participation of the mass of working people in *administration*, that for the first time puts competition on a broad basis. It is much easier to organise this in the political field than in the economic field; but for the success of socialism, it is the economic field that matters.

* * *

We have scarcely yet started on the enormous, difficult but rewarding task of organising competition between communes, of introducing accounting and publicity in the process of the production of grain, clothes and other things, of transforming dry, dead, bureaucratic accounts into living examples, some repulsive, others attractive. Under the capitalist mode of production, the significance of individual example, say the example of a co-operative workshop, was inevitably very much restricted, and only those imbued with petty-bourgeois illusions could dream of "correcting" capitalism through the example of virtuous institutions. After political power has passed to the proletariat, after the expropriators have been expropriated, the situation radically changes and—as prominent socialists have repeatedly pointed out—force of example for the first time is able to influence the people. Model communes must and will serve as educators, teachers, helping to raise the backward communes. The press must serve as an instrument of socialist construction, give publicity to the successes achieved by the model communes in all their details, must study the causes of these successes, the methods of management these communes employ, and, on the other hand, must put on the "black list" those communes which persist in the "traditions of capitalism," i.e., anarchy, laziness, disorder and profiteering. In capitalist society, statistics were entirely a matter for "government servants," or for narrow specialists; we must carry statistics to the people and make them popular so that the working people themselves may gradually learn to understand and see how long and in what way it is necessary to work, how much time and in what way one may rest, so that *the comparison of the business results* of the various communes may become a matter of general interest and study, and that the most outstanding communes may be rewarded immediately (by reducing the working day, raising remuneration, placing a larger amount of cultural or aesthetic facilities or values at their disposal, etc.).

* * *

"Harmonious Organisation" and Dictatorship

The resolution adopted by the recent Moscow Congress of Soviets advanced as the primary task of the moment the establishment of a "harmonious organisation," and the tightening of discipline. Everyone now readily "votes for" and "subscribes to" resolutions of this kind; but usually people do not think over the fact that the application of such resolutions calls for coercion—coercion precisely in the form of dictatorship. And yet it would be extremely stupid and absurdly utopian to assume that the transition from capitalism to socialism is possible without coercion and without dictatorship. Marx's theory very definitely opposed this petty-bourgeois-democratic and anarchist absurdity long ago. And Russia of 1917–18 confirms the correctness of Marx's theory in this respect so strikingly, palpably and imposingly that only those who are hopelessly dull or who have obstinately decided to turn their backs on the truth can be under any misapprehension concerning this. Either the dictatorship of Kornilov (if we take him as the Russian type of bourgeois Cavaignac), or the dictatorship of the proletariat —any other choice is *out of the question* for a country which is developing at an extremely rapid rate with extremely sharp turns and amidst desperate ruin created by one of the most horrible wars in history. Every solution that offers a middle path is either a deception of the people by the bourgeoisie—for the bourgeoisie dare not tell the truth, dare not say that they need Kornilov—or an expression of the dull-wittedness of the petty-bourgeois democrats, of the Chernovs, Tseretelis and Martovs, who chatter about the unity of democracy, the dictatorship of democracy, the general democratic front, and similar nonsense. Those whom even the progress of the Russian Revolution of 1917–18 has not taught that a middle course is impossible, must be given up for lost.

On the other hand, it is not difficult to see that during every transition from capitalism to socialism, dictatorship is necessary for two main reasons, or along two main channels. Firstly, capitalism cannot be defeated and eradicated without the ruthless suppression of the resistance of the exploiters, who cannot at once be deprived of their wealth, of their advantages of organisation and knowledge, and consequently for a fairly long period will inevitably try to overthrow the hated rule of the poor; secondly, every great revolution, and a socialist revolution in particular, even if there is no external war, is inconceivable without internal war, i.e., civil war, which is even more devastating than external war, and involves thousands and millions of cases of wavering and desertion from one side to another, implies a state of extreme indefiniteness, lack of equilibrium and chaos. And of course, all the elements of disintegration of the old society, which are inevitably very numerous and connected mainly with the petty bourgeoisie (because it is the petty bourgeoisie that every war and every crisis ruins and destroys first), are bound to "reveal themselves" during such a profound revolution. And these elements of disintegration *cannot* "reveal themselves" otherwise than in an increase of crime, hooliganism, corruption, profiteering and outrages of every kind. To put these down requires time and *requires an iron hand*.

There has not been a single great revolution in history in which the people did not instinctively realise this and did not show salutary firmness by shooting thieves on the spot. The misfortune of previous revolutions was that the revolutionary enthusiasm of the people, which sustained them in their state of tension and gave them the strength to suppress ruthlessly the elements of disintegration, did not last long. The social, i.e., the class, reason for this instability of the revolutionary enthusiasm of the people was the weakness of the proletariat, which *alone* is able (if it is sufficiently numerous, class-conscious and disciplined) to win over to its side *the majority* of the working and exploited people (the majority of the poor, to speak more simply and popularly) and retain power sufficiently long to suppress completely all the exploiters as well as all the elements of disintegration.

It was this historical experience of all revolutions, it was this world-historic—economic and political—lesson that Marx summed up when he gave his short, sharp, concise and expressive formula: dictatorship of the proletariat. And the fact that the Russian revolution has been correct in its approach to this world-historic task *has been proved* by the victorious progress of the Soviet form of organisation among all the peoples and tongues of Russia. For Soviet power is nothing but an organisational form of the dictatorship of the proletariat, the dictatorship of the advanced class, which raises to a new democracy and to independent participation in the administration of the state tens upon tens of millions of working and exploited people, who by their own experience learn to regard the disciplined and class-conscious vanguard of the proletariat as their most reliable leader.

Dictatorship, however, is a big word, and big words should not be thrown about carelessly. Dictatorship is iron rule, government that is revolutionarily bold, swift and ruthless in suppressing both exploiters and hooligans. But our government is excessively mild, very often it resembles jelly more than iron. We must not forget for a moment that the bourgeois and petty-bourgeois element is fighting against the Soviet system in two ways; on the one hand, it is operating from without, by the methods of the Savinkovs, Gotzes, Gegechkoris and Kornilovs, by conspiracies and rebellions, and by their filthy "ideological" reflection, the flood of lies and slander in the Constitutional-Democratic, Right Socialist-Revolutionary and Menshevik press; on the other hand, this element operates from within and takes advantage of every manifestation of disintegration, of every weakness, in order to bribe, to increase indiscipline, laxity and chaos. The nearer we approach the complete military suppression of the bourgeoisie, the more dangerous does the element of petty-bourgeois anarchy become. And the fight against this element cannot be waged solely with the aid of propaganda and agitation, solely by organising competition and by selecting organisers. The struggle must also be waged by means of coercion.

As the fundamental task of the government becomes, not military suppression, but administration, the typical manifestation of suppression and compulsion will be, not shooting on the spot, but trial by court. In this respect also the revolutionary people after October 25, 1917, took the right path and demonstrated the viability of the revolution by setting up their own workers' and peasants' courts, even before the decrees dissolving the bourgeois bureaucratic judiciary were passed. But our revolutionary and people's courts are extremely, incredibly weak. One feels that we have not yet done away with the people's attitude towards the courts as towards something official and alien, an attitude inherited from the yoke of the landowners and of the bourgeoisie. It is not yet sufficiently realised that the courts are an organ which enlists precisely the poor, every one of them, in the work of state administration (for the work of the courts is one of the functions of state administration), that the courts are an *organ of the power* of the proletariat and of the poor peasants, that the courts are an instrument *for inculcating discipline*. There is not yet sufficient appreciation of the simple and obvious fact that if the principal misfortunes of Russia at the present time are hunger and unemployment, these misfortunes cannot be overcome by spurts, but only by comprehensive, all-embracing, country-wide organisation and discipline in order to increase the output of bread for the people and bread for industry (fuel), to transport these in good time to the places where they are required, and to distribute them properly; and it is not fully appreciated that, consequently, it is *those* who violate labour discipline at any factory, in any undertaking, in any matter, who are *responsible* for the sufferings caused by the famine and unemployment, that we must know how to find the guilty ones, to bring them to trial and ruthlessly punish them. Where the petty-bourgeois anarchy against which we must now wage a most persistent struggle makes itself felt is in the failure to appreciate the economic and political connection between famine and unemployment, on the one hand, and general laxity in matters of organisation and discipline, on the other—in the tenacity of the *small-proprietor* outlook, namely, I'll grab all I can for myself; the rest can go hang.

In the rail transport service, which perhaps most strikingly embodies the economic ties of an organism created by large-scale capitalism, the struggle between the element of petty-bourgeois laxity and proletarian organisation is particularly evident. The "administrative" elements provide a host of saboteurs and bribe-takers; the best part of the proletarian elements fight for discipline; but among both elements there are, of course, many waverers and "weak" characters who are unable to withstand the "temptation" of profiteering, bribery, personal gain obtained by spoiling the whole apparatus, upon the proper working of which the victory over famine and unemployment depends.

The struggle that has been developing around the recent decree on the management of the railways, the decree which grants individual executives dictatorial powers (or "unlimited" powers),[2] is

2. This refers to the decree of the Council of People's Commissars "On Centralisation of Management, Protection of Roads and the Improvement of Their Carrying Capacity." The Decree was approved by the Council of People's Commissars on March 23, 1918.

characteristic. The conscious (and to a large extent, probably, unconscious) representatives of petty-bourgeois laxity would like to see in this granting of "unlimited" (i.e., dictatorial) powers to individuals a departure from the collegiate principle, from democracy and from the principles of Soviet government. Here and there, among Left Socialist-Revolutionaries, a positively hooligan agitation, i.e., agitation appealing to the base instincts and to the small proprietor's urge to "grab all he can," has been developed against the dictatorship decree. The question has become one of really enormous significance. Firstly, the question of principle, namely, is the appointment of individuals, dictators with unlimited powers, in general compatible with the fundamental principles of Soviet government? Secondly, what relation has this case—this precedent, if you will—to the special tasks of government in the present concrete situation? We must deal very thoroughly with both these questions.

That in the history of revolutionary movements the dictatorship of individuals was very often the expression, the vehicle, the channel of the dictatorship of the revolutionary classes has been shown by the irrefutable experience of history. Undoubtedly, the dictatorship of individuals was compatible with bourgeois democracy. On this point, however, the bourgeois denigrators of the Soviet system, as well as their petty-bourgeois henchmen, always display sleight of hand: on the one hand, they declare the Soviet system to be something absurd, anarchistic and savage, and carefully pass over in silence all our historical examples and theoretical arguments which prove that the Soviets are a higher form of democracy, and what is more, the beginning of a *socialist* form of democracy; on the other hand, they demand of us a higher democracy than bourgeois democracy and say: personal dictatorship is absolutely incompatible with your, Bolshevik (i.e., not bourgeois, *but socialist*), Soviet democracy.

These are exceedingly poor arguments. If we are not anarchists, we must admit that the state, *that is, coercion,* is necessary for the transition from capitalism to socialism. The form of coercion is determined by the degree of development of the given revolutionary class, and also by special circumstances, such as, for example, the legacy of a long and reactionary war and the forms of resistance put up by the bourgeoisie and the petty bourgeoisie. There is, therefore, absolutely *no* contradiction in principle between Soviet (*that is,* socialist) democracy and the exercise of dictatorial powers by individuals. The difference between proletarian dictatorship and bourgeois dictatorship is that the former strikes at the exploiting minority in the interests of the exploited majority, and that it is exercised—*also through individuals*—not only by the working and exploited people, but also by organisations which are built in such a way as to rouse these people to history-making activity. (The Soviet organisations are organisations of this kind.)

In regard to the second question, concerning the significance of individual dictatorial powers from the point of view of the specific tasks of the present moment, it must be said that large-scale machine industry—which is precisely the material source, the productive source, the foundation of socialism—calls for absolute and strict *unity of will*, which directs the joint labours of hundreds, thousands and tens of thousands of people. The technical, economic and historical necessity of this is obvious, and all those who have thought about socialism have always regarded it as one of the conditions of socialism. But how can strict unity of will be ensured? By thousands subordinating their will to the will of one.

Given ideal class-consciousness and discipline on the part of those participating in the common work, this subordination would be something like the mild leadership of a conductor of an orchestra. It may assume the sharp forms of a dictatorship if ideal discipline and class-consciousness are lacking. But be that as it may, *unquestioning subordination* to a single will is absolutely necessary for the success of processes organised on the pattern of large-scale machine industry. On the railways it is twice and three times as necessary. In this transition from one political task to another, which *on the surface* is totally dissimilar to the first, lies the whole originality of the present situation. The revolution has only just smashed the oldest, strongest and heaviest of fetters, to which the people submitted under duress. That was yesterday. Today, however, the same revolution demands—precisely in the interests of its development and consolidation, precisely in the interests of socialism—that the people *unquestioningly obey the single will* of the leaders of labour. Of course, such a transition cannot be made at one step. Clearly, it can be achieved only as a result of tremendous jolts, shocks, reversions to old ways, the enormous exertion of effort on the part of the proletarian vanguard, which is leading the people to the new ways. Those who drop into the philistine hysterics of *Novaya Zhizn* or *Vperyod*, *Dyelo Naroda* or *Nash Vek*[3] do not stop to think about this.

* * *

We have successfully fulfilled the first task of the revolution; we have seen how the mass of working people evolved in themselves

3. *Novaya Zhizn* (*New Life*): a Menshevik daily published in Petrograd from April 1917 to July 1918, when it was suppressed. *Vperyod* (*Forward*): a Moscow Menshevik daily suppressed in April 1918. *Dyelo Naroda* (*The People's Cause*): the daily organ of the Socialist-Revolutionary Party, published from March 1917 to June 1918. *Nash Vek* (*Our Age*): one of the names under which *Rech* (*Speech*), the central organ of the Cadet Party, was published (February 1906 to August 1918).

the fundamental condition for its success: they united their efforts against the exploiters in order to overthrow them. Stages like that of October 1905, February and October 1917 are of world-historic significance.

We have successfully fulfilled the second task of the revolution: to awaken, to raise those very "lower ranks" of society whom the exploiters had pushed down, and who only after October 25, 1917, obtained complete freedom to overthrow the exploiters and to begin to take stock of things and arrange life in their own way. The airing of questions at public meetings by the most oppressed and down-trodden, by the least educated mass of working people, their coming over to the side of the Bolsheviks, their setting up everywhere of their own Soviet organisations—this was the second great stage of the revolution.

The third stage is now beginning. We must consolidate what we ourselves have won, what we ourselves have decreed, made law, *labour discipline*. This is the most difficult, but the most gratifying discussed, planned—consolidate all this in stable forms of *everyday* task, because only its fulfilment will give us a socialist system. We must learn to combine the "public meeting" democracy of the working people—turbulent, surging, overflowing its banks like a spring flood—with *iron* discipline while at work, with *unquestioning obedience* to the will of a single person, the Soviet leader, while at work.

We have not yet learned to do this.

We shall learn it.

Yesterday we were menaced by the restoration of bourgeois exploitation, personified by the Kornilovs, Gotzes, Dutovs, Gegechkoris and Bogayevskys. We conquered them. This restoration, this very same restoration menaces us today in another form, in the form of the element of petty-bourgeois laxity and anarchism, or small-proprietor "it's not my business" psychology, in the form of the daily, petty, but numerous sorties and attacks of this element against proletarian discipline. We must, and we shall, vanquish this element of petty-bourgeois anarchy.

The Development of Soviet Organisation

The socialist character of Soviet, i.e., *proletarian*, democracy, as concretely applied today, lies first in the fact that the electors are the working and exploited people; the bourgeoisie is excluded. Secondly, it lies in the fact that all bureaucratic formalities and restrictions of elections are abolished; the people themselves determine the order and time of elections, and are completely free to recall any elected person. Thirdly, it lies in the creation of the best mass organisation of the vanguard of the working people, i.e., the proletariat engaged in large-scale industry, which enables it to lead the vast mass of the exploited, to draw them into independent political life, to educate them politically by their own experience; therefore for the first time a start is made by the *entire* population in learning the art of administration, and in beginning to administer.

These are the principal distinguishing features of the democracy now applied in Russia, which is a higher *type* of democracy, a break with the bourgeois distortion of democracy, transition to socialist democracy and to the conditions in which the state can begin to wither away.

It goes without saying that the element of petty-bourgeois disorganisation (which must *inevitably* be apparent to some extent in *every* proletarian revolution, and which is especially apparent in our revolution, owing to the petty-bourgeois character of our country, its backwardness and the consequences of a reactionary war) cannot but leave its impress upon the Soviets as well.

We must work unremittingly to develop the organisation of the Soviets and of the Soviet government. There is a petty-bourgeois tendency to transform the members of the Soviets into "parliamentarians," or else into bureaucrats. We must combat this by drawing *all* the members of the Soviets into the practical work of administration. In many places the departments of the Soviets are gradually merging with the Commissariats. Our aim is to draw *the whole of the poor* into the practical work of administration, and all steps that are taken in this direction—the more varied they are, the better—should be carefully recorded, studied, systematised, tested by wider experience and embodied in law. Our aim is to ensure that *every* toiler, having finished his eight hours' "task" in productive labour, shall perform state duties *without pay*; the transition to this is particularly difficult, but this transition alone can guarantee the final consolidation of socialism. Naturally, the novelty and difficulty of the change lead to an abundance of steps being taken, as it were, gropingly, to an abundance of mistakes, vacillation—without this, any marked progress is impossible. The reason why the present position seems peculiar to many of those who would like to be regarded as socialists is that they have been accustomed to contrasting capitalism with socialism abstractly, and that they profoundly put between the two the word "leap" (some of them, recalling fragments of what they have read of Engels's writings, still more profoundly add the phrase "leap from the realm of necessity into the realm of freedom"[4]). The majority of these so-called socialists,

4. Quoted from Engels's *Anti-Dühring*.

who have "read in books" about socialism but who have never seriously thought over the matter, are unable to consider that by "leap" the teachers of socialism meant turning-points on a world-historical scale, and that leaps of this kind extend over decades and even longer periods. Naturally, in such times, the notorious "intelligentsia" provides an infinite number of mourners of the dead. Some mourn over the Constituent Assembly, others mourn over bourgeois discipline, others again mourn over the capitalist system, still others mourn over the cultured landowner, and still others again mourn over imperialist Great Power policy, etc., etc.

The real interest of the epoch of great leaps lies in the fact that the abundance of fragments of the old, which sometimes accumulate more rapidly than the rudiments (not always immediately discernible) of the new, calls for the ability to discern what is most important in the line or chain of development. History knows moments when the most important thing for the success of the revolution is to heap up as large a quantity of the fragments as possible, i.e., to blow up as many of the old institutions as possible; moments arise when enough has been blown up and the next task is to perform the "prosaic" (for the petty-bourgeois revolutionary, the "boring") task of clearing away the fragments; and moments arise when the careful nursing of the rudiments of the new system, which are growing amidst the wreckage on a soil which as yet has been badly cleared of rubble, is the most important thing.

It is not enough to be a revolutionary and an adherent of socialism or a Communist in general. You must be able at each particular moment to find the particular link in the chain which you must grasp with all your might in order to hold the whole chain and to prepare firmly for the transition to the next link; the order of the links, their form, the manner in which they are linked together, the way they differ from each other in the historical chain of events, are not as simple and not as meaningless as those in an ordinary chain made by a smith.

The fight against the bureaucratic distortion of the Soviet form of organisation is assured by the firmness of the connection between the Soviets and the "people," meaning by that the working and exploited people, and by the flexibility and elasticity of this connection. Even in the most democratic capitalist republics in the world, the poor never regard the bourgeois parliament as "their" institution. But the Soviets are "theirs" and not alien institutions to the mass of workers and peasants. The modern "Social-Democrats" of the Scheidemann or, what is almost the same thing, of the Martov type are repelled by the Soviets, and they are drawn towards the respectable bourgeois parliament, or to the Constituent Assembly, in the same way as Turgenev, sixty years ago, was drawn towards a moderate monarchist and noblemen's constitution and was repelled by the peasant democracy of Dobrolyubov and Chernyshevsky.

It is the closeness of the Soviets to the "people," to the working people, that creates the special forms of recall and other means of control from below which must be most zealously developed now. For example, the Councils of Public Education, as periodical conferences of Soviet electors and their delegates called to discuss and control the activities of the Soviet authorities in this field, deserve full sympathy and support. Nothing could be sillier than to transform the Soviets into something congealed and self-contained. The more resolutely we now have to stand for a ruthlessly firm government, for the dictatorship of individuals *in definite processes of work,* in definite aspects of *purely executive* functions, the more varied must be the forms and methods of control from below in order to counteract every shadow of a possibility of distorting the principles of Soviet government, in order repeatedly and tirelessly to weed out bureaucracy.

Conclusion

An extraordinarily difficult, complex and dangerous situation in international affairs; the necessity of manoeuvring and retreating; a period of waiting for new outbreaks of the revolution which is maturing in the West at a painfully slow pace; within the country a period of slow construction and ruthless "tightening up," of prolonged and persistent struggle waged by stern, proletarian discipline against the menacing element of petty-bourgeois laxity and anarchy —these in brief are the distinguishing features of the special stage of the socialist revolution in which we are now living. This is the link in the historical chain of events which we must at present grasp with all our might in order to prove equal to the tasks that confront us before passing to the next link to which we are drawn by a special brightness, the brightness of the victories of the international proletarian revolution.

Try to compare with the ordinary everyday concept "revolutionary" the slogans that follow from the specific conditions of the present stage, namely, manoeuvre, retreat, wait, build slowly, ruthlessly tighten up, rigorously discipline, smash laxity. . . . Is it surprising that when certain "revolutionaries" hear this they are seized with noble indignation and begin to "thunder" abuse at us for forgetting the traditions of the October Revolution, for compromising with the bourgeois experts, for compromising with the bourgeoisie, for being petty bourgeois, reformists, and so on and so forth?

* * *

The social origin of such types is the small proprietor, who has been driven to frenzy by the horrors of war, by sudden ruin, by unprecedented torments of famine and devastation, who hysterically rushes about seeking a way out, seeking salvation, places his confidence in the proletariat and supports it one moment and the next gives way to fits of despair. We must clearly understand and firmly remember the fact that socialism cannot be built on such a social basis. The only class that can lead the working and exploited people is the class that unswervingly follows its path without losing courage and without giving way to despair even at the most difficult, arduous and dangerous stages. Hysterical impulses are of no use to us. What we need is the steady advance of the iron battalions of the proletariat.

The Proletarian Revolution
and the Renegade Kautsky

Karl Kautsky's pamphlet, *The Dictatorship of the Proletariat*, published in Vienna in 1918, was a criticism of the Bolshevik Revolution from the standpoint of a Social-Democratic Marxist for whom parliamentary democracy represented the proper political frame for the transition of a society from capitalism to socialism. Lenin's reply in this pamphlet written in October–November 1918 is one of the great polemical documents in the history of Marxist thought and politics, and likewise one of the ideological foundation-stones of Communist Marxism, meaning Marxism according to Lenin (or "Marxism-Leninism," as it was officially christened during the Stalin period). It is especially notable for its contention that the doctrine of proletarian dictatorship is the nub of the whole Marxist teaching (something which Marx and Engels never said, despite the importance they attached to this doctrine), and for its argument that democracy means government "for" a given class, implying that every form of government is a democracy *for* the ruling class and a dictatorship *for* the ruled.

Kautsky's pamphlet, *The Dictatorship of the Proletariat*, recently published in Vienna (Wien, 1918, Ignaz Brand, 63 pp.) is a most lucid example of that utter and ignominious bankruptcy of the Second International about which all honest socialists in all countries have been talking for a long time. The proletarian revolution is now becoming a practical issue in a number of countries, and an examination of Kautsky's renegade sophistries and his complete renunciation of Marxism is therefore essential.

* * *

In substance, the chief theoretical mistake Kautsky makes in his pamphlet on the dictatorship of the proletariat lies in those opportunist distortions of Marx's ideas on the state—the distortions which I exposed in detail in my pamphlet, *The State and Revolution*.

* * *

461

How Kautsky Turned Marx into a Common Liberal

The fundamental question that Kautsky discusses in his pamphlet is that of the very essence of proletarian revolution, namely, the dictatorship of the proletariat. This is a question that is of the greatest importance for all countries, especially for the advanced ones, especially for those at war, and especially at the present time. One may say without fear of exaggeration that this is the key problem of the entire proletarian class struggle. It is, therefore, necessary to pay particular attention to it.

Kautsky formulates the question as follows: "The contrast between the two socialist trends" (i.e., the Bolsheviks and non-Bolsheviks) "is the contrast between two radically different methods: the *dictatorial* and the *democratic*" (p. 3).

Let us point out, in passing, that when calling the non-Bolsheviks in Russia, i.e., the Mensheviks and Socialist-Revolutionaries, socialists, Kautsky was guided by their *name*, that is, by a word, and not by the *actual place* they occupy in the struggle between the proletariat and the bourgeoisie. What a wonderful understanding and application of Marxism! But more of this later.

For the moment we must deal with the main point, namely, with Kautsky's great discovery of the "fundamental contrast" between "democratic and dictatorial methods." That is the crux of the matter; that is the essence of Kautsky's pamphlet. And that is such an awful theoretical muddle, such a complete renunciation of Marxism, that Kautsky, it must be confessed, has far excelled Bernstein.

The question of the dictatorship of the proletariat is a question of the relation of the proletarian state to the bourgeois state, of proletarian democracy to bourgeois democracy. One would think that this is as plain as a pikestaff. But Kautsky, like a schoolmaster who has become as dry as dust from quoting the same old textbooks on history, persistently turns his back on the twentieth century and his face to the eighteenth century, and for the hundredth time, in a number of paragraphs, in an incredibly tedious fashion chews the old cud over the relation of bourgeois democracy to absolutism and medievalism!

It sounds just as though he were chewing rags in his sleep!

But this means he utterly fails to understand what is what! One cannot help smiling at Kautsky's effort to make it appear that there are people who preach "contempt for democracy" (p. 11) and so forth. That is the sort of twaddle Kautsky uses to befog and confuse the issue, for he talks like the liberals, speaking of democracy in general, and not of *bourgeois* democracy; he even avoids using this precise, class term, and, instead, tries to speak about "pre-socialist" democracy. This windbag devotes almost one-third of his pamphlet, twenty pages out of sixty-three, to this twaddle, which is so agreeable to the bourgeoisie, for it is tantamount to embellishing bourgeois democracy, and obscures the question of the proletarian revolution.

But, after all, the title of Kautsky's pamphlet is *The Dictatorship of the Proletariat*. Everybody knows that this is the very *essence* of Marx's doctrine; and after a lot of irrelevant twaddle Kautsky *was obliged* to quote Marx's words on the dictatorship of the proletariat.

But the *way* in which he the "Marxist" did it was simply farcical! Listen to this:

"This view" (which Kautsky dubs "contempt for democracy") "rests upon a single word of Karl Marx's." This is what Kautsky literally says on page 20. And on page 60 the same thing is repeated even in the form that they (the Bolsheviks) "opportunely recalled the little word" (that is literally what he says—*des Wörtchens*!!) "about the dictatorship of the proletariat which Marx once used in 1875 in a letter."

Here is Marx's "little word": "Between capitalist and communist society lies the period of the revolutionary transformation of the one into the other. Corresponding to this is also a political transition period in which the state can be nothing but the revolutionary dictatorship of the proletariat."[1]

First of all, to call this classical reasoning of Marx's, which sums up the whole of his revolutionary teaching, "a single word" and even "a little word," is an insult to and complete renunciation of Marxism. It must not be forgotten that Kautsky knows Marx almost by heart, and, judging by all he has written, he has in his desk, or in his head, a number of pigeon-holes in which all that was ever written by Marx is most carefully filed so as to be ready at hand for quotation. Kautsky *must know* that both Marx and Engels, in their letters as well as in their published works, *repeatedly* spoke about the dictatorship of the proletariat, before and especially after the Paris Commune. Kautsky must know that the formula "dictatorship of the proletariat" is merely a more historically concrete and scientifically exact formulation of the proletariat's task of "smashing" the bourgeois state machine, about which both Marx and Engels, in summing up the experience of the Revolution of 1848, and, still more so, of 1871, spoke *for forty years*, between 1852 and 1891.

How is this monstrous distortion of Marxism by that Marxist pedant Kautsky to be explained? As far as the philosophical roots

---

1. See Marx, *Critique of the Gotha Programme*.

of this phenomenon are concerned, it amounts to the substitution of eclecticism and sophistry for dialectics. Kautsky is a past master at this sort of substitution. Regarded from the point of view of practical politics, it amounts to subservience to the opportunists, that is, in the last analysis to the bourgeoisie. Since the outbreak of the war, Kautsky has made increasingly rapid progress in this art of being a Marxist in words and a lackey of the bourgeoisie in deeds, until he has become a virtuoso at it.

One feels even more convinced of this when examining the remarkable way in which Kautsky "interprets" Marx's "little word" about the dictatorship of the proletariat. Listen to this:

> Marx, unfortunately, neglected to show us in greater detail how he conceived this dictatorship. . . . [This is an utterly mendacious phrase of a renegade, for Marx and Engels gave us, indeed, quite a number of most detailed indications, which Kautsky, the Marxist pedant, has deliberately ignored.] Literally, the word "dictatorship" means the abolition of democracy. But, of course, taken literally, this word also means the undivided rule of a single person unrestricted by any laws—an autocracy, which differs from despotism only insofar as it is not meant as a permanent state institution, but as a transient emergency measure.
>
> The term "dictatorship of the proletariat," hence not the dictatorship of a single individual, but of a class, *ipso facto* precludes the possibility that Marx in this connection had in mind a dictatorship in the literal sense of the term.
>
> He speaks here not of a *form of government*, but of a *condition*, which must necessarily arise wherever the proletariat has gained political power. That Marx in this case did not have in mind a form of government is proved by the fact that he was of the opinion that in Britain and America the transition might take place peacefully, i.e., in a democratic way. [P. 20.]

We have deliberately quoted this argument in full so that the reader may clearly see the methods Kautsky the "theoretician" employs.

Kautsky chose to approach the question in such a way as to begin with a definition of the *"word"* dictatorship.

Very well. Everyone has a sacred right to approach a question in whatever way he pleases. One must only distinguish a serious and honest approach from a dishonest one. Anyone who wants to be serious in approaching the question in this way ought to give *his own definition* of the "word." Then the question would be put fairly and squarely. But Kautsky does not do that. "Literally," he writes, "the word 'dictatorship' means the abolition of democracy."

In the first place, this is not a definition. If Kautsky wanted to avoid giving a definition of the concept "dictatorship," why did he choose this particular approach to the question?

Secondly, it is obviously wrong. It is natural for a liberal to speak of "democracy" in general; but a Marxist will never forget to ask: "for what class?" Everyone knows, for instance (and Kautsky the "historian" knows it too), that rebellions, or even strong ferment, among the slaves in ancient times at once revealed the fact that the ancient state was essentially a *dictatorship of the slaveowners*. Did this dictatorship abolish democracy *among*, and *for*, the slaveowners? Everybody knows that it did not.

Kautsky the "Marxist" made this monstrously absurd and untrue statement because he *"forgot"* the class struggle. . . .

To transform Kautsky's liberal and false assertion into a Marxist and true one, one must say: dictatorship does not necessarily mean the abolition of democracy for the class that exercises the dictatorship over other classes; but it does mean the abolition (or very material restriction, which is also a form of abolition) of democracy for the class over which, or against which, the dictatorship is exercised.

But, however true this assertion may be, it does not give a definition of dictatorship.

Let us examine Kautsky's next sentence: ". . . But, of course, taken literally, this word also means the undivided rule of a single person unrestricted by any laws. . . ." Like a blind puppy sniffing at random first in one direction and then in another, Kautsky accidentally stumbled upon *one* true idea (namely, that dictatorship is rule unrestricted by any laws), *nevertheless*, he *failed* to give a definition of dictatorship, and, moreover, he made an obvious historical blunder, namely, that dictatorship means the rule of a single person. This is even grammatically incorrect, since dictatorship may also be exercised by a handful of persons, or by an oligarchy, or by a class, etc.

Kautsky then goes on to point out the difference between dictatorship and despotism, but, although what he says is obviously incorrect, we shall not dwell upon it, as it is wholly irrelevant to the question that interests us. Everyone knows Kautsky's inclination to turn from the twentieth century to the eighteenth, and from the eighteenth century to classical antiquity, and we hope that the German proletariat, after it has attained its dictatorship, will bear this inclination of his in mind and appoint him, say, teacher of ancient history at some high school. To try to evade a definition of the dictatorship of the proletariat by philosophising about depotism is either crass stupidity or very clumsy trickery.

As a result, we find that, having undertaken to discuss the dictatorship, Kautsky rattled off a great deal of manifest lies, but has given no definition! Yet, instead of relying on his mental faculties he could have used his memory to extract from "pigeon-holes" all those instances in which Marx speaks of dictatorship. Had he done so, he would certainly have arrived either at the following definition or at one in substance coinciding with it:

Dictatorship is rule based directly upon force and unrestricted by any laws.

The revolutionary dictatorship of the proletariat is rule won and maintained by the use of violence by the proletariat against the bourgeoisie, rule that is unrestricted by any laws.

* * *

Kautsky first committed a sleight of hand by proclaiming the obvious nonsense that the word "dictatorship," in its literal sense, means the dictatorship of a single person, and then—on the strength of this sleight of hand—he declared that "hence" Marx's words about the dictatorship of a class were *not* meant in the literal sense (but in one in which "dictatorship" does not imply revolutionary violence, but the "peaceful" winning of a majority under bourgeois —mark you—"democracy").

One must, if you please, distinguish between a "condition" and a "form of government." A wonderfully profound distinction; it is like drawing a distinction between the "condition" of stupidity of a man who reasons foolishly and the "form" of his stupidity.

Kautsky *finds it necessary* to interpret dictatorship as a "condition of domination" (this is the literal expresson he uses on the very next page, p. 21), because then *revolutionary violence, and violent revolution, disappear*. The "condition of domination" is a condition in which any majority finds itself under . . . "democracy"! Thanks to such a fraud, *revolution* happily *disappears*!

The fraud, however, is too crude and will not save Kautsky. One cannot hide the fact that dictatorship presupposes and implies a "condition," one so disagreeable to renegades, of *revolutionary violence* of one class against another. It is patently absurd to draw a distinction between a "condition" and a "form of government." To speak of forms of government in this connection is trebly stupid, for every schoolboy knows that monarchy and republic are two different forms of government. It must be explained to Mr. Kautsky that *both* these forms of government, like all transitional "forms of government" under capitalism, are only variations of the *bourgeois state*, that is, of the *dictatorship of the bourgeoisie*.

Lastly, to speak of forms of government is not only a stupid, but also a very crude falsification of Marx, who was very clearly speaking here of this or that form or type of *state*, and not of forms of government.

The proletarian revolution is impossible without the forcible destruction of the bourgeois state machine and the substitution for it of a *new one* which, in the words of Engels, is "no longer a state in the proper sense of the word."[2]

Because of his renegade position, Kautsky, however, has to befog and belie all this.

* * *

To sum up: Kautsky has in a most unparalleled manner distorted the concept "dictatorship of the proletariat," and has turned Marx into a common liberal; that is, he himself has sunk to the level of a liberal who utters banal phrases about "pure democracy," embellishing and glossing over the class content of *bourgeois* democracy, and shrinking, above all, from the use of *revolutionary violence* by the oppressed class. By so "interpreting" the concept "revolutionary dictatorship of the proletariat" as to expunge the revolutionary violence of the oppressed class against its oppressors, Kautsky has beaten the world record in the liberal distortion of Marx. The renegade Bernstein has proved to be a mere puppy compared with the renegade Kautsky.

Bourgeois and Proletarian Democracy

The question which Kautsky has so shamelessly muddled really stands as follows.

If we are not to mock at common sense and history, it is obvious that we cannot speak of "pure democracy" as long as different *classes* exist; we can only speak of *class* democracy. (Let us say in parenthesis that "pure democracy" is not only an *ignorant* phrase, revealing a lack of understanding both of the class struggle and of the nature of the state, but also a thrice-empty phrase, since in communist society democracy will *wither away* in the process of changing and becoming a habit, but will never be "pure" democracy.)

"Pure democracy" is the mendacious phrase of a liberal who wants to fool the workers. History knows of bourgeois democracy which takes the place of feudalism, and of proletarian democracy which takes the place of bourgeois democracy.

When Kautsky devotes dozens of pages to "proving" the truth that bourgeois democracy is progressive compared with medievalism, and that the proletariat must unfailingly utilise it in its struggle

<hr/>

2. See the letter of Engels to August Bebel of March 18–28, 1875 (Marx and Engels, *Selected Correspondence* [Moscow 1965], p. 293).

against the bourgeoisie, that in fact is just liberal twaddle intended to fool the workers. This is a truism, not only for educated Germany, but also for uneducated Russia. Kautsky is simply throwing "learned" dust in the eyes of the workers when, with a pompous mien, he talks about Weitling and the Jesuits of Paraguay and many other things, *in order to avoid* telling about the *bourgeois* essence of modern, i.e., *capitalist*, democracy.

Kautsky takes from Marxism what is acceptable to the liberals, to the bourgeoisie (the criticism of the Middle Ages, and the progressive historical role of capitalism in general and of capitalist democracy in particular), and discards, passes over in silence, glosses over all that in Marxism which is *unacceptable* to the bourgeoisie (the revolutionary violence of the proletariat against the bourgeoisie for the latter's destruction). That is why Kautsky, by virtue of his objective position and irrespective of what his subjective convictions may be, inevitably proves to be a lackey of the bourgeoisie.

Bourgeois democracy, although a great historical advance in comparison with medievalism, always remains, and under capitalism is bound to remain, restricted, truncated, false and hypocritical, a paradise for the rich and a snare and deception for the exploited, for the poor. It is this truth, which forms a most essential part of Marx's teaching, that Kautsky the "Marxist" has failed to understand. On this—the fundamental issue—Kautsky offers "delights" for the bourgeoisie instead of a scientific criticism of those conditions which make every bourgeois democracy a democracy for the rich.

* * *

Take the fundamental laws of modern states, take their administration, take freedom of assembly, freedom of the press, or "equality of all citizens before the law," and you will see at every turn evidence of the hypocrisy of bourgeois democracy with which every honest and class-conscious worker is familiar. There is not a single state, however democratic, which has no loopholes or reservations in its constitution guaranteeing the bourgeoisie the possibility of dispatching troops against the workers, of proclaiming martial law, and so forth, in case of a "violation of public order," and actually in case the exploited class "violates" its position of slavery and tries to behave in a non-slavish manner. Kautsky shamelessly embellishes bourgeois democracy and omits to mention, for instance, how the most democratic and republican bourgeoisie in America or Switzerland deal with workers on strike.

* * *

The learned Mr. Kautsky has "forgotten"—accidentally forgotten, probably—a "trifle," namely, that the ruling party in a bourgeois democracy extends the protection of the minority only to another *bourgeois* party, while the proletariat, on all *serious, profound and fundamental* issues, gets martial law or pogroms, instead of the "protection of the minority." *The more highly developed a democracy is, the more imminent are pogroms or civil war in connection with any profound political divergence which is dangerous to the bourgeoisie.* The learned Mr. Kautsky could have studied this "law" of bourgeois democracy in connection with the Dreyfus case in republican France, with the lynching of Negroes and internationalists in the democratic republic of America, with the case of Ireland and Ulster in democratic Britain,[3] with the baiting of the Bolsheviks and the staging of pogroms against them in April 1917 in the democratic republic of Russia. I have purposely chosen example not only from wartime but also from pre-wartime, peacetime. * * *

Take the bourgeois parliament. Can it be that the learned Kautsky has never heard that the *more highly* democracy is developed, the *more* the bourgeois parliaments are subjected by the stock exchange and the bankers? This does not mean that we must not make use of bourgeois parliament (the Bolsheviks made better use of it than probably any other party in the world, for in 1912–14 we won the entire workers' curia in the Fourth Duma). But it does mean that only a liberal can forget the *historical limitations and conventional nature* of the bourgeois parliamentary system as Kautsky does. * * *

Proletarian democracy, of which Soviet government is one of the forms, has brought a development and expansion of democracy unprecedented in the world, for the vast majority of the population, for the exploited and working people. To write a whole pamphlet about democracy, as Kautsky did, in which two pages are devoted to dictatorship and dozens to "pure democracy," and *fail to notice* this fact, means completely distorting the subject in liberal fashion.

Take foreign policy. In no bourgeois state, not even in the most democratic, is it conducted openly. The people are deceived everywhere, and in democratic France, Switzerland, America and Britain this is done on an incomparably wider scale and in an incomparably subtler manner than in other countries. The Soviet government has torn the veil of mystery from foreign policy in a revolutionary manner. Kautsky has not noticed this, he keeps silent about it, although in the era of predatory wars and secret treaties for the

3. This refers to the British reprisals against the participants in the Irish rebellion of 1916. "In Europe . . . there was a rebellion in Ireland, which the 'freedom-loving' English . . . suppressed by executions," Lenin wrote in 1916.

"division of spheres of influence" (i.e., for the partition of the world among the capitalist bandits) this is of *cardinal* importance, for on it depends the question of peace, the life and death of tens of millions of people.

Take the structure of the state. Kautsky picks at all manner of "trifles," down to the argument that under the Soviet Constitution elections are "indirect," but he misses the point. He fails to see the *class* nature of the state apparatus, of the machinery of state. Under bourgeois democracy the capitalists, by thousands of tricks —which are the more artful and effective the more "pure" democracy is developed—*drive* the people away from administrative work, from freedom of the press, freedom of assembly, etc. The Soviet government is the *first* in the world (or strictly speaking, the second, because the Paris Commune began to do the same thing) to *enlist* the people, specifically the *exploited* people, in the work of administration. The working people are *barred* from participation in bourgeois parliaments (they *never decide* important questions under bourgeois democracy, which are decided by the stock exchange and the banks) by thousands of obstacles, and the workers know and feel, see and realise perfectly well that the bourgeois parliaments are institutions *alien* to them, *instruments for the oppression* of the workers by the bourgeoisie, institutions of a hostile class, of the exploiting minority.

The Soviets are the direct organisation of the working and exploited people themselves, which *helps* them to organise and administer their own state in every possible way. And in this it is the vanguard of the working and exploited people, the urban proletariat, that enjoys the advantage of being best united by the large enterprises; it is easier for it than for all others to elect and exercise control over those elected. The Soviet form of organisation automatically *helps* to unite all the working and exploited people around their vanguard, the proletariat. The old bourgeois apparatus —the bureaucracy, the privileges of wealth, of bourgeois education, of social connections, etc. (these real privileges are the more varied the more highly bourgeois democracy is developed)—all this disappears under the Soviet form of organisation. Freedom of the press ceases to be hypocrisy, because the printing-plants and stocks of paper are taken away from the bourgeoisie. The same thing applies to the best buildings, the palaces, the mansions and manor houses. Soviet power took thousands upon thousands of the best buildings from the exploiters at one stroke, and in this way made the right of assembly—without which democracy is a fraud—*a million times* more democratic for the people. Indirect elections to non-local Soviets make it easier to hold congresses of Soviets, they make the *entire* apparatus less costly, more flexible, more accessible to the workers and peasants at a time when life is seething and it is necessary to be able very quickly to recall one's local deputy or to delegate him to a general congress of Soviets.

Proletarian democracy is a *million times* more democratic than any bourgeois democracy; Soviet power is a million times more democratic than the most democratic bourgeois republic.

* * *

We shall now examine the experience of the Russian revolution and that divergence between the Soviets of Deputies and the Constituent Assembly which led to the dissolution of the latter and to the withdrawal of the franchise from the bourgeoisie.

The Soviets Dare Not Become State Organisations

The Soviets are the Russian form of the proletarian dictatorship. If a Marxist theoretician, writing a work on the dictatorship of the proletariat, had really studied the subject (and not merely repeated the petty-bourgeois lamentations against dictatorship, as Kautsky did, singing to Menshevik tunes), he would first have given a general definition of dictatorship, and would then have examined its peculiar, national, form, the Soviets; he would have given his critique of them as one of the forms of the dictatorship of the proletariat.

It goes without saying that nothing serious could be expected from Kautsky after his liberalistic "interpretation" of Marx's teaching on dictatorship; but the manner in which he approached the question of what the Soviets are and the way he dealt with this question is highly characteristic.

The Soviets, he says, recalling their rise in 1905, created "the most all-embracing [*umfassendste*] form of proletarian organisation, for it embraced all the wage-workers" (p. 31). In 1905 they were only local bodies; in 1917 they became a national organisation. "The Soviet form of organisation," Kautsky continues,

already has a great and glorious history behind it, and it has a still mightier future before it, and not in Russia alone. It appears that everywhere the old methods of the economic and political struggle of the proletariat are inadequate [*versagen*; this German expression is somewhat stronger than "inadequate" and somewhat weaker than "impotent"] against the gigantic economic and political forces which finance capital has at its disposal. These old methods cannot be discarded; they are still indispensable for normal times; but from time to time tasks arise which they cannot cope with, tasks that can be accomplished successfully only as a result of a combination of all the political and economic instruments of force of the working class. [P. 32.]

Then follows a reasoning on the mass strike and on "trade union bureaucracy"—which is no less necessary than the trade unions—being "useless for the purpose of directing the mighty mass battles that are more and more becoming a sign of the times. . . ."

> Thus [Kautsky concludes] the Soviet form of organisation is one of the most important phenomena of our time. It promises to acquire decisive importance in the great decisive battles between capital and labour towards which we are marching.
>
> But are we entitled to demand more of the Soviets? The Bolsheviks, after the November Revolution [new style, or October, according to our style], 1917, secured in conjunction with the Left Socialist-Revolutionaries a majority in the Russian Soviets of Workers' Deputies, and after the dispersion of the Constituent Assembly, they set out to transform the Soviets from a *combat organisation* of one *class*, as they had been up to then, into a *state organisation*. They destroyed the democracy which the Russian people had won in the March [new style, or February, our style] Revolution. In line with this, the Bolsheviks have ceased to call themselves Social-*Democrats*. They call themselves *Communists*. [P. 33, Kautsky's italics.]

Those who are familiar with Russian Menshevik literature will at once see how slavishly Kautsky copies Martov, Axelrod, Stein and Co. Yes, "slavishly," because Kautsky ridiculously distorts the facts in order to pander to Menshevik prejudices. Kautsky did not take the trouble, for instance, to ask his informants (Stein of Berlin, or Axelrod of Stockholm) *when* the questions of changing the name of the Bolsheviks to Communists and of the significance of the Soviets as state organisations were first raised. Had Kautsky made this simple inquiry he would not have penned these ludicrous lines, for both these questions were raised by the Bolsheviks *in April* 1917, for example, in my "Theses" of April 4, 1917,[4] i.e., *long before* the Revolution of October 1917 (and, of course, long before the dissolution of the Constituent Assembly on January 5, 1918).

* * *

Whoever sincerely shared the Marxist view that the state is nothing but a machine for the suppression of one class by another, and who has at all reflected upon this truth, could never have reached the absurd conclusion that the proletarian organisations capable of defeating finance capital must not transform themselves into state organisations. It was this point that betrayed the petty bourgeois who believes that "after all is said and done" the state is something

---

4. See above, pp. 295–300. [*R. T.*]

outside classes or above classes. Indeed, why should the proletariat, *"one class,"* be permitted to wage unremitting war on *capital* which rules not only over the proletariat, but over the whole people, over the whole petty bourgeoisie, over all the peasants, yet this proletariat, this *"one class,"* is not to be permitted to transform its organisation into a state organisation? Because the petty bourgeois is *afraid* of the class struggle, and does not carry it to its logical conclusion, *to its main object.*

* * *

The Constituent Assembly and the Soviet Republic

The question of the Constituent Assembly and its dispersal by the Bolsheviks is the crux of Kautsky's entire pamphlet. He constantly reverts to it, and the whole of this literary production of the ideological leader of the Second International is replete with innuendoes to the effect that the Bolsheviks have "destroyed democracy" (see one of the quotations from Kautsky above). The question is really an interesting and important one, because the relation between bourgeois democracy and proletarian democracy here confronted the revolution in a *practical* form. * * *

* * *

Kautsky adopts a formal standpoint on the question of the Constituent Assembly. My theses[5] say clearly and repeatedly that the interests of the revolution are higher than the formal rights of the Constituent Assembly (see theses 16 and 17). The formal democratic point of view is precisely the point of view of the *bourgeois* democrat who refuses to admit that the interests of the proletariat and of the proletarian class struggle are supreme. As a historian, Kautsky would not have been able to deny that bourgeois parliaments are the organs of this or that class. But now (for the sordid purpose of renouncing revolution) Kautsky finds it necessary to forget his Marxism, and he *refrains from putting the question*: the organ of what *class* was the Constituent Assembly of Russia? Kautsky does not examine the concrete conditions; he does not want to face facts; he does not say a single word to his German readers about the fact that the theses contained not only a theoretical elucidation of the question of the limited character of bourgeois democracy (theses 1–3), not only a description of the concrete conditions which determined the discrepancy between the party lists of candidates in the middle of October 1917 and the real state

5. See *Theses on the Constituent Assembly*, pp. 418–22, above. [*R. T.*]

of affairs in December 1917 (theses 4–6), but also *a history of the class struggle and the Civil War* in October–December 1917 (theses 7–15). From this concrete history we drew the conclusion (thesis 14) that the slogan "All Power to the Constituent Assembly!" had, *in reality*, become the slogan of the Cadets and the Kaledin men and their abettors.

* * *

Kautsky admits that the Soviets are an excellent combat organisation of the proletariat, and that they have a great future before them. But, that being the case, Kautsky's position collapses like a house of cards, or like the dreams of a petty bourgeois that the acute struggle between the proletariat and the bourgeoisie can be avoided. For revolution is one continuous and moreover desperate struggle, and the proletariat is the vanguard class of *all* the oppressed, the focus and centre of all the aspirations of all the oppressed for their emancipation! Naturally, therefore, the Soviets, as the organ of the struggle of the oppressed people, reflected and expressed the moods and changes of opinions of these people ever so much more quickly, fully, and faithfully than any other institution (that, incidentally, is one of the reasons why Soviet democracy is the highest type of democracy).

In the period between February 28 (old style) and October 25, 1917, the Soviets managed to convene *two* all-Russia congresses of representatives of the overwhelming majority of the population of Russia, of all the workers and soldiers, and of 70 or 80 per cent of the peasants, not to mention the vast number of local, *uyezd*,[6] town, *gubernia*, and regional congresses. During this period the bourgeoisie did not succeed in convening a single institution representing the majority (except that obvious sham and mockery called the "Democratic Conference,"[7] which enraged the proletariat). The Constituent Assembly reflected *the same* popular mood and *the same* political grouping as the First (June) All-Russia Congress of Soviets. By the time the Constituent Assembly was convened (January 1918), the Second (October 1917) and Third (January 1918) Congresses of Soviets had met, both of which had *demonstrated as clear as clear could be* that the people had swung to the left, had become revolutionised, had turned away from the Mensheviks and the Socialist-Revolutionaries, and had passed over to the side of the

6. *Uyezd*: district; *gubernia*: province. [*R. T.*]

7. The All-Russia Democratic Conference was held in Petrograd from September 14 to 22 (September 27–October 5), 1917. It was convened by the Mensheviks and Socialist-Revolutionaries. The Bolsheviks took part in it in order to expose the Mensheviks and S.R.s. The Democratic Conference set up a Pre-Parliament (Provisional Council of the Republic).

On Lenin's proposal, the Central Committee of the Party adopted a decision that the Bolsheviks should walk out of the Pre-Parliament.

Bolsheviks; *that is*, had turned away from petty-bourgeois leadership, from the illusion that it was possible to reach a compromise with the bourgeoisie, and had joined the proletarian revolutionary struggle for the overthrow of the bourgeoisie.

So, even the *external history* of the Soviets shows that the Constituent Assembly was a *reactionary* body and that its dispersal was inevitable. But Kautsky sticks firmly to his "slogan": let "pure democracy" prevail though the revolution perish and the bourgeoisie triumph over the proletariat! *Fiat justitia, pereat mundus!*[8]

Here are the brief figures relating to the all-Russia congresses of Soviets in the course of the history of the Russian revolution:

All-Russia Congress of Soviets	Number of Delegates	Number of Bolsheviks	Percentage of Bolsheviks
First (June 3, 1917)	790	103	13
Second (October 25, 1917)	675	343	51
Third (January 10, 1918)	710	434	61
Fourth (March 14, 1918)	1,232	795	64
Fifth (July 4, 1918)	1,164	773	66

One glance at these figures is enough to understand why the defence of the Constituent Assembly and talk (like Kautsky's) about the Bolsheviks not having a majority of the population behind them are just ridiculed in Russia.

* * *

Bolshevism has popularised throughout the world the idea of the "dictatorship of the proletariat," has translated these words from the Latin, first into Russian, and then into *all* the languages of the world, and has shown by the example of *Soviet government* that the workers and poor peasants, *even* of a backward country, even with the least experience, education and habits of organisation, *have been able* for a whole year, amidst gigantic difficulties and amidst a struggle against the exploiters (who were supported by the bourgeoisie of the *whole* world), to maintain the power of the working people, to create a democracy that is immeasurably higher and broader than all previous democracies in the world, and to *start* the creative work of tens of millions of workers and peasants for the practical construction of socialism.

Bolshevism has actually helped to develop the proletarian revolution in Europe and America more powerfully than any party in any other country has so far succeeded in doing. While the workers of the whole world are realising more and more clearly every day that the tactics of the Scheidemanns and Kautskys have not delivered

8. Let justice be done, even though the world may perish.

them from the imperialist war and from wage-slavery to the imperialist bourgeoisie, and that these tactics cannot serve as a model for all countries, the mass of workers in all countries are realising more and more clearly every day that Bolshevism has indicated the right road of escape from the horrors of war and imperialism, that Bolshevism *can serve as a model of tactics for all.*

Not only the general European, but the world proletarian revolution is maturing before the eyes of all, and it has been assisted, accelerated and supported by the victory of the proletariat in Russia. All this is not enough for the complete victory of socialism, you say? Of course it is not enough. One country alone cannot do more. But this one country, thanks to Soviet government, has done so much that even if Soviet government in Russia were to be crushed by world imperialism tomorrow, as a result, let us say, of an agreement between German and Anglo-French imperialism—even granted that very worst possibility—it would still be found that Bolshevik tactics have brought enormous benefit to socialism and have assisted the growth of the invincible world revolution.

* * *

A Great Beginning

ON THE HEROISM OF WORKERS IN THE REAR

In May 1919, responding to a party call during the Civil War to work "in a revolutionary way," a group of workers on the Moscow-Kazan railway line decided to work an additional day on Saturdays, without pay, on behalf of victory over the White forces of Admiral Kolchak. Such Saturday work became known as a "communist *subbotnik*" (from *subbota*, the Russian word for "Saturday"), and this movement was taken under party sponsorship with wide publicity. Lenin's article of July 1919 treated it as the beginning of a revolution in the *habits* left as a heritage of the past, and is notable for its proposition—an important indicator of the further development of his political thinking—that "the dictatorship of the proletariat is not only the use of force against the exploiters, and not even mainly the use of force."

The press reports many instances of the heroism of the Red Army men. In the fight against Kolchak, Denikin and other forces of the landowners and capitalists, the workers and peasants very often display miracles of bravery and endurance, defending the gains of the socialist revolution. The guerrilla spirit, weariness and indiscipline are being overcome; it is a slow and difficult process, but it is making headway in spite of everything. The heroism of the working people making voluntary sacrifices for the victory of socialism—this is the foundation of the new, comradely discipline in the Red Army, the foundation on which that army is regenerating, gaining strength and growing.

The heroism of the workers in the rear is no less worthy of attention. In this connection, the "communist *subbotniks*" organised by the workers on their own initiative are really of enormous significance. Evidently, this is only a beginning, but it is a beginning of exceptionally great importance. It is the beginning of a revolution that is more difficult, more tangible, more radical and more decisive than the overthrow of the bourgeoisie, for it is a victory over our own conservatism, indiscipline, petty-bourgeois egoism, a victory over the habits left as a heritage to the worker and peasant by accursed capitalism. Only when *this* victory is consolidated will the new social discipline, socialist discipline, be created; then and only then will a reversion to capitalism become impossible, will communism become really invincible.

* * *

As I have had occasion to point out more than once, * * * the dictatorship of the proletariat is not only the use of force against the exploiters, and not even the mainly the use of force. The economic foundation of this use of revolutionary force, the guarantee of its effectiveness and success is the fact that the proletariat represents and creates a higher type of social organisation of labour compared with capitalism. This is what is important, this is the source of the strength and the guarantee that the final triumph of communism is inevitable.

* * *

If we translate the Latin, scientific, historico-philosophical term "dictatorship of the proletariat" into simpler language, it means just the following.

Only a definite class, namely, the urban workers and the factory, industrial workers in general, is able to lead the whole mass of the working and exploited people in the struggle to throw off the yoke of capital, in actually carrying it out, in the struggle to maintain and consolidate the victory, in the work of creating the new, socialist social system and in the entire struggle for the complete abolition of classes. (Let us observe in parenthesis that the only scientific distinction between socialism and communism is that the first term implies the first stage of the new society arising out of capitalism, while the second implies the next and higher stage.)

The mistake the "Berne" yellow International makes is that its leaders accept the class struggle and the leading role of the proletariat only in word and are afraid to think it out to its logical conclusion. They are afraid of that inevitable conclusion which particularly terrifies the bourgeoisie, and which is absolutely unacceptable to them. They are afraid to admit that the dictatorship of the proletariat is *also* a period of class struggle, which is inevitable as long as classes have not been abolished, and which changes in form, being particularly fierce and particularly peculiar in the period immediately following the overthrow of capital. The proletariat does not cease the class struggle after it has captured political power, but continues it until classes are abolished—of course, under different circumstances, in different form and by different means.

And what does the "abolition of classes" mean? All those who call themselves socialists recognise this as the ultimate goal of socialism, but by no means all give thought to its significance. Classes are large groups of people differing from each other by the place they occupy in a historically determined system of social production, by their relation (in most cases fixed and formulated in law) to the means of production, by their role in the social organisation of labour, and, consequently, by the dimensions of the share of social wealth of which they dispose and the mode of acquiring it. Classes are groups of people one of which can appropriate the labour of another owing to the different places they occupy in a definite system of social economy.

Clearly, in order to abolish classes completely, it is not enough to overthrow the exploiters, the landowners and capitalists, not enough to abolish *their* rights of ownership; it is necessary also to abolish *all* private ownership of the means of production, it is necessary to abolish the distinction between town and country, as well as the distinction between manual workers and brain workers. This requires a very long period of time. In order to achieve this an enormous step forward must be taken in developing the productive forces; it is necessary to overcome the resistance (frequently passive, which is particularly stubborn and particularly difficult to overcome) of the numerous survivals of small-scale production; it is necessary to overcome the enormous force of habit and conservatism which are connected with these survivals.

The assumption that all "working people" are equally capable of doing this work would be an empty phrase, or the illusion of an antediluvian, pre-Marxist socialist; for this ability does not come of itself, but grows historically, and grows *only* out of the material conditions of large-scale capitalist production. This ability, at the beginning of the road from capitalism to socialism, is possessed by the proletariat *alone*. It is capable of fulfilling the gigantic task that confronts it, first, because it is the strongest and most advanced class in civilised societies; secondly, because in the most developed countries it constitutes the majority of the population, and thirdly, because in backward capitalist countries, like Russia, the majority of the population consists of semi-proletarians, i.e., of people who regularly live in a proletarian way part of the year, who regularly earn a part of their means of subsistence as wage-workers in capitalist enterprises.

* * *

In order to achieve victory, in order to build and consolidate socialism, the proletariat must fulfil a twofold or dual task: first, it must, by its supreme heroism in the revolutionary struggle against capital, win over the entire mass of the working and exploited people; it must win them over, organise them and lead them in the struggle to overthrow the bourgeoisie and utterly suppress their resistance. Secondly, it must lead the whole mass of the working and exploited people, as well as all the petty-bourgeois groups, on to the road of new economic development, towards the creation of a new social bond, a new labour discipline, a new organisation of labour, which will combine the last word in science and capitalist technology with the mass association of class-conscious workers creating large-scale socialist industry.

The second task is more difficult than the first, for it cannot possibly be fulfilled by single acts of heroic fervour; it requires the most prolonged, most persistent and most difficult mass heroism in *plain, everyday* work. But this task is more essential than the first, because, in the last analysis, the deepest source of strength for victories over the bourgeoisie and the sole guarantee of the durability and permanence of these victories can only be a new and higher mode of social production, the substitution of large-scale socialist production for capitalist and petty-bourgeois production.

"Communist *subbotniks*" are of such enormous historical significance precisely because they demonstrate the conscious and voluntary initiative of the workers in developing the productivity of labour, in adopting a new labour discipline, in creating socialist conditions of economy and life.

J. Jacoby, one of the few, in fact it would be more correct to say one of the exceptionally rare, German bourgeois democrats who, after the lessons of 1870–71, went over not to chauvinism or national-liberalism, but to socialism, once said that the formation of a single trade union was of greater historical importance than the battle of Sadowa. This is true. The battle of Sadowa decided the supremacy of one of two bourgeois monarchies, the Austrian or the Prussian, in creating a German national capitalist state. The formation of one trade union was a small step towards the world victory of the proletariat over the bourgeoisie. And we may similarly say that the first communist *subbotnik*, organised by the workers of the Moscow-Kazan Railway in Moscow on May 10, 1919, was of greater historical significance than any of the victories of Hindenburg, or of Foch and the British, in the 1914–18 imperialist war. The victories of the imperialists mean the slaughter of millions of workers for the sake of the profits of the Anglo-American and French multimillionaires, they are the atrocities of doomed capitalism, bloated with over-eating and rotting alive. The communist *subbotnik* organised by the workers of the Moscow-Kazan Railway is one of the cells of the new, socialist society, which brings to all the peoples of the earth emancipation from the yoke of capital and from wars.

The bourgeois gentlemen and their hangers-on, including the Mensheviks and Socialist-Revolutionaries, who are wont to regard themselves as the representatives of "public opinion," naturally jeer at the hopes of the Communists, call those hopes "a baobab tree in a mignonette pot," sneer at the insignificance of the number of *subbotniks* compared with the vast number of cases of thieving, idleness, lower productivity, spoilage of raw materials and finished goods, etc. Our reply to these gentlemen is that if the bourgeois intellectuals had dedicated their knowledge to assisting the working people instead of giving it to the Russian and foreign capitalists in order to restore their power, the revolution would have proceeded more rapidly and more peacefully. But this is utopian, for the issue is decided by the class struggle, and the majority of the intellectuals gravitate towards the bourgeoisie. Not with the assistance of the intellectuals will the proletariat achieve victory, but in spite of their opposition (at least in the majority of cases), removing those of them who are incorrigibly bourgeois, reforming, re-educating and subordinating the waverers, and gradually winning ever larger sections of them to its side. Gloating over the difficulties and setbacks of the revolution, sowing panic, preaching a return to the past— these are all weapons and methods of class struggle of the bourgeois intellectuals. The proletariat will not allow itself to be deceived by them.

If we get down to brass tacks, however, has it ever happened in history that a new mode of production has taken root immediately, without a long succession of setbacks, blunders and relapses? Half a century after the abolition of serfdom there were still quite a number of survivals of serfdom in the Russian countryside. Half a century after the abolition of slavery in America the position of the Negroes was still very often one of semi-slavery. The bourgeois intellectuals, including the Mensheviks and Socialist-Revolutionaries, are true to themselves in serving capital and in continuing to use absolutely false arguments—before the proletarian revolution they accused us of being utopian; after the revolution they demand that we wipe out all traces of the past with fantastic rapidity!

We are not utopians, however, and we know the real value of bourgeois "arguments"; we also know that for some time after the revolution traces of the old ethics will inevitably predominate over the young shoots of the new. When the new has just been born the old always remains stronger than it for some time; this is always the case in nature and in social life. Jeering at the feebleness of the young shoots of the new order, cheap scepticism of the intellectuals and the like—these are, essentially, methods of bourgeois class struggle against the proletariat, a defence of capitalism against socialism. We must carefully study the feeble new shoots, we must devote the greatest attention to them, do everything to promote their growth and "nurse" them. Some of them will inevitably perish. We cannot vouch that precisely the "communist *subbotniks*" will play a particularly important role. But that is not the point. The point is to foster each and every shoot of the new; and life will select the most viable. If the Japanese scientist, in order to help mankind vanquish syphilis, had the patience to test six hundred and five preparations before he developed a six hundred and sixth which met definite requirements, then those who want to solve a more difficult problem, namely, to vanquish capitalism, must have the perseverance to try hundreds and thousands of new methods, means and weapons of struggle in order to elaborate the most suitable of them.

The "communist *subbotniks*" are so important because they were initiated by workers who were by no means placed in exceptionally good conditions, by workers of various specialities, and some with no speciality at all, just unskilled labourers, who are living under *ordinary*, i.e., *exceedingly hard*, conditions. We all know very well the main cause of the decline in the productivity of labour that is to be observed not only in Russia, but all over the world; it is ruin and impoverishment, embitterment and weariness caused by the imperialist war, sickness and malnutrition. The latter is first in importance. Starvation—that is the cause. And in order to do away with starvation, productivity of labour must be raised in agriculture, in transport and in industry. So, we get a sort of vicious circle: in order to raise productivity of labour we must save ourselves from starvation, and in order to save ourselves from starvation we must raise productivity of labour.

We know that in practice such contradictions are solved by breaking the vicious circle, by bringing about a radical change in the temper of the people, by the heroic initiative of the individual groups which often plays a decisive role against the background of such a radical change. The unskilled labourers and railway workers of Moscow (of course, we have in mind the majority of them, and not a handful of profiteers, officials and other whiteguards) are working people who are living in desperately hard conditions. They are constantly underfed, and now, before the new harvest is gathered, with the general worsening of the food situation, they are actually starving. And yet these starving workers, surrounded by the malicious counter-revolutionary agitation of the bourgeoisie, the Mensheviks and the Socialist-Revolutionaries, are organising "communist *subbotniks*," working overtime *without any pay*, and achieving *an enormous increase in the productivity of labour* in spite of the fact that they are weary, tormented, and exhausted by malnutrition. Is this not supreme heroism? Is this not the beginning of a change of momentous significance?

In the last analysis, productivity of labour is the most important, the principal thing for the victory of the new social system. Capitalism created a productivity of labour unknown under serfdom. Capitalism can be utterly vanquished, and will be utterly vanquished by socialism creating a new and much higher productivity of labour. This is a very difficult matter and must take a long time; but *it has been started*, and that is the main thing. If in starving Moscow, in the summer of 1919, the starving workers who had gone through four trying years of imperialist war and another year and a half of still more trying civil war could start this great work, how will things develop later when we triumph in the civil war and win peace?

Communism is the higher productivity of labour—compared with that existing under capitalism—of voluntary, class-conscious and united workers employing advanced techniques. Communist *subbotniks* are extraordinarily valuable as the *actual* beginning of *communism*; and this is a very rare thing, because we are in a stage when "only the *first* steps in the transition from capitalism to communism are being taken" (as our Party Programme quite rightly says).

Communism begins when the *rank-and-file workers* display an enthusiastic concern that is undaunted by arduous toil to increase the productivity of labour, husband *every* pood[1] *of grain, coal, iron* and other products, which do not accrue to the workers personally or to their "close" kith and kin, but to their "distant" kith and kin, i.e., to society as a whole, to tens and hundreds of millions of people united first in one socialist state, and then in a union of Soviet republics.

In *Capital*, Karl Marx ridicules the pompous and grandiloquent bourgeois-democratic great charter of liberty and the rights of man, ridicules all this phrase-mongering about liberty, equality and fraternity *in general*, which dazzles the petty bourgeois and philistines of all countries, including the present despicable heroes of the despicable Berne International. Marx contrasts these pompous declarations of rights to the plain, modest, practical, simple manner in which the question is presented by the proletariat—the legislative enactment of a shorter working day is a typical example of such treatment. The aptness and profundity of Marx's observation become the clearer and more obvious to us the more the content of the proletarian revolution unfolds. The "formulas" of genuine

---

1. A *pood* is thirty-six pounds. [*R. T.*]

communism differ from the pompous, intricate, and solemn phraseology of the Kautskys, the Mensheviks and the Socialist-Revolutionaries and their beloved "brethren" of Berne in that they reduce everything to the *conditions of labour*. Less chatter about "labour democracy," about "liberty, equality and fraternity," about "government by the people," and all such stuff; the class-conscious workers and peasants of our day see through these pompous phrases of the bourgeois intellectual and discern the trickery as easily as a person of ordinary common sense and experience, when glancing at the irreproachably "polished" features and immaculate appearance of the "fain fellow, dontcher know," immediately and unerringly puts him down as "in all probability, a scoundrel."

Fewer pompous phrases, more plain, *everyday* work, concern for the *pood* of grain and the *pood* of coal! More concern about providing this *pood* of grain and *pood* of coal needed by the hungry workers and ragged and barefoot peasants *not* by *haggling*, not in a capitalist manner, but by the conscious, voluntary, boundlessly heroic labour of plain working men like the unskilled labourers and railwaymen of the Moscow-Kazan line.

We must all admit that vestiges of the bourgeois-intellectual phrase-mongering approach to questions of the revolution are in evidence at every step, everywhere, even in our own ranks. Our press, for example, does little to fight these rotten survivals of the rotten, bourgeois-democratic past; it does little to foster the simple, modest, ordinary but viable shoots of genuine communism.

Take the position of women. In this field, not a single democratic party in the world, not even in the most advanced bourgeois republic, has done in decades so much as a hundredth part of what we did in our very first year in power. We really razed to the ground the infamous laws placing women in a position of inequality, restricting divorce and surrounding it with disgusting formalities, denying recognition to children born out of wedlock, enforcing a search for their fathers, etc., laws numerous survivals of which, to the shame of the bourgeoisie and of capitalism, are to be found in all civilised countries. We have a thousand times the right to be proud of what we have done in this field. But the more *thoroughly* we have cleared the ground of the lumber of the old, bourgeois laws and institutions, the clearer it is to us that we have only cleared the ground to build on but are not yet building.

Notwithstanding all the laws emancipating woman, she continues to be a *domestic slave*, because *petty housework* crushes, strangles, stultifies and degrades her, chains her to the kitchen and the nursery, and she wastes her labour on barbarously unproductive, petty, nerve-racking, stultifying and crushing drudgery. The real *emancipation of women*, real communism, will begin only where and when an all-out struggle begins (led by the proletariat wielding the state power) against this petty housekeeping, or rather when its *wholesale transformation* into a large-scale socialist economy begins.

Do we in practice pay sufficient attention to this question, which in theory every Communist considers indisputable? Of course not. Do we take proper care of the *shoots* of communism which already exist in this sphere? Again the answer is *no*. Public catering establishments, nurseries, kindergartens—here we have examples of these shoots, here we have the simple, everyday means, involving nothing pompous, grandiloquent or ceremonial, which can *really emancipate women*, really lessen and abolish their inequality with men as regards their role in social production and public life. These means are not new, they (like all the material prerequisites for socialism) were created by large-scale capitalism. But under capitalism they remained, first, a rarity, and secondly—which is particularly important—either *profit-making* enterprises, with all the worst features of speculation, profiteering, cheating and fraud, or "acrobatics of bourgeois charity," which the best workers rightly hated and despised.

There is no doubt that the number of these institutions in our country has increased enormously and that they are *beginning* to change in character. There is no doubt that we have far more *organising talent* among the working and peasant women than we are aware of, that we have far more people than we know of who can organise practical work, with the co-operation of large numbers of workers and of still larger numbers of consumers, without that abundance of talk, fuss, squabbling and chatter about plans, systems, etc., with which our big-headed "intellectuals" or half-baked "Communists" are "affected." But we *do not nurse* these shoots of the new as we should.

Look at the bourgeoisie. How very well they know how to advertise what *they* need! See how millions of copies of *their* newspapers extol what the capitalists regard as "model" enterprises, and how "model" bourgeois institutions are made an object of national pride! Our press does not take the trouble, or hardly ever, to describe the best catering establishments or nurseries, in order, by daily insistence, to get some of them turned into models of their kind. It does not give them enough publicity, does not describe in detail the saving in human labour, the conveniences for the consumer, the economy of products, the emancipation of women from domestic slavery, the improvement in sanitary conditions, that can be achieved with *exemplary communist work* and extended to the whole of society, to all working people.

Exemplary production, exemplary communist *subbotniks*, exemplary care and conscientiousness in procuring and distributing every *pood* of grain, exemplary catering establishments, exemplary cleanliness in such-and-such a workers' house, in such-and-such a block, should all receive ten times more attention and care from our press, as well as from *every* workers' and peasants' organisation, than they receive now. All these are shoots of communism, and it is our common and primary duty to nurse them. Difficult as our food and production situation is, in the year and a half of Bolshevik rule there has been undoubted progress *all along the line*: grain procurements have increased from 30 million *poods* (from August 1, 1917, to August 1, 1918) to 100 million *poods* (from August 1, 1918, to May 1, 1919); vegetable gardening has expanded, the margin of unsown land has diminished, railway transport has begun to improve despite the enormous fuel difficulties, and so on. Against this general background, and with the support of the proletarian state power, the shoots of communism will not wither; they will grow and blossom into complete communism.

* * *

In this respect, the "communist *subbotniks*" are a most valuable exception; for the unskilled labourers and railwaymen of the Moscow-Kazan Railway *first* demonstrated *by deeds* that they are capable of working like *Communists*, and then adopted the title of "communist subbotniks" for their undertaking. We must see to it and make sure that in future anyone who calls his enterprise, institution or undertaking a commune *without having proved* this by hard work and practical *success in prolonged effort*, by exemplary and truly communist organisation, is mercilessly ridiculed and pilloried as a charlatan or a windbag.

That great beginning, the "communist *subbotnik*," must also be utilised for another purpose, namely, to *purge* the Party. In the early period following the revolution, when the mass of "honest" and philistine-minded people was particularly timorous, and when the bourgeois intellectuals to a man, including, of course, the Mensheviks and Socialist-Revolutionaries, played the lackey to the bourgeoisie and carried on sabotage, it was absolutely inevitable that adventurers and other pernicious elements should hitch themselves to the ruling party. There never has been, and there never can be, a revolution without that. The whole point is that the ruling party should be able, relying on a sound and strong advanced class, to purge its ranks.

We started this work long ago. It must be continued steadily and untiringly. The mobilisation of Communists for the war helped us in this respect: the cowards and scoundrels fled from the Party's ranks. Good riddance! *Such* a reduction in the Party's membership means an *enormous increase* in its strength and weight. We must continue the purge, and that new beginning, the "communist *sub-botniks*," must be utilised for this purpose: members should be accepted into the Party only after six months', say, "trial," or "probation," at "working in a revolutionary way." A similar test should be demanded of *all* members of the Party who joined after October 25, 1917, and who have not proved by some special work or service that they are absolutely reliable, loyal and capable of being Communists.

The purging of the Party, through the steadily *increasing demands* it makes in regard to working in a genuinely communist way, will improve the state *apparatus* and will bring much nearer the *final transition* of the peasants to the side of the revolutionary proletariat.

Incidentally, the "communist *subbotniks*" have thrown a remarkably strong light on the class character of the state apparatus under the dictatorship of the proletariat. The Central Committee of the Party drafts a letter on "working in a revolutionary way."[2] The idea is suggested by the Central Committee of a party with from 100,000 to 200,000 members (I assume that that is the number that will remain after a thorough purging; at present the membership is larger).

The idea is taken up by the workers organised in trade unions. In Russia and the Ukraine they number about four million. The overwhelming majority of them are for the state power of the proletariat, for proletarian dictatorship. Two hundred thousand and four million—such is the ratio of the "gear-wheels," if one may so express it. Then follow the *tens of millions* of peasants, who are divided into three main groups: the most numerous and the one standing closest to the proletariat is that of the semi-proletarians or poor peasants; then come the middle peasants, and lastly the numerically very small group of kulaks or rural bourgeoisie.

As long as it is possible to trade in grain and to make profit out of famine, the peasant will remain (and this will for some time be inevitable under the dictatorship of the proletariat) a semi-working man, a semi-profiteer. As a profiteer he is hostile to us, hostile to the proletarian state; he is inclined to agree with the bourgeoisie and their faithful lackeys, up to and including the Menshevik Sher or the Socialist-Revolutionary B. Chernenkov, who stand for freedom to trade in grain. But *as a working man*, the peasant is a friend of the proletarian state, a most loyal ally of the worker in the

2. This letter, actually drafted by Lenin, was published in *Pravda* on April 12, 1919, over the signature of the party Central Committee. It called for mobilization of the masses for work as well as fighting in connection with the threat posed by Admiral Kolchak's forces on the Eastern front, and asked all party organizations and trade unions in this connection to "work in a revolutionary way, and not confine themselves to the old stereotyped methods." [*R. T.*]

struggle against the landowner and against the capitalist. As working men, the peasants, the vast mass of them, the peasant millions, support the state "machine" which is headed by the one or two hundred thousand Communists of the proletarian vanguard, and which consists of millions of organised proletarians.

* * *

The Dictatorship of the Proletariat

In September–October 1919, Lenin drafted the plan of a contemplated work on the dictatorship of the proletariat. The work itself was never written, but the portion of the plan here reproduced (roughly the first half of it) clearly sets forth Lenin's view—which was particularly characteristic of his thinking during the Civil War and War Communism—that the proletarian state is in essence the instrumentality of a continuation of class war—from above.

For treatment in the pamphlet the question falls into 4 main sections.

(A) The dictatorship of the proletariat as new forms of the class struggle of the proletariat (in other words: its new stage and new tasks).

(B) The dictatorship of the proletariat as the destruction of bourgeois democracy and the creation of proletarian democracy.

(C) The dictatorship of the proletariat and the distinguishing features of imperialism (or the imperialist stage of capitalism).

(D) The dictatorship of the proletariat and Soviet power.

Plan for the elaboration of these 4 sections:

I (A) The Dictatorship of the Proletariat as New Forms of the Class Struggle of the Proletariat

1. The chief reason why "socialists" do not understand the dictatorship of the proletariat is that they do not carry the idea of the class struggle to its logical conclusion (cf. Marx, 1852).[1]

1. Lenin's reference here is to Marx's letter of March 5, 1852, to Weydemeyer in which Marx said: "What I did that was new was to prove: (1) that the

The dictatorship of the proletariat is the *continuation* of the class struggle of the proletariat in *new* forms. That is the crux of the matter; that is what they do not understand.

The proletariat, as a *special* class, alone *continues* to wage its class struggle.

2. The state is only a *weapon* of the proletariat in its class struggle. A special kind of *cudgel, rien de plus!*[2]

Old prejudices regarding the state (cf. *The State and Revolution*). New forms of the state—the subject of section B; here only the *approach* to it.

3. The forms of the class struggle of the proletariat, under its dictatorship, cannot be what they were before. *Five* new (principal) tasks and correspondingly five new forms:

4. (1) *Suppression of the resistance of the exploiters*. This, as the task (and content) of the *epoch,* is entirely forgotten by the opportunists and "socialists."

Hence :

(*aa*) the special (higher) severity of the class struggle

(*ββ*) new forms of resistance corresponding to capitalism and its highest stage (plots + sabotage + influence on the petty bourgeoisie, etc. etc.) and, in particular,

5. (2) (*γγ*) *Civil war*.
Revolution in general and civil war (1649, 1793) (cf. Karl Kautsky, 1902, in *The Social Revolution*).

Civil war in the epoch of the international ties of capitalism.

Transformation of imperialist war into civil war. (Ignorance and despicable cowardice of the "socialists.")

The resistance of the exploiters begins *before* their overthrow and afterwards becomes *intensified* from *two* sides. A fight to a *finish*, or "talk one's way out" (Karl Kautsky, the petty bourgeoisie, the "socialists").

Civil war and the "destruction" of the party (Karl Kautsky).
Terror and civil war.

{ *a*) **Russia,** Hungary, Finland, **Germany.**
β) Switzerland and America.

---

existence of classes is only bound up with **particular, historic phases in the development of production**; (2) that the class struggle necessarily leads to the **dictatorship of the proletariat**; (3) that

this dictatorship itself only constitutes the transition to the abolition of all classes and to a *classless society*." [*R. T.*]
2. Nothing more.

Cf. Marx, 1870: give the proletariat practice in arms. The *epoch* 1871–1914 and the *epoch* of civil wars.

6. (3) *"Neutralisation" of the petty bourgeoisie, especially the peasantry.*

Communist Manifesto (reactionary and revolutionary "only in view of").

Karl Kautsky in the *Agrarfrage*.[3] The same idea of neutralisation, only *verballhornt*.[4]

"Neutralisation" in practice means
{ suppression by force (Engels, 1895) example persuasion, etc,. etc. enlisting + suppression, "only in view of."

+ Inevitability of a combination of civil war with revolutionary wars (cf. Programme of the R.C.P.).

The "ruling class." Rule precludes "liberty and equality."

"To head," "to lead," "to take with," the class meaning of these concepts.

NB | Peasant and worker. The peasant as a toiler and the peasant as an exploiter (profiteer, property-owner). "Only in view of." Vacillations in the course of the struggle. *Experience* of the struggle.

"One reactionary mass": Engels, 1875, in respect of the *Commune*.[5]

7. (4) *"Utilisation" of the bourgeoisie.*

"Specialists." Not only suppression of resistance, not only "neutralisation," but setting them to work, compelling them to serve the proletariat.

Cf. Programme of the R.C.P. "Military Specialists."

8. (5) *Inculcation of a new discipline.*

(α) The dictatorship of the proletariat and the trade unions.

(β) Bonuses and piece rates.

(γ) Party purge and its role.

(δ) "Communist *subbotniks*."

* * *

3. *The Agrarian Question.*
4. Bowdlerised.
5. In his letter of March 18–28, 1875, to Bebel, Engels objected to a statement by Ferdinand Lassalle that in relation to the working class all other classes are only "one reactionary mass," arguing that this was true only in particular and exceptional cases, e.g., in a proletarian revolution like the Paris Commune. [*R. T.*]

Communism and Electrification

Large-scale Soviet economic planning was inaugurated in February 1920 when a State Commission on the Electrification of Russia (GOELRO) was set up on Lenin's initiative to prepare a ten-year plan of electric-power development. The GOELRO plan, in the form of the commission's report, was published in December 1920 and distributed to the delegates to the Eighth Congress of Soviets, meeting in Moscow. The enthusiasm for electrification that underlay this plan is reflected in these passages from Lenin's report of December 22, 1920, to the Eighth Congress, in which he advanced his famous equation: "Communism is Soviet power plus the electrification of the whole country."

* * *

The essential feature of the present political situation is that we are now passing through a crucial period of transition, something of a zigzag transition from war to economic development. This has occurred before, but not on such a wide scale. This should constantly remind us of what the general political tasks of the Soviet government are, and what constitutes the particular feature of this transition. The dictatorship of the proletariat has been successful because it has been able to combine compulsion with persuasion. The dictatorship of the proletariat does not fear any resort to compulsion and to the most severe, decisive and ruthless forms of coercion by the state. The advanced class, the class most oppressed by capitalism, is entitled to use compulsion, because it is doing so in the interests of the working and exploited people, and because it possesses means of compulsion and persuasion such as no former classes ever possessed, although they had incomparably greater material facilities for propaganda and agitation than we have.

* * *

We have, no doubt, learnt politics; here we stand as firm as a rock. But things are bad as far as economic matters are concerned. Henceforth, less politics will be the best politics. Bring more engineers and agronomists to the fore, learn from them, keep an eye on their work, and turn our congresses and conferences, not into propaganda meetings but into bodies that will verify our economic achievements, bodies in which we can really learn the business of economic development.

You will hear the report of the State Electrification Commission, which was set up in conformity with the decision of the All-Russia Central Executive Committee of February 7, 1920. On February 21, the Presidium of the Supreme Council of the National Economy signed the final ordinance determining the composition of the commission, and a number of leading experts and workers, mainly from the Supreme Council of the National Economy, over a hundred of them, and also from the People's Commissariat of Railways and the People's Commissariat of Agriculture, are devoting their entire energy to this work. We have before us the results of the work of the State Commission for the Electrification of Russia in the shape of this small volume which will be distributed to you today or tomorrow. I trust you will not be scared by this little volume. I think I shall have no difficulty in convincing you of the particular importance of this book. In my opinion it is the second programme of our Party. We have a Party programme which has been excellently explained by Comrades Preobrazhensky and Bukharin in the form of a book which is less voluminous, but extremely useful. That is the political programme; it is an enumeration of our objectives, an explanation of the relations between classes and masses. It must, however, also be realised that the time has come to take this road in actual fact and to measure the practical results achieved. Our Party programme must not remain solely a programme of the Party. It must become a programme of our economic development, or otherwise it will be valueless even as a programme of the Party. It must be supplemented with a second Party programme, a plan of work aimed at restoring our entire economy and raising it to the level of up-to-date technical development. Without a plan of electrification, we cannot undertake any real constructive work. When we discuss the restoration of agriculture, industry and transport, and their harmonious co-ordination, we are obliged to discuss a broad economic plan. We must adopt a definite plan. Of course, it will be a plan adopted as a first approximation. This Party programme will not be as invariable as our real Party programme is, which can be modified by Party congresses alone. No, day by day this programme will be improved, elaborated, perfected and modified, in every workshop and in every *volost*.[1] We need it as a first draft, which will be submitted to the

---

1. Small rural district. [R. T.]

whole of Russia as a great economic plan designed for a period of not less than ten years and indicating how Russia is to be placed on the real economic basis required for communism. What was one of the most powerful incentives that multiplied our strength and our energies to a tremendous degree when we fought and won on the war front? It was the realisation of danger. Everybody asked whether it was possible that the landowners and capitalists might return to Russia. And the reply was that it was. We therefore multiplied our efforts a hundredfold, and we were victorious.

Take the economic front, and ask whether capitalism can be restored economically in Russia. We have combated the Sukharevka black market. The other day, just prior to the opening of the All-Russia Congress of Soviets, this not very pleasant institution was closed down by the Moscow Soviet of Workers' and Red Army Deputies. The Sukharevka black market has been closed but it is not that market that is so sinister. The old Sukharevka market on Sukharevskaya Square has been closed down, an act that presented no difficulty. The sinister thing is the "Sukharevka" that resides in the heart and behaviour of every petty proprietor. This is the "Sukharevka" that must be closed down. That "Sukharevka" is the basis of capitalism. While it exists, the capitalists may return to Russia and may grow stronger than we are. That must be clearly realised. It must serve as the mainspring of our work and as a condition and yardstick of our real success. While we live in a small-peasant country, there is a firmer economic basis for capitalism in Russia than for communism. That must be borne in mind. Anyone who has carefully observed life in the countryside, as compared with life in the cities, knows that we have not torn up the roots of capitalism and have not undermined the foundation, the basis, of the internal enemy. The latter depends on small-scale production, and there is only one way of undermining it, namely, to place the economy of the country, including agriculture, on a new technical basis, that of modern large-scale production. Only electricity provides that basis.

Communism is Soviet power plus the electrification of the whole country. Otherwise the country will remain a small-peasant country, and we must clearly realise that. We are weaker than capitalism, not only on the world scale, but also within the country. That is common knowledge. We have realised it, and we shall see to it that the economic basis is transformed from a small-peasant basis into a large-scale industrial basis. Only when the country has been electrified, and industry, agriculture and transport have been placed on the technical basis of modern large-scale industry, only then shall we be fully victorious.

We have already drawn up a preliminary plan for the electrification of the country; two hundred of our best scientific and technical men have worked on it. We have a plan which gives us estimates of materials and finances covering a long period of years, not less than a decade. * * *

I recently had occasion to attend a peasant festival held in Volokolamsk Uyezd, a remote part of Moscow Gubernia, where the peasants have electric lighting. A meeting was arranged in the street, and one of the peasants came forward and began to make a speech welcoming this new event in the lives of the peasants. "We peasants were unenlightened," he said, "and now light has appeared among us, an 'unnatural light, which will light up our peasant darkness.'" For my part, these words did not surprise me. Of course, to the non-Party peasant masses electric light is an "unnatural" light; but what we consider unnatural is that the peasants and workers should have lived for hundreds and thousands of years in such backwardness, poverty and oppression under the yoke of the landowners and the capitalists. You cannot emerge from this darkness very rapidly. What we must now try is to convert every electric power station we build into a stronghold of enlightenment to be used to make the masses electricity-conscious, so to speak. * * *

* * *

We must see to it that every factory and every electric power station becomes a centre of enlightenment; if Russia is covered with a dense network of electric power stations and powerful technical installations, our communist economic development will become a model for a future socialist Europe and Asia.

Two Resolutions on Party Policy

A milestone in the evolution of the Soviet Communist Party and the single-party political system was the Tenth Party Congress, which met in Moscow in early March 1921. The Civil War was over by then, but serious popular unrest in the war-ruined country, manifested most dramatically in the anti-Bolshevik sailors' rebellion at the naval base of Kronstadt, near Petrograd Harbor,* convinced the Bolshevik leaders of the need for the New Economic Policy (NEP), which they inaugurated at this congress.

The congress was preceded by a public intra-party debate in which various platforms of party policy toward the trade unions competed for support in the voting for delegates to the congress by the local party organizations. The "platform of the ten," reflecting Lenin's position, won a large majority and was approved by the congress. He drafted, and the congress adopted, a "Resolution on the Syndicalist and Anarchist Deviation in Our Party," which condemned the platform of the so-called Workers' Opposition group, headed by Alexander Shliapnikov. This resolution established the principle, applicable not only to the trade unions, that Soviet voluntary-membership organizations should operate under the ruling party's guidance and control—a principle never abandoned to this day.

Of no less importance was the "Resolution on Party Unity," also drafted by Lenin and adopted by the Tenth Congress. Alarmed by the spectacle of public intra-party squabbling in the trade union debate, and convinced that the need for the ruling party to tighten its internal discipline was especially acute in the present period of retreat marked by the inaugurating of the NEP, he proclaimed in this resolution the inadmissibility of "factionalism" inside the party. Clause 7, specifying sanctions for violation of the resolution, was not made public at the time.

It should not be assumed that the Resolution on Party Unity achieved its declared aim. For in fact factionalism was never eradicated from the party. The resolution did, however, tend to make factionalism more covert and also more dangerous for a losing faction—as many later expulsions and purges of losing factions were to show.

---

* The rebellion, which took place while the Tenth Party Congress was in session, was suppressed by Red Army forces. [R. T.]

Draft Resolution on the Syndicalist and Anarchist Deviation in Our Party

1. A syndicalist and anarchist deviation has been definitely revealed in our Party in the past few months. It calls for the most resolute measures of ideological struggle and also for purging the Party and restoring its health.

2. The said deviation is due partly to the influx into the Party of former Mensheviks, and also of workers and peasants who have not yet fully assimilated the communist world outlook. Mainly, however, this deviation is due to the influence exercised upon the proletariat and on the Russian Communist Party by the petty-bourgeois element, which is exceptionally strong in our country, and which inevitably engenders vacillation towards anarchism, particularly at a time when the condition of the masses has greatly deteriorated as a consequence of the crop failure and the devastating effects of war, and when the demobilisation of the army numbering millions sets loose hundreds and hundreds of thousands of peasants and workers unable immediately to find regular means of livelihood.

3. The most theoretically complete and clearly defined expression of this deviation (*or*: one of the most complete, etc., expressions of this deviation) is the theses and other literary productions of the so-called Workers' Opposition group. Sufficiently illustrative of this is, for example, the following thesis propounded by this group: "The organisation of the management of the national economy is the function of an All-Russia Congress of Producers organised in industrial unions which shall elect a central body to run the whole of the national economy of the Republic."

The ideas at the bottom of this and numerous similar statements are radically wrong in theory, and represent a complete break with Marxism and communism, with the practical experience of all semi-proletarian revolutions and of the present proletarian revolution.

First, the concept "producer" combines proletarians with semi-proletarians and small commodity producers, thus radically departing from the fundamental concept of the class struggle and from the fundamental demand that a precise distinction be drawn between classes.

Secondly, the bidding for or flirtation with the non-Party masses, which is expressed in the above-quoted thesis, is an equally radical departure from Marxism.

Marxism teaches—and this tenet has not only been formally endorsed by the whole of the Communist International in the decisions of the Second (1920) Congress of the Comintern on the role of the political party of the proletariat, but has also been confirmed in practice by our revolution—that only the political party of the working class, i.e., the Communist Party, is capable of uniting, training and organising a vanguard of the proletariat and of the whole mass of the working people that alone will be capable of withstanding the inevitable petty-bourgeois vacillations of this mass and the inevitable traditions and relapses of narrow craft unionism or craft prejudices among the proletariat, and of guiding all the united activities of the whole of the proletariat, i.e., of leading it politically, and through it, the whole mass of the working people. Without this the dictatorship of the proletariat is impossible.

The wrong understanding of the role of the Communist Party in its relation to the non-Party proletariat, and in the relation of the first and second factors to the whole mass of working people, is a radical theoretical departure from communism and a deviation towards syndicalism and anarchism, and this deviation permeates all the views of the Workers' Opposition group.

4. The Tenth Congress of the Russian Communist Party declares that it also regards as radically wrong all attempts on the part of the said group and of other persons to defend their fallacious views by referring to Paragraph 5 of the economic section of the Programme of the Russian Communist Party, which deals with the role of the trade unions. This paragraph says that "the trade unions should eventually arrive at a *de facto* concentration in their hands of the whole administration of the whole national economy, as a single economic entity," and that they will "ensure in this way indissoluble ties between the central state administration, the national economy and the broad masses of working people," "drawing" these masses "into direct economic management."

This paragraph in the Programme of the Russian Communist Party also says that a prerequisite for the state at which the trade unions "should eventually arrive" is the process whereby they increasingly "divest themselves of the narrow craft-union spirit" and embrace the majority "and eventually all" of the working people.

Lastly, this paragraph in the Programme of the Russian Communist Party emphasises that "on the strength of the laws of the R.S.F.S.R.,[1] and established practice, the trade unions participate in all the local and central organs of industrial management."

Instead of studying the practical experience of participation in administration, and instead of developing this experience further, strictly in conformity with successes achieved and mistakes rectified, the syndicalists and anarchists advance as an immediate slogan

1. Under the original Soviet Constitution of 1918, the country was officially the "Russian Soviet Federated Socialist Republic." Under the new constitution of 1924, it was renamed "Union of Soviet Socialist Republics," and the R.S.F.S.R., or Russian Federation, became one of the constituent ("union") republics along with the Ukrainian, Byelorussian, and others. [*R. T.*]

"congresses or a congress of producers" "to elect" the organs of economic management. Thus, the leading, educational and organising role of the Party in relation to the trade unions of the proletariat, and of the latter to the semi-petty-bourgeois and even wholly petty-bourgeois masses of working people, is completely evaded and eliminated, and instead of continuing and correcting the practical work of building new forms of economy already begun by the Soviet state, we get petty-bourgeois-anarchist disruption of this work, which can only lead to the triumph of the bourgeois counter-revolution.

5. In addition to the theoretical fallacies and a radically wrong attitude towards the practical experience of economic organisation already begun by the Soviet government, the Congress of the Russian Communist Party discerns in the views of this and similar groups and persons a gross political mistake and a direct political danger to the very existence of the dictatorship of the proletariat.

In a country like Russia, the overwhelming preponderance of the petty-bourgeois element and the devastation, impoverishment, epidemics, crop failures, extreme want and hardship inevitably resulting from the war, engender particularly sharp vacillations in the temper of the petty-bourgeois and semi-proletarian masses. First they incline towards a strengthening of the alliance between these masses and the proletariat, and then towards bourgeois restoration. The experience of all revolutions in the eighteenth, nineteenth, and twentieth centuries shows most clearly and convincingly that the only possible result of these vacillations—if the unity, strength and influence of the revolutionary vanguard of the proletariat is weakened in the slightest degree—will be the restoration of the power and property of the capitalists and landowners.

Hence, the views of the Workers' Opposition and of like-minded elements are not only wrong in theory, but are an expression of petty-bourgeois and anarchist wavering in practice, and actually weaken the consistency of the leading line of the Communist Party and help the class enemies of the proletarian revolution.

6. In view of all this, the Congress of the R.C.P., emphatically rejecting the said ideas, as being expressive of a syndicalist and anarchist deviation, deems it necessary:

First, to wage an unswerving and systematic struggle against these ideas;

Secondly, to recognise the propaganda of these ideas as being incompatible with membership of the R.C.P.

Instructing the C.C. of the Party strictly to enforce these decisions, the Congress at the same time points out that special publications, symposiums, etc., can and should provide space for a most comprehensive exchange of opinion between Party members on all the questions herein indicated.

Draft Resolution on Party Unity

1. The Congress calls the attention of all members of the Party to the fact that the unity and cohesion of the ranks of the Party, the guarantee of complete mutual confidence among Party members and truly harmonious work that really embodies the unanimity of will of the vanguard of the proletariat, are particularly essential at the present time, when a number of circumstances are increasing the vacillation among the petty-bourgeois population of the country.

2. Notwithstanding this, even before the general Party discussion on the trade unions, certain signs of factionalism—the formation of groups with separate platforms, striving to a certain degree to segregate and create their own group discipline—had been apparent in the Party. Such symptoms of factionalism were manifested, for example, at a Party conference in Moscow (November 1920) and at a Party conference in Kharkov, by the so-called Workers' Opposition group, and partly by the so-called Democratic Centralism group.

All class-conscious workers must clearly realise that factionalism of any kind is harmful and impermissible, for no matter how members of individual groups may desire to safeguard Party unity, factionalism in practice inevitably leads to the weakening of harmonious work and to intensified and repeated attempts by the enemies of the governing Party, who have wormed their way into it, to widen the cleavage and to use it for counter-revolutionary purposes.

The way the enemies of the proletariat take advantage of every deviation from a thoroughly consistent communist line was perhaps most strikingly shown in the case of the Kronstadt mutiny, when the bourgeois counter-revolutionaries and whiteguards in all countries of the world immediately expressed their readiness to accept the slogans of the Soviet system, if only they might thereby secure the overthrow of the dictatorship of the proletariat in Russia, and when the Socialist-Revolutionaries and the bourgeois counter-revolutionaries in general resorted in Kronstadt to slogans calling for an insurrection against the Soviet Government of Russia ostensibly in the interest of the Soviet power. These facts fully prove that the whiteguards strive, and are able, to disguise themselves as Communists, and even as the most Left-wing Communists, solely for the purpose of weakening and destroying the bulwark of the proletarian revolution in Russia. Menshevik leaflets distributed in Petrograd on the eve of the Kronstadt mutiny likewise show how the Mensheviks took advantage of the disagreements and certain rudiments of factionalism in the Russian Communist Party actually in order to egg on and support the Kronstadt mutineers, the Socialist-Revolutionaries and the whiteguards, while claiming to be opponents of mutiny and supporters of the Soviet power, only with supposedly slight modifications.

3. In this question, propaganda should consist, on the one hand, in a comprehensive explanation of the harmfulness and danger of factionalism from the standpoint of Party unity and of achieving unanimity of will among the vanguard of the proletariat as the fundamental condition for the success of the dictatorship of the proletariat; and, on the other hand, in an explanation of the peculiar features of the latest tactical devices of the enemies of the Soviet power. These enemies, having realised the hopelessness of counter-revolution under an openly whiteguard flag, are now doing their utmost to utilise the disagreements within the Russian Communist Party and to further the counter-revolution in one way or another by transferring power to a political group which is outwardly closest to recognition of the Soviet power.

Propaganda must also teach the lessons of preceding revolutions, in which the counter-revolution made a point of supporting the opposition which stood closest to the extreme revolutionary party, in order to undermine and overthrow the revolutionary dictatorship and thus pave the way for the subsequent complete victory of the counter-revolution, of the capitalists and landowners.

4. In the practical struggle against factionalism, every organisation of the Party must take strict measures to prevent all factional actions. Criticism of the Party's shortcomings, which is absolutely necessary, must be conducted in such a way that every practical proposal shall be submitted immediately, without any delay, in the most precise form possible, for consideration and decision to the leading local and central bodies of the Party. Moreover, every critic must see to it that the form of his criticism takes account of the Party's being surrounded by enemies, and that the content of his criticism is such that, by directly participating in Soviet and Party work, he can test the rectification of the errors of the Party or of individual Party members in practice. Analyses of the Party's general line, estimates of its practical experience, check-ups on the fulfilment of its decisions, studies of methods of rectifying errors, etc., must under no circumstances be submitted for preliminary discussion to groups formed on the basis of "platforms," etc., but must in all cases be submitted for discussion directly to all the members of the Party. For this purpose, the Congress orders a more regular publication of *Diskussionny Listok*[2] and special symposiums to promote unceasing efforts to ensure that criticism shall be concentrated on essentials

2. *Diskussiony Listok* (*Discussion Bulletin*) was a non-periodical publication of the party Central Committee. Two numbers had appeared, in January and February 1921, prior to the Tenth Congress. [*R. T.*]

and shall not assume a form capable of assisting the class enemies of the proletariat.

5. Rejecting in principle the deviation towards syndicalism and anarchism, which is examined in a special resolution, and instructing the Central Committee to secure the complete elimination of all factionalism, the Congress at the same time declares that every practical proposal concerning questions to which the so-called Workers' Opposition group, for example, has devoted special attention, such as purging the Party of non-proletarian and unreliable elements, combating bureaucratic practices, developing democracy and workers' initiative, etc., must be examined with the greatest care and tested in practice. The Party must know that we have not taken all the necessary measures in regard to these questions because of various obstacles, but that, while ruthlessly rejecting impractical and factional pseudo-criticism, the Party will unceasingly continue —trying out new methods—to fight with all the means at its disposal against the evils of bureaucracy, for the extension of democracy and initiative, for detecting, exposing and expelling from the Party elements that have wormed their way into its ranks, etc.

6. The Congress, therefore, hereby declares dissolved and orders the immediate dissolution of all groups without exception formed on the basis of one platform or another (such as the Workers' Opposition group, the Democratic Centralism group, etc.). Non-observance of this decision of the Congress shall entail unconditional and instant expulsion from the Party.

7. In order to ensure strict discipline within the Party and in all Soviet work and to secure the maximum unanimity in eliminating all factionalism, the Congress authorises the Central Committee, in cases of breach of discipline or of a revival or toleration of factionalism, to apply all Party penalties, including expulsion, and in regard to members of the Central Committee, reduction to the status of alternate members and, as an extreme measure, expulsion from the Party. A necessary condition for the application of such an extreme measure to members of the Central Committee, alternate members of the Central Committee and members of the Control Commission is the convocation of a plenary meeting of the Central Committee, to which all alternate members of the Central Committee and all members of the Control Commission shall be invited. If such a general assembly of the most responsible leaders of the Party deems it necessary by a two-thirds majority to reduce a member of the Central Committee to the status of alternate member, or to expel him from the Party, this measure shall be put into effect immediately.

Introducing the New Economic Policy

The central meaning of the New Economic Policy at the time of its inception was the abandonment of what had been a basic policy of War Communism—the forcible requisitioning of food products from the peasant—in favor of a graduated tax in kind as well as freedom for the peasant to trade his surplus produce freely, hence the restoration of a money economy and market relations. In this report of March 15, 1921, to the Tenth Congress, Lenin outlined the change in policy and its implications, including the implications for Soviet foreign relations.

Comrades, the question of substituting a tax for grain requisitioning is primarily and mainly a political question for it is essentially a question of the attitude of the working class to the peasantry. We are raising it because we must subject the relations of these two main classes, whose struggle or agreement determines the fate of our revolution as a whole, to a new or, I should perhaps say, a more careful and correct re-examination and some revision. There is no need for me to dwell in detail on the reasons for it. You all know very well of course what totality of causes, especially those due to the extreme want arising out of the war, ruin, demobilisation, and the disastrous crop failure—you know about the totality of circumstances that has made the condition of the peasantry especially precarious and critical and was bound to increase its swing from the proletariat to the bourgeoisie.

A word or two on the theoretical significance of, or the theoretical approach to, this issue. There is no doubt that in a country where the overwhelming majority of the population consists of small agricultural producers, a socialist revolution can be carried out only through the implementation of a whole series of special transitional measures which would be superfluous in highly developed capitalist countries where wage-workers in industry and agriculture make up the vast majority. Highly developed capitalist countries have a class of agricultural wage-workers that has taken shape over many decades. Only such a class can socially, economically, and politically support a direct transition to socialism. Only in countries where this class is sufficiently developed is it possible to pass directly from capitalism to socialism, without any special country-wide transitional measures. We have stressed in a good many written works, in all our public utterances, and all our statements in the press, that this is not the case in Russia, for here industrial workers are a minority and petty farmers are the vast majority. In such a country, the socialist revolution can triumph only on two conditions. First, if it is given timely support by a socialist revolution in one or several advanced countries. As you know, we have done very much indeed in comparison with the past to bring about this condition, but far from enough to make it a reality.

The second condition is agreement between the proletariat, which is exercising its dictatorship, that is, holds state power, and the majority of the peasant population. Agreement is a very broad concept which includes a whole series of measures and transitions. I must say at this point that our propaganda and agitation must be open and above-board. We must condemn most resolutely those who regard politics as a series of cheap little tricks, frequently bordering on deception. Their mistakes have to be corrected. You can't fool a class. We have done very much in the past three years to raise the political consciousness of the masses. They have been learning most from the sharp struggles. In keeping with our world outlook, the revolutionary experience we have accumulated over the decades, and the lessons of our revolution, we must state the issues plainly—the interests of these two classes differ, the small farmer does not want the same thing as the worker.

We know that so long as there is no revolution in other countries, only agreement with the peasantry can save the socialist revolution in Russia. And that is how it must be stated, frankly, at all meetings and in the entire press. We know that this agreement between the working class and the peasantry is not solid—to put it mildly, without entering the word "mildly" in the minutes—but, speaking plainly, it is very much worse. Under no circumstances must we try to hide anything; we must plainly state that the peasantry is dissatisfied with the form of our relations, that it does not want relations of this type and will not continue to live as it has hitherto. This is unquestionable. The peasantry has expressed its will in this respect definitely enough. It is the will of the vast masses of the working population. We must reckon with this, and we are sober enough politicians to say frankly: let us re-examine our policy in regard to the peasantry. The state of affairs that has prevailed so far cannot be continued any longer.

* * *

Difficult as our position is in regard to resources, the needs of the middle peasantry must be satisfied. There are far more middle peasants now than before, the antagonisms have been smoothed out, the land has been distributed for use far more equally, the *kulak's* position has been undermined and he has been in considerable measure expropriated—in Russia more than in the Ukraine, and less in Siberia. On the whole, however, statistics show quite definitely that there has been a levelling out, an equalisation, in the village, that is, the old sharp division into *kulaks* and cropless peasants has disappeared. Everything has become more equable, the peasantry in general has acquired the status of the middle peasant.

Can we satisfy this middle peasantry as such, with its economic peculiarities and economic roots? Any Communist who thought the economic basis, the economic roots, of small farming could be reshaped in three years was, of course, a dreamer. We need not conceal the fact that there were a good many such dreamers among us. Nor is there anything particularly bad in this. How could one start a socialist revolution in a country like ours without dreamers? Practice has, of course, shown the tremendous role all kinds of experiments and undertakings can play in the sphere of collective agriculture. But it has also afforded instances of these experiments as such playing a negative role, when people, with the best of intentions and desires, went to the countryside to set up communes but did not know how to run them because they had no experience in collective endeavour. The experience of these collective farms merely provided examples of how not to run farms: the peasants around either laughed or jeered.

You know perfectly well how many cases there have been of this kind. I repeat that this is not surprising, for it will take generations to remould the small farmer, and recast his mentality and habits. The only way to solve this problem of the small farmer—to improve, so to speak, his mentality—is through the material basis, technical equipment, the extensive use of tractors and other farm machinery and electrification on a mass scale. This would remake the small farmer fundamentally and with tremendous speed. If I say this will take generations, it does not mean centuries. But you know perfectly well that to obtain tractors and other machinery and to electrify this vast country is a matter that may take decades in any case. Such is the objective situation.

We must try to satisfy the demands of the peasants who are dissatisfied and disgruntled, and legitimately so, and who cannot be otherwise. We must say to them: "Yes, this cannot go on any longer." How is the peasant to be satisfied and what does satisfying him mean? Where is the answer? Naturally it lies in the demands of the peasantry. We know these demands. But we must verify them and examine all that we know of the farmer's economic demands from the standpoint of economic science. If we go into this, we shall see at once that it will take essentially two things to satisfy the small farmer. The first is a certain freedom of exchange, freedom for the small private proprietor, and the second is the need to obtain commodities and products. What indeed would free exchange amount to if there was nothing to exchange, and freedom of trade, if there was nothing to trade with! It would all remain on paper, and classes cannot be satisfied with scraps of paper, they want the goods. These two conditions must be clearly understood. The second—how to get commodities and whether we shall be able to obtain them— we shall discuss later. It is the first condition—free exchange—that we must deal with now.

What is free exchange? It is unrestricted trade, and that means turning back towards capitalism. Free exchange and freedom of trade mean circulation of commodities between petty proprietors. All of us who have studied at least the elements of Marxism know that this exchange and freedom of trade inevitably lead to a division of commodity producers into owners of capital and owners of labour-power, a division into capitalists and wage-workers, i.e., a revival of capitalist wage-slavery, which does not fall from the sky but springs the world over precisely from the agricultural commodity economy. This we know perfectly well in theory, and anyone in Russia who has observed the small farmer's life and the conditions under which he farms must have seen this.

How then can the Communist Party recognise freedom to trade and accept it? Does not the proposition contain irreconcilable contradictions? The answer is that the practical solution of the problem naturally presents exceedingly great difficulties. * * *

In this respect we have made many patent mistakes, and it would be a great crime not to see it, and not to realise that we have failed to keep within bounds, and have not known where to stop. There has, of course, also been the factor of necessity—until now we have been living in the conditions of a savage war that imposed an unprecedented burden on us and left us no choice but to take war-time measures in the economic sphere as well. It was a miracle that the ruined country withstood this war, yet the miracle did not come from heaven, but grew out of the economic interests of the working class and the peasantry, whose mass enthusiasm created the miracle that defeated the landowners and capitalists. But at the same time it is an unquestionable fact that we went further than was theoretically and politically necessary, and this should not be concealed in our agitation and propaganda. We can allow free local exchange to an appreciable extent, without destroying, but actually strengthening the political power of the proletariat. How this is to be done, practice will show. I only wish to prove to you that theoretically it is conceivable. The proletariat, wielding state power, can, if it has any reserves at all, put them into circulation and thereby satisfy the middle peasant to a certain extent—on the basis of local economic exchange.

* * *

We shall be asked where the goods are to come from, for unrestricted trade requires goods, and the peasants are shrewd people and very good at scoffing. Can we obtain any goods now? Today we can, for our international economic position has greatly improved. We are waging a fight against the international capitalists, who, when they were first confronted by this Republic, called us "brigands and crocodiles" (I was told by an English artist that she had heard these very words spoken by one of the most influential politicians). Crocodiles are despicable. That was the verdict of international capital. It was the verdict of a class enemy and quite correct from his point of view. However, the correctness of such conclusions has to be verified in practice. If you are world capital—a world power— and you use words like "crocodile" and have all the technical means at your disposal, why not try and shoot it! Capital did shoot—and got the worst of it. It was then that the capitalists, who are forced to reckon with political and economic realities, declared: "We must trade." This is one of our greatest victories. Let me tell you that we now have two offers of a loan to the amount of nearly one hundred million gold rubles. We have gold, but you can't sell gold, because you can't eat it. Everybody has been reduced to a state of impoverishment, currency relations between all the capitalist countries are incredibly chaotic as a result of the war. Moreover, you need a merchant marine to communicate with Europe, and we have none. It is in hostile hands. We have concluded no treaty with France; she considers that we are her debtors and, consequently, that every ship we have is hers. They have a navy and we have none. In these circumstances we have so far been in a position to make use of our gold on a limited and ridiculously insignificant scale. Now we have two offers from capitalist bankers to float a loan of one hundred million. Of course, they will charge us an exorbitant rate of interest. Still it is their first offer of this kind; so far they have said. "I'll shoot you and take everything for nothing." Now, being unable to shoot us, they are ready to trade with us. Trade agreements with America and Britain can now be said to be almost in the bag; the same applies to concessions. Yesterday I received another letter from Mr. Vanderlip, who is here and who, besides numerous complaints, sets forth a whole series of plans concerning concessions and a loan. He represents the shrewdest type of finance capitalist connected with the Western States of the U.S.A., those that are more hostile to Japan. So it is economically possible for us to obtain goods. How we shall manage to do it is another question, but a certain possibility is there.

I repeat, the type of economic relations which on top looks like a bloc with foreign capitalism makes it possible for the proletarian state power to arrange for free exchange with the peasantry below. I know—and I have had occasion to say this before—that this has evoked some sneers. There is a whole intellectual-bureaucratic stratum in Moscow, which is trying to shape "public opinion." "See what communism has come to!" these people sneer. "It's like a man on crutches and face all bandaged up—nothing but a picture puzzle." I have heard enough of gibes of this kind—they are either bureaucratic or just irresponsible. Russia emerged from the war in a state that can most of all be likened to that of a man beaten to within an inch of his life; the beating had gone on for seven years, and it's a mercy Russia can hobble about on crutches! That is the situation we are in! To think that we can get out of this state without crutches is to understand nothing! So long as there is no revolution in other countries, it would take us decades to extricate ourselves, and in these circumstances we cannot grudge hundreds of millions' or even thousands of millions' worth of our immense wealth, our rich raw material sources, in order to obtain help from the major capitalists. Later we shall recover it all and to spare. The rule of the proletariat cannot be maintained in a country laid waste as no country has ever been before—a country where the vast majority are peasants who are equally ruined—without the help of capital, for which, of course, exorbitant interest will be extorted. This we must understand. Hence, the choice is between economic relations of this type and nothing at all. He who puts the question otherwise understands absolutely nothing in practical economics and is side-stepping the issue by resorting to gibes. We must recognise the fact that the masses are utterly worn-out and exhausted. What can you expect after seven years of war in this country, if the more advanced countries still feel the effects of four years of war?!

* * *

I must say a few words about the individual exchange of commodities. When we speak of free exchange, we mean individual exchange of commodities, which in turn means encouraging the *kulaks*. What are we to do? We must not close our eyes to the fact that the switch from grain requisitioning to the tax will mean more *kulaks* under the new system. They will appear where they could not appear before. This must not be combated by prohibitive measures but by association under state auspices and by government measures from above. If you can give the peasant machines you will help him grow, and when you provide machines or electric power, tens or hundreds of thousands of small *kulaks* will be wiped out. Until you can supply all that, you must provide a certain quantity of goods. If you have the goods, you have the power; to preclude, deny or renounce any such possibility means making all exchange unfeasible and not satisfying the middle peasant, who will be impossible to get along with. A greater proportion of peasants in Russia have become middle peasants, and there is no reason to fear exchange on an individual basis. Everyone can give something in exchange to the state: one, his grain surplus; another, his garden produce; a third, his labour. Basically the situation is this: we must satisfy the middle peasantry economically and go over to free exchange; otherwise it will be impossible—economically impossible—in view of the delay in the world revolution, to preserve the rule of the proletariat in Russia. We must clearly realise this and not be afraid to say it. * * *

Why must we replace surplus appropriation by a tax? Surplus appropriation implied confiscation of all surpluses and establishment of a compulsory state monopoly. We could not do otherwise, for our need was extreme. Theoretically speaking, state monopoly is not necessarily the best system from the standpoint of the interests of socialism. A system of taxation and free exchange can be employed as a transitional measure in a peasant country possessing an industry—if this industry is running—and if there is a certain quantity of goods available.

The exchange is an incentive, a spur to the peasant. The proprietor can and will surely make an effort in his own interest when he knows that all his surplus produce will not be taken away from him and that he will only have to pay a tax, which should whenever possible be fixed in advance. The basic thing is to give the small farmer an incentive and a spur to till the soil. We must adapt our state economy to the economy of the middle peasant, which we have not managed to remake in three years, and will not be able to remake in another ten.

* * *

If there is a crop failure, surpluses cannot be collected because there will be none. They would have to be taken out of the peasants' mouths. If there is a crop, everybody will go moderately hungry and the state will be saved, or it will perish, unless we take from people who do not eat their fill as it is. This is what we must make clear in our propaganda among the peasants. A fair harvest will mean a surplus of up to five million *poods*. This will cover consumption and yield a certain reserve. The important thing is to give the peasants an economic incentive. The small proprietor must be told: "It is your job as a proprietor to produce, and the state will take a minimum tax."

* * *

We are now in a position to come to an agreement with the peasants, and this must be done in practice, skilfully, efficiently, and flexibly. We are familiar with the apparatus of the Commissariat for Food and know that it is one of the best we have. We see that it is better than that of the others and we must preserve it. Administrative machinery, however, must be subordinated to politics. The splendid apparatus of the Commissariat for Food will be useless if we cannot establish proper relations with the peasants, for otherwise this splendid apparatus will be serving Denikin and Kolchak, and not our own class. Since resolute change, flexibility and skilful transition have become politically necessary, the leaders must realise it. A strong apparatus must be suitable for any manoeuvre, but struggle is inevitable when its strength makes it unwieldy and hampers change. All efforts must, therefore, be turned to achieving our aim: the complete subordination of the apparatus to politics. Politics are relations between classes, and that will decide the fate of our Republic. The stronger the apparatus, as an auxiliary, the better and more suitable it is for manoeuvring. If it cannot manoeuvre, it is of no use to us.

I ask you to bear in mind this basic fact—it will take several months to work out the details and interpretations. The chief thing to bear in mind at the moment is that we must let the whole world know, by wireless this very night, of our decision; we must announce that this Congress of the government party is, in the main, replacing the grain requisitioning system by a tax and is giving the small farmer certain incentives to expand his farm and plant more; that by embarking on this course the Congress is correcting the system of relations between the proletariat and the peasantry and expresses its conviction that in this way these relations will be made durable.

The Importance of Gold Now and After the Complete Victory of Socialism

First published in *Pravda* on November 6–7, 1921, the fourth anniversary of the Bolshevik Revolution, this article contains Lenin's celebrated prediction that gold would one day be used to build public lavatories in the biggest cities in the world. But the article's importance lies in the succinctness and clarity with which Lenin expressed his new, NEP-born perspective on the need to proceed further—in the building of a socialist society in Soviet Russia—by "reformist," i.e., gradualist, methods rather than by revolutionary ones.

The best way to celebrate the anniversary of a great revolution is to concentrate attention on its unsolved problems. It is particularly appropriate and necessary to celebrate the revolution in this way at a time when we are faced with fundamental problems that the revolution has not yet solved, and when we must master something new (from the point of view of what the revolution has accomplished up to now) for the solution of these problems.

What is new for our revolution at the present time is the need for a "reformist," gradual, cautious and roundabout approach to the solution of the fundamental problems of economic development. This "novelty" gives rise to a number of questions, perplexities and doubts in both theory and practice.

A theoretical question. How can we explain the transition from a series of extremely revolutionary actions to extremely "reformist" actions in the same field at a time when the revolution as a whole is making victorious progress? Does it not imply a "surrender of positions," an "admission of defeat," or something of that sort? Of course, our enemies—from the semi-feudal type of reactionaries to the Mensheviks or other knights of the Two-and-a-Half International—say that it does. They would not be enemies if they did not shout something of the sort on every pretext, and even without any pretext. The touching unanimity that prevails on this question among all parties, from the feudal reactionaries to the Mensheviks, is only further proof that all these parties constitute "one reactionary mass" opposed to the proletarian revolution (as Engels foresaw in his letters to Bebel of 1875 and 1884—be it said in parenthesis).[1]

But there is "perplexity," shall we say, among friends, too.

Restore large-scale industry, organise the direct exchange of its goods for the produce of small-peasant farming, and thus assist the socialisation of the latter. For the purpose of restoring large-scale industry, borrow from the peasants a certain quantity of foodstuffs and raw materials by requisitioning—this was the plan (or method, system) that we followed for more than three years, up to the spring of 1921. This was a revolutionary approach to the problem —to break up the old social-economic system completely at one stroke and to substitute a new one for it.

Since the spring of 1921, instead of this approach, plan, method, or mode of action, we have been adopting (we have not yet "adopted" but are still "adopting," and have not yet fully realised it) a totally different method, a reformist type of method: not to *break up* the old social-economic system—trade, petty production, petty proprietorship, capitalism—but to *revive* trade, petty proprietorship, capitalism, while cautiously and gradually getting the upper hand over them, or making it possible to subject them to state regulation *only to the extent* that they revive.

That is an entirely different approach to the problem.

Compared with the previous, revolutionary, approach, it is a reformist approach (revolution is a change which breaks the old order to its very foundations, and not one that cautiously, slowly and gradually remodels it, taking care to break as little as possible).

The question that arises is this. If, after trying revolutionary methods, you find they have failed and adopt reformist methods, does it not prove that you are declaring the revolution to have been a mistake in general? Does it not prove that you should not have started with the revolution but should have started with reforms and confined yourself to them?

That is the conclusion which the Mensheviks and others like them have drawn. But this conclusion is either sophistry, a mere fraud perpetrated by case-hardened politicians, or it is the childishness of political tyros. The greatest, perhaps the only danger to the genuine revolutionary is that of exaggerated revolutionism, ignoring the limits and conditions in which revolutionary methods are appropriate and can be successfully employed. True revolutionaries have mostly come a cropper when they began to write "revolution"

1. See Marx and Engels, *Selected Correspondence* (Moscow, 1965), pp. 295, 381.

with a capital R, to elevate "revolution" to something almost divine, to lose their heads, to lose the ability to reflect, weigh and ascertain in the coolest and most dispassionate manner at what moment, under what circumstances and in which sphere of action you must act in a revolutionary manner, and at what moment, under what circumstances and in which sphere you must turn to reformist action. True revolutionaries will perish (not that they will be defeated from outside, but that their work will suffer internal collapse) only if they abandon their sober outlook and take it into their heads that the "great, victorious, world" revolution can and must solve all problems in a revolutionary manner under all circumstances and in all spheres of action. If they do this, their doom is certain.

Whoever gets such ideas into his head is lost because he has foolish ideas about a fundamental problem; and in a fierce war (and revolution is the fiercest sort of war) the penalty for folly is defeat.

What grounds are there for assuming that the "great, victorious, world" revolution can and must employ only revolutionary methods? There are none at all. The assumption is a pure fallacy; this can be proved by purely theoretical propositions if we stick to Marxism. The experience of our revolution also shows that it is a fallacy. From the theoretical point of view—foolish things are done in time of revolution just as at any other time, said Engels, and he was right. We must try to do as few foolish things as possible, and rectify those that are done as quickly as possible, and we must, as soberly as we can, estimate which problems can be solved by revolutionary methods at any given time and which cannot. From the point of view of our practical experience the Brest peace was an example of action that was not revolutionary at all; it was reformist, and even worse, because it was a retreat, whereas, as a general rule, reformist action advances slowly, cautiously, gradually, and does not move backward. The proof that our tactics in concluding the Brest peace were correct is now so complete, so obvious to all and generally admitted, that there is no need to say any more about it.

Our revolution has completed only its bourgeois-democratic work; and we have every right to be proud of this. The proletarian or socialist part of its work may be summed up in three main points: (1) The revolutionary withdrawal from the imperialist world war; the exposure and *halting* of the slaughter organised by the two world groups of capitalist predators—for our part we have done this in full; others could have done it only if there had been a revolution in a number of advanced countries. (2) The establishment of the Soviet system, as a form of the dictatorship of the proletariat. An epoch-making change has been made. The era of bourgeois-democratic parliamentarism has come to an end. A new chapter in world history—the era of proletarian dictatorship—has been opened. The Soviet system and all forms of proletarian dictatorship will have the finishing touches put to them and be completed only by the efforts of a number of countries. There is still a great deal we have not done in this field. It would be unpardonable to lose sight of this. Again and again we shall have to improve the work, re-do it, start from the beginning. Every step onward and upward that we take in developing our productive forces and our culture must be accompanied by the work of improving and altering our Soviet system—we are still low in the scale of economics and culture. Much will have to be altered, and to be "embarrassed" by this would be absurd (if not worse). (3) The creation of the economic basis of the socialist system; the main features of what is most important, most fundamental, have not yet been completed. This, however, is our soundest basis, soundest from the point of view of principle and from the practical point of view, from the point of view of the R.S.F.S.R. today and from the international point of view.

Since the main features of this basis have not yet been completed we must concentrate all our attention upon it. The difficulty here lies in the form of the transition.

In April 1918, in my *Immediate Tasks of the Soviet Government*,[2] I wrote: "It is not enough to be a revolutionary and an adherent of socialism or a Communist in general. You must be able at each particular moment to find the particular link in the chain which you must grasp with all your might in order to hold the whole chain and to prepare firmly for the transition to the next link; the order of the links, their form, the manner in which they are linked together, their difference from each other in the historical chain of events are not as simple and not as senseless as those in an ordinary chain made by a smith."

At the present time, in the sphere of activity with which we are dealing, this link is the revival of home *trade* under proper state regulation (direction). Trade is the "link" in the historical chain of events, in the transitional forms of our' socialist construction in 1921–22, which we, the proletarian government, we, the ruling Communist Party, *"must grasp with all our might."* If we "grasp" this link firmly enough *now* we shall certainly control the *whole* chain in the very near future. If we do not, we shall not control the whole chain, we shall not create the foundation for socialist social and economic relations.

2. See above, pp. 438–60. [*R. T.*]

Communism and trade?! It sounds strange. The two seem to be unconnected, incongruous, poles apart. But if we study it from the point of view of *economics*, we shall find that the one is no more remote from the other than communism is from small-peasant, patriarchal farming.

When we are victorious on a world scale I think we shall use gold for the purpose of building public lavatories in the streets of some of the largest cities in the world. This would be the most "just" and most educational way of utilising gold for the benefit of those generations which have not forgotten how, for the sake of gold, ten million men were killed and thirty million maimed in the "great war for freedom," the war of 1914–18, the war that was waged to decide the great question of which peace was the worst, that of Brest or that of Versailles; and how, for the sake of this same gold, they certainly intend to kill twenty million men and to maim sixty million in a war, say, in 1925, or 1928, between, say, Japan and the U.S.A., or between Britain and the U.S.A., or something like that.

But however "just," useful, or humane it would be to utilise gold for this purpose, we nevertheless say that we must work for another decade or two with the same intensity and with the same success as in the 1917–21 period, only in a much wider field, in order to reach this stage. Meanwhile, we must save the gold in the R.S.F.S.R., sell it at the highest price, buy goods with it at the lowest price. When you live among wolves, you must howl like a wolf, while as for exterminating all the wolves, as should be done in a rational human society, we shall act up to the wise Russian proverb: "Boast not before but after the battle."

Trade is the only possible economic link between the scores of millions of small farmers and large-scale industry *if* . . . *if* there is not alongside these farmers an excellently equipped large-scale machine industry with a network of power transmission lines, an industry whose technical equipment, organisational "superstructures" and other features are sufficient to enable it to supply the farmers with the best goods in larger quantities, more quickly and more cheaply than before. On a world scale this "if" *has already been achieved*, this condition already exists. But the country, formerly one of the most backward capitalist countries, which tried alone directly and at one stroke to create, to put into use, to organise practically the *new* links between industry and agriculture, failed to achieve this task by "direct assault," and must now try to achieve it by a number of slow, gradual, and cautious "siege" operations.

The proletarian government can control trade, direct it into definite channels, keep it within certain limits. I shall give a small, a very small example. In the Donets Basin a slight, still very slight, but undoubted revival in the economy has commenced, partly due to a rise in the productivity of labour at the large state mines, and partly due to the leasing of small mines to peasants. As a result, the proletarian government is receiving a small additional quantity (a miserably small quantity compared with what is obtained in the advanced countries, but an appreciable quantity considering our poverty-stricken condition) of coal at a cost of, say, 100; and it is selling this coal to various government departments at a price of, say, 120, and to private individuals at a price of, say, 140. (I must say in parenthesis that my figures are quite arbitrary, first because I do not know the exact figures, and, secondly, I would not now make them public even if I did.) This looks as if we are *beginning*, if only in very modest dimensions, to control *exchange* between industry and agriculture, to control wholesale trade, to cope with the task of taking in hand the available, small, backward industry, of large-scale but weakened and ruined industry; of reviving trade on the *present* economic basis; of making the ordinary middle peasant (and that is the typical peasant, the peasant in the mass, the true representative of the petty-bourgeois milieu) feel the benefit of the economic revival; of taking advantage of it for the purpose of more systematically and persistently, more widely and successfully restoring large-scale industry.

We shall not surrender to "sentimental socialism," or to the old Russian, semi-aristocratic, semi-muzhik and patriarchal mood, with their supreme contempt for trade. We can use, and, since it is necessary, we *must* learn to use, all transitional economic forms for the purpose of strengthening the link between the peasantry and the proletariat, for the purpose of immediately reviving the economy of our ruined and tormented country, of improving industry, and facilitating such future, more extensive and more deep-going, measures as electrification.

Marxism alone has precisely and correctly defined the relation of reforms to revolution, although Marx was able to see this relation only from one aspect—under the conditions preceding the first to any extent permanent and lasting victory of the proletariat, if only in one country. Under those conditions, the basis of the proper relation was that reforms are a by-product of the revolutionary class struggle of the proletariat. Throughout the capitalist world this relation is the foundation of the revolutionary tactics of the proletariat—the ABC, which is being distorted and obscured by the corrupt leaders of the Second International and the half-pedantic and half-finicky knights of the Two-and-a-Half International. After the victory of the proletariat, if only in one country, something new enters into the relation between reforms and revolution. In principle, it is the same as before, but a change in form takes place, which Marx himself could not foresee, but which can be appreciated only on the basis of the philosophy and politics of Marxism Why were we able to carry out the Brest retreat successfully? Because we had advanced so far that we had room in which to retreat. At such dizzy speed, *in a few weeks,* from October 25, 1917, to the Brest peace, we built up the Soviet state, withdrew from the imperialist war in a revolutionary manner and completed the bourgeois-democratic revolution so that *even* the great backward movement (the Brest peace) left us sufficient room in which to take advantage of the "respite" and to march forward victoriously against Kolchak, Denikin, Yudenich, Pilsudski and Wrangel.

Before the victory of the proletariat, reforms are a by-product of the revolutionary class struggle. After the victory (while still remaining a "by-product" on an international scale) they are, in addition, for the country in which victory has been achieved, a necessary and legitimate breathing space when, after the utmost exertion of effort, it becomes obvious that sufficient strength is lacking for the revolutionary accomplishment of some transition or another. Victory creates such a "reserve of strength" that it is possible to hold out even in a forced retreat, hold out both materially and morally. Holding out materially means preserving a sufficient superiority of forces to prevent the enemy from inflicting utter defeat. Holding out morally means not allowing oneself to become demoralised and disorganised, keeping a sober view of the situation, preserving vigour and firmness of spirit, even retreating a long way, but not too far, and in such a way as to stop the retreat in time and revert to the offensive.

We retreated to state capitalism, but we did not retreat too far. We are now retreating to the state regulation of trade, but we shall not retreat too far. There are visible signs that the retreat is coming to an end; there are signs that we shall be able to stop this retreat in the not too distant future. The more conscious, the more unanimous, the more free from prejudice we are in carrying out this necessary retreat, the sooner shall we be able to stop it, and the more lasting, speedy and extensive will be our subsequent victorious advance.

Communism and the New Economic Policy

The Eleventh Party Congress, held in Moscow in March–April 1922, was to be the last attended by Lenin, and his report, from which the following material is taken, gives a full picture of the further evolution of his thinking on the internal politics of the Soviet regime under the NEP as well as his overall philosophy concerning the meaning of NEP itself.

* * * I shall now proceed to deal with the issues which, in my opinion, have been the major political questions of the past year and which will be such in the ensuing year. It seems to me that the political report of the Central Committee should not merely deal with the events of the year under review, but also point out (that, at any rate, is what I usually do) the main, fundamental political lessons of the events of that year, so that we may learn something for the ensuing year and be in a position to correctly determine our policy for that year.

The New Economic Policy is, of course, the major question. This has been the dominant question throughout the year under review. * * *

First, the New Economic Policy is important for us primarily as a means of testing whether we are really establishing a link with the peasant economy. In the preceding period of development of our revolution, when all our attention and all our efforts were concentrated mainly on, or almost entirely absorbed by, the task of repelling invasion, we could not devote the necessary attention to this link; we had other things to think about. To some extent we could and had to ignore this bond when we were confronted by the absolutely urgent and overshadowing task of warding off the danger of being immediately crushed by the gigantic forces of world imperialism.

* * *

Today, as far as the New Economic Policy is concerned the main thing is to assimilate the experience of the past year correctly. That must be done, and we want to do it. And if we want to do it, come what may (and we do want to do it, and shall do it!), we must know that the problem of the New Economic Policy, the fundamental, decisive and overriding problem, is to establish a link between the new economy that we have begun to create (very badly, very clumsily, but have nevertheless begun to create, on the basis of an entirely new, socialist economy, of a new system of production and distribution) and the peasant economy, by which millions and millions of peasants obtain their livelihood.

This link has been lacking, and we must create it before anything else. Everything else must be subordinated to this. We have still to ascertain the extent to which the New Economic Policy has succeeded in creating this link without destroying what we have begun so clumsily to build.

* * *

Such is the significance of the New Economic Policy; it is the basis of our entire policy; it is the major lesson taught by the whole of the past year's experience in applying the New Economic Policy, and, so to speak, our main political rule for the coming year. The peasant is allowing us credit, and, of course, after what he has lived through, he cannot do otherwise. Taken in the mass, the peasants go on saying: "Well, if you are not able to do it yet, we shall wait; perhaps you will learn." But this credit cannot go on for ever.

This we must know; and having obtained credit we must hurry. We must know that the time is approaching when this peasant country will no longer give us credit, when it will demand cash, to use a commercial term. It will say: "You have postponed payment for so many months, so many years. But by this time, dear rulers, you must have learnt the most sound and reliable method of helping us free ourselves from poverty, want, starvation and ruin. You can do it, you have proved it." This is the test that we shall inevitably have to face; and, in the last analysis, this test will decide everything: the fate of NEP and the fate of communist rule in Russia.

Shall we accomplish our immediate task or not? Is this NEP fit for anything or not? If the retreat turns out to be correct tactics, we must link up with the peasant masses while we are in retreat, and subsequently march forward with them a hundred times more slowly, but firmly and unswervingly, in a way that will always make it apparent to them that we are really marching forward. Then our cause will be absolutely invincible, and no power on earth can vanquish us. We did not accomplish this in the first year. We must say this frankly. And I am profoundly convinced (and our New Economic Policy enables us to draw this conclusion quite definitely and firmly) that if we appreciate the enormous danger harboured by NEP and concentrate all our forces on its weak points, we shall solve this problem.

Link up with the peasant masses, with the rank-and-file working peasants, and begin to move forward immeasurably, infinitely more slowly than we expected, but in such a way that the entire mass will actually move forward with us. If we do that we shall in time progress much more quickly than we even dream of today. This, in my opinion, is the first fundamental political lesson of the New Economic Policy.

The second, more specific lesson is the test through competition between state and capitalist enterprises. * * *

* * *

We need a real test. The capitalists are operating alongside us. They are operating like robbers; they make profit; but they know how to do things. But you—you are trying to do it in a new way: you make no profit, your principles are communist, your ideals are splendid; they are written out so beautifully that you seem to be saints, that you should go to heaven while you are still alive. But can you get things done? We need a test, a real test, not the kind the Central Control Commission makes when it censures somebody and the All-Russia Central Executive Committee imposes some penalty. Yes, we want a real test from the viewpoint of the national economy.

We Communists have received numerous deferments, and more credit has been allowed us than any other government has ever been given. Of course, we Communists helped to get rid of the capitalists and landowners. The peasants appreciate this and have given us an extension of time, longer credit, but only for a certain period. After that comes the test: can you run the economy as well as the others? The old capitalist can; you cannot.

That is the first lesson, the first main part of the political report of the Central Committee. We cannot run the economy. This has been proved in the past year. I would like very much to quote the example of several Gos-trests (if I may express myself in the beautiful Russian language that Turgenev praised so highly)[1] to show how we run the economy.

Unfortunately, for a number of reasons, and largely owing to ill health, I have been unable to elaborate this part of my report and so I must confine myself to expressing my conviction, which is

1. An ironic reference to the habit, then emerging, of abbreviating the names of various institutions. Here the abbreviation stands for *state trusts*.

based on my observations of what is going on. During the past year we showed quite clearly that we cannot run the economy. That is the fundamental lesson. Either we prove the opposite in the coming year, or Soviet power will not be able to exist. And the greatest danger is that not everybody realises this. * * *

The mixed companies that we have begun to form, in which private capitalists, Russian and foreign, and Communists participate, provide one of the means by which we can learn to organise competition properly and show that we are no less able to establish a link with the peasant economy than the capitalists; that we can meet its requirements; that we can help the peasant make progress even at his present level, in spite of his backwardness; for it is impossible to change him in a brief span of time.

That is the sort of competition confronting us as an absolutely urgent task. It is the pivot of the New Economic Policy and, in my opinion, the quintessence of the Party's policy. We are faced with any number of purely political problems and difficulties. You know what they are: Genoa, the danger of intervention. The difficulties are enormous but they are nothing compared with this economic difficulty. We know how things are done in the political field; we have gained considerable experience; we have learned a lot about bourgeois diplomacy. It is the sort of thing the Mensheviks taught us for fifteen years, and we got something useful out of it. This is not new.

But here is something we must do now in the economic field. We must win the competition against the ordinary shop assistant, the ordinary capitalist, the merchant, who will go to the peasant without arguing about communism. Just imagine, he will not begin to argue about communism, but will argue in this way—if you want to obtain something, or carry on trade properly, or if you want to build, I will do the building at a high price; the Communists will, perhaps, build at a higher price, perhaps even ten times higher. It is this kind of agitation that is now the crux of the matter; herein lies the root of economics.

I repeat, thanks to our correct policy, the people allowed us a deferment of payment and credit, and this, to put it in terms of NEP, is a promissory note. But this promissory note is undated, and you cannot learn from the wording when it will be presented for redemption. Therein lies the danger; this is the specific feature that distinguishes these political promissory notes from ordinary, commercial promissory notes. We must concentrate all our attention on this, and not rest content with the fact that there are responsible and good Communists in all the state trusts and mixed companies. That is of no use, because these Communists do not know how to run the economy and, in that respect, are inferior to the ordinary capitalist salesmen, who have received their training in big factories and big firms. But we refuse to admit this; in this field communist conceit—*komchvanstvo*,[2] to use the great Russian language—still persists. The whole point is that the responsible Communists, even the best of them, who are unquestionably honest and loyal, who in the old days suffered penal servitude and did not fear death, do not know how to trade, because they are not businessmen, they have not learnt to trade, do not want to learn and do not understand that they must start learning from the beginning. Communists, revolutionaries who have accomplished the greatest revolution in the world, on whom the eyes of, if not forty pyramids, then, at all events, forty European countries are turned in the hope of emancipation from capitalism, must learn from ordinary salesmen. But these ordinary salesmen have had ten years' warehouse experience and know the business, whereas the responsible Communists and devoted revolutionaries do not know the business, and do not even realise that they do not know it.

* * *

That is how the question stands and it cannot be otherwise, for the competition will be very severe, and it will be decisive. We had many outlets and loopholes that enabled us to escape from our political and economic difficulties. We can proudly say that up to now we have been able to utilise these outlets and loopholes in various combinations corresponding to the varying circumstances. But now we have no other outlets. Permit me to say this to you without exaggeration, because in this respect it is really "the last and decisive battle," not against international capitalism—against that we shall yet have many "last and decisive battles"—but against Russian capitalism, against the capitalism that is growing out of the small-peasant economy, the capitalism that is fostered by the latter. Here we shall have a fight on our hands in the immediate future, and the date of it cannot be fixed exactly. Here the "last and decisive battle" is impending; here there are no political or any other flanking movements that we can undertake, because this is a test in competition with private capital. Either we pass this test in competition with private capital, or we fail completely. To help us pass it we have political power and a host of economic and other resources; we have everything you want except ability. We lack ability. And if we learn this simple lesson from the experience of last year and take it as our guiding line for the whole of 1922, we shall conquer this difficulty, too, in spite of the fact that it is much greater than the previous difficulty, for it rests upon ourselves. It is

2. Literally, "comconceit."

not like some external enemy. The difficulty is that we ourselves refuse to admit the unpleasant truth forced upon us; we refuse to undertake the unpleasant duty that the situation demands of us, namely, to start learning from the beginning. That, in my opinion, is the second lesson that we must learn from the New Economic Policy.

* * *

Retreat is a difficult matter, especially for revolutionaries who are accustomed to advance; especially when they have been accustomed to advance with enormous success for several years; especially if they are surrounded by revolutionaries in other countries who are longing for the time when they can launch an offensive. Seeing that we were retreating, several of them burst into tears in a disgraceful and childish manner, as was the case at the last extended plenary meeting of the Executive Committee of the Communist International. Moved by the best communist sentiments and communist aspirations, several of the comrades burst into tears because—oh horror!—the good Russian Communists were retreating. Perhaps it is now difficult for me to understand this West-European mentality, although I lived for quite a number of years in those marvellous democratic countries as an exile. Perhaps from their point of view this is such a difficult matter to understand that it is enough to make one weep. We, at any rate, have no time for sentiment. It was clear to us that because we had advanced so successfully for many years and had achieved so many extraordinary victories (and all this in a country that was in an appalling state of ruin and lacked the material resources!), to consolidate that advance, since we had gained so much, it was absolutely essential for us to retreat. We could not hold all the positions we had captured in the first onslaught. On the other hand, it was because we had captured so much in the first onslaught, on the crest of the wave of enthusiasm displayed by the workers and peasants, that we had room enough to retreat a long distance, and can retreat still further now, without losing our main and fundamental positions. On the whole, the retreat was fairly orderly, although certain panic-stricken voices, among them that of the Workers' Opposition (this was the tremendous harm it did!), caused losses in our ranks, caused a relaxation of discipline, and disturbed the proper order of retreat. The most dangerous thing during a retreat is panic. When a whole army (I speak in the figurative sense) is in retreat, it cannot have the same morale as when it is advancing. At every step you find a certain mood of depression. We even had poets who wrote that people were cold and starving in Moscow, that "everything before was bright and beautiful, but now trade and profiteering abound." We have had quite a number of poetic effusions of this sort.

Of course, retreat breeds all this. That is where the serious danger lies; it is terribly difficult to retreat after a great victorious advance, for the relations are entirely different. During a victorious advance, even if discipline is relaxed, everybody presses forward on his own accord. During a retreat, however, discipline must be more conscious and is a hundred times more necessary, because, when the entire army is in retreat, it does not know or see where it should halt. It sees only retreat; under such circumstances a few panic-stricken voices are, at times, enough to cause a stampede. The danger here is enormous. When a real army is in retreat, machine-guns are kept ready, and when an orderly retreat degenerates into a disorderly one, the command to fire is given, and quite rightly, too.

* * *

And the Mensheviks and Socialist-Revolutionaries, all of whom preach this sort of thing, are astonished when we declare that we shall shoot people for such things. They are amazed; but surely it is clear. When an army is in retreat a hundred times more discipline is required than when it is advancing, because during an advance everybody presses forward. If everybody started rushing back now, it would spell immediate and inevitable disaster.

The most important thing at such a moment is to retreat in good order, to fix the precise limits of the retreat, and not to give way to panic. And when a Menshevik says, "You are now retreating; I have been advocating retreat all the time, I agree with you, I am your man, let us retreat together," we say in reply, "For the public manifestations of Menshevism our revolutionary courts must pass the death sentence, otherwise they are not our courts, but God knows what."

* * *

The retreat has come to an end; it is now a matter of regrouping our forces. These are the instructions that the Congress must pass so as to put an end to fuss and bustle. Calm down, do not philosophise; if you do, it will be counted as a black mark against you. Show by your practical efforts that you can work no less efficiently than the capitalists. The capitalists create an economic link with the peasants in order to amass wealth; you must create a link with peasant economy in order to strengthen the economic power of our proletarian state. You have the advantage over the capitalists in that political power is in your hands; you have a number of economic weapons at your command; the only trouble is that you cannot make proper use of them. Look at things more soberly. Cast off the tinsel, the festive communist garments, learn a simple thing simply, and we shall beat the private capitalist. We possess political power; we possess a host of economic weapons. If we beat capitalism and create a link with peasant farming we shall become an absolutely invincible power. Then the building of socialism will not be the task of that drop in the ocean, called the Communist Party, but the task of the entire mass of the working people. Then the rank-and-file peasants will see that we are helping them and they will follow our lead. Consequently, even if the pace is a hundred times slower, it will be a million times more certain and more sure.

It is in this sense that we must speak of halting the retreat; and the proper thing to do is, in one way or another, to make this slogan a Congress decision.

In this connection, I should like to deal with the question: what is the Bolsheviks' New Economic Policy—evolution or tactics? This question has been raised by the *Smena Vekh* people,[3] who, as you know, are a trend which has arisen among Russian émigrés; it is a socio-political trend led by some of the most prominent Constitutional-Democrats, several Ministers of the former Kolchak government, people who have come to the conclusion that the Soviet government is building up the Russian state and therefore should be supported. They argue as follows: "What sort of state is the Soviet government building? The Communists say they are building a communist state and assure us that the new policy is a matter of tactics: the Bolsheviks are making use of the private capitalists in a difficult situation, but later they will get the upper hand. The Bolsheviks can say what they like; as a matter of fact it is not tactics but evolution, internal regeneration; they will arrive at the ordinary bourgeois state, and we must support them. History proceeds in devious ways."

Some of them pretend to be Communists; but there are others who are more straightforward, one of these is Ustryalov. I think he was a Minister in Kolchak's[4] government. He does not agree with his colleagues and says: "You can think what you like about communism, but I maintain that it is not a matter of tactics, but of evolution." I think that by being straightforward like this, Ustryalov is rendering us a great service. We, and I particularly, because of my position, hear a lot of sentimental communist lies, "com-

3. The *Smena Vekh* group arose in Russian émigré intellectual circles. It was named after the symposium of articles entitled *Smena Vekh* (*Change of Landmarks*), published in Prague in July 1921. The members of the group also published a magazine, *Smena Vekh*, in Paris, from October 1921 to March 1922. 4. Admiral Kolchak headed a White government formed in Siberia during the Civil War. [*R. T.*]

munist fibbing," every day, and sometimes we get sick to death of them. But now instead of these "communist fibs" I get a copy of *Smena Vekh*, which says quite plainly: "Things are by no means what you imagine them to be. As a matter of fact, you are slipping into the ordinary bourgeois morass with communist flags inscribed with catchwords stuck all over the place." This is very useful. It is not a repetition of what we are constantly hearing around us, but the plain class truth uttered by the class enemy. It is very useful to read this sort of thing; and it was written not because the communist state allows you to write some things and not others, but because it really is the class truth, bluntly and frankly uttered by the class enemy. "I am in favour of supporting the Soviet government," says Ustryalov, although he was a Constitutional-Democrat, a bourgeois, and supported intervention. "I am in favour of supporting Soviet power because it has taken the road that will lead it to the ordinary bourgeois state."

This is very useful, and I think that we must keep it in mind. It is much better for us if the *Smena Vekh* people write in that strain than if some of them pretend to be almost Communists, so that from a distance one cannot tell whether they believe in God or in the communist revolution. We must say frankly that such candid enemies are useful. We must say frankly that the things Ustryalov speaks about are possible. History knows all sorts of metamorphoses. Relying on firmness of convictions, loyalty, and other splendid moral qualities is anything but a serious attitude in politics. A few people may be endowed with splendid moral qualities, but historical issues are decided by vast masses, which, if the few do not suit them, may at times treat them none too politely.

There have been many cases of this kind; that is why we must welcome this frank utterance of the *Smena Vekh* people. The enemy is speaking the class truth and is pointing to the danger that confronts us, and which the enemy is striving to make inevitable. *Smena Vekh* adherents express the sentiments of thousands and tens of thousands of bourgeois, or of Soviet employees whose function it is to operate our New Economic Policy. This is the real and main danger. And that is why attention must be concentrated mainly on the question: "Who will win?" I have spoken about competition. No direct onslaught is being made on us now; nobody is clutching us by the throat. True, we have yet to see what will happen tomorrow; but today we are not being subjected to armed attack. Nevertheless, the fight against capitalist society has become a hundred times more fierce and perilous, because we are not always able to tell enemies from friends.

When I spoke about communist competition, what I had in mind were not communist sympathies but the development of economic forms and social systems. This is not competition but, if not the last, then nearly the last, desperate, furious, life-and-death struggle between capitalism and communism.

And here we must squarely put the question: Wherein lies our strength and what do we lack? We have quite enough political power. I hardly think there is anyone here who will assert that on such-and-such a practical question, in such-and-such a business institution, the Communists, the Communist Party, lack sufficient power. There are people who think only of this, but these people are hopelessly looking backward and cannot understand that one must look ahead. The main economic power is in our hands. All the vital large enterprises, the railways, etc., are in our hands. The number of leased enterprises, although considerable in places, is on the whole insignificant; altogether it is infinitesimal compared with the rest. The economic power in the hands of the proletarian state of Russia is quite adequate to ensure the transition to communism. What then is lacking? Obviously, what is lacking is culture among the stratum of the Communists who perform administrative functions. If we take Moscow with its 4,700 Communists in responsible positions, and if we take that huge bureaucratic machine, that gigantic heap, we must ask: who is directing whom? I doubt very much whether it can truthfully be said that the Communists are directing that heap. To tell the truth, they are not directing, they are being directed. Something analogous happened here to what we were told in our history lessons when we were children: sometimes one nation conquers another, the nation that conquers is the conqueror and the nation that is vanquished is the conquered nation. This is simple and intelligible to all. But what happens to the culture of these nations? Here things are not so simple. If the conquering nation is more cultured than the vanquished nation, the former imposes its culture upon the latter; but if the opposite is the case, the vanquished nation imposes its culture upon the conqueror. Has not something like this happened in the capital of the R.S.F.S.R.? Have the 4,700 Communists (nearly a whole army division, and all of them the very best) come under the influence of an alien culture? True, there may be the impression that the vanquished have a high level of culture. But that is not the case at all. Their culture is miserable, insignificant, but it is still at a higher level than ours. Miserable and low as it is, it is higher than that of our responsible Communist administrators, for the latter lack administrative ability. Communists who are put at the head of departments—and sometimes artful saboteurs deliberately put them in these positions in order to use them as a shield—are often fooled. This is a very unpleasant admission to make, or, at any rate, not a very pleasant one; but I think we must admit it, for at present this is the salient problem. I think that this is the political lesson of the past year; and it is around this that the struggle will rage in 1922.

Will the responsible Communists of the R.S.F.S.R. and of the Russian Communist Party realise that they cannot administer; that they only imagine they are directing, but are, actually, being directed? If they realise this they will learn, of course; for this business can be learnt. But one must study hard to learn it, and our people are not doing this. They scatter orders and decrees right and left, but the result is quite different from what they want.

The competition and rivalry that we have placed on the order of the day by proclaiming NEP is a serious business. It appears to be going on in all government offices; but as a matter of fact it is one more form of the struggle between two irreconcilably hostile classes. It is another form of the struggle between the bourgeoisie and the proletariat. It is a struggle that has not yet been brought to a head, and culturally it has not yet been resolved even in the central government departments in Moscow. Very often the bourgeois officials know the business better than our best Communists, who are invested with authority and have every opportunity, but who cannot make the slightest use of their rights and authority.

* * *

The idea of building communist society exclusively with the hands of the Communists is childish, absolutely childish. We Communists are but a drop in the ocean, a drop in the ocean of the people. We shall be able to lead the people along the road we have chosen only if we correctly determine it not only from the standpoint of its direction in world history. From that point of view we have determined the road quite correctly, and this is corroborated by the situation in every country. We must also determine it correctly for our own native land, for our country. But the direction in world history is not the only factor. Other factors are whether there will be intervention or not, and whether we shall be able to supply the peasants with goods in exchange for their grain. The peasants will say: "You are splendid fellows; you defended our country. That is why we obeyed you. But if you cannot run the show, get out!" Yes, that is what the peasants will say.

* * *

* * * We are living in the twentieth century, and the only nation that emerged from a reactionary war by revolutionary methods not for the benefit of a particular government, but by overthrowing it, was the Russian nation, and it was the Russian revolution that extricated it. What has been won by the Russian revolution is irrevocable. No power on earth can erase that; nor can any power on earth erase the fact that the Soviet state has been created. This is a historic victory. For hundreds of years states have been built according to the bourgeois model, and for the first time a non-bourgeois form of state has been discovered. Our machinery of government may be faulty, but it is said that the first steam engine that was invented was also faulty. No one even knows whether it worked or not, but that is not the important point; the important point is that it was invented. Even assuming that the first steam engine was of no use, the fact is that we now have steam engines. Even if our machinery of government is very faulty, the fact remains that it has been created; the greatest invention in history has been made; a proletarian type of state has been created. Therefore, let all Europe, let thousands of bourgeois newspapers broadcast news about the horrors and poverty that prevail in our country, about suffering being the sole lot of the working people in our country; the workers all over the world are still drawn towards the Soviet state. These are the great and irrevocable gains that we have achieved. But for us, members of the Communist Party, this meant only opening the door. We are now confronted with the task of laying the foundations of socialist economy. Has this been done? No, it has not. We still lack the socialist foundation. Those Communists who imagine that we have it are greatly mistaken. The whole point is to distinguish firmly, clearly and dispassionately what constitutes the historic service rendered by the Russian revolution from what we do very badly, from what has not yet been created, and what we shall have to re-do many times yet.

Political events are always very confused and complicated. They can be compared with a chain. To hold the whole chain you must grasp the main link. Not a link chosen at random. What was the central event in 1917? Withdrawal from the war. The entire nation demanded this, and it overshadowed everything. Revolutionary Russia accomplished this withdrawal from the war. It cost tremendous effort; but the major demand of the people was satisfied, and that brought us victory for many years. The people realised, the peasants saw, every soldier returning from the front understood perfectly well that the Soviet government was a more democratic government, one that stood closer to the working people. No matter how many outrageous and absurd things we may have done in other spheres, the fact that we realised what the main task was proved that everything was right.

What was the key feature of 1919 and 1920? Military resistance. The all-powerful Entente was marching against us, was at our throats. No propaganda was required there. Every non-Party peasant understood what was going on. The landowners were coming back. The Communists knew how to fight them. That is why, taken in the mass, the peasants followed the lead of the Communists; that is why we were victorious.

In 1921, the key feature was an orderly retreat. This required stern discipline. The Workers' Opposition said: "You are underrating the workers; the workers should display greater initiative." But initiative had to be displayed then by retreating in good order and by maintaining strict discipline. Anyone who introduced an undertone of panic or insubordination would have doomed the revolution to defeat; for there is nothing more difficult than retreating with people who have been accustomed to victory, who are imbued with revolutionary views and ideals, and who, in their hearts, regard every retreat as a disgraceful matter. The greatest danger was the violation of good order, and the greatest task was to maintain good order.

And what is the key feature now? The key feature now—and I would like to sum up my report with this—is not that we have changed our line of policy. An incredible lot of nonsense is being talked about this in connection with NEP. It is all hot air, pernicious twaddle. In connection with NEP some people are beginning to fuss around, proposing to reorganise our government departments and to form new ones. All this is pernicious twaddle. In the present situation the key feature is people, the proper choice of people. A revolutionary who is accustomed to struggle against petty reformists and uplift educators finds it hard to understand this. Soberly weighed up, the political conclusion to be drawn from the present situation is that we have advanced so far that we cannot hold all the positions; and we need not hold them all.

Internationally our position has improved vastly these last few years. The Soviet type of state is our achievement; it is a step forward in human progress; and the information the Communist International receives from every country every day corroborates this. Nobody has the slightest doubt about that. From the point of view of practical work, however, the position is that unless the Communists render the masses of the peasants practical assistance they will lose their support. Passing laws, passing better decrees, etc., is not now the main object of our attention. There was a time when the passing of decrees was a form of propaganda. People used to laugh at us and say that the Bolsheviks do not realise that their decrees are not being carried out; the entire whiteguard press was full of jeers on that score. But at that period this passing of decrees was quite justified. We Bolsheviks had just taken power, and we said to the peasant, to the worker: "Here is a decree; this is how we would like to have the state administered. Try it!" From the very outset we gave the ordinary workers and peasants an idea of our policy in the form of decrees. The result was the enormous confidence we enjoyed and now enjoy among the masses of the people. This was an essential period at the beginning of the revolution; without it we should not have risen on the crest of the revolutionary wave; we should have wallowed in its trough. Without it we should not have won the confidence of all the workers and peasants who wanted to build their lives on new lines. But this period has passed, and we refuse to understand this. Now the peasants and workers will laugh at us if we order this or that government department to be formed or reorganised. The ordinary workers and peasants will display no interest in this now, and they will be right, because this is not the central task today. This is not the sort of thing with which we Communists should now go to the people. Although we who are engaged in government departments are always overwhelmed with so many petty affairs, this is not the link that we must grasp, this is not the key feature. The key feature is that we have not got the right men in the right places; that responsible Communists who acquitted themselves magnificently during the revolution have been given commercial and industrial functions about which they know nothing; and they prevent us from seeing the truth, for crooks and rascals hide magnificently behind their backs. The trouble is that we have no such thing as practical control of how things have been done. This is a prosaic job, a small job; these are petty affairs. But after the greatest political change in history, bearing in mind that for a time we shall have to live in the midst of the capitalist system, the key feature now is not politics in the narrow sense of the word (what we read in the newspapers is just political fireworks; there is nothing socialist in it at all), the key feature is not resolutions, not departments and not reorganisation. As long as these things are necessary we shall do them, but don't go to the people with them. Choose the proper men and introduce practical control. That is what the people will appreciate.

In the sea of people we are after all but a drop in the ocean, and we can administer only when we express correctly what the people are conscious of. Unless we do this the Communist Party will not lead the proletariat, the proletariat will not lead the masses, and the whole machine will collapse. The chief thing the people, all the working people, want today is nothing but help in their desperate hunger and need; they want to be shown that the improvement needed by the peasants is really taking place in the form they are accustomed to. The peasant knows and is accustomed to the market and trade. We were unable to introduce direct communist distribution. We lacked the factories and their equipment for this. That being the case, we must provide the peasants with what they need through the medium of trade, and provide it as well as the capitalist did, otherwise the people will not tolerate such an administration. This is the key to the situation. * * *

* * *

Speech in Closing the Congress, April 2

Comrades, we have reached the end of our Congress.

The first difference that strikes one in comparing this Congress with the preceding one is the greater solidarity, the greater unanimity and greater organisational unity that have been displayed.

Only a small part of one of the sections of the opposition that existed at the last Congress has placed itself outside the Party.

On the trade union question and on the New Economic Policy no disagreements, or hardly any disagreements, have been revealed in our Party.

The radically and fundamentally "new" achievement of this Congress is that it has provided vivid proof that our enemies are wrong in constantly reiterating that our Party is becoming senile and is losing its flexibility of mind and body.

No. We have not lost this flexibility.

When the objective state of affairs in Russia, and all over the world, called for an advance, for a supremely bold, swift and determined onslaught on the enemy, we made that onslaught. If necessary, we shall do it again and again.

By that we raised our revolution to a height hitherto unparalleled in the world. No power on earth, no matter how much evil, hardship and suffering it may yet cause millions and hundreds of millions of people, can annul the major gains of our revolution, for these are no longer our but historic gains.

But when in the spring of 1921 it turned out that the vanguard of the revolution was in danger of becoming isolated from the masses of the people, from the masses of the peasants, whom it must skilfully lead forward, we unanimously and firmly decided to retreat. And on the whole, during the past year we retreated in good revolutionary order.

The proletarian revolutions maturing in all advanced countries of the world will be unable to solve their problems unless they combine the ability to fight heroically and to attack with the ability to retreat in good revolutionary order. The experience of the second period of our struggle, i.e., the experience of retreat, will in the future probably be just as useful to the workers of at least some countries, as the experience of the first period of our revolution, i.e., the experience of bold attack, will undoubtedly prove useful to the workers of all countries.

Now we have decided to halt the retreat.

This means that the entire object of our policy must be formulated in a new way.

The central feature of the situation now is that the vanguard must not shirk the work of educating itself, of remoulding itself, must not be afraid of frankly admitting that it is not sufficiently trained and lacks the necessary skill. The main thing now is to advance as an immeasurably wider and larger mass, and only together with the peasantry, proving to them by deeds, in practice, by experience, that we are learning, and that we shall learn to assist them, to lead them forward. In the present international situation, in the present state of the productive forces of Russia, this problem can be solved only very slowly, cautiously, in a business-like way, and by testing a thousand times in a practical way every step that is taken.

If voices are raised in our Party against this extremely slow and extremely cautious progress, these voices will be isolated ones.

The Party as a whole has understood—and will now prove by deeds that it has understood—that at the present time its work must be organised exactly along these lines, and since we have understood it, we shall achieve our goal!

I declare the Eleventh Congress of the Russian Communist Party closed.

PART V

Revolutionary Foreign Policy and Comintern Strategy

The Foreign Policy of
the Russian Revolution

Although written for *Pravda* in June 1917, before the Bolsheviks took power, this article is a useful introduction to the Leninist approach in foreign policy. Lenin's conviction about the inseparability of external and internal policy is especially noteworthy.

Despite the article's statement that the basis of a revolutionary foreign policy would be neither a separate peace with Germany nor an alliance with the Anglo-French allies, Lenin in power quickly found himself compelled to accept the former in order to avoid the destruction of his regime.

No idea could be more erroneous or harmful than to separate foreign from domestic policy. The monstrous falsity of this separation becomes even more monstrous in war-time. Yet the bourgeoisie are doing everything possible and impossible to suggest and promote this idea. Popular ignorance of foreign policy is incomparably greater than of domestic policy. The "secrecy" of diplomatic relations is sacredly observed in the freest of capitalist countries, in the most democratic republics.

Popular deception has become a real art in foreign "affairs," and our revolution suffers very badly from this deception. The poison of deception is spread far and wide by the millions of copies of bourgeois newspapers.

You must side with one of the two immensely wealthy and immensely powerful groups of imperialist predators—that is how capitalist reality poses the basic issue of present-day foreign policy. That is how this issue is posed by the capitalist class. And that, it goes without saying, is how it is posed by the broad mass of the petty bourgeoisie who have retained their old, capitalist views and prejudices.

Those whose thinking does not go beyond capitalist relations cannot understand why the workers, if they are politically conscious, cannot side with *either* group of imperialist plunderers.

Conversely, the worker cannot understand why socialists who remain true to the fraternal alliance of the workers of the world against the capitalists of the world are accused of being inclined towards a separate peace treaty with the Germans, or of virtually serving such a peace treaty. Under no circumstances can these socialists (and hence the Bolsheviks) agree to a separate peace treaty between the capitalists. The basis for the foreign policy of the politically-conscious proletariat is no separate peace treaty with the German capitalists and no alliance with the Anglo-French capitalists.

By rising up in arms against that programme because they fear a break with "Britain and France," our Mensheviks and Socialist-Revolutionaries are virtually carrying out a capitalist foreign policy programme, while embellishing it with florid and innocent phrases about "revision of treaties," declarations in support of "peace without annexations," etc. All these pious wishes are doomed to remain hollow phrases, for *capitalist* reality puts the issue bluntly: either submit to the imperialists of one of the two groups, or wage a revolutionary struggle against all imperialists.

Have we any allies for this struggle? Yes. The oppressed classes of Europe, primarily the proletariat. The peoples oppressed by imperialism, primarily our neighbours in Asia.

The Mensheviks and Socialist-Revolutionaries, who call themselves "revolutionary democrats," are in fact pursuing a counter-revolutionary and anti-democratic foreign policy. Were they revolutionaries, they would advise the workers and peasants of Russia to march at the head of all peoples oppressed by imperialism and of all the oppressed classes.

"But in that event the capitalists of all other countries would rally against Russia," the frightened philistines object. That is not impossible. No *"revolutionary"* democrat has the right to renounce revolutionary war in advance. But the practical likelihood of such a war is not very great. The British and German imperialists will not be able to "come to terms" against revolutionary Russia.

The Russian revolution, which as early as 1905 led to revolutions in Turkey, Persia and China, would have placed the German and British imperialists in a very difficult position if it had begun to establish a truly revolutionary alliance of the workers and peasants of the colonies and semi-colonies against the despots, against the khans, for expulsion of the Germans from Turkey, the British from Turkey, Persia, India, Egypt, etc.

Social-chauvinists, both French and Russian, like to refer to 1793. By this spectacular reference they try to cover up their betrayal of the revolution. But people here refuse to think that the *truly* "revolutionary" democrats in Russia could and should act *in the spirit* of 1793 towards the oppressed and backward nations.

The foreign policy of the capitalists and the petty bourgeoisie is "alliance" with the imperialists, that is, disgraceful dependence on them. The foreign policy of the proletariat is alliance with the revolutionaries of the advanced countries and with all the oppressed nations against all and any imperialists.

Decree on Peace

True to the Bolshevik-espoused policy of demanding an immediate peace without annexations, Lenin, literally on the day after the Bolshevik taking of power, November 8, 1917, drafted a "Decree on Peace" and put it before the Second Congress of Soviets, which approved it. The often-repeated Moscow claim that Soviet foreign policy began with a platform of peace rests upon this document.

The workers' and peasants' government, created by the Revolution of October 24–25 and basing itself on the Soviets of Workers', Soldiers' and Peasants' Deputies, calls upon all the belligerent peoples and their governments to start immediate negotiations for a just, democratic peace.

By a just or democratic peace, for which the overwhelming majority of the working class and other working people of all the belligerent countries, exhausted, tormented and racked by the war, are craving—a peace that has been most definitely and insistently demanded by the Russian workers and peasants ever since the overthrow of the tsarist monarchy—by such a peace the government means an immediate peace without annexations (i.e., without the seizure of foreign lands, without the forcible incorporation of foreign nations) and without indemnities.

The Government of Russia proposes that this kind of peace be immediately concluded by all the belligerent nations, and expresses its readiness to take all the resolute measures now, without the least delay, pending the final ratification of all the terms of such a peace by authoritative assemblies of the people's representatives of all countries and all nations.

In accordance with the sense of justice of democrats in general, and of the working classes in particular, the government conceives the annexation or seizure of foreign lands to mean every incorporation of a small or weak nation into a large or powerful state without the precisely, clearly and voluntarily expressed consent and wish of that nation, irrespective of the time when such forcible incorporation took place, irrespective also of the degree of development or backwardness of the nation forcibly annexed to the given state, or forcibly retained within its borders, and irrespective, finally, of whether this nation is in Europe or in distant, overseas countries.

If any nation whatsoever is forcibly retained within the borders of a given state, if, in spite of its expressed desire—no matter whether expressed in the press, at public meetings, in the decisions of parties, or in protests and uprisings against national oppression —it is not accorded the right to decide the forms of its state existence by a free vote, taken after the complete evacuation of the troops of the incorporating or, generally, of the stronger nation and without the least pressure being brought to bear, such incorporation is annexation, i.e., seizure and violence.

The government considers it the greatest of crimes against humanity to continue this war over the issue of how to divide among the strong and rich nations the weak nationalities they have conquered, and solemnly announces its determination immediately to sign terms of peace to stop this war on the terms indicated, which are equally just for all nationalities without exception.

At the same time the government declares that it does not regard the above-mentioned peace terms as an ultimatum; in other words, it is prepared to consider any other peace terms, and insists only that they be advanced by any of the belligerent countries as speedily as possible, and that in the peace proposals there should be absolute clarity and the complete absence of all ambiguity and secrecy.

The government abolishes secret diplomacy, and, for its part, announces its firm intention to conduct all negotiations quite openly in full view of the whole people. It will proceed immediately with the full publication of the secret treaties endorsed or concluded by the government of landowners and capitalists from February to October 25, 1917. The government proclaims the unconditional and immediate annulment of everything contained in these secret treaties insofar as it is aimed, as is mostly the case, at securing advantages and privileges for the Russian landowners and capitalists and at the retention, or extension, of the annexations made by the Great Russians.

* * *

Report on War and Peace

Lenin elaborated his early philosophy of Soviet foreign policy in a secret report to the Seventh Congress of the Communist Party. Delivered on March 7, 1918, the report was first published in 1923. In it Lenin gives his view of the respite gained by the "Tilsit peace" of Brest-Litovsk, underlines the legitimacy in principle of revolutionary war, and emphatically states that it would be impossible for the capitalist world to "live side by side with the Soviet Republic" for long. From this he infers that the only salvation for the Russian Revolution lies in international revolution.

---

* * *

* * * The reason we achieved such an easy victory over Kerensky's gangs, why we so easily set up our government and without the slightest difficulty passed the decrees on the socialisation of the land and on workers' control of industry, the reason why we achieved all this so easily was that a fortunate combination of circumstances protected us for a short time from international imperialism. International imperialism, with the entire might of its capital, with its highly organised military technique, which is a real force, a real fortress of international capital, could not under any circumstances, on any condition, live side by side with the Soviet Republic, both because of its objective position and because of the economic interests of the capitalist class which are embodied in it—it could not do so because of commercial connections, of international financial relations. In this sphere a conflict is inevitable. Therein lies the greatest difficulty of the Russian Revolution, its great historical problem: the necessity of solving international problems, the necessity of calling forth an international revolution, of traversing the path from our strictly national revolution to the world revolution. This problem confronts us with all its incredible difficulties. I repeat, many of our young friends who regard themselves as Lefts have begun to forget the most important thing, viz., why in the course of the weeks and months of the great triumph

542

after October we were able so easily to pass from triumph to triumph. And yet this was only due to the fact that a special combination of international circumstances temporarily protected us from imperialism. It had other things to bother about besides us. And it seemed to us that we too had other things to bother about besides imperialism. Individual imperialists had no time to bother with us, because the whole of the great social, political and military might of contemporary world imperialism was rent by internecine war into two groups. The imperialist robbers involved in this struggle had gone to such lengths, were locked in mortal combat, and to such a degree, that neither of these groups was able to concentrate serious forces against the Russian Revolution. It was in circumstances such as these that we found ourselves in October: it is paradoxical but true that our revolution broke out at such a fortunate moment when unprecedented disasters had overtaken the overwhelming majority of the imperialist countries involving the destruction of millions of human beings, when the unprecedented disasters attending the war had exhausted the nations, when in the fourth year of the war the belligerent countries had reached an *impasse*, had reached the cross-roads, when the objective question had arisen: can the nations which have been reduced to such a state continue to fight? It was only due to the fact that our revolution broke out at a fortunate moment such as this, when neither of the two gigantic groups of robbers was in a position immediately to hurl itself at the other, or to unite against us, it was only due to a situation such as this in international political and economic relations that our revolution could and did take advantage of to accomplish its brilliant triumphal march in European Russia, spread to Finland and begin the conquest of the Caucasus and Rumania. This alone explains the appearance in the leading circles of our Party of Party workers, intellectual supermen, who allowed themselves to be carried away by this triumphal march and who said: we can easily smash international imperialism; over there, there will also be a triumphal march, over there, there will be no real difficulties. There you have the divergence in the objective position of the Russian Revolution which only temporarily took advantage of the hitch in international imperialism; the engine that was supposed to have borne down on us with the force of a railway train bearing down on a truck and smashing it to splinters, was temporarily held up—and the engine was held up because two groups of robbers had clashed. Here and there the revolutionary movement grew, but in all the imperialist countries without exception it was still mostly in the initial stage. Its rate of development was entirely different from that in our country. Anyone who has given careful thought to the economic prerequisites of the socialist revolution in Europe cannot but be clear on the point that in Europe it will be immeasurably more difficult to start, whereas it was immeasurably easier for us to start; but it will be more difficult for us to continue the revolution than it will be over there. This objective situation caused us to experience an extraordinarily difficult, sharp turn in history. From the continuous triumphal march on our internal front, against our counter-revolution, against the enemies of the Soviet government in October, November and December, we had to pass to a collision with real international imperialism, in its real hostility towards us. From the period of a triumphal march we had to pass to a period in which we were confronted by an extraordinarily difficult and severe position, one which could not be brushed aside with words, with brilliant slogans—however pleasant that would have been— because in our disturbed country we had to deal with incredibly weary masses who had reached a state in which they could not possibly go on fighting, who were so shattered by three years of agonising war that they were absolutely useless from a military standpoint. Even before the October Revolution we saw representatives of the masses of the soldiers, not members of the Bolshevik Party, who did not fear to tell the whole bourgeoisie the truth that the Russian army refused to fight. This state of the army gave rise to a gigantic crisis. A small-peasant country, disorganised by war, reduced to an incredible state and placed in an extremely difficult condition; we have no army, but we have to go on living side by side with a robber who is armed to the teeth, a robber who has remained and will remain a robber and, of course, cannot be moved by agitation in favour of peace without annexations and indemnities. A tame, domesticated animal was lying side by side with a tiger and tried to persuade the latter to conclude a peace without annexations and indemnities, whereas the only way such a peace could be attained was by attacking the tiger. The top layer of our Party—intellectuals and a section of the workers' organisations— tried to brush this prospect aside primarily with phrases and excuses, such as: it must not be like that. This peace was too incredible a prospect; to think that we, who up to now have marched in open battle with flying colours and stormed the enemy's positions with "hurrahs," should now yield and accept these humilitating terms. Never! We are proud revolutionaries, we declare above all: "The Germans cannot attack."

This was the first excuse with which these people consoled themselves. History has now placed us in an extraordinarily difficult position; in the midst of organisational work of extraordinary difficulty we shall have to experience a number of tormenting setbacks. Of course, if we look at it from a world historical scale, there can be no doubt that from the standpoint of the ultimate victory of our revolution, if it were to remain alone, if there were no revolutionary movements in other countries, then our position would be hopeless. When the Bolshevik Party tackled the job alone, took it entirely into its own hands, we were convinced that the revolution was maturing in all countries and that in the end—but not at the very beginning—no matter what difficulties we experienced, no matter what defeats were in store for us, the international socialist revolution would come—because it is coming; would ripen—because it is ripening and will grow ripe. I repeat, our salvation from all these difficulties is an all-European revolution. Taking this absolutely abstract truth as our starting point, and being guided by it, we must see to it that it does not in time become a mere phrase, because every abstract truth, if it is accepted without analysis, becomes a mere phrase. If you say that every strike bears within itself the hydra of revolution, and he who fails to understand this is no socialist, you are right. Yes, every strike bears within itself the socialist revolution. But if you say that every given strike is an immediate step towards the socialist revolution, you will be uttering empty phrases. We have heard these phrases "every blessed time on this very same spot" so frequently that we are sick and tired of them, and the workers have rejected these anarchist phrases. Undoubtedly, clear as it is that every strike contains within itself the hydra of socialist revolution, it is equally clear that the assertion that every strike can develop into revolution is utter nonsense. While it is indisputable that all the difficulties of our revolution will be overcome only when the world socialist revolution matures, and it is maturing everywhere—it is absolutely absurd to declare that we must conceal every concrete difficulty of our revolution today and say: "I stake everything on the international socialist movement—I can commit any piece of folly I please." "Liebknecht will help us out, because he is going to win, anyhow." * * *

The revolution will not come as quickly as we expected. History has proved this, and we must be able to take this as a fact, reckon with the fact that the world socialist revolution cannot begin so easily in the advanced countries as the revolution began in Russia —in the land of Nicholas and Rasputin, the land in which an enormous part of the population was absolutely indifferent as to what peoples were living in the outlying regions, or to what was happening there. In such a country it was quite easy to start a revolution, as easy as lifting a feather.

But to start a revolution in a country in which capitalism is developed, in which it has produced a democratic culture and organisation, provided it to everybody—to do so without preparation would be wrong, absurd. We are only just approaching the painful period of the beginning of socialist revolutions. This is a fact. We do not know, no one knows; perhaps—it is quite possible—it will conquer within a few weeks, even within a few days, but we cannot stake everything on that. We must be prepared for extraordinary difficulties, for extraordinarily severe defeats, which are inevitable, because the revolution in Europe has not yet begun, although it may begin to-morrow, and when it does begin then, of course, we shall not be tortured by doubts, there will be no question about a revolutionary war, but just one continuous triumphal march. That will be, it will inevitably be so, but it is not so yet. This is the simple fact that history has taught us, with which she has hit us rather painfully—and a man who has been thrashed is worth two that haven't. That is why I think that after history has shattered our hope that the Germans cannot attack and that we can get everything by shouting "hurrah!" this lesson, with the help of our Soviet organizations, will very quickly sink into the minds of the masses all over Soviet Russia. They are all up and doing, gathering, preparing for the Congress, passing resolutions, thinking over what has occurred. What is taking place at the present time does not resemble the old pre-revolutionary controversies which remained within narrow Party circles; now all resolutions are discussed by the masses who demand that they be tested by experience, by deeds, and who never allow themselves to be carried away by frivolous speeches, and never allow themselves to be diverted from the path prescribed by the objective progress of events. Of course, an intellectual, or a Left Bolshevik, will try to gloss over difficulties. He can gloss over such facts as the lack of an army and the failure of the revolution to come in Germany. The vast masses—and politics begin where the masses are, not where there are thousands, but millions, that is where serious politics begin—the vast masses know what an army is, they have seen soldiers returning from the front. They know—that is, if you take, not individual persons, but real masses—that we cannot fight, that every man at the front has endured everything that it is possible to endure. The masses have understood the truth, viz., that if we have no army, and a wild beast is lying beside us, we will have to sign a distressful, humiliating peace treaty. That is inevitable until the birth of the revolution, until your army recovers, until you allow the men to return home. Until then the invalid will not recover. And we will not be able to capture the German wild beast by shouting "hurrah!"; we will not throw him off as easily as we threw off Kerensky and Kornilov. This is the lesson that the masses learned without the excuses that those who desire to evade bitter reality try to bring them.

At first a continuous triumphal march in October and November —then, suddenly, in the space of a few weeks, the Russian Revolution is defeated by the German robber; the Russian Revolution is prepared to adopt the terms of a predatory treaty. Yes, the turns of history are very sharp. All such turns affect us severely. When, in 1907, we signed the incredibly shameful internal treaty with Stolypin, when we were compelled to pass through the pig-sty of the Stolypin Duma and undertook obligations by signing monarchist documents,[1] we experienced on a small scale what we are experiencing now. At that time, people who belonged to the best vanguard of the revolution said (and they too had not the slightest doubt that they were right), "we are proud revolutionaries, we believe in the Russian Revolution, we will never enter legal Stolypin institutions." But you will. The life of the masses, history, are stronger than your protestations. If you won't go, history will compel you to do so. These were very Left people and after the first turn in history nothing remained of them as a faction but smoke. If we managed to remain revolutionaries, managed to work under terrible conditions and emerge from them, we will be able to do so now too, because it is not our caprice, it is objective inevitability created in an utterly ruined country, because in spite of our desires the European revolution dared to be late, and in spite of our desires, German imperialism dared to attack.

Here we must be able to retreat. We cannot hide the incredibly bitter, deplorable reality from ourselves with phrases; we must say: God grant that we retreat in semi-good order. We cannot retreat in perfect order, but God grant that we retreat in semi-good order, that we gain a little time in which the sick part of our organism can be absorbed at least to some extent. On the whole the organism is sound, it will overcome its sickness. But you cannot expect it to overcome it all at once, instantaneously; you cannot hold up an army in flight. When I said to one of our young friends, a would-be Left: Comrade, go to the front, see what is going on there—he took offense at this proposal. He said: "They want to deport us so as to prevent our agitating for the great principle of a revolutionary war." To tell the truth, in making this proposal I had no intention whatever of deporting factional enemies; I merely suggested that they go and see for themselves that the army was in full flight. Even before that we knew, even before that we could not close our eyes to the fact that the disintegration of the army had reached incredible proportions, to the extent of selling our guns to the Germans for next to nothing. We knew that, just as we know that the army cannot be held back, and that the excuse that the Germans will not attack was a great gamble. Since the European revolution has been delayed severe defeats await us because we lack an army, because we lack organization, because, at the moment, we

1. The reference here is to the oath of allegiance which every member of the State Duma had to sign on taking his seat.

cannot solve these two problems. If you are unable to adapt yourself, if you are not inclined to crawl in the mud on your belly, you are not a revolutionary but a chatterbox; and I propose this, not because I like it, but because we have no other road, because history has not turned out to be so pleasant as to make the revolution ripen everywhere simultaneously.

* * *

A period has set in of severe defeats, inflicted by imperialism, armed to the teeth, upon a country which has demobilised its army, which had to demobilise. What I foretold has come to pass: instead of the Brest-Litovsk Peace we have received a much more humiliating peace, and the blame for this rests upon those who refused to accept the former peace. We knew that through the fault of the army we were concluding peace with imperialism. We sat at the same table with Hoffmann[2] and not with Liebknecht—and in doing so we assisted the German revolution. But now you are assisting German imperialism, because you have surrendered wealth amounting to millions—guns and shells—and anybody who had seen the incredibly painful state of the army could have foretold this. Every conscientious man who came from the front said that had the Germans made the slightest attack we would have perished inevitably. We fell a prey to the enemy within a few days.

Having learned this lesson, we shall overcome our split, our crisis, however severe the disease may be, because an immeasurably more reliable ally will come to our assistance, viz., the world revolution. When they talk to us about ratifying this Tilsit Peace, this incredible peace, more humiliating and predatory than the Brest Peace, I say: certainly, yes. We must do this because we look at things from the point of view of the masses. Any attempt to apply the tactics of October–November in a single country—this triumphant period of the revolution—to apply them with the aid of our fantasy to the progress of events in the world revolution, is doomed to failure. * * *

* * *

Yes, of course, we are violating the treaty; we have violated it thirty or forty times. Only children can fail to understand that in an epoch like the present, when a long painful period of emancipation is setting in, which has only just created and raised the Soviet power three stages of its development—only children can fail to

2. Max Hoffmann (1869–1927), general who headed the German delegation at the peace negotiations at Brest-Litovsk in 1918.

understand that in this case there must be a long, circumspect struggle. * * *

* * *

The last war has been a bitter, painful, but serious lesson for the Russian people. It taught them to organise, to become disciplined, to obey, to create a discipline that will be exemplary discipline. Learn discipline from the Germans; if we do not, we, as a people, are doomed, we shall live in eternal slavery.

This is the way history has proceeded and no other way. History suggests that peace is a respite for another war, war is a method of obtaining a somewhat better or somewhat worse peace. At Brest the relation of forces corresponded to a peace dictated by the victor, but it was not a humiliating peace. The relation of forces at Pskov corresponded to a disgraceful, more humiliating peace; and in Petrograd and Moscow, at the next stage a peace four times more humiliating will be dictated to us. We will not say that the Soviet power is only a form, as our young Moscow friends have said, we will not say that the content can be sacrificed for this or that revolutionary principle. We will say: let the Russian people understand that they must become disciplined and organised, and then they will be able to withstand all the Tilsit peace treaties. The whole history of wars for liberation shows that when these wars involved large masses liberation came very quickly. * * *

* * *

We should have but one slogan—seriously learn the art of war, introduce order on the railways. To wage a socialist revolutionary war without railways would be the most sinister treachery. We must create order, and we must create the whole of that energy and the whole of that might which all that is best in the revolution will create.

Take advantage even of an hour's respite if it is given you, in order to maintain contact with the remote rear and there create new armies. Abandon illusions for which life has punished you and will punish you more severely in the future. An epoch of severe defeats is looming up before us, it has set in, we must be able to reckon with it, we must be prepared for persistent work in conditions of illegality, in conditions of downright slavery to the Germans; it is no use glossing this over; it is really a Peace of Tilsit. If we are able to act in this way, then, in spite of defeat, we shall be able to say with absolute certainty—victory will be ours.

"Left-Wing" Communism—
An Infantile Disorder

While *What Is to Be Done?* may have been Lenin's most historically influential writing because of its role in the rise of Bolshevism, *"Left-Wing"
Communism* has claim to be considered his political masterpiece, the dis-
tillation of a lifetime of thought and experience into a manual of revolutionary politics. A salient theme of it is the necessity for Communist
parties to pursue coalition politics ("united front tactics," as they came to
be called) for revolutionary purposes. In *World Communism*, Franz Borkenau well observed: " *'Left-Wing' Communism* is perhaps the most powerful thing Lenin has ever written. . . . It is a handbook of revolutionary
tactics and as such can sometimes be compared, for force of argument, realism, directness and convincing power, with Machiavelli's *Il Principe*. Here a
great master of politics speaks, sometimes condescendingly, sometimes
angrily, to young pupils who will not listen to reason, and makes a laughing-
stock of their 'supernatural nonsense.' "

Written in April 1920, the booklet was published in May and distributed
to the delegates of the Second Congress of the Communist International
(Comintern) when it met in Moscow in July.

I. In What Sense We Can Speak of the International
Significance of the Russian Revolution

In the first months after the proletariat in Russia had won political power (October 25 [November 7], 1917), it might have seemed
that the enormous difference between backward Russia and the
advanced countries of Western Europe would lead to the proletarian revolution in the latter countries bearing very little resemblance
to ours. We now possess quite considerable international experience, which shows very definitely that certain fundamental features
of our revolution have a significance that is not local, or peculiarly
national, or Russian alone, but international. I am not speaking
here of international significance in the broad sense of the term:
not merely several but all the primary features of our revolution,
and many of its secondary features, are of international significance

in the meaning of its effect on all countries. I am speaking of it in the narrowest sense of the word, taking international significance to mean the international validity or the historical inevitability of a repetition, on an international scale, of what has taken place in our country. It must be admitted that certain fundamental features of our revolution do possess that significance.

It would, of course, be grossly erroneous to exaggerate this truth and to extend it beyond certain fundamental features of our revolution. It would also be erroneous to lose sight of the fact that, soon after the victory of the proletarian revolution in at least one of the advanced countries, a sharp change will probably come about: Russia will cease to be the model and will once again become a backward country (in the "Soviet" and the socialist sense).

At the present moment in history, however, it is the Russian model that reveals to *all* countries something—and something highly significant—of their near and inevitable future. Advanced workers in all lands have long realised this; more often than not, they have grasped it with their revolutionary class instinct rather than realised it. Herein lies the international "significance" (in the narrow sense of the word) of Soviet power, and of the fundamentals of Bolshevik theory and tactics. The "revolutionary" leaders of the Second International, such as Kautsky in Germany and Otto Bauer and Friedrich Adler in Austria, have failed to understand this, which is why they have proved to be reactionaries and advocates of the worst kind of opportunism and social treachery. Incidentally, the anonymous pamphlet entitled *The World Revolution* (*Weltrevolution*),[1] which appeared in Vienna in 1919 (*Sozialistische Bücherei*, Heft 11; Ignaz Brand), very clearly reveals their entire thinking and their entire range of ideas, or, rather, the full extent of their stupidity, pedantry, baseness and betrayal of working-class interests—and that, moreover, under the guise of "defending" the idea of "world revolution."

We shall, however, deal with this pamphlet in greater detail some other time. We shall here note only one more point: in bygone days, when he was still a Marxist and not a renegade, Kautsky, dealing with the question as an historian, foresaw the possibility of a situation arising in which the revolutionary spirit of the Russian proletariat would provide a model to Western Europe. This was in 1902, when Kautsky worte an article for the revolutionary *Iskra*, entitled "The Slavs and Revolution." Here is what he wrote in the article:

> At the present time [in contrast with 1848] it would seem that not only have the Slavs entered the ranks of the revolutionary nations, but that the centre of revolutionary thought and revolu-

1. The pamphlet was written by Otto Bauer.

tionary action is shifting more and more to the Slavs. The revolutionary centre is shifting from the West to the East. In the first half of the nineteenth century it was located in France, at times in England. In 1848 Germany too joined the ranks of the revolutionary nations. . . . The new century has begun with events which suggest the idea that we are approaching a further shift of the revolutionary centre, namely, to Russia. . . . Russia, which has borrowed so much revolutionary initiative from the West, is now perhaps herself ready to serve the West as a source of revolutionary energy. The Russian revolutionary movement that is now flaring up will perhaps prove to be the most potent means of exorcising the spirit of flabby philistinism and coldly calculating politics that is beginning to spread in our midst, and it may cause the fighting spirit and the passionate devotion to our great ideals to flare up again. To Western Europe, Russia has long ceased to be a bulwark of reaction and absolutism. I think the reverse is true today. Western Europe is becoming Russia's bulwark of reaction and absolutism. . . . The Russian revolutionaries might perhaps have coped with the tsar long ago had they not been compelled at the same time to fight his ally—European capital. Let us hope that this time they will succeed in coping with both enemies, and that the new "Holy Alliance" will collapse more rapidly than its predecessors did. However the present struggle in Russia may end, the blood and suffering of the martyrs whom, unfortunately, it will produce in too great numbers, will not have been in vain. They will nourish the shoots of social revolution throughout the civilised world and make them grow more luxuriantly and rapidly. In 1848 the Slavs were a killing frost which blighted the flowers of the people's spring. Perhaps they are now destined to be the storm that will break the ice of reaction and irresistibly bring with it a new and happy spring for the nations. [Karl Kautsky, "The Slavs and Revolution," *Iskra*, Russian Social-Democratic revolutionary newspaper, No. 18, March 10, 1902.]

How well Karl Kautsky wrote eighteen years ago!

II. An Essential Condition of the Bolsheviks' Success

It is, I think, almost universally realised at present that the Bolsheviks could not have retained power for two and a half months, let alone two and a half years, without the most rigorous and truly iron discipline in our Party, or without the fullest and unreserved support from the entire mass of the working class, that is, from all thinking, honest, devoted and influential elements in it, capable of leading the backward strata or carrying the latter along with them. The dictatorship of the proletariat means a most determined and most ruthless war waged by the new class against a *more powerful* enemy, the bourgeoisie, whose resistance is increased *tenfold* by their overthrow (even if only in a single country), and whose power lies, not only in the strength of international capital, the strength and durability of their international connections, but also in the *force of habit*, in the strength of *small-scale production*. Unfortunately, small-scale production is still widespread in the world, and small-scale production *engenders* capitalism and the bourgeoisie continuously, daily, hourly, spontaneously, and on a mass scale. All these reasons make the dictatorship of the proletariat necessary, and victory over the bourgeoisie is impossible without a long, stubborn and desperate life-and-death struggle which calls for tenacity, discipline, and a single and inflexible will.

I repeat: the experience of the victorious dictatorship of the proletariat in Russia has clearly shown even to those who are incapable of thinking or have had no occasion to give thought to the matter that absolute centralisation and rigorous discipline in the proletariat are an essential condition of victory over the bourgeoisie.

This is often dwelt on. However, not nearly enough thought is given to what it means, and under what conditions it is possible. Would it not be better if the salutations addressed to the Soviets and the Bolsheviks were *more frequently* accompanied by a *profound analysis* of the reasons *why* the Bolsheviks have been able to build up the discipline needed by the revolutionary proletariat?

As a current of political thought and as a political party, Bolshevism has existed since 1903. Only the history of Bolshevism during the *entire* period of its existence can satisfactorily explain why it has been able to build up and maintain, under most difficult conditions, the iron discipline needed for the victory of the proletariat.

The first questions to arise are: how is the discipline of the proletariat's revolutionary party maintained? How is it tested? How is it reinforced? First, by the class-consciousness of the proletarian vanguard and by its devotion to the revolution, by its tenacity, self-sacrifice and heroism. Second, by its ability to link up, maintain the closest contact, and—if you wish—merge, in certain measure, with the broadest masses of the working people—primarily with the proletariat, *but also with the non-proletarian* masses of working people. Third, by the correctness of the political leadership exercised by this vanguard, by the correctness of its political strategy and tactics, provided the broad masses have seen, *from their own experience*, that they are correct. Without these conditions, discipline in a revolutionary party really capable of being the party of the advanced class, whose mission it is to overthrow the bourgeoisie and transform the whole of society, cannot be achieved. Without these conditions, all attempts to establish discipline inevitably fall flat and end up in phrase-mongering and clowning. On the other hand, these conditions cannot emerge at once. They are created only by prolonged effort and hard-won experience. Their creation is facilitated by a correct revolutionary theory, which, in its turn, is not a dogma, but assumes final shape only in close connection with the practical activity of a truly mass and truly revolutionary movement.

The fact that, in 1917–20, Bolshevism was able, under unprecedentedly difficult conditions, to build up and successfully maintain the strictest centralisation and iron discipline was due simply to a number of historical peculiarities of Russia.

On the one hand, Bolshevism arose in 1903 on a very firm foundation of Marxist theory. The correctness of this revolutionary theory, and of it alone, has been proved, not only by world experience throughout the nineteenth century, but especially by the experience of the seekings and vacillations, the errors and disappointments of revolutionary thought in Russia. For about half a century —approximately from the forties to the nineties of the last century—progressive thought in Russia, oppressed by a most brutal and reactionary tsarism, sought eagerly for a correct revolutionary theory, and followed with the utmost diligence and thoroughness each and every "last word" in this sphere in Europe and America. Russia achieved Marxism—the only correct revolutionary theory— through the *agony* she experienced in the course of half a century of unparalleled torment and sacrifice, of unparalleled revolutionary heroism, incredible energy, devoted searching, study, practical trial, disappointment, verification, and comparison with European experience. Thanks to the political emigration caused by tsarism, revolutionary Russia, in the second half of the nineteenth century, acquired a wealth of international links and excellent information on the forms and theories of the world revolutionary movement, such as no other country possessed.

On the other hand, Bolshevism, which had arisen on this granite foundation of theory, went through fifteen years of practical history (1903–17) unequalled anywhere in the world in its wealth of experience. During those fifteen years, no other country knew anything even approximating to that revolutionary experience, that rapid and varied succession of different forms of the movement— legal and illegal, peaceful and stormy, underground and open, local circles and mass movements, and parliamentary and terrorist forms. In no other country has there been concentrated, in so brief a period, such a wealth of forms, shades, and methods of struggle of *all* classes of modern society, a struggle which, owing to the backwardness of the country and the severity of the tsarist yoke, matured with exceptional rapidity, and assimilated most eagerly and successfully the appropriate "last word" of American and European political experience.

III. The Principal Stages of the History of Bolshevism

The years of preparation for revolution (1903–5). The approach of a great storm was sensed everywhere. All classes were in a state of ferment and preparation. Abroad, the press of the political exiles discussed the theoretical aspects of *all* the fundamental problems of the revolution. Representatives of the three main classes, of the three principal political trends—the liberal-bourgeois, the petty-bourgeois-democratic (concealed behind "social-democratic" and "social-revolutionary" labels), and the proletarian-revolutionary—anticipated and prepared the impending open class struggle by waging a most bitter struggle on issues of programme and tactics. *All* the issues on which the masses waged an armed struggle in 1905–7 and 1917–20 can (and should) be studied, in their embryonic form, in the press of the period. Among these three main trends there were, of course, a host of intermediate, transitional or half-hearted forms. It would be more correct to say that those political and ideological trends which were genuinely of a class nature crystallised in the struggle of press organs, parties, factions and groups; the classes were forging the requisite political and ideological weapons for the impending battles.

The years of revolution (1905–7). All classes came out into the open. All programmatical and tactical views were tested by the action of the masses. In its extent and acuteness, the strike struggle had no parallel anywhere in the world. The economic strike developed into a political strike, and the latter into insurrection. The relations between the proletariat, as the leader, and the vacillating and unstable peasantry, as the led, were tested in practice. The Soviet form of organisation came into being in the spontaneous development of the struggle. The controversies of that period over the significance of the Soviets anticipated the great struggle of 1917–20. The alternation of parliamentary and non-parliamentary forms of struggle, of the tactics of boycotting parliament and that of participating in parliament, of legal and illegal forms of struggle, and likewise their interrelations and connections—all this was marked by an extraordinary wealth of content. As for teaching the fundamentals of political science to masses and leaders, to classes and parties alike, each month of this period was equivalent to an entire year of "peaceful" and "constitutional" development. Without the "dress rehearsal" of 1905, the victory of the October Revolution in 1917 would have been impossible.

The years of reaction (1907–10). Tsarism was victorious. All the revolutionary and opposition parties were smashed. Depression, demoralisation, splits, discord, defection, and pornography took the place of politics. There was an ever greater drift towards philosophical idealism; mysticism became the garb of counter-revolutionary sentiments. At the same time, however, it was this great defeat that taught the revolutionary parties and the revolutionary class a real and very useful lesson, a lesson in historical dialectics, a lesson in an understanding of the political struggle, and in the art and science of waging that struggle. It is at moments of need that one learns who one's friends are. Defeated armies learn their lesson.

Victorious tsarism was compelled to speed up the destruction of the remnants of the pre-bourgeois, patriarchal mode of life in Russia. The country's development along bourgeois lines proceeded apace. Illusions that stood outside and above class distinctions, illusions concerning the possibility of avoiding capitalism, were scattered to the winds. The class struggle manifested itself in a quite new and more distinct way.

The revolutionary parties had to complete their education. They were learning how to attack. Now they had to realise that such knowledge must be supplemented with the knowledge of how to retreat in good order. They had to realise—and it is from bitter experience that the revolutionary class learns to realise this—that victory is impossible unless one has learned how to attack and retreat properly. Of all the defeated opposition and revolutionary parties, the Bolsheviks effected the most orderly retreat, with the least loss to their "army," with its core best preserved, with the least significant splits (in point of depth and incurability), with the least demoralisation, and in the best condition to resume work on the broadest scale and in the most correct and energetic manner. The Bolsheviks achieved this only because they ruthlessly exposed and expelled the revolutionary phrase-mongers, those who did not wish to understand that one had to retreat, that one had to know how to retreat, and that one had absolutely to learn how to work legally in the most reactionary of parliaments, in the most reactionary of trade unions, co-operative and insurance societies and similar organisations.

The years of revival (1910–14). At first progress was incredibly slow, then, following the Lena events of 1912,[2] it became somewhat more rapid. Overcoming unprecedented difficulties, the Bolsheviks thrust back the Mensheviks, whose role as bourgeois agents in the

2. Lenin is referring to strikes among workers in the gold fields on the Lena River, in Siberia. [R. T.]

working-class movement was clearly realised by the entire bourgeoisie after 1905, and whom the bourgeoisie therefore supported in a thousand ways against the Bolsheviks. But the Bolsheviks would never have succeeded in doing this had they not followed the correct tactics of combining illegal work with the utilisation of "legal opportunities," which they made a point of doing. In the elections to the arch-reactionary Duma, the Bolsheviks won the full support of the worker curia.

The First Imperialist World War (1914–17). Legal parliamentarianism, with an extremely reactionary "parliament," rendered most useful service to the Bolsheviks, the party of the revolutionary proletariat. The Bolshevik deputies were exiled to Siberia. All shades of social-imperialism, social-chauvinism, social-patriotism, inconsistent and consistent internationalism, pacifism, and the revolutionary repudiation of pacifist illusions found full expression in the Russian émigré press. The learned fools and the old women of the Second International, who had arrogantly and contemptuously turned up their noses at the abundance of "factions" in the Russian socialist movement and at the bitter struggle they were waging among themselves, were unable—when the war deprived them of their vaunted "legality" in *all* the advanced countries—to organise anything even approximating such a free (illegal) interchange of views and such a free (illegal) evolution of correct views as the Russian revolutionaries did in Switzerland and in a number of other countries. That was why both the avowed social-patriots and the "Kautskyites" of all countries proved to be the worst traitors to the proletariat. One of the principal reasons why Bolshevism was able to achieve victory in 1917–20 was that, since the end of 1914, it has been ruthlessly exposing the baseness and vileness of social-chauvinism and "Kautskyism" (to which Longuetism in France, the views of the Fabians and the leaders of the Independent Labour Party in Britain, of Turati in Italy, etc., correspond), the masses later becoming more and more convinced, from their own experience, of the correctness of the Bolshevik views.

The second revolution in Russia (February to October 1917). Tsarism's senility and obsoleteness had (with the aid of the blows and hardships of a most agonising war) created an incredibly destructive force directed against it. Within a few days Russia was transformed into a democratic bourgeois republic, freer—in war conditions—than any other country in the world. The leaders of the opposition and revolutionary parties began to set up a government, just as is done in the most "strictly parliamentary" republics; the fact that a man had been a leader of an opposition party in parliament—even in a most reactionary parliament—*facilitated* his subsequent role in the revolution.

In a few weeks the Mensheviks and Socialist-Revolutionaries thoroughly assimilated all the methods and manners, the arguments and sophistries of the European heroes of the Second International, of the ministerialists and other opportunist riffraff. Everything we now read about the Scheidemanns and Noskes, about Kautsky and Hilferding, Renner and Austerlitz, Otto Bauer and Fritz Adler, Turati and Longuet, about the Fabians and the leaders of the Independent Labour Party of Britain—all this seems to us (and indeed is) a dreary repetition, a reiteration, of an old and familiar refrain. We have already witnessed all this in the instance of the Mensheviks. As history would have it, the opportunists of a backward country became the forerunners of the opportunists in a number of advanced countries.

If the heroes of the Second International have all gone bankrupt and have disgraced themselves over the question of the significance and role of the Soviets and Soviet rule; if the leaders of the three very important parties which have now left the Second International (namely, the German Independent Social-Democratic Party, the French Longuetists and the British Independent Labour Party) have disgraced themselves and become entangled in this question in a most "telling" fashion; if they have all shown themselves slaves to the prejudices of petty-bourgeois democracy (fully in the spirit of the petty-bourgeois of 1848 who called themselves "Social-Democrats")—then we can only say that we have *already* witnessed *all this* in the instance of the Mensheviks. As history would have it, the Soviets came into being in Russia in 1905; from February to October 1917 they were turned to a false use by the Mensheviks, who went bankrupt because of their inability to understand the role and significance of the Soviets; today the idea of Soviet power has emerged *throughout the world* and is spreading among the proletariat of all countries with extraordinary speed. Like our Mensheviks, the old heroes of the Second International are *everywhere* going bankrupt, because they are incapable of understanding the role and significance of the Soviets. Experience has proved that, on certain very important questions of the proletarian revolution, *all* countries will inevitably have to do what Russia has done.

Despite views that are today often to be met with in Europe and America, the Bolsheviks began their victorious struggle against the parliamentary and (in fact) bourgeois republic and against the Mensheviks in a very cautious manner, and the preparations they made for it were by no means simple. At the beginning of the period mentioned, we did *not* call for the overthrow of the government but explained that it was impossible to overthrow it *without* first changing the composition and the temper of the Soviets. We did not proclaim a boycott of the bourgeois parliament, the Constituent Assembly, but said—and following the April (1917) Conference of our Party began to state officially in the name of the Party—that a bourgeois republic with a Constituent Assembly would be better than a bourgeois republic without a Constituent Assembly, but that a "workers' and peasants'" republic, a Soviet republic, would be better than any bourgeois-democratic, parliamentary republic. Without such thorough, circumspect and long preparations, we could not have achieved victory in October 1917, or have consolidated that victory.

IV. The Struggle Against Which Enemies Within the Working-Class Movement Helped Bolshevism Develop, Gain Strength, and Become Steeled

First and foremost, the struggle against opportunism, which in 1914 definitely developed into social-chauvinism and definitely sided with the bourgeoisie, against the proletariat. Naturally, this was Bolshevism's principal enemy within the working-class movement. It still remains the principal enemy on an international scale. The Bolsheviks have been devoting the greatest attention to this enemy. This aspect of Bolshevik activities is now fairly well known abroad too.

It was, however, different with Bolshevism's other enemy within the working-class movement. Little is known in other countries of the fact that Bolshevism took shape, developed and became steeled in the long years of struggle against *petty-bourgeois revolutionism*, which smacks of anarchism, or borrows something from the latter and, in all essential matters, does not measure up to the conditions and requirements of a consistently proletarian class struggle. Marxist theory has established—and the experience of all European revolutions and revolutionary movements has fully confirmed—that the petty proprietor, the small master (a social type existing on a very extensive and even mass scale in many European countries), who, under capitalism, always suffers oppression and very frequently a most acute and rapid deterioration in his conditions of life, and even ruin, easily goes to revolutionary extremes, but is incapable of perseverance, organisation, discipline and steadfastness. A petty bourgeois driven to frenzy by the horrors of capitalism is a social phenomenon which, like anarchism, is characteristic of all capitalist countries. The instability of such revolutionism, its barrenness, and its tendency to turn rapidly into submission, apathy, phantasms, and even a frenzied infatuation with one bourgeois fad or another—all this is common knowledge. However, a theoretical or abstract recognition of these truths does not at all rid revolutionary parties of old errors, which always crop up at unexpected occasions, in somewhat new forms, in a hitherto unfamiliar garb or surroundings, in an unusual—a more or less unusual—situation.

Anarchism was not infrequently a kind of penalty for the opportunist sins of the working-class movement. The two monstrosities complemented each other. And if in Russia—despite the more petty-bourgeois composition of her population as compared with the other European countries—anarchism's influence was negligible during the two revolutions (of 1905 and 1917) and the preparations for them, this should no doubt stand partly to the credit of Bolshevism, which has always waged a most ruthless and uncompromising struggle against opportunism. I say "partly," since of still greater importance in weakening anarchism's influence in Russia was the circumstance that in the past (the seventies of the nineteenth century) it was able to develop inordinately and to reveal its absolute erroneousness, its unfitness to serve the revolutionary class as a guiding theory.

When it came into being in 1903, Bolshevism took over the tradition of a ruthless struggle against petty-bourgeois, semi-anarchist (or dilettante-anarchist) revolutionism, a tradition which had always existed in revolutionary Social-Democracy and had become particularly strong in our country during the years 1900–1903, when the foundations for a mass party of the revolutionary proletariat were being laid in Russia. Bolshevism took over and carried on the struggle against a party which, more than any other, expressed the tendencies of petty-bourgeois revolutionism, namely, the "Socialist-Revolutionary" Party, and waged that struggle on three main issues. First, that party, which rejected Marxism, stubbornly refused (or, it might be more correct to say: was unable) to understand the need for a strictly objective appraisal of the class forces and their alignment, before taking any political action. Second, this party considered itself particularly "revolutionary," or "Left," because of its recognition of individual terrorism, assassination—something that we Marxists emphatically rejected. It was, of course, only on grounds of expediency that we rejected individual terrorism, whereas people who were capable of condemning "on principle" the terror of the Great French Revolution, or, in general, the terror employed by a victorious revolutionary party which is besieged by the bourgeoisie of the whole world, were ridiculed and laughed to scorn by Plekhanov in 1900–1903, when he was a Marxist and a revolutionary. Third, the "Socialist-Revolutionaries" thought it very "Left" to sneer at the comparatively insignificant opportunist sins of the German Social-Democratic Party, while they themselves imitated the extreme opportunists of that party, for example, on the agrarian question, or on the question of the dictatorship of the proletariat.

History, incidentally, has now confirmed on a vast and worldwide scale the opinion we have always advocated, namely, that German *revolutionary* Social-Democracy (note that as far back as 1900–1903 Plekhanov demanded Bernstein's expulsion from the Party, and in 1913 the Bolsheviks, always continuing this tradition, exposed Legien's baseness, vileness and treachery) *came closest* to being the party the revolutionary proletariat needs in order to achieve victory. Today, in 1920, after all the ignominious failures and crises of the war period and the early postwar years, it can be plainly seen that, of all the Western parties, the German revolutionary Social-Democrats produced the finest leaders, and recovered and gained new strength more rapidly than the others did. This may be seen in the instances both of the Spartacists and the Left, proletarian wing of the Independent Social-Democratic Party of Germany, which is waging an incessant struggle against the opportunism and spinelessness of the Kautskys, Hilferdings, Ledebours and Crispiens. If we now cast a glance to take in a complete historical period, namely, from the Paris Commune to the first Socialist Soviet Republic, we shall find that Marxism's attitude to anarchism in general stands out most definitely and unmistakably. In the final analysis, Marxism proved to be correct, and although the anarchist rightly pointed to the opportunist views on the state prevalent among most of the socialist parties, it must be said, first, that this opportunism was connected with the distortion, and even deliberate suppression, of Marx's views on the state (in my book, *The State and Revolution*, I pointed out that for thirty-six years, from 1875 to 1911, Bebel withheld a letter by Engels, which very clearly, vividly, bluntly and definitively exposed the opportunism of the current Social-Democratic views on the state); second, that the rectification of these opportunist views, and the recognition of Soviet power and its superiority to bourgeois parliamentary democracy proceeded most rapidly and extensively among those trends in the socialist parties of Europe and America that were most Marxist.

The struggle that Bolshevism waged against "Left" deviations within its own Party assumed particularly large proportions on two occasions: in 1908, on the question of whether or not to participate in a most reactionary "parliament" and in the legal workers' societies, which were being restricted by most reactionary laws; and again in 1918 (the Treaty of Brest-Litovsk), on the question of whether one "compromise" or another was permissible.

In 1908 the "Left" Bolsheviks were expelled from our Party for stubbornly refusing to understand the necessity of participating in a most reactionary "parliament." The "Lefts"—among whom there were many splendid revolutionaries who subsequently were (and still are) commendable members of the Communist Party—based themselves particularly on the successful experience of the 1905 boycott. When, in August 1905, the tsar proclaimed the convocation of a consultative "parliament," the Bolsheviks called for its boycott, in the teeth of all the opposition parties and the Mensheviks, and the "parliament" was in fact swept away by the revolution of October 1905. The boycott proved correct at the time, not because non-participating in reactionary parliaments is correct in general, but because we accurately appraised the objective situation, which was leading to the rapid development of the mass strikes first into a political strike, then into a revolutionary strike, and finally into an uprising. Moreover, the struggle centred at that time on the question of whether the convocation of the first representative assembly should be left to the tsar, or an attempt should be made to wrest its convocation from the old regime. When there was not, and could not be, any certainty that the objective situation was of a similar kind, and when there was no certainty of a similar trend and the same rate of development, the boycott was no longer correct.

The Bolsheviks' boycott of "parliament" in 1905 enriched the revolutionary proletariat with highly valuable political experience and showed that, when legal and illegal, parliamentary and non-parliamentary forms of struggle are combined, it is sometimes useful and even essential to reject parliamentary forms. It would, however, be highly erroneous to apply this experience blindly, imitatively and uncritically to *other* conditions and *other* situations. The Bolsheviks' boycott of the Duma in 1906 was a mistake, although a minor and easily remediable one.[3] The boycott of the Duma in 1907, 1908 and subsequent years was a most serious error and difficult to remedy, because, on the one hand, a very rapid rise of the revolutionary tide and its conversion into an uprising was not to be expected, and, on the other hand, the entire historical situation attendant upon the renovation of the bourgeois monarchy called for legal and illegal activities being combined. Today, when we look back at this fully completed historical period, whose connection with subsequent periods has now become quite clear, it becomes most obvious that in 1908–14 the Bolsheviks *could not have* preserved (let alone strengthened and developed) the core of the revolutionary party of the proletariat, had they not upheld, in a most strenuous struggle, the viewpoint that it was *obligatory* to

---

3. What applies to individuals also applies—with necessary modifications—to politics and parties. It is not he who makes no mistakes that is intelligent. There are no such men, nor can there be. It is he whose errors are not very grave and who is able to rectify them easily and quickly that is intelligent. [*Lenin*]

combine legal and illegal forms of struggle, and that it was *obligatory* to participate even in a most reactionary parliament and in a number of other institutions hemmed in by reactionary laws (sick benefit societies, etc.).

In 1918 things did not reach a split. At that time the "Left" Communists formed only a separate group or "faction" within our Party, and that not for long. In the same year, 1918, the most prominent representatives of "Left Communism," for example, Comrades Radek and Bukharin, openly acknowledged their error. It had seemed to them that the Treaty of Brest-Litovsk was a compromise with the imperialists, which was inexcusable on principle and harmful to the party of the revolutionary proletariat. It was indeed a compromise with the imperialists, but it was a compromise which, under the circumstances, *had to be made.*

Today, when I hear our tactics in signing the Brest-Litovsk Treaty being attacked by the Socialist-Revolutionaries, for instance, or when I hear Comrade Lansbury say, in a conversation with me, "Our British trade union leaders say that if it was permissible for the Bolsheviks to compromise, it is permissible for them to compromise too," I usually reply by first of all giving a simple and "popular" example:

Imagine that your car is held up by armed bandits. You hand them over your money, passport, revolver and car. In return you are rid of the pleasant company of the bandits. That is unquestionably a compromise. *"Do ut des"* (I "give" you money, fire-arms and a car "so that you give" me the opportunity to get away from you with a whole skin). It would, however, be difficult to find a sane man who would declare such a compromise to be "inadmissible on principle," or who would call the compromiser an accomplice of the bandits (even though the bandits might use the car and the fire-arms for further robberies). Our compromise with the bandits of German imperialism was just that kind of compromise.

But when, in 1914–18 and then in 1918–20, the Mensheviks and Socialist-Revolutionaries in Russia, the Scheidemannites (and to a large extent the Kautskyites) in Germany, Otto Bauer and Friedrich Adler (to say nothing of the Renners and Co.) in Austria, the Renaudels and Longuets and Co. in France, the Fabians, the Independents and the Labourites in Britain entered into *compromises* with the bandits of their own bourgeoisie, and sometimes of the "Allied" bourgeoisie, and *against* the revolutionary proletariat of their own countries, all these gentlemen were actually acting as *accomplices in banditry.*

The conclusion is clear: to reject compromises "on principle," to reject the permissibility of compromises in general, no matter of what kind, is childishness, which it is difficult even to consider seriously. A political leader who desires to be useful to the revolutionary proletariat must be able to distinguish *concrete* cases of compromises that are inexcusable and are an expression of opportunism and *treachery*; he must direct all the force of criticism, the full intensity of merciless exposure and relentless war, against *these concrete* compromises, and not allow the past masters of "practical" socialism and the parliamentary Jesuits to dodge and wriggle out of responsibility by means of disquisitions on "compromises in general." It is in this way that the "leaders" of the British trade unions, as well as of the Fabian society and the "Independent" Labour Party, dodge responsibility *for the treachery they have perpetrated,* for having made *a compromise* that is really tantamount to the worst kind of opportunism, treachery and betrayal.

There are different kinds of compromises. One must be able to analyse the situation and the concrete conditions of each compromise, or of each variety of compromise. One must learn to distinguish between a man who has given up his money and fire-arms to bandits so as to lessen the evil they can do and to facilitate their capture and execution, and a man who gives his money and fire-arms to bandits so as to share in the loot. In politics this is by no means always as elementary as it is in this childishly simple example. However, anyone who is out to think up for the workers some kind of recipe that will provide them with cut-and-dried solutions for all contingencies, or promises that the policy of the revolutionary proletariat will never come up against difficult or complex situations, is simply a charlatan.

To leave no room for misinterpretation, I shall attempt to outline, if only very briefly, several fundamental rules for the analysis of concrete compromises.

The party which entered into a compromise with the German imperialists by signing the Treaty of Brest-Litovsk had been evolving its internationalism in practice ever since the end of 1914. It was not afraid to call for the defeat of the tsarist monarchy and to condemn "defence of country" in a war between two imperialist robbers. The parliamentary representatives of this party preferred exile in Siberia to taking a road leading to ministerial portfolios in a bourgeois government. The revolution that overthrew tsarism and established a democratic republic put this party to a new and tremendous test—it did not enter into any agreements with its "own" imperialists, but prepared and brought about their overthrow. When it had assumed political power, this party did not leave a vestige of either landed or capitalist ownership. After making public and repudiating the imperialists' secret treaties, this party proposed peace to *all* nations, and yielded to the violence of the Brest-Litovsk robbers only after the Anglo-French imperialists had torpedoed the conclusion of a peace, and after the Bolsheviks had done everything humanly possible to hasten the revolution in Germany and other countries. The absolute correctness of this compromise, entered into by such a party in such a situation, is becoming ever clearer and more obvious with every day.

The Mensheviks and the Socialist-Revolutionaries in Russia (like all the leaders of the Second International throughout the world, in 1914–20) began with treachery—by directly or indirectly justifying "defence of country," i.e., the defence of *their own* predatory bourgeoisie. They continued their treachery by entering into a coalition with the bourgeoisie of *their own* country, and fighting, together with *their own* bourgeoisie, against the revolutionary proletariat of their own country. Their bloc, first with Kerensky and the Cadets, and then with Kolchak and Denikin in Russia—like the bloc of their *confrères* abroad with the bourgeoisie of *their* respective countries—was in fact desertion to the side of the bourgeoisie, against the proletariat. From beginning to end, *their* compromise with the bandits of imperialism meant their becoming *accomplices* in imperialist banditry.

V. "Left-Wing" Communism in Germany. The Leaders, the Party, the Class, the Masses

The German Communists we must now speak of call themselves, not "Left-wingers" but, if I am not mistaken, an "opposition on principle." From what follows below it will, however, be seen that they reveal all the symptoms of the "infantile disorder of Leftism."

Published by the "local group in Frankfurt am Main," a pamphlet reflecting the point of view of this opposition, and entitled *The Split in the Communist Party of Germany* (*The Spartacus League*), sets forth the substance of this opposition's views most saliently, and with the utmost clarity and concision. A few quotations will suffice to acquaint the reader with that substance:

> The Communist Party is the party of the most determined class struggle. . . .
> . . . Politically, the transitional period [between capitalism and socialism] is one of the proletarian dictatorship. . . .
> . . . The question arises: who is to exercise this dictatorship: *the Communist Party or the proletarian class?* . . . *Fundamentally*, should we strive for a dictatorship of the Communist Party, or for a dictatorship of the proletarian class? . . . [All italics as in the original.]

The author of the pamphlet goes on to accuse the Central Committee of the Communist Party of Germany of seeking ways of achieving a *coalition with the Independent Social-Democratic Party of Germany*, and of raising *"the question of recognising, in principle, all political means"* of struggle, including parliamentarianism, with the sole purpose of concealing its actual and main efforts to form a coalition with the Independents. The pamphlet goes on to say:

> The opposition have chosen another road. They are of the opinion that the question of the rule of the Communist Party and of the dictatorship of the Party is merely one of tactics. In any case, rule by the Communist Party is the ultimate form of any party rule. *Fundamentally*, we must work for the dictatorship of the proletarian class. And all the measures of the Party, its organisations, methods of struggle, strategy and tactics should be directed to that end. Accordingly, all compromise with other parties, all reversion to parliamentary forms of struggle, which have become historically and politically obsolete, and any policy of manoeuvring and compromise must be emphatically rejected. . . . Specifically proletarian methods of revolutionary struggle must be strongly emphasised. New forms of organisation must be created on the widest basis and with the widest scope in order to enlist the most extensive proletarian circles and strata to take part in the revolutionary struggle under the leadership of the Communist Party. A *Workers' Union*, based on factory organisations, should be the rallying point for all revolutionary elements. This should unite all workers who follow the slogan: 'Get out of the trade unions!' It is here that the militant proletariat musters its ranks for battle. Recognition of the class struggle, of the Soviet system and of the dictatorship should be sufficient for enrolment. All subsequent political education of the fighting masses and their political orientation in the struggle are the task of the Communist Party, which stands outside the Workers' Union. . . .
>
> . . . Consequently, two Communist parties are now arrayed against each other:
>
> *One is a party of leaders*, which is out to organise the revolutionary struggle and to direct it from *above*, accepting compromises and parliamentarianism so as to create a situation enabling it to join a coalition government exercising a dictatorship.
>
> *The other is a mass party*, which expects an upsurge of the revolutionary struggle from *below*, which knows and applies a single method in this struggle—a method which clearly leads to the goal—and rejects all parliamentary and opportunist methods. That single method is the unconditional *overthrow of the bourgeoisie*, so as then to set up the proletarian class dictatorship for the accomplishment of socialism. . . .
>
> . . . There—the dictatorship of leaders; here—the dictatorship of the masses! That is our slogan.

Such are the main features characterising the views of the opposition in the German Communist Party.

Any Bolshevik who has consciously participated in the development of Bolshevism since 1903 or has closely observed that development will at once say, after reading these arguments, "What old and familiar rubbish! What 'Left-wing' childishness!"

But let us examine these arguments a little more closely.

The mere presentation of the question—"dictatorship of the party *or* dictatorship of the class: dictatorship (party) of the leaders, *or* dictatorship (party) of the masses?"—testifies to most incredibly and hopelessly muddled thinking. These people want to *invent* something quite out of the ordinary, and, in their effort to be clever, make themselves ridiculous. It is common knowledge that the masses are divided into classes; that the masses can be contrasted with classes only by contrasting the vast majority in general, regardless of division according to status in the social system of production, with categories holding a definite status in the social system of production; that as a rule and in most cases—at least in present-day civilised countries—classes are led by political parties; that political parties, as a general rule, are run by more or less stable groups composed of the most authoritative, influential and experienced members, who are elected to the most responsible positions, and are called leaders. All this is elementary. All this is clear and simple. Why replace this with some kind of rigmarole, some new Volapük?[4] On the one hand, these people seem to have got muddled when they found themselves in a predicament, when the party's abrupt transition from legality to illegality upset the customary, normal and simple relations between leaders, parties and classes. In Germany, as in other European countries, people had become too accustomed to legality, to the free and proper election of "leaders" at regular party congresses, to the convenient method of testing the class composition of parties through parliamentary elections, mass meetings, the press, the sentiments of the trade unions and other associations, etc. When, instead of this customary procedure, it become necessary, because of the stormy development of the revolution and the development of the civil war, to go over rapidly from legality to illegality, to combine the two, and to adopt the "inconvenient" and "undemocratic" methods of selecting, or forming, or preserving "groups of leaders"—people lost their bearings and began to think up some unmitigated nonsense. Certain members of the Communist Party of Holland, who were unlucky enough to be born in a small country with traditions and conditions of highly privileged and highly stable legality, and who had never seen a transition from legality to illegality, probably fell into confusion, lost their heads, and helped create these absurd inventions.

On the other hand, one can see simply a thoughtless and inco-

4. Literally, "world's speech"; a language, intended to be international, based largely on English, and invented by Johann Martin Schleyer around 1879. [*R. T.*]

herent use of the now "fashionable" terms: "masses" and "leaders." These people have heard and memorised a great many attacks on "leaders," in which the latter have been contrasted with the "masses"; however, they have proved unable to think matters out and gain a clear understanding of what it was all about.

The divergence between "leaders" and "masses" was brought out with particular clarity and sharpness in all countries at the end of the imperialist war and following it. The principal reason for this was explained many times by Marx and Engels between the years 1852 and 1892, from the example of Britain. That country's exclusive position led to the emergence, from the "masses," of a semi-petty bourgeois, opportunist "labour aristocracy." The leaders of this labour aristocracy were constantly going over to the bourgeoisie, and were directly or indirectly on its pay roll. Marx earned the honour of incurring the hatred of these disreputable persons by openly branding them as traitors. Present-day (twentieth-century) imperialism has given a few advanced countries an exceptionally privileged position, which, everywhere in the Second International, has produced a certain type of traitor, opportunist, and social-chauvinist leaders, who champion the interests of their own craft, their own section of the labour aristocracy. The opportunist parties have become separated from the "masses," i.e., from the broadest strata of the working people, their majority, the lowest-paid workers. The revolutionary proletariat cannot be victorious unless this evil is combated, unless the opportunist, social-traitor leaders are exposed, discredited and expelled. That is the policy the Third International has embarked on.

To go so far, in this connection, as to contrast, *in general*, the dictatorship of the masses with a dictatorship of the leaders is ridiculously absurd, and stupid. What is particularly amusing is that, in fact, instead of the old leaders, who hold generally accepted views on simple matters, *new leaders* are brought forth (under cover of the slogan "Down with the leaders!"), who talk rank stuff and nonsense. Such are Laufenberg, Wolffheim, Horner, Karl Schröder, Friedrich Wendel and Karl Erler,[5] in Germany. Erler's attempts to give the question more "profundity" and to proclaim

---

5. Karl Erler, "The Dissolution of the Party," *Kommunistische Arbeiterzeitung*, Hamburg, February 7, 1920, No. 32: "The working class cannot destroy the bourgeois state without destroying bourgeois democracy, and it cannot destroy bourgeois democracy without destroying parties."

The more muddle-headed of the syndicalists and anarchists in the Latin countries may derive "satisfaction" from the fact that solid Germans, who evidently consider themselves Marxists (by

their articles in the above-mentioned paper K. Erler and K. Horner have shown most plainly that they consider themselves sound Marxists, but talk incredible nonsense in a most ridiculous manner and reveal their failure to understand the ABC of Marxism), go to the length of making utterly inept statements. Mere acceptance of Marxism does not save one from errors. We Russians know this especially well, because Marxism has been very often the "fashion" in our country. [*Lenin*]

that in general political parties are unnecessary and "bourgeois" are so supremely absurd that one can only shrug one's shoulders. It all goes to drive home the truth that a minor error can always assume monstrous proportions if it is persisted in, if profound justifications are sought for it, and if it is carried to its logical conclusion.

Repudiation of the Party principle and of Party discipline—that is what the opposition has *arrived at*. And this is tantamount to completely disarming the proletariat *in the interests of the bourgeoisie*. It all adds up to that petty-bourgeois diffuseness and instability, that incapacity for sustained effort, unity and organised action, which, if encouraged, must inevitably destroy any proletarian revolutionary movement. From the standpoint of communism, repudiation of the Party principle means attempting to leap from the eve of capitalism's collapse (in Germany), not to the lower or the intermediate phase of communism, but to the higher. We in Russia (in the third year since the overthrow of the bourgeoisie) are making the first steps in the transition from capitalism to socialism or the lower stage of communism. Classes still remain, and will remain everywhere *for years after* the proletariat's conquest of power. Perhaps in Britain, where there is no peasantry (but where petty proprietors exist), this period may be shorter. The abolition of classes means, not merely ousting the landowners and the capitalists—that is something we accomplished with comparative ease; it also means *abolishing the small commodity producers*, and they *cannot be ousted*, or crushed; we *must learn to live* with them. They can (and must) be transformed and re-educated only by means of very prolonged, slow, and cautious organisational work. They surround the proletariat on every side with a petty-bourgeois atmosphere, which permeates and corrupts the proletariat, and constantly causes among the proletariat relapses into petty-bourgeois spinelessness, disunity, individualism, and alternating moods of exaltation and dejection. The strictest centralisation and discipline are required within the political party of the proletariat in order to counteract this, in order that the *organisational* role of the proletariat (and that is its *principal* role) may be exercised correctly, successfully and victoriously. The dictatorship of the proletariat means a persistent struggle—bloody and bloodless, violent and peaceful, military and economic, educational and administrative—against the forces and traditions of the old society. The force of habit in millions and tens of millions is a most formidable force. Without a party of iron that has been tempered in the struggle, a party enjoying the confidence of all honest people in the class in question, a party capable of watching and influencing the mood of the masses, such a struggle cannot be waged successfully. It is a thousand times easier to vanquish the centralised big bourgeoisie than to "vanquish" the millions upon millions of petty proprietors; however, through their ordinary, everyday, imperceptible, elusive and demoralising activities, they produce the *very* results which the bourgeoisie need and which tend to *restore* the bourgeoisie. Whoever brings about even the slightest weakening of the iron discipline of the party of the proletariat (especially during its dictatorship), is actually aiding the bourgeoisie against the proletariat.

Parallel with the question of the leaders—the party—the class—the masses, we must pose the question of the "reactionary" trade unions. But first I shall take the liberty of making a few concluding remarks based on the experience of our Party. There *have always been* attacks on the "dictatorship of leaders" in our Party. The first time I heard such attacks, I recall, was in 1895, when, officially, no party yet existed, but a central group was taking shape in St. Petersburg, which was to assume the leadership of the district groups. At the Ninth Congress of our Party (April 1920) there was a small opposition, which also spoke against the "dictatorship of leaders," against the "oligarchy," and so on.[6] There is therefore nothing surprising, new, or terrible in the "infantile disorder" of "Left-wing communism" among the Germans. The ailment involves no danger, and after it the organism even becomes more robust. In our case, on the other hand, the rapid alternation of legal and illegal work, which made it necessary to keep the general staff—the leaders—under cover and cloak them in the greatest secrecy, sometimes gave rise to extremely dangerous consequences. The worst of these was that in 1912 the *agent provocateur* Malinovsky got into the Bolshevik Central Committee. He betrayed scores and scores of the best and most loyal comrades, caused them to be sentenced to penal servitude, and hastened the death of many of them. That he did not cause still greater harm was due to the correct balance between legal and illegal work. As member of the Party's Central Committee and Duma deputy, Malinovsky was forced, in order to gain our confidence, to help us establish legal daily papers, which even under tsarism were able to wage a struggle against the Menshevik opportunism and to spread the fundamentals of Bolshevism in a suitably disguised form. While, with one hand, Malinovsky sent scores and scores of the finest Bolsheviks to penal servitude and death, he was obliged, with the other, to assist in the education of scores and scores of thousands of new Bolsheviks through the

6. Lenin is referring to the democratic centralism group (T. Sapronov, N. Osinsky, V. Smirnov, and others). They denied the leading role of the Party in the Soviets and trade unions, rejected the need for one-man management and personal responsibility in guiding the enterprises, opposed Lenin's policy in organisational questions, and demanded freedom for factions and groupings in the Party. The Ninth Congress of the R.C.P.(B.) condemned the Democratic Centralists as an anti-Party group.

medium of the legal press. Those German (and also British, American, French and Italian) comrades who are faced with the task of learning how to conduct revolutionary work within the reactionary trade unions would do well to give serious thought to this fact.[7]

In many countries, including the most advanced, the bourgeoisie are undoubtedly sending *agents provocateurs* into the Communist parties and will continue to do so. A skilful combining of illegal and legal work is one of the ways to combat this danger.

VI. Should Revolutionaries Work in Reactionary Trade Unions?

The German "Lefts" consider that, as far as they are concerned, the reply to this question is an unqualified negative. In their opinion, declamations and angry outcries (such as uttered by K. Horner in a particularly "solid" and particularly stupid manner) against "reactionary" and "counter-revolutionary" trade unions are sufficient "proof" that it is unnecessary and even inexcusable for revolutionaries and Communists to work in yellow, social-chauvinist, compromising and counter-revolutionary trade unions of the Legien type.

However firmly the German "Lefts" may be convinced of the revolutionism of such tactics, the latter are in fact fundamentally wrong, and contain nothing but empty phrases.

To make this clear, I shall begin with our own experience, in keeping with the general plan of the present pamphlet, which is aimed at applying to Western Europe whatever is universally practicable, significant and relevant in the history and the present-day tactics of Bolshevism.

In Russia today, the connection between leaders, party, class and masses, as well as the attitude of the dictatorship of the proletariat and its party to the trade unions, are concretely as follows: the dictatorship is exercised by the proletariat organised in the Soviets; the proletariat is guided by the Communist Party of Bolsheviks, which, according to the figures of the latest Party Congress (April 1920), has a membership of 611,000. The membership varied

7. Malinovsky was a prisoner of war in Germany. On his return to Russia when the Bolsheviks were in power he was instantly put on trial and shot by our workers. The Mensheviks attacked us most bitterly for our mistake—the fact that an *agent provocateur* had become a member of the Central Committee of our Party. But when, under Kerensky, we demanded the arrest and trial of Rodzyanko, the Chairman of the Duma, because he had known, even before the war, that Malinovsky was an *agent provocateur* and *had not informed* the Trudoviks and the workers in the Duma, neither the Mensheviks nor the Socialist-Revolutionaries in the Kerensky government supported our demand, and Rodzyanko remained at large and made off unhindered to join Denikin. [*Lenin*]

greatly both before and after the October Revolution, and used to be much smaller, even in 1918 and 1919.[8] We are apprehensive of an excessive growth of the Party, because careerists and charlatans, who deserve only to be shot, inevitably do all they can to insinuate themselves into the ranks of the ruling party. The last time we opened wide the doors of the Party—to workers and peasants only—was when (in the winter of 1919) Yudenich was within a few versts of Petrograd, and Denikin was in Orel (about 350 versts from Moscow), i.e., when the Soviet Republic was in mortal danger, and when adventurers, careerists, charlatans and unreliable persons generally could not possibly count on making a profitable career (and had more reason to expect the gallows and torture) by joining the Communists. The Party, which holds annual congresses (the most recent on the basis of one delegate per 1,000 members), is directed by a Central Committee of nineteen elected at the Congress, while the current work in Moscow has to be carried on by still smaller bodies, known as the Organising Bureau and the Political Bureau, which are elected at plenary meetings of the Central Committee, five members of the Central Committee to each bureau. This, it would appear, is a full-fledged "oligarchy." No important political or organisational question is decided by any state institution in our republic without the guidance of the Party's Central Committee.

In its work, the Party relies directly on the *trade unions*, which, according to the data of the last congress (April 1920), now have a membership of over four million and are formally *non-Party*. Actually, all the directing bodies of the vast majority of the unions, and primarily, of course, of the all-Russia general trade union centre or bureau (the All-Russia Central Council of Trade Unions), are made up of Communists and carry out all the directives of the Party. Thus, on the whole, we have a formally non-communist, flexible and relatively wide and very powerful proletarian apparatus, by means of which the Party is closely linked up with the *class* and the *masses*, and by means of which, under the leadership of the Party, the *class dictatorship* is exercised. Without close contacts with the trade unions, and without their energetic support and devoted efforts, not only in economic, *but also in military* affairs, it would of course have been impossible for us to govern the country and to maintain the dictatorship for two and a half months, let

8. The Party membership after the February revolution in 1917 and up to 1919 changed as follows: at the time of the Seventh (April) All-Russia Conference of the R.S.D.L.P.(B.) in 1917 the Party numbered 80,000 members; at the time of the Sixth Congress of the R.S.D.L.P.(B.) in July-August 1917 there were about 240,000 members; at the time of the Seventh Congress of the R.C.P.(B.) in March 1918 there were about 300,000, and at the time of the Eighth Congress of the R.C.P.(B.) in March 1919 there were 313,766 Party members.

alone two and a half years. In practice, these very close contacts naturally call for highly complex and diversified work in the form of propaganda, agitation, timely and frequent conferences, not only with the leading trade union workers, but with influential trade union workers generally; they call for a determined struggle against the Mensheviks, who still have a certain though very small following to whom they teach all kinds of counter-revolutionary machinations, ranging from an ideological defence of (*bourgeois*) democracy and the preaching that the trade unions should be "independent" (independent of proletarian state power!) to sabotage of proletarian discipline, etc., etc.

We consider that contacts with the "masses" through the trade unions are not enough. In the course of our revolution, practical activities have given rise to such institutions as *non-Party workers' and peasants' conferences*, and we strive by every means to support, develop and extend this institution in order to be able to observe the temper of the masses, come closer to them, meet their requirements, promote the best among them to state posts, etc. Under a recent decree on the transformation of the People's Commissariat of State Control into the Workers' and Peasants' Inspection, non-Party conferences of this kind have been empowered to select members of the State Control to carry out various kinds of investigations, etc.

Then, of course, all the work of the Party is carried on through the Soviets, which embrace the working masses, irrespective of occupation. The district congresses of Soviets are *democratic* institutions, the like of which even the best of the democratic republics of the bourgeois world have never known; through these congresses (whose proceedings the Party endeavours to follow with the closest attention), as well as by continually appointing class-conscious workers to various posts in the rural districts, the proletariat exercises its role of leader of the peasantry, gives effect to the dictatorship of the urban proletariat, wages a systematic struggle against the rich, bourgeois, exploiting and profiteering peasantry, etc.

Such is the general mechanism of the proletarian state power viewed "from above," from the standpoint of the practical implementation of the dictatorship. We hope that the reader will understand why the Russian Bolshevik, who has known this mechanism for twenty-five years and has seen it develop out of small, illegal and underground circles, cannot help regarding all this talk about "from above" *or* "from below," about the dictatorship of leaders *or* the dictatorship of the masses, etc., as ridiculous and childish nonsense, something like discussing whether a man's left leg or right arm is of greater use to him.

We cannot but regard as equally ridiculous and childish nonsense the pompous, very learned, and frightfully revolutionary disquisitions of the German Lefts to the effect that Communists cannot and should not work in reactionary trade unions, that it is permissible to turn down such work, that it is necessary to withdraw from the trade unions and create a brand-new and immaculate "Workers' Union" invented by very pleasant (and, probably, for the most part very youthful) Communists, etc., etc.

Capitalism inevitably leaves socialism the legacy, on the one hand, of the old trade and craft distinctions among the workers, distinctions evolved in the course of centuries; on the other hand, trade unions, which only very slowly, in the course of years and years, can and will develop into broader industrial unions with less of the craft union about them (embracing entire industries, and not only crafts, trades and occupations), and later proceed, through these industrial unions, to eliminate the division of labour among people, to educate and school people, give them *all-round development and an all-round* training, so that they *are able to do everything*. Communism is advancing and must advance towards that goal, and *will reach it*, but only after very many years. To attempt in practice, today, to anticipate this future result of a fully developed, fully stabilised and constituted, fully comprehensive and mature communism would be like trying to teach higher mathematics to a child of four.

We can (and must) begin to build socialism, not with abstract human material, or with human material specially prepared by us, but with the human material bequeathed to us by capitalism. True, that is no easy matter, but no other approach to this task is serious enough to warrant discussion.

The trade unions were a tremendous step forward for the working class in the early days of capitalist development, inasmuch as they marked a transition from the workers' disunity and helplessness to the *rudiments* of class organisation. When the *revolutionary party of the proletariat*, the *highest* form of proletarian class organisation, began to take shape (and the Party will not merit the name until it learns to weld the leaders into one indivisible whole with the class and the masses), the trade unions inevitably began to reveal *certain* reactionary features, a certain craft narrow-mindedness, a certain tendency to be non-political, a certain inertness, etc. However, the development of the proletariat did not, and could not, proceed anywhere in the world otherwise than through the trade unions, through reciprocal action between them and the party of the working class. The proletariat's conquest of political power is a gigantic step forward for the proletariat as a class, and the Party must more than ever and in a new way, not only in the old, educate and guide the trade unions, at the same time bearing in mind that they are and will long remain an indispensable "school of communism" and a preparatory school that trains proletarians to exercise their dictatorship, an indispensable organisation of the workers for the gradual transfer of the management of the whole economic life of the country to the working *class* (and not to the separate trades), and later to all the working people.

In the sense mentioned above, a *certain* "reactionism" in the trade unions is *inevitable* under the dictatorship of the proletariat. Not to understand this means a complete failure to understand the fundamental conditions of the *transition* from capitalism to socialism. It would be egregious folly to fear *this* "reactionism" or to try to *evade* or leap over it, for it would mean fearing that function of the proletarian vanguard which consists in training, educating, enlightening and drawing into the new life the most backward strata and masses of the working class and the peasantry. On the other hand, it would be a still graver error to postpone the achievement of the dictatorship of the proletariat until a time when there will not be a single worker with a narrow-minded craft outlook, or with craft and craft-union prejudices. The art of politics (and the Communist's correct understanding of his tasks) consists in correctly gauging the conditions and the moment when the vanguard of the proletariat can successfully assume power, when it is able—during and after the seizure of power—to win adequate support from sufficiently broad strata of the working class and of the non-proletarian working masses, and when it is able thereafter to maintain, consolidate and extend its rule by educating, training and attracting ever broader masses of the working people.

Further. In countries more advanced than Russia, a certain reactionism in the trade unions has been and was bound to be manifested in a far greater measure than in our country. Our Mensheviks found support in the trade unions (and to some extent still do so in a small number of unions), as a result of the latter's craft narrow-mindedness, craft selfishness and opportunism. The Mensheviks of the West have acquired a much firmer footing in the trade unions; there the *craft-union, narrow-minded, selfish, case-hardened, covetous, and petty-bourgeois "labour aristocracy," imperialist-minded, and imperialist-corrupted*, has developed into a much stronger section than in our country. That is incontestable. The struggle against the Gomperses, and against the Jouhaux, Hendersons, Merrheims, Legiens and Co. in Western Europe is much more difficult than the struggle against our Mensheviks, who are an *absolutely homogeneous* social and political type. This struggle must be waged ruthlessly, and it must unfailingly be brought—as we brought it—to a point when all the incorrigible leaders of opportunism and social-chauvinism are completely discredited and driven out of the trade unions. Political power cannot be captured (and the attempt to capture it should not be made) until the struggle has reached a *certain* stage. This "certain stage" will be *different* in different countries and in different circumstances; it can be correctly gauged only by thoughtful, experienced and knowledgeable political leaders of the proletariat in each particular country. (In Russia the elections to the Constituent Assembly in November 1917, a few days after the proletarian revolution of October 25, 1917, were one of the criteria of the success of this struggle. In these elections the Mensheviks were utterly defeated; they received 700,000 votes—1,400,000 if the vote in Transcaucasia is added—as against 9,000,000 votes polled by the Bolsheviks. See my article, "The Constituent Assembly Elections and the Dictatorship of the Proletariat," in the *Communist International*, No. 7–8.)

We are waging a struggle against the "labour aristocracy" in the name of the masses of the workers and in order to win them over to our side; we are waging the struggle against the opportunist and social-chauvinist leaders in order to win the working class over to our side. It would be absurd to forget this most elementary and most self-evident truth. Yet it is this very absurdity that the German "Left" Communists perpetrate when, *because* of the reactionary and counter-revolutionary character of the trade union *top leadership*, they jump to the conclusion that . . . we must withdraw from the trade unions, refuse to work in them, and create new and *artificial* forms of labour organisation! This is so unpardonable a blunder that it is tantamount to the greatest service Communists could render the bourgeoisie. Like all the opportunist, social-chauvinist, and Kautskyite trade union leaders, our Mensheviks are nothing but "agents of the bourgeoisie in the working-class movement" (as we have always said the Mensheviks are), or "labour lieutenants of the capitalist class," to use the splendid and profoundly true expression of the followers of Daniel De Leon in America. To refuse to work in the reactionary trade unions means leaving the insufficiently developed or backward masses of workers under the influence of the reactionary leaders, the agents of the bourgeoisie, the labour aristocrats, or "workers who have become completely bourgeois" (cf. Engels's letter to Marx in 1858 about the British workers[9]).

This ridiculous "theory" that Communists should not work in reactionary trade unions reveals with the utmost clarity the frivolous attitude of the "Left" Communists towards the question of influencing the "masses," and their misuse of clamour about the

9. Marx and Engels, *Selected Correspondence* (Moscow 1965), p. 110.

"masses." If you want to help the "masses" and win the sympathy and support of the "masses," you should not fear difficulties, or pinpricks, chicanery, insults and persecution from the "leaders" (who, being opportunists and social-chauvinists, are in most cases directly or indirectly connected with the bourgeoisie and the police), but must absolutely *work wherever the masses are to be found.* You must be capable of any sacrifice, of overcoming the greatest obstacles, in order to carry on agitation and propaganda systematically, perseveringly, persistently and patiently in those institutions, societies and associations—even the most reactionary— in which proletarian or semi-proletarian masses are to be found. The trade unions and the workers' cooperatives (the latter sometimes, at least) are the very organisations in which the masses are to be found. According to figures quoted in the Swedish paper *Folkets Dagblad—Politiken* of March 10, 1920, the trade union membership in Great Britain increased from 5,500,000 at the end of 1917 to 6,600,000 at the end of 1918, an increase of 19 per cent. Towards the close of 1919, the membership was estimated at 7,500,000. I have not got the corresponding figures for France and Germany to hand, but absolutely incontestable and generally known facts testify to a rapid rise in the trade union membership in these countries too.

These facts make crystal clear something that is confirmed by thousands of other symptoms, namely, that class-consciousness and the desire for organisation are growing among the proletarian masses, among the rank and file, among the backward elements. Millions of workers in Great Britain, France and Germany are *for the first time* passing from a complete lack of organisation to the elementary, lowest, simplest, and (to those still thoroughly imbued with bourgeois-democratic prejudices) most easily comprehensible form of organisation, namely, the trade unions; yet the revolutionary but imprudent Left Communists stand by, crying out "the masses," "the masses!" but *refusing to work within the trade unions,* on the pretext that they are "reactionary," and invent a brandnew, immaculate little "Workers' Union," which is guiltless of bourgeois-democratic prejudices and innocent of craft or narrowminded craft-union sins, a union which, they claim, will be (!) a broad organisation. "Recognition of the Soviet system and the dictatorship" will be the *only* (!) condition of membership. (See the passage quoted above.)

It would be hard to imagine any greater ineptitude or greater harm to the revolution than that caused by the "Left" revolutionaries! Why, if we in Russia today, after two and a half years of unprecedented victories over the bourgeoisie of Russia and the Entente, were to make "recognition of the dictatorship" a condition of trade union membership, we would be doing a very foolish thing, damaging our influence among the masses, and helping the Mensheviks. The task devolving on Communists is to *convince* the backward elements, to work *among* them, and not to *fence themselves off* from them with artificial and childishly "Left" slogans.

There can be no doubt that the Gomperses, the Hendersons, the Jouhaux and the Legiens are very grateful to those "Left" revolutionaries who, like the German opposition "on principle" (heaven preserve us from such "principles"!), or like some of the revolutionaries in the American Industrial Workers of the World advocate quitting the reactionary trade unions and refusing to work in them. These men, the "leaders" of opportunism, will no doubt resort to every device of bourgeois diplomacy and to the aid of bourgeois governments, the clergy, the police and the courts, to keep Communists out of the trade unions, oust them by every means, make their work in the trade unions as unpleasant as possible, and insult, bait and persecute them. We must be able to stand up to all this, agree to make any sacrifice, and even—if need be—to resort to various stratagems, artifices and illegal methods, to evasions and subterfuges, as long as we get into the trade unions, remain in them, and carry on communist work within them at all costs. Under tsarism we had no "legal opportunities" whatsoever until 1905. However, when Zubatov, agent of the secret police, organised Black-Hundred workers' assemblies and workingmen's societies for the purpose of trapping revolutionaries and combating them, we sent members of our Party to these assemblies and into these societies (I personally remember one of them, Comrade Babushkin, a leading St. Petersburg factory worker, shot by order of the tsar's generals in 1906). They established contacts with the masses, were able to carry on their agitation, and succeeded in wresting workers from the influence of Zubatov's agents.[1] Of course, in Western Europe, which is imbued with most deep-rooted legalistic, constitutionalist and bourgeois-democratic prejudices, this is more difficult of achievement. However, it can and must be carried out, and systematically at that.

The Executive Committee of the Third International must, in my opinion, positively condemn, and call upon the next congress of the Communist International to condemn both the policy of refusing to work in reactionary trade unions in general (explaining in detail why such refusal is unwise, and what extreme harm it does to the cause of the proletarian revolution) and, in particular, the line of

---

1. The Gomperses, Hendersons, Jouhaux and Legiens are nothing but Zubatovs, differing from our Zubatov only in their European garb and polish, and the civilised, refined and democratically suave manner of conducting their despicable policy. [*Lenin*]

conduct of some members of the Communist Party of Holland, who—whether directly or indirectly, overtly or covertly, wholly or partly, it does not matter—have supported this erroneous policy. The Third International must break with the tactics of the Second International; it must not evade or play down points at issue, but must pose them in a straightforward fashion. The whole truth has been put squarely to the "Independents" (the Independent Social-Democratic Party of Germany); the whole truth must likewise be put squarely to the "Left" Communists.

VII. Should We Participate in Bourgeois Parliaments?

It is with the utmost contempt—and the utmost levity—that the German "Left" Communists reply to this question in the negative. Their arguments? In the passage quoted above we read: ". . . All reversion to parliamentary forms of struggle, which have become historically and politically obsolete, must be emphatically rejected. . . ." This is said with ridiculous pretentiousness, and is patently wrong. "Reversion" to parliamentarianism, forsooth! Perhaps there is already a Soviet republic in Germany? It does not look like it! How, then, can one speak of "reversion"? Is this not an empty phrase?

Parliamentarianism has become "historically obsolete." That is true in the propaganda sense. However, everybody knows that this is still a far cry from overcoming it in *practice*. Capitalism could have been declared—and with full justice—to be "historically obsolete" many decades ago, but that does not at all remove the need for a very long and very persistent struggle *on the basis* of capitalism. Parliamentarianism is "historically obsolete" from the standpoint of *world history*, i.e., the *era* of bourgeois parliamentarianism is over, and the *era* of the proletarian dictatorship has *begun*. That is incontestable. But world history is counted in decades. Ten or twenty years earlier or later makes no difference when measured with the yardstick of world history; from the standpoint of world history it is a trifle that cannot be considered even approximately. But for that very reason, it is a glaring theoretical error to apply the yardstick of world history to practical politics.

Is parliamentarianism "politically obsolete"? That is quite a different matter. If that were true, the position of the "Lefts" would be a strong one. But it has to be proved by a most searching analysis, and the "Lefts" do not even know how to approach the matter. In the "Theses on Parliamentarianism," published in the *Bulletin of the Provisional Bureau in Amsterdam of the Communist International* No. 1, February 1920, and obviously expressing the Dutch-

Left or Left-Dutch strivings, the analysis, as we shall see, is also hopelessly poor.

In the first place, contrary to the opinion of such outstanding political leaders as Rosa Luxemburg and Karl Liebknecht, the German "Lefts," as we know, considered parliamentarianism "politically obsolete" even in January 1919. We know that the "Lefts" were mistaken. This fact alone utterly destroys, at a single stroke, the proposition that parliamentarianism is "politically obsolete." It is for the "Lefts" to prove why their error, indisputable at that time, is no longer an error. They do not and cannot produce even a shred of proof. A political party's attitude towards its own mistakes is one of the most important and surest ways of judging how earnest the party is and how it fulfils *in practice* its obligations towards its *class* and the *working people*. Frankly acknowledging a mistake, ascertaining the reasons for it, analysing the conditions that have led up to it, and thrashing out the means of its rectification—that is the hallmark of a serious party; that is how it should perform its duties, and how it should educate and train its *class*, and then the *masses*. By failing to fulfil this duty and give the utmost attention and consideration to the study of their patent error, the "Lefts" in Germany (and in Holland) have proved that they are not a *party of a class*, but a circle, not a *party of the masses*, but a group of intellectualists and of a few workers who ape the worst features of intellectualism.

Second, in the same pamphlet of the Frankfurt group of "Lefts," which we have already cited in detail, we read: ". . . The millions of workers who still follow the policy of the Centre [the Catholic "Centre" Party] are counter-revolutionary. The rural proletarians provide the legions of counter-revolutionary troops." (Page 3 of the pamphlet.) Everything goes to show that this statement is far too sweeping and exaggerated. But the basic fact set forth here is incontrovertible, and its acknowledgement by the "Lefts" is particularly clear evidence of their mistake. How can one say that "parliamentarianism is politically obsolete," when "millions" and "legions" of *proletarians* are not only still in favour of parliamentarianism in general, but are downright "counter-revolutionary"!? It is obvious that parliamentarianism in Germany is *not yet* politically obsolete. It is obvious that the "Lefts" in Germany have mistaken *their desire*, their politico-ideological attitude, for objective reality. That is a most dangerous mistake for revolutionaries to make. In Russia —where, over a particularly long period and in particularly varied forms, the most brutal and savage yoke of tsarism produced revolutionaries of diverse shades, revolutionaries who displayed amazing devotion, enthusiasm, heroism and will power—in Russia we have observed this mistake of the revolutionaries at very close quarters; we have studied it very attentively and have a first-hand knowledge of it; that is why we can also see it especially clearly in others. Parliamentarianism is of course "politically obsolete" to the Communists in Germany; but—and that is the whole point—we must *not* regard what is obsolete *to us* as something obsolete *to a class, to the masses*. Here again we find that the "Lefts" do not know how to reason, do not know how to act as the party of a *class*, as the party of the *masses*. You must not sink to the level of the masses, to the level of the backward strata of the class. That is incontestable. You must tell them the bitter truth. You are in duty bound to call their bourgeois-democratic and parliamentary prejudices what they are— prejudices. But at the same time you must *soberly* follow the *actual* state of the class-consciousness and preparedness of the entire class (not only of its communist vanguard), and of all the *working people* (not only of their advanced elements.)

Even if only a fairly large *minority* of the industrial workers, and not "millions" and "legions," follow the lead of the Catholic clergy —and a similar minority of rural workers follow the land-owners and *kulaks* (*Grossbauern*)—it *undoubtedly* signifies that parliamentarianism in Germany has *not yet* politically outlived itself, that participation in parliamentary elections and in the struggle on the parliamentary rostrum is *obligatory* on the party of the revolutionary proletariat *specifically* for the purpose of educating the backward strata of *its own class*, and for the purpose of awakening and enlightening the undeveloped, downtrodden and ignorant rural *masses*. Whilst you lack the strength to do away with the bourgeois parliaments and every other type of reactionary institution, you *must* work within them because *it is there* that you will still find workers who are duped by the priests and stultified by the conditions of rural life; otherwise you risk turning into nothing but windbags.

Third, the "Left" Communists have a great deal to say in praise of us Bolsheviks. One sometimes feels like telling them to praise us less and to try to get a better knowledge of the Bolsheviks' tactics. We took part in the elections to the Constituent Assembly, the Russian bourgeois parliament, in September–November 1917. Were our tactics correct or not? If not, then this should be clearly stated and proved, for it is necessary in evolving the correct tactics for international communism. If they were correct, then certain conclusions must be drawn. Of course, there can be no question of placing conditions in Russia on a par with conditions in Western Europe. But as regards the particular question of the meaning of the concept that "parliamentarianism has become politically obsolete," due account should be taken of our experience, for unless concrete experience is taken into account such concepts very easily turn into empty phrases. In September–November 1917, did we, the Russian Bolsheviks, not have *more* right than any Western

Communists to consider that parliamentarianism was politically obsolete in Russia? Of course we did, for the point is not whether bourgeois parliaments have existed for a long time or a short time, but how far the masses of the working people are *prepared* (ideologically, politically and practically) to accept the Soviet system and to dissolve the bourgeois-democratic parliament (or allow it to be dissolved). It is an absolutely incontestable and fully established historical fact that, in September–November 1917, the urban working class and the soldiers and peasants of Russia were, because of a number of special conditions, exceptionally well prepared to accept the Soviet system and to disband the most democratic of bourgeois parliaments. Nevertheless, the Bolsheviks did *not* boycott the Constituent Assembly, but took part in the elections both before *and after* the proletariat conquered political power. That these elections yielded exceedingly valuable (and to the proletariat, highly useful) political results has, I make bold to hope, been proved by me in the above-mentioned article, which analyses in detail the returns of the elections to the Constituent Assembly in Russia.

The conclusion which follows from this is absolutely incontrovertible: it has been proved that, far from causing harm to the revolutionary proletariat, participation in a bourgeois-democratic parliament, even a few weeks before the victory of a Soviet republic and even *after* such a victory, actually helps that proletariat to *prove* to the backward masses why such parliaments deserve to be done away with; it *facilitates* their successful dissolution, and *helps* to make bourgeois parliamentarianism "politically obsolete." To ignore this experience, while at the same time claiming affiliation to the Communist *International*, which must work out its tactics internationally (not as narrow or exclusively national tactics, but as international tactics), means committing a gross error and actually abandoning internationalism in deed, while recognising it in word.

Now let us examine the "Dutch-Left" arguments in favour of non-participation in parliaments. The following is the text of Thesis No. 4, the most important of the above-mentioned "Dutch" theses:

> When the capitalist system of production has broken down, and society is in a state of revolution, parliamentary action gradually loses importance as compared with the action of the masses themselves. When, in these conditions, parliament becomes the centre and organ of the counter-revolution, whilst, on the other hand, the labouring class builds up the instruments of its power in the Soviets, it may even prove necessary to abstain from all and any participation in parliamentary action.

The first sentence is obviously wrong, since action by the masses, a big strike, for instance, is more important than parliamentary activity at *all* times, and not only during a revolution or in a revolutionary situation. This obviously untenable and historically and politically incorrect argument merely shows very clearly that the authors completely ignore both the general European experience (the French experience before the revolutions of 1848 and 1870; the German experience of 1878–90, etc.) and the Russian experience (see above) of the importance of *combining* legal and illegal struggle. This question is of immense importance both in general and in particular, because in *all* civilised and advanced countries the time is rapidly approaching when such a combination will more and more become— and has already partly become—mandatory on the party of the revolutionary proletariat, inasmuch as civil war between the proletariat and the bourgeoisie is maturing and is imminent, and because of savage persecution of the Communists by republican governments and bourgeois governments generally, which resort to any violation of legality (the example of America is edifying enough), etc. The Dutch, and the Lefts in general, have utterly failed to understand this highly important question.

The second sentence is, in the first place, historically wrong. We Bolsheviks participated in the most counter-revolutionary parliaments, and experience has shown that this participation was not only useful but indispensable to the party of the revolutionary proletariat, after the first bourgeois revolution in Russia (1905), so as to pave the way for the second bourgeois revolution (February 1917), and then for the socialist revolution (October 1917). In the second place, this sentence is amazingly illogical. If a parliament becomes an organ and a "centre" (in reality it never has been and never can be a "centre," but that is by the way) of counter-revolution, while the workers are building up the instruments of their power in the form of the Soviets, then it follows that the workers must prepare—ideologically, politically and technically—for the struggle of the Soviets against parliament, for the dispersal of parliament by the Soviets. But it does not at all follow that this dispersal is hindered, or is not facilitated, by the presence of a Soviet opposition *within* the counter-revolutionary parliament. In the course of our victorious struggle against Denikin and Kolchak, we never found that the existence of a Soviet and proletarian opposition in their camp was immaterial to our victories. We know perfectly well that the dispersal of the Constituent Assembly on January 5, 1918, was not hampered but was actually facilitated by the fact that, within the counter-revolutionary Constituent Assembly which was about to be dispersed, there was a consistent Bolshevik, as well as an inconsistent Left Socialist-Revolutionary, Soviet opposition. The authors of the theses are engaged in muddled thinking; they have forgotten the experience of many, if not all, revolutions, which shows the great usefulness, during a revolution, of a *combination* of mass action outside a reactionary parliament with an opposition sympathetic to (or, better still, directly supporting) the revolution within it. The Dutch, and the "Lefts" in general, argue in this respect like doctrinaires of the revolution, who have never taken part in a real revolution, have never given thought to the history of revolutions, or have naïvely mistaken subjective "rejection" of a reactionary institution for its actual destruction by the combined operation of a number of objective factors. The surest way of discrediting and damaging a new political (and not only political) idea is to reduce it to absurdity on the plea of defending it. For any truth, if "overdone" (as Dietzgen Senior put it), if exaggerated, or if carried beyond the limits of its actual applicability, can be reduced to an absurdity, and is even bound to become an absurdity under these conditions. That is just the kind of disservice the Dutch and German Lefts are rendering to the new truth of the Soviet form of government being superior to bourgeois-democratic parliaments. Of course, anyone would be in error who voiced the outmoded viewpoint or in general considered it impermissible, in all and any circumstances, to reject participation in bourgeois parliaments. I cannot attempt here to formulate the conditions under which a boycott is useful, since the object of this pamphlet is far more modest, namely, to study Russian experience in connection with certain topical questons of international communist tactics. Russian experience has provided us with one successful and correct instance (1905), and another that was incorrect (1906), of the use of a boycott by the Bolsheviks. Analysing the first case, we see that we succeeded in *preventing* a reactionary government from *convening* a reactionary parliament in a situation in which extra-parliamentary revolutionary mass action (strikes in particular) was developing at great speed, when not a single section of the proletariat and the peasantry could support the reactionary government in any way, and when the revolutionary proletariat was gaining influence over the backward masses through the strike struggle and through the agrarian movement. It is quite obvious that *this* experience is not applicable to present-day European conditions. It is likewise quite obvious—and the foregoing arguments bear this out—that the advocacy, even if with reservations, by the Dutch and the other "Lefts" of refusal to participate in parliaments is fundamentally wrong and detrimental to the cause of the revolutionary proletariat.

In Western Europe and America, parliament has become most odious to the revolutionary vanguard of the working class. That cannot be denied. It can readily be understood, for it is difficult to imagine anything more infamous, vile or treacherous than the behaviour of the vast majority of socialist and Social-Democratic parliamentary deputies during and after the war. It would, however,

be not only unreasonable but actually criminal to yield to this
mood when deciding *how* this generally recognised evil should be
fought. In many countries of Western Europe, the revolutionary
mood, we might say, is at present a "novelty," or a "rarity," which
has all too long been vainly and impatiently awaited; perhaps that
is why people so easily yield to that mood. Certainly, without a
revolutionary mood among the masses, and without conditions facilitating the growth of this mood, revolutionary tactics will never
develop into action. In Russia, however, lengthy, painful and san-
guinary experience has taught us the truth that revolutionary tactics
cannot be built on a revolutionary mood alone. Tactics must be
based on a sober and strictly objective appraisal of *all* the class
forces in a particular state (and of the states that surround it, and
of all states the world over) as well as of the experience of revolutionary movements. It is very easy to show one's "revolutionary"
temper merely by hurling abuse at parliamentary opportunism, or
merely by repudiating participation in parliaments; its very ease,
however, cannot turn this into a solution of a difficult, a very
difficult, problem. It is far more difficult to create a really revolutionary parliamentary group in a European parliament than it was
in Russia. That stands to reason. But it is only a particular expression of the general truth that it was easy for Russia, in the specific
and historically unique situation of 1917, to *start* the socialist revolution, but it will be more difficult for Russia than for the European
countries to *continue* the revolution and bring it to its consummation. I had occasion to point this out already at the beginning of
1918, and our experience of the past two years has entirely confirmed the correctness of this view. Certain specific conditions, viz.,
(1) the possibility of linking up the Soviet revolution with the
ending, as a consequence of this revolution, of the imperialist war,
which had exhausted the workers and peasants to an incredible
degree; (2) the possibility of taking temporary advantage of the
mortal conflict between the world's two most powerful groups of
imperialist robbers, who were unable to unite against their Soviet
enemy; (3) the possibility of enduring a comparatively lengthy civil
war, partly owing to the enormous size of the country and to the
poor means of communication; (4) the existence of such a profound bourgeois-democratic revolutionary movement among the
peasantry that the party of the proletariat was able to adopt the
revolutionary demands of the peasant party (the Socialist-Revolutionary Party, the majority of whose members were definitely hostile
to Bolshevism) and realise them at once, thanks to the conquest of
political power by the proletariat—all these specific conditions do
not at present exist in Western Europe, and a repetition of such or
similar conditions will not occur so easily. Incidentally, apart from

a number of other causes, that is why it is more difficult for Western Europe to *start* a socialist revolution than it was for us. To attempt to "circumvent" this difficulty by "skipping" the arduous job of utilising reactionary parliaments for revolutionary purposes is absolutely childish. You want to create a new society, yet you fear the difficulties involved in forming a good parliamentary group made up of convinced, devoted and heroic Communists, in a reactionary parliament! Is that not childish? If Karl Liebknecht in Germany and Z. Höglund in Sweden were able, even without mass support from below, to set examples of the truly revolutionary utilisation of reactionary parliaments, why should a rapidly growing revolutionary mass party, in the midst of the post-war disillusionment and embitterment of the masses, be unable to *forge* a communist group in the worst of parliaments? It is because, in Western Europe, the backward masses of the workers and—to an even greater degree—of the small peasants are much more imbued with bourgeois-democratic and parliamentary prejudices than they were in Russia; because of that, it is *only* from within such institutions as bourgeois parliaments that Communists can (and must) wage a long and persistent struggle, undaunted by any difficulties, to expose, dispel and overcome these prejudices.

The German "Lefts" complain of bad "leaders" in their party, give way to despair, and even arrive at a ridiculous "negation" of "leaders." But in conditions in which it is often necessary to hide "leaders" underground, the *evolution* of good "leaders," reliable, tested and authoritative, is a very difficult matter; these difficulties *cannot* be successfully overcome without combining legal and illegal work, and *without testing the "leaders," among other ways*, in parliaments. Criticism—the most keen, ruthless and uncompromising criticism—should be directed, not against parliamentarianism or parliamentary activities, but against those leaders who are unable—and still more against those who are *unwilling*—to utilise parliamentary elections and the parliamentary rostrum in a revolutionary and communist manner. Only such criticism—combined, of course, with the dismissal of incapable leaders and their replacement by capable ones—will constitute useful and fruitful revolutionary work that will simultaneously train the "leaders" to be worthy of the working class and of all working people, and train the masses to be able properly to understand the political situation and the often very complicated and intricate tasks that spring from that situation.[2]

2. I have had too little opportunity to acquaint myself with "Left-wing" communism in Italy. Comrade Bordiga and his faction of Abstentionist Communists (*Comunista astensionista*) are certainly wrong in advocating non-participation in parliament. But on one point, it seems to me, Comrade Bordiga is right—as far as

VIII. No Compromises?

In the quotation from the Frankfurt pamphlet, we have seen how emphatically the "Lefts" have advanced this slogan. It is sad to see people who no doubt consider themselves Marxists, and want to be Marxists, forget the fundamental truths of Marxism. This is what Engels—who, like Marx, was one of those rarest of authors whose every sentence in every one of their fundamental works contains a remarkably profound content—wrote in 1874, against the manifesto of the thirty-three Blanquist Communards:

"We are Communists" [the Blanquist Communards wrote in their manifesto], "because we want to attain our goal without stopping at intermediate stations, without any compromises, which only postpone the day of victory and prolong the period of slavery."

The German Communists are Communists because, through all the intermediate stations and all compromises created, not by them but by the course of historical development, they clearly perceive and constantly pursue the final aim—the abolition of classes and the creation of a society in which there will no longer be private ownership of land or of the means of production. The thirty-three Blanquists are Communists just because they imagine that, merely because *they* want to skip the intermediate stations and compromises, the matter is settled, and if "it begins" in the next few days—which they take for granted—and they take over power, "communism will be introduced" the day after tomorrow. If that is not immediately possible, they are not Communists.

What childish innocence it is to present one's own impatience as a theoretically convincing argument! [Frederick Engels, "Programme of the Blanquist Communards," from the German Social-Democratic newspaper *Volksstaat*, 1874, No. 73, given in the Russian translation, *Articles, 1871–1875*, Petrograd, 1919, pp. 52–53.]

can be judged from two issues of his paper, *Il Soviet* (Nos. 3 and 4, January 18 and February 1, 1920), from four issues of Comrade Serrati's excellent periodical, *Comunismo* (Nos. 1–4, October 1–November 30, 1919), and from separate issues of Italian bourgeois papers which I have seen. Comrade Bordiga and his group are right in attacking Turati and his partisans, who remain in a party which has recognised Soviet power and the dictatorship of the proletariat, and yet continue their former pernicious and opportunist policy as members of parliament. Of course, in tolerating this, Comrade Serrati and the entire Italian Socialist Party are making a mistake which threatens to do as much harm and give rise to the same dangers as it did in Hungary, where the Hungarian Turatis sabotaged both the party and the Soviet government from within. Such a mistaken, inconsistent, or spineless attitude towards the opportunist parliamentarians gives rise to "Left-wing" communism, on the one hand, and *to a certain extent* justifies its existence, on the other. Comrade Serrati is obviously wrong when he accuses Deputy Turati of being "inconsistent" (*Comunismo* No. 3), for it is the Italian Socialist Party itself that is inconsistent in tolerating such opportunist parliamentarians as Turati and Co. [*Lenin*]

In the same article, Engels expresses his profound esteem for Vaillant, and speaks of the "unquestionable merit" of the latter (who, like Guesde, was one of the most prominent leaders of international socialism until their betrayal of socialism in August 1914). But Engels does not fail to give a detailed analysis of an obvious error. Of course, to very young and inexperienced revolutionaries, as well as to petty-bourgeois revolutionaries of even very respectable age and great experience, it seems extremely "dangerous," incomprehensible and wrong to "permit compromises." Many sophists (being unusually or excessively "experienced" politicians) reason exactly in the same way as the British leaders of opportunism mentioned by Comrade Lansbury: "If the Bolsheviks are permitted a certain compromise, why should we not be permitted any kind of compromise?" However, proletarians schooled in numerous strikes (to take only this manifestation of the class struggle) usually assimilate in admirable fashion the very profound truth (philosophical, historical, political and psychological) expounded by Engels. Every proletarian has been through strikes and has experienced "compromises" with the hated oppressors and exploiters, when the workers have had to return to work either without having achieved anything or else agreeing to only a partial satisfaction of their demands. Every proletarian—as a result of the conditions of the mass struggle and the acute intensification of class antagonisms he lives among—sees the difference between a compromise enforced by objective conditions (such as lack of strike funds, no outside support, starvation and exhaustion)—a compromise which in no way minimises the revolutionary devotion and readiness to carry on the struggle on the part of the workers who have agreed to such a compromise—and, on the other hand, a compromise by traitors who try to ascribe to objective causes their self-interest (strike-breakers also enter into "compromises"!), their cowardice, desire to toady to the capitalists, and readiness to yield to intimidation, sometimes to persuasion, sometimes to sops, and sometimes to flattery from the capitalists. (The history of the British labour movement provides a very large number of instances of such treacherous compromises by British trade union leaders, but, in one form or another, almost all workers in all countries have witnessed the same sort of thing.)

Naturally, there are individual cases of exceptional difficulty and complexity, when the greatest efforts are necessary for a proper assessment of the actual character of this or that "compromise," just as there are cases of homicide when it is by no means easy to establish whether the homicide was fully justified and even necessary (as, for example, legitimate self-defence), or due to unpardonable negligence, or even to a cunningly executed perfidious plan. Of course, in politics, where it is sometimes a matter of extremely complex relations—national and international—between classes and parties, very many cases will arise that will be much more difficult than the question of a legitimate "compromise" in a strike or a treacherous "compromise" by a strike-breaker, treacherous leader, etc. It would be absurd to formulate a recipe or general rule ("No compromises!") to suit all cases. One must use one's own brains and be able to find one's bearings in each particular instance. It is, in fact, one of the functions of a party organisation and of party leaders worthy of the name, to acquire, through the prolonged, persistent, variegated and comprehensive efforts of all thinking representatives of a given class,[3] the knowledge, experience and—in addition to knowledge and experience—the political flair necessary for the speedy and correct solution of complex political problems.

Naïve and quite inexperienced people imagine that the permissibility of compromise *in general* is sufficient to obliterate any distinction between opportunism, against which we are waging, and must wage, an unremitting struggle, and revolutionary Marxism, or communism. But if such people do not yet know that in nature and in society *all* distinctions are fluid and up to a certain point conventional, nothing can help them but lengthy training, education, enlightenment, and political and everyday experience. In the practical questions that arise in the politics of any particular or specific historical moment, it is important to single out those which display the principal type of intolerable and treacherous compromises, such as embody an opportunism that is fatal to the revolutionary class, and to exert all efforts to explain them and combat them. During the 1914–18 imperialist war between two groups of equally predatory countries, social-chauvinism was the principal and fundamental type of opportunism, i.e., support of "defence of country," which in *such* a war was really equivalent to defence of the predatory interests of one's "own" bourgeoisie. After the war, defence of the robber League of Nations, defence of direct or indirect alliances with the bourgeoisie of one's own country against the revolutionary proletariat and the "Soviet" movement, and defence of bourgeois democracy and bourgeois parliamentarianism against "Soviet power" became the principal manifestations of those intolerable

---

3. Within every class, even in the conditions prevailing in the most enlightened countries, even within the most advanced class, and even when the circumstances of the moment have aroused all its spiritual forces to an exceptional degree, there always are—and inevitably *will be* as long as classes exist, as long as a classless society has not fully consolidated itself, and has not developed on its own foundations—representatives of the class who do *not* think, and are incapable of thinking, for themselves. Capitalism would not be the oppressor of the masses that it actually is, if things were otherwise. [*Lenin*]

and treacherous compromises, whose sum total constituted an opportunism fatal to the revolutionary proletariat and its cause.

". . . All compromise with other parties . . . any policy of manoeuvring and compromise must be emphatically rejected," the German Lefts write in the Frankfurt pamphlet. It is surprising that, with such views, these Lefts do not emphatically condemn Bolshevism! After all, the German Lefts cannot but know that the entire history of Bolshevism, both before and after the October Revolution, is *full* of instances of changes of tack, conciliatory tactics and compromises with other parties, including bourgeois parties!

To carry on a war for the overthrow of the international bourgeoisie, a war which is a hundred times more difficult, protracted and complex than the most stubborn of ordinary wars between states, and to renounce in advance any change of tack, or any utilisation of a conflict of interests (even if temporary) among one's enemies, or any conciliation or compromise with possible allies (even if they are temporary, unstable, vacillating or conditional allies)—is that not ridiculous in the extreme? Is it not like making a difficult ascent of an unexplored and hitherto inaccessible mountain and refusing in advance ever to move in zigzags, ever to retrace one's steps, or ever to abandon a course once selected, and to try others? And yet people so immature and inexperienced (if youth were the explanation, it would not be so bad; young people are preordained to talk such nonsense for a certain period) have met with support—whether direct or indirect, open or covert, whole or partial, it does not matter—from some members of the Communist Party of Holland.

After the first socialist revolution of the proletariat, and the overthrow of the bourgeoisie in some country, the proletariat of that country remains *for a long time weaker* than the bourgeoisie, simply because of the latter's extensive international links, and also because of the spontaneous and continuous restoration and regeneration of capitalism and the bourgeoisie by the small commodity producers of the country which has overthrown the bourgeoisie. The more powerful enemy can be vanquished only by exerting the utmost effort, and by the most thorough, careful, attentive, skilful and *obligatory* use of any, even the smallest, rift between the enemies, any conflict of interests among the bourgeoisie of the various countries and among the various groups or types of bourgeoisie within the various countries, and also by taking advantage of any, even the smallest, opportunity of winning a mass ally, even though this ally is temporary, vacillating, unstable, unreliable and conditional. Those who do not understand this reveal a failure to understand even the smallest grain of Marxism, of modern scientific socialism *in general*. Those who have not proved *in practice*, over a fairly considerable period of time and in fairly varied political situations, their ability to apply this truth in practice have not yet learned to help the revolutionary class in its struggle to emancipate all toiling humanity from the exploiters. And this applies equally to the period *before* and *after* the proletariat has won political power.

Our theory is not a dogma, but a *guide to action*, said Marx and Engels.[4] The greatest blunder, the greatest crime, committed by such "out-and-out" Marxists as Karl Kautsky, Otto Bauer, etc., is that they have not understood this and have been unable to apply it at crucial moments of the proletarian revolution. "Political activity is not like the pavement of Nevsky Prospect" (the well-kept, broad and level pavement of the perfectly straight principal thoroughfare of St. Petersburg), N. G. Chernyshevsky, the great Russian socialist of the pre-Marxist period, used to say. Since Chernyshevsky's time, disregard or forgetfulness of this truth has cost Russian revolutionaries countless sacrifices. We must strive at all costs to *prevent* the Left Communists and West-European and American revolutionaries that are devoted to the working class from paying *as dearly* as the backward Russians did to learn this truth.

Prior to the downfall of tsarism, the Russian revolutionary Social-Democrats made repeated use of the services of the bourgeois liberals, i.e., they concluded numerous practical compromises with the latter. In 1901–2, even prior to the appearance of Bolshevism, the old editorial board of *Iskra* (consisting of Plekhanov, Axelrod, Zasulich, Martov, Potresov and myself) concluded (not for long, it is true) a formal political alliance with Struve, the political leader of bourgeois liberalism, while at the same time being able to wage an unremitting and most merciless ideological and political struggle against bourgeois liberalism and against the slightest manifestations of its influence in the working-class movement. The Bolsheviks have always adhered to this policy. Since 1905 they have systematically advocated an alliance between the working class and the peasantry, against the liberal bourgeoisie and tsarism, never, however, refusing to support the bourgeoisie against tsarism (for instance, during second rounds of elections, or during second ballots) and never ceasing their relentless ideological and political struggle against the Socialist-Revolutionaries, the bourgeois-revolutionary peasant party, exposing them as petty-bourgeois democrats who have falsely described themselves as socialists. During the Duma elections of 1907, the Bolsheviks entered briefly into a formal political bloc with the Socialist-Revolutionaries. Between 1903 and

4. Lenin is referring to a passage in Engels's letter to F. A. Sorge of November 29, 1886, where, in criticising the German Social-Democrat exiles in America, Engels said that for them theory was "a credo, not a guide to action." See Marx and Engels, *Selected Correspondence* (Moscow, 1965), p. 395.

1912, there were periods of several years in which we were formally united with the Mensheviks in a single Social-Democratic Party, but we *never stopped* our ideological and political struggle against them as opportunists and vehicles of bourgeois influence on the proletariat. During the war, we concluded certain compromises with the Kautskyites, with the Left Mensheviks (Martov), and with a section of the Socialist-Revolutionaries (Chernov and Natanson); we were together with them at Zimmerwald and Kienthal, and issued joint manifestos. However, we never ceased and never relaxed our ideological and political struggle against the Kautskyites, Martov and Chernov (when Natanson died in 1919, a "Revolutionary-Communist" Narodnik, he was very close to and almost in agreement with us). At the very moment of the October Revolution, we entered into an informal but very important (and very successful) political bloc with the petty-bourgeois peasantry by adopting the *Socialist-Revolutionary* agrarian programme *in its entirety*, without a single alteration—i.e., we effected an undeniable compromise in order to prove to the peasants that we wanted, not to "steamroller" them but to reach agreement with them. At the same time we proposed (and soon after effected) a formal political bloc, including participation in the government, with the Left Socialist-Revolutionaries, who dissolved this bloc after the conclusion of the Treaty of Brest-Litovsk and then, in July 1918, went to the length of armed rebellion, and subsequently of an armed struggle, against us.

It is therefore understandable why the attacks made by the German Lefts against the Central Committee of the Communist Party of Germany for entertaining the idea of a bloc with the Independents (the Independent Social-Democratic Party of Germany—the Kautskyites) are absolutely inane, in our opinion, and clear proof that the "Lefts" are in the *wrong*. In Russia, too, there were Right Mensheviks (participants in the Kerensky government), who corresponded to the German Scheidemanns, and Left Mensheviks (Martov), corresponding to the German Kautskyites and standing in opposition to the Right Mensheviks. A gradual shift of the worker masses from the Mensheviks over to the Bolsheviks was to be clearly seen in 1917. At the First All-Russian Congress of Soviets, held in June 1917, we had only 13 per cent of the votes; the Socialist-Revolutionaries and the Mensheviks had a majority. At the Second Congress of Soviets (October 25, 1917, old style) we had 51 per cent of the votes. Why is it that in Germany the *same* and absolutely *identical* shift of the workers from Right to Left did not immediately strengthen the Communists, but first strengthened the midway Independent Party, although the latter never had independent political ideas or an independent policy, but merely wavered between the Scheidemanns and the Communists?

One of the evident reasons was the *erroneous* tactics of the German Communists, who must fearlessly and honestly admit this error and learn to rectify it. The error consisted in their denial of the need to take part in the reactionary bourgeois parliaments and in the reactionary trade unions; the error consisted in numerous manifestations of the "Left-wing" infantile disorder which has now come to the surface and will consequently be cured the more thoroughly, the more rapidly and with greater advantage to the organism.

The German Independent Social-Democratic Party is obviously not a homogeneous body. Alongside the old opportunist leaders (Kautsky, Hilferding and apparently, to a considerable extent, Crispien, Ledebour and others)—these have revealed their inability to understand the significance of Soviet power and the dictatorship of the proletariat, and their inability to lead the proletariat's revolutionary struggle—there has emerged in this party a Left and proletarian wing, which is growing most rapidly. Hundreds of thousands of members of this party (which has, I think, a membership of some three-quarters of a million) are proletarians who are abandoning Scheidemann and are rapidly going over to communism. This proletarian wing has already proposed—at the Leipizig Congress of the Independents (1919)—immediate and unconditional affiliation to the Third International. To fear a "compromise" with this wing of the party is positively ridiculous. On the contrary, it is the *duty* of Communists to seek *and find* a suitable form of compromise with them, a compromise which, on the one hand, will facilitate and accelerate the necessary complete fusion with this wing and, on the other, will in no way hamper the Communists in their ideological and political struggle against the opportunist Right wing of the Independents. It will probably be no easy matter to devise a suitable form of compromise—but only a charlatan could promise the German workers and the German Communists an "easy" road to victory.

Capitalism would not be capitalism if the proletariat *pur sang* were not surrounded by a large number of exceedingly motley types intermediate between the proletarian and the semi-proletarian (who earns his livelihood in part by the sale of his labour-power), between the semi-proletarian and the small peasant (and petty artisan, handicraft worker and small master in general), between the small peasant and the middle peasant, and so on, and if the proletariat itself were not divided into more developed and less developed strata, if it were not divided according to territorial origin, trade, sometimes according to religion, and so on. From all this follows the necessity, the absolute necessity, for the Communist Party, the vanguard of the proletariat, its class-conscious section, to resort to changes of tack, to conciliation and compromises with the various groups of proletarians, with the various parties of the workers and small masters. It is entirely a matter of *knowing how* to apply these tactics in order to *raise*—not lower—the *general* level of proletarian class-consciousness, revolutionary spirit, and ability to fight and win. Incidentally, it should be noted that the Bolsheviks' victory over the Mensheviks called for the application of tactics of changes of tack, conciliation and compromises, not only before *but also after* the October Revolution of 1917, but the changes of tack and compromises were, of course, such as assisted, boosted and consolidated the Bolsheviks at the expense of the Mensheviks. The petty-bourgeois democrats (including the Mensheviks) inevitably vacillate between the bourgeoisie and the proletariat, between bourgeois democracy and the Soviet system, between reformism and revolutionism, between love for the workers and fear of the proletarian dictatorship, etc. The Communists' proper tactics should consist in *utilising* these vacillations, not ignoring them; utilising them calls for concessions to elements that are turning towards the proletariat —whenever and in the measure that they turn towards the proletariat—in addition to fighting those who turn towards the bourgeoisie. As a result of the application of the correct tactics, Menshevism began to disintegrate, and has been disintegrating more and more in our country; the stubbornly opportunist leaders are being isolated, and the best of the workers and the best elements among the petty-bourgeois democrats are being brought into our camp. This is a lengthy process, and the hasty "decision"—"No compromises, no manoeuvres"—can only prejudice the strengthening of the revolutionary proletariat's influence and the enlargement of its forces.

Lastly, one of the undoubted errors of the German "Lefts" lies in their downright refusal to recognise the Treaty of Versailles. The more "weightily" and "pompously," the more "emphatically" and peremptorily this viewpoint is formulated (by K. Horner, for instance), the less sense it seems to make. It is not enough, under the present conditions of the international proletarian revolution, to repudiate the preposterous absurdities of "National Bolshevism" (Laufenberg and others), which has gone to the length of advocating a bloc with the German bourgeoisie for a war against the Entente. One must realise that it is utterly false tactics to refuse to admit that a Soviet Germany (if a German Soviet republic were soon to arise) would have to recognise the Treaty of Versailles for a time, and to submit to it. From this it does not follow that the Independents—at a time when the Scheidemanns were in the government, when the Soviet government in Hungary had not yet been overthrown, and when it was still possible that a Soviet revolution in Vienna would support Soviet Hungary—were right, *under the circumstances*, in putting forward the demand that the Treaty of

Versailles should be signed. At that time the independents tacked and manoeuvred very clumsily, for they more or less accepted responsibility for the Scheidemann traitors, and more or less backslid from advocacy of a ruthless (and most calmly conducted) class war against the Scheidemanns, to advocacy of a "classless" or "above-class" standpoint.

In the present situation, however, the German Communists should obviously not deprive themselves of freedom of action by giving a positive and categorical promise to repudiate the Treaty of Versailles in the event of communism's victory. That would be absurd. They should say: the Scheidemanns and the Kautskyites have committed a number of acts of treachery hindering (and in part quite ruining) the chances of an alliance with Soviet Russia and Soviet Hungary. We Communists will do all we can to *facilitate* and *pave the way* for such an alliance. However, we are in no way obligated to repudiate the Treaty of Versailles, come what may, or to do so at once. The possibility of its successful repudiation will depend, not only on the German, but also on the international successes of the Soviet movement. The Scheidemanns and the Kautskyites have hampered this movement; we are helping it. That is the gist of the matter; therein lies the fundamental difference. And if our class enemies, the exploiters and their Scheidemann and Kautskyite lackeys, have missed many an opportunity of strengthening both the German and the international Soviet movement, of strengthening both the German and the international Soviet revolution, the blame lies with them. The Soviet revolution in Germany will strengthen the international Soviet movement, which is the strongest bulwark (and the only reliable, invincible and worldwide bulwark) against the Treaty of Versailles and against international imperialism in general. To give absolute, categorical and immediate precedence to liberation from the Treaty of Versailles and to give it *precedence over the question* of liberating *other* countries oppressed by imperialism, from the yoke of imperialism, is philistine nationalism (worthy of the Kautskys, the Hilferdings, the Otto Bauers and Co.), not revolutionary internationalism. The overthrow of the bourgeoisie in any of the large European countries, including Germany, would be such a gain for the international revolution that, for its sake, one can, and if necessary should, tolerate a *more prolonged existence of the Treaty of Versailles*. If Russia, standing alone, could endure the Treaty of Brest-Litovsk for several months, to the advantage of the revolution, there is nothing impossible in a Soviet Germany, allied with Soviet Russia, enduring the existence of the Treaty of Versailles for a longer period, to the advantage of the revolution.

The imperialists of France, Britain, etc., are trying to provoke and ensnare the German Communists: "Say that you will not sign the Treaty of Versailles!" they urge. Like babes, the Left Communists fall into the trap laid for them, instead of skilfully manoeuvring against the crafty and, *at present*, stronger enemy, and instead of telling him, "We shall sign the Treaty of Versailles now." It is folly, not revolutionism, to deprive ourselves in advance of any freedom of action, openly to inform an enemy who is at present better armed than we are whether we shall fight him, and when. To accept battle at a time when it is obviously advantageous to the enemy, but not to us, is criminal; political leaders of the revolutionary class are absolutely useless if they are incapable of "changing tack, or offering conciliation and compromise" in order to take evasive action in a patently disadvantageous battle.

IX. "Left-Wing" Communism in Great Britain

There is no Communist Party in Great Britain as yet, but there is a fresh, broad, powerful and rapidly growing communist movement among the workers, which justifies the best hopes. There are several political parties and organisations (the British Socialist Party, the Socialist Labour Party, the South Wales Socialist Society, the Workers' Socialist Federation), which desire to form a Communist Party and are already negotiating among themselves to this end. In its issue of February 21, 1920, Vol. VI, No. 48, *The Workers' Dreadnought*, weekly organ of the last of the organisations mentioned, carried an article by the editor, Comrade Sylvia Pankhurst, entitled "Towards a Communist Party." The article outlines the progress of the negotiations between the four organisations mentioned, for the formation of a united Communist Party, on the basis of affiliation to the Third International, the recognition of the Soviet system instead of parliamentarianism, and the recognition of the dictatorship of the proletariat. It appears that one of the greatest obstacles to the immediate formation of a united Communist Party is presented by the disagreement on the questions of participation in Parliament and on whether the new Communist Party should affiliate to the old, trade-unionist, opportunist and social-chauvinist Labour Party, which is mostly made up of trade unions. The Workers' Socialist Federation and the Socialist Labour Party[5] are opposed to taking part in parliamentary elections and in Parliament, and they are opposed to affiliation to the Labour Party; in this they disagree with all or with most of the members of the

---

5. I believe this party is opposed to affiliation to the Labour Party but not all its members are opposed to participation in Parliament. [*Lenin*]

British Socialist Party, which they regard as the "Right wing of the Communist parties" in Great Britain. (Page 5, Sylvia Pankhurst's article.)

Thus, the main division is the same as in Germany, notwithstanding the enormous difference in the forms in which the disagreements manifest themselves (in Germany the form is far closer to the "Russian" than it is in Great Britain), and in a number of other things. Let us examine the arguments of the "Lefts."

On the question of participation in Parliament, Comrade Sylvia Pankhurst refers to an article in the same issue, by Comrade Gallacher, who writes in the name of the Scottish Workers' Council in Glasgow.

> The above council [he writes] is definitely anti-parliamentarian, and has behind it the Left wing of the various political bodies. We represent the revolutionary movement in Scotland, striving continually to build up a revolutionary organisation within the industries [in various branches of production], and a Communist Party based on social committees, throughout the country. For a considerable time we have been sparring with the official parliamentarians. We have not considered it necessary to declare open warfare on them, and they are *afraid* to open an attack on us.
>
> But this state of affairs cannot long continue. We are winning all along the line.
>
> The rank and file of the I.L.P. in Scotland is becoming more and more disgusted with the thought of Parliament, and the Soviets [the Russian word transliterated into English is used] or Workers' Councils are being supported by almost every branch. This is very serious, of course, for the gentlemen who look to politics for a profession, and they are using any and every means to persuade their members to come back into the parliamentary fold. Revolutionary comrades *must not* [all italics are the author's] give any support to this gang. Our fight here is going to be a difficult one. One of the worst features of it will be the treachery of those whose personal ambition is a more impelling force than their regard for the revolution. Any support given to parliamentarism is simply assisting to put power into the hands of our British Scheidemanns and Noskes. Henderson, Clynes and Co. are hopelessly reactionary. The official I.L.P. is more and more coming under the control of middle-class Liberals, who . . . have found their "spiritual home" in the camp of Messrs. MacDonald, Snowden and Co. The official I.L.P. is bitterly hostile to the Third International, the rank and file is for it. Any support to the parliamentary opportunists is simply playing into the hands of the former. The B.S.P. doesn't count at all here. . . . What is wanted here is a sound revolutionary industrial organisation, and a Communist Party working along clear, well-defined, scientific lines. If our comrades can assist us in building these, we will take their

help gladly; if they cannot, for God's sake let them keep out altogether, lest they betray the revolution by lending their support to the reactionaries, who are so eagerly clamouring for parliamentary "honours" (?) [the query mark is the author's] and who are so anxious to prove that they *can rule* as effectively as the "boss" class politicians themselves.

In my opinion, this letter to the editor expresses excellently the temper and point of view of the young Communists, or of rank-and-file workers who are only just beginning to accept communism. This temper is highly gratifying and valuable; we must learn to appreciate and support it for, in its absence, it would be hopeless to expect the victory of the proletarian revolution in Great Britain, or in any other country for that matter. People who can give expression to this temper of the masses, and are able to evoke such a temper (which is very often dormant, unconscious and latent) among the masses, should be appreciated and given every assistance. At the same time, we must tell them openly and frankly that a state of mind is *by itself* insufficient for leadership of the masses in a great revolutionary struggle, and that the cause of the revolution may well be harmed by certain errors that people who are most devoted to the cause of the revolution are about to commit, or are committing. Comrade Gallacher's letter undoubtedly reveals the rudiments of *all* the mistakes that are being made by the German "Left" Communists and were made by the Russian "Left" Bolsheviks in 1908 and 1918.

The writer of the letter is full of a noble and working-class hatred for the bourgeois "class politicians" (a hatred understood and shared, however, not only by proletarians but by all working people, by all *Kleinen Leuten*,[6] to use the German expression). In a representative of the oppressed and exploited masses, this hatred is truly the "beginning of all wisdom," the basis of any socialist and communist movement and of its success. The writer, however, has apparently lost sight of the fact that politics is a science and an art that does not fall from the skies or come gratis, and that, if it wants to overcome the bourgeoisie, the proletariat must train its *own* proletarian "class politicians," of a kind in no way inferior to bourgeois politicians.

The writer of the letter fully realises that only workers' Soviets, not parliament, can be the instrument enabling the proletariat to achieve its aims; those who have failed to understand this are, of course, out-and-out reactionaries, even if they are most highly educated people, most experienced politicians, most sincere socialists, most erudite Marxists, and most honest citizens and fathers of

6. Little people.

families. But the writer of the letter does not even ask—it does not occur to him to ask—whether it is possible to bring about the Soviets' victory over parliament without getting pro-Soviet politicians *into* parliament, without disintegrating parliamentarianism from *within*, without working within parliament for the success of the Soviets in their forthcoming task of dispersing parliament. Yet the writer of the letter expresses the absolutely correct idea that the Communist Party in Great Britain must act on *scientific* principles. Science demands, first, that the experience of other countries be taken into account, especially if these other countries, which are also capitalist, are undergoing, or have recently undergone, a very similar experience; second, it demands that account be taken of *all* the forces, groups, parties, classes and masses operating in a given country, and also that policy should not be determined only by the desires and views, by the degree of class-consciousness and the militancy of one group or party alone.

It is true that the Hendersons, the Clyneses, the MacDonalds and the Snowdens are hopelessly reactionary. It is equally true that they want to assume power (though they would prefer a coalition with the bourgeoisie), that they want to "rule" along the old bourgeois lines, and that when they are in power they will certainly behave like the Scheidemanns and Noskes. All that is true. But it does not at all follow that to support them means treachery to the revolution; what does follow is that, in the interests of the revolution, working-class revolutionaries should give these gentlemen a certain amount of parliamentary support. To explain this idea, I shall take two contemporary British political documents: (1) the speech delivered by Prime Minister Lloyd George on March 18, 1920 (as reported in *The Manchester Guardian* of March 19, 1920), and (2) the arguments of a "Left" Communist, Comrade Sylvia Pankhurst, in the article mentioned above.

In his speech Lloyd George entered into a polemic with Asquith (who had been especially invited to this meeting but declined to attend) and with those Liberals who want, not a coalition with the Conservatives, but closer relations with the Labour Party. (In the above-quoted letter, Comrade Gallacher also points to the fact that Liberals are joining the Independent Labour Party.) Lloyd George argued that a coalition—and a *close* coalition at that—between the Liberals and the Conservatives was essential, otherwise there might be a victory for the Labour Party, which Lloyd George prefers to call "Socialist" and which is working for the "common ownership" of the means of production. "It is . . . known as communism in France," the leader of the British bourgeoisie said, putting it popularly for his audience, Liberal M.P.s who probably never knew it before. In Germany it was called socialism, and in Russia it is called Bolshevism, he went on to say. To Liberals this is unacceptable on principle, Lloyd George explained, because they stand in principle for private property. "Civilisation is in jeopardy," the speaker declared, and consequently Liberals and Conservatives must unite. . . .

. . . If you go to the agricultural areas [said Lloyd George] I agree you have the old party divisions as strong as ever. They are removed from the danger. It does not walk their lanes. But when they see it they will be as strong as some of these industrial constituencies are now. Four-fifths of this country is industrial and commercial; hardly one-fifth is agricultural. It is one of the things I have constantly in my mind when I think of the dangers of the future here. In France the population is agricultural, and you have a solid body of opinion which does not move very rapidly, and which is not very easily excited by revolutionary movements. That is not the case here. This country is more top-heavy than any country in the world, and if it begins to rock, the crash here, for that reason, will be greater than in any land.

From this the reader will see that Mr. Lloyd George is not only a very intelligent man, but one who has also learned a great deal from the Marxists. We too have something to learn from Lloyd George.

Of definite interest is the following episode, which occurred in the course of the discussion after Lloyd George's speech:

MR. WALLACE, M.P.: I should like to ask what the Prime Minister considers the effect might be in the industrial constituencies upon the industrial workers, so many of whom are Liberals at the present time and from whom we get so much support. Would not a possible result be to cause an immediate overwhelming accession of strength to the Labour Party from men who at present are our cordial supporters?

THE PRIME MINISTER: I take a totally different view. The fact that Liberals are fighting among themselves undoubtedly drives a very considerable number of Liberals in despair to the Labour Party, where you get a considerable body of Liberals, very able men, whose business it is to discredit the Government. The result is undoubtedly to bring a good accession of public sentiment to the Labour Party. It does not go to the Liberals who are outside, it goes to the Labour Party, the by-elections show that.

It may be said, in passing, that this argument shows in particular how muddled even the most intelligent members of the bourgeoisie have become and how they cannot help committing irreparable blunders. That, in fact, is what will bring about the downfall of the bourgeoisie. Our people, however, may commit blunders (provided, of course, that they are not too serious and are rectified in time) and yet, in the long run, will prove the victors.

The second political document is the following argument advanced by Comrade Sylvia Pankhurst, a "Left" Communist:

> . . . Comrade Inkpin [the General Secretary of the British Socialist Party] refers to the Labour Party as "the main body of the working-class movement." Another comrade of the British Socialist Party, at the Third International, just held, put the British Socialist Party position more strongly. He said: "We regard the Labour Party as the organised working class."
>
> We do not take this view of the Labour Party. The Labour Party is very large numerically though its membership is to a great extent quiescent and apathetic, consisting of men and women who have joined the trade unions because their workmates are trade unionists, and to share the friendly benefits.
>
> But we recognise that the great size of the Labour Party is also due to the fact that it is the creation of a school of thought beyond which the majority of the British working class has not yet emerged, though great changes are at work in the mind of the people which will presently alter this state of affairs. . . .
>
> The British Labour Party, like the social-patriotic organisations of other countries, will, in the natural development of society, inevitably come into power. It is for the Communists to build up the forces that will overthrow the social patriots, and in this country we must not delay or falter in that work.
>
> We must not dissipate our energy in adding to the strength of the Labour Party; its rise to power is inevitable. We must concentrate on making a communist movement that will vanquish it. The Labour Party will soon be forming a government; the revolutionary opposition must make ready to attack it. . . .

Thus the liberal bourgeoisie are abandoning the historical system of "two parties" (of exploiters), which has been hallowed by centuries of experience and has been extremely advantageous to the exploiters, and consider it necessary for these two parties to join forces against the Labour Party. A number of Liberals are deserting to the Labour Party like rats from a sinking ship. The Left Communists believe that the transfer of power to the Labour Party is inevitable and admit that it now has the backing of most workers. From this they draw the strange conclusion which Comrade Sylvia Pankhurst formulates as follows: "The Communist Party must not compromise. . . . The Communist Party must keep its doctrine pure, and its independence of reformism inviolate; its mission is to lead the way, without stopping or turning, by the direct road to the communist revolution."

On the contrary, the fact that most British workers still follow the lead of the British Kerenskys or Scheidemanns and have not yet had experience of a government composed of these people—an experience which was necessary in Russia and Germany so as to secure the mass transition of the workers to communism—undoubtedly indicates that the British Communists *should* participate in parliamentary action, that they should, from *within* parliament, help the masses of the workers see the results of a Henderson and Snowden government in practice, and that they should help the Hendersons and Snowdens defeat the united forces of Lloyd George and Churchill. To act otherwise would mean hampering the cause of the revolution, since revolution is impossible without a change in the views of the majority of the working class, a change brought about by the political experience of the masses, never by propaganda alone. "To lead the way without compromises, without turning"—this slogan is obviously wrong if it comes from a patently impotent minority of the workers who know (or at all events should know) that given a Henderson and Snowden victory over Lloyd George and Churchill, the majority will soon become disappointed in their leaders and will begin to support communism (or at all events will adopt an attitude of neutrality, and, in the main, of sympathetic neutrality, towards the Communists). It is as though 10,000 soldiers were to hurl themselves into battle against an enemy force of 50,000, when it would be proper to "halt," "take evasive action," or even effect a "compromise" so as to gain time until the arrival of the 100,000 reinforcements that are on their way but cannot go into action immediately. That is intellectualist childishness, not the serious tactics of a revolutionary class.

The fundamental law of revolution, which has been confirmed by all revolutions and especially by all three Russian revolutions in the twentieth century, is as follows: for a revolution to take place it is not enough for the exploited and oppressed masses to realise the impossibility of living in the old way, and demand changes; for a revolution to take place it is essential that the exploiters should not be able to live and rule in the old way. It is only when the *"lower classes" do not want* to live in the old way and the "upper classes" *cannot carry on in the old way* that the revolution can triumph. This truth can be expressed in other words: revolution is impossible without a nation-wide crisis (affecting both the exploited and the exploiters). It follows that, for a revolution to take place, it is essential, first, that a majority of the workers (or at least a majority of the class-conscious, thinking, and politically active workers) should fully realise that revolution is necessary, and that they should be prepared to die for it; second, that the ruling classes should be going through a governmental crisis, which draws even the most backward masses into politics (symptomatic of any genuine revolution is a rapid, tenfold and even hundredfold increase in the size of the working and oppressed masses—hitherto apathetic—

who are capable of waging the political struggle), weakens the government, and makes it possible for the revolutionaries to rapidly overthrow it.

Incidentally, as can also be seen from Lloyd George's speech, both conditions for a successful proletarian revolution are clearly maturing in Great Britain. The errors of the Left Communists are particularly dangerous at present, because certain revolutionaries are not displaying a sufficiently thoughtful, sufficiently attentive, sufficiently intelligent and sufficiently shrewd attitude toward each of these conditions. If we are the party of the revolutionary *class*, and not merely a revolutionary group, and if we want the *masses* to follow us (and unless we achieve that, we stand the risk of remaining mere windbags), we must, first, help Henderson or Snowden to beat Lloyd George and Churchill (or, rather, compel the former to beat the latter, because the former *are afraid of their victory*!); second, we must help the majority of the working class to be convinced by their own experience that we are right, i.e., that the Hendersons and Snowdens are absolutely good for nothing, that they are petty-bourgeois and treacherous by nature, and that their bankruptcy is inevitable; third, we must bring nearer the moment when, *on the basis* of the disappointment of most of the workers in the Hendersons, it will be possible, with serious chances of success, to overthrow the government of the Hendersons at once; because of the most astute and solid Lloyd George, that big, not petty, bourgeois, is displaying consternation and is more and more weakening himself (and the bourgeoisie as a whole) by his "friction" with Churchill today and with Asquith tomorrow, how much greater will be the consternation of a Henderson government!

I will put it more concretely. In my opinion, the British Communists should unite their four parties and groups (all very weak, and some of them very, very weak) into a single Communist Party on the basis of the principles of the Third International and of *obligatory* participation in parliament. The Communist Party should propose the following "compromise" election agreement to the Hendersons and Snowdens: let us jointly fight against the alliance between Lloyd George and the Conservatives; let us share parliamentary seats in proportion to the number of workers' votes polled for the Labour Party and for the Communist Party (not in elections, but in a special ballot), and let us retain *complete freedom* of agitation, propaganda and political activity. Of course, without this latter condition, we cannot agree to a bloc, for that would be treachery; the British Communists must demand and get complete freedom to expose the Hendersons and the Snowdens in the same way as (*for fifteen years*—1903–17) the Russian Bolsheviks demanded and got it in respect of the Russian Hendersons and Snowdens, i.e., the Mensheviks.

If the Hendersons and the Snowdens accept a bloc on these terms, we shall be the gainers, because the number of parliamentary seats is of no importance to us; we are not out for seats. We shall yield on this point (whilst the Hendersons and especially their new friends—or new masters—the Liberals who have joined the Independent Labour Party are most eager to get seats). We shall be the gainers, because we shall carry on *our* agitation among the *masses* at a time when Lloyd George *himself* has "incensed" them, and we shall not only be helping the Labour Party to establish its government sooner, but shall also be helping the masses sooner to understand the communist propaganda that we shall carry on against the Hendersons, without any reticence or omission.

If the Hendersons and the Snowdens reject a bloc with us on these terms, we shall gain still more, for we shall at once have shown the *masses* (note that, even in the purely Menshevik and completely opportunist Independent Labour Party, the *rank and file* are in favour of Soviets) that the Hendersons prefer *their* close relations with the capitalists to the unity of all the workers. We shall immediately gain in the eyes of the masses, who, particularly after the brilliant, highly correct and highly useful (to communism) explanations given by Lloyd George, will be sympathetic to the idea of uniting all the workers against the Lloyd George-Conservative alliance. We shall gain immediately, because we shall have demonstrated to the masses that the Hendersons and the Snowdens are afraid to beat Lloyd George, afraid to assume power alone, and are striving to secure the *secret* support of Lloyd George, who is *openly* extending a hand to the Conservatives, against the Labour Party. It should be noted that in Russia, after the revolution of February 27, 1917 (old style), the Bolsheviks' propaganda against the Mensheviks and Socialist-Revolutionaries (i.e., the Russian Hendersons and Snowdens) derived benefit precisely from a circumstance of this kind. We said to the Mensheviks and the Socialist-Revolutionaries: assume full power without the bourgeoisie, because you have a majority in the Soviets (at the First All-Russia Congress of Soviets, in June 1917, the Bolsheviks had only 13 per cent of the votes). But the Russian Hendersons and Snowdens were afraid to assume power without the bourgeoisie, and when the bourgeoisie held up the elections to the Constituent Assembly, knowing full well that the elections would give a majority to the Socialist-Revolutionaries and the Mensheviks[7] (who formed a close

7. The results of the November 1917 elections to the Constituent Assembly in Russia, based on returns embracing over 36,000,000 voters, were as follows: the Bolsheviks obtained 25 per cent of the votes; the various parties of the land-owners and the bourgeoisie obtained 13 per cent, and the petty-bourgeois-democratic parties, i.e., the Social-Revolutionaries, Mensheviks and a number of similar groups obtained 62 per cent. [*Lenin*]

political bloc and in fact represented *only* petty-bourgeois democracy), the Socialist-Revolutionaries and the Mensheviks were unable energetically and consistently to oppose these delays.

If the Hendersons and the Snowdens reject a bloc with the Communists, the latter will immediately gain by winning the sympathy of the masses and discrediting the Hendersons and Snowdens; if, as a result, we do lose a few parliamentary seats, it is a matter of no significance to us. We would put up our candidates in a very few but absolutely safe constituencies, namely, constituencies where our candidatures would not give any seats to the Liberals at the expense of the Labour candidates. We would take part in the election campaign, distribute leaflets agitating for communism, and, in *all* constituencies where we have no candidates, we would urge the electors *to vote for the Labour candidate and against the bourgeois candidate.* Comrades Sylvia Pankhurst and Gallacher are mistaken in thinking that this is a betrayal of communism, or a renunciation of the struggle against the social-traitors. On the contrary, the cause of communist revolution would undoubtedly gain thereby.

At present, British Communists very often find it hard even to approach the masses, and even to get a hearing from them. If I come out as a Communist and call upon them to vote for Henderson and against Lloyd George, they will certainly give me a hearing. And I shall be able to explain in a popular manner, not only why the Soviets are better than a parliament and why the dictatorship of the proletariat is better than the dictatorship of Churchill (disguised with the signboard of bourgeois "democracy"), but also that, with my vote, I want to support Henderson in the same way as the rope supports a hanged man—that the impending establishment of a government of the Hendersons will prove that I am right, will bring the masses over to my side, and will hasten the political death of the Hendersons and the Snowdens just as was the case with their kindred spirits in Russia and Germany.

If the objection is raised that these tactics are too "subtle" or too complex for the masses to understand, that these tactics will split and scatter our forces, will prevent us from concentrating them on Soviet revolution, etc., I will reply to the "Left" objectors: don't ascribe your doctrinairism to the masses! The masses in Russia are no doubt no better educated than the masses in Britain; if anything, they are less so. Yet the masses understood the Bolsheviks, and the fact that, in September 1917, *on the eve* of the Soviet revolution, the Bolsheviks put up their candidates for a bourgeois parliament (the Constituent Assembly) and *on the day after* the Soviet revolution, in November 1917, took part in the elections to this Constituent Assembly, which they got rid of on January 5, 1918—this did not hamper the Bolsheviks, but, on the contrary, helped them.

I cannot deal here with the second point of disagreement among the British Communists—the question of affiliation or non-affiliation to the Labour Party. I have too little material at my disposal on this question, which is highly complex because of the unique character of the British Labour Party, whose very structure is so unlike that of the political parties usual in the European continent. It is beyond doubt, however, first, that in this question, too, those who try to deduce the tactics of the revolutionary proletariat from principles such as: "The Communist Party must keep its doctrine pure, and its independence of reformism inviolate; its mission is to lead the way, without stopping or turning, by the direct road to the communist revolution"—will inevitably fall into error. Such principles are merely a repetition of the mistake made by the French Blanquist Communards, who, in 1874, "repudiated" all compromises and all intermediate stages. Second, it is beyond doubt that, in this question too, as always, the task consists in learning to apply the general and basic principles of communism to the *specific relations* between classes and parties, to the *specific features* in the objective development towards communism, which are different in each country and which we must be able to discover, study, and predict.

This, however, should be discussed, not in connection with British communism alone, but in connection with the general conclusions concerning the development of communism in all capitalist countries. We shall now proceed to deal with this subject.

X. Several Conclusions

The Russian bourgeois revolution of 1905 revealed a highly original turn in world history: in one of the most backward capitalist countries, the strike movement attained a scope and power unprecedented anywhere in the world. In the *first month* of 1905 *alone*, the number of strikers was ten times the *annual* average for the previous decade (1895–1904); from January to October 1905, strikes grew all the time and reached enormous proportions. Under the influence of a number of unique historical conditions, backward Russia was the first to show the world, not only the growth, by leaps and bounds, of the independent activity of the oppressed masses in time of revolution (this had occurred in all great revolutions), but also that the significance of the proletariat is infinitely greater than its proportion in the total population; it showed a combination of the economic strike and the political strike, with the latter developing into an armed uprising, and the birth of the Soviets, a new form of mass struggle and mass organisation of the classes oppressed by capitalism.

The revolutions of February and October 1917 led to the all-round development of the Soviets on a nation-wide scale and to their victory in the proletarian socialist revolution. In less than two years, the international character of the Soviets, the spread of this form of struggle and organisation to the world working-class movement and the historical mission of the Soviets as the grave-digger, heir and successor of bourgeois parliamentarianism and of bourgeois democracy in general, all became clear.

But that is not all. The history of the working-class movement now shows that, in all countries, it is about to go through (and is already going through) a struggle waged by communism—emergent, gaining strength and advancing towards victory—against, primarily, Menshevism, i.e., opportunism and social-chauvinism (the home brand in each particular country), and then as a complement, so to say, Left-wing communism. The former struggle has developed in all countries, apparently without any exception, as a duel between the Second International (already virtually dead) and the Third International. The latter struggle is to be seen in Germany, Great Britain, Italy, America (at any rate, a certain *section* of the Industrial Workers of the World and of the anarcho-syndicalist trends uphold the errors on Left-wing communism alongside of an almost universal and almost unreserved acceptance of the Soviet system), and in France (the attitude of a section of the former syndicalists towards the political party and parliamentarianism, also alongside of the acceptance of the Soviet system); in other words, the struggle is undoubtedly being waged, not only on an international, but even on a world-wide scale.

But while the working-class movement is everywhere going through what is actually the same kind of preparatory school for victory over the bourgeoisie, it is achieving that development in its *own way* in each country. The big and advanced capitalist countries are travelling this road *far more rapidly* than did Bolshevism, to which history granted fifteen years to prepare itself for victory, as an organised political trend. In the brief space of a year, the Third International has already scored a decisive victory; it has defeated the yellow, social-chauvinist Second International, which only a few months ago was incomparably stronger than the Third International, seemed stable and powerful, and enjoyed every possible support—direct and indirect, material (cabinet posts, passports, the press) and ideological—from the world bourgeoisie.

It is now essential that Communists of every country should quite consciously take into account both the fundamental objectives of the struggle against opportunism and "Left" doctrinairism, and the *concrete features* which this struggle assumes and must inevitably assume in each country, in conformity with the specific character of its economics, politics, culture, and national composition (Ireland, etc.), its colonies, religious divisions, and so on and so forth. Dissatisfaction with the Second International is felt everywhere and is spreading and growing, both because of its opportunism and because of its inability or incapacity to create a really centralised and really leading centre capable of directing the international tactics of the revolutionary proletariat in its struggle for a world Soviet republic. It should be clearly realised that such a leading centre can never be built up on stereotyped, mechanically equated, and identical tactical rules of struggle. As long as national and state distinctions exist among peoples and countries—and these will continue to exist for a very long time to come, even after the dictatorship of the proletariat has been established on a world-wide scale—the unity of the International tactics of the communist working-class movement in all countries demands, not the elimination of variety or the suppression of national distinctions (which is a pipe dream at present), but the application of the *fundamental* principles of communism (Soviet power and the dictatorship of the proletariat), which will *correctly modify* these principles in certain *particulars*, correctly adapt and apply them to national and national-state distinctions. To seek out, investigate, predict, and grasp that which is nationally specific and nationally distinctive, in the *concrete manner* in which each country should tackle a *single* international task: victory over opportunism and Left doctrinairism within the working-class movement; the overthrow of the bourgeoisie; the establishment of a Soviet republic and a proletarian dictatorship—such is the basic task in the historical period that all the advanced countries (and not they alone) are going through. The chief thing—though, of course, far from everything—the chief thing, has already been achieved: the vanguard of the working class has been won over, has ranged itself on the side of Soviet government and against parliamentarianism, on the side of the dictatorship of the proletariat and against bourgeois democracy. All efforts and all attention should now be concentrated on the *next* step, which may seem—and from a certain viewpoint actually is—less fundamental, but, on the other hand, is actually closer to a practical accomplishment of the task. That step is: the search after forms of the *transition* or the *approach* to the proletarian revolution.

The proletarian vanguard has been won over ideologically. That is the main thing. Without this, not even the first step towards victory can be made. But that is still quite a long way from victory. Victory cannot be won with a vanguard alone. To throw only the vanguard into the decisive battle, before the entire class, the broad masses, have taken up a position either of direct support for the vanguard, or at least of sympathetic neutrality towards it and of precluded support for the enemy, would be, not merely foolish but criminal. Propaganda and agitation alone are not enough for an entire class, the broad masses of the working people, those oppressed by capital, to take up such a stand. For that, the masses must have their own political experience. Such is the fundamental law of all great revolutions, which has been confirmed with compelling force and vividness, not only in Russia but in Germany as well. To turn resolutely towards communism, it was necessary, not only for the ignorant and often illiterate masses of Russia, but also for the literate and well-educated masses of Germany, to realise from their own bitter experience the absolute impotence and spinelessness, the absolute helplessness and servility to the bourgeoisie, and the utter vileness of the government of the paladins of the Second International; they had to realise that a dictatorship of the extreme reactionaries (Kornilov in Russia; Kapp and Co. in Germany) is inevitably the only alternative to a dictatorship of the proletariat.

The immediate objective of the class-conscious vanguard of the international working-class movement, i.e., the Communist parties, groups and trends, is to be able to *lead* the broad masses (who are still, for the most part, apathetic, inert, dormant, habit-ridden, and unawakened) to their new position, or, rather, to be able to lead, *not only* their own party but also these masses in their advance and transition to the new position. While the first historical objective (that of winning over the class-conscious vanguard of the proletariat to the side of Soviet power and the dictatorship of the working class) could not have been reached without a complete ideological and political victory over opportunism and social-chauvinism, the second and immediate objective, which consists in being able to lead the *masses* to a new position ensuring the victory of the vanguard in the revolution, cannot be reached without the liquidation of Left doctrinairism, and without a full elimination of its errors.

As long as it was (and inasmuch as it still is) a question of winning the proletariat's vanguard over to the side of communism, priority went and still goes to propaganda work; even propaganda circles, with all their parochial limitations, are useful under these conditions, and produce good results. But when it is a question of practical action by the masses, of the disposition, if one may so put it, of vast armies, of the alignment of *all* the class forces in a given society *for the final and decisive battle*, then propagandist methods alone, the mere repetition of the truths of "pure" communism, are of no avail. In these circumstances, one must not count in thousands, like the propagandist belonging to a small group that has not yet given leadership to the masses; in these circumstances one must count in millions and tens of millions. In these circumstances, we must ask ourselves, not only whether we have convinced the vanguard of the revolutionary class, but also whether the historically effective forces of *all* classes—positively of all the classes in a given society, without exception—are arrayed in such a way that the decisive battle is at hand—in such a way that: (1) all the class forces hostile to us have become sufficiently entangled, are sufficiently at loggerheads with each other, have sufficiently weakened themselves in a struggle which is beyond their strength; (2) all the vacillating and unstable, intermediate elements—the petty bourgeoisie and the petty-bourgeois democrats, as distinct from the bourgeoisie—have sufficiently exposed themselves in the eyes of the people, have sufficiently disgraced themselves through their practical bankruptcy, and (3) among the proletariat, a mass sentiment favouring the most determined, bold and dedicated revolutionary action against the bourgeoisie has emerged and begun to grow vigorously. Then revolution is indeed ripe; then, indeed, if we have correctly gauged all the conditions indicated and summarised above, and if we have chosen the right moment, our victory is assured.

The differences between the Churchills and Lloyd Georges—with insignificant national distinctions, these political types exist in *all* countries—on the one hand, and between the Hendersons and the Lloyd Georges on the other, are quite minor and unimportant from the standpoint of pure (i.e., abstract) communism, i.e., communism that has not yet matured to the stage of practical political action by the masses. However, from the standpoint of this practical action by the masses, these differences are most important. To take due account of these differences, and to determine the moment when the inevitable conflicts between these "friends," which weaken and enfeeble *all the "friends" taken together*, will have come to a head—that is the concern, the task, of a Communist who wants to be, not merely a class-conscious and convinced propagandist of ideas, but a practical leader of the *masses* in the revolution. It is necessary to link the strictest devotion to the ideas of communism with the ability to effect all the necessary practical compromises, tacks, conciliatory manoeuvres, zigzags, retreats and so on, in order to speed up the achievement and then loss of political power by the Hendersons (the heroes of the Second International, if we are not to name individual representatives of petty-bourgeois democracy who call themselves socialists); to accelerate their inevitable bankruptcy in practice, which will enlighten the masses in the spirit of our ideas, in the direction of communism; to accelerate the inevitable friction, quarrels, conflicts and complete disintegration among the Hendersons, the Lloyd Georges and the Churchills (the Mensheviks, the Socialist-Revolutionaries, the Constitutional-Democrats, the monarchists; the Scheidemanns, the bourgeoisie and the Kappists,[8] etc.); to select the proper moment when the discord among these "pillars of sacrosanct private property" is at its height, so that, through a decisive offensive, the proletariat will defeat them all and capture political power.

History as a whole, and the history of revolutions in particular, is always richer in content, more varied, more multiform, more lively and ingenious than is imagined by even the best parties, the most class-conscious vanguards of the most advanced classes. This can readily be understood, because even the finest of vanguards express the class-consciousness, will, passion and imagination of tens of thousands, whereas at moments of great upsurge and the exertion of all human capacities, revolutions are made by the class-consciousness, will, passion and imagination of tens of millions, spurred on by a most acute struggle of classes. Two very important practical conclusions follow from this: first, that in order to accomplish its task the revolutionary class must be able to master *all* forms or aspects of social activity without exception (completing after the capture of political power—sometimes at great risk and with very great danger—what it did not complete before the capture of power); second, that the revolutionary class must be prepared for the most rapid and brusque replacement of one form by another.

One will readily agree that any army which does not train to use all the weapons, all the means and methods of warfare that the enemy possesses, or may possess, is behaving in an unwise or even criminal manner. This applies to politics even more than it does to the art of war. In politics it is even harder to know in advance which methods of struggle will be applicable and to our advantage in certain future conditions. Unless we learn to apply all the methods of struggle, we may suffer grave and sometimes even decisive defeat, if changes beyond our control in the position of the other classes bring to the forefront a form of activity in which we are especially weak. If, however, we learn to use all the methods of struggle, victory will be certain, because we represent the interests of the really foremost and really revolutionary class, even if circumstances do not permit us to make use of weapons that are most dangerous to the enemy, weapons that deal the swiftest mortal blows. Inexperienced revolutionaries often think that legal methods of struggle are opportunist because, in this field, the bourgeoisie has most frequently deceived and duped the workers (particularly in

---

8. Participants in the monarchist *coup d'état* in Germany which was headed by Wolfgang Kapp and became known as the "Kapp Putsch." On March 13, 1920, army units under the Kappists advanced against Berlin; encountering no resistance from the Social-Democratic government, they declared the latter overthrown and set up a new government. A general strike in Berlin led to the fall of the Kapp government on March 17.

"peaceful" and non-revolutionary times), while illegal methods of struggle are revolutionary. That, however, is wrong. The truth is that those parties and leaders are opportunists and traitors to the working class that are unable or unwilling (do not say, "I can't"; say, "I shan't") to use illegal methods of struggle in conditions such as those which prevailed, for example, during the imperialist war of 1914–18, when the bourgeoisie of the freest democratic countries most brazenly and brutally deceived the workers, and smothered the truth about the predatory character of the war. But revolutionaries who are incapable of combining illegal forms of struggle with *every* form of legal struggle are poor revolutionaries indeed. It is not difficult to be a revolutionary when revolution has already broken out and is in spate, when all people are joining the revolution just because they are carried away, because it is the vogue, and sometimes even from careerist motives. After its victory, the proletariat has to make most strenuous efforts, even the most painful, so as to "liberate" itself from such pseudo-revolutionaries. It is far more difficult—and far more precious—to be a revolutionary when the conditions for direct, open, really mass and really revolutionary struggle *do not yet exist*, to be able to champion the interests of the revolution (by propaganda, agitation and organisation) in non-revolutionary bodies, and quite often in downright reactionary bodies, in a non-revolutionary situation, among the masses who are incapable of immediately appreciating the need for revolutionary methods of action. To be able to seek, find and correctly determine the specific path or the particular turn of events that will *lead* the masses to the real, decisive and final revolutionary struggle—such is the main objective of communism in Western Europe and in America today.

Britain is an example. We cannot tell—no one can tell in advance—how soon a real proletarian revolution will flare up there, and *what immediate cause* will most serve to rouse, kindle, and impel into the struggle the very wide masses, who are still dormant. Hence, it is our duty to carry on all our preparatory work in such a way as to be "well shod on all four feet" (as the late Plekhanov, when he was a Marxist and revolutionary, was fond of saying). It is possible that the breach will be forced, the ice broken, by a parliamentary crisis, or by a crisis arising from colonial and imperialist contradictions, which are hopelessly entangled and are becoming increasingly painful and acute, or perhaps by some third cause, etc. We are not discussing the kind of struggle that will *determine* the fate of the proletarian revolution in Great Britain (no Communist has any doubt on that score; for all of us this is a foregone conclusion): what we are discussing is the *immediate cause* that will bring into motion the now dormant proletarian masses, and lead them right up to revolution. Let us not forget that in the French bourgeois republic, for example, in a situation which, from both the international and the national viewpoints, was a hundred times less revolutionary than it is today, such an "unexpected" and "petty" cause as one of the many thousands of fraudulent machinations of the reactionary military caste (the Dreyfus case) was enough to bring the people to the brink of civil war!

In Great Britain the Communists should constantly, unremittingly and unswervingly utilise parliamentary elections and all the vicissitudes of the Irish, colonial and world-imperialist policy of the British Government, and all other fields, spheres and aspects of public life, and work in all of them in a new way, in a communist way, in the spirit of the Third, not the Second, International. I have neither the time nor the space here to describe the "Russian" "Bolshevik" methods of participation in parliamentary elections and in the parliamentary struggle; I can, however, assure foreign Communists that they were quite unlike the usual West-European parliamentary campaigns. From this the conclusion is often drawn: "Well, that was in Russia; in our country parliamentarianism is different." This is a false conclusion. Communists, adherents of the Third International in all countries, exist for the purpose of *changing*—all along the line, in all spheres of life—the old socialist, trade unionist, syndicalist, and parliamentary type of work into a *new* type of work, the communist. In Russia, too, there was always an abundance of opportunism, purely bourgeois sharp practices and capitalist rigging in the elections. In Western Europe and in America, the Communists must learn to create a new, uncustomary, non-opportunist, and non-careerist parliamentarianism; the Communist parties must issue their slogans; true proletarians, with the help of the unorganised and downtrodden poor, should distribute leaflets, canvass workers' houses and cottages of the rural proletarians and peasants in the remote villages (fortunately there are many times fewer remote villages in Europe than in Russia, and in Britain the number is very small); they should go into the public houses, penetrate into unions, societies and chance gatherings of the common people, and speak to the people, not in learned (or very parliamentary) language; they should not at all strive to "get seats" in parliament, but should everywhere try to get people to think, and draw the masses into the struggle, to take the bourgeoisie at its word and utilise the machinery it has set up, the elections it has appointed, and the appeals it has made to the people; they should try to explain to the people what Bolshevism is, in a way that was never possible (under bourgeois rule) outside of election times (exclusive, of course, of times of big strikes, when in Russia a *similar* apparatus for widespread popular agitation worked even more intensively). It is very difficult to do this in Western Europe and extremely difficult in America, but it can and must be done, for the objectives of communism cannot be achieved without effort. We must work to accomplish *practical* tasks, ever more varied and ever more closely connected with all branches of social life, *winning* branch after branch, and sphere after sphere *from the bourgeoisie*.

In Great Britain, further, the work of propaganda, agitation and organisation among the armed forces and among the oppressed and underprivileged nationalities in their "own" state (Ireland, the colonies) must also be tackled in a new fashion (one that is not socialist, but communist; not reformist, but revolutionary). That is because, in the era of imperialism in general and especially today after a war that was a sore trial to the peoples and has quickly opened their eyes to the truth (i.e., the fact that tens of millions were killed and maimed for the sole purpose of deciding whether the British or the German robbers should plunder the largest number of countries), all these spheres of social life are heavily charged with inflammable material and are creating numerous causes of conflicts, crises and an intensification of the class struggle. We do not and cannot know which spark—of the innumerable sparks that are flying about in all countries as a result of the world economic and political crisis—will kindle the conflagration, in the sense of raising up the masses; we must, therefore, with our new and communist principles, set to work to stir up all and sundry, even the oldest, mustiest and seemingly hopeless spheres, for otherwise we shall not be able to cope with our tasks, shall not be comprehensively prepared, shall not be in possession of all the weapons and shall not prepare ourselves either to gain victory over the bourgeoisie (which arranged all aspects of social life—and has now disarranged them—in its bourgeois fashion), or to bring about the impending communist reorganisation of every sphere of life, following that victory.

Since the proletarian revolution in Russia and its victories on an international scale, expected neither by the bourgeoisie nor the philistines, the entire world has become different, and the bourgeoisie everywhere has become different too. It is terrified of "Bolshevism," exasperated by it almost to the point of frenzy, and for that very reason it is, on the one hand, precipitating the progress of events and, on the other, concentrating on the forcible suppression of Bolshevism, thereby weakening its own position in a number of other fields. In their tactics the Communists in all the advanced countries must take both these circumstances into account.

When the Russian Cadets and Kerensky began furiously to hound the Bolsheviks—especially since April 1917, and more particularly in June and July 1917—they overdid things. Millions of copies of bourgeois papers, clamouring in every key against the Bolsheviks, helped the masses to make an appraisal of Bolshevism; apart from the newspapers, all public life was full of discussions about Bolshevism, as a result of the bourgeoisie's "zeal." Today the millionaires of all countries are behaving on an international scale in a way that deserves our heartiest thanks. They are hounding Bolshevism with the same zeal as Kerensky and Co. did; they, too, are overdoing things and *helping* us just as Kerensky did. When the French bourgeoisie makes Bolshevism the central issue in the elections, and accuses the comparatively moderate or vacillating socialists of being Bolsheviks; when the American bourgeoisie, which has completely lost its head, seizes thousands and thousands of people on suspicion of Bolshevism, creates an atmosphere of panic, and broadcasts stories of Bolshevik plots; when, despite all its wisdom and experience, the British bourgeoisie—the most "solid" in the world—makes incredible blunders, founds richly endowed "anti-Bolshevik societies," creates a special literature on Bolshevism, and recruits an extra number of scientists, agitators and clergymen to combat it, we must salute and thank the capitalists. They are working for us. They are helping us to get the masses interested in the essence and significance of Bolshevism, and they cannot do otherwise, for they have *already* failed to ignore Bolshevism and stifle it.

But at the same time, the bourgeoisie sees practically only one aspect of Bolshevism—insurrection, violence, and terror; it therefore strives to prepare itself for resistance and opposition primarily in *this* field. It is possible that, in certain instances, in certain countries, and for certain brief periods, it will succeed in this. We must reckon with such an eventuality, and we have absolutely nothing to fear if it does succeed. Communism is emerging in positively every sphere of public life; its beginnings are to be seen literally on all sides. The "contagion" (to use the favourite metaphor of the bourgeoisie and the bourgeois police, the one most to their liking) has very thoroughly penetrated the organism and has completely permeated it. If special efforts are made to block one of the channels, the "contagion" will find another one, sometimes very unexpectedly. Life will assert itself. Let the bourgeoisie rave, work itself into a frenzy, go to extremes, commit follies, take vengeance on the Bolsheviks in advance, and endeavour to kill off (as in India, Hungary, Germany, etc.) more hundreds, thousands, and hundreds of thousands of yesterday's and tomorrow's Bolsheviks. In acting thus, the bourgeoisie is acting as all historically doomed classes have done. Communists should know that, in any case, the future belongs to them; therefore, we can (and must) combine the most intense passion in the great revolutionary struggle, with the coolest and most sober appraisal of the frenzied ravings of the bourgeoisie. The Russian revolution was cruelly defeated in 1905; the Russian Bolsheviks were defeated in July 1917; over 15,000 German Communists were killed as a result of the wily provocation and cunning manoeuvres of Scheidemann and Noske, who were working hand in glove with the bourgeoisie and the monarchist generals; White terror is raging in Finland and Hungary. But in all cases and in all countries, communism is becoming steeled and is growing; its roots are so deep that persecution does not weaken or debilitate it, but only strengthens it. Only one thing is lacking to enable us to march forward more confidently and firmly to victory, namely, the universal and thorough awareness of all Communists in all countries, of the necessity to display the utmost *flexibility* in their tactics. The communist movement, which is developing magnificently, now lacks, especially in the advanced countries, this awareness and the ability to apply it in practice.

That which happened to such leaders of the Second International, such highly erudite Marxists devoted to socialism as Kautsky, Otto Bauer and others, could (and should) provide a useful lesson. They fully appreciated the need for flexible tactics; they themselves learned Marxist dialectic and taught it to others (and much of what they have done in this field will always remain a valuable contribution to socialist literature); however, *in the application* of this dialectic they committed such an error, or proved to be so *un*dialectical in practice, so incapable of taking into account the rapid change of forms and the rapid acquisition of new content by the old forms, that their fate is not much more enviable than that of Hyndman, Guesde and Plekhanov. The principal reason for their bankruptcy was that they were hypnotised by a definite form of growth of the working-class movement and socialism, forgot all about the one-sidedness of that form, were afraid to see the break-up which objective conditions made inevitable, and continued to repeat simple and, at first glance, incontestable axioms that had been learned by rote, like: "three is more than two." But politics is more like algebra than arithmetic, and still more like higher than elementary mathematics. In reality, all the old forms of the socialist movement have acquired a new content, and, consequently, a new symbol, the "minus" sign, has appeared in front of all the figures; our wiseacres, however, have stubbornly continued (and still continue) to persuade themselves and others that "minus three" is more than "minus two."

We must see to it that Communists do not make a similar mistake, only in the opposite sense, or rather, we must see to it that a *similar mistake*, only made in the opposite sense by the "Left" Communists, is corrected as soon as possible and eliminated as rapidly and painlessly as possible. It is not only Right doctrinairism that is erroneous; Left doctrinairism is erroneous too. Of course, the mistake of Left doctrinairism in communism is at present a thousand times less dangerous and less significant than that of Right doctrinairism (i.e., social-chauvinism and Kautskyism); but, after all, that is only due to the fact that Left communism is a very young trend, is only just coming into being. It is only for this reason that, under certain conditions, the disease can be easily eradicated, and we must set to work with the utmost energy to eradicate it.

The old forms burst asunder, for it turned out that their new content—anti-proletarian and reactionary—had attained an inordinate development. From the standpoint of the development of international communism, our work today has such a durable and powerful content (for Soviet power and the dictatorship of the proletariat) that it can *and must* manifest itself in any form, both new and old; it can and must regenerate, conquer and subjugate all forms, not only the new, but also the old—not for the purpose of reconciling itself with the old, but for the purpose of making all and every form—new and old—a weapon for the complete and irrevocable victory of communism.

The Communists must exert every effort to direct the working-class movement and social development in general along the straightest and shortest road to the victory of Soviet power and the dictatorship of the proletariat on a world-wide scale. That is an incontestable truth. But it is enough to take one little step farther—a step that might seem to be in the same direction—and truth turns into error. We have only to say, as the German and British Left Communists do, that we recognise only one road, only the direct road, and that we will not permit tacking, conciliatory manoeuvres, or compromising—and it will be a mistake which may cause, and in part has already caused and is causing, very grave prejudice to communism. Right doctrinairism persisted in recognising only the old forms, and became utterly bankrupt, for it did not notice the new content. Left doctrinairism persists in the unconditional repudiation of certain old forms, failing to see that the new content is forcing its way through all and sundry forms, that it is our duty as Communists to master all forms, to learn how, with the maximum rapidity, to supplement one form with another, to substitute one for another, and to adapt our tactics to any such change that does not come from our class or from our efforts.

World revolution has been so powerfully stimulated and accelerated by the horrors, vileness and abominations of the world imperialist war and by the hopelessness of the situation created by it, this revolution is developing in scope and depth with such splendid rapidity, with such a wonderful variety of changing forms, with such an instructive practical refutation of all doctrinairism, that there is every reason to hope for a rapid and complete recovery of the international communist movement from the infantile disorder of "Left-wing" communism.

Communism and the East: Theses on the National and Colonial Questions

Although the statement often attributed to Lenin, that "the road to Paris runs through Peking [or New Delhi]," appears apocryphal, his analysis of the contemporary international system in *Imperialism* did imply that successful national-independence or liberation movements in the colonies and dependencies could, by detaching markets for export of capital from the imperialist countries, aggravate internal class antagonisms in the latter and thereby render European proletarian revolutions more likely. So in an interview of June 1920 with a Japanese journalist, K. Fujii, who asked: "Where has communism the greater chance of success, in the West or in the East?," Lenin said: "Real communism can so far have success only in the West. But the West, after all, lives at the expense of the East. The European imperialist powers get rich mainly in the Eastern colonies. But at the same time they are arming their colonies and training them to fight, and thereby the West is digging itself a grave in the East." (*Polnoe sobranie sochinenii*, Vol. 41, p. 133.)

From this it followed that a Soviet policy of alliance with and encouragement of national-independence movements in the colonial world (what would nowadays be called the Third World) could indirectly assist the progress of socialist revolution in the West. Such a policy was elaborated in the set of "Theses on the National and Colonial Questions" which Lenin drafted in June 1920 for the Second Comintern Congress.

In submitting for discussion by the Second Congress of the Communist International the following draft theses on the national and the colonial questions I would request all comrades, especially those who possess concrete information on any of these very complex problems, to let me have their opinions, amendments, addenda and concrete remarks *in the most concise form* (*no more than two or three pages*), particularly on the following points:

Austrian experience;
Polish-Jewish and Ukrainian experience;
Alsace-Lorraine and Belgium;

619

Ireland;
Danish-German, Italo-French and Italo-Slav relations;
Balkan experience;
Eastern peoples;
The struggle against Pan-Islamism;
Relations in the Caucasus;
The Bashkir and Tatar Republics;
Kirghizia;
Turkestan, its experience;
Negroes in America;
Colonies;
China-Korea-Japan.

June 5, 1920   *Lenin*

1) An abstract or formal posing of the problem of equality in general and national equality in particular is in the very nature of bourgeois democracy. Under the guise of the equality of the individual in general, bourgeois democracy proclaims the formal or legal equality of the property-owner and the proletarian, the exploiter and the exploited, thereby grossly deceiving the oppressed classes. On the plea that all men are absolutely equal, the bourgeoisie is transforming the idea of equality, which is itself a reflection of relations in commodity production, into a weapon in its struggle against the abolition of classes. The real meaning of the demand for equality consists in its being a demand for the abolition of classes.

2) In conformity with its fundamental task of combating bourgeois democracy and exposing its falseness and hypocrisy, the Communist Party, as the avowed champion of the proletarian struggle to overthrow the bourgeois yoke, must base its policy, in the national question too, not on abstract and formal principles but, first, on a precise appraisal of the specific historical situation and, primarily, of economic conditions; second, on a clear distinction between the interests of the oppressed classes, of working and exploited people, and the general concept of national interests as a whole, which implies the interests of the ruling class; third, on an equally clear distinction between the oppressed, dependent and subject nations and the oppressing, exploiting and sovereign nations, in order to counter the bourgeois-democratic lies that play down this colonial and financial enslavement of the vast majority of the world's population by an insignificant minority of the richest and advanced capitalist countries, a feature characteristic of the era of finance capital and imperialism.

3) The imperialist war of 1914–18 has very clearly revealed to all nations and to the oppressed classes of the whole world the

falseness of bourgeois-democratic phrases, by practically demonstrating that the Treaty of Versailles of the celebrated "Western democracies" is an even more brutal and foul act of violence against weak nations than was the Treaty of Brest-Litovsk of the German Junkers and the Kaiser. The League of Nations and the entire postwar policy of the Entente reveal this truth with even greater clarity and distinctness. They are everywhere intensifying the revolutionary struggle both of the proletariat in the advanced countries and of the toiling masses in the colonial and dependent countries. They are hastening the collapse of the petty-bourgeois nationalist illusions that nations can live together in peace and equality under capitalism.

4) From these fundamental premises it follows that the Communist International's entire policy on the national and the colonial question should rest primarily on a closer union of the proletarians and the working masses of all nations and countries for a joint revolutionary struggle to overthrow the landowners and the bourgeoisie. This union alone will guarantee victory over capitalism, without which the abolition of national oppression and inequality is impossible.

5) The world political situation has now placed the dictatorship of the proletariat on the order of the day. World political developments are of necessity concentrated on a single focus—the struggle of the world bourgeoisie against the Soviet Russian Republic, around which are inevitably grouped, on the one hand, the Soviet movements of the advanced workers in all countries, and, on the other, all the national liberation movements in the colonies and among the oppressed nationalities, who are learning from bitter experience that their only salvation lies in the Soviet system's victory over world imperialism.

6) Consequently, one cannot at present confine oneself to a bare recognition or proclamation of the need for closer union between the working people of the various nations; a policy must be pursued that will achieve the closest alliance, with Soviet Russia, of all the national and colonial liberation movements. The form of this alliance should be determined by the degree of development of the communist movement in the proletariat of each country, or of the bourgeois-democratic liberation movement of the workers and peasants in backward countries or among backward nationalities.

7) Federation is a transitional form to the complete unity of the working people of different nations. The feasibility of federation has already been demonstrated in practice both by the relations between the R.S.F.S.R. and other Soviet Republics (the Hungarian, Finnish and Latvian in the past, and the Azerbaijan and Ukrainian at present), and by the relations within the R.S.F.S.R. in respect of

nationalities which formerly enjoyed neither statehood nor autonomy (e.g., the Bashkir and Tatar autonomous republics in the
R.S.F.S.R., founded in 1919 and 1920 respectively).

8) In this respect, it is the task of the Communist International
to further develop and also to study and test by experience these
new federations, which are arising on the basis of the Soviet system
and the Soviet movement. In recognising that federation is a transitional form to complete unity, it is necessary to strive for ever
closer federal unity, bearing in mind, first, that the Soviet republics,
surrounded as they are by the imperialist powers of the whole
world—which from the military standpoint are immeasurably
stronger—cannot possibly continue to exist without the closest alliance; second, that a close economic alliance between the Soviet
republics is necessary, otherwise the productive forces which have
been ruined by imperialism cannot be restored and the well-being
of the working people cannot be ensured; third, that there is a
tendency towards the creation of a single world economy, regulated
by the proletariat of all nations as an integral whole and according
to a common plan. This tendency has already revealed itself quite
clearly under capitalism and is bound to be further developed and
consummated under socialism.

9) The Communist International's national policy in the sphere
of relations within the state cannot be restricted to the bare, formal,
purely declaratory and actually non-committal recognition of the
equality of nations to which the bourgeois democrats confine themselves—both those who frankly admit being such, and those who
assume the name of socialists (such as the socialists of the Second
International).

In all their propaganda and agitation—both within parliament
and outside it—the Communist parties must consistently expose
that constant violation of the equality of nations and of the guaranteed rights of national minorities which is to be seen in all capitalist
countries, despite their "democratic" constitutions. It is also necessary, first, constantly to explain that only the Soviet system is
capable of ensuring genuine equality of nations, by uniting first the
proletarians and then the whole mass of the working population in
the struggle against the bourgeoisie; and, second, that all Communist parties should render direct aid to the revolutionary movements
among the dependent and under-privileged nations (for example,
Ireland, the American Negroes, etc.) and in the colonies.

Without the latter condition, which is particularly important, the
struggle against the oppression of dependent nations and colonies,
as well as recognition of their right to secede, are but a false
signboard, as is evidenced by the parties of the Second International.

10) Recognition of internationalism in word, and its replacement in deed by petty-bourgeois nationalism and pacifism, in all propaganda, agitation and practical work, is very common, not only among the parties of the Second International, but also among those which have withdrawn from it, and often even among parties which now call themselves communist. The urgency of the struggle against this evil, against the most deep-rooted petty-bourgeois national prejudices, looms ever larger with the mounting exigency of the task of converting the dictatorship of the proletariat from a national dictatorship (i.e., existing in a single country and incapable of determining world politics) into an international one (i.e., a dictatorship of the proletariat involving at least several advanced countries, and capable of exercising a decisive influence upon world politics as a whole). Petty-bourgeois nationalism proclaims as internationalism the mere recognition of the equality of nations, and nothing more. Quite apart from the fact that this recognition is purely verbal, petty-bourgeois nationalism preserves national self-interest intact, whereas proletarian internationalism demands, first, that the interests of the proletarian struggle in any one country should be subordinated to the interests of that struggle on a world-wide scale, and, second, that a nation which is achieving victory over the bourgeoisie should be able and willing to make the greatest national sacrifices for the overthrow of international capital.

Thus, in countries that are already fully capitalist and have workers' parties that really act as the vanguard of the proletariat, the struggle against opportunist and petty-bourgeois pacifist distortions of the concept and policy of internationalism is a primary and cardinal task.

11) With regard to the more backward states and nations, in which feudal or patriarchal and patriarchal-peasant relations predominate, it is particularly important to bear in mind:

first, that all Communist parties must assist the bourgeois-democratic liberation movement in these countries, and that the duty of rendering the most active assistance rests primarily with the workers of the country the backward nation is colonially or financially dependent on;

second, the need for a struggle against the clergy and other influential reactionary and medieval elements in backward countries;

third, the need to combat Pan-Islamism and similiar trends, which strive to combine the liberation movement against European and American imperialism with an attempt to strengthen the positions of the khans, landowners, mullahs, etc.;

fourth, the need, in backward countries, to give special support to the peasant movement against the landowners, against landed proprietorship, and against all manifestations or survivals of feudalism, and to strive to lend the peasant movement the most revolutionary character by establishing the closest possible alliance between the West-European communist proletariat and the revolutionary peasant movement in the East, in the colonies, and in the backward countries generally. It is particularly necessary to exert every effort to apply the basic principles of the Soviet system in countries where pre-capitalist relations predominate—by setting up "working people's Soviets," etc.;

fifth, the need for a determined struggle against attempts to give a communist colouring to bourgeois-democratic liberation trends in the backward countries; the Communist International should support bourgeois-democratic national movements in colonial and backward countries only on condition that, in these countries, the elements of future proletarian parties, which will be communist not only in name, are brought together and trained to understand their special tasks, i.e., those of the struggle against the bourgeois-democratic movements within their own nations. The Communist International must enter into a temporary alliance with bourgeois democracy in the colonial and backward countries, but should not merge with it, and should under all circumstances uphold the independence of the proletarian movement even if it is in its most embryonic form;

sixth, the need constantly to explain and expose among the broadest working masses of all countries, and particularly of the backward countries, the deception systematically practised by the imperialist powers, which, under the guise of politically independent states, set up states that are wholly dependent upon them economically, financially and militarily. Under present-day international conditions there is no salvation for dependent and weak nations except in a union of Soviet republics.

12) The age-old oppression of colonial and weak nationalities by the imperialist powers has not only filled the working masses of the oppressed countries with animosity towards the oppressor nations, but has also aroused distrust in these nations in general, even in their proletariat. The despicable betrayal of socialism by the majority of the official leaders of this proletariat in 1914–19, when "defence of country" was used as a social-chauvinist cloak to conceal the defence of the "right" of their "own" bourgeoisie to oppress colonies and fleece financially dependent countries, was certain to enhance this perfectly legitimate distrust. On the other hand, the more backward the country, the stronger is the hold of small-scale agricultural production, patriarchalism and isolation, which inevitably lend particular strength and tenacity to the deepest of petty-bourgeois prejudices, i.e., to national egoism and national

narrow-mindedness. These prejudices are bound to die out very slowly, for they can disappear only after imperialism and capitalism have disappeared in the advanced countries, and after the entire foundation of the backward countries' economic life has radically changed. It is therefore the duty of the class-conscious communist proletariat of all countries to regard with particular caution and attention the survivals of national sentiments in the countries and among nationalities which have been oppressed the longest; it is equally necessary to make certain concessions with a view to more rapidly overcoming this distrust and these prejudices. Complete victory over capitalism cannot be won unless the proletariat and, following it, the mass of working people in all countries and nations throughout the world voluntarily strive for alliance and unity.

Foreign Communist Parties
and the Russian Spirit

The Soviet Communist Party was factually the dominant force in the Comintern, and through its representatives' influence the Second Comintern Congress adopted a set of twenty-one conditions for a Communist party to meet as one of the world revolutionary organization's national "sections." These twenty-one points amounted in effect to a Russification of the international Communist movement. Thus, Point 12 enjoined centralization and "iron discipline" along with supreme authority for a party's Central Committee, and Point 13 called for periodical purges of a party's membership. At the Third Comintern Congress, in 1921, a further resolution was adopted along these lines.

In his report to the Fourth Comintern Congress, on November 13, 1922, Lenin showed in the following passage both an awareness of the extent to which the "Russian spirit" had been instilled in the foreign parties and a feeling that this had not in all respects been a sound course to follow.

* * *

At the Third Congress, in 1921, we adopted a resolution on the organisational structure of the Communist Parties and on the methods and content of their activities. The resolution is an excellent one, but it is almost entirely Russian, that is to say, everything in it is based on Russian conditions. This is its good point, but it is also its failing. It is its failing because I am sure that no foreigner can read it. I have read it again before saying this. In the first place, it is too long, containing fifty or more points. Foreigners are not usually able to read such things. Secondly, even if they read it, they will not understand it because it is too Russian. Not because it is written in Russian—it has been excellently translated into all languages—but because it is thoroughly imbued with the Russian spirit. And thirdly, if by way of exception some foreigner does understand it, he cannot carry it out. This is its third defect. I have talked with a few of the foreign delegates and hope to discuss matters in detail with a large number of delegates from different

626

countries during the Congress, although I shall not take part in its
proceedings, for unfortunately it is impossible for me to do that. I
have the impression that we made a big mistake with this resolution, namely, that we blocked our own road to further success. As I
have said already, the resolution is excellently drafted; I am prepared to subscribe to every one of its fifty or more points. But we
have not learnt how to present our Russian experience to foreigners. All that was said in the resolution has remained a dead letter. If
we do not realise this, we shall be unable to move ahead. I think
that after five years of the Russian revolution the most important
thing for all of us, Russian and foreign comrades alike, is to sit
down and study. We have only now obtained the opportunity to do
so. I do not know how long this opportunity will last. I do not
know for how long the capitalist powers will give us the opportunity to study in peace. But we must take advantage of every moment of respite from fighting, from war, to study, and to study
from scratch.

* * *

Capitalist Discords and
the Concessions Policy

As the Civil War ended and reconstruction of the war-ruined economy loomed as the revolutionary regime's supreme internal task, a policy of concessions to foreign commercial interests was adopted. Timber concessions in the far North, agricultural concessions in Western Siberia and the Don River region, and concessions to develop the mineral wealth of Siberia were discussed in this report by Lenin to the party group at the Eighth Congress of Soviets on December 21, 1920. Of special interest is the way in which he related the concessions policy to the basic principle of Soviet foreign policy —exploiting conflicts or discords between capitalist states as a means of forestalling a combined onslaught upon Soviet Russia.

---

* * *

* * * The main subject of this talk is to offer proof of two premises: first, that any war is merely the continuation of peacetime politics by other means, and second, that the concessions which we are giving, which we are forced to give, are a continuation of war in another form, using other means. To prove these two premises, or rather to prove only the second because the first does not require any special proof, I shall begin with the political aspect of the question. I shall dwell on those relations existing between the present-day imperialist powers, which are important for an understanding of present-day foreign policy in its entirety, and of our reasons for adopting this policy.

The American Vanderlip sent a letter to the Council of People's Commissars in which he said that the Republicans, members of the Republican Party of America, the party of the banking interests, which is linked with memories of the war against the Southern States for liberation, were not in power at the time. He wrote this before the November elections, which he hoped the Republicans would win (they have won them) and have their own president in March. The Republicans' policy, he went on, would not repeat the follies that had involved America in European affairs, they would look after their own interests. American interests would lead them to a clash with Japan, and they would fight Japan. It might interest you to know, he went on, that in 1923 the U.S. navy would be stronger than Britain's. To fight, they needed control of oil, without which they could not wage a modern war. They not only needed oil, but also had to take steps to ensure that the enemy did not get any. Japan was in a bad way in that respect. Somewhere near Kamchatka there is an inlet (whose name he had forgotten) with oil deposits, and they did not want the Japanese to get that oil. If we sold them that land, Vanderlip could vouch that the Americans would grow so enthusiastic that the U.S. would immediately recognise our government. If we offered a concession, and did not sell them the land, he could not say that they would refuse to examine the project, but he could not promise the enthusiasm that would guarantee recognition of the Soviet Government.

Vanderlip's letter is quite outspoken; with unparalleled cynicism he outlines the point of view of an imperialist who clearly sees that a war with Japan is imminent, and poses the question openly and directly—enter into a deal with us and you will get certain advantages from it. The issue is the following: the Far East, Kamchatka and a piece of Siberia are *de facto* in the possession of Japan insofar as her troops are in control there, and circumstances made necessary the creation of a buffer state, the Far Eastern Republic. We are well aware of the unbelievable sufferings that the Siberian peasants are enduring at the hands of the Japanese imperialists and the atrocities the Japanese have committed in Siberia. The comrades from Siberia know this; their recent publications have given details of it. Nevertheless, we cannot go to war with Japan and must make every effort, not only to put off a war with Japan but, if possible, to avert it because, for reasons known to you, it is beyond our strength. At the same time Japan is causing us tremendous losses by depriving us of our links with world trade through the Pacific Ocean. Under such conditions, when we are confronted with a growing conflict, an imminent clash between America and Japan—for a most stubborn struggle has been going on for many decades between Japan and America over the Pacific Ocean and the mastery of its shores, and the entire diplomatic, economic and trade history of the Pacific Ocean and its shores is full of quite definite indications that the struggle is developing and making war between America and Japan inevitable—we return to a situation we were in for three years: we are a Socialist Republic surrounded by imperialist countries that are far stronger than us in the military sense, are using every means of agitation and propaganda to increase hatred for the Soviet Republic, and will never miss an opportunity for military intervention, as they put it, i.e., to strangle Soviet power.

If, remembering this, we cast a glance over the history of the past three years from the point of view of the international situation of the Soviet Republic, it becomes clear that we have been able to hold out and have been able to defeat the Entente powers—an alliance of unparalleled might that was supported by our white-guards—only because there has been no unity among these powers. We have so far been victorious only because of the most profound discord among the imperialist powers, and only because that discord has not been a fortuitous and internal dissension between parties, but a most deep-seated and ineradicable conflict of economic interests among the imperialist countries which, based on private property in land and capital, cannot but pursue a predatory policy which has stultified their efforts to unite their forces against the Soviets. I take Japan, which controlled almost the whole of Siberia and could, of course, have helped Kolchak at any time. The main reason she did not do so was that her interests differ radically from those of America, and she did not want to pull chestnuts out of the fire for U.S. capital. Knowing this weakness, we could of course pursue no other policy than that of taking advantage of this enmity between America and Japan so as to strengthen ourselves and delay any possibility of an agreement between Japan and America against us. * * *

* * *

When I told a meeting of leading executives what I am now telling you, a comrade just back from America where he had worked in Vanderlip's factories, said he had been horrified; nowhere had he seen such exploitation as at Vanderlip's factories. And now in the person of this capitalist shark we have won a propagandist for trade relations with Soviet Russia, and even if we do not get anything except the proposed agreement on concessions we shall still be able to say that we have gained something. We have received a number of reports, secret ones, of course, to the effect that the capitalist countries have not given up the idea of launching a new war against Soviet Russia in the spring. We have learnt that preliminary steps are being taken by some capitalist states, while whiteguard elements are, it may be said, making preparations in all countries. Our chief interest therefore, lies in achieving the re-establishment of trade relations, and for that purpose we need to have at least a section of the capitalists on our side.

* * *

* * * Is it the correct policy for us to use the discord between the imperialist bandits to make it more difficult for them to unite

against us, who are doing everything in our power to accelerate that revolution, but are in the position of a weak socialist republic that is being attacked by imperialist bandits? Of course, it is the correct policy. We have pursued that policy for four years. The Treaty of Brest-Litovsk was the chief expression of this policy. While the German imperialists were offering resistance, we were able to hold out even when the Red Army had not yet been formed, by using the contradictions existing between the imperialists.

* * *

* * * At present, after having burnt their fingers in the armed invasion of Russia, they cannot think of an immediate resumption of the war. We must seize the opportunity and bend every effort to achieve trade relations even at the cost of maximum concessions, for we cannot for a moment believe in lasting trade relations with the imperialist powers; the respite will be temporary. The experience of the history of revolutions and great conflicts teaches us that wars, a series of wars, are inevitable. The existence of a Soviet Republic alongside of capitalist countries—a Soviet Republic surrounded by capitalist countries—is so intolerable to the capitalists that they will seize any opportunity to resume the war. The peoples are weary of the imperialist war and threaten to make their indignation felt if war continues, but the possibility of the capitalists being able to resume it in a few years is not precluded. That is why we must exert every effort to utilise the opportunity, since it exists, and conclude trade agreements. I can say the following here (this is not for the record). I think that we shall ultimately emerge on top as a result of our firm stand that the Communist International is not a governmental institution. That is the more probable for the British bourgeoisie having to realise the ridiculousness of rising up against the Third International. The Third International was formed in March 1919. Its Second Congress was held in July 1920, following which the terms proposed in Moscow were made publicly known in all countries. An open struggle is going on for adhesion to the Communist International. The organisational foundations for the formation of Communist parties exist everywhere. In these circumstances, any attempt to present us seriously with an ultimatum that we get rid of the Communist International is inexcusable. However, the emphasis laid on the matter shows where the shoe pinches and what displeases them in our policy. Even without that, we have known what it is in our policy that is not to their liking. The East is another question that can be spoken of at a Party meeting, and is alarming Britain. The latter wants us to give assurances that we will do nothing against Britain's interests in the East. We are willing and ready to give such an undertaking. As an example I might mention that the Congress of Peoples of the East, a Communist congress, took place, not in the R.S.F.S.R. but in Baku, in the independent republic of Azerbaijan.[1] The British Government will have no reason to accuse us of doing anything against British interests. In their ignorance of our Constitution, they sometimes confuse the Azerbaijan Republic with the Russian Soviet Republic. Our laws are definite and precise on that score, and it will be easy to refute the false interpretations of the British ministers. * * *

* * *

I now come to the question of the relations between Britain and France. These are confused. On the one hand, Britain and France belong to the League of Nations and are obliged to act jointly; on the other hand, whenever any tension arises they fail to do so. * * * Concessions are more acceptable to Britain than to France, which still aspires to get her debts paid back, while in Britain capitalists with any business sense no longer think about it. From that angle, too, it is to our advantage to use the dissension between Britain and France, and we must therefore insist on the political proposal of concessions to Britain. We now have a draft agreement on timber concessions in the Far North. Since there is no political unity between Britain and France, our position imposes on us the duty of even incurring a certain risk, if only we succeed in hampering a military alliance between Britain and France against us. * * *

Last, the final aspect of the matter is the attitude of Britain and the entire Entente to Germany. If we exclude America, Germany is the most advanced country. In the development of electricity her technical level is even higher than America's. The conditions obtaining in Germany in consequence of the Treaty of Versailles make her existence impossible. Because of that situation it is natural for Germany to be prompted towards an alliance with Russia. When the Russian troops were approaching Warsaw, all Germany was seething. An alliance between Russia and Germany, a country that has been strangled, a country that is able to set gigantic productive forces in motion—this situation has led to a political mix-up in Germany: the German Black Hundreds sympathise with the Russian Bolsheviks in the same way as the Spartacus League does. This can well be understood because it derives from economic causes, and is the basis of the entire economic situation and of our foreign policy.

While we stand alone and the capitalist world is strong, our foreign policy consists, on the one hand, in our having to utilise disagreements (to vanquish all the imperialist powers would, of

1. Lenin is referring to the *Soviet* Republic of Azerbaijan. [*R. T.*]

course, be a most pleasant thing, but for a fairly long time we shall not be in a position to do so). On the one hand, our existence depends on the presence of radical differences between the imperialist powers, and, on the other, on the Entente's victory and the Peace of Versailles having thrown the vast majority of the German nation into a situation it is impossible for them to live in. The Peace of Versailles has created a situation in which Germany cannot even dream of a breathing-space, or of not being plundered, of not having the means of subsistence taken away from her, of her people not being doomed to starvation and extinction; Germany cannot even dream of any of these things, so that, naturally, her only means of salvation lies in an alliance with Soviet Russia, a country towards which her eyes are therefore turning. They are furiously opposing Soviet Russia; they detest the Bolsheviks, and shoot down their own Communists in the manner of real whiteguards. The German bourgeois government has an implacable hatred of the Bolsheviks, but such is its international position that, against its own desires, the government is driven towards peace with Soviet Russia. That, comrades, is the second corner-stone of our international policy, our foreign policy; it is to show peoples that are conscious of the bourgeois yoke that there is no salvation for them without the Soviet Republic. Since the Soviet Republic withstood the onslaught of the imperialists for three years, this goes to show that one country, and that country alone, has been successful in hurling back this imperialist yoke. That country has been called a country of "robbers," "plunderers," "bandits," Bolsheviks, etc.—let that be so, but still it is impossible to improve the economic situation without that country.

* * *

Our economic interest in timber concessions in the Far North of European Russia is obvious; there are tens and even hundreds of millions of *dessiatines*[1] of forest land which we are quite unable to exploit because we lack the railways, the means of production and the possibility of providing the workers there with food, but which could be exploited by a country that owns a big merchant fleet and could fell and saw timber properly and export it in tremendous quantities.

If we want to trade with foreign countries—and we do want to, because we realise its necessity—our chief interest is in obtaining as quickly as possible, from the capitalist countries, the means of production (locomotives, machinery, and electrical equipment) without which we cannot more or less seriously rehabilitate our

---

1. A *dessiatine* is about 2.7 acres. [*R. T.*]

industry, or perhaps may even be unable to do so at all, because the machinery needed by our factories cannot be made available. It is with the motive of extra profit that we must attract the capitalist. He will get surplus profit—well, let him have that surplus profit; we shall obtain the fundamentals that will help strengthen us; we shall stand firmly on our own feet, and shall win in the economic field. * * *

* * *

* * * There is no doubt that concessions are a new kind of war. The capitalists are coming to us to wage a new kind of war—the very existence of the capitalists is in itself a war against the socialist world surrounding them. Capitalist enterprises in a socialist state are in the economic sense a war for freedom of trade, against the policy of compulsory deliveries, a war for private property against a republic that has abolished that property. * * * I think we shall agree that the concessions policy is a policy of continuation of the war, but we must also agree that it is our task to ensure the continued existence of an isolated socialist republic surrounded by capitalist enemies, to preserve a republic that is infinitely weaker than the capitalist enemies surrounding it, thereby eliminating any possibility of our enemies forming an alliance among themselves for the struggle against us, and to hamper their policies and not give them an opportunity to win a victory. It is our task to secure for Russia the necessary machinery and funds for the restoration of the economy; when we have obtained that, we shall stand so firmly on our own feet that no capitalist enemies can overawe us. That is the point of view which has guided us in our policy on concessions, the policy I have outlined.

Soviet Economic Development
and World Revolution

This was Lenin's closing speech at the Tenth All-Russia Party Conference, held in late May 1921. The conference was devoted to the implementation of the NEP, and the closing speech may be seen as the adumbrating of a Soviet foreign policy for the NEP era, based on the postulate that a certain "equilibrium" had been established between Soviet Russia and the capitalist world. He did not call it "coexistence," although in an interview of February 18, 1920, with a Western journalist, Karl Wiegand, published in the *New York Evening Journal* on February 21, he had spoken of "peaceful cohabitation (*sozhitel'stvo*) with the peoples" as a Soviet *aim*. NEP in Soviet foreign policy was to find expression in the spring of 1922 in the Soviet-German agreement at Rapallo, under which the new Russia in a sense re-entered the European system. Lenin's statement in the Tenth Conference speech that "we are now exercising our main influence on the international revolution through our economic policy" was to provide a text for a future Soviet leader, Nikita Khrushchev, when he expounded his foreign policy of competitive coexistence in the nineteen-fifties.

Comrades, I think I can confine myself to a very short speech. As you are aware, we convened this special conference mainly for the purpose of achieving complete understanding on economic policy between the centre and the localities, among Party and all Soviet workers. I think that the conference has fully achieved its object. Some speakers noted that Comrade Osinsky gave the correct expression to the feelings of very many, probably the majority of, local Party workers when he said that we must remove all doubt about the fact that the policy adopted by the Tenth Party Congress and subsequently reinforced by decrees and orders has unquestionably been accepted by the Party in earnest and for a long time. This is what the conference most emphatically expressed and amplified by a number of points. When the comrades return to their localities, not the slightest possibility of wrong interpretation will remain. Of course, in adopting a policy to be pursued over a number of years we do not for a moment forget that everything may be altered by the international revolution, its rate of development and the circumstances accompanying it. The current international situation is such that some sort of a temporary, unstable equilibrium, but equilibrium for all that, has been established; it is the kind of equilibrium under which the imperialist powers have been compelled to abandon their desire to hurl themselves at Soviet Russia, despite their hatred for her, because the disintegration of the capitalist world is steadily progressing, unity is steadily diminishing, while the onslaught of the forces of the oppressed colonies, which have a population of over a thousand million, is increasing from year to year, month to month, and even week to week. But we can make no conjectures on this score. We are now exercising our main influence on the international revolution through our economic policy. The working people of all countries without exception and without exaggeration are looking to the Soviet Russian Republic. This much has been achieved. The capitalists cannot hush up or conceal anything. That is why they so eagerly catch at our every economic mistake and weakness. The struggle in this field has now become global. Once we solve this problem, we shall have certainly and finally won on an international scale. That is why for us questions of economic development become of absolutely exceptional importance. On this front, we must achieve victory by a steady rise and progress which must be gradual and necessarily slow. I think that as a result of the work of our conference we shall certainly achieve this goal.

PART VI

Revolution and Culture

On Marxism and Philosophy

Lenin's Marxism was to a great extent a Marxism of practice: a body of thought on the Marxist politics of revolution and related questions. He did, however, concern himself at various times with problems of Marxist philosophy, with Marxism as a world-view, and with dialectics; the following four selections reflect these concerns and their development.

"The Three Sources and Three Component Parts of Marxism" is a general characterization of classical Marxism, or the thought of Marx and Engels, as Lenin viewed it. The article appeared in the party journal *Prosveshchenie* (*Enlightenment*) in 1913, on the occasion of the thirtieth anniversary of the death of Marx.

The highly doctrinaire, not to say religious-dogmatic, nature of Lenin's earlier approach to Marxist philosophy is clearly evident in his major treatise of 1908, *Materialism and Empirio-criticism*, which was written to combat and condemn the attempts of a number of Russian Marxists of that time (Bazarov, Bogdanov, Lunacharsky, Valentinov, and others) to supplement Marxist philosophical materialism with an "empirio-criticist" theory of knowledge derived largely from the German philosophical thinkers Ernst Mach and R. H. L. Avenarius. The passage given here, entitled "Parties in Philosophy and Philosophical Blockheads," is taken from the concluding chapter and expresses Lenin's view of the history of philosophy as a "party" struggle between idealist and materialist positions, no middle position being possible.

The volume known as *Philosophical Notebooks*, originally published in the nineteen-thirties, is a compendium of Lenin's conspectuses of philosophical works and other preparatory materials dating from between 1895 and 1916. The bulk of it consists of conspectuses prepared in 1914–16 of Hegel's *The Science of Logic* and other writings, and Lenin's notes by way of commentary. These materials show signs of a development of his philosophical thinking away from *Materialism and Empirio-criticism's* naïve realism (and its "copy" theory of perception) to a dialectical view of reality deeply influenced by Hegel's thought. Symptomatic of this development is Lenin's comment at one point: "It is impossible to understand completely Marx's *Capital*, and especially its first chapter, without having thoroughly studied and understood the *whole* of Hegel's *Logic*. Consequently, half a century later none of the Marxists understood Marx!!" Again, "Cognition is the eternal, endless approximation of thought to the object. The *reflection* of nature in man's thought must be understood not 'lifelessly,' not 'abstractly,' not devoid of movement, NOT WITHOUT CONTRADICTIONS, but in the eternal PROCESS of movement, the arising of contradictions and their solution." In the course of the work on Hegel, and evidently under his inspiration, Lenin in 1915 wrote "On the Question of Dialectics," an essay which appears here unabridged. First published in 1925 in the Soviet party journal *Bolshevik*, this essay subsequently was included in the *Philosophical Notebooks*.

The last of the four philosophical selections included here was written in March 1922 for a new Soviet philosophical journal, *Pod Znamenem Marksizma* (*Under the Banner of Marxism*), and shows the influence of the *Philosophical Notebooks* in its advice to the contributors to engage in the systematic study of Hegelian dialectics from a materialist standpoint and to constitute themselves a kind of "Society of Materialist Friends of Hegelian Dialectics."

The Three Sources and Three Component Parts of Marxism

Throughout the civilised world the teachings of Marx evoke the utmost hostility and hatred of all bourgeois science (both official and liberal), which regards Marxism as a kind of "pernicious sect." And no other attitude is to be expected, for there can be no "impartial" social science in a society based on class struggle. In one way or another, *all* official and liberal science *defends* wage slavery, whereas Marxism has declared relentless war on that slavery. To expect science to be impartial in a wage-slave society is as foolishly naïve as to expect impartiality from manufacturers on the question of whether workers' wages ought not to be increased by decreasing the profits of capital.

But this is not all. The history of philosophy and the history of social science show with perfect clarity that there is nothing resembling "sectarianism" in Marxism, in the sense of its being a hidebound, petrified doctrine, a doctrine which arose *away from* the highroad of the development of world civilisation. On the contrary, the genius of Marx consists precisely in his having furnished answers to questions already presented by the foremost minds of mankind. His doctrine emerged as the direct and immediate *continuation* of the teachings of the greatest representatives of philosophy, political economy and socialism.

The Marxist doctrine is omnipotent because it is true. It is comprehensive and harmonious, and provides men with an integral world outlook irreconcilable with any form of superstition, reaction, or defence of bourgeois oppression. It is the legitimate successor to the best that man produced in the nineteenth century, as represented by German philosophy, English political economy and French socialism.

It is these three sources of Marxism, which are also its component parts, that we shall outline in brief.

I

The philosophy of Marxism is *materialism*. Throughout the modern history of Europe, and especially at the end of the eighteenth century in France, where a resolute struggle was conducted against every kind of medieval rubbish, against serfdom in institutions and ideas, materialism has proved to be the only philosophy that is consistent, true to all the teachings of natural science and hostile to superstition, cant and so forth. The enemies of democracy have, therefore, always exerted all their efforts to "refute," undermine and defame materialism, and have advocated various forms of philosophical idealism, which always, in one way or another, amounts to the defence or support of religion.

Marx and Engels defended philosophical materialism in the most determined manner and repeatedly explained how profoundly erroneous is every deviation from this basis. Their views are most clearly and fully expounded in the works of Engels, *Ludwig Feuerbach* and *Anti-Dühring*, which, like the *Communist Manifesto*, are handbooks for every class-conscious worker.

But Marx did not stop at eighteenth-century materialism: he developed philosophy to a higher level. He enriched it with the achievements of German classical philosophy, especially of Hegel's system, which in its turn had led to the materialism of Feuerbach. The main achievement was *dialectics*, i.e., the doctrine of development in its fullest, deepest and most comprehensive form, the doctrine of the relativity of the human knowledge that provides us with a reflection of eternally developing matter. The latest discoveries of natural science—radium, electrons, the transmutation of elements—have been a remarkable confirmation of Marx's dialectical materialism, despite the teachings of the bourgeois philosophers with their "new" reversions to old and decadent idealism.

Marx deepened and developed philosophical materialism to the full, and extended the cognition of nature to include the cognition of *human society*. His *historical materialism* was a great achievement in scientific thinking. The chaos and arbitrariness that had previously reigned in views on history and politics were replaced by a strikingly integral and harmonious scientific theory, which shows how, in consequence of the growth of productive forces, out of one system of social life another and higher system develops—how capitalism, for instance, grows out of feudalism.

Just as man's knowledge reflects nature (i.e., developing matter), which exists independently of him, so man's *social knowledge* (i.e., his various views and doctrines—philosophical, religious, political and so forth) reflects the *economic system* of society. Political institutions are a superstructure on the economic foundation. We see, for example, that the various political forms of the modern European states serve to strengthen the domination of the bourgeoisie over the proletariat.

Marx's philosophy is a consummate philosophical materialism which has provided mankind, and especially the working class, with powerful instruments of knowledge.

II

Having recognised that the economic system is the foundation on which the political superstructure is erected, Marx devoted his greatest attention to the study of this economic system. Marx's principal work, *Capital,* is devoted to a study of the economic system of modern, i.e., capitalist, society.

Classical political economy, before Marx, evolved in England, the most developed of the capitalist countries. Adam Smith and David Ricardo, by their investigations of the economic system, laid the foundations of the *labour theory of value.* Marx continued their work; he provided a proof of the theory and developed it consistently. He showed that the value of every commodity is determined by the quantity of socially necessary labour time spent on its production.

Where the bourgeois economists saw a relation between things (the exchange of one commodity for another) Marx revealed a *relation between people.* The exchange of commodities expresses the connections between individual producers through the market. *Money* signifies that the connection is becoming closer and closer, inseparably uniting the entire economic life of the individual producers into one whole. *Capital* signifies a further development of this connection: man's labour power becomes a commodity. The wage worker sells his labour power to the owner of land, factories and instruments of labour. The worker spends one part of the day covering the cost of maintaining himself and his family (wages), while the other part of the day he works without remuneration, creating for the capitalist *surplus-value,* the source of profit, the source of the wealth of the capitalist class.

The doctrine of surplus-value is the corner-stone of Marx's economic theory.

Capital, created by the labour of the worker, crushes the worker, ruining small proprietors and creating an army of unemployed. In industry, the victory of large-scale production is immediately apparent, but the same phenomenon is also to be observed in agriculture, where the superiority of large-scale capitalist agriculture is enhanced, the use of machinery increases and the peasant economy, trapped by money-capital, declines and falls into ruin under the burden of its backward technique. The decline of small-scale production assumes different forms in agriculture, but the decline itself is an indisputable fact.

By destroying small-scale production, capital leads to an increase in productivity of labour and to the creation of a monopoly position for the associations of big capitalists. Production itself becomes more and more social—hundreds of thousands and millions of workers become bound together in a regular economic organism —but the product of this collective labour is appropriated by a handful of capitalists. Anarchy of production, crises, the furious chase after markets and the insecurity of existence of the mass of the population are intensified.

By increasing the dependence of the workers on capital, the capitalist system creates the great power of united labour.

Marx traced the development of capitalism from embryonic commodity economy, from simple exchange, to its highest forms, to large-scale production.

And the experience of all capitalist countries, old and new, year by year demonstrates clearly the truth of this Marxian doctrine to increasing numbers of workers.

Capitalism has triumphed all over the world, but this triumph is only the prelude to the triumph of labour over capital.

III

When feudalism was overthrown, and *"free"* capitalist society appeared in the world, it at once became apparent that this freedom meant a new system of oppression and exploitation of the working people. Various socialist doctrines immediately emerged as a reflection of and protest against this oppression. Early socialism, however, was *utopian* socialism. It criticised capitalist society, it condemned and damned it, it dreamed of its destruction, it had visions of a better order and endeavoured to convince the rich of the immorality of exploitation.

But utopian socialism could not indicate the real solution. It could not explain the real nature of wage-slavery under capitalism, it could not reveal the laws of capitalist development, or show what *social force* is capable of becoming the creator of a new society.

Meanwhile, the stormy revolutions which everywhere in Europe, and especially in France, accompanied the fall of feudalism, of serfdom, more and more clearly revealed the *struggle of classes* as the basis and the driving force of all development.

Not a single victory of political freedom over the feudal class was won except against desperate resistance. Not a single capitalist country evolved on a more or less free and democratic basis except by a life-and-death struggle between the various classes of capitalist society.

The genius of Marx lies in his having been the first to deduce from this the lesson world history teaches and to apply that lesson consistently. The deduction he made is the doctrine of the *class struggle*.

People always have been the foolish victims of deception and self-deception in politics, and they always will be until they have learnt to seek out the *interests* of some class or other behind all moral, religious, political and social phrases, declarations and promises. Champions of reforms and improvements will always be fooled by the defenders of the old order until they realise that every old institution, however barbarous and rotten it may appear to be, is kept going by the forces of certain ruling classes. And there is *only one* way of smashing the resistance of those classes, and that is to find, in the very society which surrounds us, the forces which can—and, owing to their social position, *must*—constitute the power capable of sweeping away the old and creating the new, and to enlighten and organise those forces for the struggle.

Marx's philosophical materialism alone has shown the proletariat the way out of the spiritual slavery in which all oppressed classes have hitherto languished. Marx's economic theory alone has explained the true position of the proletariat in the general system of capitalism.

Independent organisations of the proletariat are multiplying all over the world, from America to Japan and from Sweden to South Africa. The proletariat is becoming enlightened and educated by waging its class struggle; it is ridding itself of the prejudices of bourgeois society; it is rallying its ranks ever more closely and is learning to gauge the measure of its successes; it is steeling its forces and is growing irresistibly.

Parties in Philosophy and Philosophical Blockheads

It remains for us to examine the relation between Machism and religion. But this broadens into the question of whether there are parties generally in philosophy, and what is meant by non-partisanship in philosophy.

Throughout the preceding exposition, in connection with every problem of epistemology touched upon and in connection with every philosophical question raised by the new physics, we traced

the struggle between *materialism* and *idealism*. Behind the mass of
new terminological devices, behind the litter of erudite scholasti-
cism, we invariably discerned *two* principal alignments, two fundamental trends in the solution of philosophical problems. Whether
nature, matter, the physical, the external world be taken as primary, and mind, spirit, sensation (experience—as the *widespread*
terminology of our time has it), the psychical, etc., be regarded as
secondary—that is the root question which *in fact* continues to
divide the philosophers into *two great camps*. The source of thousands upon thousands of mistakes and of the confusion reigning in
this sphere is the fact that beneath the envelope of terms, definitions, scholastic devices and verbal artifices, these two fundamental
trends are *overlooked*. (Bogdanov, for instance, refuses to ac-
knowledge his idealism, because, you see, instead of the "metaphysical" concepts "nature" and "mind," he has taken the "experi-
ential" physical and psychical. A word has been changed!)

The genius of Marx and Engels consisted in the very fact that in
the course of a long period, *nearly half a century*, they developed
materialism, that they further advanced one fundamental trend in
philosophy, that they did not confine themselves to reiterating epistemological problems that had already been solved, but consistently
applied—and showed *how* to apply—*this same* materialism in the
sphere of the social sciences, mercilessly brushing aside as litter and
rubbish the pretentious rigmarole, the innumerable attempts to
"discover" a "new" line in philosophy, to invent a "new" trend and
so forth. The verbal nature of such attempts, the scholastic play
with new philosophical "isms," the clogging of the issue by pretentious devices, the inability to comprehend and clearly present the
struggle between the two fundamental epistemological trends—this
is what Marx and Engels persistently pursued and fought against
throughout their entire activity.

We said, "nearly half a century." And, indeed, as far back as
1843, when Marx was only becoming Marx, i.e., the founder of
scientific socialism, the founder of *modern materialism*, which is
immeasurably richer in content and incomparably more consistent
than all preceding forms of materialism, even at that time Marx
pointed out with amazing clarity the basic trends in philosophy.
Karl Grün quotes a letter from Marx to Feuerbach dated October
20, 1843, in which Marx invites Feuerbach to write an article for
the *Deutsch-Französische Jahrbücher* against Schelling. This Schelling, writes Marx, is a shallow braggart with his claims to having
embraced and transcended all previous philosophical trends. "To
the French romanticists and mystics he [Schelling] says: I am the
union of philosophy and theology; to the French materialists: I am
the union of the flesh and the idea; to the French sceptics: I am the

destroyer of dogmatism."[1] That the "sceptics," be they called Humeans or Kantians (or, in the twentieth century, Machians), cry out against the "dogmatism" of both materialism and idealism, Marx at that time already realised; and, without letting himself be diverted by any one of a thousand wretched little philosophical systems, he was able with the help of Feuerbach to take the direct materialist road as against idealism. Thirty years later, in the afterword to the second edition of the first volume of *Capital*, Marx just as clearly and definitely contrasted *his materialism* to Hegel's *idealism*, the most consistent and developed idealism of all; he contemptuously brushed Comtian "positivism" aside and dubbed as wretched epigoni the contemporary philosophers who imagined that they had destroyed Hegel when in reality they had reverted to a repetition of the pre-Hegelian errors of Kant and Hume. In the letter to Kugelmann of June 27, 1870, Marx refers contemptuously to "Büchner, Lange, Dühring, Fechner, etc.," because they understood nothing of Hegel's dialectics and treated him with scorn.[2] And finally, take the various philosophical utterances by Marx in *Capital* and other works, and you will find an *invariable* basic motif, viz., insistence upon *materialism* and contemptuous derision of all obscurity, of all confusion and all deviations towards *idealism*. All Marx's philosophical utterances revolve within these fundamental opposites, and, in the eyes of professorial philosophy, their defect lies in this "narrowness" and "one-sidedness." As a matter of fact, this refusal to recognise the hybrid projects for reconciling materialism and idealism constitutes the great merit of Marx, who moved *forward* along a sharply-defined philosophical road.

Entirely in the spirit of Marx, and in close collaboration with him, Engels in all his philosophical works briefly and clearly contrasts the materialist and idealist line in regard to *all* questions, without, either in 1878, 1888, or 1892, taking seriously the endless attempts to "transcend" the "one-sidedness" of materialism and idealism, to proclaim a *new* trend—"positivism," "realism," or some other professorial charlatanism. * * *

* * *

Marx and Engels were partisans in philosophy from start to finish; they were able to detect the deviations from materialism and

1. Karl Grün, *Ludwig Feuerbach in seinem Briefwechsel und Nachlass, sowie in seiner philosophischen Charakterentwicklung*, Bd. I (Leipzig, 1874), S. 361. [*Lenin*]
2. Of the positivist, Beesly, Marx, in the letter (to Kugelmann—*Trans.*) of December 13, 1870, speaks as follows:

"Professor Beesly is a Comtist and is as such obliged to support all sorts of crotchets." Compare this with the opinion given of the positivists of the Huxley type by Engels in 1892. [*Lenin*] The work referred to is Engels's *Socialism: Utopian and Scientific*.

concessions to idealism and fideism in each and every "new" tendency. They therefore appraised Huxley *exclusively* from the standpoint of his materialist consistency. They therefore rebuked Feuerbach for not pursuing materialism to the end, for renouncing materialism because of the errors of individual materialists, for combating religion in order to renovate it or invent a new religion, for being unable, in sociology, to rid himself of idealist phraseology and become a materialist.

And whatever particular mistakes he committed in his exposition of dialectical materialism, J. Dietzgen[3] fully appreciated and took over this great and most precious tradition of his teachers. Dietzgen sinned much by his clumsy deviations from materialism, but he never attempted to dissociate himself from it in principle, he never attempted to hoist a "new" standard, and always at the decisive moment he firmly and categorically declared: I am a materialist; our philosophy is a materialist philosophy. "Of all parties," our Joseph Dietzgen justly said,

> the middle party is the most repulsive. . . . Just as parties in politics are more and more becoming divided into two camps . . . so science too is being divided into two general classes [*Generalklassen*]: metaphysicians on the one hand, and physicists, or materialists, on the other.[4] The intermediate elements and conciliatory quacks, with their various appellations—spiritualists, sensationalists, realists, etc., etc.,—fall into the current on their way. We aim at definition and clarity. The reactionaries who sound a retreat call themselves idealists,[5] and materialists should be the name for all who are striving to liberate the human mind from the metaphysical spell. . . . If we compare the two parties respectively to solid and liquid, between them there is a mush."[6]

True! The "realists," etc., including the "positivists," the Machians, etc., are all a wretched mush; they are a contemptible *middle party* in philosophy, who confuse the materialist and idealist trends on every question. The attempt to escape these two basic trends in philosophy is nothing but "conciliatory quackery."

* * *

3. Joseph Dietzgen (1828–88), a German worker and socialist, arrived independently at basic propositions of dialectical materialism. [*R. T.*]
4. Here again we have a clumsy and inexact expression: instead of "metaphysicians," he should have said "idealists." Elsewhere Dietzgen himself contrasts the metaphysicians and the dialecticians. [*Lenin*]
5. Note that Dietzgen has corrected himself and now explains *more precisely* which is the party of the enemies of materialism. [*Lenin*]
6. See the article, "Social-Democratic Philosophy," written in 1876, *Kleinere philosophische Schriften*, 1903, S. 135. [*Lenin*]

On the Question of Dialectics

The splitting of a single whole and the cognition of its contradictory parts (see the quotation from Philo on Heraclitus at the beginning of Section III, "On Cognition," in Lassalle's book on Heraclitus) is the *essence* (one of the "essentials," one of the principal, if not the principal, characteristics or features) of dialectics. That is precisely how Hegel, too, put the matter (Aristotle in his *Metaphysics* continually *grapples* with it and *combats* Heraclitean ideas).

The correctness of this aspect of the content of dialectics must be tested by the history of science. This aspect of dialectics (e.g., in Plekhanov) usually receives inadequate attention: the identity of opposites is taken as the sum-total of *examples* ["for example, a seed," "for example, primitive communism." The same is true of Engels. But it is "in the interests of popularisation . . ."] and not as a *law of cognition* (*and* as a law of the objective world).

In mathematics: + and −. Differential and integral.

In mechanics: action and reaction.

In physics: positive and negative electricity.

In chemistry: the combination and dissociation of atoms.

In social science: the class struggle.

The identity of opposites (it would be more correct, perhaps, to say their "unity"—although the difference between the terms identity and unity is not particularly important here. In a certain sense both are correct) is the recognition (discovery) of the contradictory, *mutually exclusive*, opposite tendencies in *all* phenomena and processes of nature (*including* mind and society). The condition for the knowledge of all processes of the world in their *"self-movement,"* in their spontaneous development, in their real life, is the knowledge of them as a unity of opposites. Development is the "struggle" of opposites. The two basic (or two possible? or two historically observable?) conceptions of development (evolution) are: development as decrease and increase, as repetition, *and* development as a unity of opposites (the division of a unity into mutually exclusive opposites and their reciprocal relation).

In the first conception of motion, *self*-movement, its *driving* force, its source, its motive, remains in the shade (or this source is made *external*—God, subject, etc.). In the second conception the chief attention is directed precisely to knowledge of the *source* of *"self"*-movement.

The first conception is lifeless, pale and dry. The second is living. The second *alone* furnishes the key to the "self-movement" of everything existing; it alone furnishes the key to the "leaps," to the "break in continuity," to the "transformation into the opposite," to the destruction of the old and the emergence of the new.

The unity (coincidence, identity, equal action) of opposites is conditional, temporary, transitory, relative. The struggle of mutually exclusive opposites is absolute, just as development and motion are absolute.

> *NB:* The distinction between subjectivism (scepticism, sophistry, etc.) and dialectics, incidentally, is that in (objective) dialectics the difference between the relative and the absolute is itself relative. For objective dialectics there *is* an absolute *within* the relative. For subjectivism and sophistry the relative is only relative and excludes the absolute.

In his *Capital*, Marx first analyses the simplest, most ordinary and fundamental, most common and everyday *relation* of bourgeois (commodity) society, a relation encountered billions of times, viz. the exchange of commodities. In this very simple phenomenon (in this "cell" of bourgeois society) analysis reveals *all* the contradictions (or the germs of *all* the contradictions) of modern society. The subsequent exposition shows us the development (*both* growth *and* movement) of these contradictions and of this society in the Σ^1 of its individual parts, from its beginning to its end.

Such must also be the method of exposition (or study) of dialectics in general (for with Marx the dialectics of bourgeois society is only a particular case of dialectics). To begin with what is the simplest, most ordinary, common, etc., with any *proposition*: the leaves of a tree are green; John is a man; Fido is a dog, etc. Here already we have *dialectics* (as Hegel's genius recognised): the **individual** is the *universal* (cf. Aristoteles, *Metaphysik*, translation by Schwegler, Bd. II, S. 40, 3. Buch, 4. Kapitel, 8–9: "denn natürlich kann man nicht der Meinung sein, daß es ein Haus (a house in general) gebe außer den sichtbaren Häusern," "οὐ γὰρ ἂν θείημεν εἶναί τινα οἰκίαν παρὰ τὰς τινὰς οἰκίας").[2] Consquently, the opposites (the individual is opposed to the universal) are identical: the individual exists only in the connection that leads to the universal. The universal exists only in the individual and through the individual. Every individual is (in one way or another) a universal. Every universal is (a fragment, or an aspect, or the essence of) an individual. Every universal only approximately embraces all the individual objects. Every individual enters incompletely into the universal, etc., etc. Every individual is connected by thousands of transitions with other kinds of individuals (things, phenomena, processes), etc. *Here already* we have the elements, the germs, the

1. Summation.
2. "For, of course, one cannot hold the opinion that there can be a house (in general) apart from visible houses."

concepts of *necessity,* of objective connection in nature, etc. Here already we have the contingent and the necessary, the phenomenon and the essence; for when we say: John is a man, Fido is a dog, *this* is a leaf of a tree, etc., we *disregard* a number of attributes as *contingent*; we separate the essence from the appearance, and counterpose the one to the other.

Thus in *any* proposition we can (and must) disclose as in a "nucleus" ("cell") the germs of *all* the elements of dialectics, and thereby show that dialectics is a property of all human knowledge in general. And natural science shows us (and here again it must be demonstrated in *any* simple instance) objective nature with the same qualities, the transformation of the individual into the universal, of the contingent into the necessary, transitions, modulations, and the reciprocal connection of opposites. Dialectics *is* the theory of knowledge of (Hegel and) Marxism. This is the "aspect" of the matter (it is not "an aspect" but the *essence* of the matter) to which Plekhanov, not to speak of other Marxists, paid no attention.

Knowledge is represented in the form of a series of circles both by Hegel (see *Logic*) and by the modern "epistemologist" of natural science, the eclectic and foe of Hegelianism (which he did not understand!), Paul Volkmann (see his *Erkenntnistheoretische Grundzüge,*[3] S.)

"Circles" in philosophy: is a chronology of *persons* essential? No!

Ancient: from Democritus to Plato and the dialectics of Heraclitus.
Renaissance: Descartes versus Gassendi (Spinoza?)
Modern: Holbach-Hegel (via Berkeley, Hume, Kant).
Hegel—Feuerbach—Marx.

Dialectics as *living,* many-sided knowledge (with the number of sides eternally increasing), with an infinite number of shades of every approach and approximation to reality (with a philosophica system growing into a whole out of each shade)—here we have an immeasurably rich content as compared with "metaphysical" ma terialism, the fundamental *misfortune* of which is its inability to apply dialectics to the *Bildertheorie,*[4] to the process and development of knowledge.

Philosophical idealism is *only* nonsense from the standpoint of

---

3. P. Volkmann, *Erkenntnistheoretische* (Leipzig-Berlin, 1910), p. 35.
Grundzüge der Naturwissenschaften 4. Theory of reflection.

crude, simple, metaphysical materialism. From the standpoint of *dialectical* materialism, on the other hand, philosophical idealism is a *one-sided*, exaggerated, *überschwengliches* (Dietzgen) development (inflation, distention) of one of the features, aspects, facets of knowledge into an absolute, *divorced* from matter, from nature, apotheosised. Idealism is clerical obscurantism. True. But philosophical idealism is (*"more correctly"* and *"in addition"*) a *road* to clerical obscurantism *through* one of the shades of the infinitely complex *knowledge* (dialectical) of man. NB this aphorism

Human knowledge is not (or does not follow) a straight line, but a curve, which endlessly approximates a series of circles, a spiral. Any fragment, segment, section of this curve can be transformed (transformed one-sidedly) into an independent, complete, straight line, which then (if one does not see the wood for the trees) leads into the quagmire, into clerical obscurantism (where it is *anchored* by the class interests of the ruling classes). Rectilinearity and one-sidedness, woodenness and petrification, subjectivism and subjective blindness—voilà the epistemological roots of idealism. And clerical obscurantism [= philosophical idealism], of course, has *epistemological* roots, it is not groundless; it is a *sterile flower* undoubtedly, but a sterile flower that grows on the living tree of living, fertile, genuine, powerful, omnipotent, objective, absolute human knowledge.

On the Significance of Militant Materialism

Comrade Trotsky has already said everything necessary, and said it very well, about the general purposes of *Pod Znamenem Marksizma* in issue No. 1–2 of that journal. I should like to deal with certain questions that more closely define the content and programme of the work which its editors have set forth in the introductory statement in this issue.

This statement says that not all those gathered round the journal *Pod Znamenem Marksizma* are Communists but that they are all consistent materialists. I think that this alliance of Communists and non-Communists is absolutely essential and correctly defines the purposes of the journal. One of the biggest and most dangerous mistakes made by Communists (as generally by revolutionaries who have successfully accomplished the beginning of a great revolution) is the idea that a revolution can be made by revolutionaries alone. On the contrary, to be successful, all serious revolutionary work requires that the idea that revolutionaries are capable of playing the part only of the vanguard of the truly virile and advanced class must be understood and translated into action. A vanguard performs its task as vanguard only when it is able to avoid being isolated from the mass of the people it leads and is able really to lead the whole mass forward. Without an alliance with non-Communists in the most diverse spheres of activity there can be no question of any successful communist construction.

This also applies to the defence of materialism and Marxism, which has been undertaken by *Pod Znamenem Marksizma*. Fortunately, the main trends of advanced social thinking in Russia have a solid materialist tradition. Apart from G. V. Plekhanov, it will be enough to mention Chernyshevsky, from whom the modern Narodniks (the Popular Socialists, Socialist-Revolutionaries, etc.) have frequently retreated in quest of fashionable reactionary philosophical doctrines, captivated by the tinsel of the so-called last word in European science, and unable to discern beneath this tinsel some variety of servility to the bourgeoisie, to bourgeois prejudice and bourgeois reaction.

At any rate, in Russia we still have—and shall undoubtedly have for a fairly long time to come—materialists from the non-communist camp, and it is our absolute duty to enlist all adherents of consistent and militant materialism in the joint work of combating philosophical reaction and the philosophical prejudices of so-called educated society. * * *

* * *

Pod Znamenem Marksizma, which sets out to be an organ of militant materialism, should devote much of its space to atheist propaganda, to reviews of the literature on the subject and to correcting the immense shortcomings of our governmental work in this field. It is particularly important to utilise books and pamphlets which contain many concrete facts and comparisons showing how the class interests and class organisations of the modern bourgeoisie are connected with the organisations of religious institutions and religious propaganda.

* * *

In addition to the alliance with consistent materialists who do not belong to the Communist Party, of no less and perhaps even of more importance for the work which militant materialism should perform is an alliance with those modern natural scientists who incline towards materialism and are not afraid to defend and preach it as against the modish philosophical wanderings into idealism and scepticism which are prevalent in so-called educated society.

* * *

For our attitude towards this phenomenon to be a politically conscious one, it must be realised that no natural science and no materialism can hold its own in the struggle against the onslaught of bourgeois ideas and the restoration of the bourgeois world outlook unless it stands on solid philosophical ground. In order to hold his own in this struggle and carry it to a victorious finish, the natural scientist must be a modern materialist, a conscious adherent of the materialism represented by Marx, i.e., he must be a dialectical materialist. In order to attain this aim, the contributors to *Pod Znamenem Marksizma* must arrange for the systematic study of Hegelian dialectics from a materialist standpoint, i.e., the dialectics which Marx applied practically in his *Capital* and in his historical and political works, and applied so successfully that now every day of the awakening to life and struggle of new classes in the East (Japan, India, and China)—i.e., the hundreds of millions of human beings who form the greater part of the world population and whose historical passivity and historical torpor have hitherto conditioned the stagnation and decay of many advanced European countries—every day of the awakening to life of new peoples and new classes serves as a fresh confirmation of Marxism.

Of course, this study, this interpretation, this propaganda of Hegelian dialectics is extremely difficult, and the first experiments in this direction will undoubtedly be accompanied by errors. But only he who never does anything never makes mistakes. Taking as our basis Marx's method of applying materialistically conceived Hegelian dialectics, we can and should elaborate this dialectics from all aspects, print in the journal excerpts from Hegel's principal works, interpret them materialistically and comment on them with the help of examples of the way Marx applied dialectics, as well as of examples of dialectics in the sphere of economic and political relations, which recent history, especially modern imperialist war and revolution, provides in unusual abundance. In my opinion, the editors and contributors of *Pod Znamenem Marksizma* should be a kind of "Society of Materialist Friends of Hegelian Dialectics." Modern natural scientists (if they know how to seek, and if we learn to help them) will find in the Hegelian dialectics, materialistically interpreted, a series of answers to the philosophical problems which are being raised by the revolution in natural science and which make the intellectual admirers of bourgeois fashion "stumble" into reaction.

Unless it sets itself such a task and systematically fulfils it, materialism cannot be militant materialism. * * *

Two Cultures in
Every National Culture

The following discussion of national cultures is taken from Lenin's essay "Critical Remarks on the National Question," which was written in late 1913 and published that year in *Prosveshchenie*. It is notable for its contention that there are "two cultures in every national culture" and for its extended remarks on the moot issue of a national Jewish culture. As the reader will see, Lenin, arguing from a Marxist position, took a strongly assimilationist view, based in part on his belief that the Jews in America were undergoing cultural assimilation into a common American culture.

* * *

The *elements* of democratic and socialist culture are present, if only in rudimentary form, in *every* national culture, since in *every* nation there are toiling and exploited masses, whose conditions of life inevitably give rise to the ideology of democracy and socialism. But *every* nation also possesses a bourgeois culture (and most nations a reactionary and clerical culture as well) in the form, not merely of "elements," but of the *dominant* culture. Therefore, the general "national culture" *is* the culture of the landlords, the clergy and the bourgeoisie. * * *

In advancing the slogan of "the international culture of democracy and of the world working-class movement," we take *from each* national culture *only* its democratic and socialist elements; we take them *only* and *absolutely* in opposition to the bourgeois culture and the bourgeois nationalism of *each* nation. * * *

* * *

Those who seek to serve the proletariat must unite the workers of all nations, and unswervingly fight bourgeois nationalism, *domestic* and foreign. The place of those who advocate the slogan of national culture is among the nationalist petty bourgeois, not among the Marxists.

Take a concrete example. Can a Great-Russian Marxist accept the slogan of national, Great-Russian, culture? No, he cannot. Anyone who does that should stand in the ranks of the nationalists, not of the Marxists. Our task is to fight the dominant, Black-Hundred and bourgeois national culture of the Great Russians, and to develop, exclusively in the internationalist spirit and in the closest alliance with the workers of other countries, the rudiments also existing in the history of our democratic and working-class movement. Fight your own Great-Russian landlords and bourgeoisie, fight their "culture" in the name of internationalism, and, in so fighting, "adapt" yourself to the special features of the Purishke-viches[1] and Struves—that is your task, not preaching or tolerating the slogan of national culture.

The same applies to the most oppressed and persecuted nation—the Jews. Jewish national culture is the slogan of the rabbis and the bourgeoisie, the slogan of our enemies. But there are other elements in Jewish culture and in Jewish history as a whole. Of the ten and a half million Jews in the world, somewhat over a half live in Galicia and Russia, backward and semi-barbarous countries, where the Jews are *forcibly* kept in the status of a caste. The other half lives in the civilised world, and there the Jews do not live as a segregated caste. There the great world-progressive features of Jewish culture stand clearly revealed: its internationalism, its identification with the advanced movements of the epoch (the percentage of Jews in the democratic and proletarian movements is everywhere higher than the percentage of Jews among the population).

Whoever, directly or indirectly, puts forward the slogan of Jewish "national culture" is (whatever his good intentions may be) an enemy of the proletariat, a supporter of all that is *outmoded* and connected with *caste* among the Jewish people; he is an accomplice of the rabbis and the bourgeoisie. On the other hand, those Jewish Marxists who mingle with the Russian, Lithuanian, Ukrainian and other workers in international Marxist organisations, and make their contribution (both in Russian and in Yiddish) towards creating the international culture of the working-class movement—those Jews, despite the separatism of the Bund,[2] uphold the best traditions of Jewry by fighting the slogan of "national culture."

Bourgeois nationalism and proletarian internationalism—these are the two irreconcilably hostile slogans that correspond to the two great class camps throughout the capitalist world, and express the *two* policies (nay, the two world outlooks) in the national question. In advocating the slogan of national culture and building up on it an entire plan and practical programme of what they call "cultural-

1. See note 5, p. 178, above. [*R. T.*]   2. See Introduction, p. xxxvii [*R. T.*]

national autonomy," the Bundists are *in effect* instruments of bourgeois nationalism among the workers.

* * *

It is the Jewish nationalists in Russia in general, and the Bundists in particular, who vociferate most about Russian orthodox Marxists being "assimilators." And yet, as the aforementioned figures show, out of the ten and a half million Jews all over the world, *about half* that number live in the *civilised* world, where conditions favouring "assimilation" are *strongest*, whereas the unhappy, downtrodden, disfranchised Jews in Russia and Galicia, who are crushed under the heel of the Purishkeviches (Russian and Polish), live where conditions for "assimilation" *least* prevail, where there is most segregation, and even a "Pale of Settlement," a *numerus clausus* and other charming features of the Purishkevich regime.

The Jews in the civilised world are not a nation, they have in the main become assimilated, say Karl Kautsky and Otto Bauer. The Jews in Galicia and in Russia are not a nation; unfortunately (through *no* fault of their own but through that of the Purishkeviches), they are still a *caste* here. Such is the incontrovertible judgment of people who are undoubtedly familiar with the history of Jewry and take the above-cited facts into consideration.

What do these facts prove? It is that only Jewish reactionary philistines, who want to turn back the wheel of history, and make it proceed, not from the conditions prevailing in Russia and Galicia to those prevailing in Paris and New York, but in the reverse direction—only they can clamour against "assimilation."

The best Jews, those who are celebrated in world history, and have given the world foremost leaders of democracy and socialism, have never clamoured against assimilation. It is only those who contemplate the "rear aspect" of Jewry with reverential awe that clamour against assimilation.

A rough idea of the scale which the general process of assimilation of nations is assuming under the present conditions of advanced capitalism may be obtained, for example, from the immigration statistics of the United States of America. During the decade between 1891–1900, Europe sent 3,700,000 people there, and during the nine years between 1901 and 1909, 7,200,000. The 1900 census in the United States recorded over 10,000,000 foreigners. New York State, in which, according to the same census, there were over 78,000 Austrians, 136,000 Englishmen, 20,000 Frenchmen, 480,000 Germans, 37,000 Hungarians, 425,000 Irish, 182,-000 Italians, 70,000 Poles, 166,000 people from Russia (mostly Jews), 43,000 Swedes, etc., grinds down national distinctions. And what is taking place on a grand, international scale in New York is also to be seen in *every* big city and industrial township.

No one unobsessed by nationalist prejudices can fail to perceive that this process of assimilation of nations by capitalism means the greatest historical progress, the breakdown of hidebound national conservatism in the various backwoods, especially in backward countries like Russia.

Take Russia and the attitude of Great Russians towards the Ukrainians. Naturally, every democrat, not to mention Marxists, will strongly oppose the incredible humiliation of Ukrainians, and demand complete equality for them. But it would be a downright betrayal of socialism and a silly policy *even* from the standpoint of the bourgeois "national aims" of the Ukrainians to *weaken* the ties and the alliance between the Ukrainian and Great-Russian proletariat that now exist within the confines of a single state.

* * *

* * * For several decades a well-defined process of accelerated economic development has been going on in the South, i.e., the Ukraine, attracting hundreds of thousands of peasants and workers from Great Russia to the capitalist farms, mines, and cities. The "assimilation"—within these limits—of the Great-Russian and Ukrainian proletariat is an indisputable fact. *And this* fact is *undoubtedly* progressive. Capitalism is replacing the ignorant, conservative, settled muzhik of the Great-Russian or Ukrainian backwoods with a mobile proletarian whose conditions of life break down specifically national narrow-mindedness, both Great-Russian and Ukrainian. Even if we assume that, in time, there will be a state frontier between Great Russia and the Ukraine, the historically progressive nature of the "assimilation" of the Great-Russian and Ukrainian workers will be as undoubted as the progressive nature of the grinding down of nations in America. The freer the Ukraine and Great Russia become, the *more extensive and more rapid* will be the development of capitalism, which will still more powerfully attract the workers, the working masses of *all* nations from all regions of the state and from all the neighbouring states (should Russia become a neighbouring state in relation to the Ukraine) to the cities, the mines, and the factories.

* * *

Contraposing Ukrainian culture as a whole to Great-Russian culture as a whole, when speaking of the proletariat, is a gross betrayal of the proletariat's interests for the benefit of bourgeois nationalism.

There are two nations in every modern nation—we say to all

nationalist-socialists. There are two national cultures in every national culture. There is the Great-Russian culture of the Purishkeviches, Guchkovs[3] and Struves—but there is also the Great-Russian culture typified in the names of Chernyshevsky and Plekhanov. There are *the same two* cultures in the Ukraine as there are in Germany, in France, in England, among the Jews, and so forth. If the majority of the Ukrainian workers are under the influence of Great-Russian culture, we also know definitely that the ideas of Great-Russian democracy and Social-Democracy operate parallel with the Great-Russian clerical and bourgeois culture. In fighting the latter kind of "culture," the Ukrainian *Marxist* will always bring the former into focus, and say to his workers: "We must snatch at, make use of, and develop to the utmost every opportunity for intercourse with the Great-Russian class-conscious workers, with their literature and with their range of ideas; the fundamental interests of *both* the Ukrainian and the Great-Russian working-class movements demand it."

If a Ukrainian Marxist allows himself to be swayed by his *quite legitimate and natural* hatred of the Great-Russian oppressors *to such a degree* that he transfers even a particle of this hatred, even if it be only estrangement, to the proletarian culture and proletarian cause of the Great-Russian workers, then such a Marxist will get bogged down in bourgeois nationalism. Similarly, the Great-Russian Marxists will be bogged down, not only in bourgeois, but also in Black-Hundred nationalism, if he loses sight, even for a moment, of the demand for complete equality for the Ukrainians, or of their *right* to form an independent state.

The Great-Russian and Ukrainian workers must work together, and, as long as they live in a single state, act in the closest organisational unity and concert, towards a common or international culture of the proletarian movement, displaying absolute tolerance in the question of the language in which propaganda is conducted, and in the purely local or purely national *details* of that propaganda. This is the imperative demand of Marxism. All advocacy of the segregation of the workers of one nation from those of another, all attacks upon Marxist "assimilation," or attempts, where the proletariat is concerned, to contrapose one national culture as a whole to another allegedly integral national culture, and so forth, is *bourgeois* nationalism, against which it is essential to wage a ruthless struggle.

* * *

3. A. I. Guchkov (1862–1936) was a prominent Russian conservative who be- came an émigré after the Revolution. [R. T.]

Against Great-Russian Chauvinism

In the early post-revolutionary intra-party debates on nationality policy, Lenin was at odds periodically with a "Left Communist" view (one of whose spokesmen was Piatakov) that national differences should be submerged in a general *class* approach to political questions. Lenin feared that such an approach could provide a cover for a nationalism of the dominant Great-Russian national group in their relations with the minority peoples of the Soviet Republic. His fear found vivid expression in the following passage from his speech of March 19, 1919, closing the debate on the party program at the Eighth Party Congress.

* * *

* * * When Comrade Piatakov said that the Ukrainian Communists act in conformity with the instructions of the Central Committee of the R.C.P.(B.), I was not sure about the tone in which he said it. Was it regret? I do not suspect Comrade Pyatakov of that, but what he said was tantamount to asking what was the good of all this self-determination when we have a splendid Central Committee in Moscow. This is a childish point of view. The Ukraine was separated from Russia by exceptional circumstances, and the national movement did not take deep root there. Whatever there was of such a movement the Germans killed. This is a fact, but an exceptional fact. Even as regards the language it is not clear whether the Ukrainian language today is the language of the common people or not. The mass of working people of the other nations greatly distrusted the Great Russians, whom they regarded as a *kulak* and oppressor nation. That is a fact. A Finnish representative told me that among the Finnish bourgeoisie, who hated the Great Russians, voices are to be heard saying: "The Germans proved to be more savage brutes, the Entente proved to be more savage, we had better have the Bolsheviks." This is the tremendous victory we have gained over the Finnish bourgeoisie in the national question. This does not in the least prevent us from fighting it as our class enemy and from choosing the proper methods for the purpose. The

659

Soviet Republic, which has been established in the country where tsarism formerly oppressed Finland, must declare that it respects the right of nations to independence. We concluded a treaty with the short-lived Red Finnish Government and agreed to certain territorial concessions, to which I heard quite a number of utterly chauvinistic objections, such as: "There are excellent fisheries there, and you have surrendered them." These are the kind of objections which induce me to say, "Scratch some Communists and you will find Great-Russian chauvinists."

I think that the case of Finland, as well as of the Bashkirs, shows that in dealing with the national question one cannot argue that economic unity should be effected under all circumstances. Of course, it is necessary! But we must endeavour to secure it by propaganda, by agitation, by a voluntary alliance. The Bashkirs distrust the Great Russians because the Great Russians are more cultured and have utilised their culture to rob the Bashkirs. That is why the term Great Russian is synonymous with the terms "oppressor," "rogue" to Bashkirs in those remote places. This must be taken into account, it must be combated, but it will be a lengthy process. It cannot be eliminated by a decree. We must be very cautious in this matter. Exceptional caution must be displayed by a nation like the Great Russians, who earned the bitter hatred of all the other nations: we have only just learned how to remedy the situation, and then, not entirely. For instance, at the Commissariat of Education, or connected with it, there are Communists, who say that our schools are uniform schools, and therefore don't dare to teach in any language but Russian! In my opinion, such a Communist is a Great-Russian chauvinist. Many of us harbour such sentiments and they must be combated.

* * *

The Tasks of the Youth Leagues

The communist revolution in relation to culture is the main theme of this speech of October 2, 1920, to the Third All-Russia Congress of the Russian Young Communist League (Komsomol). Notable in it is Lenin's conception of the building of a communist society as a long-range task comprising the work of an entire generation, and his contention that no one can become a Communist in the intellectual sense without "assimilating the wealth of knowledge amassed by mankind." This speech is also important as Lenin's principal statement on the theme of "communist morality," which he defines in terms of the good of the revolution or the interests of the proletarian class struggle.

Comrades, today I would like to talk on the fundamental tasks of the Young Communist League and, in this connection, on what the youth organisations in a socialist republic should be like in general.

It is all the more necessary to dwell on this question because in a certain sense it may be said that it is the youth that will be faced with the actual task of creating a communist society. For it is clear that the generation of working people brought up in capitalist society can, at best, accomplish the task of destroying the foundations of the old, the capitalist way of life, which was built on exploitation. At best it will be able to accomplish the tasks of creating a social system that will help the proletariat and the working classes retain power and lay a firm foundation, which can be built on only by a generation that is starting to work under the new conditions, in a situation in which relations based on the exploitation of man by man no longer exist.

And so, in dealing from this angle with the tasks confronting the youth, I must say that the tasks of the youth in general, and of the Young Communist Leagues and all other organisations in particular, might be summed up in a single word: learn.

Of course, this is only a "single word." It does not reply to the principal and most essential questions: what to learn, and how to learn? And the whole point here is that, with the transformation of the old, capitalist society, the upbringing, training and education of the new generations that will create the communist society cannot be conducted on the old lines. The teaching, training and education of the youth must proceed from the material that has been left to us by the old society. We can build communism only on the basis of the totality of knowledge, organisations and institutions, only by using the stock of human forces and means that have been left to us by the old society. Only by radically remoulding the teaching, organisation and training of the youth shall we be able to ensure that the efforts of the younger generation will result in the creation of a society that will be unlike the old society, i.e., in the creation of a communist society. That is why we must deal in detail with the question of what we should teach the youth and how the youth should learn if it really wants to justify the name of communist youth, and how it should be trained so as to be able to complete and consummate what we have started.

I must say that the first and most natural reply would seem to be that the Youth League, and the youth in general, who want to advance to communism, should learn communism.

But this reply—"learn communism"—is too general. What do we need in order to learn communism? What must be singled out from the sum of general knowledge so as to acquire a knowledge of communism? Here a number of dangers arise, which very often manifest themselves whenever the task of learning communism is presented incorrectly, or when it is interpreted in too one-sided a manner.

Naturally, the first thought that enters one's mind is that learning communism means assimilating the sum of knowledge that is contained in communist manuals, pamphlets and books. But such a definition of the study of communism would be too crude and inadequate. If the study of communism consisted solely in assimilating what is contained in communist books and pamphlets, we might all too easily obtain communist text-jugglers or braggarts, and this would very often do us harm, because such people, after learning by rote what is set forth in communist books and pamphlets, would prove incapable of combining the various branches of knowledge, and would be unable to act in the way communism really demands.

One of the greatest evils and misfortunes left to us by the old, capitalist society is the complete rift between books and practical life; we have had books explaining everything in the best possible manner, yet in most cases these books contained the most pernicious and hypocritical lies, a false description of capitalist society.

That is why it would be most mistaken merely to assimilate book knowledge about communism. No longer do our speeches and articles merely reiterate what used to be said about communism, because our speeches and articles are connected with our daily work in all fields. Without work and without struggle, book knowledge of communism obtained from communist pamphlets and works is absolutely worthless, for it would continue the old separation of theory and practice, the old rift which was the most pernicious feature of the old, bourgeois society.

It would be still more dangerous to set about assimilating only communist slogans. Had we not realised this danger in time, and had we not directed all our efforts to averting this danger, the half million or million young men and women who would have called themselves Communists after studying communism in this way would only greatly prejudice the cause of communism.

The question arises: how is all this to be blended for the study of communism? What must we take from the old schools, from the old kind of science? It was the declared aim of the old type of school to produce men with an all-round education, to teach the sciences in general. We know that this was utterly false, since the whole of society was based and maintained on the division of people into classes, into exploiters and oppressed. Since they were thoroughly imbued with the class spirit, the old schools naturally gave knowledge only to the children of the bourgeoisie. Every word was falsified in the interests of the bourgeoisie. In these schools the younger generation of workers and peasants were not so much educated as drilled in the interests of that bourgeoisie. They were trained in such a way as to be useful servants of the bourgeoisie, able to create profits for it without disturbing its peace and leisure. That is why, while rejecting the old type of schools, we have made it our task to take from it only what we require for genuine communist education.

This brings me to the reproaches and accusations which we constantly hear levelled at the old schools, and which often lead to wholly wrong conclusions. It is said that the old school was a school of purely book knowledge, of ceaseless drilling and grinding. That is true, but we must distinguish between what was bad in the old school and what is useful to us, and we must be able to select from it what is necessary for communism.

The old schools provided purely book knowledge; they compelled their pupils to assimilate a mass of useless, superfluous and barren knowledge, which cluttered up the brain and turned the younger generation into bureaucrats regimented according to a single pattern. But it would mean falling into a grave error for you to try to draw the conclusion that one can become a Communist without assimilating the wealth of knowledge amassed by mankind. It would be mistaken to think it sufficient to learn communist slogans and the conclusions of communist science, without acquiring that sum of knowledge of which communism itself is a result. Marxism is an example which shows how communism arose out of the sum of human knowledge.

You have read and heard that communist theory—the science of communism created in the main by Marx, this doctrine of Marxism —has ceased to be the work of a single socialist of the nineteenth century, even though he was a genius, and that it has become the doctrine of millions and tens of millions of proletarians all over the world, who are applying it in their struggle against capitalism. If you were to ask why the teachings of Marx have been able to win the hearts and minds of millions and tens of millions of the most revolutionary class, you would receive only one answer: it was because Marx based his work on the firm foundation of the human knowledge acquired under capitalism. After making a study of the laws governing the development of human society, Marx realised the inevitability of capitalism developing towards communism. What is most important is that he proved this on the sole basis of a most precise, detailed and profound study of this capitalist society, by fully assimilating all that earlier science had produced. He critically reshaped everything that had been created by human society, without ignoring a single detail. He reconsidered, subjected to criticism, and verified on the working-class movement everything that human thinking had created, and therefrom formulated conclusions which people hemmed in by bourgeois limitations or bound by bourgeois prejudices could not draw.

We must bear this in mind when, for example, we talk about proletarian culture. We shall be unable to solve this problem unless we clearly realise that only a precise knowledge and transformation of the culture created by the entire development of mankind will enable us to create a proletarian culture. The latter is not clutched out of thin air; it is not an invention of those who call themselves experts in proletarian culture. That is all nonsense. Proletarian culture must be the logical development of the store of knowledge mankind has accumulated under the yoke of capitalist, landowner and bureaucratic society. All these roads have been leading, and will continue to lead up to proletarian culture, in the same way as political economy, as reshaped by Marx, has shown us what human society must arrive at, shown us the passage to the class struggle, to the beginning of the proletarian revolution.

When we so often hear representatives of the youth, as well as certain advocates of a new system of education, attacking the old schools, claiming that they used the system of cramming, we say to them that we must take what was good in the old schools. We must not borrow the system of encumbering young people's minds with an immense amount of knowledge, nine-tenths of which was useless and one-tenth distorted. This, however, does not mean that we can restrict ourselves to communist conclusions and learn only communist slogans. You will not create communism that way. You can become a Communist only when you enrich your mind with a knowledge of all the treasures created by mankind.

We have no need of cramming, but we do need to develop and perfect the mind of every student with a knowledge of fundamental facts. Communism will become an empty word, a mere signboard, and a Communist a mere boaster, if all the knowledge he has acquired is not digested in his mind. You should not merely assimilate this knowledge, but assimilate it critically, so as not to cram your mind with useless lumber, but enrich it with all those facts that are indispensable to the well-educated man of today. If a Communist took it into his head to boast about his communism because of the cut-and-dried conclusions he had acquired, without putting in a great deal of serious and hard work and without understanding facts he should examine critically, he would be a deplorable Communist indeed. Such superficiality would be decidedly fatal. If I know that I know little, I shall strive to learn more; but if a man says that he is a Communist and that he need not know anything thoroughly, he will never become anything like a Communist.

The old schools produced servants needed by the capitalists; the old schools turned men of science into men who had to write and say whatever pleased the capitalists. We must therefore abolish them. But does the fact that we must abolish them, destroy them, mean that we should not take from them everything mankind has accumulated that is essential to man? Does it mean that we do not have to distinguish between what was necessary to capitalism and what is necessary to communism?

We are replacing the old drill-sergeant methods practised in bourgeois society, against the will of the majority, with the class-conscious discipline of the workers and peasants, who combine hatred of the old society with a determination, ability and readiness to unite and organise their forces for this struggle so as to forge the wills of millions and hundreds of millions of people—disunited, and scattered over the territory of a huge country—into a single will, without which defeat is inevitable. Without this solidarity, without this conscious discipline of the workers and peasants, our cause is hopeless. Without this, we shall be unable to vanquish the capitalists and landowners of the whole world. We shall not even consolidate the foundation, let alone build a new, communist society on that foundation. Likewise, while condemning the old schools, while harbouring an absolutely justified and necessary hatred for the old schools, and appreciating the readiness to destroy them, we must realise that we must replace the old system of instruction, the old cramming and the old drill, with an ability to acquire the sum total of human knowledge, and to acquire it in such a way that communism shall not be something to be learned by rote, but something that you yourselves have thought over, something that will embody conclusions inevitable from the standpoint of present-day education.

That is the way the main tasks should be presented when we speak of the aim: learn communism.

I shall take a practical example to make this clear to you, and to demonstrate the approach to the problem of how you must learn. You all know that, following the military problems, those of defending the republic, we are now confronted with economic tasks. Communist society, as we know, cannot be built unless we restore industry and agriculture, and that, not in the old way. They must be re-established on a modern basis, in accordance with the last word in science. You know that electricity is that basis, and that only after electrification of the entire country, of all branches of industry and agriculture, only when you have achieved that aim, will you be able to build for yourselves the communist society which the older generation will not be able to build. Confronting you is the task of economically reviving the whole country, of reorganising and restoring both agriculture and industry on modern technical lines, based on modern science and technology, on electricity. You realise perfectly well that illiterate people cannot tackle electrification, and that elementary literacy is not enough either. It is insufficient to understand what electricity is; what is needed is the knowledge of how to apply it technically in industry and agriculture, and in the individual branches of industry and agriculture. This has to be learnt for oneself, and it must be taught to the entire rising generation of working people. That is the task confronting every class-conscious Communist, every young person who regards himself as a Communist and who clearly understands that, by joining the Young Communist League, he has pledged himself to help the Party build communism and to help the whole younger generation create a communist society. He must realise that he can create it only on the basis of modern education, and if he does not acquire this education communism will remain merely a pious wish.

It was the task of the older generation to overthrow the bourgeoisie. The main task then was to criticise the bourgeoisie, arouse hatred of the bourgeoisie among the masses, and foster class-consciousness and the ability to unite their forces. The new generation is confronted with a far more complex task. Your duty does not lie only in assembling your forces so as to uphold the workers' and peasants' government against an invasion instigated by the capitalists. Of course, you must do that; that is something you clearly realise, and is distinctly seen by the Communist. However, that is not enough. You have to build up a communist society. In many respects half of the work has been done. The old order has been destroyed, just as it deserved, it has been turned into a heap of ruins, just as it deserved. The ground has been cleared, and on this ground the younger communist generation must build a communist society. You are faced with the task of construction, and you can accomplish that task only by assimilating all modern knowledge, only if you are able to transform communism from cut-and-dried and memorised formulas, counsels, recipes, prescriptions and programmes into that living reality which gives unity to your immediate work, and only if you are able to make communism a guide in all your practical work.

That is the task you should pursue in educating, training and rousing the entire younger generation. You must be foremost among the millions of builders of a communist society in whose ranks every young man and young woman should be. You will not build a communist society unless you enlist the mass of young workers and peasants in the work of building communism.

This naturally brings me to the question of how we should teach communism and what the specific features of our methods should be.

I first of all shall deal here with the question of communist ethics.

You must train yourselves to be Communists. It is the task of the Youth League to organise its practical activities in such a way that, by learning, organising, uniting and fighting, its members shall train both themselves and all those who look to it for leadership; it should train Communists. The entire purpose of training, educating and teaching the youth of today should be to imbue them with communist ethics.

But is there such a thing as communist ethics? Is there such a thing as communist morality? Of course, there is. It is often suggested that we have no ethics of our own; very often the bourgeoisie accuse us Communists of rejecting all morality. This is a method of confusing the issue, of throwing dust in the eyes of the workers and peasants.

In what sense do we reject ethics, reject morality?

In the sense given to it by the bourgeoisie, who based ethics on God's commandments. On this point we, of course, say that we do not believe in God, and that we know perfectly well that the clergy, the landowners and the bourgeoisie invoked the name of God so as to further their own interests as exploiters. Or, instead of basing ethics on the commandments of morality, on the commandments of God, they based it on idealist or semi-idealist phrases, which always amounted to something very similar to God's commandments.

We reject any morality based on extra-human and extra-class concepts. We say that this is deception, dupery, stultification of the workers and peasants in the interests of the landowners and capitalists.

We say that our morality is entirely subordinated to the interests of the proletariat's class struggle. Our morality stems from the interests of the class struggle of the proletariat.

The old society was based on the oppression of all the workers and peasants by the landowners and capitalists. We had to destroy all that and overthrow them, but to do that we had to create unity. That is something that God cannot create.

This unity could be provided only by the factories, only by a proletariat trained and roused from its long slumber. Only when that class was formed did a mass movement arise which has led to what we have now—the victory of the proletarian revolution in one of the weakest of countries, which for three years has been repelling the onslaught of the bourgeoisie of the whole world. We can see how the proletarian revolution is developing all over the world. On the basis of experience, we now say that only the proletariat could have created the solid force which the disunited and scattered peasantry are following and which has withstood all onslaughts by the exploiters. Only this class can help the working masses unite, rally their ranks and conclusively defend, conclusively consolidate and conclusively build up a communist society.

That is why we say that to us there is no such thing as a morality that stands outside human society; that is a fraud. To us morality is subordinated to the interests of the proletariat's class struggle.

What does that class struggle consist in? It consists in overthrowing the tsar, overthrowing the capitalists, and abolishing the capitalist class.

What are classes in general? Classes are that which permits one section of society to appropriate the labour of another section. If one section of society appropriates all the land, we have a landowner class and a peasant class. If one section of society owns the factories, shares and capital, while another section works in these factories, we have a capitalist class and a proletarian class.

It was not difficult to drive out the tsar—that required only a few days. It was not very difficult to drive out the landowners—that was done in a few months. Nor was it very difficult to drive out the capitalists. But it is incomparably more difficult to abolish classes; we still have the division into workers and peasants. If the peasant is installed on his plot of land and appropriates his surplus grain, that is, grain that he does not need for himself or for his cattle, while the rest of the people have to go without bread, then the peasant becomes an exploiter. The more grain he clings to, the more profitable he finds it; as for the rest, let them starve: "The more they starve, the dearer I can sell this grain." All should work according to a single common plan, on common land, in common factories and in accordance with a common system. Is that easy to attain? You see that it is not as easy as driving out the tsar, the landowners and the capitalists. What is required is that the proletariat re-educate a section of the peasantry; it must win over the working peasants in order to crush the resistance of those peasants who are rich and are profiting from the poverty and want of the rest. Hence the task of the proletarian struggle is not quite completed after we have overthrown the tsar and driven out the landowners and capitalists; to accomplish that is the task of the system we call the dictatorship of the proletariat.

The class struggle is continuing; it has merely changed its forms. It is the class struggle of the proletariat to prevent the return of the old exploiters, to unite in a single union the scattered masses of unenlightened peasants. The class struggle is continuing and it is our task to subordinate all interests to that struggle. Our communist morality is also subordinated to that task. We say: morality is what serves to destroy the old exploiting society and to unite all the working people around the proletariat, which is building up a new, a communist society.

Communist morality is that which serves this struggle and unites the working people against all exploitation, against all petty private property; for petty property puts into the hands of one person that which has been created by the labour of the whole of society. In our country the land is common property.

But suppose I take a piece of this common property and grow on it twice as much grain as I need, and profiteer on the surplus? Suppose I argue that the more starving people there are, the more they will pay? Would I then be behaving like a Communist? No, I would be behaving like an exploiter, like a proprietor. That must be combated. If that is allowed to go on, things will revert to the rule of the capitalists, to the rule of the bourgeoisie, as has more than once happened in previous revolutions. To prevent the restoration of the rule of the capitalists and the bourgeoisie, we must not allow profiteering; we must not allow individuals to enrich themselves at the expense of the rest; the working people must unite with the proletariat and form a communist society. This is the principal feature of the fundamental task of the League and the organisation of the communist youth.

The old society was based on the principle: rob or be robbed;

work for others or make others work for you; be a slave-owner or a slave. Naturally, people brought up in such a society assimilate with their mother's milk, one might say, the psychology, the habit, the concept which says: you are either a slave-owner or a slave, or else, a small owner, a petty employee, a petty official, or an intellectual—in short, a man who is concerned only with himself, and does not care a rap for anybody else.

If I work this plot of land, I do not care a rap for anybody else; if others starve, all the better, I shall get the more for my grain. If I have a job as a doctor, engineer, teacher, or clerk, I do not care a rap for anybody else. If I toady to and please the powers that be, I may be able to keep my job, and even get on in life and become a bourgeois. A Communist cannot harbour such a psychology and such sentiments. When the workers and peasants proved that they were able, by their own efforts, to defend themselves and create a new society—that was the beginning of the new and communist education, education in the struggle against the exploiters, education in alliance with the proletariat against the self-seekers and petty proprietors, against the psychology and habits which say: I seek my own profit and don't care a rap for anything else.

That is the reply to the question of how the young and rising generation should learn communism.

It can learn communism only by linking up every step in its studies, training and education with the continuous struggle the proletarians and the working people are waging against the old society of exploiters. When people tell us about morality, we say: to a Communist all morality lies in this united discipline and conscious mass struggle against the exploiters. We do not believe in an eternal morality, and we expose the falseness of all the fables about morality. Morality serves the purpose of helping human society rise to a higher level and rid itself of the exploitation of labour.

To achieve this we need that generation of young people who began to reach political maturity in the midst of a disciplined and desperate struggle against the bourgeoisie. In this struggle that generation is training genuine Communists; it must subordinate to this struggle, and link up with it, each step in its studies, education and training. The education of the communist youth must consist, not in giving them suave talks and moral precepts. This is not what education consists in. When people have seen the way in which their fathers and mothers lived under the yoke of the landowners and capitalists; when they have themselves experienced the sufferings of those who began the struggle against the exploiters; when they have seen the sacrifices made to keep what has been won, and seen what deadly enemies the landowners and capitalists are—they are taught by these conditions to become Communists. Communist morality is based on the struggle for the consolidation and completion of communism. That is also the basis of communist training, education, and teaching. That is the reply to the question of how communism should be learnt.

We could not believe in teaching, training and education if they were restricted only to the schoolroom and divorced from the ferment of life. As long as the workers and peasants are oppressed by the landowners and capitalists, and as long as the schools are controlled by the landowners and capitalists, the young generation will remain blind and ignorant. Our schools must provide the youth with the fundamentals of knowledge, the ability to evolve communist views independently; they must make educated people of the youth. While they are attending school, they must learn to become participants in the struggle for emancipation from the exploiters. The Young Communist League will justify its name as the League of the young communist generation only when every step in its teaching, training and education is linked up with participation in the common struggle of all working people against the exploiters. You are well aware that, as long as Russia remains the only workers' republic and the old, bourgeois system exists in the rest of the world, we shall be weaker than they are, and be constantly threatened with a new attack; and that only if we learn to be solidly united shall we win in the further struggle and—having gained strength—become really invincible. Thus, to be a Communist means that you must organise and unite the entire young generation and set an example of training and discipline in this struggle. Then you will be able to start building the edifice of communist society and bring it to completion.

To make this clearer to you, I shall quote an example. We call ourselves Communists. What is a Communist? "Communist" is a Latin word. *Communis* is the Latin for "common." Communist society is a society in which all things—the land, the factories—are owned in common and the people work in common. That is communism.

Is it possible to work in common if each one works separately on his own plot of land? Work in common cannot be brought about all at once. That is impossible. It does not drop from the skies. It comes through toil and suffering; it is created in the course of struggle. The old books are of no use here; no one will believe them. One's own experience of life is needed. When Kolchak and Denikin were advancing from Siberia and the South, the peasants were on their side. They did not like Bolshevism because the Bolsheviks took their grain at a fixed price. But when the peasants in Siberia and the Ukraine experienced the rule of Kolchak and Denikin, they realised that they had only one alternative: either to go to the capitalists, who would at once hand them over into slavery under the landowners; or to follow the workers, who, it is true, did not promise a land flowing with milk and honey, and demanded iron discipline and firmness in an arduous struggle, but would lead them out of enslavement by the capitalists and landowners. When even the ignorant peasants saw and realised this from their own experience, they became conscious adherents of communism, who had gone through a severe school. It is such experience that must form the basis of all the activities of the Young Communist League.

I have replied to the questions of what we must learn, what we must take from the old schools and from the old science. I shall now try to answer the question of how this must be learnt. The answer is: only by inseparably linking each step in the activities of the schools, each step in training, education and teaching, with the struggle of all the working people against the exploiters.

I shall quote a few examples from the experience of the work of some of the youth organisations so as to illustrate how this training in communism should proceed. Everybody is talking about abolishing illiteracy. You know that a communist society cannot be built in an illiterate country. It is not enough for the Soviet government to issue an order, or for the Party to issue a particular slogan, or to assign a certain number of the best workers to this task. The young generation itself must take up this work. Communism means that the youth, the young men and women who belong to the Youth League, should say: this is our job; we shall unite and go into the rural districts to abolish illiteracy, so that there shall be no illiterates among our young people. We are trying to get the rising generation to devote their activities to this work. You know that we cannot rapidly transform an ignorant and illiterate Russia into a literate country. But if the Youth League sets to work on the job, and if all young people work for the benefit of all, the League, with a membership of 400,000 young men and women, will be entitled to call itself a Young Communist League. It is also a task of the League, not only to acquire knowledge itself, but to help those young people who are unable to extricate themselves by their own efforts from the toils of illiteracy. Being a member of the Youth League means devoting one's labour and efforts to the common cause. That is what a communist education means. Only in the course of such work do young men and women become real Communists. Only if they achieve practical results in this work will they become Communists.

Take, for example, work in the suburban vegetable gardens. Is that not a real job of work? It is one of the tasks of the Young Communist League. People are starving; there is hunger in the factories. To save ourselves from starvation, vegetable gardens must be developed. But farming is being carried on in the old way. Therefore, more class-conscious elements should engage in this work, and then you will find that the number of vegetable gardens will increase, their acreage will grow, and the results will improve. The Young Communist League must take an active part in this work. Every League and League branch should regard this as its duty.

The Young Communist League must be a shock force, helping in every job and displaying initiative and enterprise. The League should be an organisation enabling any worker to see that it consists of people whose teachings he perhaps does not understand, and whose teachings he may not immediately believe, but from whose practical work and activity he can see that they are really people who are showing him the right road.

If the Young Communist League fails to organise its work in this way in all fields, it will mean that it is reverting to the old bourgeois path. We must combine our education with the struggle of the working people against the exploiters, so as to help the former accomplish the tasks set by the teachings of communism.

The members of the League should use every spare hour to improve the vegetable gardens, or to organise the education of young people at some factory, and so on. We want to transform Russia from a poverty-stricken and wretched country into one that is wealthy. The Young Communist League must combine its education, learning and training with the labour of the workers and peasants, so as not to confine itself to schools or to reading communist books and pamphlets. Only by working side by side with the workers and peasants can one become a genuine Communist. It has to be generally realised that all members of the Youth League are literate people and at the same time are keen at their jobs. When everyone sees that we have ousted the old drill-ground methods from the old schools and have replaced them with conscious discipline, that all young men and women take part in *subbotniks*, and utilise every suburban farm to help the population—people will cease to regard labour in the old way.

It is the task of the Young Communist League to organise assistance everywhere, in village or city block, in such matters as—and I shall take a small example—public hygiene or the distribution of food. How was this done in the old, capitalist society? Everybody worked only for himself and nobody cared a straw for the aged and the sick, or whether housework was the concern only of the women, who, in consequence, were in a condition of oppression and servitude. Whose business is it to combat this? It is the business of the Youth Leagues, which must say: we shall change all this; we shall organise detachments of young people who will help to assure public hygiene or distribute food, who will conduct systematic house-to-house inspections, and work in an organised way for the benefit of the whole of society, distributing their forces properly and demonstrating that labour must be organised.

The generation of people who are now at the age of fifty cannot expect to see a communist society. This generation will be gone before then. But the generation of those who are now fifteen will see a communist society, and will itself build this society. This generation should know that the entire purpose of their lives is to build a communist society. In the old society, each family worked separately and labour was not organised by anybody except the landowners and capitalists, who oppressed the masses of the people. We must organise all labour, no matter how toilsome or messy it may be, in such a way that every worker and peasant will be able to say: I am part of the great army of free labour, and shall be able to build up my life without the landowners and capitalists, able to help establish a communist system. The Young Communist League should teach all young people to engage in conscious and disciplined labour from an early age. In this way we can be confident that the problems now confronting us will be solved. We must assume that no less than ten years will be required for the electrification of the country, so that our impoverished land may profit from the latest achievements of technology. And so, the generation of those who are now fifteen years old, and will be living in a communist society in ten or twenty years' time, should tackle all its educational tasks in such a way that every day, in every village and city, the young people shall engage in the practical solution of some problem of labour in common, even though the smallest or the simplest. The success of communist construction will be assured when this is done in every village, as communist emulation develops, and the youth prove that they can unite their labour. Only by regarding your every step from the standpoint of the success of that construction, and only by asking ourselves whether we have done all we can to be united and politically-conscious working people will the Young Communist League succeed in uniting its half a million members into a single army of labour and win universal respect.

On Proletarian Culture

Lenin's view that a communist culture must embody the entire store of knowledge accumulated in the pre-revolutionary past placed him in opposition to some exponents of the "Proletcult" (proletarian culture) movement, which developed on the eve of the October Revolution and subsequently was given organizational form under the Department of Proletarian Culture of the People's Commissariat of Education. Some leading figures of the Proletcult movement advocated a proletarian culture divorced from past culture. At the First All-Russia Congress of Proletcult, held in Moscow in early October 1920, the commissar of education, A. V. Lunacharsky, supported the autonomy of the Proletcult in the system of the People's Commissariat and brought on himself the following reply and draft resolution by Lenin, which was taken by the congress as guidance in drawing up its own subsequently formulated resolution.

We see from *Izvestia* of October 8 that, in his address to the Proletcult Congress, Comrade Lunacharsky said things that were *diametrically opposite* to what he and I had agreed upon yesterday.

It is necessary that a draft resolution (of the Proletcult Congress) should be drawn up with the utmost urgency, and that it should be endorsed by the Central Committee, in time to have it put to the vote *at this very* session of the Proletcult. On behalf of the Central Committee it should be submitted not later than today, for endorsement both by the Collegium of the People's Commissariat of Education and by the Proletcult Congress, because the Congress is closing today.

Draft Resolution

1) All educational work in the Soviet Republic of workers and peasants, in the field of political education in general and in the field of art in particular, should be imbued with the spirit of the class struggle being waged by the proletariat for the successful

achievement of the aims of its dictatorship, i.e., the overthrow of the bourgeoisie, the abolition of classes, and the elimination of all forms of exploitation of man by man.

2) Hence, the proletariat, both through its vanguard—the Communist Party—and through the many types of proletarian organisations in general, should display the utmost activity and play the leading part in all the work of public education.

3) All the experience of modern history and, particularly, the more than half-century-old revolutionary struggle of the proletariat of all countries since the appearance of the *Communist Manifesto* has unquestionably demonstrated that the Marxist world outlook is the only true expression of the interests, the viewpoint, and the culture of the revolutionary proletariat.

4) Marxism has won its historic significance as the ideology of the revolutionary proletariat because, far from rejecting the most valuable achievements of the bourgeois epoch, it has, on the contrary, assimilated and refashioned everything of value in the more than two thousand years of the development of human thought and culture. Only further work on this basis and in this direction, inspired by the practical experience of the proletarian dictatorship as the final stage in the struggle against every form of exploitation, can be recognised as the development of a genuine proletarian culture.

5) Adhering unswervingly to this stand of principle, the All-Russian Proletcult Congress rejects in the most resolute manner, as theoretically unsound and practically harmful, all attempts to invent one's own particular brand of culture, to remain isolated in self-contained organisations, to draw a line dividing the field of work of the People's Commissariat of Education and the Proletcult, or to set up a Proletcult "autonomy" within establishments under the People's Commissariat of Education and so forth. On the contrary, the Congress enjoins all Proletcult organisations to fully consider themselves in duty bound to act as auxiliary bodies of the network of establishments under the People's Commissariat of Education, and to accomplish their tasks under the general guidance of the Soviet authorities (specifically, of the People's Commissariat of Education) and of the Russian Communist Party, as part of the tasks of the proletarian dictatorship.

Comrade Lunacharsky says that his words have been distorted. In that case this resolution is needed *all the more* urgently.

Against Futurism

The cultural conservatism that led Lenin to look askance at the Proletcult idea of creating a proletarian culture detached from the past was also evident in his literary tastes. Vladimir Mayakovsky, one of the leading poets of the revolutionary period and an exponent of the "futurist" movement, had written a poem in 1920 called *150 Millions* in which "Ivan is the symbol of the Russian Revolution, while Woodrow Wilson is the incarnation of world capitalism: the latter squats in his wondrous palace in Chicago—a city built on a gigantic screw and operated by a dynamo. At the end of this utopian and highly romantic epic written in a crude, highly pitched, half-surrealistic, half-slapstick style, America is being won over to Communism by 150,000,000 Ivans; a hundred years hence the centenary of this event is celebrated in a Sahara that by then is blooming." (Marc Slonim, *Soviet Russian Literature* [London, 1967], p. 24.)

Lenin's letter of May 6, 1921, to Lunacharsky castigating him for agreeing to publish an edition of *150 Millions* in five thousand copies, and his simultaneous letter to M. N. Pokrovsky, the deputy commissar of education, express his reaction not only to this poem but to the literary style and movement that it reflected.

Letter to A. V. Lunacharsky

Aren't you ashamed to vote for publication of Mayakovsky's *150 Millions* in five thousand copies?

Rubbish, stupidity, double-dyed stupidity and pretentiousness.

In my opinion, we should print only one out of ten such things, and *not more than fifteen hundred copies*, for libraries and odd people.

And flog Lunacharsky for futurism.

Lenin

Letter to M. N. Pokrovsky

Comrade Pokrovsky! Again and again I beseech your assistance in the struggle against futurism and so forth.

(1) Lunacharsky put through in the collegium (alas!) the publication of Mayakovsky's 150 *Millions*.

Can't this be stopped? It must be stopped. Let's agree that these futurists are not to be printed more than two times a year *and not more than fifteen hundred copies*.

(2) Information has it that Lunacharsky has once again squeezed out Kiselis, who is said to be a *"realist"* artist, in his effort to make way, both directly and *indirectly*, for a futurist.

Can't we find reliable *anti*-futurists?

Lenin

On the Emancipation of Women

Lenin, like Marx and Engels, took a materialist view of women's oppression, believing it to be rooted in the economic arrangements of the larger society. Thus, while recognizing the fact of women's inferior status and even calling attention to the prevalence of male chauvinism in all sectors of society, Lenin held that only a socialist transformation of society could make possible both the change in personal consciousness and the widened economic opportunities necessary for women's emancipation. This view runs through all of his writings on the subject, a selection of which are given here.

"Women and Capitalist Production" consists of excerpts from Chapters VI and VII of Lenin's book *The Development of Capitalism in Russia* (1899). Especially notable is his statement that factory work, even under capitalism, is a progressive development for women because it leads to their independence from the stifling isolation of the rural patriarchal family. "Capitalism and Female Labour," an article written in 1913, discusses the effects of home production on women's status and on the entire labor market. The 1913 article on "The Fifth International Congress Against Prostitution" denounces the "bourgeois hypocrisy" of condemning prostitution as a moral evil without attempting to change the economic conditions from which it arises.

Lenin's own conservatism on the subject of sexual behavior is displayed in his letter of January 17, 1915, to Inessa Armand, who was both a party comrade and a very close personal friend of his.* She had informed him of her intention to write a pamphlet for working women in which she would defend the "demand for free love." Lenin's negative reaction to the latter point was the theme of his reply. (They continued the argument in a further exchange of letters, but the pamphlet was never written.)

The prominent German revolutionary Clara Zetkin recorded her 1920 conversation with Lenin on many aspects of the "woman question" in her pamphlet *My Recollections of Lenin*. The "Dialogue with Lenin" given below is notable for, among other things, his comment on Freud and his acid criticism of the then much-discussed glass-of-water theory of relations between the sexes.**

---

* On their relationship see Robert H. McNeal, *Bride of the Revolution: Krupskaya and Lenin* (Ann Arbor, Mich., 1972), pp. 135–43, 209–11; and Louis Fischer, *The Life of Lenin* (New York, 1964), pp. 74–81.

** This headnote and the following selections were prepared with the assistance of Emily Garlin.

Women and Capitalist Production

The Home

* * * Capitalist domestic industry inevitably entails extremely insanitary working conditions. The utter poverty of the worker, the utter impossibility of controlling working conditions by regulations of any kind, and the combination of the living and working premises, such are the conditions that convert the dwellings of the home workers into hotbeds of infection and occupational disease. In the large establishments one can fight such things; domestic industry, however, is in this respect the most "liberal" form of capitalist exploitation.

An excessively long working day is also an essential feature of domestic work for the capitalist and of the small industries in general. Instances have been given illustrating the comparative length of the working day in the "factories" and among the "handicraftsmen."

The drawing of women and of children of the tenderest age into production is nearly always observed in domestic industry. To illustrate this, let us cite some facts from a description of the women's industries of Moscow Gubernia. There are 10,004 women engaged in cotton winding; children start work at the age of 5 or 6 (!); daily earnings are 10 kopeks, yearly 17 rubles. The working day in the women's industries in general is as much as 18 hours. In the knitting industry children start work from the age of six, daily earnings are 10 kopeks, yearly 22 rubles. Altogether 37,514 females are employed in the women's industries; they begin working from the age of 5 or 6 (in 6 out of 19 industries, which 6 industries account for 32,400 female workers); the average daily earnings are 13 kopeks, yearly 26 rubles 20 kopeks.[1]

One of the most pernicious aspects of capitalist domestic industry is that it leads to a reduction in the level of the worker's requirements. The employer is able to recruit workers in remote districts where the people's standard of living is particularly low and where the worker's connection with the land enables him to work for a bare pittance. For example, the owner of a village stocking establishment explains that in Moscow rents are high and that, besides, the knitters "have to be . . . supplied with white bread, . . . whereas here the workers do the job in their own cottages and eat

1. Mme. Gorbunova, who has described the women's industries, wrongly gives the earnings as 18 kopeks and 37 rubles 77 kopeks respectively, for she takes only the average figures for each industry and leaves out of account the different numbers of women working in the different industries. [*Lenin*]

black bread. . . . Now how can Moscow compete with us!"[2] In the cotton-winding industry the explanation of the very low wages is that for the peasants' wives, daughters, etc., this is merely a supplementary source of income. "Thus, the system prevailing in this trade forces down to the utmost limit the wages of those for whom it is the sole means of livelihood, reduces the wages of those who obtain their livelihood exclusively by factory labour below their minimum needs, or retards the raising of their standard of living. In both cases it creates extremely abnormal conditions."[3] "The factory seeks cheap weavers," says Mr. Kharizomenov, "and it finds them in their native villages, far from the centres of industry. . . . That wages drop steadily as one moves from the industrial centres to the outer regions is an undoubted fact."[4] Hence, the employers are perfectly well able to take advantage of the conditions which artificially tie the population to the rural districts.

The Factory

Large-scale machine industry, which concentrates masses of workers who often come from various parts of the country, absolutely refuses to tolerate survivals of patriarchalism and personal dependence, and is marked by a truly "contemptuous attitude to the past." It is this break with obsolete tradition that is one of the substantial conditions which have created the possibility and evoked the necessity of regulating production and of public control over it. In particular, speaking of the transformation brought about by the factory in the conditions of life of the population, it must be stated that the drawing of women and juveniles into production[5] is, at bottom, progressive. It is indisputable that the capitalist factory places these categories of the working population in particularly hard conditions, and that for them it is particularly necessary to regulate and shorten the working day, to guarantee hygienic conditions of labour, etc.; but endeavours to ban completely the work of women and juveniles in industry, or to maintain the patriarchal manner of life that ruled out such work, would be reactionary and utopian. By destroying the patriarchal isolation of these categories of the population who formerly never emerged from the narrow circle of domestic, family relationships, by drawing them into direct participation in social production, large-scale machine industry

2. *Statistical Returns for Moscow Gubernia*, Vol. VII, Pt. II, p. 104. [*Lenin*]
3. *Ibid.*, p. 285. [*Lenin*]
4. *Industries of Vladimir Gubernia*, III, 63; *ibid.*, 250. [*Lenin*]
5. According to the *Directory*, the facto-ries of European Russia in 1890 employed a total of 875,764 workers, of whom 210,207 (24 per cent) were women, 17,793 (2 percent) boys, and 8,216 (1 percent) girls. [*Lenin*]

stimulates their development and increases their independence, in other words, creates conditions of life that are incomparably superior to the patriarchal immobility of pre-capitalist relations.[6]

Capitalism and Female Labour

Modern capitalist society is the hiding place of numerous cases of poverty and oppression that are not immediately visible. The scattered families of middle-class people, artisans, factory workers, clerks and the lower civil servants, are indescribably poor and barely make ends meet in the *best* of times. Millions and millions of women in such families live (or rather drag out an existence) as household slaves, striving with a desperate daily effort to feed and clothe their families on a few coppers, economising in everything except their own labour.

It is from among these women that the capitalists are most eager to engage workers who work at home and who are prepared for a monstrously low wage to "earn" an extra crust of bread for themselves and their families. It is from among them that the capitalists of all countries (like the slave-owners of antiquity and the feudal lords of the Middle Ages) choose any number of concubines at the most "favourable" price. No "moral indignation" (hypocritical in ninety-nine cases out of a hundred) about prostitution can do anything to prevent this commerce in women's bodies; as long as

6. "The poor woman weaver follows her father and husband to the factory and works alongside of them and independently of them. She is as much a breadwinner as the man is." "In the factory . . . the woman is quite an independent producer, apart from her husband." Literacy spreads among the women factory workers with remarkable rapidity. (*Industries of Vladimir Gubernia*, III, 113, 118, 112 and elsewhere.) Mr. Kharizomenov is perfectly right in drawing the following conclusion: industry has destroyed "the economic dependence of the woman on the family . . . and on the husband. . . . At the factory, the woman is the equal of the man; this is the equality of the proletarian. . . . The capitalisation of industry is an important factor in the woman's struggle for her independence in the family." "Industry creates a new position for the woman in which she is completely independent of her family and husband." (*Yuridichesky Vestnik*, 1883, No. 12, pp. 582, 596.) In the *Statistical Returns for Moscow Gubernia* (Vol. VII, Pt. II, [Moscow, 1882], pp. 152, 138–39), the investigators compare the position of women engaged in making stockings by hand and by machine. The daily earnings of hand workers is about 8 kopeks, and of machine workers, 14 to 30 kopeks. The working woman's conditions under machine production are described as follows: ". . . Before us is a free young woman, hampered by no obstacles, emancipated from the family and from all that constitutes the peasant woman's conditions of life, a young woman who at any moment may leave one place for another, one employer for another, and may at any moment find herself without a job . . . without a crust of bread. . . . Under hand production, the knitters' earnings are very meagre, insufficient to cover the cost of her food, earnings only acceptable if she, as a member of an allotment-holding and farming family, enjoys in part the product of that land; under machine production the working woman, in addition to food and tea, gets earnings which enable . . . her to live away from the family and to do without the family's income from the land. . . . Moreover, the woman worker's earnings in machine industry, under present conditions, are more secure." [*Lenin*]

wage slavery exists, prostitution must inevitably continue. Through-out the history of society all the oppressed and exploited classes have always been compelled (their exploitation consists in this) to hand over to the oppressors, first, their unpaid labour and, sec-ondly, their women to be the concubines of the "masters."

Slavery, feudalism and capitalism are alike in this respect. Only the *form* of the exploitation changes, the exploitation remains.

In Paris, the world capital, the center of civilization, an *exhibi-tion* is now being held of the work of "exploited women workers employed in their homes."

Every exhibit bears a ticket showing how much the woman working at home *received* for making it and how much she could earn per day and per hour.

How does this work out? A woman working at home *cannot earn* more than one and a quarter francs, i.e., 50 kopeks, *on any article*. Most of the jobs pay wages that are immeasurably lower. Take lampshades, for instance—four kopeks a dozen. Or paper bags at 15 kopeks a thousand giving a wage of *six* kopeks an hour. And then there are little toys with ribbons, etc.—two and a half kopeks an hour; artificial flowers that bring in *two or three* kopeks an hour; and men's and women's underclothes—from *two* to six kopeks an hour. And so on ad infinitum.

Our workers' associations and trade unions should organise a similar "exhibition." It will not produce the tremendous profits obtained by bourgeois-organised exhibitions. An exhibition of pro-letarian women's poverty and want will bring benefits of another kind—it will help wage slaves, both men and women, to realise their condition, to take a look at their own "lives" and think about how to deliver themselves from this eternal oppression of poverty, want, prostitution and other humiliations suffered by the poor.

The Fifth International Congress Against Prostitution

The *fifth* international congress for the suppression of the white slave traffic recently ended in London.

Duchesses, countesses, bishops, priests, rabbis, police officials and all sorts of bourgeois philanthropists were well to the fore! How many festive luncheons and magnificent official receptions were given! And how many solemn speeches on the harm and infamy of prostitution!

What means of struggle were proposed by the elegant bourgeois delegates to the congress? Mainly two methods—religion and po-lice. They are, it appears, the most valid and reliable methods of combating prostitution. One English delegate boasted, according to the London correspondent of the *Leipziger Volkszeitung,* that he had introduced a bill into parliament providing for *corporal punishment* for pimps. See the sort he is, this modern "civilised" hero of the struggle against prostitution!

One lady from Canada waxed enthusiastic over the police and the supervision of "fallen" women by policewomen, but as far as raising wages was concerned, she said that women workers did not deserve better pay.

One German pastor reviled present-day materialism, which, he said, is taking hold among the people and promoting the spread of free love.

When the Austrian delegate Gärtner tried to raise the question of the social causes of prostitution, of the need and poverty experienced by working-class families, of the exploitation of child labour, of unbearable housing conditions, etc., he was forced to silence by hostile shouts!

But the things that were said about highly-placed personages—among groups of delegates—were instructive and sublime. When, for example, the German Empress visits a maternity hospital in Berlin, *rings are placed on the fingers* of mothers of "illegitimate" children in order that this august individual may not be shocked by the sight of unmarried mothers!

We may judge from this of the disgusting bourgeois hypocrisy that reigns at these aristocratic-bourgeois congresses. Acrobats in the field of philanthropy and police defenders of this mockery of poverty and need gather "to struggle against prostitution," which is supported precisely by the aristocracy and the bourgeoisie. . . .

Letter to Inessa Armand

Dear Friend,

I advise you to write the plan of your pamphlet in greater detail. Otherwise there is much that is unclear.

I feel bound to make one point right away. I suggest you delete altogether §3 dealing with "the demand (on the part of women) for free love."

This is, in fact, a bourgeois, not a proletarian, demand.

What do you really mean by it? What *can* it be understood to mean?

1. Freedom *from* material (financial) considerations in love?
2. *From* material cares as well?
3. From religious prejudices?

4. From the ban imposed by one's father, etc.?
5. From the prejudices of "society"?
6. From the narrow surroundings of the (peasant or petty-bourgeois or intellectual-bourgeois) environment?
7. From the shackles of the law, the court and the police?
8. From earnestness in love?
9. From childbirth?
10. Freedom to commit adultery, etc.?

I have listed many (not all, of course) shades of meaning. You do not mean, of course, Nos. 8–10, but Nos. 1–7 or *something like* Nos. 1–7.

But for Nos. 1–7 another definition should be chosen, for free love does not express the idea exactly.

And the public at large, the readers will *inevitably* understand "free love" to mean in general something along the lines of Nos. 8–10, even *against your will.*

Precisely because in modern society the most talkative and noisy "top strata" mean by "free love" Nos. 8–10, this demand for free love is a bourgeois, not a proletarian demand.

Nos. 1 and 2 are most important to the proletariat, and then Nos. 1–7, but this, properly speaking, is not "free love."

What you *subjectively* "want to understand" by it does not matter. What matters is *the objective logic* of class relations in affairs of love.

Friendly shake hands![1]
V. I.

Dialogue with Clara Zetkin

Comrade Lenin repeatedly discussed with me the problem of women's rights. He obviously attached great importance to the women's movement, which was to him an essential component of the mass movement that in certain circumstances might become decisive. Needless to say he saw full social equality of women as a principle which no Communist could dispute.

We had our first lengthy talk on this subject in the autumn of 1920, in Lenin's big study in the Kremlin. Lenin sat at his desk, which was covered with books and papers, indicating study and work without the "brilliant disorder" associated with genius.

"We must by all means set up a powerful international women's movement on a clear-cut theoretical basis," he began after greeting

---

1. In English in the original.

me. "It is clear that without Marxist theory we cannot have proper practice. Here, too, we Communists need the greatest clarity of principle. We must draw a sharp line between us and all other parties. Our Second International Congress[1] unfortunately did not come up to expectations in discussing the question of women. It posed the question but did not get around to taking a definite stand. A committee is still in charge of the matter. It is to draft a resolution, theses and directives but has made little progress so far. You must help it."

I had already heard from others what Lenin was now telling me and I expressed my amazement. I was full of enthusiasm for everything Russian women had done during the revolution and what they were doing now for its defence and further development. As for the standing and activity of women in the Bolshevik Party, I thought that it was a model party—indeed, *the* model party. It alone supplied the international Communist women's movement with a valuable trained and experienced force and set a great example for history.

"That is true, it's wonderful," Lenin remarked with a faint smile. "In Petrograd, here in Moscow, and in other cities and industrial centres, proletarian women showed up splendidly during the revolution. We would not have won without them, or hardly. That is my opinion. What courage they showed and how courageous they still are! Imagine the suffering and privation they are enduring. But they are holding out because they want to defend the Soviets, because they want freedom and communism. Yes, our working women are magnificent class fighters. They are worthy of admiration and love. In general, it must be acknowledged that even the ladies of the 'Constitutional Democrats' in Petrograd showed greater courage in fighting us than those wretched military Cadets.

"It's true that we have reliable, intelligent and tireless women in our Party. They hold important posts in the Soviets, Executive Committees, People's Commissariats, and public offices of every kind. Many of them work day and night either in the Party or among the workers and peasants or in the Red Army. That is of great value to us. It is important for women all over the world, as it is evidence of the capacity of women, of the great value of the work they do for society. The first proletarian dictatorship is truly paving the way for the complete social equality of women. It eradicates more prejudice than volumes of feminist literature. However, in spite of all this, we do not yet have an international Communist women's movement and we must have one without fail. We must

---

1. The Second Congress of the Communist International met from July 19 to August 7, 1920.

immediately set about starting it. Without such a movement, the work of our International and of its parties is incomplete and never will be complete. Yet our revolutionary work has to be fulfilled in its entirety. Tell me how Communist work is getting on abroad."

I did—as well as I could at the time, with the links between the Comintern parties still very loose and irregular. * * *

Naturally, I spoke in great detail about the state of affairs in Germany. * * *

"Not bad, not bad at all," Lenin said. "The Communist women's energy, devotion and enthusiasm, their courage and intelligence during the illegal and semi-legal periods, promise well for the development of our work. It would be useful for the expansion of the Party and the growth of its strength to win over the masses and carry through actions. But how about giving all the comrades a clear understanding of the fundamentals of this question and training them—how are you getting along in this respect? This is what counts most in the work among the masses. It is very important in terms of the ideas we convey to the masses, and of the things we want the masses to adopt and take inspiration from. I cannot remember at the moment who said 'It takes inspiration to do great deeds.' We and the working people of the whole world still have really great deeds to perform. What inspires your comrades, the proletarian women of Germany? What about their proletarian class-consciousness? Do their interests and activities centre on the political demands of the moment? What is the focal point of their thoughts?

"I have heard strange things about that from Russian and German comrades. I must tell you what I mean. I understand that in Hamburg a gifted Communist woman is bringing out a newspaper for prostitutes, and is trying to organise them for the revolutionary struggle. Now Rosa,[1] a true Communist, felt and acted like a human being when she wrote an article in defence of prostitutes who have landed in jail for violating a police regulation concerning their sad trade. They are unfortunate double victims of bourgeois society. Victims, first, of its accursed system of property and, secondly, of its accursed moral hypocrisy. There's no doubt about this. Only a coarse-grained and short-sighted person could forget this. To understand this is one thing, but it is quite another thing—how shall I put it?—to organise the prostitutes as a special revolutionary guild contingent and publish a trade union paper for them. Are there really no industrial working women left in Germany who need organising, who need a newspaper, who should be enlisted in your struggle? This is a morbid deviation. It strongly reminds me of the

---

1. Rosa Luxemburg. [*R. T.*]

literary vogue which made a sweet madonna out of every prostitute. Its origin was sound too: social sympathy, and indignation against the moral hypocrisy of the honourable bourgeoisie. But the healthy principle underwent bourgeois corrosion and degenerated. The question of prostitution will confront us even in our country with many a difficult problem. Return the prostitute to productive work, find her a place in the social economy—that is the thing to do. But the present state of our economy and all the other circumstances make it a difficult and complicated matter. Here you have an aspect of the women problem which faces us in all its magnitude, after the proletariat has come to power, and demands a practical solution. It will still require a great deal of effort here in Soviet Russia. But to return to your special problem in Germany. Under no circumstances should the Party look calmly upon such improper acts of its members. It causes confusion and splits our forces. Now what have *you* done to stop it?"

Before I could answer Lenin continued:

"The record of your sins, Clara, is even worse. I have been told that at the evenings arranged for reading and discussion with working women, sex and marriage problems come first. They are said to be the main objects of interest in your political instruction and educational work. I could not believe my ears when I heard that. The first state of proletarian dictatorship is battling with the counter-revolutionaries of the whole world. The situation in Germany itself calls for the greatest unity of all proletarian revolutionary forces, so that they can repel the counter-revolution which is pushing on. But active Communist women are busy discussing sex problems and the forms of marriage—'past, present and future.' They consider it their most important task to enlighten working women on these questions. It is said that a pamphlet on the sex question written by a Communist authoress from Vienna enjoys the greatest popularity. What rot that booklet is! The workers read what is right in it long ago in Bebel. Only not in the tedious, cut-and-dried form found in the pamphlet but in the form of gripping agitation that strikes out at bourgeois society. The mention of Freud's hypotheses is designed to give the pamphlet a scientific veneer, but it is so much bungling by an amateur. Freud's theory has now become a fad. I mistrust sex theories expounded in articles, treatises, pamphlets, etc.—in short, the theories dealt with in that specific literature which sprouts so luxuriantly on the dung heap of bourgeois society. I mistrust those who are always absorbed in the sex problems, the way an Indian saint is absorbed in the contemplation of his navel. It seems to me that this superabundance of sex theories, which for the most part are mere hypotheses, and often quite arbitrary ones, stems from a personal need. It springs from the desire to justify one's own abnormal or excessive sex life before bourgeois morality and to plead for tolerance towards oneself. This veiled respect for bourgeois morality is as repugnant to me as rooting about in all that bears on sex. No matter how rebellious and revolutionary it may be made to appear, it is in the final analysis thoroughly bourgeois. Intellectuals and others like them are particularly keen on this. There is no room for it in the Party, among the class-conscious, fighting proletariat."

I interposed that where private property and the bourgeois social order prevail, questions of sex and marriage gave rise to manifold problems, conflicts and suffering for women of all social classes and strata. As far as women are concerned, the war and its consequences exacerbated the existing conflicts and suffering to the utmost precisely in the sphere of sexual relations. Problems formerly concealed from women were now laid bare. To this was added the atmosphere of incipient revolution. The world of old emotions and thoughts was cracking up. Former social connections were loosening and breaking. The makings of new relations between people were appearing. Interest in the relevant problems was an expression of the need for enlightnment and a new orientation. It was also a reaction against the distortions and hypocrisy of bourgeois society. Knowledge of the modifications of the forms of marriage and family that took place in the course of history, and of their dependence on economics, would serve to rid the minds of working women of their preconceived idea of the eternity of bourgeois society. The critically historical attitude to this had to lead to an unrelenting analysis of bourgeois society, an exposure of its essence and its consequences, including the branding of false sex morality. All roads led to Rome. Every truly Marxist analysis of an important part of the ideological superstructure of society, of an outstanding social phenomenon, had to lead to an analysis of bourgeois society and its foundation, private property. It should lead to the conclusion that "Carthage must be destroyed."

Lenin nodded with a smile.

"There you are! You defend your comrades and your Party like a lawyer. What you say is of course true. But that can at best excuse, not justify, the mistake made in Germany. It remains a mistake. Can you assure me in all sincerity that during those reading and discussion evenings, questions of sex and marriage are dealt with from the point of view of mature, vital historical materialism? This presupposes wide-ranging, profound knowledge, and the fullest Marxist mastery of a vast amount of material. Do you now have the forces you need for that? Had you had them, a pamphlet like the one we spoke about would not have been used for instruction during reading and discussion evenings. It is being recommended and disseminated instead of being criticised. Why is the approach to this problem inadequate and un-Marxist? Because sex and marriage problems are not treated as only part of the main social problem. Conversely, the main social problem is presented as a part, an appendage to the sex problem. The important point recedes into the background. Thus not only is this question obscured, but also thought, and the class-consciousness of working women in general, is dulled.

"Besides, and this isn't the least important point, Solomon the Wise said there is a time for everything. I ask you, is this the time to keep working women busy for months at a stretch with such questions as how to love or be loved, how to woo or be wooed? This, of course, with regard to the "past, present and future," and among the various races. And it is proudly styled historical materialism. Nowadays all the thoughts of Communist women, of working women, should be centred on the proletarian revolution, which will lay the foundation, among other things, for the necessary revision of marital and sexual relations. Just now we must really give priority to problems other than the forms of marriage prevalent among Australia's aborigines, or marriage between brother and sister in ancient times. For the German proletariat, the problem of the Soviets, of the Versailles Treaty and its impact on the lives of women, the problem of unemployment, of falling wages, of taxes and many other things remain the order of the day. To be brief, I am still of the opinion that this sort of political and social education of working women is wrong, absolutely wrong. How could you keep quiet about it? You should have set your authority against it."

I told my fervent friend that I had never failed to criticise and to remonstrate with the leading women comrades in various places. But, as he knew, no prophet is honoured in his own country or in his own house. By my criticism I had drawn upon myself the suspicion that "survivals of a Social-Democratic attitude and old-fashioned philistinism were still strong" in my mind. However, in the end my criticism had proved effective. Sex and marriage were no longer the focal point in lectures at discussion evenings. Lenin resumed the thread of his argument.

"Yes, yes, I know that," he said. "Many people rather suspect *me* of philistinism on this account, although such an attitude is repugnant to me—it conceals so much narrow-mindedness and hypocrisy. Well, I'm unruffled by it. Yellow-beaked fledgelings newly hatched from their bourgeois-tainted eggs are all so terribly clever. We have to put up with that without mending our ways. The youth movement is also affected with the modern approach to the sex problem and with excessive interest in it."

Lenin emphasised the word "modern" with an ironical, deprecating gesture.

"I was also told that sex problems are a favourite subject in your youth organisations too, and that there are hardly enough lecturers on this subject. This nonsense is especially dangerous and damaging to the youth movement. It can easily lead to sexual excesses, to overstimulation of sex life and to wasted health and strength of young people. You must fight that too. There is no lack of contact between the youth movement and the women's movement. Our Communist women everywhere should co-operate methodically with young people. This will be a continuation of motherhood, will elevate it and extend it from the individual to the social sphere. Women's incipient social life and activities must be promoted, so that they can outgrow the narrowness of their philistine, individualistic psychology centred on home and family. But this is incidental.

"In our country, too, considerable numbers of young people are busy 'revising bourgeois conceptions and morals' in the sex question. And let me add that this involves a considerable section of our best boys and girls, of our truly promising youth. It is as you have just said. In the atmosphere created by the aftermath of war and by the revolution which has begun, old ideological values, finding themselves in a society whose economic foundations are undergoing a radical change, perish, and lose their restraining force. New values crystallise slowly, in the struggle. With regard to relations between people, and between man and woman, feelings and thoughts are also becoming revolutionised. New boundaries are being drawn between the rights of the individual and those of the community, and hence also the duties of the individual. Things are still in complete, chaotic-ferment. The direction and potentiality of the various contradictory tendencies can still not be seen clearly enough. It is a slow and often very painful process of passing away and coming into being. All this applies also to the field of sexual relations, marriage, and the family. The decay, putrescence, and filth of bourgeois marriage with its difficult dissolution, its licence for the husband and bondage for the wife, and its disgustingly false sex morality and relations fill the best and most spiritually active of people with the utmost loathing.

"The coercion of bourgeois marriage and bourgeois legislation on the family enhance the evil and aggravate the conflicts. It is the coercion of 'sacrosanct' property. It sanctifies venality, baseness, and dirt. The conventional hypocrisy of 'respectable' bourgeois society takes care of the rest. People revolt against the prevailing abominations and perversions. And at a time when mighty nations are being destroyed, when the former power relations are being disrupted, when a whole social world is beginning to decline, the sensations of the individual undergo a rapid change. A stimulating thirst for different forms of enjoyment easily acquires an irresistible force. Sexual and marriage reforms in the bourgeois sense will not do. In the sphere of sexual relations and marriage, a revolution is approaching—in keeping with the proletarian revolution. Of course, women and young people are taking a deep interest in the complex tangle of problems which have arisen as a result of this. Both the former and the latter suffer greatly from the present messy state of sex relations. Young people rebel against them with the vehemence of their years. This is only natural. Nothing could be falser than to preach monastic self-denial and the sanctity of the filthy bourgeois morals to young people. However, it is hardly a good thing that sex, already strongly felt in the physical sense, should at such a time assume so much prominence in the psychology of young people. The consequences are nothing short of fatal. Ask Comrade Lilina about it. She ought to have had many experiences in her extensive work at educational institutions of various kinds and you know that she is a Communist through and through, and has no prejudices.

"Youth's altered attitude to questions of sex is of course 'fundamental,' and based on theory. Many people call it 'revolutionary' and 'communist.' They sincerely believe that this is so. I am an old man, and I do not like it. I may be a morose ascetic, but quite often this so-called 'new sex life' of young people—and frequently of the adults too—seems to me purely bourgeois and simply an extension of the good old bourgeois brothel. All this has nothing in common with free love as we Communists understand it. No doubt you have heard about the famous theory that in communist society satisfying sexual desire and the craving for love is as simple and trivial as 'drinking a glass of water.' A section of our youth has gone mad, absolutely mad, over this 'glass-of-water theory.' It has been fatal to many a young boy and girl. Its devotees assert that it is a Marxist theory. I want no part of the kind of Marxism which infers all phenomena and all changes in the ideological superstructure of society directly and blandly from its economic basis, for things are not as simple as all that. A certain Frederick Engels has established this a long time ago with regard to historical materialism.

"I consider the famous 'glass-of-water' theory as completely un-Marxist and, moreover, as anti-social. It is not only what nature has given but also what has become culture, whether of a high or low level, that comes into play in sexual life. Engels pointed out in his *Origin of the Family* how significant it was that the common sexual relations had developed into individual sex love and thus became purer. The relations between the sexes are not simply the expression of a mutual influence between economics and a physical want deliberately singled out for physiological examination. It would be rationalism and not Marxism to attempt to refer the change in these relations directly to the economic basis of society in isolation from its connection with the ideology as a whole. To be sure, thirst has to be quenched. But would a normal person normally lie down in the gutter and drink from a puddle? Or even from a glass whose edge has been greased by many lips? But the social aspect is more important than anything else. The drinking of water is really an individual matter. But it takes two people to make love, and a third person, a new life, is likely to come into being. This deed has a social complexion and constitutes a duty to the community.

"As a Communist I have no liking at all for the 'glass-of-water' theory, despite its attractive label: 'emancipation of love.' Besides, emancipation of love is neither a novel nor a communistic idea. You will recall that it was advanced in fine literature around the middle of the past century as 'emancipation of the heart.' In bourgeois practice it materialised into emancipation of the flesh. It was preached with greater talent than now, though I cannot judge how it was practised. Not that I want my criticism to breed asceticism. That is farthest from my thoughts. Communism should not bring asceticism, but joy and strength, stemming, among other things, from a consummate love life. Whereas today, in my opinion, the obtaining plethora of sex life yields neither joy nor strength. On the contrary, it impairs them. This is bad, very bad, indeed, in the epoch of revolution.

"Young people are particularly in need of joy and strength. Healthy sports, such as gymnastics, swimming, hiking, physical exercises of every description and a wide range of intellectual interests are what they need, as well as learning, study and research, and as far as possible collectively. This will be far more useful to young people than endless lectures and discussions on sex problems and the so-called living by one's nature. *Mens sana in corpore sano.* Be neither monk nor Don Juan, but not anything in between either, like a German philistine. You know the young comrade X. He is a splendid lad, and highly gifted. For all that, I am afraid that he will never amount to anything. He has one love affair after another. This is not good for the political struggle and for the revolution. I will not vouch for the reliability or the endurance of women whose love affair is intertwined with politics, or for the men who run after every petticoat and let themselves in with every young female. No, no, that does not go well with revolution."

Lenin sprang to his feet, slapped the table with his hand and paced up and down the room.

"The revolution calls for concentration and rallying of every nerve by the masses and by the individual. It does not tolerate orgiastic conditions so common among D'Annunzio's decadent heroes and heroines. Promiscuity in sexual matters is bourgeois. It is a sign of degeneration. The proletariat is a rising class. It does not need an intoxicant to stupefy or stimulate it, neither the intoxicant of sexual laxity or of alcohol. It should not and will not forget the vileness, the filth and the barbarity of capitalism. It derives its strongest inspiration to fight from its class position, from the communist ideal. What it needs is clarity, clarity, and more clarity. Therefore, I repeat, there must be no weakening, no waste and no dissipation of energy. Self-control and self-discipline are not slavery; not in matters of love either. But excuse me, Clara, I have strayed far from the point which we set out to discuss. Why have you not called me to order? Worry has set me talking. I take the future of our youth very close to heart. It is part and parcel of the revolution. Whenever harmful elements appear, which creep from bourgeois society to the world of the revolution and spread like the roots of prolific weeds, it is better to take action against them quickly. The questions we have dealt with are also part of the women's problems."

* * *

Lenin consulted his watch.

"Half of the time I have at my disposal for you," he said, "has already expired. I have chatted too long. You are to work out the leading theses on communist work among women. I know your principled approach and practical experience. So our talk about this will be brief; you had better get busy. What do you think the theses should be?"

I gave him a concise account on this score. Lenin nodded approvingly a few times without interrupting. When I was through I looked at him questioningly.

"Right," he remarked. "It would also be a good thing if you were to inform a meeting of responsible women Party comrades about it and to discuss it with them. Too bad Comrade Inessa[2] is not here. She is sick and has gone to the Caucasus. Put the theses in writing after the discussion. A committee will look them over and the Executive Committee will make the final decision. I give my opinion on only some of the main points, on which I fully share your views. They seem important to me also for our present agitation and propaganda work if it is to pave the way for action, for successful fighting.

2. Inessa Armand. [*R. T.*]

"The theses must emphasise strongly that true emancipation of women is not possible except through communism. You must lay stress on the unbreakable connection between woman's human and social position and the private ownership of the means of production. This will draw a strong, ineradicable line against the bourgeois movement for the 'emancipation of women.' This will also give us a basis for examining the woman question as part of the social, working-class question, and to bind it firmly with the proletarian class struggle and the revolution. The communist women's movement itself must be a mass movement, a part of the general mass movements; and not only of the proletarians, but of all the exploited and oppressed, of all victims of capitalism or of the dominant class. Therein, too, lies the significance of the women's movement for the class struggle of the proletariat and its historic mission, the creation of a communist society. We can be legitimately proud that we have the flower of revolutionary womanhood in our Party, in the Comintern. But this is not decisive, we have to win over the millions of working women in town and country for our struggle and, particularly, for the communist reconstruction of society. There can be no real mass movement without the women.

"We derive our organisational ideas from our ideological conceptions. We want no separate organisations of communist women! She who is a Communist belongs as a member to the Party, just as he who is a Communist. They have the same rights and duties. There can be no difference of opinion on that score. However, we must not shut our eyes to the facts. The Party must have organs—working groups, commissions, committees, sections or whatever else they may be called—with the specific purpose of rousing the broad masses of women, bringing them into contact with the Party and keeping them under its influence. This naturally requires that we carry on systematic work among the women. We must teach the awakened women, win them over for the proletarian class struggle under the leadership of the Communist Party, and equip them for it. When I say this I have in mind not only proletarian women, whether they work in mills or cook the family meal. I also have in mind the peasant women and the women of the various sections of the lower middle class. They, too, are victims of capitalism, and more than ever since the war. The lack of interest in politics and the otherwise anti-social and backward psychology of these masses of women, the narrow scope of their activities and the whole pattern of their lives are undeniable facts. It would be silly to ignore them, absolutely silly. We must have our own groups to work among them, special methods of agitation, and special forms of organisation. This is not bourgeois 'feminism'; it is a practical revolutionary expediency."

I told Lenin that his arguments were a valuable encouragement for me. Many comrades, very good ones, too, vehemently opposed the Party's setting up special groups for planned work among women. They denounced it as a return to the notorious "emancipation of women" movement, to Social-Democratic traditions. They claimed that since the Communist Parties gave equality to women they should, consequently, carry on work without differentiation among all the working people in general. The approach to men and to women should be the same. Any attempt to consider the circumstances which Lenin had noted concerning agitation and organisation would be branded by the exponents of this view as opportunism, as renunciation and betrayal of fundamental principles.

"This is not new and not conclusive," Lenin said. "Do not let it mislead you. Why are there nowhere as many women in the Party as men, not even in Soviet Russia? Why is the number of women in the trade unions so small? These facts give one food for thought. Denial of the indispensable special groups for work among the masses of women is part of the very principled, very radical attitude of our dear friends of the Communist Workers' Party.[3] They are of the opinion that only one form of organisation should exist—a workers' union. I know about it. Principles are invoked by many revolutionary-minded but confused people whenever there is a lack of understanding, i.e., whenever the mind refuses to grasp the obvious facts that ought to be heeded. How do such guardians of the 'purity of principles' cope with the historical necessities of our revolutionary policy? All their talk collapses in face of the inexorable necessities. We cannot exercise the dictatorship of the proletariat without having millions of women on our side. Nor can we engage in communist construction without them. We must find a way to reach them. We must study and search in order to find this way.

"It is therefore perfectly right for us to put forward demands for the benefit of women. This is not a minimum programme, nor a programme of reform in the Social-Democratic sense, in the sense of the Second International. It does not go to show that we believe the bourgeoisie and its state will last forever, or even for a long time. Nor is it an attempt to pacify the masses of women with reforms and to divert them from the path of revolutionary struggle. It is nothing of the sort, and not any sort of reformist humbug either. Our demands are no more than practical conclusions, drawn by us from the crying needs and disgraceful humiliations that weak and underprivileged woman must bear under the bourgeois system. We demonstrate thereby that we are aware of these needs and of

3. A German anarcho-syndicalist group formed in 1919 by members who split off from the Communist Party of Germany.

the oppression of women, that we are conscious of the privileged position of the men, and that we hate—yes, hate—and want to remove whatever oppresses and harasses the working woman, the wife of the worker, the peasant woman, the wife of the little man, and even in many respects the woman of the propertied classes. The rights and social measures we demand of bourgeois society for women are proof that we understand the position and interests of women and that we will take note of them under the proletarian dictatorship. Naturally, not as soporific and patronising reformists. No, by no means. But as revolutionaries who call upon the women to take a hand as equals in the reconstruction of the economy and of the ideological superstructure."

* * *

* * * But let us not deceive ourselves. Our national sections still lack the proper understanding of this question. They adopt a passive, wait-and-see attitude when it comes to creating a mass movement of working women under communist leadership. They do not realise that developing and leading such a mass movement is an important part of all Party activity, as much as half of all the Party work. Their occasional recognition of the need and value of a purposeful, strong and numerous communist women's movement is but platonic lip-service rather than a steady concern and task of the Party.

"They regard agitation and propaganda among women and the task of rousing and revolutionising them as of secondary importance, as the job of just the women Communists. None but the latter are rebuked because the matter does not move ahead more quickly and strongly. This is wrong, fundamentally wrong! It is outright separatism. It is equality of women *à rebours*, as the French say, i.e., equality reversed. What is at the bottom of the incorrect attitude of our national sections? (I am not speaking of Soviet Russia.) In the final analysis, it is an underestimation of women and of their accomplishments. That's just what it is! Unfortunately, we may still say of many of our comrades, 'Scratch the Communist and a philistine appears.' To be sure, you have to scratch the sensitive spots—such as their mentality regarding women. Could there be any more palpable proof than the common sight of a man calmly watching a woman wear herself out with trivial, monotonous, strength- and time-consuming work, such as her housework, and watching her spirit shrinking, her mind growing dull, her heartbeat growing faint, and her will growing slack? It goes without saying that I am not referring to the bourgeois ladies who dump all housework and the care for their children on the hired help. What I say applies to the vast majority of women, including the wives of workers, even if these spend the day at the factory and earn money.

"Very few husbands, not even the proletarians, think of how much they could lighten the burdens and worries of their wives, or relieve them entirely, if they lent a hand in this 'women's work.' But no, that would go against the 'privilege and dignity of the husband.' He demands that he have rest and comfort. The domestic life of the woman is a daily sacrifice of self to a thousand insignificant trifles. The ancient rights of her husband, her lord and master, survive unnoticed. Objectively, his slave takes her revenge. Also in concealed form. Her backwardness and her lack of understanding for her husband's revolutionary ideals act as a drag on his fighting spirit, on his determination to fight. They are like tiny worms, gnawing and undermining imperceptibly, slowly but surely. I know the life of the workers, and not only from books. Our communist work among the masses of women, and our political work in general, involves considerable educational work among the men. We must root out the old slave-owner's point of view, both in the Party and among the masses. That is one of our political tasks, a task just as urgently necessary as the formation of a staff composed of comrades, men and women, with thorough theoretical and practical training for Party work among working women."

To my question about present-day conditions in Soviet Russia, Lenin replied:

"The government of the proletarian dictatorship—jointly with the Communist Party and the trade unions of course—makes every effort to overcome the backward views of men and women and thus uproot the old, non-communist psychology. It goes without saying that men and women are absolutely equal before the law. A sincere desire to give effect to this equality is evident in all spheres. We are enlisting women to work in the economy, the administration, legislation and government. All courses and educational institutions are open to them, so that they can improve their professional and social training. We are organising community kitchens and public dining-rooms, laundries and repair shops, crèches, kindergartens, children's homes and educational institutions of every kind. In brief, we are quite in earnest about carrying out the requirements of our programme to shift the functions of house-keeping and education from the individual household to society. Woman is thus being relieved from her old domestic slavery and all dependence on her husband. She is enabled to give her capabilities and inclinations full play in society. Children are offered better opportunities for their development than at home. We have the most progressive female labour legislation in the world, and it is enforced by authorised representatives of organised labour. We are establishing maternity homes, mother-and-child homes, mothers' health centres, courses for infant and child care, exhibitions of mother and child care, and the like. We are making every effort to provide for needy and unemployed women.

"We know perfectly well that all this is still too little, considering the needs of the working women, and that it is still far from sufficient for their real emancipation. Yet it is an immense stride forward from what there was in tsarist and capitalist Russia. Moreover, it is a lot as compared with the state of affairs where capitalism still holds undivided sway. It is a good start in the right direction, and we shall continue to develop it consistently, and with all available energy, too. You abroad may rest assured. Because with each day that passes it becomes clearer that we cannot make progress without the millions of women. Think what this means in a country where the peasants comprise a solid 80 per cent of the population. Small peasant farming implies individual housekeeping and the bondage of women. * * * Under the proletarian dictatorship the emancipation of women through the realisation of communism will proceed also in the countryside. In this respect I expect much from the electrification of our industry and agriculture. That is a grand scheme! The difficulties in its way are great, monstrously great. Powerful forces latent in the masses will have to be released and trained to overcome them. Millions of women must take part in this."4 * * *

* * *

4. See also "A Great Beginning," pp. 484–85, above. [*R. T.*]

PART VII

The Fate of
the Revolution

Our Revolution

(APROPOS OF N. SUKHANOV'S NOTES)

After the strokes that he suffered in December 1922, Lenin doubtless realized that he had not long to live, and the materials that he was able to
write or dictate toward the end of that month and in January–March 1923
represented his effort to provide guidance for the ruling party in the event
of his early death. Some had to do with the overall direction of future
policy, and some with the problem of the leadership succession.

"Our Revolution," written in mid-January 1923, was a general defense
of the Bolshevik Revolution in the form of a comment on Nikolai Sukhanov's *Zapiski o Revoliutsii* (*Notes on the Revolution*), an eyewitness
account of events of 1917 in Petrograd by a non-Bolshevik observer and
critic of Lenin's party. The *Zapiski* were published and widely read in
Soviet Russia in 1922.

I

I have lately been glancing through Sukhanov's notes on the
revolution. What strikes one most is the pedantry of all our petty-
bourgeois democrats and of all the heroes of the Second International. Apart from the fact that they are all extremely faint-hearted,
that when it comes to the minutest deviation from the German
model even the best of them fortify themselves with reservations—
apart from this characteristic, which is common to all petty-bourgeois democrats and has been abundantly manifested by them
throughout the revolution, what strikes one is their slavish imitation
of the past.

They all call themselves Marxists, but their conception of Marxism is impossibly pedantic. They have completely failed to understand what is decisive in Marxism, namely, its revolutionary dialectics. They have even absolutely failed to understand Marx's plain
statements that in times of revolution the utmost flexibility[1] is

---

1. Lenin is apparently referring here to
Marx's words in his work *The Civil War
in France* and in his letter to Kugelmann

dated April 12, 1871 (*Selected Works*,
Vol. 1 [Moscow, 1958], p. 522; Vol. 2,
p. 463).

demanded, and have even failed to notice, for instance, the statements Marx made in his letters—I think it was in 1856—expressing
the hope of combining a peasant war in Germany, which might
create a revolutionary situation, with the working-class movement[2]
—they avoid even this plain statement and walk around and about
it like a cat around a bowl of hot porridge.

Their conduct betrays them as cowardly reformists who are
afraid to deviate from the bourgeoisie, let alone break with it, and
at the same time they disguise their cowardice with the wildest
rhetoric and braggartry. But what strikes one in all of them even
from the purely theoretical point of view is their utter inability to
grasp the following Marxist considerations: up to now they have
seen capitalism and bourgeois democracy in Western Europe follow
a definite path of development, and cannot conceive that this path
can be taken as a model only *mutatis mutandis*, only with certain
amendments (quite insignificant from the standpoint of the general
development of world history).

First—the revolution connected with the first imperialist world
war. Such a revolution was bound to reveal new features, or variations, resulting from the war itself, for the world has never seen
such a war in such a situation. We find that since the war the
bourgeoisie of the wealthiest countries have to this day been unable
to restore "normal" bourgeois relations. Yet our reformists—petty
bourgeois who make a show of being revolutionaries—believed,
and still believe, that normal bourgeois relations are the limit (thus
far shalt thou go and no farther). And even their conception of
"normal" is extremely stereotyped and narrow.

Secondly, they are complete strangers to the idea that while the
development of world history as a whole follows general laws it is
by no means precluded, but, on the contrary, presumed, that certain periods of development may display peculiarities in either the
form or the sequence of this development. For instance, it does not
even occur to them that because Russia stands on the border-line
between the civilised countries and the countries which this war has
for the first time definitely brought into the orbit of civilisation—all
the Oriental, non-European countries—she could and was, indeed,
bound to reveal certain distinguishing features; although these, of
course, are in keeping with the general line of world development,
they distinguish her revolution from those which took place in the
West-European countries and introduce certain partial innovations
as the revolution moves on to the countries of the East.

Infinitely stereotyped, for instance, is the argument they learned

2. See the letter of Marx and Engels of   cow, 1965], pp. 110–11).
April 16, 1856 (*Selected Letters* [Mos-

by rote during the development of West-European Social-Democracy, namely, that we are not yet ripe for socialism, that, as certain "learned" gentlemen among them put it, the objective economic premises of socialism do not exist in our country. It does not occur to any of them to ask: but what about a people that found itself in a revolutionary situation such as that created during the first imperialist war? Might it not, influenced by the hopelessness of its situation, fling itself into a struggle that would offer it at least some chance of securing conditions for the further development of civilisation that were somewhat unusual?

"The development of the productive forces of Russia has not attained the level that makes socialism possible." All the heroes of the Second International, including, of course, Sukhanov, beat the drums about this proposition. They keep harping on this incontrovertible proposition in a thousand different keys, and think that it is the decisive criterion of our revolution.

But what if the situation, which drew Russia into the imperialist world war that involved every more or less influential West-European country and made her a witness of the eve of the revolutions maturing or partly already begun in the East, gave rise to circumstances that put Russia and her development in a position which enabled us to achieve precisely that combination of a "peasant war" with the working-class movement suggested in 1856 by no less a Marxist than Marx himself as a possible prospect for Prussia?

What if the complete hopelessness of the situation, by stimulating the efforts of the workers and peasants tenfold, offered us the opportunity to create the fundamental requisites of civilisation in a different way from that of the West-European countries? Has that altered the general line of development of world history? Has that altered the basic relations between the basic classes of all the countries that are being, or have been, drawn into the general course of world history?

If a definite level of culture is required for the building of socialism (although nobody can say just what that definite "level of culture" is, for it differs in every West-European country), why cannot we begin by first achieving the prerequisites for that definite level of culture in a revolutionary way, and *then*, with the aid of the workers' and peasants' government and the Soviet system, proceed to overtake the other nations?

II

You say that civilisation is necessary for the building of socialism. Very good. But why could we not first create such prerequisites of civilisation in our country as the expulsion of the landowners and the Russian capitalists, and then start moving towards socialism? Where, in what books, have you read that such variations of the customary historical sequence of events are impermissible or impossible?

Napoleon, I think, wrote: *"On s'engage et puis . . . on voit."* Rendered freely this means: "First engage in a serious battle and then see what happens." Well, we did first engage in a serious battle in October 1917, and then saw such details of development (from the standpoint of world history they were certainly details) as the Brest peace, the New Economic Policy, and so forth. And now there can be no doubt that in the main we have been victorious.

Our Sukhanovs, not to mention Social-Democrats still farther to the right, never even dream that revolutions cannot be made in any other way. Our European philistines never even dream that the subsequent revolutions in Oriental countries, which possess much vaster populations and a much vaster diversity of social conditions, will undoubtedly display even greater distinctions than the Russian revolution.

It need hardly be said that a textbook written on Kautskyan lines was a very useful thing in its day. But it is time, for all that, to abandon the idea that it foresaw all the forms of development of subsequent world history. It would be timely to say that those who think so are simply fools.

On Cooperation

Written in early January 1923, this short article shows the further development of Lenin's thinking along the lines already suggested in "The Importance of Gold" and other writings of the NEP period. He finds the
ideas of such nineteenth-century designers of cooperative communities as
Robert Owen relevant to the party's problem of bringing the peasant population of Soviet Russia into cooperatives through long-range cultural and
educational efforts that would comprise what Lenin here calls a "cultural
revolution." In the post-Lenin period this line of thought was developed
further (under the heading of "agrarian-cooperative socialism") by Nikolai
Bukharin, editor of *Pravda* and intellectual leader of a group of Bolshevik
moderates who were politically defeated by Stalin in 1929 and stigmatized
as representatives of a "right-wing deviation." Very likely Lenin would have
shared much of the position that Bukharin and others of his group elaborated in the mid-twenties.

I

It seems to me that not enough attention is being paid to the co-
operative movement in our country. Not everyone understands that
now, since the time of the October Revolution and quite apart from
NEP (on the contrary, in this connection we must say—because of
NEP), our co-operative movement has become one of great significance. There is a lot of fantasy in the dreams of the old co-operators. Often they are ridiculously fantastic. But why are they
fantastic? Because people do not understand the fundamental, the
rock-bottom significance of the working-class political struggle for
the overthrow of the rule of the exploiters. We have overthrown the
rule of the exploiters, and much that was fantastic, even romantic,
even banal in the dreams of the old co-operators is now becoming
unvarnished reality.

Indeed, since political power is in the hands of the working class,
since this political power owns all the means of production, the
only task, indeed, that remains for us is to organise the population
in co-operative societies. With most of the population organised in

co-operatives, the socialism which in the past was legitimately treated with ridicule, scorn and contempt by those who were rightly convinced that it was necessary to wage the class struggle, the struggle for political power, etc., will achieve its aim automatically. But not all comrades realise how vastly, how infinitely important it is now to organise the population of Russia in co-operative societies. By adopting NEP we made a concession to the peasant as a trader, to the principle of private trade; it is precisely for this reason (contrary to what some people think) that the co-operative movement is of such immense importance. All we actually need under NEP is to organise the population of Russia in co-operative societies on a sufficiently large scale, for we have now found that degree of combination of private interest, of private commercial interest, with state supervision and control of this interest, that degree of its subordination to the common interests which was formerly the stumbling-block for very many socialists. Indeed, the power of the state over all large-scale means of production, political power in the hands of the proletariat, the alliance of this proletariat with the many millions of small and very small peasants, the assured proletarian leadership of the peasantry, etc.—is this not all that is necessary to build a complete socialist society out of co-operatives, out of co-operatives alone, which we formerly ridiculed as huckstering and which from a certain aspect we have the right to treat as such now, under NEP? Is this not all that is necessary to build a complete socialist society? It is still not the building of socialist society, but it is all that is necessary and sufficient for it.

It is this very circumstance that is underestimated by many of our practical workers. They look down upon our co-operative societies, failing to appreciate their exceptional importance, first, from the standpoint of principle (the means of production are owned by the state), and, second, from the standpoint of transition to the new system by means that are the *simplest, easiest and most acceptable to the peasant*.

But this again is of fundamental importance. It is one thing to draw up fantastic plans for building socialism through all sorts of workers' associations, and quite another to learn to build socialism in practice in such a way that *every* small peasant could take part in it. That is the very stage we have now reached. And there is no doubt that, having reached it, we are taking too little advantage of it.

We went too far when we introduced NEP, but not because we attached too much importance to the principle of free enterprise and trade—we went too far because we lost sight of the co-operatives, because we now underrate the co-operatives, because we are already beginning to forget the vast importance of the co-operatives from the above two points of view.

I now propose to discuss with the reader what can and must at once be done practically on the basis of this "co-operative" principle. By what means can we, and must we, start at once to develop this "co-operative" principle so that its socialist meaning may be clear to all?

Co-operation must be politically so organised that it will not only generally and always enjoy certain privileges, but that these privileges should be of a purely material nature (a favourable bank-rate, ect.). The co-operatives must be granted state loans that are greater, if only by a little, than the loans we grant to private enterprises, even to heavy industry, etc.

A social system emerges only if it has the financial backing of a definite class. There is no need to mention the hundreds of millions of rubles that the birth of "free" capitalism cost. At present we have to realise that the co-operative system is the social system we must now give more than ordinary assistance, and we must actually give that assistance. But it must be assistance in the real sense of the word, i.e., it will not be enough to interpret it to mean assistance for any kind of co-operative trade; by assistance we must mean aid to co-operative trade in which *really large masses of the population actually take part*. It is certainly a correct form of assistance to give a bonus to peasants who take part in co-operative trade; but the whole point is to verify the nature of this participation, to verify the awareness behind it, and to verify its quality. Strictly speaking, when a co-operator goes to a village and opens a co-operative store, the people take no part in this whatever; but at the same time guided by their own interests they will hasten to try to take part in it.

There is another aspect to this question. From the point of view of the "enlightened" (primarily, literate) European there is not much left for us to do to induce absolutely everyone to take not a passive, but an active part in co-operative operations. Strictly speaking, there is *"only"* one thing we have left to do and that is to make our people so "enlightened" that they understand all the advantages of everybody participating in the work of the co-operatives, and organise this participation. *"Only"* that. There are now no other devices needed to advance to socialism. But to achieve this "only," there must be a veritable revolution—the entire people must go through a period of cultural development. Therefore, our rule must be: as little philosophising and as few acrobatics as possible. In this respect NEP is an advance, because it is adjustable to the level of the most ordinary peasant and does not demand anything higher of him. But it will take a whole historical epoch to get the entire population into the work of the co-operatives through NEP. At best we can achieve this in one or two decades. Nevertheless, it will be a distinct historical epoch, and without this historical epoch, without universal literacy, without a proper degree of efficiency, without training the population sufficiently to acquire the habit of book-reading, and without the material basis for this, without a certain sufficiency to safeguard against, say, bad harvests, famine, etc.—without this we shall not achieve our object. The thing now is to learn to combine the wide revolutionary range of action, the revolutionary enthusiasm which we have displayed, and displayed abundantly, and crowned with complete success—to learn to combine this with (I am almost inclined to say) the ability to be an efficient and capable trader, which is quite enough to be a good co-operator. By ability to be a trader I mean the ability to be a cultured trader. Let those Russians, or peasants, who imagine that since they trade they are good traders, get that well into their heads. This does not follow at all. They do trade, but that is far from being cultured traders. They now trade in an Asiatic manner, but to be a good trader one must trade in the European manner. They are a whole epoch behind in that.

In conclusion: a number of economic, financial and banking privileges must be granted to the co-operatives—this is the way our socialist state must promote the new principle on which the population must be organised. But this is only the general outline of the task; it does not define and depict in detail the entire content of the practical task, i.e., we must find what form of "bonus" to give for joining the co-operatives (and the terms on which we should give it), the form of bonus by which we shall assist the co-operatives sufficiently, the form of bonus that will produce the civilised co-operator. And given social ownership of the means of production, given the class victory of the proletariat over the bourgeoisie, the system of civilised co-operators is the system of socialism.

II

Whenever I wrote about the New Economic Policy I always quoted the article on state capitalism[1] which I wrote in 1918. This has more than once aroused doubts in the minds of certain young comrades. But their doubts were mainly on abstract political points.

It seemed to them that the term "state capitalism" could not be applied to a system under which the means of production were owned by the working class, a working class that held political power. They did not notice, however, that I used the term "state capitalism," *firstly*, to connect historically our present position with the position adopted in my controversy with the so-called Left Communists; also, I argued at the time that state capitalism would

---

1. The reference is to his article " 'Left-wing' Childishness and Petty-Bourgeois Mentality." See Lenin, *Selected Works* (Moscow, 1970), Vol. 2, pp. 685–709.

be superior to our existing economy. It was important for me to show the continuity between ordinary state capitalism and the unusual, even very unusual, state capitalism to which I referred in introducing the reader to the New Economic Policy. *Secondly,* the practical purpose was always important to me. And the practical purpose of our New Economic Policy was to lease out concessions. In the prevailing circumstances, concessions in our country would unquestionably have been a pure type of state capitalism. That is how I argued about state capitalism.

But there is another aspect of the matter for which we may need state capitalism, or at least a comparison with it. It is the question of co-operatives.

In the capitalist state, co-operatives are no doubt collective capitalist institutions. Nor is there any doubt that under our present economic conditions, when we combine private capitalist enterprises—but in no other way than on nationalised land and in no other way than under the control of the working-class state—with enterprises of a consistently socialist type (the means of production, the land on which the enterprises are situated, and the enterprises as a whole belonging to the state), the question arises about a third type of enterprise, the co-operatives, which were not formerly regarded as an independent type differing fundamentally from the others. Under private capitalism, co-operative enterprises differ from capitalist enterprises as collective enterprises differ from private enterprises. Under state capitalism, co-operative enterprises differ from state capitalist enterprises, firstly, because they are private enterprises, and, secondly, because they are collective enterprises. Under our present system, co-operative enterprises differ from private capitalist enterprises because they are collective enterprises, but do not differ from socialist enterprises if the land on which they are situated and the means of production belong to the state, i.e., the working class.

This circumstance is not considered sufficiently when co-operatives are discussed. It is forgotten that owing to the special features of our political system, our co-operatives acquire an altogether exceptional significance. If we exclude concessions, which, incidentally, have not developed on any considerable scale, co-operation under our conditions nearly always coincides fully with socialism.

Let me explain what I mean. Why were the plans of the old co-operators, from Robert Owen onwards, fantastic? Because they dreamed of peacefully remodelling contemporary society into socialism without taking account of such fundamental questions as the class struggle, the capture of political power by the working class, the overthrow of the rule of the exploiting class. That is why we are right in regarding as entirely fantastic this "co-operative" socialism, and as romantic, and even banal, the dream of transforming class enemies into class collaborators and class war into class peace (so-called class truce) by merely organising the population in co-operative societies.

Undoubtedly we were right from the point of view of the fundamental task of the present day, for socialism cannot be established without a class struggle for political power in the state.

But see how things have changed now that political power is in the hands of the working class, now that the political power of the exploiters is overthrown and all the means of production (except those which the workers' state voluntarily abandons on specified terms and for a certain time to the exploiters in the form of concessions) are owned by the working class.

Now we are entitled to say that for us the mere growth of cooperation (with the "slight" exception mentioned above) is identical with the growth of socialism, and at the same time we have to admit that there has been a radical modification in our whole outlook on socialism. The radical modification is this; formerly we placed, and had to place, the main emphasis on the political struggle, on revolution, on winning political power, etc. Now the emphasis is changing and shifting to peaceful, organisational, "cultural" work. I should say the emphasis is shifting to educational work, were it not for our international relations, were it not for the fact that we have to fight for our position on a world scale. If we leave that aside, however, and confine ourselves to internal economic relations, the emphasis in our work is certainly shifting to education.

Two main tasks confront us, which constitute the epoch—to reorganise our machinery of state, which is utterly useless, and which we took over in its entirety from the preceding epoch; during the past five years of struggle we did not, and could not, drastically reorganise it. Our second task is educational work among the peasants. And the economic object of this educational work among the peasants is to organise the latter in co-operative societies. If the whole of the peasantry had been organised in cooperatives, we would by now have been standing with both feet on the soil of socialism. But the organisation of the entire peasantry in co-operative societies presupposes a standard of culture among the peasants (precisely among the peasants as the overwhelming mass) that cannot, in fact, be achieved without a cultural revolution.

Our opponents told us repeatedly that we were rash in undertaking to implant socialism in an insufficiently cultured country. But they were misled by our having started from the opposite end to that prescribed by theory (the theory of pedants of all kinds), because in our country the political and social revolution preceded the cultural revolution, that very cultural revolution which nevertheless now confronts us.

This cultural revolution would now suffice to make our country a completely socialist country; but it presents immense difficulties of a purely cultural (for we are illiterate) and material character (for to be cultured we must achieve a certain development of the material means of production, must have a certain material base).

On Bureaucracy:
From Lenin's Correspondence

Lenin's hatred of Russian bureaucratic ways had been one of the powerful motivating forces in his resolve to revolutionize Russia. But as premier in the revolutionary regime he found himself, to his horror, confronted with Russian bureaucratic ways in the Soviet framework. His strong reactions, and his concern over what this might mean for the future of the Revolution, are evident in the five following letters drawn from his inter-office and personal correspondence between 1919 and 1922.

Letter of March 1919 to L. B. Krasin[1]

Maria Fedorovna has transmitted the attached papers to me. Grzhebin does not express himself clearly. Who in the world is *Pravbum?* Cannot copies of its permit and the annulment of it be obtained? To whom is *Pravbum* subordinated? I shall have to demand a response from it, and incidentally to find out in more detail what books and pamphlets *World Literature* is requesting.

Letter of January 1920 to M. P. Tomsky[2]

To Comrade Tomsky, and for the ARCCTU and the Communist Fraction of ARCCTU

Dear Comrades! I hereby transmit to you information on an astonishing manifestation of *red-tape*, negligence, bureaucratism,

1. L. B. Krasin was at that time a high official in the Supreme Council of National Economy. Maria Fedorovna Andreeva, to whom Lenin refers, was the wife of the writer Maxim Gorky. She had evidently solicited Lenin's help in obtaining the release of a stock of paper for the magazine *World Literature*. The bureaucratic agency called *Pravbum* for short was the Petrograd department of the Chief Administration of State Enterprises of the Paper Industry. [R. T.]

2. M. P. Tomsky was chairman of the All-Russia Central Council of Trade Unions (ARCCTU). At the end of 1919, evidently in response to a request from a trade union official named Melnichansky, Lenin had arranged for the transfer

and heavy-handedness in a most important *practical* matter.

I never doubted that there was still very much bureaucratism in our commissariats, all of them.

But that there was no less bureaucratism in the trade unions—that I did not expect.

This is a colossal disgrace. I very much request you to read all the attached documents in the Communist fraction in ARCCTU and work out *practical* ways of combating bureaucratism, red-tape, inaction and heavy-handedness.

Please do not fail to inform me of the results.

Melnichansky *himself* phoned me about those ten thousand metal workers. I raised a big fuss with the People's Commissariat of Railways, and now Comrade Melnichansky has made a fool out of me.

With Communist greetings.

V. *Ulyanov* (*Lenin*)

Letter of July 1920 to F. A. Rothstein[3]

Dear Comrade! Many thanks for your letters, which always contain highly valuable information. I enclose a letter from my wife and ask you to convey my greetings to your wife and family, with whom I used to visit when I came to see you in London.

As for your trip to Russia, I hesitate. You are very important for the cause in London. * * *

Regarding the dispatch of literature to you, I have taken special measures. You must know that one has to swear at Russians twenty times and check up on them thirty times in order to get the simplest thing done in the right way. Follow up on the matter and let us know more often (if need be sometimes directly to me), and I will apply pressure to see that what you have failed to receive arrives regularly.

I think that your guiding participation (possible both by pen and secretly) in the Anglo-Saxon movement is especially valuable. The rectifying of the line there is doubly important. You will receive my pamphlet against the "left-wingers" and (draft) resolutions for the

of ten thousand skilled metal workers to do repair work on the railways, but the ARCCTU leadership had failed to work out terms for their assignment to the Moscow rail junction. The "Communist fraction" referred to was the group of party members employed in the ARCCTU. [*R. T.*]

3. F. A. Rothstein was an old party comrade of Lenin's who had emigrated to London in 1890. He was active in the founding of the British Communist Party in 1920. He had thoughts then about returning to Russia, but Lenin discouraged him from doing that. The pamphlet against the "left-wingers" mentioned in the letter is Lenin's "*Left-Wing*" Communism (above, pp. 550–618). [*R. T.*]

Second Congress of the Third International and I would very much like to know your opinion.

I firmly shake your hand and send you very best wishes.

Your Lenin

Letter of May 1921 to M. F. Sokolov[4]

* * * You write:

"The spontaneous activity of the masses is *possible* only if we *sweep from the face* of the earth the carbuncle called bureaucratic chief administrations and centers."

Although I have not had local experience, I do know this bureaucratism and all the harm that it does. Your mistake is to think that it can be destroyed immediately, "swept from the face of the earth," like a "carbuncle."

That is wrong. The tsar can be sent packing, the landed proprietors sent packing, the capitalists sent packing. That we did. But bureaucratism cannot be "sent packing" from a peasant country, cannot be "swept from the face of the earth." One can only *reduce* it by slow, stubborn effort.

To "throw off" the "bureaucratic boil," as you put it in another passage, is a wrong way to put the problem. It reflects a failure to comprehend the issue. A boil of that kind *cannot* be "thrown off." It can only be *cured*. In *this* matter surgery is an absurdity, an *impossibility*; only *slow cure*—all else is charlatanism or naïveté.

Naïve is what you are, if you will excuse my frankness. But you yourself write about your youthfulness.

It is naïve to dismiss cure with a wave of the hand and a statement that you two or three times tried to fight the bureaucrats but lost out. In the first place, runs my response to your unsuccessful experience—in the first place, you have to try not two or three times but twenty or thirty times, try and go on trying, start all over again.

In the second place, where has it been shown that you have fought in the right way, fought skilfully? Bureaucrats are tricky types; there are many rascals among them, arch-opportunists. You will not catch them with bare hands. Did you fight in the right way? Did you *surround* the "enemy" by all the rules of military art? I don't know.

4. M. F. Sokolov was then a young (twenty-eight-year-old) official of the Foreign Affairs Commissariat, where he served as secretary of the Administration for Affairs of Evacuation of Property and Archives from Poland. He had sent Lenin—with a request for comments—the draft of a report on Soviet economic policy which he intended to present before a meeting of the party cell of the Commissariat before the end of May. [*R. T.*]

Your reference to Engels is to no purpose.[5] Wasn't it some "intellectual" who prompted you to make it? A pointless reference, if not worse than pointless. It smacks of doctrinaire thinking. Sounds like desperation. And for us to give way to despair is either comical or shameful.

The fight against bureaucratism in an utterly worn-out peasant country takes a long time and has to be carried on tenaciously without losing heart at the first setback.

"Sweep away" the "chief administrations"? Nonsense. What are you going to put *in their place*? You don't know. Not to *sweep away* but to cleanse, cure, cure and cleanse ten times and a hundred times. And not to lose heart.

If you do give your report (I absolutely have no objection to that), please also read them this letter of mine to you.

I shake your hand and ask you not to give way to the "spirit of despondency."

Lenin

Letter of January 1922 to A. D. Tsiurupa[6]

Comrade Tsiurupa!

In connection with your telephone conversation of yesterday and your promise to observe a strict regime, it is necessary for us to talk in detail about the whole system of work and think it though very carefully.

The most fundamental defect of the Council of People's Commissars and the Council of Labour and Defence is the lack of check-up on fulfilment. The vile bureaucratic bog *draws us* into the writing of papers, endless talkfests about decrees, the writing of decrees, and real live work drowns in that sea of paper.

Clever saboteurs deliberately draw us into this paper swamp. The majority of people's commissars and other government dignitaries unwittingly "walk into the trap."

You must make use of the strict medical regime to cut yourself

5. The reference in Sokolov's draft was to Engels's statement in *The Peasant War in Germany*: "The worst fate that can befall the leader of an extreme party is the forced necessity to take power at a time when the movement has not yet sufficiently matured to rule the class that it represents and to carry out measures for consolidating its rule." [*R. T.*]

6. In December 1921, by Politburo decision, A. D. Tsiurupa was appointed second vice president of the Council of Labour and Defence and deputy chairman of the Council of People's Commissars, of which the Council of Labour and Defense was a commission. It is apparent from this letter that Lenin had arranged for Tsiurupa to take medical leave in order to have leisure and the necessary freedom from current work to think out ways of combating bureaucracy in the work of the supreme organs of the Soviet government. In 1922 Tsiurupa replaced Stalin as commissar of the Workers' and Peasants' Inspection, an organ which Lenin conceived as a force for popular control over the bureaucratic apparatus. [*R. T.*]

off *at all cost* from the hurly-burly, the hullabaloo, the commissions, the talking about and the writing of papers, cut yourself off and *think through* the system of work and *revise it radically*.

The center of gravity of your work must be just this remaking of our repulsive-bureaucratic mode of work, the fight against bureaucratism and red tape, *check up on fulfilment*.

Check up on fulfilment, check up on what actually happens—that's your chief and basic task; set up for this purpose a very small (four to six people) apparatus consisting of arch-experienced and tested assistants (an office manager, his assistants, a secretary, etc.). * * *

The Question of Nationalities
or "Autonomisation"

As the reader is aware from earlier selections (e.g., "Against Great-Russian Chauvinism," pp. 659–60, above), Lenin was seriously concerned over indications of a trend of Great-Russian nationalism in the Soviet regime's dealings with minority nations of the country. In part, as the document below shows, he was worried that a failure to demonstrate to the world how the Soviet Revolution had benefited the minority nations of the former Tsarist Empire might inhibit its influence upon the awakening peoples of the East.

In time, Lenin became aware that the Georgian Bolshevik whom he had placed in the key post of commissar for nationality affairs, Stalin, was himself infected by the Great-Russian nationalist trend and that he had shown this in his harsh treatment of his Georgian countrymen after Georgia's forcible sovietization in 1921. He and Stalin had also disagreed about the structure of the Soviet federal state, a problem under discussion in 1922, with Stalin favoring "autonomization" (meaning the incorporation of the non-Russian Soviet republics in the Russian Federation—the RSFSR—as "autonomous" republics) while Lenin favored their unification with the RSFSR on a formal plane of equality in a "Union of Soviet Socialist Republics" (the version adopted in the Soviet Constitution adopted in 1923).

In these notes dictated on December 30–31, 1922, to "M. V." (his secretary, M. A. Volodicheva), Lenin set forth his conclusions on these matters in a document meant for the forthcoming Twelfth Party Congress (then scheduled for March 1923, although it in fact was held in April). The harsh criticism of Stalin was intended as part of the substantiation of Lenin's plan to request the congress to remove Stalin from the powerful post of general secretary of the party Central Committee.*

I suppose I have been very remiss with respect to the workers of Russia for not having intervened energetically and decisively enough in the notorious question of autonomisation, which, it ap-

* For a more detailed analysis of the document and its background, see Tucker, *Stalin as Revolutionary*, pp. 250–66.

pears, is officially called the question of the union of Soviet socialist republics.

When this question arose last summer, I was ill; and then in autumn I relied too much on my recovery and on the October and December plenary meetings[1] giving me an opportunity of intervening in this question. However, I did not manage to attend the October Plenary Meeting (when this question came up) or the one in December, and so the question passed me by almost completely.

I have only had time for a talk with Comrade Dzerzhinsky, who came from the Caucasus and told me how this matter stood in Georgia. I have also managed to exchange a few words with Comrade Zinoviev and express my apprehensions on this matter. From what I was told by Comrade Dzerzhinsky, who was at the head of the commission sent by the C.C. to "investigate" the Georgian incident, I could only draw the greatest apprehensions. If matters had come to such a pass that Ordzhonikidze could go to the extreme of applying physical violence, as Comrade Dzerzhinsky informed me, we can imagine what a mess we have got ourselves into. Obviously the whole business of "autonomisation" was radically wrong and badly timed.

It is said that a united apparatus was needed. Where did that assurance come from? Did it not come from that same Russian apparatus which, as I pointed out in one of the preceding sections of my diary, we took over from tsarism and slightly anointed with Soviet oil?

There is no doubt that that measure should have been delayed somewhat until we could say that we vouched for our apparatus as our own. But now, we must, in all conscience, admit the contrary; the apparatus we call ours is, in fact, still quite alien to us; it is a bourgeois and tsarist hotch-potch and there has been no possibility of getting rid of it in the course of the past five years without the help of other countries and because we have been "busy" most of the time with military engagements and the fight against famine.

It is quite natural that in such circumstances the "freedom to secede from the union" by which we justify ourselves will be a mere scrap of paper, unable to defend the non-Russians from the onslaught of that true-Russian man, the Great-Russian chauvinist, in substance a true brute and a scoundrel, such as the typical Russian bureaucrat is. There is no doubt that the infinitesimal percentage of Soviet and sovietised workers will drown in that tide of chauvinistic Great-Russian riffraff like a fly in milk.

It is said in defence of this measure that the People's Commis-

---

1. The reference is to meetings of the Central Committee of the party in October and December 1922, at which questions of federalism under the Soviet Constitution were discussed. [*R. T.*]

sariats directly concerned with national psychology and national education were set up as separate bodies. But there the question arises: can these People's Commissariats be made quite independent? and secondly: were we careful enough to take measures to provide the non-Russians with a real safeguard against the truly Russian bully? I do not think we took such measures although we could and should have done so.

I think that Stalin's haste and his love of issuing orders, together with his malice against the notorious "social-nationalism,"[2] played a fatal role here. In general, malice plays the very worst role in politics.

I also fear that Comrade Dzerzhinsky, who went to the Caucasus to investigate the "crime" of those "social-nationals," distinguished himself there by his true-Russianism (it is common knowledge that people of other nationalities who have become Russified overdo it on the side of true-Russianism) and that the impartiality of his whole commission was typified well enough by Ordzhonikidze's "laying on of hands." I think that no provocation or even insult can justify such Russian "laying on of hands" and that Comrade Dzerzhinsky was inexcusably guilty in adopting a light-hearted attitude towards it.

For all the citizens in the Caucasus Ordzhonikidze was the authority. Ordzhonikidze had no right to display that irritability to which he and Dzerzhinsky referred. On the contrary, Ordzhonikidze should have behaved with a restraint which cannot be demanded of any ordinary citizen, still less of a man accused of a "political" crime. And, to tell the truth, those "social-nationals" were citizens who were accused of a political crime, and the terms of the accusation were such that it could not be described otherwise.

Here we have an important question of principle: how is internationalism to be understood?[3]

Lenin

December 30, 1922
Taken down by M. V.

---

2. This phrase, a variation on the earlier Leninist term "social-chauvinism," was the epithet used by Stalin and his associates to stigmatize the Georgian Bolsheviks, who, in Stalin's opinion, wanted to follow a nationalist policy. [*R. T.*]

3. After this the following phrase was crossed out in the shorthand text: "It seems to me that our comrades have not studied this important question of principle sufficiently."

Continuation of the Notes (December 31, 1922)

In my writings on the national question I have already said that an abstract presentation of the question of nationalism in general is of no use at all. A distinction must necessarily be made between the nationalism of an oppressor nation and that of an oppressed nation, the nationalism of a big nation and that of a small nation.

In respect of the second kind of nationalism we, nationals of a big nation, have nearly always been guilty, in historic practice, of an infinite number of cases of violence; furthermore, we commit violence and insult an infinite number of times without noticing it. It is sufficient to recall my Volga reminiscences of how non-Russians are treated; how the Poles are not called by any other name than Polyachishka, how the Tatar is nicknamed Prince, how the Ukrainians are always Khokhols and the Georgians and other Caucasian nationals always Kapkasians.

That is why internationalism on the part of oppressors or "great" nations, as they are called (though they are great only in their violence, great only as bullies), must consist not only in the observance of the formal equality of nations but even in an inequality of the oppressor nation, the great nation, that must make up for the inequality which obtains in actual practice. Anybody who does not understand this has not grasped the real proletarian attitude to the national question, he is still essentially petty bourgeois in his point of view and is, therefore, sure to descend to the bourgeois point of view.

What is important for the proletarian? For the proletarian it is not only important, it is absolutely essential that he should be assured that the non-Russians place the greatest possible trust in the proletarian class struggle. What is needed to ensure this? Not merely formal equality. In one way or another, by one's attitude or by concessions, it is necessary to compensate the non-Russians for the lack of trust, for the suspicion and the insults to which the government of the "dominant" nation subjected them in the past.

I think it is unnecessary to explain this to Bolsheviks, to Communists, in greater detail. And I think that in the present instance, as far as the Georgian nation is concerned, we have a typical case in which a genuinely proletarian attitude makes profound caution, thoughtfulness and a readiness to compromise a matter of necessity for us. The Georgian who is neglectful of this aspect of the question, or who carelessly flings about accusations of "social-nationalism" (whereas he himself is a real and true "social-nationalist," and even a vulgar Great-Russian bully), violates, in substance, the interests of proletarian class solidarity, for nothing holds up the development and strengthening of proletarian class solidarity so much as national injustice; "offended" nationals are not sensitive to anything so much as to the feeling of equality and the violation of this equality, if only through negligence or jest—to the violation of that equality by their proletarian comrades. That is why in this case it is better to overdo rather than underdo the concessions and leniency towards the national minorities. That is why, in this case, the fundamental interest of proletarian solidarity, and consequently of the proletarian class struggle, requires that we never adopt a formal attitude to the national question, but always take into account the specific attitude of the proletarian of the oppressed (or small) nation toward the oppressor (or great) nation.

Lenin

December 31, 1922
Taken down by M. V.

Continuation of the Notes (December 31, 1922)

What practical measures must be taken in the present situation?

Firstly, we must maintain and strengthen the union of socialist republics. Of this there can be no doubt. This measure is necessary for us and it is necessary for the world communist proletariat in its struggle against the world bourgeoisie and its defence against bourgeois intrigues.

Secondly, the union of socialist republics must be retained for its diplomatic apparatus. By the way, this apparatus is an exceptional component of our state apparatus. We have not allowed a single influential person from the old tsarist apparatus into it. All sections with any authority are composed of Communists. That is why it has already won for itself (this may be said boldly) the name of a reliable communist apparatus purged to an incomparably greater extent of the old tsarist, bourgeois and petty-bourgeois elements than that which we have had to make do with in other People's Commissariats.

Thirdly, exemplary punishment must be inflicted on Comrade Ordzhonikidze (I say this all the more regretfully as I am one of his personal friends and have worked with him abroad) and the investigation of all the material which Dzerzhinsky's commission has collected must be completed or started over again to correct the enormous mass of wrongs and biased judgments which it doubtlessly contains. The political responsibility for all this truly Great-Russian nationalist campaign must, of course, be laid on Stalin and Dzerzhinsky.

Fourthly, the strictest rules must be introduced on the use of the national language in the non-Russian republics of our union, and these rules be checked with special care. There is no doubt that our apparatus being what it is, there is bound to be, on the pretext of unity in the railway service, unity in the fiscal service and so on, a mass of truly Russian abuses. Special ingenuity is necessary for the struggle against these abuses, not to mention special sincerity on the part of those who undertake this struggle. A detailed code will be required, and only the nationals living in the republic in question can draw it up at all successfully. And then we cannot be sure in advance that as a result of this work we shall not take a step backward at our next Congress of Soviets, i.e., retain the union of Soviet socialist republics only for military and diplomatic affairs, and in all other respects restore full independence to the individual People's Commissariats.

It must be borne in mind that the decentralisation of the People's Commissariats and the lack of co-ordination in their work as far as Moscow and other centres are concerned can be compensated sufficiently by Party authority, if it is exercised with sufficient prudence and impartiality; the harm that can result to our state from a lack of unification between the national apparatuses and the Russian apparatus is infinitely less than that which will be done not only to us, but to the whole International, and to the hundreds of millions of the peoples of Asia, which is destined to follow us on to the stage of history in the near future. It would be unpardonable opportunism if, on the eve of the debut of the East, just as it is awakening, we undermined our prestige with its peoples, even if only by the slighest crudity or injustice towards our own non-Russian nationalities. The need to rally against the imperialists of the West, who are defending the capitalist world, is one thing. There can be no doubt about that and it would be superfluous for me to speak about my unconditional approval of it. It is another thing when we ourselves lapse, even if only in trifles, into imperialist attitudes towards oppressed nationalities, thus undermining all our principled sincerity, all our principled defence of the struggle against imperialism. But the morrow of world history will be a day when the awakening peoples oppressed by imperialism are finally aroused and the decisive, long and hard struggle for their liberation begins.

Lenin

December 31, 1922
Taken down by M. V.

Letter to the Congress

First published in the Soviet Union in the aftermath of the Twentieth Party Congress of 1956, this document had long since become informally known as "Lenin's testament." Although portions of it deal with organizational plans designed, in Lenin's mind, to avert the danger of a split in the party, the most significant portion of the document historically is that in which Lenin went over the qualifications of six prominent associates for future leadership of the party; and the postscript of January 4, 1923, in which he recommended Stalin's removal from the post of general secretary.

Although the notes comprising this "Letter to the Congress" were kept secret by Lenin and treated as though they might become in fact a political testament to be opened after his death, the document's title, combined with other circumstances, indicate that he was hoping to communicate the letter to the *forthcoming* party congress along with the notes on nationalities and other materials, with a view to unseating Stalin in the near future rather than after his own death. However, the drastic worsening of Lenin's health in early March 1923 brought his active political life to an end, and the "Letter" was not opened until after he died. The congress to which it was then communicated was the Thirteenth, which took place in May 1924. There the party leaders, meeting in private, decided against the removal of Stalin.*

I

I would urge strongly that at this Congress a number of changes be made in our political structure.

I want to tell you of the considerations to which I attach most importance.

At the head of the list I set an increase in the number of Central Committee members to a few dozen or even a hundred. It is my opinion that without this reform our Central Committee would be in great danger if the course of events were not quite favourable for us (and that is something we cannot count on).

* For a more detailed presentation of the argument that the "Letter" was intended by Lenin for the Twelfth Congress, for which he hoped to be still alive and active, see Tucker, *Stalin as Revolutionary*, pp. 267–77.

Then, I intend to propose that the Congress should on certain conditions invest the decisions of the State Planning Commission with legislative force, meeting, in this respect, the wishes of Comrade Trotsky—to a certain extent and on certain conditions.

As for the first point, i.e., increasing the number of C.C. members, I think it must be done in order to raise the prestige of the Central Committee, to do a thorough job of improving our administrative machinery and to prevent conflicts between small sections of the C.C. from acquiring excessive importance for the future of the Party.

It seems to me that our Party has every right to demand from the working class 50 to 100 C.C. members, and that it could get them from it without unduly taxing the resources of that class.

Such a reform would considerably increase the stability of our Party and ease its struggle in the encirclement of hostile states, which, in my opinion, is likely to, and must, become much more acute in the next few years. I think that the stability of our Party would gain a thousandfold by such a measure.

Lenin

December 23, 1922
Taken down by M. V.

Continuation of the Notes (December 24, 1922)

II

By stability of the Central Committee, of which I spoke above, I mean measures against a split, as far as such measures can at all be taken. For, of course, the whiteguard in *Russkaya Mysl* (it seems to have been S.S. Oldenburg) was right when, first, in the whiteguards' game against Soviet Russia he banked on a split in our Party, and when, secondly, he banked on grave differences in our Party to cause that split.

Our Party relies on two classes and therefore its instability would be possible and its downfall inevitable if there were no agreement between those two classes. In that event this or that measure, and generally all talk about the stability of our C.C., would be futile. No measures of any kind could prevent a split in such a case. But I hope that this is too remote a future and too improbable an event to talk about.

I have in mind stability as a guarantee against a split in the immediate future, and I intend to deal here with a few ideas concerning personal qualities.

I think that from this standpoint the prime factors in the question of stability are such members of the C.C. as Stalin and Trotsky. I think relations between them make up the greater part of the danger of a split, which could be avoided, and this purpose, in my opinion, would be served, among other things, by increasing the number of C.C. members to 50 or 100.

Comrade Stalin, having become secretary-general, has boundless power concentrated in his hands, and I am not sure whether he will always be capable of using that power with sufficient caution. Comrade Trotsky, on the other hand, as his struggle against the C.C. on the question of the People's Commissariat for Communications has already proved, is distinguished not only by outstanding ability. He is personally perhaps the most capable man in the present C.C., but he has displayed excessive self-assurance and shown excessive preoccupation with the purely administrative side of the work.

These two qualities of the two outstanding leaders of the present C.C. can inadvertently lead to a split, and if our Party does not take steps to avert this, the split may come unexpectedly.

I shall not give any further appraisals of the personal qualities of other members of the C.C. I shall just recall that the October episode with Zinoviev and Kamenev[1] was, of course, no accident, but neither can the blame for it be laid upon them personally, any more than non-Bolshevism can upon Trotsky.

Speaking of the young C.C. members, I wish to say a few words about Bukharin and Pyatakov. They are, in my opinion, the most outstanding figures (among the youngest ones), and the following must be borne in mind about them: Bukharin is not only a most valuable and major theorist of the Party; he is also rightly considered the favourite of the whole Party, but his theoretical views can be classified as fully Marxist only with great reserve, for there is something scholastic about him (he has never made a study of dialectics, and, I think, never fully understood it).

December 25. As for Pyatakov, he is unquestionably a man of outstanding will and outstanding ability, but shows too much zeal for administrating and the administrative side of the work to be relied upon in a serious political matter.

Both of these remarks, of course, are made only for the present, on the assumption that both these outstanding and devoted Party workers fail to find an occasion to enhance their knowledge and amend their one-sidedness.

Lenin

December 25, 1922
Taken down by M. V.

---

1. The reference is to their opposition to the plan for an immediate armed uprising in 1917 and their revelation of the plan in a statement that appeared on October 18 in the Menshevik paper *Novaya Zhizn* (*New Life*). [R. T.]

Addition to the Letter of December 24, 1922

Stalin is too rude and this defect, although quite tolerable in our midst and in dealings among us Communists, becomes intolerable in a secretary-general. That is why I suggest that the comrades think about a way of removing Stalin from that post and appointing another man in his stead who in all other respects differs from Comrade Stalin in having only one advantage, namely, that of being more tolerant, more loyal, more polite and more considerate to the comrades, less capricious, etc. This circumstance may appear to be an insignificant trifle. But I think that from the standpoint of safeguards against a split and from the standpoint of what I wrote above about the relationship between Stalin and Trotsky it is not a trifle, or it is a trifle which can assume decisive significance.

Lenin

January 4, 1923
Taken down by L. F.

How We Should Reorganise the Workers' and Peasants' Inspection

RECOMMENDATION TO THE TWELFTH PARTY CONGRESS

This article of January 23, 1923, which was printed in *Pravda* on January 25, was one more document in the case that Lenin was building against Stalin—as well as a further expression of his general desire to combat Soviet bureaucracy. The People's Commissariat of Workers' and Peasants' Inspection (familiarly known in Soviet jargon as Rabkrin) was headed by Stalin from 1919 until 1922, when he took over the party post of general secretary. Although he had recently been succeeded in the Rabkrin post by A. D. Tsiurupa, Lenin's strong criticism of the institution in this article was an implied criticism of Stalin's failure to make it the instrument of popular control over the bureaucracy that Lenin had designed it to be.

It is beyond question that the Workers' and Peasants' Inspection is an enormous difficulty for us, and that so far this difficulty has not been overcome. I think that the comrades who try to overcome the difficulty by denying that the Workers' and Peasants' Inspection is useful and necessary are wrong. But I do not deny that the problem presented by our state apparatus and the task of improving it is very difficult, that it is far from being solved, and is an extremely urgent one.

With the exception of the People's Commissariat of Foreign Affairs, our state apparatus is to a considerable extent a survival of the past and has undergone hardly any serious change. It has only been slightly touched up on the surface, but in all other respects it is a most typical relic of our old state machine. And so, to find a method of really renovating it, I think we ought to turn for experience to our Civil War.

How did we act in the more critical moments of the Civil War?

We concentrated our best Party forces in the Red Army; we mobilised the best of our workers; we looked for new forces at the deepest roots of our dictatorship.

I am convinced that we must go to the same source to find the means of reorganising the Workers' and Peasants' Inspection. I recommend that our Twelfth Party Congress adopt the following plan of reorganisation, based on some enlargement of our Central Control Commission.

The Plenary Meetings of the Central Committee of our Party are already revealing a tendency to develop into a kind of supreme Party conference. They take place, on the average, not more than once in two months, while the routine work is conducted, as we know, on behalf of the Central Committee by our Political Bureau, our Organising Bureau, our Secretariat, and so forth. I think we ought to follow the road we have thus taken to the end and definitely transform the Plenary Meetings of the Central Committee into supreme Party conferences convened once in two months jointly with the Central Control Commission. The Central Control Commission should be amalgamated with the main body of the reorganised Workers' and Peasants' Inspection on the following lines.

I propose that the Congress should elect 75 to 100 new members to the Central Control Commission. They should be workers and peasants, and should go through the same Party screening as ordinary members of the Central Committee, because they are to enjoy the same rights as the members of the Central Committee.

On the other hand, the staff of the Workers' and Peasants' Inspection should be reduced to three or four hundred persons, specially screened for conscientiousness and knowledge of our state apparatus. They must also undergo a special test as regards their knowledge of the principles of scientific organisation of labour in general, and of administrative work, office work, and so forth, in particular.

In my opinion, such an amalgamation of the Workers' and Peasants' Inspection with the Central Control Commission will be beneficial to both these institutions. On the one hand, the Workers' and Peasants' Inspection will thus obtain such high authority that it will certainly not be inferior to the People's Commissariat of Foreign Affairs. On the other hand, our Central Committee, together with the Central Control Commission, will definitely take the road of becoming a supreme Party conference, which in fact it has already taken, and along which it should proceed to the end so as to be able to fulfil its functions properly in two respects: in respect to *its own* methodical, expedient and systematic organisation and work, and in respect to maintaining contacts with the broad masses through the medium of the best of our workers and peasants.

I foresee an objection that, directly or indirectly, may come from those spheres which make our state apparatus antiquated, i.e., from those who urge that its present utterly impossible, indecently pre-revolutionary form be preserved (incidentally, we now have an opportunity which rarely occurs in history of ascertaining the period necessary for bringing about radical social changes; we now see clearly *what* can be done in five years, and what requires much more time).

The objection I foresee is that the change I propose will lead to nothing but chaos. The members of the Central Control Commission will wander around all the institutions, not knowing where, why or to whom to apply, causing disorganisation everywhere and distracting employees from their routine work, etc., etc.

I think that the malicious source of this objection is so obvious that it does not warrant a reply. It goes without saying that the Presidium of the Central Control Commission, the People's Commissar of the Workers' and Peasants' Inspection and his collegium (and also, in the proper cases, the Secretariat of our Central Committee) will have to put in years of persistent effort to get the Commissariat properly organised, and to get it to function smoothly in conjunction with the Central Control Commission. In my opinion, the People's Commissar of the Workers' and Peasants' Inspection, as well as the whole collegium, can (and should) remain and guide the work of the entire Workers' and Peasants' Inspection, including the work of all the members of the Central Control Commission who will be "placed under his command." The three or four hundred employees of the Workers' and Peasants' Inspection that are to remain, according to my plan, should, on the one hand, perform purely secretarial functions for the other members of the Workers' and Peasants' Inspection and for the supplementary members of the Central Control Commission; and, on the other hand, they should be highly skilled, specially screened, particularly reliable, and highly paid, so that they may be relieved of their present truly unhappy (to say the least) position of Workers' and Peasants' Inspection officials.

I am sure that the reduction of the staff to the number I have indicated will greatly enhance the efficiency of the Workers' and Peasants' Inspection personnel and the quality of all its work, enabling the People's Commissar and the members of the collegium to concentrate their efforts entirely on organising work and on systematically and steadily improving its efficiency, which is so absolutely essential for our workers' and peasants' government, and for our Soviet system.

On the other hand, I also think that the People's Commissar of the Workers' and Peasants' Inspection should work on partly amalgamating and partly co-ordinating those higher institutions for the organisation of labour (the Central Institute of Labour, the Institute for the Scientific Organisation of Labour, etc.), of which there are now no fewer than twelve in our Republic. Excessive uniformity and a consequent desire to amalgamate will be harmful. On the contrary, what is needed here is a reasonable and expedient mean between amalgamating all these institutions and properly delimiting them, allowing for a certain independence for each of them.

Our own Central Committee will undoubtedly gain no less from this reorganisation than the Workers' and Peasants' Inspection. It will gain because its contacts with the masses will be greater and because the regularity and effectiveness of its work will improve. It will then be possible (and necessary) to institute a stricter and more responsible procedure of preparing for the meetings of the Political Bureau, which should be attended by a definite number of members of the Central Control Commission determined either for a definite period or by some organisational plan.

In distributing work to the members of the Central Control Commission, the People's Commissar of the Workers' and Peasants' Inspection, in conjunction with the Presidium of the Central Control Commission, should impose on them the duty either of attending the meetings of the Political Bureau for the purpose of examining all the documents appertaining to matters that come before it in one way or another; or of devoting their working time to theoretical study, to the study of scientific methods of organising labour; or of taking a practical part in the work of supervising and improving our machinery of state, from the higher state institutions to the lower local bodies, etc.

I also think that in addition to the political advantages accruing from the fact that the members of the Central Committee and the Central Control Commission will, as a consequence of this reform, be much better informed and better prepared for the meetings of the Political Bureau (all the documents relevant to the business to be discussed at these meetings should be sent to all the members of the Central Committee and the Central Control Commission not later than the day before the meeting of the Political Bureau, except in absolutely urgent cases, for which special methods of informing the members of the Central Committee and the Central Control Commission and of settling these matters must be devised), there will also be the advantage that the influence of purely personal and incidental factors in our Central Committee will diminish, and this will reduce the danger of a split.

Our Central Committee has grown into a strictly centralised and highly authoritative group, but the conditions under which this group is working are not commensurate with its authority. The reform I recommend should help to remove this defect, and the members of the Central Control Commission, whose duty it will be to attend all meetings of the Political Bureau in a definite number, will have to form a compact group which should not allow anybody's authority without exception, neither that of the General Secretary nor of any other member of the Central Committee, to prevent them from putting questions, verifying documents, and, in general, from keeping themselves fully informed of all things and from exercising the strictest control over the proper conduct of affairs.

Of course, in our Soviet Republic, the social order is based on the collaboration of two classes: the workers and peasants, in which the "Nepmen,"[1] i.e., the bourgeoisie, are now permitted to participate on certain terms. If serious class disagreements arise between these classes, a split will be inevitable. But the grounds for such a split are not inevitable in our social system, and it is the principal task of our Central Committee and Central Control Commission, as well as of our Party as a whole, to watch very closely over such circumstances as may cause a split, and to forestall them, for in the final analysis the fate of our Republic will depend on whether the peasant masses will stand by the working class, loyal to their alliance, or whether they will permit the "Nepmen," i.e., the new bourgeoisie, to drive a wedge between them and the working class, to split them off from the working class. The more clearly we see this alternative, the more clearly all our workers and peasants understand it, the greater are the chances that we shall avoid a split, which would be fatal for the Soviet Republic.

---

1. The term "Nepmen" was used to designate the private entrepreneurs who were permitted to function in the service trades and small-scale industry under the NEP. [R. T.]

Better Fewer, But Better

Dictated in early February 1923, this was Lenin's last article. Although it did not mention Stalin by name, its savage criticism of Rabkrin, coupled with the comment about bureaucracy "not only in Soviet institutions but in party institutions as well"—a clear allusion to Stalin—made the article so embarrassing for Stalin that an effort was made in the Politburo to prevent its publication. Stalin's supporter Valerian Kuibyshev suggested in the Politburo's discussion that the article be withheld from publication save in a single copy of *Pravda* made up especially for Lenin (whose strict medical regime could have kept him from learning of the deception). This proposal was rejected, however, by Trotsky, with Kamenev's support, and *Pravda* carried the article on March 4, 1923.

Apart from its significance in the drama of Lenin's final campaign against Stalin, the article is of interest for its general reflections on policy and its statement that the coming into movement of the Eastern peoples would be decisive in the final outcome of the world revolutionary process initiated by the Russian Revolution.

In the matter of improving our state apparatus, the Workers' and Peasants' Inspection should not, in my opinion, either strive after quantity or hurry. We have so far been able to devote so little thought and attention to the efficiency of our state apparatus that it would now be quite legitimate if we took special care to secure its thorough organisation, and concentrated in the Workers' and Peasants' Inspection a staff of workers really abreast of the times, i.e., not inferior to the best West-European standards. For a socialist republic this condition is, of course, too modest. But our experience of the first five years has fairly crammed our heads with mistrust and scepticism. These qualities assert themselves involuntarily when, for example, we hear people dilating at too great length and too flippantly on "proletarian" culture. For a start, we should be satisfied with real bourgeois culture; for a start, we should be glad to dispense with the cruder types of pre-bourgeois culture, i.e., bureaucratic culture or serf culture, etc. In matters of culture, haste and sweeping measures are most harmful. Many of our young writers and Communists should get this well into their heads.

Thus, in the matter of our state apparatus we should now draw the conclusion from our past experience that it would be better to proceed more slowly.

Our state apparatus is so deplorable, not to say wretched, that we must first think very carefully how to combat its defects, bearing in mind that these defects are rooted in the past, which, although it has been overthrown, has not yet been overcome, has not yet reached the stage of a culture that has receded into the distant past. I say culture deliberately, because in these matters we can only regard as achieved what has become part and parcel of our culture, of our social life, our habits. We might say that the good in our social system has not been properly studied, understood, and taken to heart; it has been hastily grasped at; it has not been verified or tested, corroborated by experience, and not made durable, etc. Of course, it could not be otherwise in a revolutionary epoch, when development proceeded at such breakneck speed that in a matter of five years we passed from tsarism to the Soviet system.

It is time we did something about it. We must show sound scepticism for too rapid progress, for boastfulness, etc. We must give thought to testing the steps forward we proclaim every hour, take every minute and then prove every second that they are flimsy, superficial and misunderstood. The most harmful thing here would be haste. The most harmful thing would be to rely on the assumption that we know at least something, or that we have any considerable number of elements necessary for the building of a really new state apparatus, one really worthy to be called socialist, Soviet, etc.

No, we are ridiculously deficient of such an apparatus, and even of the elements of it, and we must remember that we should not stint time on building it, and that it will take many, many years.

What elements have we for building this apparatus? Only two. First, the workers who are absorbed in the struggle for socialism. These elements are not sufficiently educated. They would like to build a better apparatus for us, but they do not know how. They cannot build one. They have not yet developed the culture required for this; and it is culture that is required. Nothing will be achieved in this by doing things in a rush, by assault, by vim or vigour, or in general, by any of the best human qualities. Secondly, we have elements of knowledge, education and training, but they are ridiculously inadequate compared with all other countries.

Here we must not forget that we are too prone to compensate (or imagine that we can compensate) our lack of knowledge by zeal, haste, etc.

In order to renovate our state apparatus we must at all costs set out, first, to learn, secondly, to learn, and thirdly, to learn, and then see to it that learning shall not remain a dead letter, or a fashionable catch-phrase (and we should admit in all frankness that this happens very often with us), that learning shall really become part of our very being, that it shall actually and fully become a constituent element of our social life. In short, we must not make the demands that are made by bourgeois Western Europe, but demands that are fit and proper for a country which has set out to develop into a socialist country.

The conclusions to be drawn from the above are the following: we must make the Workers' and Peasants' Inspection a really exemplary institution, an instrument to improve our state apparatus.

In order that it may attain the desired high level, we must follow the rule: "Measure your cloth seven times before you cut."

For this purpose, we must utilise the very best of what there is in our social system, and utilise it with the greatest caution, thoughtfulness and knowledge, to build up the new People's Commissariat.

For this purpose, the best elements that we have in our social system—such as, first, the advanced workers, and, second, the really enlightened elements for whom we can vouch that they will not take the word for the deed, and will not utter a single word that goes against their conscience—should not shrink from admitting any difficulty and should not shrink from any struggle in order to achieve the object they have seriously set themselves.

We have been bustling for five years trying to improve our state apparatus, but it has been mere bustle, which has proved useless in these five years, or even futile, or even harmful. This bustle created the impression that we were doing something, but in effect it was only clogging up our institutions and our brains.

It is high time things were changed.

We must follow the rule: Better fewer, but better. We must follow the rule: Better get good human material in two or even three years than work in haste without hope of getting any at all.

I know that it will be hard to keep to this rule and apply it under our conditions. I know that the opposite rule will force its way through a thousand loopholes. I know that enormous resistance will have to be put up, that devilish persistence will be required, that in the first few years at least work in this field will be hellishly hard. Nevertheless, I am convinced that only by such effort shall we be able to achieve our aim; and that only by achieving this aim shall we create a republic that is really worthy of the name of Soviet, socialist, and so on, and so forth.

Many readers probably thought that the figures I quoted by way of illustration in my first article[1] were too small. I am sure that many calculations may be made to prove that they are. But I think that we must put one thing above all such and other calculations, i.e., our desire to obtain really exemplary quality.

I think that the time has at last come when we must work in real earnest to improve our state apparatus and in this there can scarcely be anything more harmful than haste. That is why I would sound a strong warning against inflating the figures. In my opinion, we should, on the contrary, be especially sparing with figures in this matter. Let us say frankly that the People's Commissariat of the Workers' and Peasants' Inspection does not at present enjoy the slightest authority. Everybody knows that no other institutions are worse organised than those of our Workers' and Peasants' Inspection, and that under present conditions nothing can be expected from this People's Commissariat. We must have this firmly fixed in our minds if we really want to create within a few years an institution that will, first, be an exemplary institution, secondly, win everybody's absolute confidence, and, thirdly, prove to all and sundry that we have really justified the work of such a highly placed institution as the Central Control Commission. In my opinion, we must immediately and irrevocably reject all general figures for the size of office staffs. We must select employees for the Workers' and Peasants' Inspection with particular care and only on the basis of the strictest test. Indeed, what is the use of establishing a People's Commissariat which carries on anyhow, which does not enjoy the slightest confidence, and whose word carries scarcely any weight? I think that our main object in launching the work of reconstruction that we now have in mind is to avoid all this.

The workers whom we are enlisting as members of the Central Control Commission must be irreproachable Communists, and I think that a great deal has yet to be done to teach them the methods and objects of their work. Furthermore, there must be a definite number of secretaries to assist in this work, who must be put to a triple test before they are appointed to their posts. Lastly, the officials whom in exceptional cases we shall accept directly as employees of the Workers' and Peasants' Inspection must conform to the following requirements:

First, they must be recommended by several Communists.

Second, they must pass a test for knowledge of our state apparatus.

Third, they must pass a test in the fundamentals of the theory of our state apparatus, in the fundamentals of management, office routine, etc.

1. The reference is to "How We Should Reorganise the Workers' and Peasants' Inspection," above, pp. 729–33. [*R. T.*]

Fourth, they must work in such close harmony with the members of the Central Control Commission and with their own secretariat that we could vouch for the work of the whole apparatus.

I know that these requirements are extraordinarily strict, and I am very much afraid that the majority of the "practical" workers in the Workers' and Peasants' Inspection will say that these requirements are impracticable, or will scoff at them. But I ask any of the present chiefs of the Workers' and Peasants' Inspection, or anyone associated with that body, whether they can honestly tell me the practical purpose of a People's Commissariat like the Workers' and Peasants' Inspection. I think this question will help them recover their sense of proportion. Either it is not worth while having another of the numerous reorganisations that we have had of this hopeless affair, the Workers' and Peasants' Inspection, or we must really set to work, by slow, difficult and unusual methods, and by testing these methods over and over again, to create something really exemplary, something that will win the respect of all and sundry for its merits, and not only because of its rank and title.

If we do not arm ourselves with patience, if we do not devote several years to this task, we had better not tackle it at all.

In my opinion we ought to select a minimum number of the higher labour research institutes, etc., which we have baked so hastily, see whether they are organised properly, and allow them to continue working, but only in a way that conforms to the high standards of modern science and gives us all its benefits. If we do that it will not be utopian to hope that within a few years we shall have an institution that will be able to perform its functions, to work systematically and steadily on improving our state apparatus, an institution backed by the trust of the working class, of the Russian Communist Party, and the whole population of our Republic.

The spade-work for this could be begun at once. If the People's Commissariat of the Workers' and Peasants' Inspection accepted the present plan of reorganisation, it could now take preparatory steps and work methodically until the task is completed, without haste, and not hesitating to alter what has already been done.

Any half-hearted solution would be extremely harmful in this matter. A measure for the size of the staff of the Workers' and Peasants' Inspection based on any other consideration would, in fact, be based on the old bureaucratic considerations, on old prejudices, on what has already been condemned, universally ridiculed, etc.

In substance, the matter is as follows:

Either we prove now that we have really learned something about state organisation (we ought to have learned something in five years), or we prove that we are not sufficiently mature for it. If the latter is the case, we had better not tackle the task.

I think that with the available human material it will not be immodest to assume that we have learned enough to be able systematically to rebuild at least one People's Commissariat. True, this one People's Commissariat will have to be the model for our entire state apparatus.

We ought at once to announce a contest in the compilation of two or more textbooks on the organisation of labour in general, and on management in particular. We can take as a basis the book already published by Yermansky, although it should be said in parentheses that he obviously sympathises with Menshevism and is unfit to compile textbooks for the Soviet system. We can also take as a basis the recent book by Kerzhentsev, and some of the other partial textbooks available may be useful too.

We ought to send several qualified and conscientious people to Germany, or to Britain, to collect literature and to study this question. I mention Britain in case it is found impossible to send people to the U.S.A. or Canada.

We ought to appoint a commission to draw up the preliminary programme of examinations for prospective employees of the Workers' and Peasants' Inspection; ditto for candidates to the Central Control Commission.

These and similar measures will not, of course, cause any difficulties for the People's Commissar or the collegium of the Workers' and Peasants' Inspection, or for the Presidium of the Central Control Commission.

Simultaneously, a preparatory commission should be appointed to select candidates for membership of the Central Control Commission. I hope that we shall now be able to find more than enough candidates for this post among the experienced workers in all departments, as well as among the students of our Soviet higher schools. It would hardly be right to exclude one or another category beforehand. Probably preference will have to be given to a mixed composition for this institution, which should combine many qualities, and dissimilar merits. Consequently, the task of drawing up the list of candidates will entail a considerable amount of work. For example, it would be least desirable for the staff of the new People's Commissariat to consist of people of one type, only of officials, say, or for it to exclude people of the propagandist type, or people whose principal quality is sociability or the ability to penetrate into circles that are not altogether customary for officials in this field, etc.

I think I shall be able to express my idea best if I compare my plan with that of academic institutions. Under the guidance of their

Presidium, the members of the Central Control Commission should systematically examine all the papers and documents of the Political Bureau. Moreover, they should divide their time correctly between various jobs in investigating the routine in our institutions, from the very small and privately-owned offices to the highest state institutions. And lastly, their functions should include the study of theory, i.e., the theory of organisation of the work they intend to devote themselves to, and practical work under the guidance either of older comrades or of teachers in the higher institutes for the organisation of labour.

I do not think, however, that they will be able to confine themselves to this sort of academic work. In addition, they will have to prepare themselves for work which I would not hesitate to call training to catch, I will not say rogues, but something like that, and working out special ruses to screen their movements, their approach, etc.

If such proposals were made in West-European government institutions they would rouse frightful resentment, a feeling of moral indignation, etc.; but I trust that we have not become so bureaucratic as to be capable of that. NEP has not yet succeeded in gaining such respect as to cause any of us to be shocked at the idea that somebody may be caught. Our Soviet Republic is of such recent construction, and there are such heaps of the old lumber still lying around that it would hardly occur to anyone to be shocked at the idea that we should delve into them by means of ruses, by means of investigations sometimes directed to rather remote sources or in a roundabout way. And even if it did occur to anyone to be shocked by this, we may be sure that such a person would make himself a laughing-stock.

Let us hope that our new Workers' and Peasants' Inspection will abandon what the French call *pruderie*, which we may call ridiculous primness, or ridiculous swank, and which plays entirely into the hands of our Soviet and Party bureaucracy. Let it be said in parentheses that we have bureaucrats in our Party offices as well as in Soviet offices.

When I said above that we must study and study hard in institutes for the higher organisation of labour, etc., I did not by any means imply "studying" in the schoolroom way, nor did I confine myself to the idea of studying only in the schoolroom way. I hope that not a single genuine revolutionary will suspect me of refusing, in this case, to understand "studies" to include resorting to some semi-humorous trick, cunning device, piece of trickery or something of that sort. I know that in the staid and earnest states of Western Europe such an idea would horrify people and that not a single decent official would even entertain it. I hope, however, that we have not yet become as bureaucratic as all that and that in our midst the discussion of this idea will give rise to nothing more than amusement.

Indeed, why not combine pleasure with utility? Why not resort to some humorous or semi-humorous trick to expose something ridiculous, something harmful, something semi-ridiculous, semi-harmful, etc.?

It seems to me that our Workers' and Peasants' Inspection will gain a great deal if it undertakes to examine these ideas, and that the list of cases in which our Central Control Commission and its colleagues in the Workers' and Peasants' Inspection achieved a few of their most brilliant victories will be enriched by not a few exploits of our future Workers' and Peasants' Inspection and Central Control Commission members in places not quite mentionable in prim and staid textbooks.

How can a Party institution be amalgamated with a Soviet institution? Is there not something improper in this suggestion?

I do not ask these questions on my own behalf, but on behalf of those I hinted at above when I said that we have bureaucrats in our Party institutions as well as in the Soviet institutions.

But why, indeed, should we not amalgamate the two if this is in the interests of our work? Do we not all see that such an amalgamation has been very beneficial in the case of the People's Commissariat of Foreign Affairs, where it was brought about at the very beginning? Does not the Political Bureau discuss from the Party point of view many questions, both minor and important, concerning the "moves" we should make in reply to the "moves" of foreign powers in order to forestall their, say, cunning, if we are not to use a less respectable term? Is not this flexible amalgamation of a Soviet institution with a Party institution a source of great strength in our politics? I think that what has proved its usefulness, what has been definitely adopted in our foreign politics and has become so customary that it no longer calls forth any doubt in this field, will be at least as appropriate (in fact, I think it will be much more appropriate) for our state apparatus as a whole. The functions of the Workers' and Peasants' Inspection cover our state apparatus as a whole, and its activities should affect all and every state institution without exception: local, central, commercial, purely administrative, educational, archive, theatrical, etc.—in short, all without any exception.

Why then should not an institution, whose activities have such wide scope, and which moreover requires such extraordinary flexibility of forms, be permitted to adopt this peculiar amalgamation of a Party control institution with a Soviet control institution?

I see no obstacles to this. What is more, I think that such an amalgamation is the only guarantee of success in our work. I think that all doubts on this score arise in the dustiest corners of our government offices, and that they deserve to be treated with nothing but ridicule.

Another doubt: is it expedient to combine educational activities with official activities? I think that it is not only expedient, but necessary. Generally speaking, in spite of our revolutionary attitude towards the West-European form of state, we have allowed ourselves to become infected with a number of its most harmful and ridiculous prejudices; to some extent we have been deliberately infected with them by our dear bureaucrats, who counted on being able again and again to fish in the muddy waters of these prejudices. And they did fish in these muddy waters to so great an extent that only the blind among us failed to see how extensively this fishing was practised.

In all spheres of social, economic and political relationships we are "frightfully" revolutionary. But as regards precedence, the observance of the forms and rites of office management, our "revolutionariness" often gives way to the mustiest routine. On more than one occasion, we have witnessed the very interesting phenomenon of a great leap forward in social life being accompanied by amazing timidity whenever the slightest changes are proposed.

This is natural, for the boldest steps forward were taken in a field which was long reserved for theoretical study, which was promoted mainly, and even almost exclusively, in theory. The Russian, when away from work, found solace from bleak bureaucratic realities in unusually bold theoretical constructions, and that is why in our country these unusually bold theoretical constructions assumed an unusually lopsided character. Theoretical audacity in general constructions went hand in hand with amazing timidity as regards certain very minor reforms in office routine. A great nation-wide agrarian revolution was worked out with an audacity unexampled in any other country, and at the same time the imagination failed when it came to working out a tenth-rate reform in office routine; the imagination, or patience, was lacking to apply to this reform the general propositions that produced such brilliant results when applied to general problems.

That is why in our present life reckless audacity goes hand in hand, to an astonishing degree, with timidity of thought even when it comes to very minor changes.

I think that this has happened in all really great revolutions, for really great revolutions grow out of the contradictions between the old, between what is directed towards developing the old, and the very abstract striving for the new, which must be so new as not to contain the tiniest particle of the old.

And the more abrupt the revolution, the longer will many of these contradictions last.

The general feature of our present life is the following: we have destroyed capitalist industry and have done our best to raze to the ground the medieval institutions and landed proprietorship, and thus created a small and very small peasantry, which is following the lead of the proletariat because it believes in the results of its revolutionary work. It is not easy for us, however, to keep going until the socialist revolution is victorious in more developed countries merely with the aid of this confidence, because economic necessity, especially under NEP, keeps the productivity of labour of the small and very small peasants at an extremely low level. Moreover, the international situation, too, threw Russia back and, by and large, reduced the labour productivity of the people to a level considerably below pre-war. The West-European capitalist powers, partly deliberately and partly unconsciously, did everything they could to throw us back, to utilise the elements of the Civil War in Russia in order to spread as much ruin in the country as possible. It was precisely this way out of the imperialist war that seemed to have many advantages. They argued somewhat as follows: "If we fail to overthrow the revolutionary system in Russia, we shall, at all events, hinder its progress towards socialism." And from their point of view they could argue in no other way. In the end, their problem was half-solved. They failed to overthrow the new system created by the revolution, but they did prevent it from at once taking the step forward that would have justified the forecasts of the socialists, that would have enabled the latter to develop the productive forces with enormous speed, to develop all the potentialities which, taken together, would have produced socialism; socialists would thus have proved to all and sundry that socialism contains within itself gigantic forces and that mankind had now entered into a new stage of development of extraordinarily brilliant prospects.

The system of international relationships which has now taken shape is one in which a European state, Germany, is enslaved by the victor countries. Furthermore, owing to their victory, a number of states, the oldest states in the West, are in a position to make some insignificant concessions to their oppressed classes—concessions which, insignificant though they are, nevertheless retard the revolutionary movement in those countries and create some semblance of "class truce."

At the same time, as a result of the last imperialist war, a number of countries of the East, India, China, etc., have been completely jolted out of the rut. Their development has definitely shifted to general European capitalist lines. The general European ferment has begun to affect them, and it is now clear to the whole world that they have been drawn into a process of development that must lead to a crisis in the whole of world capitalism.

Thus, at the present time we are confronted with the question— shall we be able to hold on with our small and very small peasant production, and in our present state of ruin, until the West-European capitalist countries consummate their development towards socialism? But they are consummating it not as we formerly expected. They are not consummating it through the gradual "maturing" of socialism, but through the exploitation of some countries by others, through the exploitation of the first of the countries vanquished in the imperialist war combined with the exploitation of the whole of the East. On the other hand, precisely as a result of the first imperialist war, the East has been definitely drawn into the revolutionary movement, has been definitely drawn into the general maelstrom of the world revolutionary movement.

What tactics does this situation prescribe for our country? Obviously the following. We must display extreme caution so as to preserve our workers' government and to retain our small and very small peasantry under its leadership and authority. We have the advantage that the whole world is now passing to a movement that must give rise to a world socialist revolution. But we are labouring under the disadvantage that the imperialists have succeeded in splitting the world into two camps; and this split is made more complicated by the fact that it is extremely difficult for Germany, which is really a land of advanced, cultured, capitalist development, to rise to her feet. All the capitalist powers of what is called the West are pecking at her and preventing her from rising. On the other hand, the entire East, with its hundreds of millions of exploited working people, reduced to the last degree of human suffering, has been forced into a position where its physical and material strength cannot possibly be compared with the physical, material and military strength of any of the much smaller West-European states.

Can we save ourselves from the impending conflict with these imperialist countries? May we hope that the internal antagonisms and conflicts between the thriving imperialist countries of the West and the thriving imperialist countries of the East will give us a second respite as they did the first time, when the campaign of the West-European counter-revolution in support of the Russian counter-revolution broke down owing to the antagonisms in the camp of the counter-revolutionaries of the West and the East, in the camp of the Eastern and Western exploiters, in the camp of Japan and the U.S.A.?

I think the reply to this question should be that the issue depends upon too many factors, and that the outcome of the struggle as a whole can be forecast only because in the long run capitalism itself is educating and training the vast majority of the population of the globe for the struggle.

In the last analysis, the outcome of the struggle will be determined by the fact that Russia, India, China, etc., account for the overwhelming majority of the population of the globe. And during the past few years it is this majority that has been drawn into the struggle for emancipation with extraordinary rapidity, so that in this respect there cannot be the slightest doubt what the final outcome of the world struggle will be. In this sense, the complete victory of socialism is fully and absolutely assured.

But what interests us is not the inevitability of this complete victory of socialism, but the tactics which we, the Russian Communist Party, we, the Russian Soviet Government, should pursue to prevent the West-European counter-revolutionary states from crushing us. To ensure our existence until the next military conflict between the counter-revolutionary imperialist West and the revolutionary and nationalist East, between the most civilised countries of the world and the orientally backward countries which, however, comprise the majority, this majority must become civilised. We, too, lack enough civilisation to enable us to pass straight on to socialism, although we do have the political requisites for it. We should adopt the following tactics, or pursue the following policy, to save ourselves.

We must strive to build up a state in which the workers retain the leadership of the peasants, in which they retain the confidence of the peasants, and by exercising the greatest economy remove every trace of extravagance from our social relations.

We must reduce our state apparatus to the utmost degree of economy. We must banish from it all traces of extravagance, of which so much has been left over from tsarist Russia, from its bureaucratic capitalist state machine.

Will not this be a reign of peasant limitations?

No. If we see to it that the working class retains its leadership over the peasantry, we shall be able, by exercising the greatest possible thrift in the economic life of our state, to use every saving we make to develop our large-scale machine industry, to develop electrification, the hydraulic extraction of peat, to complete the Volkhov Power Project,[1] etc.

In this, and in this alone, lies our hope. Only when we have done this shall we, speaking figuratively, be able to change horses, to

1. The first of the big hydroelectric power stations built on the Volkhov River. Construction began in 1918.

change from the peasant, *muzhik* horse of poverty, from the horse of an economy designed for a ruined peasant country, to the horse which the proletariat is seeking and must seek—the horse of large-scale machine industry, of electrification, of the Volkhov Power Station, etc.

That is how I link up in my mind the general plan of our work, of our policy, of our tactics, of our strategy, with the functions of the reorganised Workers' and Peasants' Inspection. This is what, in my opinion, justifies the exceptional care, the exceptional attention that we must devote to the Workers' and Peasants' Inspection in raising it to an exceptionally high level, in giving it a leadership with Central Committee rights, etc., etc.

And this justification is that only by thoroughly purging our government machine, by reducing to the utmost everything that is not absolutely essential in it, shall we be certain of being able to keep going. Moreover, we shall be able to keep going not on the level of a small-peasant country, not on the level of universal limitation, but on a level steadily advancing to large-scale machine industry.

These are the lofty tasks that I dream of for our Workers' and Peasants' Inspection. That is why I am planning for it the amalgamation of the most authoritative Party body with an "ordinary" People's Commissariat.

Last Letters

These three short letters, dictated on March 5 and 6, 1923, were elements of Lenin's plan to purge Stalin at the forthcoming party congress. The first, dated March 5, enlisted Trotsky's support for an attack in the party Central Committee's pre-congress plenary meeting on Stalin's handling of the Georgian affair, and the letter of March 6 to Mdivani and Makharadze was a promise to Stalin's Bolshevik opponents in Georgia to rally to their side in their dispute with him. But Lenin's incapacitation as his health worsened on March 6 and 10 decisively altered the course of events, and Stalin weathered the Twelfth Congress discussion of the Georgian affair without great difficulty—in part because of Trotsky's willingness to make a compromise with him over the issue.

Lenin's curt note of March 5 to Stalin demanding an apology for his rudeness to Krupskaya was evidently designed to elicit from Stalin an admission of his rudeness—the charge made against him in the postscript to the "Letter to the Congress." It may therefore be seen as a deliberate effort on Lenin's part to document the case he was planning to make for Stalin's removal from the General Secretaryship. Stalin did immediately produce a note of apology, but that document has never been published.

Strictly secret
Personal

Respected Comrade Trotsky:

I would request you very much to take upon yourself the defense of the George case in the party Central Committee. This case is now under "persecution" by Stalin and Dzerzhinsky, and I cannot rely upon their impartiality. Even quite to the contrary. If you would consent to take upon yourself the defense of it, I could be serene. If for some reason you do not agree, return the whole file to me. I will take that as a sign of your non-agreement.

With very best comradely greetings,

Lenin

747

Strictly secret
Copies to Comrades Trotsky and Kamenev

To Comrades Mdivani, Makharadze and others

Respected Comrades:

With all my heart I am following your case. Am outraged by Ordzhonikidze's rudeness and the little indulgences of Stalin and Dzerzhinsky. Am preparing notes and a speech for you.

With respect,

Lenin

Strictly secret
Personal
Copies to Comrades Kamenev and Zinoviev

Respected Comrade Stalin:

You had the rudeness to call my wife on the telephone and berate her. Although she expressed her willingness to forget what was said, this fact nevertheless became known, through her, to Zinoviev and Kamenev. I do not intend to forget so easily what was done against me, and there is no need to point out that what is done against my wife I consider to be against me also. Therefore, I ask you to consider whether you agree to take back what you said and apologize, or whether you prefer to break relations between us.

With respect,

Lenin

Bibliographical Note

The literature about Lenin is large in all major languages, especially Russian. The following titles represent only a small personal selection of books available in English. No attempt has been made at a complete coverage of works of significance even in this limited category. Books marked with an asterisk are available as paperbacks.

BIOGRAPHICAL WORKS

There is still no adequate full-scale biography of Lenin in English. *Louis Fischer, *The Life of Lenin* (New York, 1964) is the fullest available narrative biography and includes much factual material first published in Russia in the Khrushchev era, but is less than adequate in the interpretive aspect. Of greater value interpretively, though limited in factual terms because of its small size, is Rolf H. W. Theen, *Lenin: Genesis and Development of a Revolutionary* (Philadelphia, 1973). An earlier narrative biography, abridged in its paperback edition, is *David Shub, *Lenin* (New York, 1948). See also *Bertram D. Wolfe, *Three Who Made a Revolution* (Boston, 1962), Robert H. McNeal, *Bride of the Revolution: Krupskaya and Lenin* (Ann Arbor, 1972); and *Adam B. Ulam, *The Bolsheviks* (New York, 1965).

For Lenin's early life, see Isaac Deutscher, *Lenin's Childhood* (London, 1970); Leon Trotsky, *The Young Lenin*, translation and introduction by Max Eastman (Garden City, 1972); and N. Valentinov, *The Early Years of Lenin*, translated and edited by Rolf H. W. Theen (Ann Arbor, 1969). For his final period see *Moshe Lewin, *Lenin's Last Struggle*, translated by A. M. Sheridan (New York, 1968); and *Robert C. Tucker, *Stalin as Revolutionary, 1879–1929* (New York, 1973).

MEMOIRS

For a portrait of Lenin in the early nineteen-hundreds, and an interpretation of his political personality, the most valuable existing work is N. Valentinov, *Encounters with Lenin*, translated by Paul Rosta and Brian Pearce, foreword by Leonard Schapiro (London, 1968). Other standard memoir works include: N. K. Krupskaya, *Reminiscences of Lenin* (New York, 1970); Maxim Gorky, *Days with Lenin* (New York, 1932); *Angelica Balabanoff, *Impressions of Lenin*, translated by Isotta Cesari, foreword by Bertram Wolfe (Ann Arbor, 1968); *Leon Trotsky, *Lenin: Notes for a Biographer*, translated by Tamara Deutscher (New York, 1973); Clara Zetkin, *Reminiscences of Lenin* (London, 1929). See also *Reminiscences of Lenin by His Relatives* (Moscow, 1956) and *Recollections of Lenin* (Moscow, 1956).

LENIN'S THOUGHT

For Lenin's roots in the Russian revolutionary tradition, see (in addition to works mentioned above) *Franco Venturi, *Roots of Revolution: A History of the Populist and Socialist Movements in Nineteenth-Century Russia* (New York, 1960); *Theodore Dan, *The Origins of Bolshevism*, translated and edited by Joel Carmichael (New York, 1964); and *Avrahm Yarmolinsky, *Road to Revolution: A Century of Russian Radicalism* (New York, 1962).

On Leninism and Leninist Marxism, see also *Leon Trotsky, *The New Course* (Ann Arbor, 1965); Joseph Stalin, *Problems of Leninism* (Moscow, many editions); *Georg Lukacs, *Lenin: A Study on the Unity of His Thought*, translated by Nicholas Jacobs (Cambridge, Mass., 1971); Raya Dunayevskaya, *Marxism and Freedom* (New York, 1958) and her chapter on "Hegelian Leninism" in Bart Grahl and Paul Piccone, eds., *Towards a New Marxism* (St. Louis, 1973); Stephen F. Cohen, *Bukharin and the Bolshevik Revolution* (New York, 1973); *L. H. Haimson, *The Russian Marxists and the Origins of Bolshevism* (Cambridge, Mass., 1955); *Alfred Meyer, *Leninism* (New York, 1957); and *Robert C. Tucker, *The Soviet Political Mind*, second ed. (New York, 1971) and *The Marxian Revolutionary Idea* (New York, 1969).

LENIN'S POLITICS

In addition to relevant works cited above, studies of interest include: *E. H. Carr, *The Bolshevik Revolution, 1917–1923*, 3 vols. (New York, 1951–53); Donald W. Treadgold, *Lenin and His Rivals: The Struggle for Russia's Future, 1898–1906* (New York, 1955); Leonard Schapiro and P. Reddaway, eds., *Lenin: The Man, the Theorist, the Leader* (New York, 1968); *Robert V. Daniels, *The Conscience of the Revolution: Communist Opposition in Soviet Russia* (Cambridge, Mass., 1960); Leonard Schapiro, *The Origin of the Communist Autocracy* (Cambridge, Mass., 1955); Sheila Fitzpatrick, *The Commissariat of Enlightenment* (New York, 1971); *Stanley W. Page, *Lenin and World Revolution* (New York, 1959); Branko Lazitch and Milorad Drachkovitch, *Lenin and the Comintern*, Vol. I (Stanford, 1972); *F. Borkenau, *World Communism: A History of the Communist International* (Ann Arbor, 1962); and *George F. Kennan, *Russia and the West under Lenin and Stalin* (Boston, 1961).

Index